ANTIQUE FIREARMS

ASSEMBLY/DISASSEMBLY

David R. Chicoine

Published by

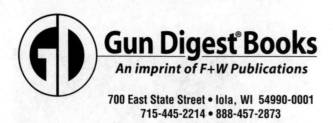

Gun Digest® Books

An imprint of F+W Publications

700 East State Street • Iola, WI 54990-0001
715-445-2214 • 888-457-2873

Our toll-free number to place an order or obtain
a free catalog is (800) 258-0929.

Library of Congress Catalog Number: 2005931346
ISBN: 0-87349-767-8

Designed by Paul Birling
Edited by Dan Shideler

Printed in United States of America

Dedication and Acknowledgments

I would like to dedicate this book to John M. Tyler, a dear friend and teacher, for his untiring, selfless sharing of wisdom and compassion.

That this book was written at all, I owe a tremendous debt of gratitude to my wife Kathy and also to my family who, during the time this was being written, got to see much less of me than they are used to. Thank you for your patience, your generosity, your support, your help on so many levels, and for just being who you are: my dear family.

There were also many individuals and businesses, both in and out of the firearms industry, who were generous enough to offer help with the writing of this book. Without the efforts of these people and companies, it would not have been possible to complete a work of this scope in such a short period of time. I would like to offer my sincere thanks and gratitude to all of you for what you have done to insure that this project would be a success:

Gloria Ardesi at Davide Pedersoli & C. in Italy. Duff Armfield. Frank Brownell at Brownells Inc. David T. Chicoine. Reid Coffield. Boyd Davis at EMF Co.. Cristie Gates at Stoeger Industries. Gary Germaine at U.S. Firearms Co. Frank Gregg. Mike Harvey at Cimarron Firearms. Lisa Keller at VTI Replica Gun Parts. Keith Lawrence at American Gunsmith. Giacomo Merlino at A. Uberti srl in Italy. Diana Morin at Marlin Firearms Co. Amy Navitsky at Colt Firearms. Walt Penner. Allesandro Pietta in Italy. Margaret Sheldon at Sturm, Ruger & Co. Jim Supica at Old Town Station. Ed Wade. John Watts. Suzanne Webb at A. Uberti Srl. in Italy. Will at EMF Company. Larry Weeks at Brownells Inc. and the late Butch Winter at Dixie Gun Works.

Thank you all!

About The Author

David R. Chicoine is a gunsmith and author who has spent most of his adult life working with and around older firearms. For the last 30 years, he has specialized in the repair, restoration and conservation of antique firearms, especially Smith & Wesson, Colt, and Winchester. Chicoine's expertise with 19th century firearms is so widely known and well thought of that since 1976 firearms companies including S&W, U.S. Repeating Arms and Remington regularly refer customers with antique and obsolete arms to him for repair or restoration.

Other printed works by David R. Chicoine include *Gunsmithing Guns of the Old West* (Krause Publications, 2001 & 2004), *Smith & Wesson Sixguns of the Old West* (Mowbray, 2004) and *Guns of the New West* (K-P Books, 2005). David is the editor/publisher of *Bullet 'N Press* as well as a contributing editor to the *American Rifleman* "Dope Bag." He has published many articles in *American Gunsmith*, Dixie Gun Works *"Black Powder Annual,"* *Winchester Collector, Smith & Wesson Collectors Journal, Man at Arms*, and others.

Table Of Contents

Table Of Contents

Introduction

Well over 25 years ago a gentleman came into my gunsmith shop in western North Carolina. He had an early 32-20 Smith and Wesson revolver. His son had been shooting it using old ammunition. One of the rounds did not fire properly and the bullet lodged in the barrel. His son continued to fire the revolver and ended up stacking at least three more bullets behind the first stuck bullet. This ruined the barrel with both a crack and a sizeable bulge. He asked me to replace the barrel but he wanted one that matched the original which had a special target front sight.

I was unsure if I could find such a barrel for this 50-year-old revolver but I promised I would do my best. Fortunately, I had seen a small ad for a fellow up in Maine who sold antique Smith and Wesson parts. The company was Liberty Antique Gun Works and the fellow was Dave Chicoine. I sent away for the catalog and upon receipt I saw that he had what I needed. Just to be sure, I called him and had a most pleasant and enjoyable conversation. This resulted in two things. First, I got the barrel I needed. Secondly, I began an enduring friendship with a wonderful guy.

Dave is one of those rare individuals who possess exceptional talent, skill and knowledge. At the same time he is one of the friendliest, most open and sharing men I have ever known. Unlike some "experts," Dave does not hoard knowledge or have any secrets. He has always been willing to share his experience and knowledge with anyone interested in firearms. It makes no difference to Dave whether the person is a major figure in the firearms trade, a hobbyist, or some small town gunsmith from the hills of North Carolina – he always responds in a helpful, courteous manner. He is a true gentleman in every sense of the word.

This book is a reflection of Dave. It provides great information not available anywhere else. While there are several assembly/disassembly manuals currently in print, none offers information on many of the wonderful old guns that Dave so obviously loves. The information he provides is presented in a clear, concise, easily understood manner, with a logical, systematic approach. In addition to takedown and assembly instructions, Dave shares lots of nuggets of information that only a true expert would know.

This is one of those "must have" books that any amateur or professional gunsmith or anyone who just wants to care for his firearms will want to add to his library. It's an exceptional book from an exceptional guy.

Reid Coffield
Gunsmithing Editor
Shooting Times
Shotgun News
Contributing Editor, *The American Rifleman*

Foreword

L ooking back over the years, I guess I have worked in the gun trades for most of my adult life and I think it has been a true blessing to have had a job that I love. Early on, as a young inexperienced gunsmith, I became painfully aware that any gunsmith, armorer, serious tinkerer or even the general sportsman just can't get enough good information about how old guns are put together.

I still remember my initial taste of this, trying to disassemble my first Browning A-5 semi-automatic shotgun so I could give the gun a detailed cleaning. Without any written instructions in hand I began, honestly fearful of the outcome. This "little" job took me almost nine hours to finish. Now, it did turn out successfully, but if success were measured by time spent, then I certainly did not make a profit on this one! The only saving grace for me and what got me through the job at all was ol' John Browning's perfectly sensible, easy-to-grasp design. Also, I can remember phoning the late Bob Brownell for help with that one. Bob was a dear old gunsmith friend, the same Bob B. who founded the gunsmithing supply company called Brownell's in rural Iowa. Bob didn't have a large "technical staff" manning the phones back then; in fact, he was "it"! Nevertheless, he always offered the best information he could, for free and regardless of how much time it took from his busy schedule, a wonderful service that his company still provides to the trade today.

On the other end of the spectrum, if all firearms were as simple as the Remington Rolling Block or the Sharps 4-barrel pepperbox (about 20 parts in all), then most of us could probably get by just fine without any instructions. Alas, such is not the case and if you have even a little experience trying to disassemble various kinds of firearms, you already understand that. Indeed, there are so many different firearms designs, with more being designed almost daily, that if you somehow could combine all the factory owner's-manuals . . . well, the sentence doesn't need to be finished – the key word here is "if." When disassembling a firearm you haven't had any experience with before, sometimes the hard part is finding the exact set of instructions, preferably with an exploded drawing, that explains just how that odd and rare old gun laying on your bench can be safely taken apart. Having good instructional material is a boon to the average sportsman, but it is vital if you are a working professional.

Thus, when this work was begun, it was with the thought of presenting a good, easy to read manual to aid those who had the need to disassemble antique firearms, taking care to include some of the more unusual older weapons, ones that are not normally covered. It was also our intention to present the material in such a way that the reader would more quickly become familiar with the subject than with earlier presentations.

As the book progressed, it became apparent to me that if we were going to meet the practical needs of today's collector, cowboy action shooter and re-enactor, then we had better include several of the popular modern-made replicas along with the genuine antique weapons. In that light, we have taken the liberty of writing instructions that in many cases will be found suitable for use with both the replica and an original. Today it is a fact that some replica weapons are being used in greater numbers than originals are; it is for that reason more than any other that in some cases we thought it more appropriate to use internal photos of replica weapons within the instructions.

By taking the approach of combining exploded firearms drawings and photographs, along with newly written text instructions and a brief historical sketch tracing the highlights and history of the weaponry included in this book, it is the author's hope the reader will come away with a deeper understanding of each firearm's mechanism. I only wish we had more space, so we could have included a hundred more of these great old guns!

David R. Chicoine
North Carolina, January 2005

SECTION I
DISASSEMBLY

Disassembling Old Guns:
TIPS, TOOLS & TECHNIQUES

In the new millennium, firearms are commonly made from space-age polymers, sophisticated aluminum, fiberglass resin, high-tech stainless steel and even titanium. The key words are low-maintenance, no-rust, non-organic and low-glare. Flat ugly is considered to be okay, as long as pure functionality is the goal. Machine work, where there is any, is performed largely by computer-controlled, automated machines and many complicated parts are now precision investment castings that require very little, if any, final machining in order to function. Often these modern marvels have rough looking surfaces, finished off with matte, low-glare coatings that are as modern as the parent materials. In many instances, modern weapons can be completely disassembled in short order, using few or sometimes even no tools.

It was not so very long ago that weapons were built very differently from how they are today. In days past, firearms were manufactured in a labor-intensive environment, using mostly finely machined carbon steel. This was brought to a brilliant luster by hand and beautifully finished in various types of blue or nickel plating. The former was an oxide of the steel surface itself, while the latter was a thin coating on top of the steel surface. Older guns were stocked, for the most part, with closely fitted, often decorated, hand-finished hardwoods, with a decided preference given to walnut. Older firearms were (usually) a homogenous blend of vulnerable organic beauty and function. Of compelling forms, they were generally held together by screws and pins, combined sometimes with ingeniously machined joint-work. More often than not, older weapons also required the use of special tools, a good set of instructions and quite a bit of time to disassemble.

While covering so many different kinds of older weapons, this book is by no means a factory service manual; rather, it is a guide to help lead you through the different nuances of disassembling the individual types covered. We can offer some basic advice that pertains to the normal methods used to hold most older firearms together; screws and drivers; pins and punches. We will also touch on wood-to-metal fit and the kind of care the disassembly technician (you) should give to these areas.

Need I say that a comfortable, safe place to work is essential? For most, a workshop with a wooden work bench would be best, but for the casual tinkerer that place might be a kitchen table with good light, the latter being a necessary ingredient for this work, no matter who you are. Just be sure the location is in an area that is secured from the curious hands of small children or from an indignant walk-through by the family feline (the "actual" owner of your home, a fact that cat owners already know).

This special tool is called a mainspring vise. If you work on old shotguns or muzzle-loaders, this is a handy tool for safely compressing the huge V-shaped mainsprings found in many of these weapons. Tool courtesy of Dixie Gun Works.

The screw in this old Remington-Keene had its slot damaged long ago by someone who tried to turn it using the incorrect kind of screwdriver.

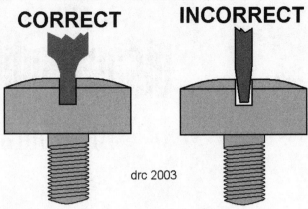

This illustration shows the difference between how hollow-ground and taper-bladed screwdrivers fit into gun screw slots.

Disassembling handguns doesn't require much bench space, but for rifles and shotguns, a work bench at least four feet long and two feet deep will prove to be a handy size for a work area. A rifle vise or gun cradle is a piece of equipment that can help you hold the weapon while you are working on it, that is, at least until you get to the point where the wood is removed. Think ahead. Have a place, better yet a container, with a closable lid to put small parts in. If you are disassembling a double gun, a fine idea is to use three containers, one for the right hand parts, one for left and one for everything else. Work carefully. Try not to extend what you are unscrewing over the edge or even near the edge of a work bench; losing irreplaceable, tiny parts from a 100-year-old gun is not my idea of a fun time, and if you do it even once it won't be yours either.

When disassembling things that are under spring tension, make it a habit to hold that portion of the gun captive so small parts don't take off flying when you release something. To do this, you can use your hand, an old towel to cover the area, or you can actually work with the weapon placed down inside a cardboard box to hold everything inside a captive environment. The latter method is a lot of trouble but I use it for disassembling and assembling old guns with complex parts, parts that I know I would never be able to replace if I lost them.

Finally, take your time and never use brute force on an old gun. If anything on an old firearm seems to require more force than is comfortable, just stop. Carefully examine the situation, look at it from every angle, read more about it, then if you still can't figure it out, by all means let a gunsmith have a look. In the medical professions, an MD's oath evolves along the lines of "first, do no harm." That is what we are after here: to take the weapon apart and get it back together, but to *do no harm* in the process.

Removing old gun screws and pins

I mentioned above that older firearms were held together, for the most part, by screws and pins. Two kinds of screws were commonly used: machine screws and wood screws. Either type almost always used straight slots; we seldom see Philips or Allen headed screws except on some guns produced in the post WW2 era. Gun pins were usually straight and non-tapered and often had domed or rounded heads to compliment the surrounding surface area and to match nearby screw heads.

Anyone who has ever worked on old firearms knows this already, but for those that haven't, removing screws without doing damage to either the screw or to the gun itself, is often a huge challenge to the person trying to disassemble the firearm. Whatever the reason is that we want to remove the screws, whether to repair some broken part inside or simply to clean and inspect the weapon, those screws will have to be removed.

Why are gun screws so hard to remove? There are several reasons and these are usually compound. Gun screws that have been there for a long time may be stuck fast by a coating of rust and/or old grease and oils that can harden into a tough, varnish-like cement over time. Complicating that is the idea that gun screws, especially in well made guns, were closely fitted to exacting tolerances and the screw heads were often countersunk into the side of the receiver. All of those factors considered together increase the potential surface area of the screw, which translates into more area that is subject to being rusted together with a resulting increase in resistance to the screw being turned. In the old days, some gun screws were installed by factory assemblers who used a bit and brace. This offered the installer an big advantage of leverage when tightening the screw and it saved a lot

The screwdriver shown here is a tapered, general purpose blade; notice how poorly it fits the gun screw slot.

This is the same screw as above. This time the gunsmith is using the correct, hollow-ground driver blade.

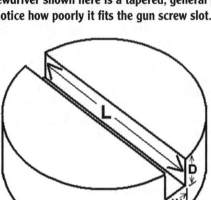

Here is how screw slots are measured.

of time. Unfortunately, this practice also caused many small screws to get tightened way past the point where they should have been.

On top of all this, older gun screws mostly had straight screw slots (some folks now call these old-fashioned slots). Being easily damaged and broken, this kind of slot is terribly inadequate in cases where the screw is really tight. However, these poor little slots offer you the only easy means of removing the screw, so it would seem that you have not been left with many options. I hate to be the bearer of bad news, but to compound the situation even more, many older guns used screws that were hardened in order to help prevent wear. The trouble is that some screws got hardened too much, taking them to the point of being brittle. Those sorts of screws need to be handled with special care; you don't want the screw head to shear off before the screw can turn in its threads.

This is the portion of this section that I really hope the reader will pay attention to. It is largely because of those dainty screw slots and from over-tightening or rusting in place, or all the above, that there is such a high chance of damaging the gun's exterior while you are trying to remove the screws. Make no mistake,

this is where the real damage can be done. Having established that removal of gun screws is a highly critical area, there are some steps you can take to help you safely remove the screws from older firearms.

The first sensible step in turning gun screws is to always use a high-quality, hollow-ground gunsmith screwdriver. Choose a screwdriver blade that fits the screw slots as perfectly as possible. Why hollow-ground? Because hollow-ground, gunsmith screwdrivers have straight sided blades that are meant to fit all the way down into the bottom of a gun screw slot, which is also straight sided. Making sure the bit fits the screw slot is the all-important part of turning gun screws. Finding the correct size blade might mean you will have to do some grinding or filing on the screwdriver bit itself. What you want to end up with, before you turn a screw, is for the screwdriver you are using to fill up the screw slot.

But before you can fill up the slot, it will first have to be emptied. That means you have to clean the screw slot of any and all hardened grease, dirt and rust deposits. Those cruddy deposits can be quite hard, especially in weapons that are a hundred or more years old. Deposits like this are capable of keeping even the perfectly sized screwdriver from completely entering the screw slot. I like to soften the deposits by soaking them in solvents like Hoppe's #9 or white kerosene and then use strong dental picks of various shapes and sizes to clean the slots, scraping away any hardened deposits right down to the bottom of the slot.

After you have the screw slot emptied and cleaned, we can "fill the slot" with a proper-fitting screwdriver blade. We will select a blade that fits from side to side in the slot, not one that is so wide that it touches the sides and scratches or mars the metal surrounding the screw, but wide enough to fill the slot from side to side about 95%. The blade should also fit the slot perfectly

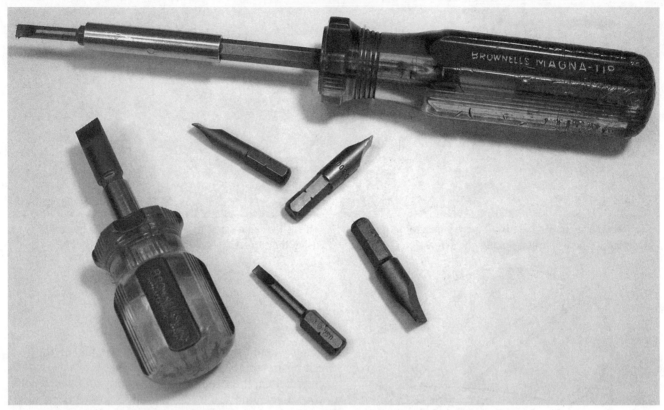

Brownells excellent Magna-Tip screwdrivers use replaceable blades that come is a wide variety of sizes.

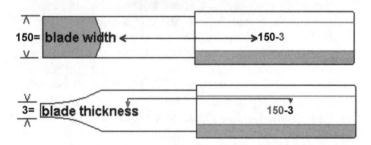

Here is what the size numbers denote on Magna-Tip driver blades.

for width. We want the fit just tight enough so that we have to tap it just once, very lightly, with a hammer to make it drop all the way down into the bottom of the slot. If your screwdriver blade fits all the above criteria, you have the perfect fitting screwdriver.

Screwdrivers themselves are probably the single most important tool in your kit. We won't be messing around those fancy colored screwdrivers you can buy at the local hardware store. They may be "pretty" tools, but they do not work in gun screws because their blades are tapered to allow them to fit into a wide variety of different generic screw slot sizes. The truth is they probably never fit into any screw slot very well. As we mentioned, old gun screws have precision ground slots that are square-sided, and to turn them without damage you have to use screwdrivers that are made specifically to fit into this kind of screw slot.

Old gun screws also came in different sizes and they used various width and breadth driver slots. Choosing the correct size hollow-ground screwdriver that perfectly fits the slot of the screw you want to loosen is the first concern during firearms disassembly and assembly. Fitting perfectly means just that, not a little bit too small or too big. Many years ago gunsmiths had to make up all their screwdrivers on a custom, as-needed basis, but in more recent decades they took to altering store-bought screwdrivers to suit a particular gun screw. By the late 1940s, special hollow-ground gun screwdrivers like the ones we are familiar with became commercially available. The hard part about old guns is that gun screws come in a huge array of sizes with a great variety of different length and width of screw slots. Until fairly recently any well equipped gunsmith who had been in business for a few years could accumulate hundreds of different screwdrivers,

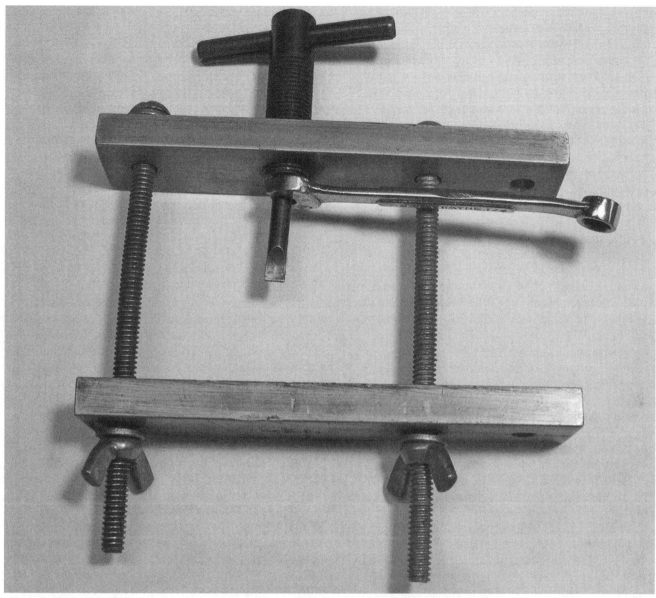

Made by B-Square, this screw jack is a great tool for removing some really stuck gun screws.

every one of them in different custom sizes and shapes. Often the smith owned so many screwdrivers they occupied several drawers of his tool chest.

Today we have access to a neater, more accurate and compact alternative to all of these different size screwdrivers. This is a unique screwdriver set intended for the professional or the amateur gunsmith and sold by Brownell's, Inc. under their trade name "Magna-Tip." The Magna-Tip system is basically one screwdriver handle assembly (several handle sizes and types are available) equipped with a 1/4-inch hex drive that allows the one handle to accept a large variety of factory-made, quickly replaceable, accessory screw driver-bit tips of various thicknesses, widths and breadths. Magna-Tip bits are hollow-ground and sized to fit many of the more common and some uncommon gun screws. I have found that a set like this is exactly what you want for this kind of work. The replaceable

bits allow you to cover just about any screw slot that you might come in contact with. With the larger sets, you have the capability to drive more than a hundred different size screws. The bits are stored in a space that would be covered by the span of a hand.

If you prefer them, there are also several brands of good quality, conventional looking screwdrivers on the market that are made for gunsmith use and have hollow-ground blades. Whichever method you chose, if you are serious about taking old guns apart and you want to do it the right way, then by all means, invest in good screwdrivers

Believe it or not, there is a right way to hold a screwdriver. What? Heck, everyone knows how to hold a screwdriver! Yep, sure they do and that's exactly why we see so many nice old guns with buggered up screw slots. Think about it: straight or conventional screw slots really don't offer the screw turner (you) a lot of options. Look at the shape of the slot: it's basically a shallow, rectangular trench with square sides. The "rules" for screw turning are very simple, but very important. First of all, you are going to be bearing down hard and turning, so be sure to support your work (the gun) so it cannot slide, tip or move. Stand over the screw slot and face it, looking straight down. The screwdriver has to be held straight down, right into the screw slot in alignment with the screw, not tipped or angled even a little, but straight down.

If you tilt or angle the driver blade while you are trying to turn it, you are decreasing, sometimes drastically, the amount of surface area the blade has to bear on in the screw slot. Then, if you aren't pushing straight down, when you turn the driver the blade will probably slip up and out of the slot, tearing up the slot and the surrounding area up in the process. Make it a conscious habit to push the driver down with even more force than you will use to turn the driver and maintain that downward force as you turn, never letting up.

For screws that have been in there for a long time, the application of heat and light penetrating oil can be the ingredients used in our next steps. Should the screw we have to remove be located in an area where there is organic material such as wood or rubber (the stock or grip areas), using heat may be out of the question lest we damage the stock. Small amounts of heat may be applied without damaging either of those materials by using a hair dryer set on a medium to high setting, using care not to heat the area any hotter than you can comfortably touch. Once you have the area around the screw head warmed up, try applying small amounts of a good penetrating oil, let it sit a few minutes and then re-heat the area. It's often a good idea to repeat this several times before attempting to use the screwdriver.

In those instances when there is nothing nearby that the heat will damage, we can make the area hotter, an effective method of loosening a stuck gun screw. Where it is safe to, we can use a propane torch to heat the screw head and the area around it, and sometimes when you can reach it, the threaded area can be heated as well. Don't use so much heat you damage the metal finishes; try to keep the temperature of the metal around 250 to 300 degrees Fahrenheit. That's the point where a drop of water will just "spatter and spit." We will do no damage or harm to metal finishes at these temperature levels, whether blue or plating, but we might if we go any hotter. Once the metal is heated to the desired point, remove the flame and quickly apply a small amount of penetrating oil, wait a few moments, then re-heat the area as before. As the metal re-heats, you may see bubbles popping up around the screw head or threads. This is an indication that the oil is seeping around the screw and that's a good thing. Repeat the process several times before you attempt to loosen the screw.

For really tightly stuck screws that may be in places

where you have a flat area surrounding both ends of the screw, consider using a tool called a screw-jack. The screw-jack, when you are able to use it, gives the you the ability to apply the maximum amount of turning force, but more importantly, it does this along with the most possible downward force, holding the driver in the slot as well as supplying great side to side stability for the driver blade. B-Square makes a screw jack that works very well, or you may make one yourself. The tool is useful for removing some extremely stubborn screws but they should still have a slot that is in at least decent condition. Screw-jacks cannot be used everywhere – the contours of some firearms prevent it. Made like a clamp, the tool is made up of two pieces of heavy aluminum or steel plate held with machine screws and nuts at either end. One of the plates has an adjustable device at its center to fit Brownell's Magna-Tip bits.

In use, the screw-jack is clamped around the firearm with its center, which contains the Magna-Tip screwdriver blade, over the top of the frozen screw. It is then tightened in place. Once tight, the adjustment at the blade is tightened enough to hold the blade down firmly into the screw slot. A quarter-inch, open-ended wrench can then be used to turn the Magna-Tip bit, and hopefully the great amount of torque provided by the wrench, along with the fact that the bit is clamped tightly and straight into the screw slot, will either cause the screw to turn or the bit will break. If the screw stays stuck, you might rip the head out of the screw – the tool gives you that much torque potential. The screw-jack has so much torque that it is not a tool that should be used lightly or before you have done some of the screw removal prep-work as mentioned above. The screw jack is used to break the screw loose initially; once the screw has broken loose, it is then unscrewed with the bit in the normal way.

To repeat: When you make the first attempt to loosen the screw, be sure the driver blade fills the screw slot. Always hold the screwdriver down straight into the screw with even more force than you will use to try and turn it. It is much more important that your driver blade stays securely inside of that screw slot than it is for the screw to turn! Should the bit slip up out of the screw slot, it will probably tear out the slot, and then you are all done here. If the screw absolutely refuses to budge: Just stop! Making further attempts to turn it will probably only bring frustration. Face the fact that the screw simply is not ready to turn yet. Once again, try the heat and oil process as outlined above, this time trying Chrysler Heat Riser Valve Penetrant or Corrosion X in place of whatever penetrating oil you were using before. You have to be patient with this. It may take several more attempts before you get that penetrating oil into the threads and up under the screw head enough for it finally to let go. However much time this takes, whenever you start to get mad, think about how much less time this is taking than the amount of

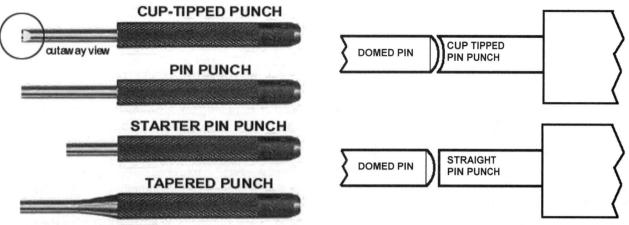

CUP-TIPPED PUNCH

cutaway view

PIN PUNCH

STARTER PIN PUNCH

TAPERED PUNCH

DOMED PIN | CUP TIPPED PIN PUNCH

DOMED PIN | STRAIGHT PIN PUNCH

A few common gunsmith punches.

In this drawing you can readily see how the cup-tipped punch would be the ideal tool for removing domed gun pins.

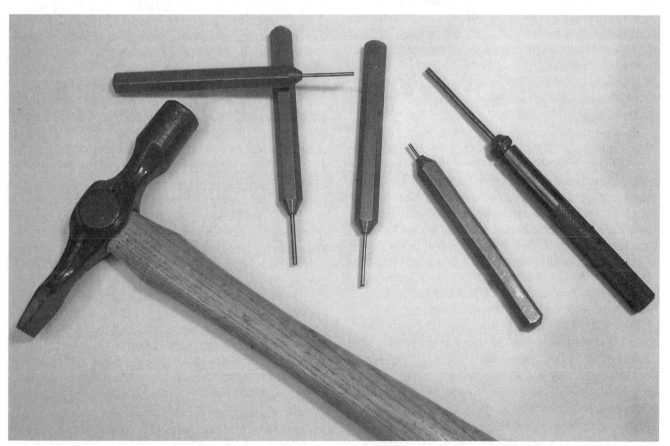

Shown with a Brownells cross-pane hammer are a few cup-tipped punches and a replaceable tip pin punch (right.)

time you might have to spend if you were trying to drill out that same screw after you tore its slot up.

Okay, the screw head is badly messed-up already and it won't hold any driver. What do you do now? It's time to visit your friendly gunsmith. A gunsmith will have several ways to get frozen and broken screws out, most of which are beyond the capabilities of the amateur smith. His last resort, which requires sophisticated tooling, would be drilling or milling the old screw out.

Pins and punches

Let's have a look at pins and the punches that are used to move them. Most guns make use of cross-pins to hold parts together. Many times pins act as a pivot-point or an axle of some kind. To remove and install pins we cause them to move in and out by indirect impact, that is, with punches that are driven by hammer blows. Moving pins this way is called driving or drifting.

Most old gun pins were straight sided, not tapered, and they can be driven out in either direction. A few old guns did use tapered pins and almost all of these kinds of pins would normally be driven out from left to right (looking down the barrel from the rear.) Some modern guns use pins that have one slightly enlarged end with striations (small teeth) in it that dig into the metal of the firearm as the pin is bottomed out. This locks the pin in place. Whether the pins are tapered, striated or straight, it is a safe practice for the gunsmith to learn to drive all pins from left to right, unless of course you are absolutely certain that the pin is not tapered. To drive a gun pin out of a hole from one side to another you need a kind of punch called a pin-punch. Pin-punches are punches with straight sides, and you will regularly use them instead of tapered punches to drive pins out of holes because the tapered punch would stick in the hole. All pin punches are sized from the manufacturer so their diameters are just slightly smaller than the pins which they are intended to drive. For example, a pin punch intended to drive a 1/8-inch pin would actually be a tad smaller in diameter than 1/8 inch, allowing it to slip all the way through the pin hole without binding.

Some gun pins are very tightly in place, either from a much-too-tight factory fit or the result of years of rust or dried up, hardened oil. Those tight pins will require yet another type of punch called a starter pin punch, a conventional pin punch made with an extra-short shank so it is less likely to bend or break than a normal-length pin punch. This is used only to get the stubborn pin moving. Persuading stuck pins to start moving can be a tricky job if the pin is really stuck, because both the punch and the pin will have to be hit much harder to make the pin start moving. This increases the likelihood of slipping off the pin, of breaking a punch, and of scratching or marring the surrounding finish of the gun.

We have talked about straight-sided pin punches of different lengths, for various functions. These kinds of pin punches have been commonly available in solid form; in other words the punch is made from one piece of steel. Brownells Inc. also sells replaceable-tip pin punches. These have a two-piece handle with replaceable, hardened steel pins.

For the very few pins that are extremely stubborn, a tapered starter punch may be the tool of choice. As its name implies, the punch is tapered, not straight-sided, and made short and stubby to give it much more rigidity. Because of their tapered shape, these are useful only to get a stubborn pin moving initially; after that a starter pin punch or a conventional pin punch would be used to finish driving the pin. Tapered starter punches come in several sizes, and you will want select a punch with a head that is slightly smaller than the head of the pin you want to drive so that as the pin begins to move, the head of the starter punch will fit

down into the pin hole just slightly without damaging either the hole or the surrounding metal.

You have probably noticed that many of the pins in older guns with exposed heads are rounded on their ends. Gun manufacturers and gunsmiths call this a domed head, and this matches most older gun screws, which also had a domed shape. In order to correctly remove these domed headed pins without damage, we should be using cup-tipped punches. These punches are made to perfectly fit the corresponding sizes of domed pin heads. If you use a conventional flat-tipped pin punch to remove the domed pins, the flat tip would flatten out and ruin those nice rounded domes, which would defeat our purpose and detract from the overall appearance of the firearm. This is especially true with tight fitting domed pins, where it would be too easy to flatten and mushroom the pin's head by using a flat pin punch. When that happens, once the domed pin head has been beaten into a mushroom shape, it enlarges and tears up the edges of the pin hole. As you can see, it is important to keep the shape of the pin head intact as it is being driven. Cup-tipped pin punches to suit this need are also available from Brownells, Inc. They are a bit expensive as far as punches go, but they are a worthwhile investment. Personally, I consider a set of these punches a mandatory part of my disassembly-assembly kit to work on nineteenth-century firearms.

On the other side of the job, starting a small pin back into its hole during reassembly is a difficult chore that can be made much easier by using another specialized punch known as a magnetic starter punch. These starter punches are hollow and they have been magnetized. There is a blind hole at the front-center of the punch, made just deep enough to hold enough of the pin so that it remains straight and stable while you are starting the pin in the hole. Starter punches allow you to "set" the pin into the hole slightly by giving the punch a couple of light taps with a small hammer. The same pin is then driven into the hole with the cup-tipped pin punch if the pin is domed, or a flat tipped pin punch if it is not.

When you have to install sub-assemblies back into a firearm that have one or more separate parts or springs attached with them, you sometimes have to use a kind of assembly pin known as a "dummy" or "slave" pin. The slave pin is made so that it is the same diameter but shorter than the normal cross pin, so it won't extend all the way through the gun. The only function of the slave pin is to hold all the small parts of the sub-assembly in order while the sub-assembly is being held in alignment with the pin holes in the gun for reassembly. The regular pin is then driven into the gun through the holes and as it passes through the sub-assembly, the cross pin replaces the slave pin, which it drives out the other side of the hole. A good example of when a slave pin is used is to reassemble the trigger guard to the receiver on the 1897 Winchester.

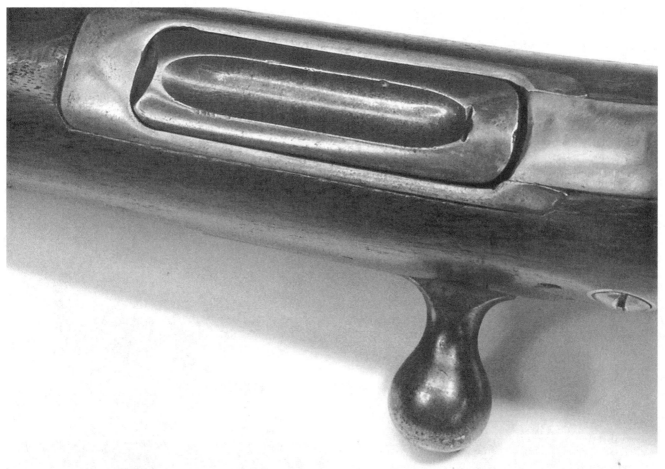

This photo shows the triggerguard area of a Remington-Keene carbine. This is an area where wood to metal fit is critical, so be very careful when accomplishing this segment of the disassembly process.

Punches that aren't used to drive pins.

Alignment punches are another specialized item. They appear to be long, mildly tapered punches. Actually, they are not used as punches at all. Alignment punches are tools that are used when one or more loose parts held by the same screw or pin within a hole need to be aligned before pin or screw can be inserted.

When you need to move sights from side to side or in and out of a dovetail in a gun barrel, you need a punch that won't scratch or mar the ends of the sight while it is being driven. Special purpose punches for this delicate sight work are available in brass, aluminum and plastic and are called soft punches, intended for just this purpose. They come in round, square and rectangular shapes.

Wood and metal

Taking the wood off a gun or perhaps we should say, removing the metal from the wood, especially on older arms, requires special care and attention to detail. There are so many different kinds of wood-to-metal fits on rifles and shotguns as well as handgun grips that it would be virtually impossible to cover them all. We can however come up with some general rules of thumb and following them can prevent you from possibly damaging or breaking an old gunstock or grip made from wood or hard rubber.

Handgun grips first. The one-piece kind such as used on Colts are pretty straightforward: remove the three backstrap screws and lift off the backstrap with the grip. Most take-down instructions say you can then separate the grip from the backstrap. But what happens when the grip seems to be stuck on the backstrap? Look over all the edges very well; sometimes rust has bonded the wood to the metal. You may see indications of this in places where the wood seems "proud" or higher than the metal. Try giving all the seams a soaking with Break-Free spray and letting them sit overnight. In the morning warm the whole

The Colt 1860 Army one piece grip shown with the backstrap still installed. Notice how tightly fitted those seams are? Proceed gently.

Here the single-edged industrial blade has been carefully slipped in between the grip frame and the wood grip.

thing up with a hair dryer and within a short time the grip will usually come free of the metal.

Two-piece grips were often fitted very tightly by the factory, a tightness that will generally increase with age. Old-school thought was that you loosened the grip screw and then pounded it back in to drive the opposite side grip off. That may work fine for a while, that is until you run into a really tight grip and end up driving out the escutcheon nut (the metal piece in the grip that the screw threads into) which in turn can rip a chunk of wood or a chip of hard rubber out with it! Now you have a damaged grip that is still stuck in place.

I use a couple of time-tried methods to remove tight two-piece grips, either wood or hard rubber. The first is after removing the screw, I use the very edge of a single edge industrial razor blade to locate a tiny seam or gap somewhere around the butt of the gun. I try to very carefully slip the razor blade in between the wood and metal. Once a substantial portion of the blade is in, very slowly and gently I try to rock the blade in order to lever-up the grip from the grip frame. When I have the grip up about 1/16-inch, I remove the blade and use the end of a stainless rule in the same

manner until the grip is up high enough to pull off with my fingers. Now, I reach through the open grip frame and hold a three-inch long piece of 3/8-inch hardwood dowel against the inside of the other grip near the bottom where the locating pin is, and carefully tap the dowel to remove that grip.

The other method is to remove the grip screw and spray some Break-Free through the grip screw hole. Slosh it around so the Break-Free gets around all the seams and let it sit a few hours. Now heat the area up with a hair dryer and insert a long skinny punch back through the grip screw hole. Cant the punch on a slight angle as you do this so it comes into contact with the back side of the other grip. Gently tap the punch. The idea is to cause the other side grip to start to separate from the grip frame. Don't hit hard, especially if the grips are hard rubber. If the grip(s) won't budge with either method, then you have done about all you can and should take the project to a pro.

With old long-gun stocks, especially old military rifles and ones from the big factories like Winchester and Remington, the stocks will be very tightly fitted to the metal. Being organic, over long periods of time the wood swells up with moisture to the point where it

If you look hard enough you can usually find the tiniest of seams between the wood and metal where a thin razor blade can be inserted without harm to either.

An alternate method of getting tight fitting grips off. Be sure you use great caution when tapping the punch, especially with hard rubber grips, which are frequently brittle.

actually "puckers" up proud. It becomes higher than the surrounding surface and sometimes slightly wraps itself around the metal. At the same time, rust caused by this moisture literally glues the wood to the steel. To say the least, removing the metal from the wood in such areas is a very delicate job. Indeed, areas with 100% inletting like that around some old military sling swivel bases and some lock-plates can present a true challenge, so much so that on a few occasions I have left such areas completely alone, knowing I might just do more harm than good if I persisted.

Think about the job in front of you before you jump in with both feet. When disassembling antique guns where the wood and metal have been married for 75 years or more, we must use extra care as we remove the wood from the metal. Having said that, move at extra slow speed and in your lowest gear, paying attention to every detail. Rushing will only get you into trouble. One idea that has helped is to spray tight fitting areas such as the tangs and lock-plate areas with WD-40 or Break Free. Do this after you loosen the screws and a few hours before attempting to actually remove the wood. When some time has passed, heat the affected areas up, so they are hot to

the touch, using a hair dryer. Then, proceeding ever so gently, begin to move the stock while applying only a light pulling tension in the direction of removal. The idea is that the otherwise harmless solvent will get down in the seams and loosen up some of the rust and hardened crud that is bonding the two materials together.

When trying to loosen a tight butt-stock on a gun with a two-piece stock, after loosening the screws, it sometimes helps to lay a round piece of hardwood (like the side of a baseball bat), on the buttplate and strike the hardwood a light blow toward the front with a mallet. This to simulate the recoil of firing. The small shock will not split or damage the wood but it may help to break the wood free of its bond with the steel.

Sometimes, but always with great caution, you may be able to insert a craft-knife blade in around the seams of wood-to-metal fit while you are beginning to loosen the wood. If you try this, please do it very gingerly, thoughtfully and carefully, cutting away only rust or dried up grease and oils that may be bonding the metal to the wood, being mindful not to cut into the wood itself. If you see an area of wood start to splinter off or lift up as the metal moves away, stop right there

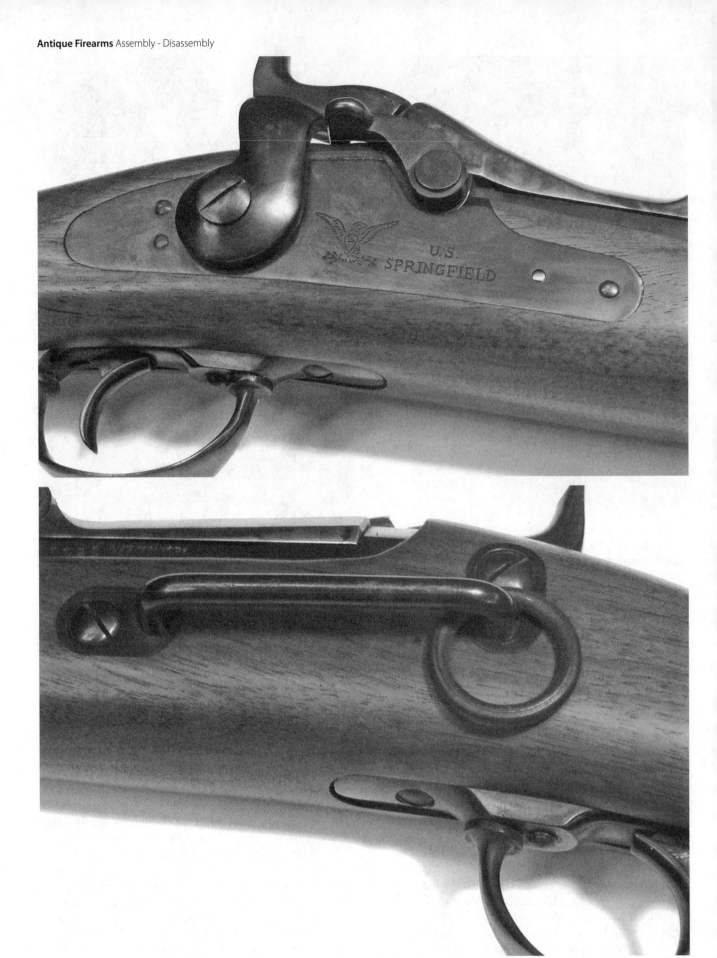

These two photos show opposite sides of a replica trapdoor Springfield and areas that are always a concern during disassembly. Yes, even modern replicas may have very tight wood to metal seams and if you are not careful they can splinter out.

When wood surrounds 100% of the steel, such as on this nineteenth-century sling plate, extra caution is urged. This particular one doesn't look too bad but sometimes, when the wood has been extremely moist and badly puckered up around the metal, it may be best to leave the part right where it is.

These special tools are nipple wrenches used for removing the nipples from various percussion weapons. Tools courtesy of Dixie Gun Works.

and survey the situation. These little flaps or splinters are occurring because the wood has swelled around the metal and to some degree the metal has rusted to the wood, as we mentioned before. Slivers like this can be cleaned up and glued back down as long as you are very careful to notice exactly where they came from and that you do this right away. If you fix it while the break is fresh the chances are excellent that you can make an invisible repair.

Dummies

Sometimes it is necessary to use cartridges to check one form of function or another. To avoid the obvious dangers involved, you should make it an absolute law that you never allow live ammunition on your workbench. What you can use on the bench for testing and trying are dummy cartridges. Dummies – that is, high quality inert cartridges –are available from Brownells. They come in many popular calibers for rifle, handgun and shotgun. I think every gunsmith, tinkerer, gun owner who displays his firearms ought to have a good supply on of dummies on hand. Dummies ought to be the only cartridges that are ever kept near your firearms unless you are shooting them. They are the only safe way to use cartridges to determine how a gun is feeding or ejecting, how a revolver cylinder is indexing and for many other uses around the shop.

Last but not least, when working on old or antique firearms, we are dealing with pieces of history. Always go slow and be deliberate, and above all don't be afraid to stop before you get in over your head. If you find that happening, take the gun to a professional. When it comes to disassembling old guns, gunsmiths have a thousand and one tricks up their sleeves. After all, it's what they do for a living.

SECTION II
HANDGUNS

Colt Paterson
Percussion Revolvers & Their Replicas

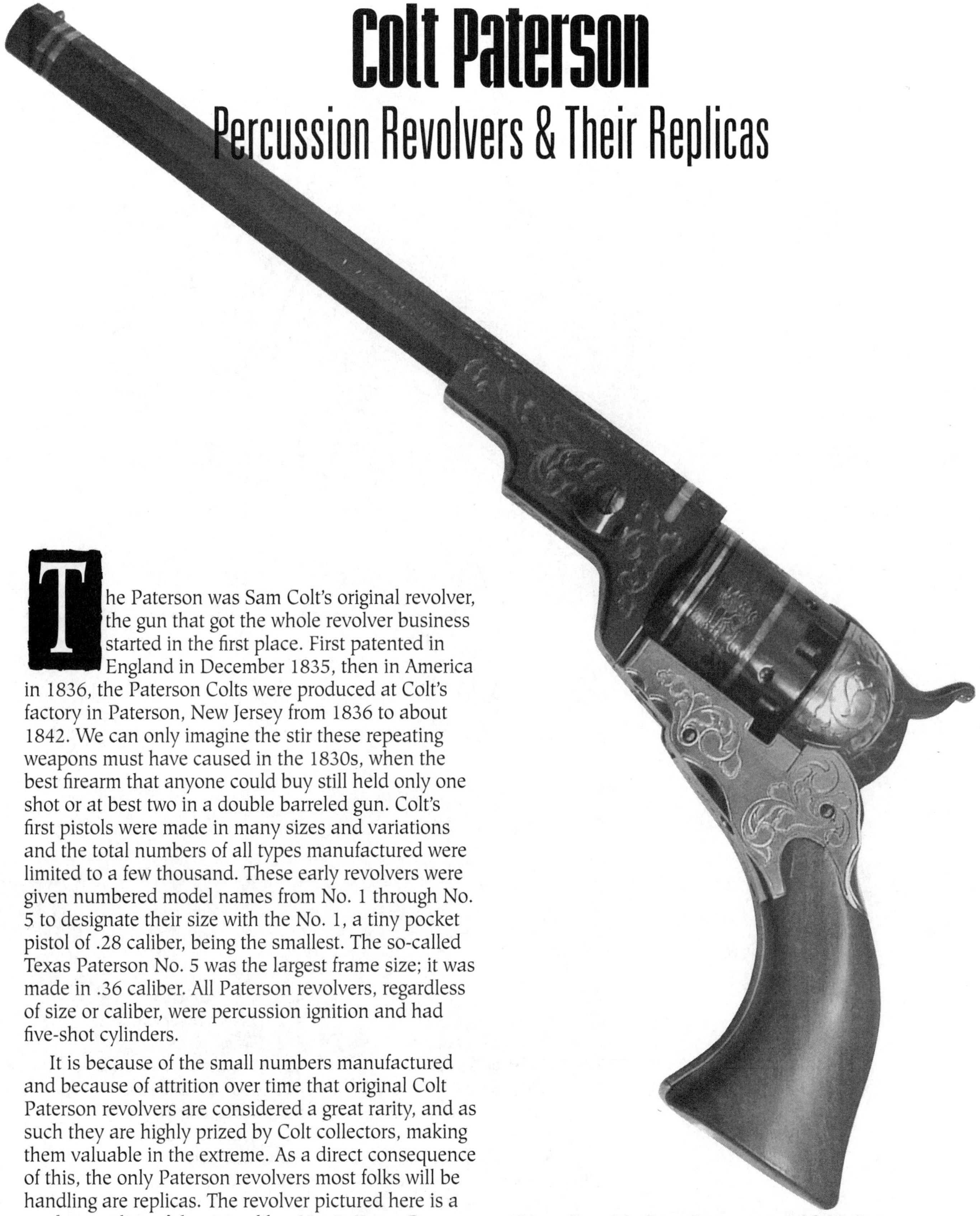

T he Paterson was Sam Colt's original revolver, the gun that got the whole revolver business started in the first place. First patented in England in December 1835, then in America in 1836, the Paterson Colts were produced at Colt's factory in Paterson, New Jersey from 1836 to about 1842. We can only imagine the stir these repeating weapons must have caused in the 1830s, when the best firearm that anyone could buy still held only one shot or at best two in a double barreled gun. Colt's first pistols were made in many sizes and variations and the total numbers of all types manufactured were limited to a few thousand. These early revolvers were given numbered model names from No. 1 through No. 5 to designate their size with the No. 1, a tiny pocket pistol of .28 caliber, being the smallest. The so-called Texas Paterson No. 5 was the largest frame size; it was made in .36 caliber. All Paterson revolvers, regardless of size or caliber, were percussion ignition and had five-shot cylinders.

It is because of the small numbers manufactured and because of attrition over time that original Colt Paterson revolvers are considered a great rarity, and as such they are highly prized by Colt collectors, making them valuable in the extreme. As a direct consequence of this, the only Paterson revolvers most folks will be handling are replicas. The revolver pictured here is a modern replica of the .36-caliber No. 5, Texas Paterson manufactured in Italy by Pietta. It has a nine-inch barrel and is made without a loading lever.

This replica of the Texas Paterson, one of Colt's first revolvers, is made in Italy by Pietta. Revolver courtesy of EMF. Author photo.

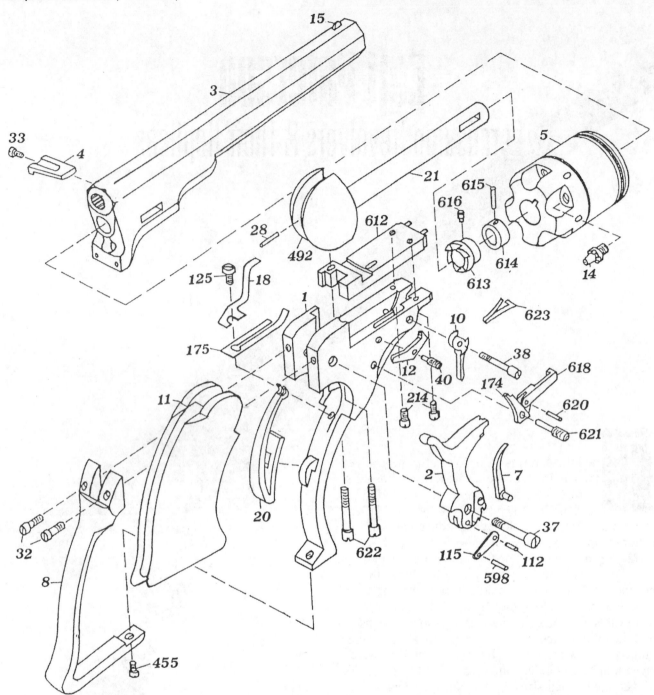

Parts List, Uberti nomenclature

1	Frame	20	Mainspring	455	Connect Screw
2	Hammer	21	Base Pin	492	Breech Assembly
3	Barrel	28	Cylinder Pin Lock Pin	612	Frame plate
4	Wedge	32	Backstrap Screw	613	Toothed Rack (Ratchet)
5	Cylinder	33	Wedge Screw	614	Toothed Rack Link
7	Hand	37	Hammer Screw	615	Toothed Rack Link Pin
8	Backstrap	38	Screw	616	Toothed Rack Latch
10	Trigger	112	Stirrup Plug (Pin)	618	Sear Lever
11	Grip	115	Stirrup	620	Sear Pin
12	Bolt	125	Hand and Sear Spring Screw	621	Sear Screw
14	Nipple	174	Sear	622	Breech Screw
15	Front Sight	175	Sear Spring	623	Trigger Spring
18	Hand Spring	214	Frame Plate Screw		

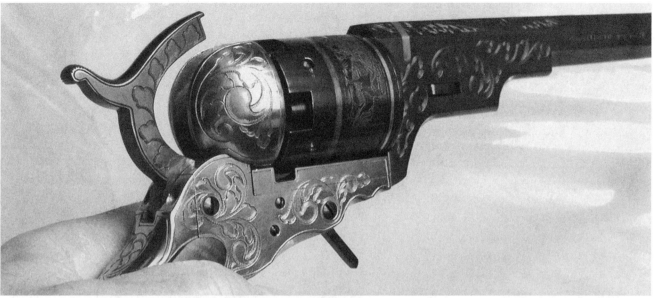

With any percussion revolver, always look at the nipples to be sure there are no percussion caps on them. Without caps the revolver can't be fired.

The Paterson barrel and cylinder are removed in the same manner used as any later Colt percussion revolver: by removing the wedge.

DISASSEMBLY INSTRUCTIONS

Uberti Paterson parts nomenclature is used within the text.

1 Before starting, be absolutely sure this revolver is unloaded. Grasp the revolver firmly around its grip, being careful to always keep your fingers away from the trigger (#10). Be sure to point and hold the muzzle in a safe direction, facing away from any person, pet, vehicle or dwelling. Pull the hammer (#2) back one audible click to the loading position and check to be certain that the revolver's cylinder (#5) is unloaded before attempting any disassembly or before handling the revolver. Perform this check by carefully examining the rear of the cylinder at each chamber to be certain that there are no percussion caps on any of the nipples (#14). Also, you should

always look at the front of the cylinder to make sure that there are no charges in the cylinder chambers (a good indication that a chamber is most likely loaded would be bullets or balls showing at the front end of the chamber). If percussion caps are present on the nipples, you should consider this a loaded firearm; do not attempt any further disassembly. A loaded cylinder may be emptied by taking the gun to a range and firing it until it is empty or the cylinder itself may be carefully removed without firing the revolver in order to render the revolver safe for further operations by following the instructions in 2) below.

2 To remove the barrel and cylinder: The barrel (#3) may be separated from the frame (#1) by pushing the wedge (#4) out toward the left side of

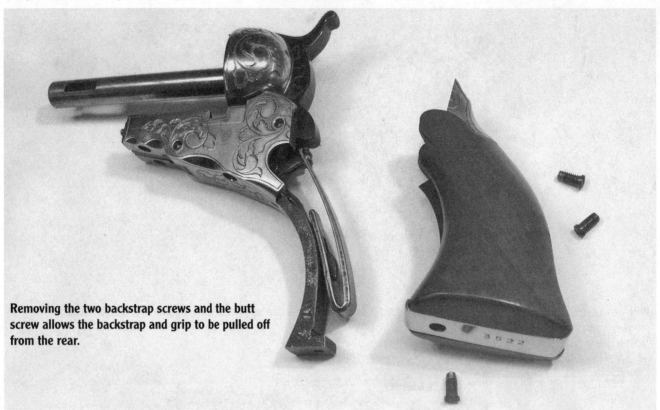

Removing the two backstrap screws and the butt screw allows the backstrap and grip to be pulled off from the rear.

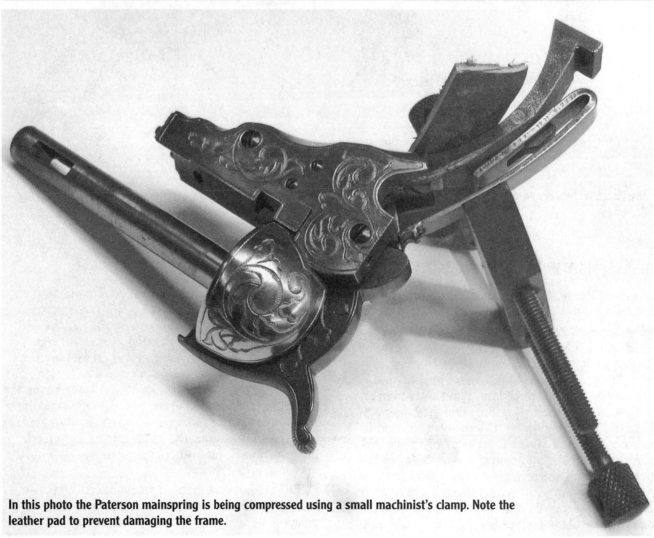

In this photo the Paterson mainspring is being compressed using a small machinist's clamp. Note the leather pad to prevent damaging the frame.

Just two screws hold the breech assembly onto the frame.

the barrel as far as it will move. If the wedge is so tight that it will not move by hand pressure, you may have to use a small nylon drift punch (nylon is used in order to lessen the chance of damaging either the wedge or the surrounding metal) with a small hammer to break the wedge free. The hammer should still be in the loading position so that the cylinder will spin freely. If the revolver is equipped with a loading lever (not shown), turn the cylinder so that the rammer pin (not shown) will contact the cylinder in between two chambers, then operate the rammer so that the barrel loosens and moves forward from the frame forward slightly. The barrel may now be removed from the frame by pulling it straight forward. The cylinder assembly is likewise removed from the frame by pulling it straight forward off the base pin (#21), which Colt called the "arbor."

3 To disassemble the barrel and cylinder: The wedge (#4) may be removed from the barrel by first removing the wedge screw (#33) from the left side of the barrel and then withdrawing the wedge. If so equipped, the loading lever may be removed from the barrel by first removing the loading lever screw. The only disassembly that will be possible on the cylinder would be the removal of the percussion nipples (#14) and this step should be accomplished with a special tool called a nipple wrench. Percussion nipples are screwed in with right-hand threads, which means that they unscrew in a counter-clockwise direction. Original Colt and other vintage percussion revolvers may have nipples that are hand fitted to each specific chamber and care should always be taken that these are re-installed in exactly the chamber they were removed from.

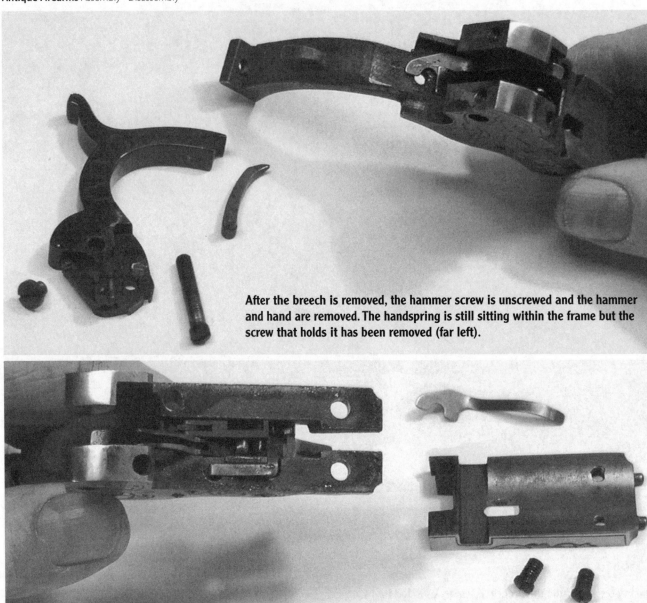

After the breech is removed, the hammer screw is unscrewed and the hammer and hand are removed. The handspring is still sitting within the frame but the screw that holds it has been removed (far left).

The frame plate has been removed; notice the trigger spring is still sitting in the frame, just behind the lower frame plate hole. The leaf spring above the frame is the hand spring, which fits in from the rear (left).

4 To remove the grip, grip strap and mainspring: Pull the hammer (#2) all the way to the rear and hold it with your thumb. Pull the trigger (#10) and allow the hammer to ease all the way forward, slowing its motion with your thumb. Unscrew and remove the two backstrap screws (#32) from the top-rear of the backstrap (#8) and remove the single connect screw (#455) from the butt of the backstrap. The backstrap and the one-piece grip (#11) may be removed by carefully pulling them down and to the rear as a unit. Once off the frame, the grip itself may be pulled down slightly at the top to separate it slightly from the backstrap and then straight forward off the backstrap. The mainspring (#20) must be detached from the stirrup (#115) before it can be removed from the

mainspring seat on the frame. This is done by pressing down on the upper portion of the mainspring using both thumbs. In some cases the spring may be so stiff that a small machinist's clamp is necessary; notice the frame is padded with a leather strip in the illustration. Once the mainspring is compressed enough, the stirrup is pivoted forward and the spring released. Now the spring can be slid down far enough to be unhooked from the mainspring seat and taken off.

5 To disassemble the action: Carefully note the positioning of all parts for reassembly. Unscrew and remove the two breech screws (#622). One breech screw runs straight up from the bottom of the frame just behind and to the left of the trigger; the other runs up at an angle and it may be accessed inside the right

· 28 ·

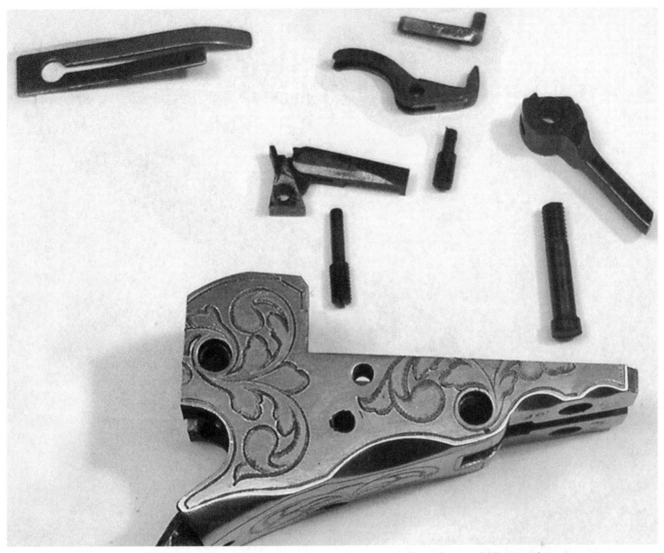

Once the frame plate is off, the remainder of the action parts can be removed. Here they are laid out as they were disassembled with the frame.

hand grip circle at the lower rear of the frame. The breech assembly (#492) with the base pin attached may be removed by pulling it straight up off the frame. Further disassembly of the breech is not recommended unless performed by a skilled gunsmith. Loosen the hand and sear spring screw (#125) located just behind and below the hammer facing up. Unscrew and remove the hammer screw (#37) and lift the hammer straight up out the top of the frame. The hand (#7) will come with it. The handspring (#18) may now be slid to the side and lifted up out of the frame opening.

6 To disassemble the bolt and trigger: Unscrew and remove the two frame plate screws (#214) from the bottom-front of the frame, at the same time keeping downward pressure on the frame plate (#612). After the screws are out, turn the frame right side up. The frame plate is now lifted straight up off the frame, exposing the bolt and trigger mechanisms. The trigger spring (#623) is loose and may be lifted up and out of

its seat with the frame; pay attention to its position for reassembly. Loosen the bolt screw (#40), the tiny screw nearest the top of the frame. The bolt (#12) may now lifted straight up out of the frame opening. The rear and lowest of the two tiny screws in the right side of the frame is the sear screw (#621), which may now be loosened several turns. The sear/trigger bar assembly (#618 & #174) may now be lifted out of the top of the frame. Unscrew and remove the trigger screw (#38), which is the forward-most screw in the right side of the frame. The trigger (#10) may be lifted out of and removed from the frame. Unscrew and remove the hand and sear spring screw and lift the hand and sear spring (#19) out of the frame.

REASSEMBLY

Reassemble the revolver in reverse order.

Colt Walker

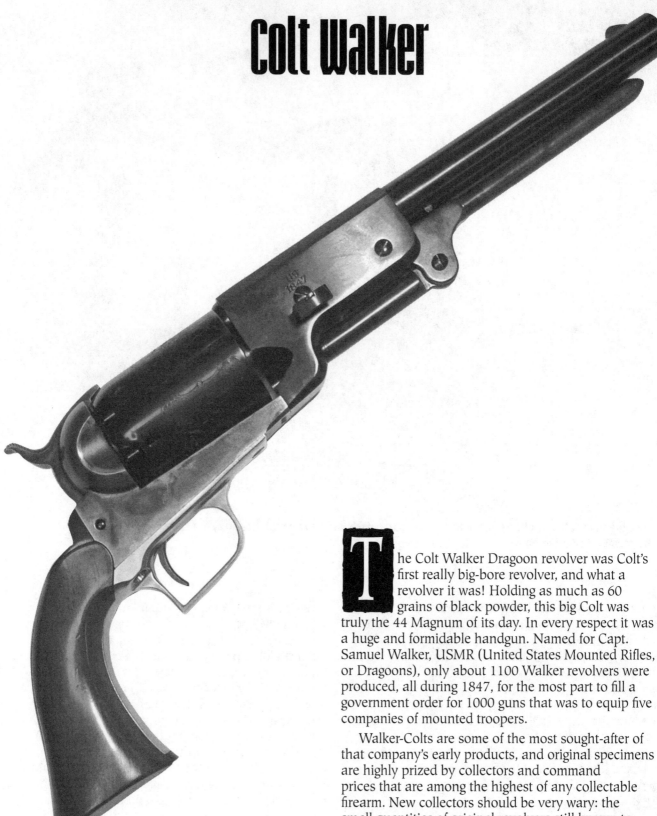

The Colt Walker was a truly massive handgun. This is a beautifully made replica by A. Uberti in Italy. Revolver courtesy Stoeger Industries. Author photos.

The Colt Walker Dragoon revolver was Colt's first really big-bore revolver, and what a revolver it was! Holding as much as 60 grains of black powder, this big Colt was truly the 44 Magnum of its day. In every respect it was a huge and formidable handgun. Named for Capt. Samuel Walker, USMR (United States Mounted Rifles, or Dragoons), only about 1100 Walker revolvers were produced, all during 1847, for the most part to fill a government order for 1000 guns that was to equip five companies of mounted troopers.

Walker-Colts are some of the most sought-after of that company's early products, and original specimens are highly prized by collectors and command prices that are among the highest of any collectable firearm. New collectors should be very wary: the small quantities of original revolvers still known to exist, coupled with the fact that they have held very high values for many years, have tempted some unscrupulous souls to create faked Walkers. Some of these fakes are very good, making them difficult even for an expert to tell apart from an original.

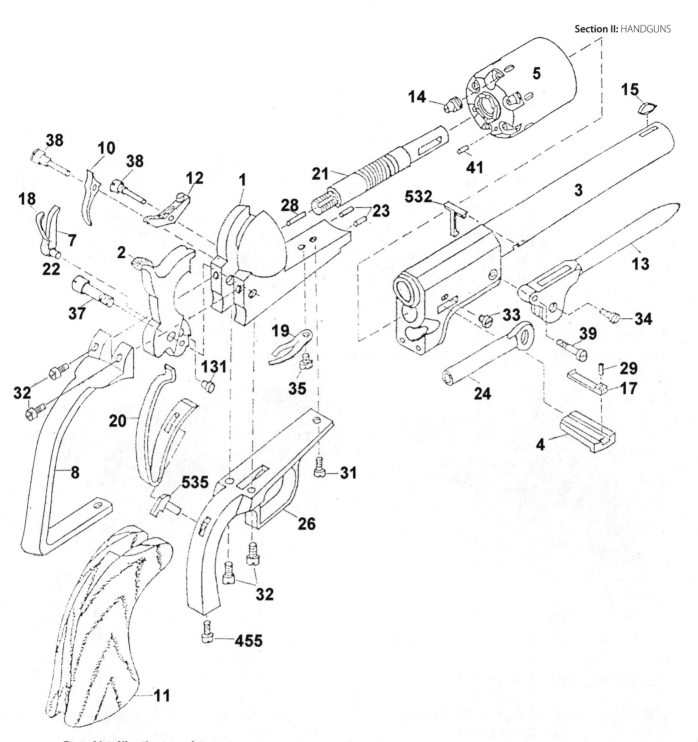

Parts List, Uberti nomenclature

1	Frame	17	Wedge Spring	34	Plunger Screw
2	Hammer	18	Hand Spring	35	Trigger-bolt Spring Screw
3	Barrel	19	Trigger-bolt Spring	37	Hammer Screw
4	Wedge	20	Mainspring	38	Trigger-bolt Screw
5	Cylinder	21	Base pin	39	Loading Lever Screw
7	Hand Assembly	22	Hand Spring Pin	41	Cylinder Pin
8	Backstrap	23	Barrel Pin	131	Hammer Latch
10	Trigger	24	Plunger	455	Connect. Screw
11	Grip	26	Triggerguard	532	Loading Lever Latch
12	Bolt	28	Cylinder Lock Pin	535	Mainspring Latch
13	Loading Lever	29	Wedge Pin		
14	Nipple	31	Front Triggerguard Screw		
15	Sight	32	Rear Backstrap Screw		
16	Cylinder Lock Pin	33	Wedge Screw		

Place the hammer at the loading position (the first click) and spin the cylinder to make certain there are no percussion caps on the nipples.

The Walker with its barrel and cylinder removed.

DISASSEMBLY INSTRUCTIONS

1 Begin by making absolutely sure the revolver is not loaded. Hold the revolver firmly by its grip (#11), while consciously keeping your fingers away from the trigger (#10). Point and hold the muzzle in a safe direction, away from any person, pet, vehicle or dwelling. Now place the hammer (#2) in the loading position by pulling it to the rear until one audible click is heard. Now check to be certain that the revolver's cylinder (#5) is unloaded before attempting any disassembly or before handling the revolver. This check is performed by carefully examining the rear of the cylinder at each chamber to be certain that there are no percussion caps on any of the nipples (#14). If percussion caps are present on the nipples then you should consider this a loaded firearm. Do not attempt any further disassembly. Also, you should always look at the front of the cylinder to make sure that there are

no charges in the cylinder chambers (a good indication that a chamber may be loaded would be if bullets or balls show at the front end of the chamber). Never look directly into the barrel or chambers; instead, view the chambers by looking down into them from the side. A loaded cylinder may be emptied by taking the gun to a range and firing it until it is empty. Alternately, the loaded cylinder may be carefully removed without firing the revolver in order to render the revolver safe for further operations by following the instructions at 2) below. Note: Once the loaded cylinder has been removed from the revolver, set it aside, away from the remainder of the firearm.

2 To remove the barrel and cylinder: The barrel (#3) may be separated from the frame (#1) by first pushing out the wedge (#4) out toward the right side of the barrel as far as it will move. Barrel

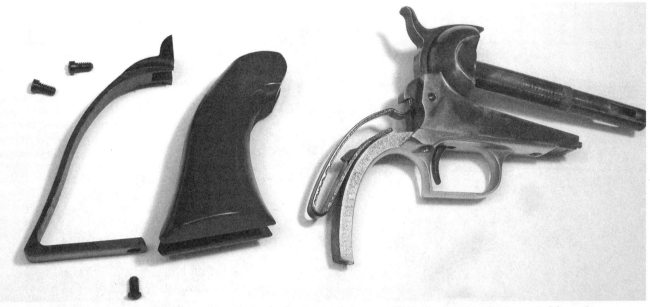

To remove the one-piece grip the three screws in the backstrap are taken out. The grip may then be separated from the backstrap.

wedges are equipped with a wedge lock spring (#17) with a lock that grasps the right side of the barrel. Before the wedge can be moved, this lock must first be depressed. If the wedge is so tight that it will not move by hand pressure, you may use a small nylon drift punch (nylon is used in order to lessen the chance of damaging either the wedge or the surrounding metal) with a hammer to break the wedge free. Place the hammer (#2) in the loading position so that the cylinder will spin freely. Turn the cylinder (#5) so that the plunger (#24) will contact the cylinder in-between two chambers, then pull the rammer lever down. This will cause the barrel to loosen and move forward from the frame (#1) slightly. The barrel is now removed from the frame by pulling it straight forward. The cylinder assembly (#5) is likewise removed from the frame by pulling it straight forward, off the cylinder pin (i.e., base pin or arbor, #21).

3 To disassemble the barrel and cylinder: Remove the rammer pin screw (#34) from the rammer and if so equipped, remove the loading lever screw (#39) from the left side of the barrel. The rammer (or loading lever, #13) and its plunger (#24) may be removed from the front. The wedge (#4) may be removed from the barrel by first removing the wedge screw (#33) from the right side of the barrel and then withdrawing the wedge. The only disassembly that will be required, or that is indeed possible on the unloaded cylinder (#5), is the removal of the percussion nipples (#14). This step should be accomplished with a special tool called a nipple wrench. Percussion nipples are screwed into the rear of the cylinder and have right-hand threads, which means that they unscrew in a counter-clockwise direction. Original Colt and other vintage percussion revolvers often have nipples that were hand-fitted to

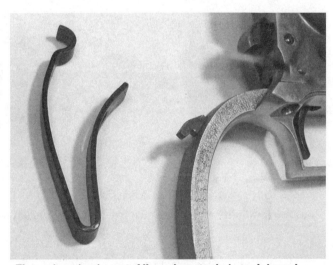

The mainspring is next. All you have to do is push in and down, and the spring slides out the bottom.

each specific chamber, so care should always be taken that these are re-installed in the chamber they were removed from.

4 To remove the grip, mainspring and triggerguard: These revolvers are equipped with one-piece grips and are disassembled thus: Unscrew and remove the two backstrap screws (#32) from the top-rear of the backstrap (#8) and remove the single butt screw (#455) from the butt of the backstrap. The backstrap (#8) and the one-piece grip (#11) may be removed by pulling them down and to the rear as a unit. Once off the frame, the grip may be pulled straight forward and off the backstrap. Compress the top of the mainspring (#20) and push down at the same time to disengage the mainspring from its latch (#535) on the rear of

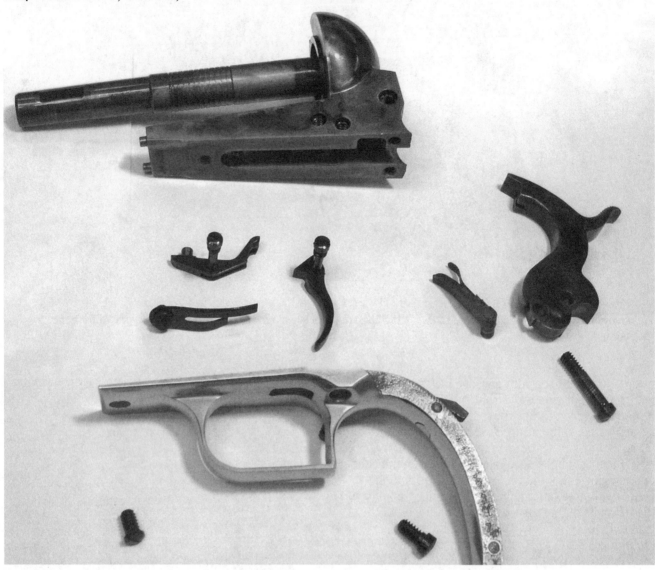

The Walker with its entire action removed. Notice the similarities to all later single action Colt products.

the triggerguard. The mainspring #20) will now lift out. Assembly note: This same mainspring design is used on First and early Second Model Hartford Dragoon pistols. The top of the spring must be partially compressed and then slid upwards to engage it with its mount on the rear of the triggerguard.

Unscrew and remove the two triggerguard screws (#32) and the front triggerguard screw (#31) and the triggerguard (#26) may be removed from the bottom.

5 To disassemble the action: Unscrew and remove the trigger and bolt spring screw (#35). This is the only screw inside the frame that faces straight up from the underside of the frame. Now the trigger and bolt spring (#19) may be lifted out the bottom of the frame. Unscrew and remove the trigger screw (#38). This is the center screw of the three screws on the left frame side and the trigger (#10). Next, remove the forwardmost of the three screws on the left side of the frame; this is the bolt screw (#40) that holds the bolt

(#12) in place. The bolt may now be removed from the bottom. Be sure you keep the bolt screw (#40) with the bolt (#12) and the trigger screw together with the trigger while they are removed because the trigger screw may easily be mistaken for the bolt screw, which is slightly shorter. The hammer screw (#37) may now be unscrewed and removed, after which the hammer assembly (#2) may be rotated slightly to the rear and pulled down and out of the frame. The hand assembly (#7) is connected to the hammer and will withdraw with the hammer. Once the hammer assembly (#2) is out, the hand assembly (#7) can be removed by lifting it up out of its socket hole on the left side of the hammer.

REASSEMBLY

Reassemble the revolver in reverse order of above.

· 34 ·

Colt Percussion Revolvers
Models 1848-1862

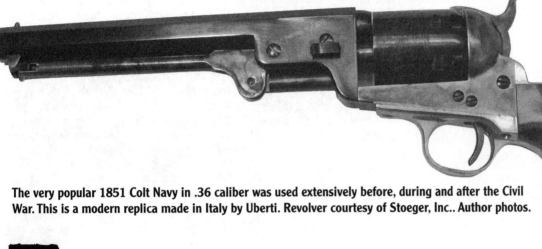

The very popular 1851 Colt Navy in .36 caliber was used extensively before, during and after the Civil War. This is a modern replica made in Italy by Uberti. Revolver courtesy of Stoeger, Inc.. Author photos.

Sam Colt's open-top revolvers have been around since he first introduced his Paterson five-shot revolver in 1836. Despite its detractors, the open-top has been a very successful design. Used to fight the American Civil war and several foreign wars, it lasted throughout the percussion era and for a short time into the cartridge era with Colt's cartridge conversions and finally with the 1871-1872 Open-Top revolvers. Over the years, a great many objections to these revolvers have been voiced. They have been roundly condemned for the lack of a top-strap and for their seemingly crude method of fastening the barrel to the frame by means of a tapered steel wedge. Nevertheless, these pistols were fashioned with quick disassembly in mind, not just for ease of cleaning in an era where black powder fouling was a genuine concern, but for fast reloading with a spare pre-loaded cylinder, an attribute at which these pistols excel. What is more, these revolvers were beautifully made, their wonderful craftsmanship compensating, to a degree at least, for some of the inherent weakness of the open-top design. The fact is that much of the world gladly adopted it and used it successfully long before anyone knew there would be something better.

From 1836 until 1848 Colt sold comparatively small numbers of his revolvers, but his revolver designs were quickly evolving and were gradually improved into what became a very reliable, timeless mechanism. By 1848, with the introduction of the Baby Dragoon pocket revolver, and the next year's introduction of the 1849 Pocket Model, Colt's revolvers became more universally accepted and they began to sell on a much larger scale. The 1848-49 pattern revolvers remained basically the same until 1860, their sizes varying from the tiny five-shot .31 caliber Pocket Models on up to the huge six-shot Dragoon .44s. However, all these Colt percussion revolvers used the now-familiar Colt single action internal mechanism, along with octagon barrels and hinged loading levers that pivoted on a screw.

Changes came with the 1860 Army which introduced the more efficient "creeping" loading lever and a streamlined, round barrel shape. Probably the most popular feature of the 1860 was that it was a six-shot .44 caliber revolver that was

Colt's 1860 Army .44 was built on the .36 Navy frame and saw heavy use during the American Civil War. Here is a modern replica by Uberti; it has an extra screw on each side of the frame for mounting a detachable shoulder stock. Revolver courtesy of Stoeger, Inc.

built on the smaller 1851 Navy .36-caliber frame. This combination offered the shooter a real powerhouse .44-caliber revolver on a medium-sized frame that was far easier to tote in a belt holster than the massive .44 Dragoon. Colt accomplished this feat by making use of a new rebated or stepped cylinder design. The following years saw the release of a .36 caliber Model 1861 Navy, also built on the 1851 Navy frame and making use of the new creeping loading system and round barrel, and the 1862 Pocket Police, a five-shot .36 caliber revolver with the 1860 pattern changes built on the tiny 1849 Pocket .31-caliber frame.

All the above models retained that same, incredibly reliable internal action mechanism introduced with the Model 1848 Baby Dragoon. Modern day revolver aficionados will quickly recognize that the actions used in all these previous percussion revolvers are pretty much identical to that of the more familiar Colt Single Action Army of 1873. That's right, William Mason, the designer of the Peacemaker, knew a good thing when he saw it. Today we are graced with a large variety of good quality, modern-made replicas of most of the Colt percussion models and most of these share that same excellent Sam Colt single action mechanism.

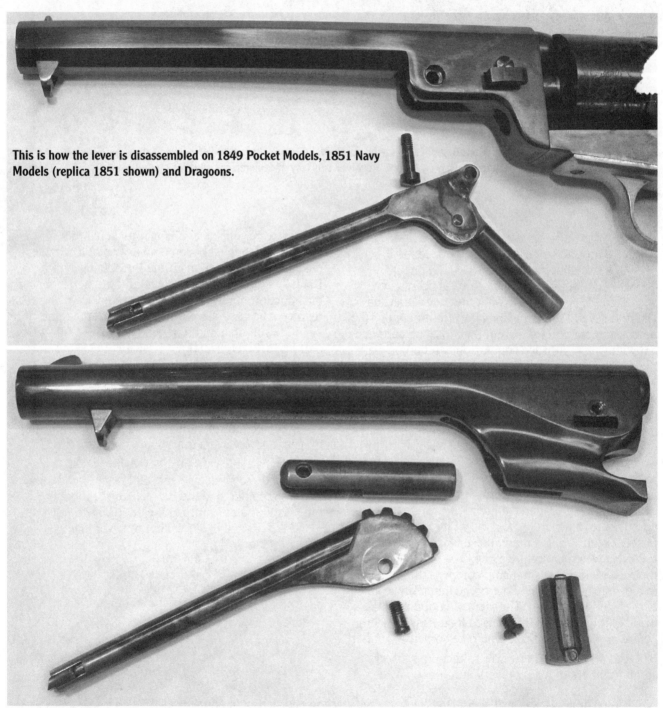

This is how the lever is disassembled on 1849 Pocket Models, 1851 Navy Models (replica 1851 shown) and Dragoons.

The so-called "creeping" lever mechanism lever disassembled. This is from an 1860 Army replica and is typical of those used on the 1861 Navy, 1862 Police models and the 1855 side-hammer models.

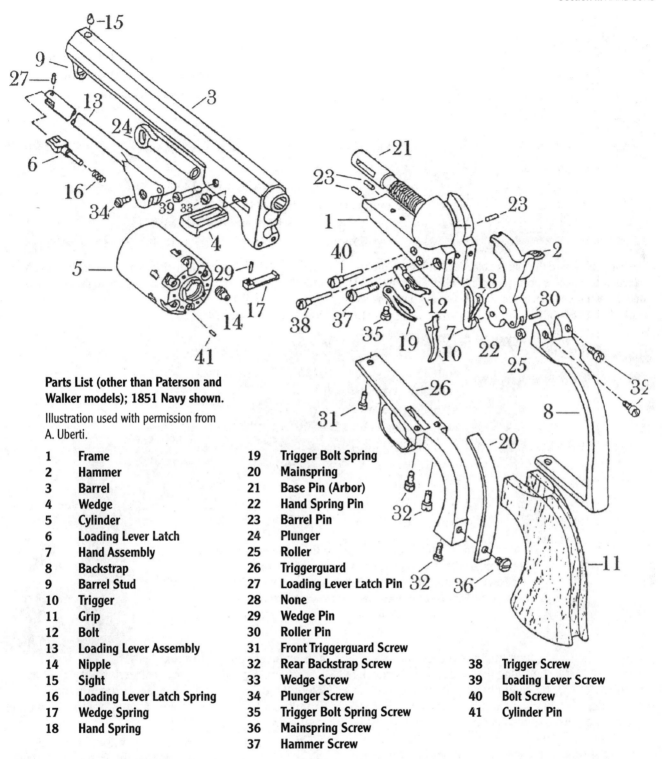

Parts List (other than Paterson and Walker models); 1851 Navy shown.

Illustration used with permission from A. Uberti.

1	Frame	19	Trigger Bolt Spring		
2	Hammer	20	Mainspring		
3	Barrel	21	Base Pin (Arbor)		
4	Wedge	22	Hand Spring Pin		
5	Cylinder	23	Barrel Pin		
6	Loading Lever Latch	24	Plunger		
7	Hand Assembly	25	Roller		
8	Backstrap	26	Triggerguard		
9	Barrel Stud	27	Loading Lever Latch Pin		
10	Trigger	28	None		
11	Grip	29	Wedge Pin		
12	Bolt	30	Roller Pin		
13	Loading Lever Assembly	31	Front Triggerguard Screw		
14	Nipple	32	Rear Backstrap Screw	38	Trigger Screw
15	Sight	33	Wedge Screw	39	Loading Lever Screw
16	Loading Lever Latch Spring	34	Plunger Screw	40	Bolt Screw
17	Wedge Spring	35	Trigger Bolt Spring Screw	41	Cylinder Pin
18	Hand Spring	36	Mainspring Screw		
		37	Hammer Screw		

DISASSEMBLY INSTRUCTIONS

With only minor variations, the following instructions can be suitable for use with nearly all of the percussion ignition, open-top-frame Colt and Colt-type revolvers based on the late Second Model and Third Model Dragoon, and the 1848, 1849, 1851, 1860, 1861 and 1862 patterns.

1 Begin by making absolutely sure the revolver is not loaded. Hold the revolver firmly by its grip (#11), while consciously keeping your fingers away from the trigger (#10). Point and hold the muzzle in a safe direction, facing away from any person, pet, vehicle or dwelling. Now place the hammer (#2) in the loading position by pulling it to the rear until one audible click is heard. You may now check to be certain that the revolver's cylinder (#5) is unloaded

Checking to be sure the gun is unloaded. With the hammer placed in the loading position, here is what a nipple should look like without a percussion cap. Pictured is a well-worn original Colt 1860 Model Army.

Look down into the cylinder chambers from above and off to the side to be certain there are no bullets in the chambers.

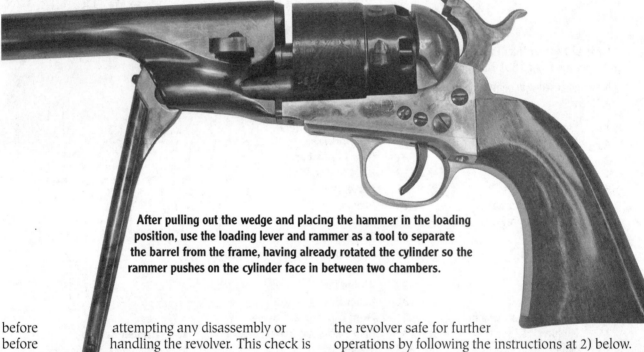

After pulling out the wedge and placing the hammer in the loading position, use the loading lever and rammer as a tool to separate the barrel from the frame, having already rotated the cylinder so the rammer pushes on the cylinder face in between two chambers.

before attempting any disassembly or before handling the revolver. This check is performed by carefully examining the rear of the cylinder at each chamber to be certain that there are no percussion caps on any of the nipples (#14). If percussion caps are present on the nipples then you should consider this a loaded firearm. Do not attempt any further disassembly. Also you should always look at the front of the cylinder to make sure that there are no charges in the cylinder chambers (a good indication that a chamber is most likely loaded would be bullets or balls showing at the front end of the chamber). Never look directly into the barrel or chambers; instead, view the chambers by looking down into them from the side. A loaded cylinder may be emptied by taking the gun to a range and firing it until it is empty, or the loaded cylinder may be carefully removed without firing the revolver in order to render

the revolver safe for further operations by following the instructions at 2) below. Note: Once the loaded cylinder has been removed from the revolver, set it aside, away from the remainder of the firearm.

2 To remove the barrel and cylinder: The barrel (#3) may be separated from the frame (#1) by first pushing out the wedge (#4) out toward the left side of the barrel as far as it will move. Some barrel wedges are equipped with a wedge lock spring (#17) with a lock that grasps the right side of the barrel, and before the wedge can be moved this lock must first be depressed. If the wedge is so tight that it will not move by hand pressure, you may use a small nylon (nylon is used in order to lessen the chance of damaging either the wedge, or the surrounding metal) drift punch with a hammer to break the wedge free. Place the hammer (#2) in the loading position so that the cylinder will spin freely. If

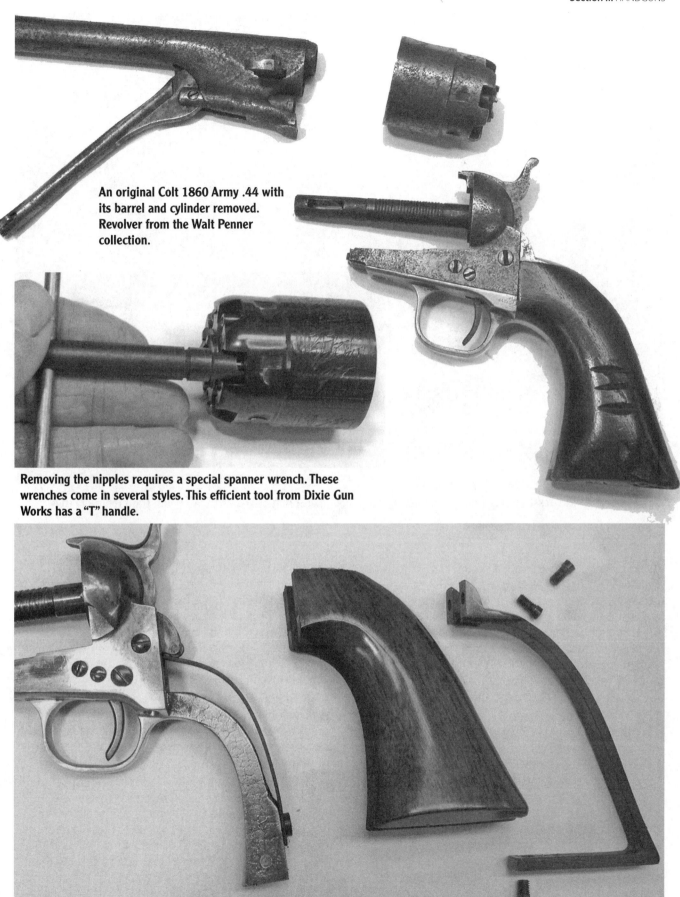

An original Colt 1860 Army .44 with its barrel and cylinder removed. Revolver from the Walt Penner collection.

Removing the nipples requires a special spanner wrench. These wrenches come in several styles. This efficient tool from Dixie Gun Works has a "T" handle.

After removing the two screws from the upper portion of the backstrap and the one screw from the butt, the backstrap and one-piece grip can be pulled off the frame to the rear. The grip is then slid off the backstrap.

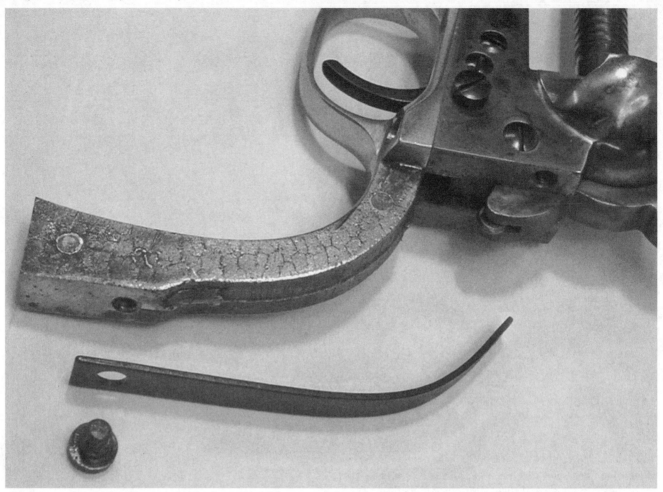

After removing the backstrap and grip, the mainspring screw and mainspring are removed. A replica 1860 replica is shown.

the revolver is equipped with a rammer (#13), turn the cylinder (#5) so that the rammer pin (#24) will contact the cylinder in between two chambers and then pull the rammer lever down. This will cause the barrel to loosen and move forward from the frame (#1) slightly. The barrel is now removed from the frame by pulling it off straight forward. The cylinder assembly (#5) is likewise removed from the frame by pulling it straight forward, off the cylinder pin (i.e., base pin or arbor, #21).

3 To disassemble the barrel and cylinder: Remove the rammer pin screw (#34) from the rammer and if so equipped, remove the rammer screw (#39) from the left side of the barrel. (1860 Army/1861 Navy and 1862 Pocket Police types do not use a rammer screw but have male gears on their tops which engage female gear teeth on the underside of the barrel.) The rammer (or rammer lever, #13) and its rammer pin (#24) may be removed from the front. The wedge (#4) may be removed from the barrel by first removing the wedge screw (#33) from the left side of the barrel and then withdrawing the wedge. The only disassembly that will be required, or that is indeed possible on the unloaded cylinder (#5), would be the removal of the percussion nipples (#14). This step should be accomplished with

a special tool called a nipple wrench. Percussion nipples are screwed in and have right-hand threads, which means that they unscrew in a counter-clockwise direction. Original Colt and other vintage percussion revolvers may have nipples which have been hand fitted to each specific chamber, so care should always be taken that these are re-installed in the chamber they were removed from.

4 To remove the grip and grip straps: 4a) If the revolver is equipped with two-piece grips, first remove the grip screw from the center of the grip and then remove the two grips. Now proceed to step 4b.

In the great majority of cases, however, these revolvers will be equipped with one-piece grips and are disassembled thus: Unscrew and remove the two backstrap screws (#32) from the top-rear of the backstrap (#8) and remove the single butt-screw from the butt of the backstrap. The backstrap (#8) and the one-piece grip (#11) may be removed by pulling them down and to the rear as a unit. Once off the frame, the grip may be pulled straight forward and off the backstrap. Unscrew and remove the mainspring screw (#36) from the inside-lower area of the triggerguard (#26). The mainspring (#20) will now lift out.

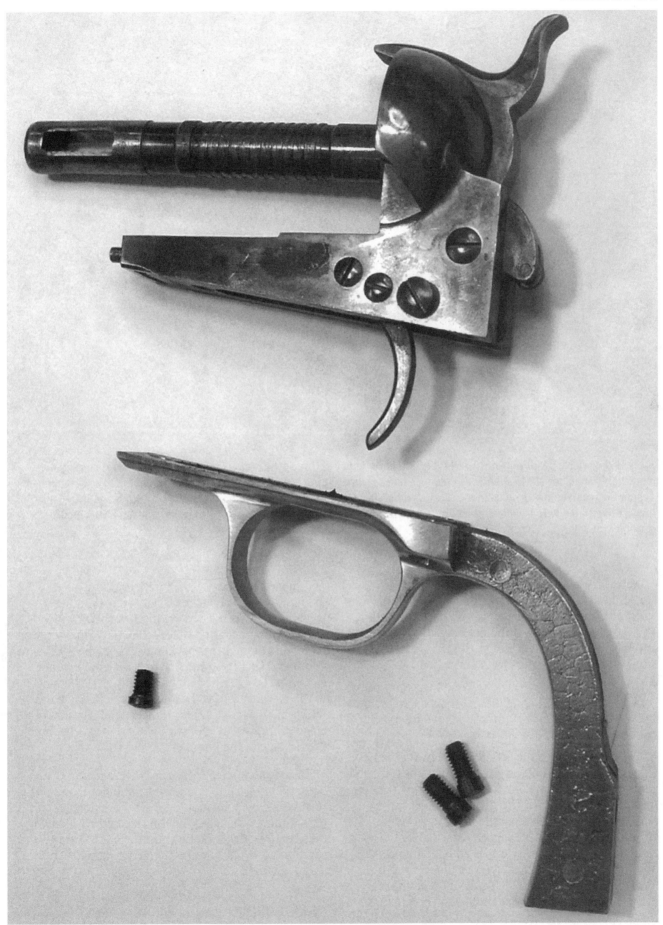

Removing the three screws in the triggerguard allows it to be pulled off the frame from the bottom.

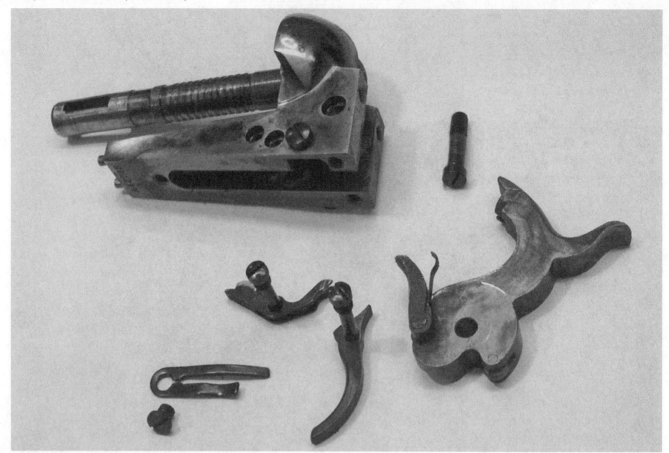

Here is the replica 1860 shown with all its action parts removed. The screw remaining in the frame is for mounting a detachable shoulder stock, a feature found on some specimens of the 1860. This extra screw does not hold any components inside the revolver and there is an identical screw on the opposite side of the frame. Note: the grip strap and internal action design illustrated here is typical of all Colt single action pistols from 1848 through 1873 except the Model 1855 side hammer models.

Note: First and early Second Model Hartford Dragoon pistols use a V-shaped mainspring that requires a somewhat different disassembly procedure. The top of the spring must be partially compressed and then slid upwards slightly to disengage it from its mount on the rear of the triggerguard.

4b Unscrew and remove the two triggerguard screws (#32) and the front triggerguard screw (#31). The triggerguard (#26) will remove from the bottom.

5 To disassemble the action: Unscrew and remove the trigger and bolt spring screw (#35 – the only screw inside the frame that faces straight up) from the underside of the frame. The trigger and bolt spring (#19) may now be lifted out the bottom of the frame. Unscrew and remove the trigger screw (#38 – this is the centermost of the three screws on the left frame side) and the trigger (#10). Next, remove the forwardmost of the three screws on the left side of the frame; this is the bolt screw (#40), which holds the bolt (#12) in place. The bolt may now be removed from the bottom. Be sure you keep the bolt screw (#40), the bolt (#12)

and the trigger screw close by the trigger while they are removed because the trigger screw (#38) may easily be mistaken for the bolt screw (#40), which is slightly shorter. The hammer screw (#37) may now be removed, after which the hammer assembly (#2) may be rotated slightly to the rear and pulled down and out of the frame. The hand assembly (#7) is connected to the hammer and will withdraw with it. Once the hammer assembly (#2) is out, the hand assembly (#7) can be removed by lifting it up out of its socket hole on the left side of the hammer.

Disassembly note: Some 1860s were factory equipped to accept a detachable shoulder stock. These revolvers have two additional screws, one in each side of the frame. The stock locating screws are located between the trigger screw and the hammer screw and serve no function other than the mounting of the shoulder stock.

REASSEMBLY

Reassemble the revolver in reverse order of above.

Colt Richards-Mason
Cartridge Conversion Revolver And Replicas

A fter the Civil War, the big revolver makers, including Colt, were left with thousands of percussion revolvers left over from the war. At that time, the late 1860s to early 1870s, these revolvers were being made obsolete by the new metallic cartridge revolvers so the gun companies were trying to find ways of salvaging these weapons. One solution was to come up with a means of converting them so they could accept metallic cartridges. The problem in this for Colt and others was that Smith & Wesson already held the rights to a patent covering the concept of loading a rimmed cartridge into a cylinder from the rear and the patent would not expire until 1869. Colt tried to evade the patent by adopting an invention by Alexander Thuer, a conversion for percussion Colts that enabled them to accept a very unconventional, tapered metallic cartridge that loaded from the front of the cylinder. The Thuer system did not prove to be a very practical idea, but it did give Colt a stop-gap design and with that they managed to sell about 5000 converted percussion revolvers that they otherwise may not have be able to sell.

A Colt employee and inventor by the name of Charles Richards patented a better method of converting Colt percussion pistols to use metallic cartridge revolvers in 1871. These so-called Richards' cartridge conversions were performed on the 1860 Army model and chambered a conventional rimmed, centerfire .44-caliber cartridge called the 44 Colt. Richards added a loading gate to the revolver by using a conversion ring. This steel ring was attached to the revolver frame via some intricate machine work. Within the conversion ring were a fixed rear sight and a spring-loaded firing pin. Another part of the Richards conversion was the addition of a barrel-mounted ejector rod assembly that fit up into the recess where the percussion rammer once worked.

Colt's next step forward in conversions was the Richards-Mason. This conversion was a combination of the efforts of Richards and the patents of William Mason, who among other things contributed a simpler ejector assembly that was also less expensive to manufacture. Richards-Mason conversions retained the rear sight on the percussion hammer nose, and they also used a hammer-mounted firing pin. These features shaved expenses for Colt and that helped the bottom line since the R-M was more refined and easier to manufacture conversion than the Richards. Today's shooters can enjoy firing faithful copies of the Colt Richards-Mason conversion revolver manufactured in Italy by Uberti and sold in the USA by Cimarron Firearms and others.

This newly-manufactured replica of the Colt Richards-Mason conversion revolver is produced by Uberti and sold in the U.S. by Cimarron Firearms in several calibers. This one is in 44 Colt CF. Author photos.

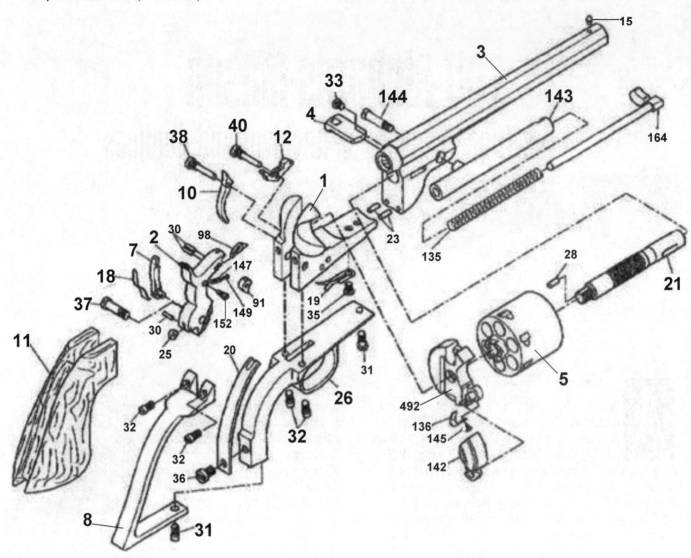

Parts List

1	Frame	21	Base Pin	98	Firing Pin
2	Hammer Assembly	23	Barrel Pin	135	Ejector Spring
3	Barrel	25	Roller	136	Gate Spring
4	Wedge	26	Triggerguard	142	Gate
5	Cylinder	30	Hammer Pin	143	Ejector Rod Tube
7	Hand	31	Front Triggerguard Screw	144	Ejector Rod Tube Screw
8	Backstrap	32	Backstrap & Triggerguard Screw	145	Gate Catch Screw
10	Trigger	33	Wedge Screw	147	Hammer Safety Spring
11	Grip	35	Trigger Bolt Spring Screw	149	Safety Pin
12	Bolt	36	Main Spring Screw	152	Hammer Safety Stop Screw
15	Sight Octagon Barrel	37	Hammer Screw	164	Ejector Nut Assembly
18	Hand Spring	38	Trigger Screw	492	Breech Ring
19	Trigger Bolt Spring	40	Bolt Screw	455	Connect Screw (not shown)
20	Mainspring	91	Hammer Safety Bar		

As with all revolver disassembly procedures, the first step is always to visibly check to make certain the cylinder chambers are empty.

Here you can see the wedge screw has been loosened so the flat spot on its head faces the wedge; this frees the wedge for removal.

Once the wedge is removed, the barrel and then the cylinder are simply pulled off to the front for removal.

DISASSEMBLY INSTRUCTIONS

These instructions will work with Colt and Uberti Richards-Mason revolvers and replicas thereof based on the traditional Colt design.

1 Be sure this weapon is unloaded by opening the loading gate (#142) and pulling the hammer (#2) slowly to the rear until you have heard one audible click. This should place the hammer in the half-cock or loading position and the cylinder (#5) should spin freely in a clockwise direction. Remember to keep your fingers away from the trigger during this entire operation. Slowly rotate the cylinder two full revolutions by hand, all the while examining the cylinder's chambers through the opening that has been presented by the opened loading gate at the rear of the frame (#1) in order to make absolutely certain that the cylinder chambers have no cartridges in them.

If cartridges are present, keep the muzzle pointed in a safe direction. Leave the hammer right where it is, in the half-cock or loading position, and with the loading gate opened. Using your left hand to hold the revolver securely by the grip, still keeping your fingers away from that trigger, tilt the revolver so that the barrel's muzzle (front) is facing away from you and upwards, in a direction that you determine is safe (so that if the gun did accidentally fire no one would be harmed). Next, use your right hand to rotate the cylinder (#5) slowly, one chamber at a time, pausing at each click to allow each successive cartridge to fall out of its chamber. If any cartridge will not fall out of its own weight, manually operate the ejector by pushing the ejector rod (#164 – located under the front of the barrel) to the rear with your right hand until the ejector rod has forced that cartridge out of the chamber. When you are absolutely certain that there are no more cartridges left in the cylinder chambers, the revolver may now be safely disassembled.

Removing the three screws that hold the backstrap enables it and the one-piece grip to be removed.

The mainspring is held on by one screw and it should be removed before you take off the triggerguard.

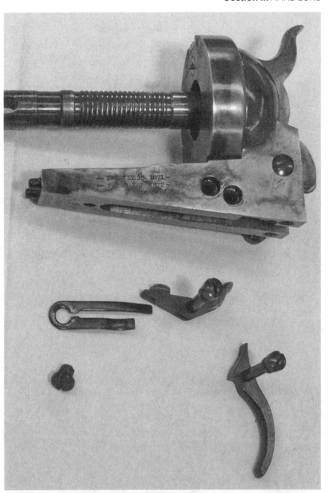

Once the mainspring is removed, the three screws holding the triggerguard can be removed, allowing the guard to come off from the bottom; this exposes the action parts.

This view shows the sear and bolt spring, bolt and trigger disassembled along with their respective screws.

2 To remove the barrel and cylinder: The hammer should still be resting in the loading or half-cocked position and the loading gate should still be open for this operation. Turn the wedge screw (#33) so that the flat portion of its head faces the wedge (#4). This frees the wedge for removal. Use a wooden drift and hammer to drive out the wedge (#4) from right to left. Pull the barrel (#3) to the front and remove it. Next, pull the cylinder (#5) to the front and remove it.

3 To remove the grip and grip straps: These revolvers are equipped with one-piece grips that may be disassembled thus: Unscrew and remove the two backstrap screws (#32) from the top-rear of the backstrap (#8) and, remove the single butt-screw (#31) from the butt or bottom of the backstrap. The backstrap (#8) and the one-piece grip (#11) are now removed by pulling them down and to the rear as a unit. Once the subassembly is off the frame, the grip itself (#11) may be pulled straight forward off the backstrap. Unscrew and remove the mainspring screw (#36) from the inside-lower area of triggerguard (#26). The mainspring (#20)

is now loose. Remove the two triggerguard screws (#32) from the rear of the triggerguard and the one front triggerguard screw (#31) and the triggerguard (#26) will come off from the bottom.

4 To disassemble the action: Notice how the sear and bolt spring bears on the trigger and bolt for re-assembly. Unscrew and remove the sear and bolt spring screw (#35 – this is the only screw facing straight up within the frame from the underside); the sear and bolt spring (#19) will fall out the bottom of the frame. Now remove the trigger screw (#38 – this is the center screw of the three screws that pass through the frame) and remove the trigger (#10). Next, remove the forwardmost of the three screws on the left side of the frame. This is the bolt screw (#40), which holds the bolt (#12) in place; the bolt may now be removed from the bottom. Be sure to keep the bolt screw (#40) with the bolt (#12) while they are removed because the trigger screw (#38) may easily be mistaken for the bolt screw, which is shorter. The hammer screw (#37) may now be unscrewed and removed, after which the hammer assembly (#2) may be

The hammer and hand assembly come out as a unit but once the hammer is out the hand assembly can be simply lifted off the hammer.

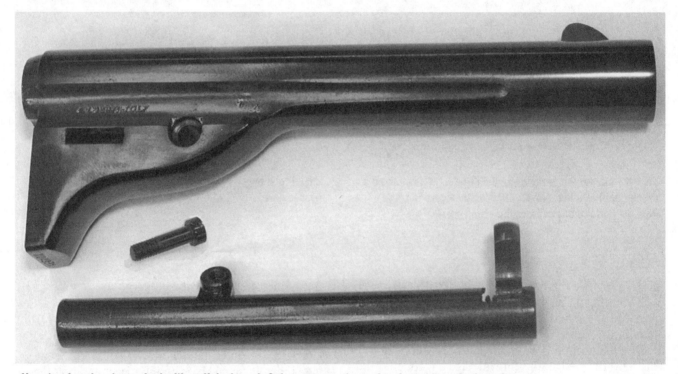

Here is what the ejector looks like off the barrel. Only one screw is used to fasten it to the barrel.

rotated slightly to the rear and pulled down and out of the frame. The hand assembly (#7) is connected to the hammer and will come out with it. Once the hammer assembly (#2) is out, the hand assembly (#7) may be removed by lifting it up out of its socket hole on the left side of the hammer.

5 Peripheral disassembly: To disassemble the ejector assembly from the barrel: The ejector rod tube screw (#144) is removed from the left side of the barrel (#3) and the entire ejector tube assembly

(#143), (#164) and (#135) may be pulled to the right side until it separates from the barrel. The ejector rod (not numbered) is removed by pushing the rod to the rear and clamping it in a padded vise or holding it with a padded pair of pliers. Now unscrew the ejector rod from the assembly by turning it counterclockwise until the rod unscrews from the head (#164). Using a small screwdriver to hold the ejector spring (#135) captive, slide the ejector head (#164) forward, noting its position for reassembly. Pull it out through the slot in the ejector tube (#143). The spring (#135) may be

The arrow points to the gate catch (spring) screw under the conversion ring.

removed out the front of the tube and the rod pulled out the rear of the tube.

To disassemble the loading gate: Under the conversion ring (#492) on the right side, you will notice a small screw; this is the gate spring screw (#145). Unscrew and remove the screw (#145) and remove the gate spring (#136). The loading gate itself may not be removed without removing the conversion ring, an operation that is not recommended except to factory-trained gunsmiths.

To disassemble the Uberti-Cimarron hammer (#2): The hammer safety bar (#91) may be removed by unscrewing and removing the hammer safety stop screw (#152) and lifting out the hammer safety bar (#91) and the safety pin and spring (#149). Pay careful attention of the relationship of these parts for later reassembly. The roll (#25) may be removed by drifting out its pin (#30). Further disassembly of the hammer is not recommended.

REASSEMBLY

Reassemble the revolver in the reverse order.

Colt Open-Top
1871-72 Revolver

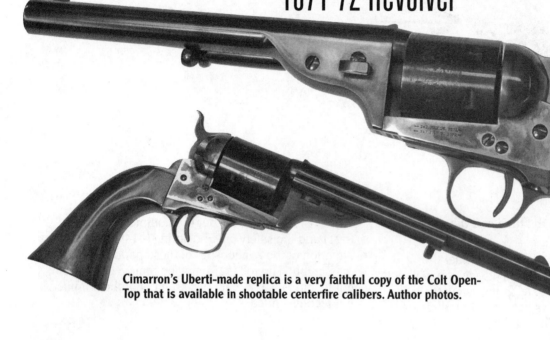

Cimarron's Uberti-made replica is a very faithful copy of the Colt Open-Top that is available in shootable centerfire calibers. Author photos.

The revolver we know today as the Colt Open-Top was the Colt company's first revolver to be made expressly for metallic cartridges and it was the immediate predecessor of the famous Single Action Army of 1873. Colt's Open-Top used a frame that was specifically intended to fire metallic cartridges in that its frame was machined to accept a loading gate and it did not need to use a separate conversion ring such as those on converted cap-n-ball pistols. Another first-time feature seen on the Open-Top was the addition of a gas ring seal to the front of its cylinder. This unique attribute (first seen on the Smith & Wesson 44 American Model of 1870) helped prevent black powder fouling from entering the cylinder axis hole. Powder fouling was a major cause of revolver cylinders binding or seizing, sometimes after only a few shots were fired, so the gas ring was an important addition.

This revolver was still a throwback in that it retained the open-top frame with no topstrap along with a barrel that was held in place by a wedge as in earlier

Colt percussion pistols. The Colt Richards and Richards-Mason conversion revolvers were chambered to fire the 44 Colt centerfire cartridge, but all of the 7000 original Open-Top revolvers were manufactured to use the 44 Henry Rimfire cartridge. William Mason's patented ejector was also used on the Open-Top, just as it had been on the former Richards-Mason conversions, and was fastened through the barrel's underlug in the same manner as the former.

The new Uberti replicas as offered by Cimarron Firearms are available in several centerfire calibers, including the popular 44 S&W Special. Unlike the original Colt Open-Top, the Uberti's hammer is equipped with a unique safety device. The safety is manually operated after placing the hammer at half-cock by turning a screw on the hammer side. This causes a solid steel block to rotate down so the block actually protrudes from the hammer face. With the safety placed in the "on" position, the hammer is prevented from falling all the way down, preventing the firing pin from reaching the primer.

gas ring →

This photo shows the gas ring, one of the unique features that sets the Open-Top apart from previous Colt conversion revolvers.

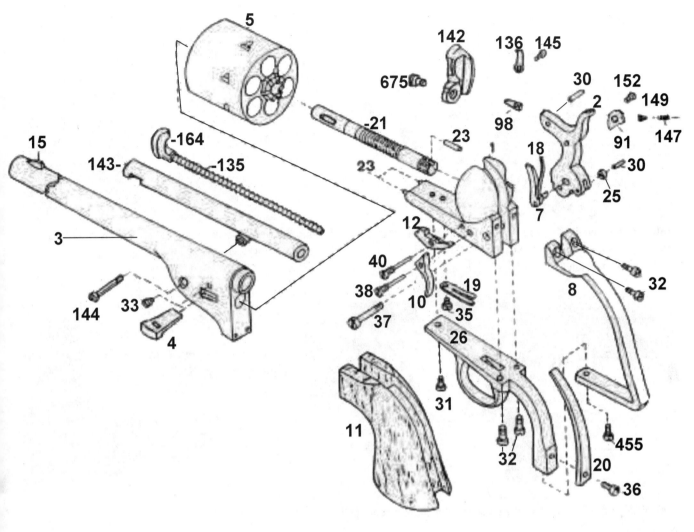

Parts List

#		#		#	
1	Frame	21	Base Pin	91	Hammer Safety Bar
2	Hammer	23	Barrel Pin	98	Firing Pin
3	Barrel	25	Roller	135	Ejector Spring
4	Wedge	26	Triggerguard	136	Gate Spring
5	Cylinder	30	Hammer Pin	142	Gate
7	Hand	31	Front Triggerguard Screw	143	Ejector Rod Tube
8	Backstrap	32	Backstrap and	144	Ejector Rod Tube Screw
10	Trigger		Triggerguard Screw	145	Gate Catch Screw
11	Grip	33	Wedge Screw	147	Hammer Safety Spring
12	Bolt	35	Trigger Bolt Spring Screw	149	Safety Spring
15	Sight	36	Mainspring Screw	152	Hammer Safety Stop Screw
18	Hand Spring	37	Hammer Screw	164	Ejector Rod and Head
19	Trigger Bolt Spring	38	Trigger Screw	455	Connect Screw
20	Mainspring	40	Bolt Screw	675	Gate Screw

Always open the loading gate, bring the hammer into the loading position and check to be sure each chamber is empty before handling the revolver.

Turning the wedge screw so the flat spot on its head faces the wedge unlocks the wedge for removal.

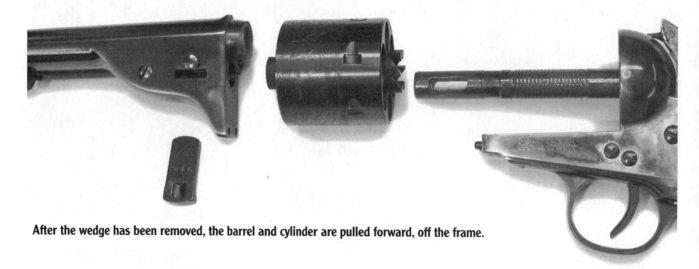

After the wedge has been removed, the barrel and cylinder are pulled forward, off the frame.

DISASSEMBLY INSTRUCTIONS

These instructions will work with Colt and Uberti Open-Top revolvers and replicas thereof that are based on the traditional Colt design.

1 Be sure the gun is unloaded. Point and hold the muzzle away from any person, pet, vehicle or dwelling. Always check first to make absolutely sure this weapon is unloaded by opening the loading gate (#142) and pulling the hammer (#2) slowly to the rear until you hear a click. This should place the hammer in the half-cock or loading position and the cylinder (#5) should spin freely in a clockwise direction. Remember to keep your fingers away from the trigger during this entire operation! Slowly rotate the cylinder two full revolutions by hand, all the while examining the cylinder's chambers through the opening that has been created by the opened loading gate at the rear of the frame (#1) to make absolutely certain that the cylinder chambers have no cartridges in them.

If cartridges are present, keep the muzzle pointed in a safe direction. Leave the hammer right where it is, in the half-cock or loading position and with the loading gate opened. Using your left hand to hold the revolver securely by the grip, still keeping your fingers away from that trigger, tilt the revolver so that the barrel's muzzle (front) is facing away from you and upwards, in a direction that you determine is safe (so that if the gun did accidentally fire no one would be harmed). Next, use your right hand to rotate the cylinder (#5) slowly, one chamber at a time, pausing at each click to allow each successive cartridge to fall out of its chamber and onto your workbench. If any cartridge will not fall out of its own weight, manually operate the ejector by pushing the ejector rod (#164) located under the front of the barrel to the rear with your right hand until the ejector rod has forced that cartridge out of the chamber. When you are absolutely certain that there are no more cartridges left in the cylinder chambers, the revolver may now be safely disassembled.

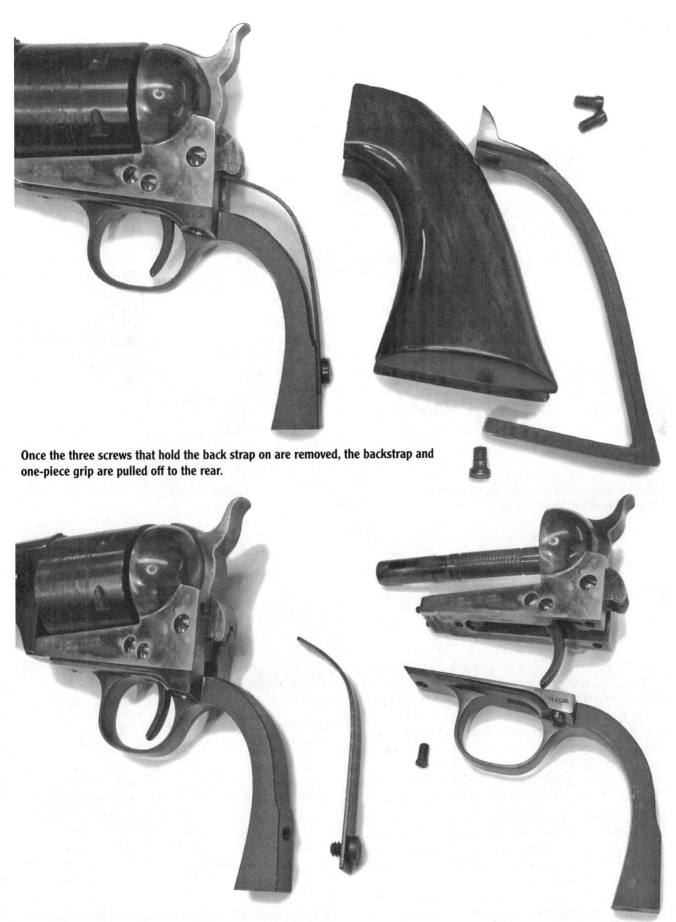

Once the three screws that hold the back strap on are removed, the backstrap and one-piece grip are pulled off to the rear.

Unscrewing the mainspring screw allows the mainspring to be removed. This should be done before the attempting to remove the triggerguard.

After the three screws that face straight-up are removed, the triggerguard will come off toward the bottom.

After the guard is off, you have full access to all the action components shown here.

This view shows the loading gate catch (spring) screw. Removing it allows the loading gate catch to come out.

2 To remove the barrel and cylinder: The hammer should still be resting in the loading or half-cocked position and the loading gate should still be open for this operation. Turn the wedge screw (#33) so that the flat portion of its head faces the wedge (#4). This frees the wedge for removal. Use a wooden drift and hammer to drive out the wedge (#4) from right to left. Pull the barrel (#3) to the front and remove it. Next, pull the cylinder (#5) to the front and remove it.

3 To remove the grip and grip straps: These revolvers are equipped with one-piece grips that may be disassembled thus: Unscrew and remove the two backstrap screws (#32) from the top-rear of the backstrap (#8) and remove the single connect-screw (#455) from the butt or bottom of the backstrap. The backstrap (#8) and the one-piece grip (#11) are now removed by pulling them down and to the rear as a unit. Once the subassembly is off the frame, the grip itself (#11) may be pulled straight forward off

the backstrap. Unscrew and remove the mainspring screw (#36) from the inside-lower area of triggerguard (#26). The mainspring (#20) is now loose. Remove the two triggerguard screws (#32) from the rear of the triggerguard and the one front triggerguard screw (#31) and the triggerguard (#26) will come off from the bottom.

4 To disassemble the action: Notice how the sear and bolt spring bears on the trigger and bolt for re-assembly. Unscrew and remove the sear and bolt spring screw (#35) – this is the only screw facing

By removing the ejector tube screw that passes through the barrel, you can access the entire ejector tube assembly.

straight up within the frame from the underside – and the sear and bolt spring (#19) will fall out the bottom of the frame. Now remove the trigger screw (#38), the center screw of the three screws that pass through the frame, and remove the trigger (#10). Next, remove the forwardmost of the three screws on the left side of the frame. This is the bolt screw (#40), which holds the bolt (#12) in place. The bolt may now be removed from the bottom. Be sure to keep the bolt screw (#40) with the bolt (#12) while they are removed because the trigger screw (#38) may easily be mistaken for the bolt screw, which is shorter. The hammer screw (#37) may now be unscrewed and removed, after which the hammer assembly (#2) may be rotated slightly to the rear and pulled down and out of the frame. The hand assembly (#7) is connected to the hammer and can be withdrawn with it. Once the hammer assembly (#2) is out, the hand assembly (#7 and #18) may be removed by lifting it up out of its socket hole on the left side of the hammer.

5 Peripheral disassembly: To disassemble the ejector assembly from the barrel, the ejector rod tube screw (#144) is removed from the left side of the barrel (#3). Now the entire ejector tube assembly (#143), (#164) and (#135) may be pulled to the right side until it separates from the barrel. The ejector rod (not numbered) is removed by pushing the rod to the rear and clamping it in a padded vise or holding it with a padded pair of pliers. Now unscrew the ejector rod

from the assembly by turning it counterclockwise until the rod unscrews from the head (#164). Use a small screwdriver to hold the ejector spring (#135) captive and slide the ejector head (#164) forward, noting its position for reassembly. Pull it out through the slot in the ejector tube (#143). The spring (#135) may be removed out the front of the tube and the rod pulled out the rear of the tube.

The loading gate: Under the frame bulge on the right side you will notice a small screw. This is the gate spring screw (#145). Unscrew and remove the screw (#145) and remove the gate spring (#136). Unscrew and remove the gate screw (#675) and the loading gate itself (#142) will come off toward the front.

To disassemble the Uberti-Cimarron hammer (#2): The hammer safety bar (#91) may be removed by unscrewing and removing the hammer safety stop screw (#152) and lifting out the hammer safety bar (#91) and the safety pin and spring (#149 and #147). Pay careful attention to the relationship of these parts for later reassembly. The roll (#25) may be removed by drifting out its pin (#30). Further disassembly of the hammer is not recommended.

REASSEMBLY

Reassemble the revolver in reverse order of above.

Colt Single Action Army
Model 1873 and Replicas

The Peacemaker, Frontier Six Shooter, and Model P are a few of the well-known names given the legendary Single Action Army revolver introduced by Colt in 1873. The revolver was adopted by the U.S. Army and used extensively in the Indian Wars period. Colt Peacemakers were also used in use by outlaws, lawmen, cowboys and other characters who played important roles in the winning of the west. The Colt SAA has also been a great favorite of the Hollywood western movie throughout the twentieth century and it is largely because of this that the Colt is, arguably, at least one of the most the most recognizable firearms all over the world.

There were three production runs or manufacturing periods for the Single Action Army or, as the Colt factory calls it, the "Model P." The first of these is the original production run, which ran from 1873 through 1940 and totaled 357,859 revolvers (including both Bisley and SAA Target models). This lot has become known as the First Generation. In 1956 Colt introduced the "Second Generation" Single Action Army, which was produced until 1978, when some engineering changes (denoted by the letters SA after the serial number) were made that resulted in the "Third Generation" SAA, which is still in production. A variant of the SAA was produced during the first production called the Bisley Model (1894 to 1915). The Bisley had a radically different hammer, trigger and grip shape but was built on the same basic Model P frame configuration as the SAA. There were also target versions of both the SAA (made from 1888 to 1896) and the Bisley (made from 1894 to 1913) available during that early production, and these special revolvers are termed by collectors as the "Flattop Target Models."

Colt's time-tested Single Action Army has a huge following. This newly-manufactured Third Generation SAA has a 5-1/2-inch barrel and is chambered in 45 Colt.

The Single Action Army was designed based on the ultra-dependable 1851 Navy percussion lock frame by William Mason and the design has proven itself to be unusually rugged. In fact it will still work in a pinch, even with several critical parts broken or missing. One drawback of the SAA's design has always has been its awkward method of loading and unloading, which is accomplished one shell at a time. However, as some of our more "rapid" shooters have shown us, the old hogleg Colt is capable of being operated with much greater speed than might seem possible for a revolver with such a simple, almost crude action.

Many cartridges have been chambered in the SAA since it was introduced, including the 32/20, 357 Magnum and 44/40 Winchester. The standard chambering, and by far most popular chambering, has always been the time-tried 45 Colt. Standard revolvers were cataloged with barrel lengths of 4-3/4, 5-1/2 and 7-1/2 inches, although in the early days Colt would supply just about any custom barrel length the buyer was willing to pay for.

For years now there have been many replicas of the Single Action Army, called by some "clones," being imported into the USA from factories in Europe,

especially Germany and Italy. In the main, these revolvers are less expensive than Colts, and they have found a waiting market in the many American shooters and Colt SAA fanciers. Many of the early copies acquired poor reputations because they were crudely made, fitted with parts that were prone to break, and usually required the services of a skilled gunsmith before they could be used for any serious competition shooting. For the most part our modern copies today have improved in quality vastly to the point where (with very few exceptions) most off-the-shelf SAA replicas are serviceable weapons as purchased, with many of the newer Uberti and Pietta revolvers showing workmanship that rivals their American parent.

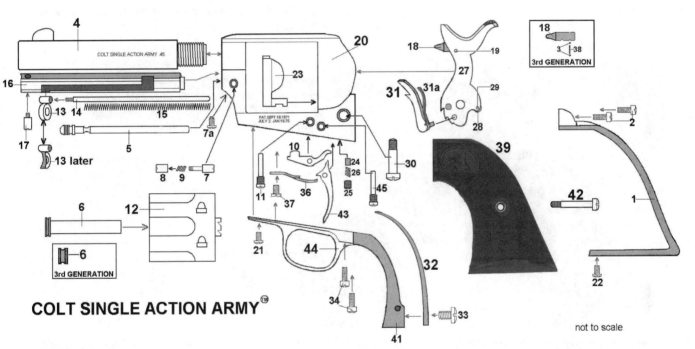

COLT SINGLE ACTION ARMY™

Parts List

1	Backstrap	17	Ejector Housing Screw	33	Mainspring Screw
2	Backstrap Screw, Upper (2)	18	Firing Pin	34	Triggerguard Screw, Rear (2)
3	Detent Ball (2)	19	Firing Pin Rivet	35	Recoil Plate (not shown)
4	Barrel	20	Frame	36	Sear and Bolt Spring
5	Base Pin	21	Triggerguard Screw, Front	37	Sear and Bolt Spring Screw
6	Base Pin Bushing	22	Backstrap Screw, Lower	38	Firing Pin Detent Spring
7	Base Pin Lock Screw	23	Loading Gate	39	Grip, Left
8	Base Pin Lock Nut	24	Loading Gate Detent	40	Grip, Right (not shown)
9	Base Pin Lock Spring	25	Loading Gate Detent Screw	41	Grip Locating Pin
10	Bolt	26	Loading Gate Detent Spring	42	Grip Screw
11	Bolt Screw	27	Hammer	43	Trigger
12	Cylinder	28	Hammer Roll	44	Triggerguard
13	Ejector Rod Head	29	Hammer Roll Pin	45	Trigger Screw
14	Ejector Rod	30	Hammer Screw	46	Washer, Hammer Screw (not shown)
15	Ejector Spring	31	Hand Assembly	47	Washers, No. 8 (not shown)
16	Ejector Housing	32	Mainspring		

Before you begin, always check to make certain the revolver is empty.

Here you can see the base pin nut being depressed by the gunsmith's thumb. Under the barrel the base pin is partially withdrawn.

The hammer remains at half-cock with the loading gate open. Note that the base pin and cylinder have been removed and that the base pin bushing is partially withdrawn from the cylinder.

DISASSEMBLY INSTRUCTIONS

1 First, make sure the gun is unloaded. Begin by holding the revolver around its grip with the left hand, being careful to always keep your finger away from the trigger (#43). Be sure that the revolver is always being pointed toward a direction where no one would be harmed if it were accidentally fired. Use your thumb to roll the loading gate (#23) open to the right, and then cautiously pull the hammer (#27) slowly toward the rear until you have heard two audible clicks. Doing this should have placed the hammer in the half-cock or loading position and the cylinder (#12) will now spin freely in a clockwise direction. Once more, keep your fingers away from the trigger

during the course of this entire operation. Slowly rotate the cylinder by hand, all the while examining the cylinder's chambers through the opening presented by the opened loading gate at the rear of the frame (#20) to make absolutely certain that the cylinder chambers have no cartridges in them.

If you can see cartridges in the chambers, you have a loaded gun. What you see might be fired cartridge cases, but you should always treat this kind of situation as if the gun were loaded with live ammunition. Leave the hammer right where it is, still in the half-cock or loading position, and leave the loading gate opened. Still using your left hand

Two-piece grips are easily removed by removing the grip screw.

to hold the revolver securely by its grip and keeping your fingers away from the trigger, tilt the revolver so the barrel is facing away from you and upwards. The gun should be facing generally in a direction that you determine is safe, so that if the gun did accidentally discharge, no one would be harmed. Using your right hand, rotate the cylinder slowly, one chamber at a time, pausing as you hear each audible click to allow each cartridge to fall out of its chamber and onto the bench. If a cartridge does not fall out of the chamber of its own accord, you should manually operate the ejector by pushing the ejector rod head (#13) located under the front of the barrel to the rear with your right

hand until the ejector forces the cartridge out of the chamber. When you are certain there are no more cartridges left in the cylinder chambers, you may consider the revolver empty and proceed with the disassembly. Remove any live cartridges from the area and store them in a secure location before moving on to the next step.

2 Removing the cylinder: The hammer should still be at rest in the loading or half-cocked position and the loading gate should still be open for this operation. Colt Single Action Army cylinders rotate on the base pin (#5), which must first be removed through the front of the frame before the cylinder can

Removing the three screws in the triggerguard allows the guard to be removed from the bottom of the frame.

Once the backstrap is out of the way, the mainspring screw is unscrewed to remove the mainspring.

Next the sear and bolt spring screw are removed and the sear and bolt spring taken out.

be removed from the revolver. The Colt company, and some Colt clonemakers, have used two methods of retaining the base pin over the years. The first method was used on Colts up to about serial number 165,000: the so-called black powder method where the base pin was restrained by a single locking-screw located at the front of the frame, just under the barrel and forward of the triggerguard bow. In order to remove the base pin you have to remove this lock-screw (#7A), and then the base pin (#5) can be pulled straight out through the front of the frame (#20). The second method requires no tools for base pin removal and uses a sliding,

spring-powered crossbolt to hold the base pin in place. The base pin is removed by depressing this crossbolt, which Colt calls the base pin screw (#7), and then pulling the base pin straight out the front of the frame (#20). The cylinder (#12) is now loose and may be carefully rolled out from the right side (the loading gate side) of the frame.

3 Removing the grips and grip straps: If the revolver is equipped with two-piece grip, unscrew and remove the grip screw (#42) from the center of the grip and then lift off the two grips.

The trigger, bolt and hammer along with the hand assembly have been removed, leaving the frame almost empty.

In some cases these revolvers will be equipped with one-piece grips and these are disassembled thus: Remove the two backstrap screws (#2) located at the top rear of the backstrap (#1), then unscrew and remove the single butt-screw (#22) from the bottom front of the backstrap. The backstrap (#1) and the one-piece grip (if so equipped) are removed by pulling them down and to the rear as one unit. Once they are off the frame, the grip itself is pulled straight forward off the backstrap. Next, for either grip type, unscrew and remove the mainspring screw (#33) from the inside-lower area of triggerguard (#44). The mainspring (#32) can now be lifted off. Unscrew and remove the two rear guard screws (#34, these are facing straight up) as well as the front triggerguard screw (#21). The

triggerguard (#44) is now loose and will come off toward the bottom.

4 Disassembling the action: Unscrew and remove the sear and bolt spring screw (#37) from the underside of the frame. (This is the screw that faces straight up, located just forward of the trigger.) The sear and bolt spring (#36) will fall out the bottom of the frame. Now remove the trigger screw (#45) – this is the center screw of the three screws in the left side of the frame – and the trigger (#43). Next, remove the forwardmost of the three screws from the left side of the frame. This is the bolt screw (#11) that holds the bolt (#10) in place, and once it has been removed, the bolt may now be taken out the bottom of the frame. Be sure you keep the bolt screw (#11) with the

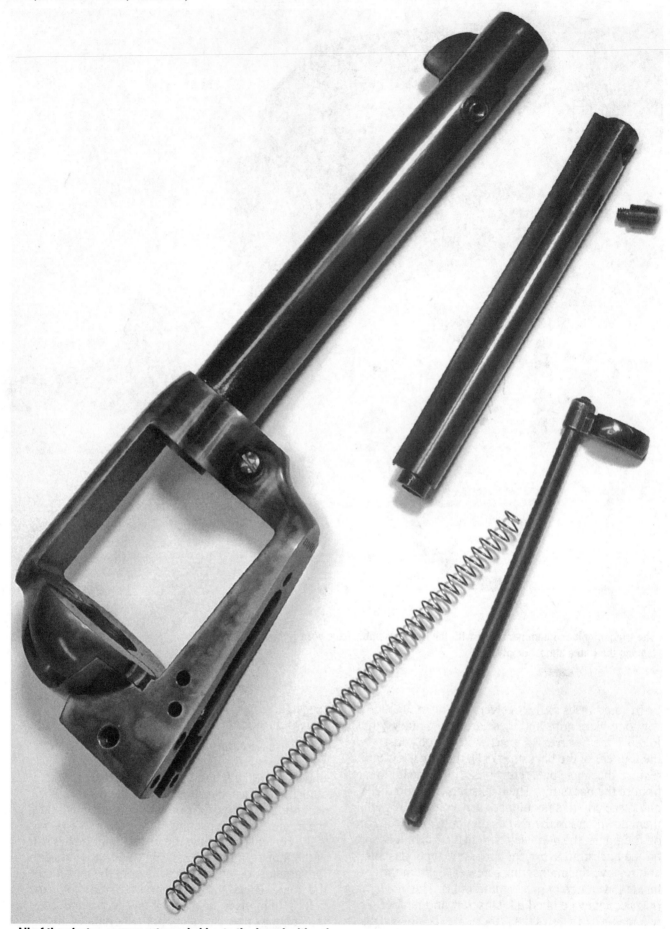

All of the ejector components are held onto the barrel with only one screw.

By using opposing screwdrivers, the base pin screw and nut assembly may be removed from the frame. Notice the gate catch screw in the lower-left leg of the frame.

bolt (#10) while they are out of the gun because the trigger screw (#45) might easily be mistaken for the bolt screw (#11), which is essentially the same screw, just slightly shorter. The hammer screw (#30) is now unscrewed and removed. The hammer (#27) is then rotated slightly to the rear and pulled down and out of the frame. The hand assembly (#31 and #31A) is connected to the hammer and will come out of the gun with the hammer. Once the hammer (#27) is out of the frame, the hand assembly (#31) is removed by lifting it up out of its pivot hole on the left side of the hammer.

5 Peripheral disassembly: The ejector tube screw (#17) is now unscrewed and removed from the front of the ejector tube (#16). The ejector tube assembly may be pulled to the side by its front until it is slightly away from the barrel. In this position the entire assembly may be withdrawn forward and off the barrel. The ejector rod (#14), the ejector head (#13)

and its spring (#15) are removed by pulling them both straight back and out of the ejector tube except on early revolvers; with these you have to unscrew the ejector rod (#14) from the ejector head (#13) and then remove each part separately.

On the underside of the frame in the right side frame rail you will notice a small headless screw facing up. This is the gate catch screw (#25). Remove this screw and its plunger and the gate spring (#26) out through the screw hole. The loading gate may now be removed by pulling it out into the cylinder opening toward the front of the frame.

REASSEMBLY

Reverse the order above for reassembly of the revolver.

Colt Single Action
Frontier Scout

Colt's Scout and Frontier Scout revolvers are scaled-down, .22 rimfire versions of the familiar Single Action Army. Introduced in 1957, the Scout was a six-shot single action with an aluminum frame using a steel barrel, cylinder and ejector tube. Primarily chambered to accept 22 Short, Long and Long Rifle, a 22 Magnum version was made available about 1959, with dual cylinder versions available a few years later. The Scout was offered in 4-1/4-, 4-3/4- and 9-1/2-inch (Buntline Scout) barrels.

Internally and externally, Colt simplified the single action with the introduction of the Scout, which used a one-piece backstrap cast of aluminum and a semi-captive leaf mainspring. Seeming to mimic the early Remington single actions, the Scout also used only two side frame screws, utilizing only one screw to act as the pivot for both the bolt and the trigger. Colt discontinued the Scout in 1970 or 1971, replacing the line with the steel-framed Peacemaker Scout and New Frontier Scout revolvers.

Illustration from *The Gun Digest Book of Exploded Firearms Drawings,* Second Edition, edited by Harold A. Murtz ©DBI Books Inc., 1977. Reproduced with permission of the publisher, K-P Books, 700 E. State St., Iola, WI 54990-0001. Retouched and renumbered by the author.

The Colt Scout is a scaled-down version of the full sized Peacemaker. Because of the accurate scaling, this .22 Scout revolver with a 4-3/4-inch barrel has the appearance of a full-size 5-1/2-inch SAA. Author photos.

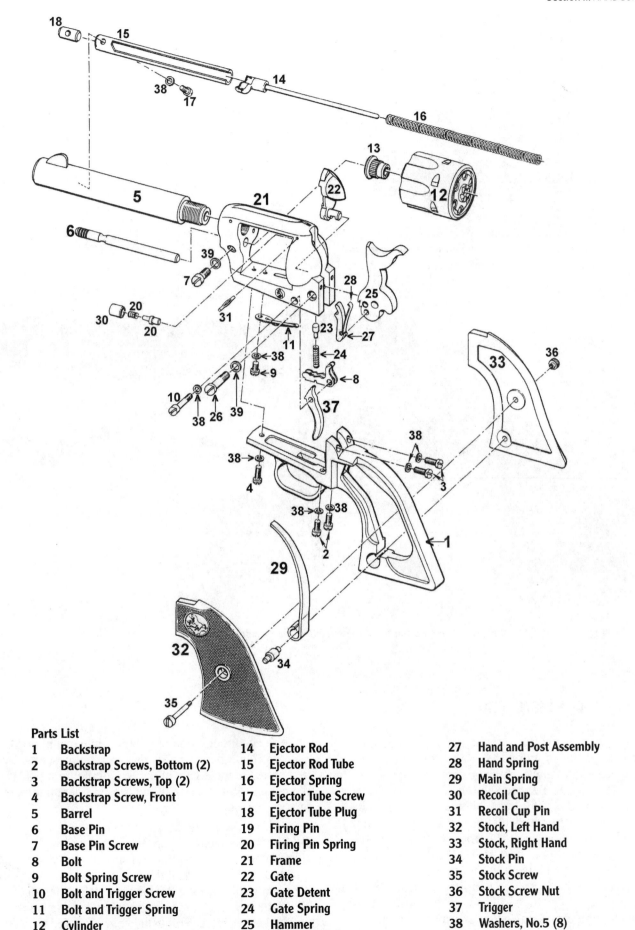

Parts List

1	Backstrap	14	Ejector Rod	27	Hand and Post Assembly
2	Backstrap Screws, Bottom (2)	15	Ejector Rod Tube	28	Hand Spring
3	Backstrap Screws, Top (2)	16	Ejector Spring	29	Main Spring
4	Backstrap Screw, Front	17	Ejector Tube Screw	30	Recoil Cup
5	Barrel	18	Ejector Tube Plug	31	Recoil Cup Pin
6	Base Pin	19	Firing Pin	32	Stock, Left Hand
7	Base Pin Screw	20	Firing Pin Spring	33	Stock, Right Hand
8	Bolt	21	Frame	34	Stock Pin
9	Bolt Spring Screw	22	Gate	35	Stock Screw
10	Bolt and Trigger Screw	23	Gate Detent	36	Stock Screw Nut
11	Bolt and Trigger Spring	24	Gate Spring	37	Trigger
12	Cylinder	25	Hammer	38	Washers, No.5 (8)
13	Cylinder Bushing	26	Hammer Screw	39	Washers, No. 10 (2)

To check if the Scout is loaded, pull back the hammer two clicks and open the gate to expose the cylinder chambers.

Removing the base pin screw allows the base pin to be removed and the cylinder rolled out.

DISASSEMBLY INSTRUCTIONS

1 Begin by making sure the gun is unloaded. Hold the revolver around its grip with your left hand, being careful to always keep your finger away from the trigger (#37). Be sure that the revolver is always being pointed in a direction where no one would be harmed if it were accidentally fired. Use your thumb to roll the loading gate (#22) open to the right and then cautiously pull the hammer (#25) slowly toward the rear until you have heard two clicks. This places the hammer in the half-cock or loading position. From here the cylinder (#12) will spin freely in a clockwise direction. Again, keep your fingers away from the trigger during the course of this entire operation. Slowly rotate the cylinder by hand, all the while examining the cylinder's chambers through the opening presented by the opened loading gate at the rear of the frame (#21) to make absolutely certain that the cylinder chambers have no cartridges in them.

If you can see cartridges in the chambers, you probably have a loaded gun. What you see might be fired cartridge cases, but you should always treat this kind of situation as if the gun were loaded with live ammunition. Leave the hammer right where it is, still in the half-cock or loading position and leave the loading gate opened. Still using your left hand to hold the revolver securely by its grip, tilt the revolver so the

The grips and one-piece backstrap removed. The mainspring can stay in place for normal disassembly.

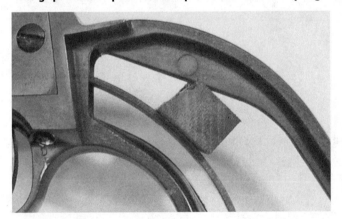

Before the backstrap is removed, a block of wood is inserted here to take the mainspring tension off the hammer.

muzzle is facing away from you and upwards. The gun should be facing in a safe direction.

Using your right hand, rotate the cylinder slowly, one chamber at a time, pausing as you hear each click, to allow each cartridge to fall out of its chamber and onto the bench. If a cartridge does not fall out of the chamber of its own accord, you should manually operate the ejector by pushing the ejector rod head (#14) located under the front of the barrel to the rear with your right hand until the ejector forces the cartridge out of the chamber. When you are certain there are no more cartridges left in the cylinder chambers, you may consider the revolver empty

and proceed with the disassembly. Remove any live cartridges from the area and store them in a secure location before moving on to the next step.

2 To remove the cylinder: The hammer should still be at rest in the loading or half-cocked position and the loading gate should still be open for this operation. Colt single action cylinders rotate on the base pin (#6), which must first be remove through the front of the frame before the cylinder can be removed from the revolver. The base pin is restrained by a single locking screw located at the front-left side of the frame, just forward of the cylinder and above the triggerguard bow. In order to remove the base pin you have to

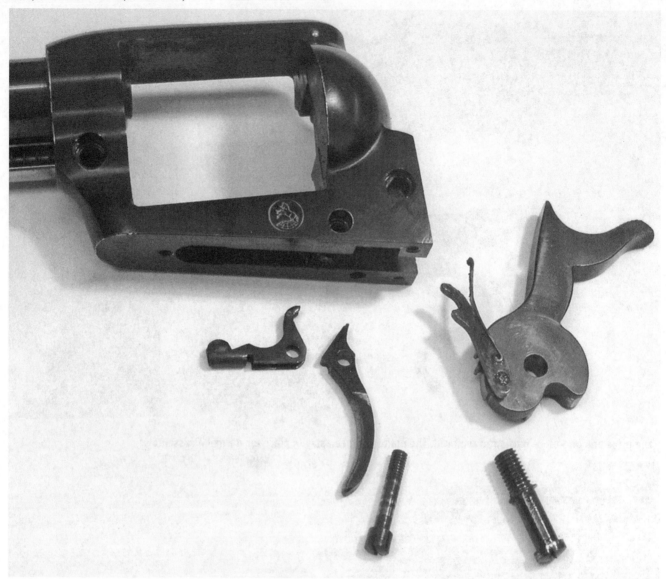

The Scout is simplified by having only one screw for the bolt and trigger. In this respect it is like the early Remington single action revolvers.

remove this screw (#7) so the base pin (#6) can be pulled straight out through the front of the frame. The cylinder is now loose and may be carefully rolled out from the right side (the loading gate side) of the frame. Notice that the screws in these revolvers all have nylon washers (#38) and (#39) under their heads to help keep them from loosening.

3 To remove the grips and backstrap: Unscrew and remove the grip screw (#35) from the center of the left grip (#32) and then lift off the two grips. Cock the hammer and insert a small block of wood about 3/8-inch square or a small piece of dowel between the top area of the mainspring and the inside of the backstrap and release the hammer, allowing it to fall forward. The wood will hold the mainspring compressed, relieving tension from the hammer. You may leave this wood block in place for later reassembly. Unscrew and remove the two rear backstrap screws (#3) – these are facing straight forward – as well as the front triggerguard screw (#4) and the bottom backstrap screws (#2). The backstrap assembly (#1) is now loose and will come off toward the bottom. Make note of the gate spring (#24) in the bottom of the frame that is now loose. Remove the gate spring and the gate spring detent (#23) through the bottom of the frame and slide the opened gate (#22) out toward the front of the frame.

4 To disassemble the action: Unscrew and remove the bolt spring screw (#9) – this is the screw that faces straight up, located just forward of the trigger – from the underside of the frame. The sear and bolt spring (#11) will fall out the bottom of the frame. Now

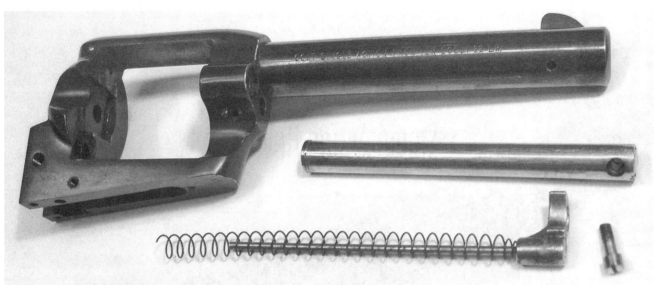

One screw holds the ejector assembly on the barrel. The tube slides back into that round hole in the front of the frame to the left of the base pin hole.

Scouts don't have a gate detent screw as the SAA does. The spring is held in by the backstrap itself; here the gate is shown disassembled and the bolt spring has been removed.

remove the trigger screw (#10) – the forwardmost screw of the two screws in the left side of the frame – and the trigger (#37). The bolt (#8) will drop out through the frame bottom. The hammer screw (#26), the larger and rearmost of the two screws in the left side of the frame, is now unscrewed and removed. The hammer (#25) may be rotated slightly to the rear and pulled down and out of the frame. The hand assembly (#27) and (#28) is connected to the hammer and will come out of the gun with the hammer. Once the hammer is out of the frame, the hand assembly is removed by lifting it up out of its pivot hole on the left side of the hammer.

5 Peripheral disassembly: The ejector tube screw (#17) is unscrewed and removed from the front of the ejector tube (#15). The ejector tube assembly may be pulled to the side by its front until it is slightly away

from the barrel. The entire assembly is now withdrawn forward and off the barrel. The ejector rod assembly (#14) and the ejector spring (#16) are removed by pulling them both straight back and out of the ejector tube. The ejector tube plug (#18) may be taken out the front of the ejector tube. Further disassembly is not required for normal maintenance.

REASSEMBLY

Reverse the order above to reassemble the revolver.

Colt Cowboy
Single Action Revolver

In order to fill public demand for a less expensive version of the famous Single Action Army, that is, to offer the public a genuine Colt but at a price that was in the range of the imported copies, Colt introduced the single action Cowboy model in 1999. The primary intended market for the Cowboy was, of course, to be cowboy action shooters. As some Colt collectors are already aware, the company actually made and sold 140 Cowboys prior to the official beginning of production in 1998 but the serious advertising and sales started in 1999.

Colt's Cowboy models were not as highly polished as the standard blue and case-hardened Single Action Army model Ps. The Cowboy's color case hardening was also done using a different process that did not give the gun the beautiful Colt bone and charcoal colors. Cowboy case colors have a look reminiscent of some of the older Italian imports more than of Colt's older case coloring. Hand-fitting in areas such as the junction of the grip straps to the frame and grips to the grip straps wasn't given the normal careful attention. Other areas, including the front edges of the cylinder where the flutes used to be cleanly chamfered, were not finished as well. It is for those reasons that many Cowboy models are found with sharp edges. Colt's factory model numbers for the Cowboy models were

Colt's Cowboy was also manufactured for four years, during which time nearly 14,000 were produced.

CB1840 for 4-3/4-inch barrel, CB1850 for 5-1/2-inch barrel, and CB1870 for the 7-1/2-inch barrel length. The official name for the Cowboy's standard finish was called "casehardened," but in actuality these guns were furnished with color casehardened frame and with a blued barrel, cylinder and grip straps similar to the Model P, while the hammer appeared to be parkerized.

The first cock notch, which was also known as the so-called safety notch, is not used on Cowboy's hammer; gone along with it are the hammer-mounted firing pin we are so used to seeing on Colt single actions. In their place the Cowboy used a modern, transfer bar ignition with a frame-mounted, floating firing pin. For loading and unloading the hammer must still be pulled back into the half-cock position, so the Cowboy is officially a "two clicker." Cowboy barrel tops are stamped with the Colt factory name and address, and barrel sides are marked "COLT COWBOY .45 COLT." Unlike the Single Action Army, the left frame side has no patent dates. The hammer spur is very practical and equipped with some of the most positive, non-slip checkering we have ever seen on a Colt single action revolver.

In a letter from Amy Navitsky of Colt, the author learned that the Colt Custom Shop also did custom work on some Cowboys, to which they assigned a "Z" model number designation, signifying Custom Shop work. "I have seen nickel Cowboys and engraved Cowboys, and Cowboys with wood grips. All of these deviations of the standard models were done through the custom shop," says Navitsky. There was also a Cowboy Buntline manufactured, along with a few Cowboys chambered in 38 Special. Alas, the American cowboy shooter did not respond to the Cowboy model as well as Colt would have liked, and in 2003 the Colt factory discontinued the model. Their official reason for discontinuing the Cowboy is, "Colt was responding to market signals." A total of 13,984 Cowboys were manufactured.

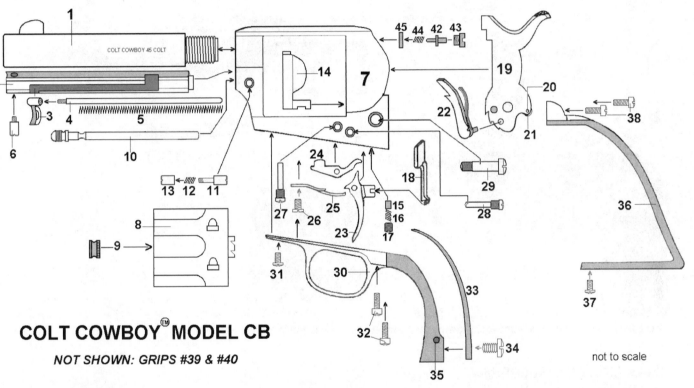

COLT COWBOY™ MODEL CB

NOT SHOWN: GRIPS #39 & #40

not to scale

Parts List

1	Barrel	16	Gate Spring	31	Front Strap Screw
2	Ejector Tube	17	Gate Catch Screw	32	Rear Guard Screw (2)
3	Ejector Head	18	Transfer Bar	33	Main Spring
4	Ejector Rod	19	Hammer Assembly	34	Main Spring Screw
5	Ejector Spring	20	Hammer Roll Pin	35	Stock Pin
6	Ejector Tube Screw	21	Hammer Roll	36	Backstrap
7	Frame	22	Hand	37	Backstrap, Lower Screw
8	Cylinder	23	Trigger	38	Backstrap Screw (2)
9	Base Pin Bushing	24	Bolt	39	Stock Left
10	Base Pin	25	Sear & Bolt Spring	40	Stock Right
11	Base Pin Screw	26	Sear & Bolt Spring Screw	41	Stock Screw (not shown)
12	Base Pin Spring	27	Bolt Screw	42	Firing Pin
13	Base Spring Screw Nut	28	Trigger Screw	43	Firing Pin Retainer
14	Gate	29	Hammer Screw	44	Firing Pin Spring
15	Gate Catch	30	Triggerguard	45	Firing Pin Spacer

Shown here with its hammer in the loading position and the loading gate opened, the shooter is in the act of pushing the ejector rod back to certify this chamber is unloaded.

Here the base pin has been removed, allowing the cylinder to be rolled out the right side of the frame.

DISASSEMBLY INSTRUCTIONS

1 Always check to be sure the weapon is unloaded. Grasp the revolver around the grip firmly, pointing the muzzle in a safe direction. Keep your fingers away from the trigger and open the loading gate (#14). Next pull the hammer (#19) slowly to the rear until you hear one audible click; this should place the hammer in the half-cock or loading position and the cylinder (#8) should now be able to spin freely in a clockwise direction. Remember during this entire operation to keep your fingers away from the trigger (#23). Slowly rotate the cylinder two full revolutions by hand, all the while examining the cylinder's chambers through the opening that has been presented by the opened loading gate at the rear of the frame (#7) to make certain that the cylinder chambers have no cartridges in them.

If cartridges are present in the chambers, this as a loaded gun. Leave the hammer right where it is, in the half-cock or loading position, and with the loading gate still opened. Using your left hand to hold the revolver securely by its grip, keeping your fingers away from the trigger; tilt the revolver so that the barrel's muzzle is facing in a direction that you determine is safe (so that if the gun did accidentally fire, no one would be injured). Use your right hand to rotate the cylinder slowly, one chamber at a time, in a clockwise direction (viewed from the rear), pausing at each audible click to allow each successive cartridge to fall out of its chamber and onto the workbench. If any cartridge will not fall out of its own weight, manually operate the ejector by pushing the ejector rod head (#6), located under the front of the barrel, to the rear with your right

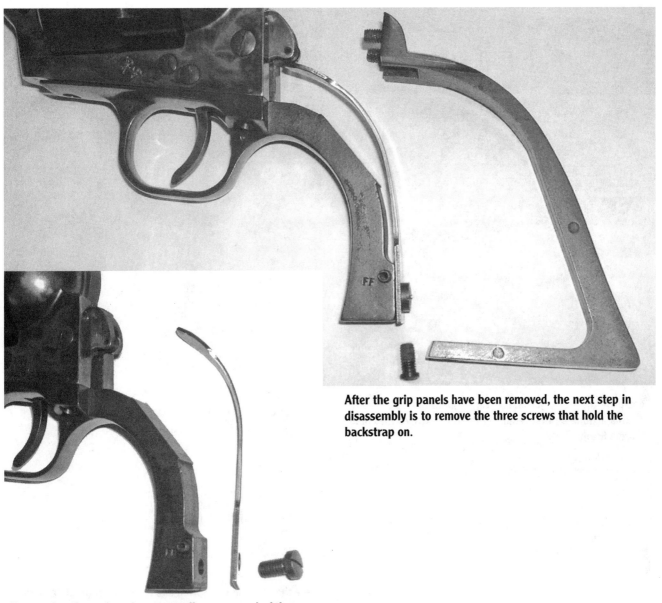

After the grip panels have been removed, the next step in disassembly is to remove the three screws that hold the backstrap on.

Unscrewing the mainspring screw allows removal of the mainspring.

hand until the ejector rod has forced that cartridge out of the chamber. Repeat this operation for each chamber. When you are certain that there are no more cartridges left in the cylinder chambers, the revolver is empty and ready to be safely disassembled.

2 Cylinder removal: The hammer should still be resting in the loading or half-cocked position and the loading gate should still be open for this operation. The Cowboy cylinder rotates on a part called the base pin (#10), and this part must first be removed through the front of the frame before the cylinder can be taken out. The base pin is held in place by a sliding, spring-powered crossbolt called the base pin screw (#11). The base pin is removed by first depressing this screw, and then pulling the base pin (#10) straight out the front of the frame (#20). The cylinder (#8) may now be

carefully rolled out sideways through the right side of the frame.

3 Grip and grip strap removal: First remove the grip screw (#41) from the center of the grip and then remove the two grips (#39) and (#40). Unscrew and remove the two backstrap screws (#38) from the top rear of the backstrap (#36) and remove the single butt screw (#37) from the butt of the backstrap. The backstrap (#36) may be removed by pulling it off to the rear. Unscrew and remove the mainspring screw (#34) from the inside-lower area of triggerguard (#30). The mainspring (#32) will now lift out. Unscrew and remove the two rear triggerguard screws (#32) (facing straight up) and the front triggerguard screw (also facing up, #31) and the triggerguard (#30) can be removed from the bottom.

To expose the action parts, the triggerguard must be taken off. This is done by first removing the three screws that hold it to the frame.

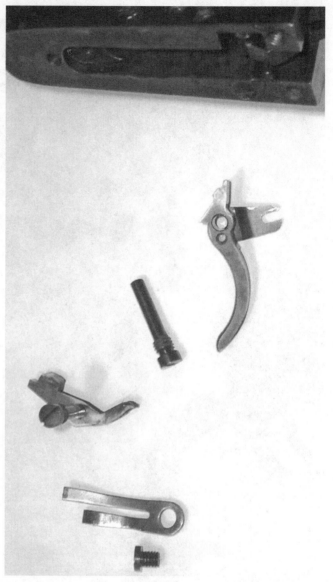

Here the sear and bolt spring and its screw (bottom) lie on the bench just below the bolt and its screw. The top screw is the one the trigger pivots on. You should try to keep these screws with the parts they hold in; because of the frame's taper, the bolt screw is shorter than the trigger screw.

4 Disassembling the action: Unscrew and remove the sear and bolt spring screw (#26) – this is the only screw that faces straight-up on the inside of the lock frame – from the underside of the frame. The sear and bolt spring (#25) can now be lifted out from the bottom of the frame. Next, unscrew and remove the trigger screw (#28), the centermost of the three screws that pass through the frame side. The trigger (#23) may be removed through the bottom of the frame. Notice how the trigger connects with the transfer bar (#18). The hammer screw (#29), the rearmost of the three screws in the frame side, can now be unscrewed and removed, after which the hammer (#19) is rotated slightly to the rear and then pulled down and out of the frame.

You will find that the hand assembly (#22) is connected to the hammer and it can be withdrawn from the frame along with the hammer. Once the hammer (#19) is out, the hand assembly (#22) is removed by lifting it up out of its socket hole on the left side of the hammer. The transfer bar (#18) may be slid down out the bottom of the frame. Be sure to make note of its relative positioning for reassembly. Unscrew and remove the bolt screw (#27), the forwardmost of the three screws on the left side of the frame and the one that holds the bolt (#24) in place. The bolt may now be removed from the bottom. Be sure you keep the bolt screw (#27) with the bolt (#24) while they are removed from the gun because the trigger screw (#28)

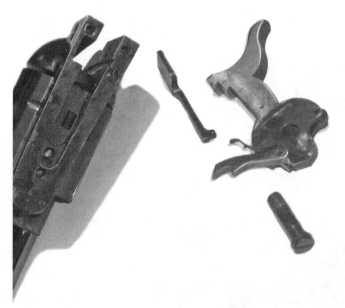

Next, the hammer and its screw, along with the hand assembly and transfer bar, are removed from the bottom of the frame. Now all the major action parts have been removed.

The loading gate and its component parts after removal from the frame.

All the ejector parts are held onto the barrel by one screw.

may easily be mistaken for the bolt screw, which is similar but slightly shorter.

5 Peripheral disassembly: The ejector tube screw (#6) is unscrewed and removed from the front of the ejector tube (#2), thus leaving the entire ejector tube assembly loose so it may be pulled to the side by its front until it moves slightly away from the barrel. At this position, the assembly may be withdrawn forward and off the barrel. The ejector rod (#4) and the ejector head (#6) and its spring (#5) are removed by pushing them both straight back and removing them out the rear of the ejector tube.

Removing the loading gate: Under the frame in the right side frame rail you will notice a small screw. This is the gate catch screw (#17). Unscrew and remove the screw, the gate spring (#16) and its plunger (#15) through the same screw hole. The loading gate itself (#14) may now be removed by pulling it out towards the front of the frame. At reassembly, the gate catch screw should be turned in until it is just barely below flush with the frame.

REASSEMBLY

Further disassembly is not recommended for normal maintenance. Reassemble the revolver in the reverse order of above.

Colt Model 1878
Double Action Army

Colt's first large-bore DA was the 1878 Double Action Army, designed by the company's own William Mason. Author photos.

I n physical size and shape, Colt's 1878 Double Action Army revolver is very close to the more familiar and very popular Single Action Army. In fact, the two are kissin'-cousin revolvers, at least in size. They even share the same barrels, ejector parts and, except for the bolt notches, the same cylinders. At one time, the factory actually altered Model 1878 double action cylinders and used them in production models of the Single Action Army in an attempt to use up spare parts.

Many people have incorrectly assumed that the 1878 is a nightmare to repair, that it is easily damaged and that its parts are nearly impossible to locate. While these statements are true of its smaller relative, the Colt 1877 .38 Lightning and .41 Thunderer models, they really cannot be applied to the big Double Action Army. The large-frame 1878 has by far the better internal mechanism of these two designs; in fact, it uses an entirely different mechanism, one that once understood is possible to restore with far less effort than you may have imagined.

One thing that scares some folks is the 1878's complete lack of a cylinder stop or bolt, so it's just hard to imagine what in the world locks the cylinder in correct alignment with the barrel. The truth is that the design uses a rather ingenious idea of William Mason's that binds two ratchet teeth against the hand when the trigger is held all the way to the rear, effectively indexing the cylinder chamber to the barrel. In an 1878 that is still in good mechanical shape the system works perfectly, although worn 1878 revolvers are well known for their habit of throwing lead out the barrel/cylinder gap due to misalignment.

Some 51,210 of this robust double action model were manufactured between 1878 and 1905, the majority being chambered in standard 45 Colt caliber. Other calibers offered in this model were 32-20, 38 Colt, 38-40, 41 Colt, 44-40 and 476 Eley as well as a few others. The 1878 was made both without ejectors in 3-, 3-1/2- or 4-inch barrels and with ejectors in 4-3/4, 5-1/2 and 7-1/2 barrels, just as the SAA was. Colt used a medium-large size birds-head-shaped grip on a rounded butt and capped it off with checkered hard rubber grips for the majority of production, although some of the early revolvers were equipped with checkered walnut stocks.

The 1878 double actions are well known for their very long trigger pull lengths and hard double action trigger pulls. An odd variation of the Model 1878 is the so-called Model 1902 Alaskan or Philippine Model in 45 Colt with a 6-inch barrel, about 4,600 of which were produced for a U.S. Army contract. These awkward-looking pistols were equipped with an extra-long trigger surrounded by an equally oversized and awkward-looking triggerguard that people have assumed was intended for use with gloved hands. In fact, this was a crude effort to at last do something about the 1878's reputation for heavy double action trigger pulls. By providing a longer trigger, the shooter had greater leverage over the action – hence the perception of a reduced trigger pull.

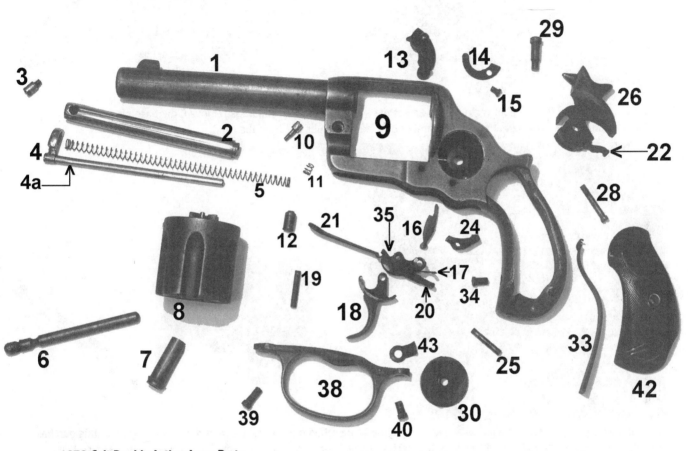

1878 Colt Double Action Army Parts

1	Barrel	15	Loading Gate Spring Screw	31	Hammer Stirrup
2	Ejector Tube	16	Hand	32	Hammer Stirrup Pin
3	Ejector Tube Screw	17	Hand Spring	33	Mainspring
4	Ejector Rod Head	18	Trigger	34	Mainspring Screw
4A	Ejector Rod	19	Trigger Pin	35	Trigger Saddle
5	Ejector Spring	20	Strut	36	Lanyard Ring (not shown)
6	Cylinder Pin	21	Trigger Spring	37	Lanyard Ring Pin (not shown)
7	Cylinder Bushing	22	Trigger Stirrup	38	Triggerguard
8	Cylinder	23	Trigger Stirrup Pin	39	Front Triggerguard Screw
9	Frame	24	Sear	40	Rear Triggerguard Screw
10	Cylinder Pin Catch Screw	25	Sear Pin	41	Grip Pin
11	Cylinder Pin Catch Spring	26	Hammer	42	Grip
12	Cylinder Pin Catch Nut	28	Grip Screw	43	Sear Spring
13	Loading Gate	29	Hammer Screw	44	Escutcheons
14	Loading Gate Spring	30	Sideplate	45	Recoil Plate

Always make certain there are no cartridges in any of the cylinder chambers before attempting any gunsmithing work.

After the cylinder is removed, the base pin bushing simply pulls out from the front.

Here the base pin has been removed, allowing the cylinder to be rolled out the right side of the frame. Note that this gun has had its ejector removed and the frame where the ejector would fit has been ground away. The hammer spur has also been shortened.

DISASSEMBLY INSTRUCTIONS

1 The first step you should take before starting disassembly should always be to make certain that your weapon is unloaded.

Begin by holding the revolver around its grip with the left hand, being careful to always keep your fingers away from the trigger (#18). Be sure that the muzzle is always being pointed in a direction where no one would be harmed if the gun were accidentally discharged. Using a thumb, roll the loading gate (#13) open to the right and then cautiously pull the hammer (#26) slowly toward the rear until you have heard two clicks. Doing this should have placed the hammer in the half-cock, or loading position. (It should be located about half-way back in its travel.) From here,

the cylinder (#8) should spin freely in a clockwise direction. Once more, keep your fingers away from the trigger during this entire operation. Slowly rotate the cylinder by hand while examining the cylinder's chambers through the opening presented by the opened loading gate at the rear of the frame (#9) and make absolutely certain that the cylinder chambers have no cartridges in them.

If you can see cartridges in the chambers, then this is very likely a loaded gun. Leave the hammer right where it is, still in the half-cock or loading position, and leave the loading gate opened. Using your right hand, rotate the cylinder slowly, one chamber at a time, pausing as you hear each click to allow each

When you remove the sideplate, notice the small "nub" on its edge and the corresponding notch in the frame. These must be aligned for reassembly.

cartridge to fall out of its chamber and onto the bench. If a cartridge does not fall out of the cylinder of its own accord, then you will have to manually operate the ejector by pushing the ejector rod head (#4), located under the front of the barrel, to the rear with your right hand until the ejector rod forces the cartridge out of the chamber. Repeat this until there are no more cartridges in the cylinder and when you are certain of this, you may consider the revolver empty and proceed with the disassembly. It is also a good habit to remove any live cartridges from the area and store them in a secure location before moving along to the next step.

2 To remove the cylinder: The hammer (#26) should remain resting in the loading or half-

cocked position. Leave the loading gate (#13) open. The Colt Double Action Army cylinder rotates on a part called the base pin (#6). Just as with its single action cousin, this base pin must be removed through the front of the frame before the cylinder can be taken out. The base pin is held in place in the frame by a sliding, spring-powered crossbolt located at the front of the frame and just below the barrel. The base pin may be removed by depressing this crossbolt, which Colt calls the base pin screw (#10), and then pulling the base pin (#6) straight out through the front of the frame (#9). The cylinder (#8) can now be carefully rolled out sideways toward the right side of the frame.

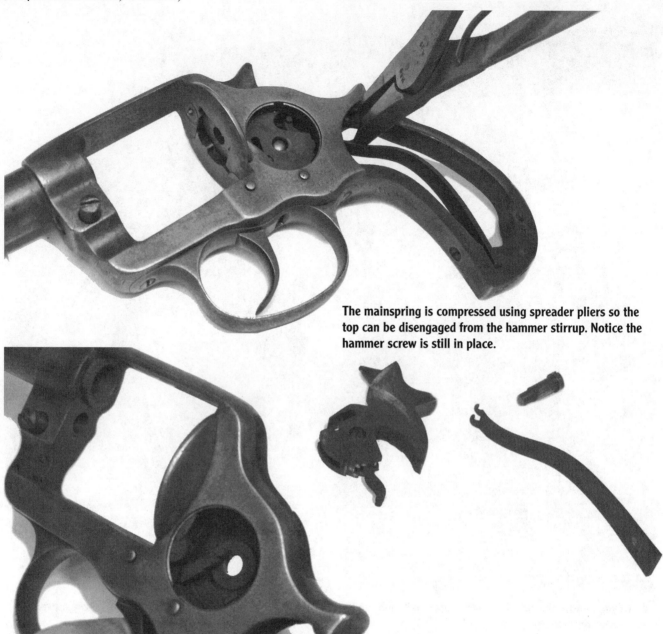

The mainspring is compressed using spreader pliers so the top can be disengaged from the hammer stirrup. Notice the hammer screw is still in place.

Here the mainspring, hammer screw and hammer are shown removed.

3 To remove the grips and the sideplate: Pull the hammer all the way to the rear. Taking hold of the hammer spur with your thumb, pull the trigger and allow the hammer to gently fall forward all the way, controlling its fall with your thumb, then release the trigger. Unscrew and remove the grip screw (#25) from the center of the grip and then lift off the two grips (#42.) The sideplate (#30), which is round in shape and located on the left side of the revolver frame, is held in place by a single screw (#29) that passes from the right side of the frame. (This same screw also serves as a pivot for the hammer.) The sideplate screw (#29) has a left-hand thread, so it must be turned clockwise in order to be removed.

During the screw's removal, hold the screwdriver tightly into the screw, so that the head stays within its recess in the frame. This will cause the sideplate (#30) to be pushed up out of its seat on the left side of the frame. As the sideplate lifts out, make note of the small lug on one side of the inside of the sideplate and of where that lug fits within its machined seat in the frame for reassembly. Once you have gotten the sideplate off the frame, leave the sideplate screw where it is.

4 To remove the mainspring and hammer: With the hammer forward, compress the top of the mainspring (#33) with a pair of spreader-type pliers just enough so that its top-fingers may be disengaged from the hammer stirrup (#31) by pivoting the stirrup

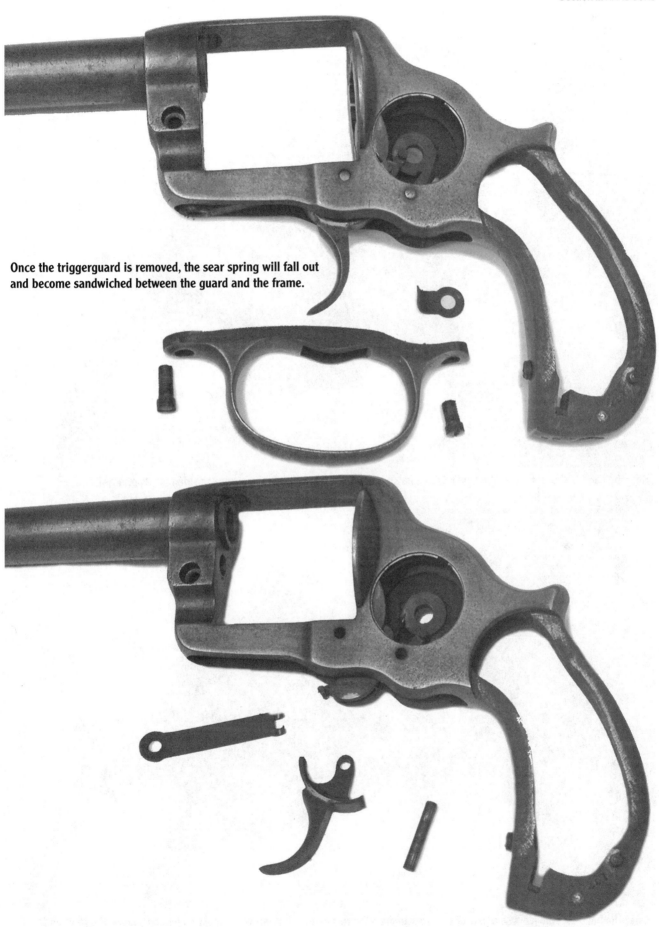

Once the triggerguard is removed, the sear spring will fall out and become sandwiched between the guard and the frame.

Removing the trigger pin frees the trigger and its spring to be removed. The rocker assembly is now also loose.

Here the hand is shown properly aligned with the notch in the sideplate window, the correct position for its removal.

Once the hand is removed, use a pair of tweezers to grab the rocker, lifting it out the sideplate opening. Notice the strut and handspring sticking straight up.

By driving out the sear pin, the sear may be dropped out the bottom. (The sear works for single action only.) Note its position for later reassembly.

forward. Loosen the strain screw (#34) and remove the mainspring (#33) out through the side of the grip frame opening. Pull the trigger so the hammer (#26) cycles all the way to the rear, to the point where it disengages from the DA sear. Now push the hammer forward while continuing to hold the trigger (#16) all the way to the rear. With the trigger held to the rear and the hammer (#26) in the forward position, push out the sideplate screw (#29) and rotate the hammer (#26) to the rear slightly while at the same time pulling it up and out of the frame. You may now release the trigger.

5 To remove the triggerguard and disassemble the action: Unscrew, then remove the two triggerguard screws (#39) and (#40) from the front and rear of the triggerguard (#38). Notice that the front screw is longer than the rear screw. Now, pull the triggerguard straight down and off the frame. At this point, notice the positioning of the single action sear spring (#43), which will fall out from the rear of the guard since it is held in place by being sandwiched between the guard and the frame. (The rear guard screw also passes through this spring.) Using a cup-tipped pin punch and hammer, drive out the sear pin (#25), the rearmost of the two cross pins that pass

side to side through the frame. Remove the sear (#24) through the frame bottom via the triggerguard opening. Use the same cup-tipped pin punch and hammer to drive out the trigger pin (#19), the forwardmost of the two pins passing side to side through the frame. The trigger (#18) is now loose and may be pulled straight out the bottom.

Take note of the relative positions of the following parts as you disassemble them for ease of assembly later: the trigger spring (#21) may be unhooked from the trigger stirrup (#22), which is the part that connects it to the rocker (#35). Remove the trigger stirrup. The rocker assembly may now be pushed slightly up and to the rear until it reaches a point where the hand (#16) may be aligned with the notch in the sideplate opening and lifted up out of its seat in the rocker (#35) through the round sideplate opening. Once the hand has been removed from the rocker, the rocker assembly may be removed through the sideplate opening. If it is necessary to remove the strut/hand spring assembly from the rocker, support the side of the rocker and use a small pin punch and hammer to drive out the strut pin. You will notice that the handspring is semi-permanently mounted on the strut with a rivet.

Only one screw secures the loading gate spring and the loading gate.

6 To remove the ejector assembly: Unscrew and remove the ejector tube screw (#3) from the front of the ejector tube (#2). This will allow the entire ejector tube assembly to be pulled out to the right side by its front until it moves slightly away from the barrel. At this position the assembly is withdrawn forward and off the barrel. The ejector rod (#4A), rod head (#4) and its spring (#5) may be removed as an assembly by pulling and working them both back and out through the rear of the ejector tube.

7 To remove the loading gate: Looking through the sideplate opening into the inside of the frame, you will notice a small screw just below the hole where the sideplate screw goes through. This is the gate spring screw (#15). Unscrew and remove this screw. The gate spring (#14) is now free to be removed by lifting it up out of its recess in the frame. The loading gate itself (#13) is now loose and can be removed by pulling it out toward the front of the frame

REASSEMBLY

Reverse the order of disassembly exactly to reassemble the revolver.

Colt Double Action
Official Police; Army Special;

Medium-framed Colt Revolvers including Commando, Officers Model Match, Trooper, .357 Magnum and pre-1969 Python; and Smaller-Framed Colt Double Action Revolvers

Colt's Official Police was a very popular revolver that was manufactured from 1908 through 1969. This particular gun is a 5-inch 38 Special made in 1947. From the Frank Gregg collection. Author photos.

The Official Police is a medium-framed, six-shot revolver that was Colt's equivalent of the S&W Military and Police model, although the Colt is actually a slightly larger gun. This model was a direct improvement over their former 1889 - 1892 New Army and New Navy models. Originally introduced to the public in 1908 (some sources say 1907) as the Army Special, the revolver was available in 32-20, 38 Special and 41 Colt. The expectation was that the military would be interested in the revolver, but by then the Army had set its sights on a .45-caliber weapon.

Colt had no worries, though, for this excellent handgun very quickly gained popularity with law enforcement, so much so that the Army Special was renamed the Official Police in 1928. In 1930 a 22 Long Rifle version was introduced and the 41 Colt chambering was discontinued, while the 32-20 chambering was retained until 1942. The standard 38 Special chambering was used through the entire production.

Army Special and Official Police revolvers were made with barrel lengths of 2, 4, 5 and 6 inches.

Roughly 50,000 unusual Official Police revolvers were manufactured during WWII. These were called the Commando Model. Manufactured with a rough-looking parkerized finish, the Commando was chambered in 38 Special with 2- (scarce), 4- and 6-inch barrels. Colt made the Official Police right up until 1969, having produced nearly a million revolvers on this frame size. The crane lock on all these models was changed during the 1950s to a spring-loaded detent, and over its 60-odd-year life span, the grips were made variously from hard rubber, plastic and walnut. Many target revolvers based on the Official

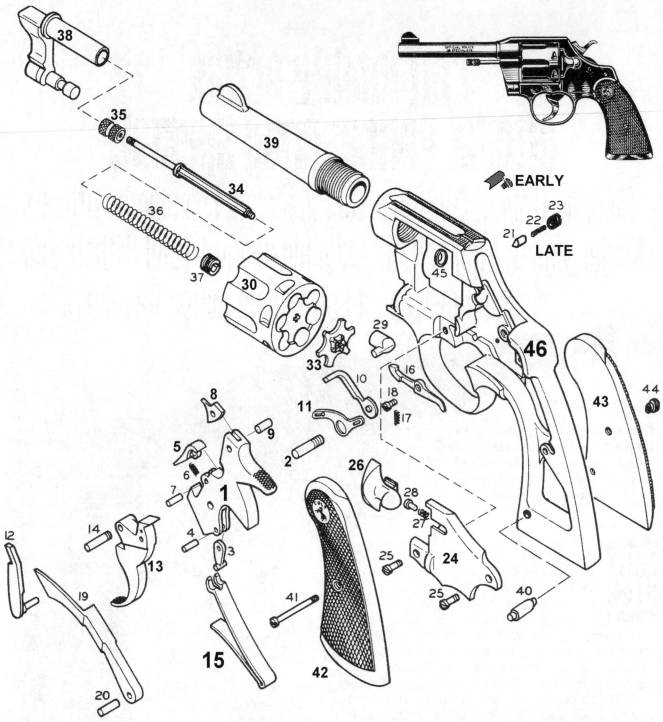

EARLY

LATE

Note: Nomenclature and drawing are taken from 1955 Colt catalog.

Colt Official Police parts

1	Hammer
2	Hammer Pin
3	Hammer Stirrup
4	Hammer Stirrup Pin
5	Strut
6	Strut Spring
7	Strut Pin
8	Firing Pin
9	Firing Pin Rivet
10	Safety
11	Safety Lever.
12	Hand
13	Trigger
14	Trigger Pin
15	Main Spring
16	Bolt
17	Bolt Spring.
18	Bolt Screw
19	Rebound Lever
20	Rebound Lever Pin
21	Crane Lock Detent
22	Crane Lock Spring
23	Crane Lock Screw
23A	Crane lock
24	Side Plate
25	Side Plate Screws (2)
26	Latch
27	Latch Spring
28	Latch Spring Guide
29	Latch Pin
30	Cylinder
31	Cylinder Bushing
32	Cylinder Bushing Pin
33	Ratchet
34	Ejector Rod
35	Ejector Rod Head
36	Ejector Spring
37	Crane Bushing
38	Crane
39	Barrel
40	Stock Pin
41	Stock Screw
42	Stock--Left Hand
43	Stock -Right Hand
44	Stock Screw Nut
45	Recoil Plate
46	Main Frame

Police frame were also manufactured by Colt (e.g., the Officers Model Match). When Colt introduced its premium revolver in 1955, the famous 357 Magnum Python, they built it using a specially heat-treated Official Police size frame, a design and frame size so popular that even S&W eventually mimicked it with its now popular .357 "L" frame series revolvers.

There are strong similarities in action designs between the Official Police, the smaller Police Positive and Police Positive Special, and the larger New Service Colt revolvers. Except for the obvious physical size differences, the mechanical design of all these revolvers is virtually identical, as are loading, unloading, operational and disassembly procedures for all of them. These disassembly instructions will work equally well with these other sizes of Colt revolvers, including those built on the small Police Positive/ Police Positive Special/Banker's Special/Detective Special size frame, as well as the much larger framed New Service, 1917 and Shooting Master.

In order to open a Colt DA cylinder, the latch is pulled to the rear.

DISASSEMBLY INSTRUCTIONS

1 First, make sure the gun is unloaded. Grasp the revolver firmly around its grip, being careful to keep your fingers away from the trigger (#13) and making sure that the muzzle is always pointed in a safe direction. Use your shooting hand's thumb to pull rearward on the latch (#26) and push the cylinder (#30) open toward the left side of the revolver. At this point, check to be certain that all the cylinder chambers are unloaded. If cartridges are present, tilt the revolver so the rear of the cylinder faces the bench top and push the ejector rod head (#35) toward the rear of the gun. This will cause the ejector to expel the cartridges from the cylinder. Remove any live ammunition from the work area.

2 To remove the cylinder: Unscrew and remove the crane lock screw (#23) and the crane lock (#23A). On later-production (post-mid-1950s) revolvers, unscrew and remove the crane lock screw (the only screw on the right side of the frame), detent and spring (#21, #22, #23). Open the cylinder as above and line up one of the cylinder flutes with the bottom front of the crane (#38), and withdraw the cylinder-extractor-crane assembly out toward the front of the main frame (#46).

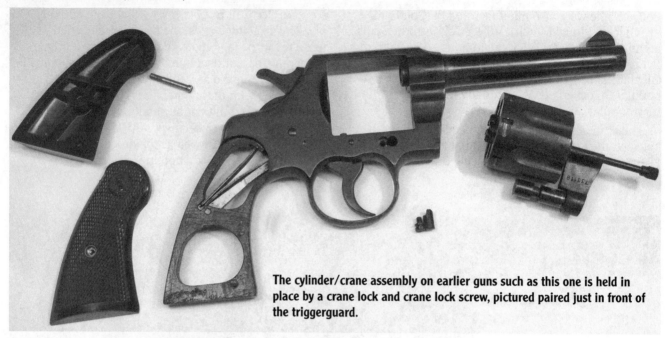

The cylinder/crane assembly on earlier guns such as this one is held in place by a crane lock and crane lock screw, pictured paired just in front of the triggerguard.

The Colt DA sideplate is off and the latch and its spring and guide have been removed. Once the plate is off you have complete access to the action.

The mainspring, hand and rebound lever are taken out next, in that order.

3 To remove the grips and sideplate: Remove the grip screw (#41) and lift off the grips (#42) and (#43). Unscrew and remove the two sideplate screws (#25). Turn the gun on its side with the sideplate facing up and hold the revolver by the barrel over a well-padded bench-top. Use a wooden or plastic mallet to strike the grip frame one or more sharp blows. This will cause the sideplate (#24) to jump up and out of its seat with the frame. Never attempt to pry off the sideplate as damage to the frame or sideplate may result. As you are removing the sideplate, hold your thumb over the latch to keep it from jumping out. Remove the latch

(#26) by pulling it forward out of the sideplate. Remove the latch spring guide (#28) and latch spring (#27) from the latch opening in the sideplate. Take care to notice how the hole in the rear of the latch fits over the little leg on the latch pin (#29) for later reassembly.

4 To remove the mainspring, rebound lever, hand and hammer: Pull the hammer (#1) back about one-quarter inch and use a screwdriver to push the rear of the mainspring (#15) down so it may be separated from the hammer stirrup (#3). Push the hammer forward and pull the mainspring out to the left. Lift the hand (#12) up out of its seat in the trigger

Here the remainder of the Colt DA action is removed. Pay special attention to how those safety parts fit onto the back side of the trigger. The only part remaining inside the frame is the bolt, which is held on with one screw.

(#13). Use a pin punch and hammer to push out the rebound lever pin (#20) and slip the rebound lever (#19) out of the frame. Pull the hammer back slightly and withdraw the hammer by lifting it straight up and off its pin (#2) in the frame.

5 To remove the trigger and safety component parts: Once the hammer is out, the trigger, along with the safety (#10) and safety lever (#11), may be lifted straight up out of the frame. Pay special attention to the relationship of the safety and safety lever to the trigger for reassembly later. The latch pin (#29) may now be pulled straight out to the rear of the main frame.

6 To remove the bolt: Unscrew and remove the bolt screw (#18). Carefully pry the bottom of the bolt spring (#17) away from the frame to release its tension and remove the bolt (#16).

7 To disassemble the cylinder: Insert six fired cartridge casings or dummy cartridges into the cylinder chambers. Grasp the ejector rod head (#35) in a padded vise and unscrew it from the ejector rod (#34) by turning in a counterclockwise direction. Remove the dummy cartridges and, using a special tool such as the one shown in the photograph (courtesy Brownells), push the ejector rod in slightly to hold the ejector (#33) up off the cylinder. (As you do, notice the witness

The ejector ratchet or star is unscrewed using a special tool like the multi-tool shown here from Brownells. The hex hole fits the Official Police; the other end has two screw heads that will unscrew New Service or Police Positive ejectors. The large hole is for the 1911 barrel bushing. Once the star is off, the cylinder is pulled back off the crane.

In order to disassemble the crane, the crane bushing must be unscrewed, and that requires a special spanner tool. The tool pictured is from Brownells and works on several Colt DA frame sizes.

Colt DA hammers are easy to disassemble. There isn't much to them.

Notice that at the rear of the Colt ejector there are witness marks (about 7 o'clock) and two notches at the top of the star legs (at about 11:30 and 5:30 o'clock). These must align at reassembly.

mark and cutouts at the ends of two of the "star legs" of the ejector and make note of these for alignment during assembly). Unscrew the ejector from the rod by turning it in a counterclockwise direction. The cylinder (#30) may now be pulled to the rear and off the crane assembly.

8 To disassemble the crane: Use a special spanner wrench like the one pictured (courtesy Brownells) to unscrew the crane bushing (#37) from the rear of the crane (#38). Remove the ejector rod and the ejector spring (#36) via the rear of the crane.

9 To disassemble the hammer: Support the hammer sides for this operation. Use a straight

pin punch and hammer to drive out the strut pin (#7) and lift off the strut (#5) and its spring (#6). To remove the stirrup, simply use a pin punch and hammer to drive out the stirrup pin (#4). The firing pin (#8) is held in place by a solid rivet (#9) that may be driven out by using a straight punch and hammer if necessary. A new rivet will be required for reassembly.

REASSEMBLY

Further disassembly is not required for normal cleaning and maintenance of the revolver mechanism. Reassemble in the reverse order of above.

Colt Third Model Deringer

Colt's 41 rimfire Third Model Deringer designed by Alexander Thuer was manufactured from about 1871 through 1912. From the Ed Wade collection.

The famous Colt Third Model Deringer was a single-shot, metallic cartridge pistol with a barrel that rotated sideways for loading and unloading. Chambered in 41 rimfire caliber, the so-called No. 3 was designed in 1870 by Colt employee Alexander Thuer. One of its novel features was the automatic ejection of the fired cartridge casing as the barrel was opened. The barrel seemingly had no actual lock to hold it shut, but it depended on a machined lip or rim at its base which was fitted tightly into a machined groove in the frame when the barrel was closed, preventing the breech from springing open. Further, a spring-loaded barrel latch/ejector was designed to snap into a depressed steel bushing in the frame as the barrel was swung closed, serving as a detent to lock the barrel in the closed position. The barrel actually became locked (side to side) when the gun was fired, at which point the solid steel hammer nose or firing pin fell into a machined

notch at the rear of the barrel, preventing the barrel from being swung out.

The Third Model Deringer used a bronze frame that was generally either silver or nickel plated. The barrel and the remainder of the gun were made from steel, often blued. As the result of their acquiring the National Fire Arms Co. of New York in 1870, Colt also introduced a different single-shot, Deringer-type pistol around the same time. That pistol was based on a National Fire Arms design using a Daniel Moore patent and was called the First Model Deringer. A slightly different version of the National became known as the No. 2; hence the Thuer, introduced only a short time later, became the Third Model Deringer. A popular pocket pistol, the Third Model Deringer weighed in at a scant 6-1/2 ounces and was by far the most successful of the three types, with Colt selling about 48,000 of the tiny pistols from about 1871 to 1912.

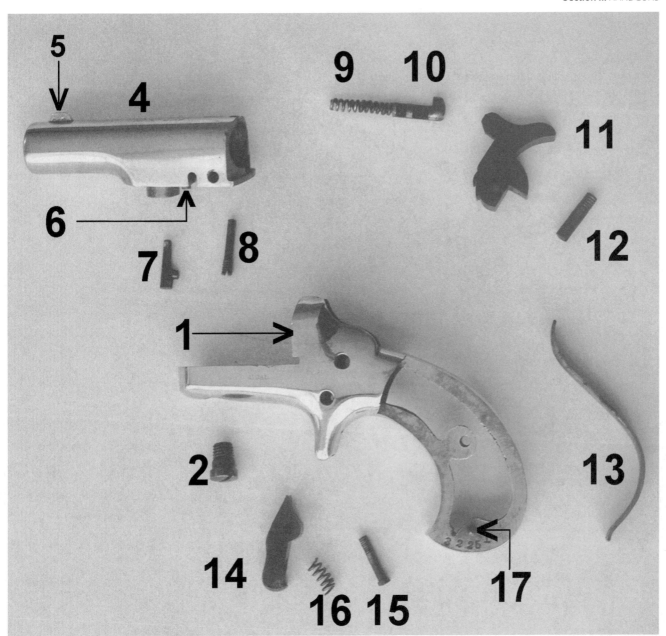

Parts List

1	Frame	11	Hammer
2	Barrel Screw	12	Hammer Screw
3	Barrel Latch Bushing	13	Mainspring
4	Barrel	14	Trigger
5	Front Sight	15	Trigger screw
6	Barrel Stop Pin	16	Trigger Spring
7	Barrel Latch Release Pin	17	Grip Pin
8	Barrel Latch & Ejector Screw	18	Escutcheon
9	Barrel Latch & Ejector Spring	19	Grip Screw
10	Barrel Latch & Ejector	20	Grips

The procedure to find out if the single shot Colt Deringer is empty or not is very simple.

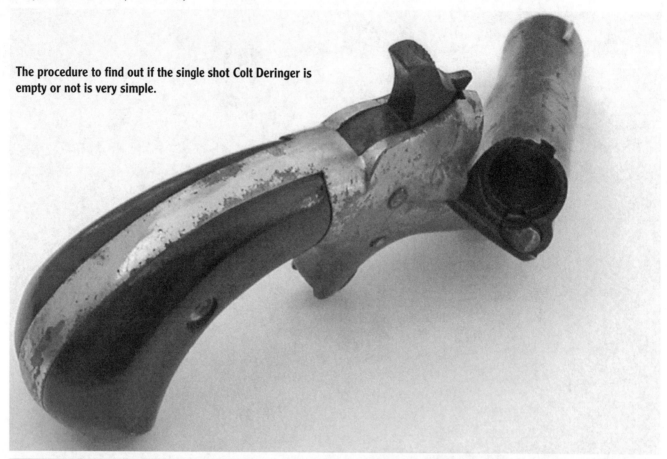

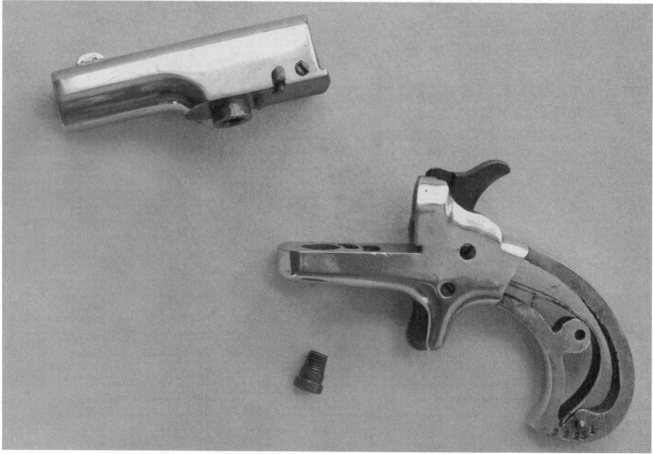

Once the barrel screw is removed, removing the barrel is a simple matter of swinging the barrel open and lifting it up and off the frame.

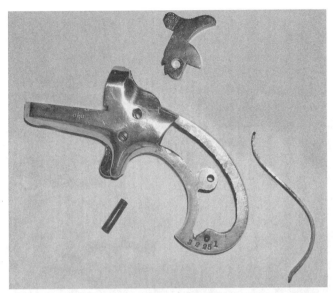

Here the mainspring and hammer are shown after removal.

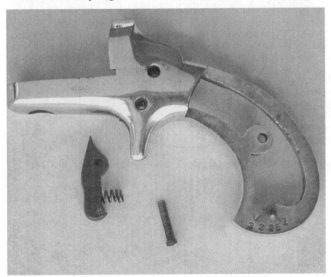

Removing the trigger and its spring completes the very simple disassembly of the Colt Deringer frame.

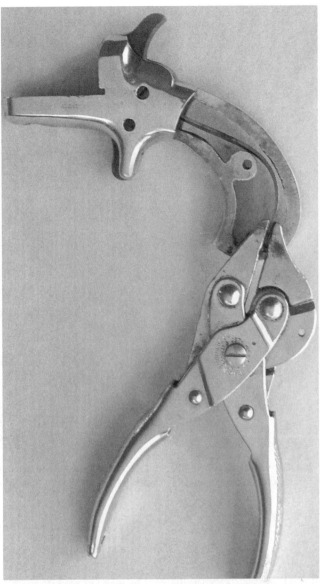

The mainspring can be removed by tapping out its base to the side or, as shown here, by grasping its base with a small, strong pair of pliers. This step is highly recommended for easing reassembly.

DISASSEMBLY INSTRUCTIONS

1 Before you begin, always be certain the weapon is unloaded. Pick up the pistol, holding it by the grip, being careful to keep your fingers away from the trigger (#14) and to keep the muzzle pointing in a safe direction. Pull the hammer (#11) back one click, into the loading position, so it comes to rest just slightly to the rear of its forward position. Twist the barrel (#4) to the side so the rear of the barrel pivots out to the right, exposing the chamber. If a cartridge is present it will be ejected from the barrel automatically. Even so,

it is wise to take the time to visibly check the chamber to make absolutely sure it is empty; once you have, return the barrel to the closed position.

2 To remove the barrel (#4): Holding the gun by the barrel, bottom side up, unscrew and remove the large screw at the bottom of the frame (#1). This is located directly under the barrel and is called the barrel screw (#2). Turn the pistol right-side-up and once again and swing the barrel open as before, but this time when it is all the way open, lift the barrel up and off the frame.

· 95 ·

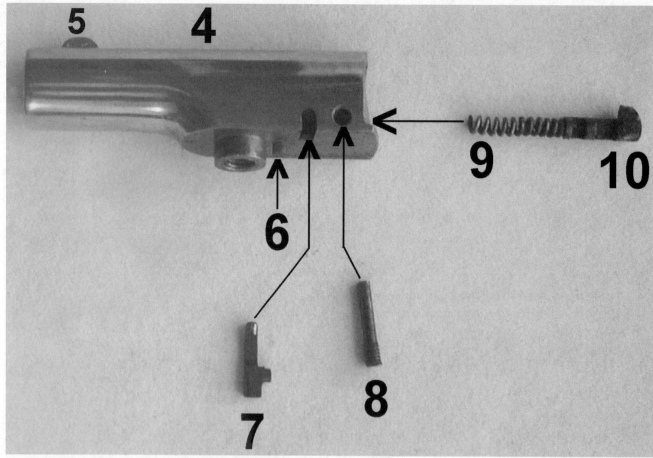

The Colt Deringer barrel after disassembly showing the various parts in their relative locations. The barrel stop pin (#6) and front sight (#5) have not been removed, and normally they do not have to be.

3 To remove the grips and disassemble the action: Unscrew and remove the grip screw (#19) from the left side and lift off the grip panels (#20). Use a small brass punch and hammer to tap the base of the mainspring (#13) out to the side and remove it from the frame. Unscrew and remove the hammer screw (#12) from the left side of the frame and, while holding the trigger (#14) to the rear, lift the hammer out through the top of the frame. Release the trigger. Unscrew and remove the trigger screw (#15) from the left side of the frame. The trigger (#14) and its spring (#16) will come out through the bottom of the frame. Note: Some earlier guns used a V leaf-type spring; the drawing shows the later, coil-type trigger spring.

4 To disassemble the barrel (#4): Hold your thumb over the rear of the barrel to cover the barrel latch & ejector (#10). Unscrew and remove the barrel latch & ejector screw (#8) from the left side of the barrel and remove the barrel latch & ejector (#10) and its spring (#9) out the rear of the barrel. The barrel latch release pin (#7) may be lifted out the left side of the barrel.

REASSEMBLY

Reassemble the pistol in the reverse order of above.

The LeMat® Revolver

The incredible LeMat revolver was both a nine-shot revolver and a single-barreled shotgun. This excellent copy made in Italy by Pietta is courtesy of Dixie Gun Works. Author photos.

A mong its titles, the LeMat revolver has been called "the most awesome hand-held weapon ever produced," and anyone who has ever fired one will agree there is more than a little truth in that statement. The LeMat was an unusual two-barreled percussion revolver that was used to some extent by the Confederacy during the American Civil War. Some called the LeMat the "Grapeshot Revolver," largely because LeMat revolvers were equipped with a nine-shot, .42-caliber cylinder and, as if that weren't enough, the cylinder rotated on a .63-caliber (about 20-gauge) smoothbore shot barrel. That brought the concept of the percussion revolver as a personal weapon to never-before-imagined levels. The LeMat's hammer used a moveable hammer nose that enabled the user to fire the center-shotgun barrel separately from the cylinder. It is believed that a total of about 2900 Le Mat revolvers were manufactured from about 1856 through 1865. Production took place in several countries: in the USA (about 1859); Liege, Belgium (1862); Paris, France (1864-64); and in Birmingham, England (1865.) The Union Naval blockade of the south created tremendous difficulties and those revolvers made in Belgium and France were sent to England for proofing and then shipped on to Bermuda. From there the guns were run through the Union blockade and on to Confederate ports.

The design for this unique revolver was first patented in the U.S. in 1856 by Dr. Jean Alexandre Francois LeMat of New Orleans, who later patented the weapon in several European countries. Early in its production, LeMat was assisted in the manufacture and sale (some say, in its design as well) of his revolver by P.G.T. Beauregard, the man who would later emerge as one of the Confederacy's best known and most flamboyant general officers. Roughly twenty-five prototype LeMat revolvers were produced in 1859 by John Krider in Philadelphia. It is reported that a substantial number of LeMats were sold to the Confederate States of America. Several well known officers, including the famous General J.E.B. Stuart, were very fond of its nine-shot capacity and that nice little "surprise" tenth round in the shotgun barrel. According to Flayderman's, 900 of the Belgian production went to the Confederate Army and 600 to the Navy.

A shooting replica of the LeMat is available today, manufactured in Italy by F.F.L. Pietta and sold in the US by several importers, including Dixie Gun Works. These modern Pietta-made replicas are chambered to accept a .451″ ball, making this modern copy an even more formidable revolver than the original with nine shots in .45 caliber plus a 20-gauge shot barrel.

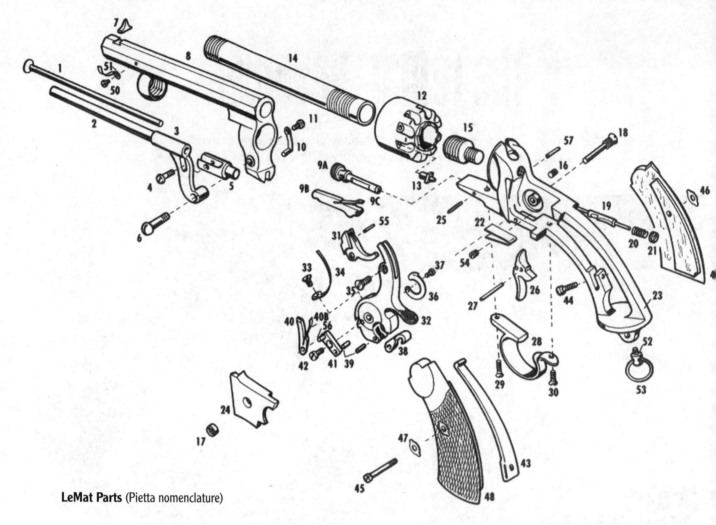

LeMat Parts (Pietta nomenclature)

1	Shot Barrel Ramrod	19	Cylinder Stop	38	Mainspring Retainer
2	Loading Lever Tube	20	Cylinder Stop Return Spring	39	Mainspring Retainer Pin
3	Loading Lever	21	Cylinder Stop Retaining Nut	40	Hand & Spring
4	Plunger Screw	22	Trigger Spring	41	Hand Bracket
5	Plunger	23	Frame	42	Hand Bracket Screw
6	Loading Lever Screw	24	Side Plate	43	Mainspring
7	Front Sight	25.	Takedown Lever Pin	44	Mainspring Screw
8	Barrel	26	Trigger	45	Grip Screw
9A	Takedown Pin (Army/Navy)	27	Trigger Pin	46	Right Grip Locking Nut
9B	Takedown Lever (Cavalry)	28	Trigger Guard	47	Left Grip Nut
9	Takedown Lever Spring	29	Front Trigger Guard Screw	48	Left Grip
10	Takedown Pin Spring	30	Rear Trigger Guard Screw	49	Right Grip
11	Takedown Pin Spring Screw	31	Hammer Nose	50	Loading Lever Retaining Spring Screw
12	Cylinder	32	Hammer	51	Loading Lever Retaining Spring
13	Nipple	33	Hammer Nose Spring Screw	52	Lanyard Base
14	Shot Barrel .20 Ga.	3	Hammer Nose Spring	53	Lanyard Ring
15	Breech Plug	35	Hammer Nose Screw	54	Cylinder Stop Screw
16	Tension Spring Adj. Screw	36	Cylinder Stop Tension Spring	55	Hammer Nose Pin
17	Side Plate Nut	37	Cylinder Stop Tension Spring Screw		
18	Hammer Screw				

To make sure a percussion revolver is safe to handle, always examine the percussion nipples and be sure there are no caps present.

Unlatching the Lemat barrel so it may be unscrewed from the frame.

DISASSEMBLY INSTRUCTIONS

Pietta parts nomenclature is used within the text. With only minor variations, the following instructions can be suitable for use with original Le Mat percussion ignition type revolvers, and copies thereof based on this pattern.

1 First, be absolutely certain the firearm is not loaded! Always keep your finger away from the trigger. Point the muzzle in a safe direction, then pull the hammer (#32) back until it rests in the loading position (the first audible click). Now check to be sure that the revolver cylinder (#12) is unloaded before attempting any disassembly or handling the revolver. Perform this check while rotating the cylinder by carefully examining the front and the rear of the cylinder at *each chamber* to be sure there are no bullets showing in the front and at the rear of the center barrel. Also, make certain that there are no percussion caps on any of the nipples.

If percussion caps are present on any of the cylinder nipples, you should consider this a loaded firearm. Do not attempt any further disassembly and you should always look at the front of the cylinder to make sure that there are no charges in the cylinder chambers. If examining the gun to see if any bullets have been chambered, never look directly down the bore or into

the barrel – always examine the front of the cylinder with your head and body held well off to the side, safely away from any potential danger from the muzzle. A loaded cylinder could be emptied by taking the gun to a range and firing it until it is empty, or the cylinder may be carefully removed without firing the revolver in order to render the revolver itself safe for further operations by following the instructions at 2) below.

Note: If there is a percussion cap on the nipple of the center barrel, you should assume that the barrel is loaded. Point the muzzle in a safe direction, always pointing away from yourself or anyone else, and while holding the grip tightly, always taking care to keep your finger away from the trigger: Move the hammer nose (#31) into the "up" position, so if the hammer did fall, it would not contact the center barrel percussion cap. Slowly and cautiously remove the percussion cap from the barrel nipple. NEVER DROP A LOADED, CAPPED CYLINDER! It can fire with the same effect as a short-barreled pistol!

Once the barrel is unscrewed, the cylinder is simply slid forward, off the shotgun barrel, which also serves as its axle.

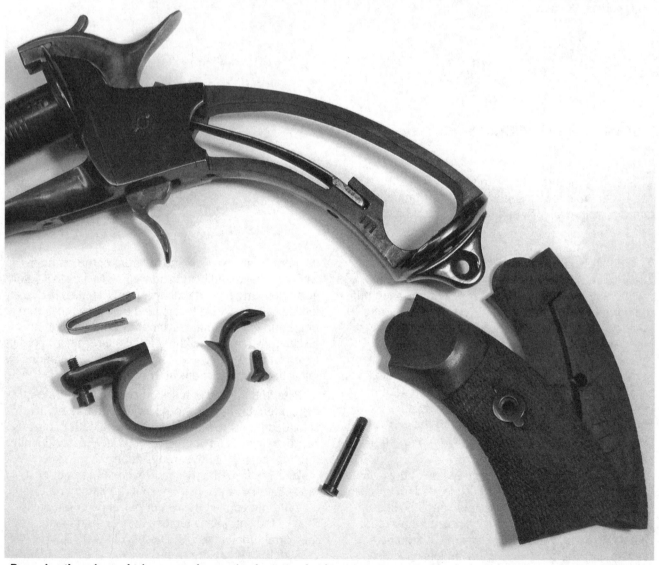

Removing the grips and trigger guard are a simple matter, but be sure you pay attention to how that trigger spring came out.

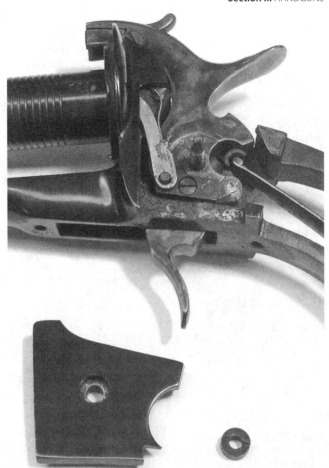

Here you can see we have ground a Brownells Magna-Tip screwdriver bit into a spanner to fit the sideplate nut.

Once the sideplate is removed, the LeMat's action is very easy to disassemble.

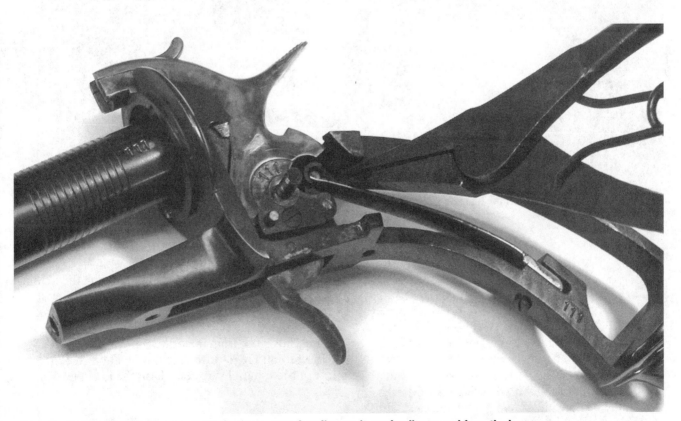

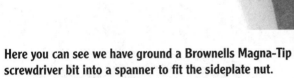

Here, the mainspring is being compressed using a spreader pliers so it can be disengaged from the hammer.

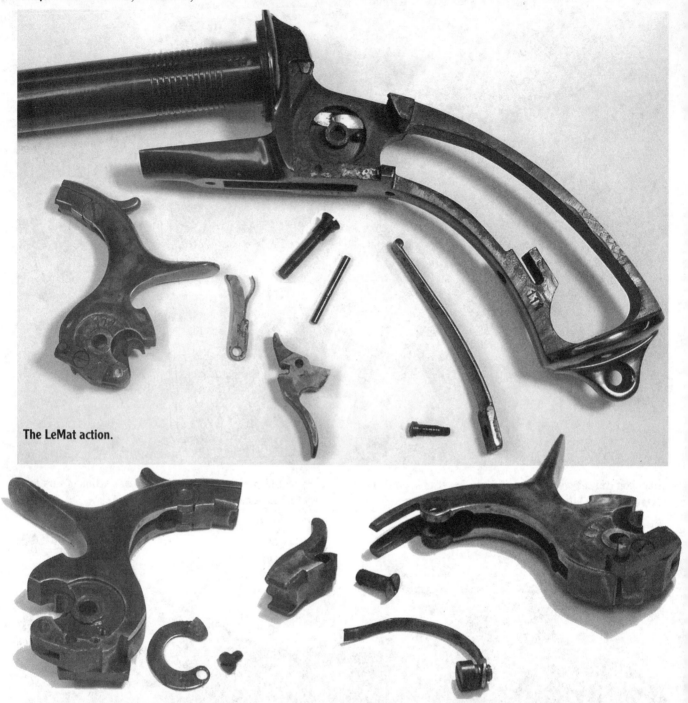

The LeMat action.

These two photos show (right) the hammer top and its components apart and (left) the cylinder stop tension spring removed.

2 To remove the barrel and cylinder (Army/Navy Models): With the hammer still in the loading position, pull the take down pin (#9A) forward. Cavalry Models: Pivot the takedown lever (#9B) down until it is perpendicular with the barrel. Looking from the rear of the gun, twist the barrel assembly (#8) in a clockwise direction and unscrew it several turns until it pulls forward and off the shot barrel (#20). The cylinder (#12) may be now pulled straight forward also and taken off the shot barrel.

2a To disassemble the barrel: Unlatch the loading lever tube (#2) by pulling it up to unsnap it from the loading lever retaining spring (#51) located on the front left side of the barrel. Pull the shotgun barrel ramrod (#1) out from the front of the loading lever. Unscrew and remove the loading lever screw (#6) from the left-rear barrel side and lift off the loading lever.

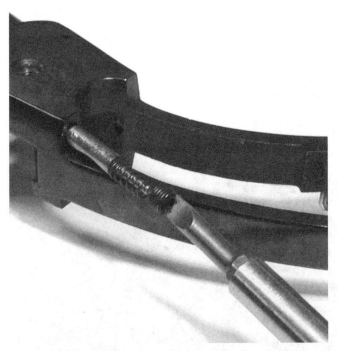

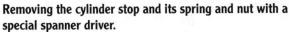

Removing the cylinder stop and its spring and nut with a special spanner driver.

Removing the nipples using a nipple wrench.

3 To remove the grips and trigger guard: Unscrew and remove the grip screw (#45). The grip panels (#46) right and (#47) left can now be lifted off each side of the frame (#23.) Remove the trigger guard (#28) by unscrewing and removing the front (#29) and rear (#30) trigger guard screws. The guard will drop off the bottom of the frame. The trigger spring (#22) is now loose and may be removed. Make note of its position for reassembly.

4 To remove the sideplate and mainspring: Lower the hammer all the way forward. Using a special spanner-driver, unscrew and remove the sideplate nut (#17). Never attempt to pry off a sideplate, but instead hold the frame by the front with one hand and strike the grip frame area several smart, but not too heavy, blows with a wooden or plastic mallet. This will cause the sideplate (#24) to be shocked up out of its seat in the frame. Using a pair of spreader pliers, compress the top of the mainspring (#43) downward, and then disengage it from the mainspring retainer (#38), releasing the spring. Unscrew and remove the mainspring screw (#44) and lift the mainspring out through the left side of the frame.

5 To remove the hand and hammer: Push on the top of the hand (#40) to pivot it toward the rear and lift the hand (#40) and its assembled handspring off the hand bracket (#41) on the hammer. Next, move the hammer slightly to the rear and lift it out of the frame. The trigger (#26) may be removed by using a pin punch and hammer to drift out the trigger pin (#27). To remove the hammer nose: Unscrew and remove the hammer nose spring screw (#33) and the hammer nose spring (#34) from the front of the hammer. Unscrew and remove the hammer nose screw (#35) from the left side of the hammer and lift out the hammer nose (#31).

6 To remove the cylinder stop assembly: Unscrew and remove the cylinder stop tension screw spring (#37) from the inside of the frame at the hammer cut and lift out the cylinder stop tension spring (#36). Use a specially-made spanner driver to unscrew and remove the cylinder stop retaining nut (#21) from the right-rear of the grip frame. The cylinder stop return spring (#20) and cylinder stop #19) may now be withdrawn to the rear out the same hole. Note their positions for reassembly.

REASSEMBLY

Further disassembly is not suggested. Reassemble the revolver in the reverse order.

Merwin-Hulbert
Single Action Revolvers

This Merwin-Hulbert Pocket Army in 44-40 caliber is severely worn and has seen more than its share of home-gunsmithing work. The grips are not original. These M-H revolvers were beautifully machined pieces of the gunmaker's art. From the Walt Penner collection. Author photos.

The Merwin-Hulbert company was a firearms dealer-distributor who listed their address as New York City. They were the successors of Merwin & Bray of Worcester, Mass.; they were not firearms manufacturers. Merwin-Hulbert were the primary sales agents for Hopkins & Allen and their revolvers were manufactured by the Hopkins & Allen company at Norwich, Conn., with a surprisingly high degree of quality. The story is that quite a few of the engineers and gunsmiths working at the Hopkins & Allen plant during that period were fellows who had formerly worked for Smith & Wesson, Colt and the U.S. armory at Springfield. If that is true, it would certainly help to explain the quality found in M-H revolvers.

These unique revolvers used an advanced design that was, in many ways, simply ingenious. Among other features, they sported a redundant, selective-simultaneous ejection system that effectively had no moving parts. When the gun was unlatched its barrel was twisted ninety degrees to the right and then pulled forward. The cylinder moved forward along with the barrel but the cartridges (which were held in place by a steel ring on the breech that engaged the cartridge rims) stayed were they were. After the cylinder was moved all the way forward to the extent of its travel, only the fired cartridge cases would fall away, but because of their extra length any loaded cartridges (which of course, still had bullets) would remain supported by the cylinder so they could not fall out. Very cool!

The revolver was loaded with the barrel latched in place, one cartridge at a time, similar to the Colt

Single Action Army, through a sliding loading gate at the right side of the frame's recoil shield. Merwin-Hulbert twist-barrel revolvers were offered in three frame sizes and in .32, .38 and .44 calibers, very similar to the frame size and caliber offerings of Smith & Wesson – who, by the way, were at Springfield, just up the Connecticut River from Hopkins and Allen's factory at Norwich. Merwin-Hulberts were offered in quite a variety: with or without barrel topstraps, with square or round butts, and in both single and double action. Some models even came with a very neat little folding hammer spur.

Merwin-Hulbert sold their unusual and innovative twist-barrel revolvers during the 1870s and 1880s. We do not know the exact quantities of these guns manufactured, since the factory records were lost in a fire in the late 1880s; however, one source indicates that large quantities of the large framed "Army" revolvers were manufactured between 1876 to perhaps as late as 1885. Another source gives 1887 or possible even later as the date of M-H's last production revolvers. Author Mike Venturino thinks that between 10,000 and 20,000 large-framed revolvers were manufactured.

It is the large-framed .44-caliber M-Hs that most shooters are interested in, and these were made from around 1876 up into the 1880s. Those full-sized revolvers were chambered in both 44-40 Winchester and .44 Merwin-Hulbert (similar to the .44 S&W American) and were known as the "Army" or "Frontier" models. The model name Frontier may not be correct, but collectors like to use the term to discriminate between the "Army" model in 44 M-H caliber and 44-40 "Frontier" models.

Army models were offered in 7-inch barrel length (later, with a 5-1/2-inch barrel) and they were made with or without topstraps, in single and double action and with rounded or square butt shapes. There was also a shorter-barreled version of the same revolver

that they called the "Pocket Army" which was offered only with the rounded birds-head butt shape, though we have seen some longer barreled "Army" models with this same butt shape. An interesting feature of the Pocket Army is that the grips were made shorter than the length of the butt, leaving a fairly substantial steel "tail" hanging down. I always thought these were intended to be used as a club that you could hit someone over the head with, but so designed that the grips wouldn't break in the process. As a matter of fact, the name skull-crusher is often used when referring to these Pocket Army grip shapes.

not to scale

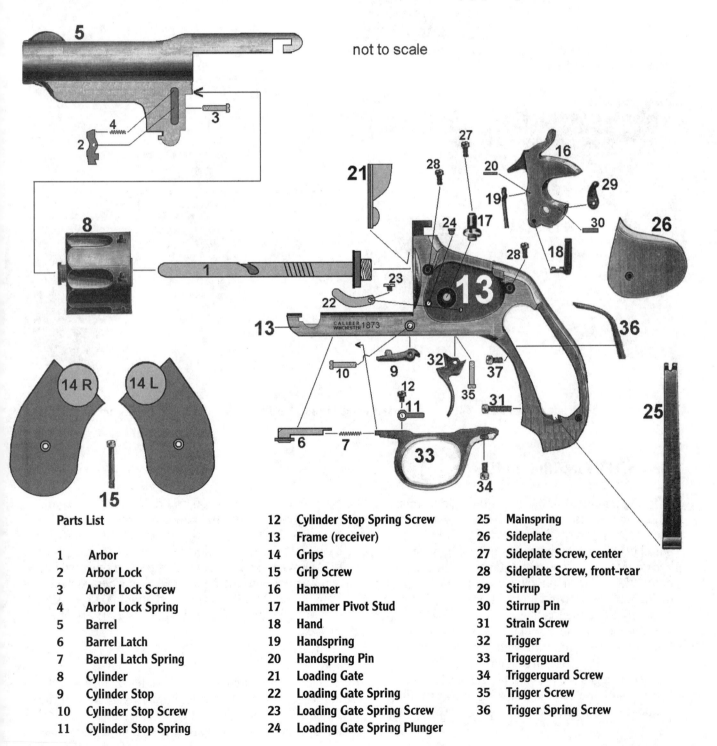

Parts List

1	Arbor	12	Cylinder Stop Spring Screw	25	Mainspring
2	Arbor Lock	13	Frame (receiver)	26	Sideplate
3	Arbor Lock Screw	14	Grips	27	Sideplate Screw, center
4	Arbor Lock Spring	15	Grip Screw	28	Sideplate Screw, front-rear
5	Barrel	16	Hammer	29	Stirrup
6	Barrel Latch	17	Hammer Pivot Stud	30	Stirrup Pin
7	Barrel Latch Spring	18	Hand	31	Strain Screw
8	Cylinder	19	Handspring	32	Trigger
9	Cylinder Stop	20	Handspring Pin	33	Triggerguard
10	Cylinder Stop Screw	21	Loading Gate	34	Triggerguard Screw
11	Cylinder Stop Spring	22	Loading Gate Spring	35	Trigger Screw
		23	Loading Gate Spring Screw	36	Trigger Spring Screw
		24	Loading Gate Spring Plunger		

The M-H with its barrel slid forward and opened up; notice that the gunsmith's finger is not in the triggerguard.

Removing the barrel and cylinder on an M-H is a simple matter of depressing the arbor lock and pulling them forward, off the arbor.

DISASSEMBLY INSTRUCTIONS

1 First, make sure the gun is unloaded. Grasp the revolver around its grip, being very careful to keep your fingers off the trigger (#32). Pointing the barrel (#5) in a safe direction, pull the hammer (#16) back only far enough so that it rests in the half-cock notch (this is the first audible click encountered as the hammer is drawn rearward from the fully forward position). Slide the loading gate (#21) down to expose the chambers at the rear of the cylinder and rotate the cylinder (#8) one full turn while visibly examining each chamber, making certain that each chamber is empty. If any cartridges are present, tilt the barrel up and slowly rotate the cylinder, allowing each cartridge to fall out onto the workbench.

2 To open the weapon and remove the barrel and cylinder: With the hammer remaining in the half-cock position, open the barrel (#5) by pushing the barrel latch (#6) located just forward of the triggerguard (#33) toward the rear. Now, at the same time, twist the revolver barrel to the right (clockwise when viewed from the rear) until it has turned about 90 degrees, then pull the barrel forward on the arbor (#1) until it is fully extended.

To remove the barrel and cylinder: Grasp the barrel and cylinder as an assembly, depress the arbor lock (#2) located on the left side of the barrel and pull the barrel along with the cylinder forward and off the arbor. The cylinder may now be pulled straight down out of its seat with the barrel. Take note of how the

Here you can see the cylinder ring and how it fits into the barrel recess under the bore. Merwins had a wonderfully effective gas-ring system!

The round "ring" at the center of the breech engages the cartridge rims for extraction.

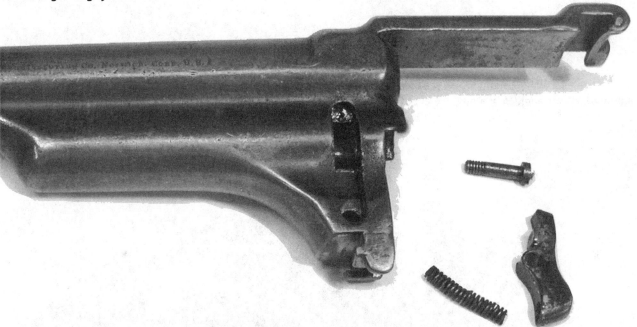

The arbor lock is shown disassembled. There is nothing else on the barrel to take apart.

machined ring at the front of the cylinder fits up into the recess at the rear of the barrel.

2a To remove the arbor lock: The arbor lock (#2) may be removed by unscrewing and removing the arbor lock screw (#3), located on the rear face of the barrel flat, just below the hole the arbor fits into. Once the arbor lock screw is out, the arbor lock (#2) and arbor lock spring (#4) may be lifted out of their opening in the barrel's side.

3 To remove the grips, sideplate and mainspring: Place the hammer in the fully down position. Unscrew and remove the grip screw (#15) and lift off the grips (#14). Unscrew and remove the three sideplate screws (#27) and (#28), there being two of the latter. Turn the frame (#13) on its side, holding it

by the front end with the sideplate (#26) facing up over a padded bench-top surface. Strike the grip frame a sharp blow or two using a plastic or hardwood mallet; the resulting shock will cause the sideplate to jump up out of its seat in the frame for removal. Never attempt to pry off the sideplate. Using a pair of spreader-type pliers, pry down on the top-rear of the mainspring (#25) and disengage its ears from the hammer's stirrup (#29). Loosen the mainspring strain screw (#31). The mainspring (#25) may be now removed out through the side of the grip frame.

4 To remove the hammer: Using your off-hand, pull the trigger to the rear and hold it there. Using the tip of a small screwdriver, rotate the hand (#18) to the rear and hold it there while you draw the hammer

With the sideplate and grips off you can see how similar the M-H action is to the S&W Model No. 3. Note: The repaired mainspring and the addition of a machine nut to hold the trigger spring in are not original M-H parts!

This is how to compress the mainspring to disengage it from the hammer stirrup.

The hammer and mainspring removed from the frame.

After the hammer is removed, only one screw holds the triggerguard on the frame. The barrel latch comes off with the guard.

Once the guard is off, the trigger and cylinder stop are exposed for easy removal.

about half way to the rear and lift it straight up off the hammer pivot stud (#17) and out of the frame (#13) through the sideplate opening.

5 To remove the triggerguard and latch: Unscrew and remove the triggerguard screw (#34) from the rear of the triggerguard (#33); this allows the guard to pivot down at the rear. Pull the triggerguard down and to the rear until its front has disengaged from the frame. The barrel latch (#6) may now be removed through the bottom of the frame. Unscrew and remove the cylinder stop spring screw (#12) from the inside of the guard. The cylinder stop spring (#11) may now be lifted off. Next, pull the barrel latch spring (#7) out from its hole in the front of the guard.

6 To remove the trigger and cylinder stop: Remove the cylinder stop screw (#10) from the left side of the frame and withdraw the cylinder stop (#9) through the bottom of the frame. The trigger screw (#35) may now be removed from the right side of the frame and the trigger (#32) can be withdrawn through the frame bottom.

7 To remove the loading gate and trigger spring: Remove the loading gate spring screw (#23) from inside the sideplate opening in the frame and lift out the loading gate spring (#22) and the tiny loading gate spring plunger (#24). The loading gate (#21) may now be pulled straight down and out of its mortise cut in the frame. The trigger spring (#36) is retained by a small screw that passes through the front grip strap,

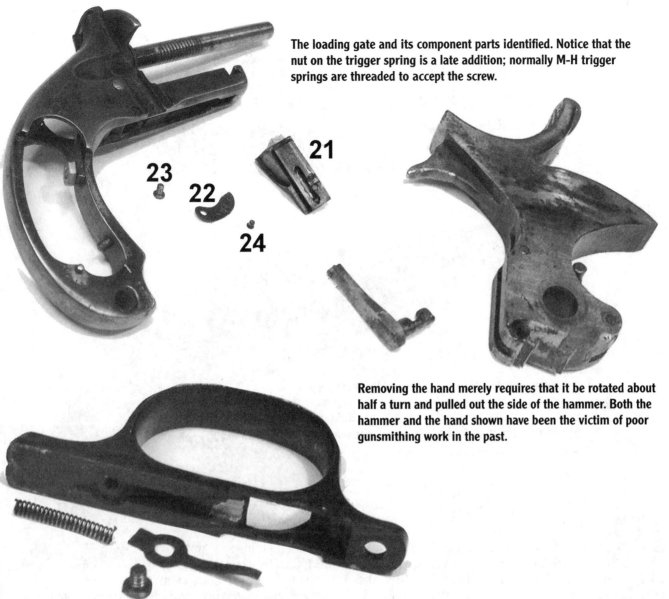

The loading gate and its component parts identified. Notice that the nut on the trigger spring is a late addition; normally M-H trigger springs are threaded to accept the screw.

23

22

21

24

Removing the hand merely requires that it be rotated about half a turn and pulled out the side of the hammer. Both the hammer and the hand shown have been the victim of poor gunsmithing work in the past.

The coil spring on the left is the barrel latch spring while the leaf spring (front) is the cylinder stop spring.

just behind the triggerguard opening. Remove the trigger spring screw (#37) and the trigger spring (#36) will lift out of the frame.

8 To disassemble the hammer: Rotate the hand (#18) about 180 degrees forward and lift it out of its hole in the hammer. Note: The step cut on the right side of the hand's shank is used during reassembly to re-engage the handspring (#19) so that the hand may be installed without the aid of tools. Support the hammer by laying it on a flat steel block with holes drilled through it to accept pins. Use a small pin punch and hammer to drift out the handspring pin (#20), which passes through the front of the hammer from side to side. The handspring may now be lifted out of its mortise cut at the front of the hammer. Drift out the

stirrup pin (#30) which passes through the rear of the hammer from side to side and the stirrup (#29) can be removed. Make note of the position of the stirrup for correct reassembly.

REASSEMBLY

Further disassembly is not required for normal maintenance. Reassemble the revolver in the reverse order of the above.

Remington Large-Caliber Percussion Revolvers

The Remington New Model Army was one of the most popular designs used in the civil war and its replicas remain popular to this day. This is a modern replica in .44 caliber built in Italy by A. Uberti from stainless steel. Revolver courtesy Stoeger Industries. Author photos.

Remington's first martial-caliber revolvers were single-action percussion types that were based on the Beals patent of 1858. The Remington-Beals revolvers were introduced in 1860, and they participated heavily in the American Civil War, first as the .36-caliber Navy model and soon thereafter in an Army Model in .44 caliber. The Union army procured many thousands of Remington's revolvers. The largest quantities of large-frame Remington percussion single action revolvers produced were the New Model Army in .44 caliber, of which about 132,000 were manufactured from 1863 to 1873.

Unlike the more familiar Colt revolvers that used an open-topped frame, Remington's revolvers used a full frame with a topstrap into which the barrel was permanently screwed. This frame layout proved itself more rugged than the Colt's, laying the ground work for modern revolver frame design. The Remington revolver also offered the shooter a fixed rear sight machined into the lock frame in place of the "V" notch on the top of Colt's hammer. Remington did away with several parts and manufacturing steps by using grip straps that were machined integrally with the lock frame. The triggerguard was held in place by a machined mortise and tenon, requiring only one screw to hold it in place.

The Remington was simpler mechanically as well: the extra screw that held the Colt's cylinder bolt was eliminated from the frame side because the Remington-Beals design used the same pivot screw to mount the bolt and the trigger.

Today, several replica arms makers produce copies of the Remingtons revolvers, most especially of the New Model Army percussion revolvers, and these are being sold in the USA under various trade names. Apparently the most popular of the Remington replicas has been the replica sold by Navy Arms of the New Model Army .44 percussion, which is manufactured in Italy by Pietta. Val Forgett of Arms informed the author in 1997 they had sold over 200,000 of these, in this case actually exceeding the original Remington production of the parent revolver. A. Uberti also manufactures a high-quality copy of the New Model Army and, as shown in these photos, a very modern stainless steel version. For the record, most of these replicas are sold as being the "1858 Remington New Model Army," but in fact 1858 is the date of the original Remington-Beals patent. The New Model Army revolver was actually introduced in 1863, and it is this latter model which most of the replica companies are copying.

Parts List

1	Frame	20	Mainspring	46	Left Grip
2	Hammer	21	Base Pin	47	Link
3	Barrel	24	Plunger	49	Link Pin
5	Cylinder	25	Roller	50	Plunger Pin
6	Loading Lever Latch	26	Trigger Guard	51	Grip Pin
7	Hand Assembly	27	Loading Lever Latch Pin	52	Hand Screw
9	Barrel Stud	30	Roller Pin	53	Mainspring Screw
10	Trigger	31	Triggerguard Screw	54	Grip Screw
12	Bolt	35	Trigger-Bolt Spring Screw		
13	Loading Lever Assembly	37	Hammer Screw		
14	Nipple	38	Trigger Screw		
15	Sight	39	Loading Lever Screw		
16	Loading Lever Latch Spring	43	Right Grip Nut		
18	Hand Spring	44	Left Grip Nut		
19	Trigger & Bolt Spring	45	Right Grip		

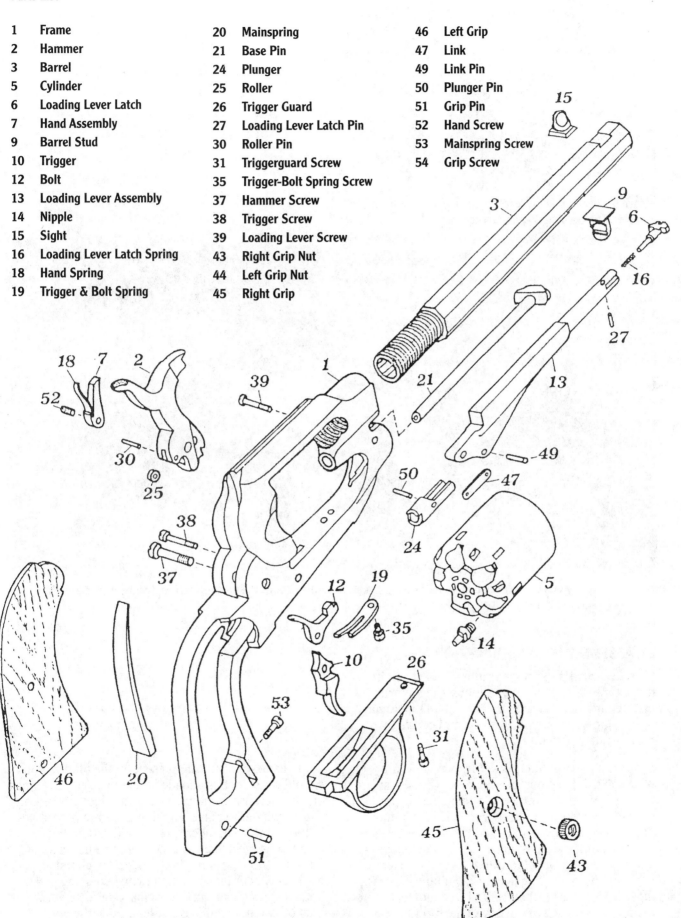

Place the hammer in the loading position and check the nipples to make sure they are uncapped.

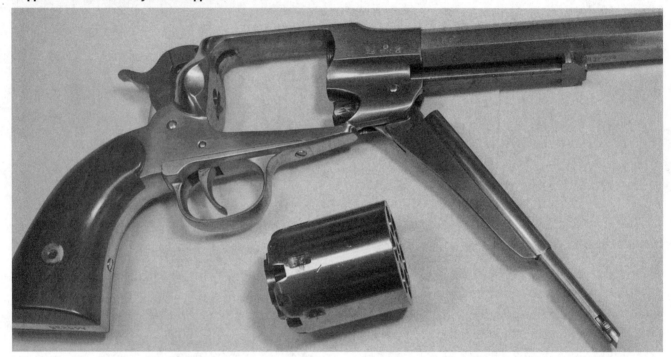

Removing the cylinder on the Remington revolvers is a real snap. Just unlatch the loading lever and pull out the base pin.

DISASSEMBLY INSTRUCTIONS

Note: Uberti parts nomenclature is used within the text. With only minor variations, the following instructions can be used for nearly all of the Remington percussion ignition type revolvers and copies thereof based on this pattern.

1 First, be absolutely sure the revolver is not loaded. Hold the revolver by its grip, being careful to point the muzzle in a safe direction and keep your finger away from the trigger. Place the hammer (#2) in the loading position and check to be certain that the cylinder (#5) is unloaded before attempting any disassembly or before handling the revolver. Perform this check by carefully examining the rear of the cylinder at each chamber to be certain that there are no percussion caps on any of the nipples.

If percussion caps are present on the nipples you should consider this a loaded firearm; do not attempt any further disassembly. Also, always look at the front of the cylinder to make sure that there are no charges in the cylinder chambers; a good indication that a chamber is most likely loaded would be if bullets or balls are showing at the front end of the chamber. A loaded cylinder may be emptied by taking the gun to a range and firing it until it is empty, or the cylinder may be carefully removed without firing the revolver

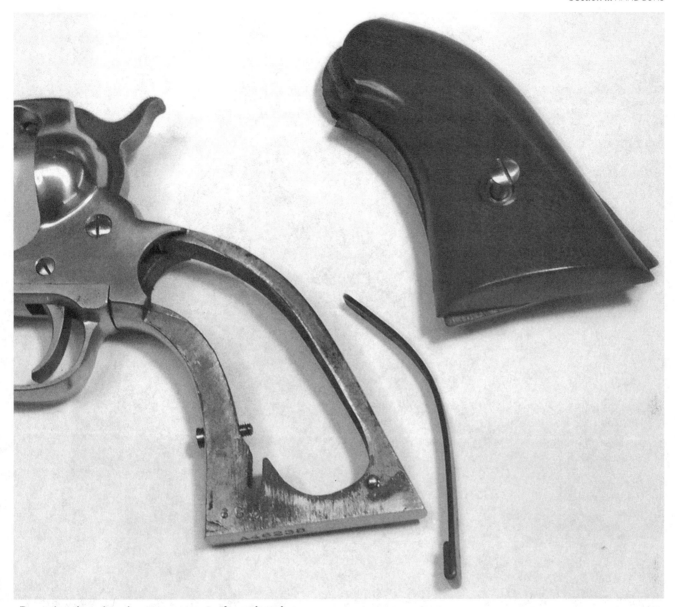

Removing the grips gives you access to the mainspring.

in order to render the revolver itself safe for further operations by following the instructions at 2) below.

2 To remove the cylinder: With the hammer (#2) in the loading position so that the cylinder spins freely, unlatch the loading lever (#13) by pulling the loading lever latch (#6) to the rear and allow the loading lever to drop so it is pointing at the floor. Pull forward on the base pin (#21) and withdraw the base pin as far as it will go. The cylinder assembly (#5) may now be removed from the frame by rolling it out the right side of the frame (#1).

3 To disassemble the cylinder: The only disassembly that will be required, or that is indeed possible, on the cylinder (#5) is the removal of the percussion nipples (#14). This step should be accomplished with a special tool called a nipple wrench. Percussion nipples are screwed in and have right-hand threads, which means that they unscrew in a counter-clockwise direction. Original Remington and other vintage percussion revolvers may have nipples which have been hand fitted to each specific chamber and care should always be taken that these are reinstalled in the chamber they were removed from.

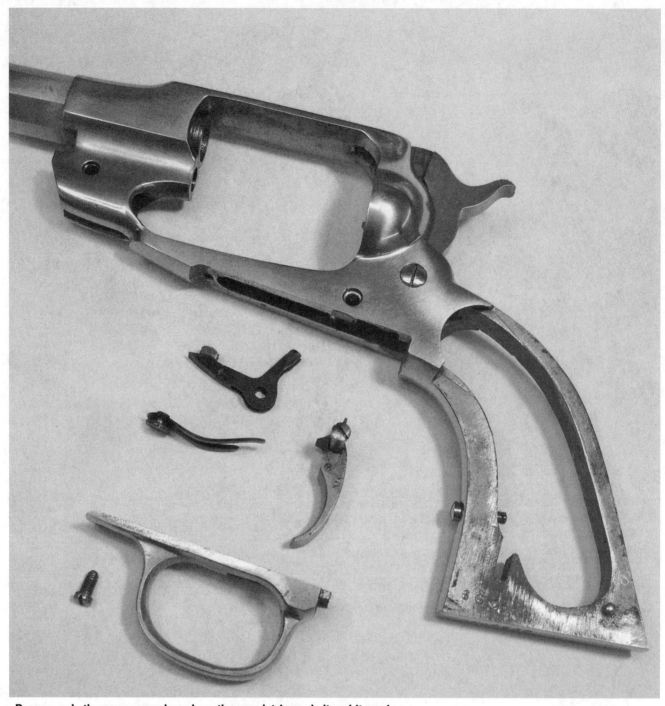

Remove only three screws and you have the guard, trigger, bolt and its spring.

4 To remove the grip, mainspring and guard removal: The revolver is equipped with two-piece grips. First remove the grip screw (#54) from the center of the left hand grip (#46) and then remove the two grips (#46) and (#45). Loosen the mainspring screw (#53). The bottom of the mainspring (#20) may now be tapped sideways out of its slot in the grip frame in either direction by using a small hammer against a 1/8" pin punch. Unscrew and remove the trigger guard screw (#31) from the front of the guard bow. The trigger guard (#26) may now be tilted down from the front

and pulled forward and down, off the frame. Note: To reinstall the mainspring, hold its top up against the bottom of the roller (#25) at the lower-rear side of the hammer, grasp the spring by its bottom side with a strong pair of pliers and push upwards, causing the spring to bend just far enough for you to re-seat it in its slot in the frame. Once you have the spring started into the slot, you can release your grip with the pliers and then use the small punch and hammer to reseat the spring fully into the frame slot.

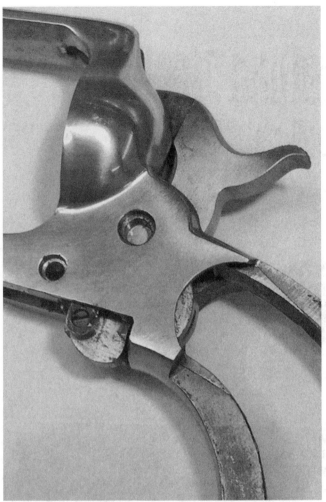

Remove the hammer screw and slide the hammer down to gain access to the hand screw, which is now removed.

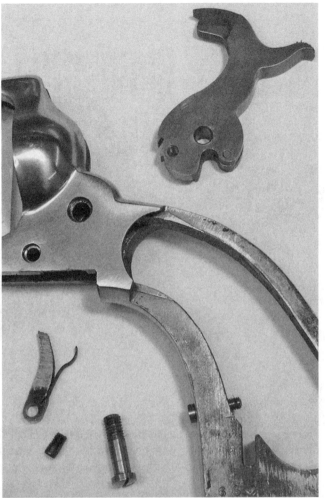

Once the hand screw is removed from the hammer, it can be pulled out the hammer opening in the frame, while the hand assembly comes out the bottom.

5 To disassemble the action: Unscrew and remove the trigger bolt spring screw (#35), which is the only screw inside the action that is facing straight up, from the underside of the frame. The trigger bolt spring (#19) will fall out the bottom of the frame. Next, remove the forwardmost of the two screws on the right side of the frame. This is also the smaller of the two and is called the trigger screw (#38); it holds the bolt (#12) and the trigger (#10) in place. The trigger and the bolt may now be removed from the bottom. The hammer screw (#37) can now be removed, after which the hammer assembly (#2) can be pushed down far enough so that the hand screw (#52) becomes fully exposed. Remove the hand screw and push the hammer (#2) back up through the frame and remove

it through the hammer opening at the frame top. The hand assembly (#7) may now be withdrawn through the bottom of the frame.

6 Peripheral disassembly: The loading lever assembly (#13) may be removed by removing the loading lever screw (#39) from the front left side of the frame and pulling the loading lever assembly forward and out the front of the frame. Once the loading lever is out of the frame, the base pin (#21) may be fully withdrawn from the front.

REASSEMBLY

Reassemble the revolver in the reverse order.

Remington Rolling Block
.50-caliber Single-shot Pistol, 1870 Pattern

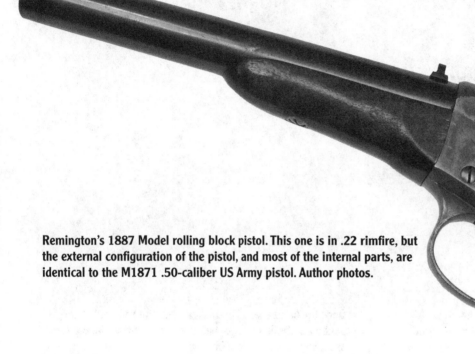

Remington's 1887 Model rolling block pistol. This one is in .22 rimfire, but the external configuration of the pistol, and most of the internal parts, are identical to the M1871 .50-caliber US Army pistol. Author photos.

R emington produced single shot pistols based on the rolling block pistol action from 1866 to around 1909. The design of the first pistol of this type (sometimes called the Model 1867) was modified in 1870 for the U.S. Navy and this became a long-lived, rolling block pistol pattern. Remington's rolling block action was noted for its great strength, its simplicity and utter reliability. The majority of these pistols were furnished in .50-caliber centerfire, although in later years considerable quantities were produced in .22, .25 and .32 rimfire.

This design includes:

Model 1867 Navy, .50-caliber centerfire, 7-inch round barrel, walnut grip and forearm, blue finish, case-hardened frame. Manufactured in unknown quantities from 1870 to 1875.

Model 1871 Army, .50-caliber center fire, 8-inch round barrel, walnut grip and forearm, blue finish case-hardened frame. Over 6,000 were manufactured from 1871 to 1872, of which about 5,000 went to the U.S. Army.

Model 1887 Target, .22 and .25 rimfire, .32- and .50-caliber center fire, 8-inch round barrel, walnut grip and forearm, blue finish, case-hardened frame. Also called the "Plinker Model of 1887." Around 900 of these pistols were manufactured from 1887 to 1891.

Model 1891 Target, .22 and .25 rimfire and .32 centerfire calibers, 10-inch part octagon-part round barrel, smooth walnut grip and forearm, blue finish, case-hardened frame. Around 116 were manufactured from 1891 to 1900.

Model 1901 Target, 22 Short and Long and .25 rimfire and .32 and 44 S&W Russian centerfire calibers, 10-inch octagon/round barrel, checkered walnut grip and forearm, blue finish. More than 700 were manufactured from 1900 to 1909.

This is the Model 1887 .22 rimfire Remington Rolling Block pistol disassembled. The part numbers shown are the same used in the accompanying Uberti drawing.

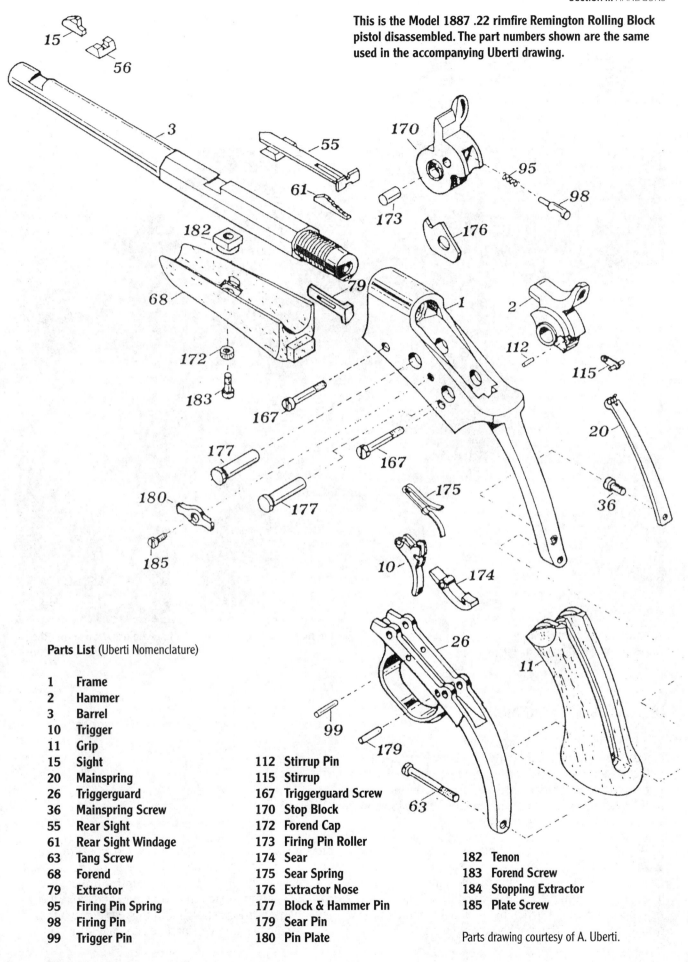

Parts List (Uberti Nomenclature)

1	Frame	
2	Hammer	
3	Barrel	
10	Trigger	
11	Grip	
15	Sight	
20	Mainspring	
26	Triggerguard	
36	Mainspring Screw	
55	Rear Sight	
61	Rear Sight Windage	
63	Tang Screw	
68	Forend	
79	Extractor	
95	Firing Pin Spring	
98	Firing Pin	
99	Trigger Pin	

112	Stirrup Pin
115	Stirrup
167	Triggerguard Screw
170	Stop Block
172	Forend Cap
173	Firing Pin Roller
174	Sear
175	Sear Spring
176	Extractor Nose
177	Block & Hammer Pin
179	Sear Pin
180	Pin Plate

182	Tenon
183	Forend Screw
184	Stopping Extractor
185	Plate Screw

Parts drawing courtesy of A. Uberti.

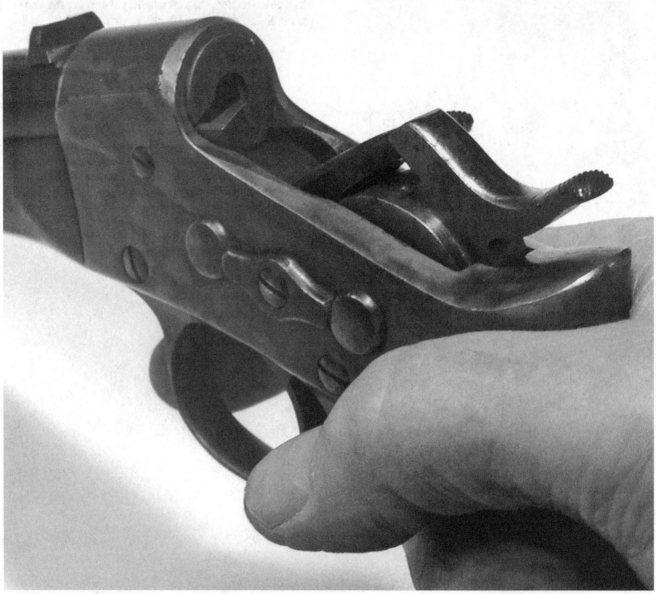

It's easy to check whether the rolling block is unloaded. Pull the hammer back and pull open the breechblock. Notice that the handler's finger is not in the triggerguard.

DISASSEMBLY INSTRUCTIONS

Please note that in the following section modern Uberti nomenclature and parts numbering are used. Some variations will be encountered between original Remington rolling block pistols and Uberti replica pistols and between rimfire and centerfire versions of each make.

1 Make sure the pistol is unloaded. Grasp the pistol around the wooden grip and keep your fingers away from the trigger at all times. Point the muzzle in a safe direction, holding it by the grip with your right hand. Open the action by pulling the hammer (#2) all the way to the rear and then pulling back the breechblock lever (#170) all the way to "roll" the breech open. Look into the barrel and check to be certain there is not a cartridge in the barrel's chamber. If there is a cartridge present, reach in and manually remove it by pulling the cartridge straight out the rear of the barrel. Remove all live ammunition to a separate location.

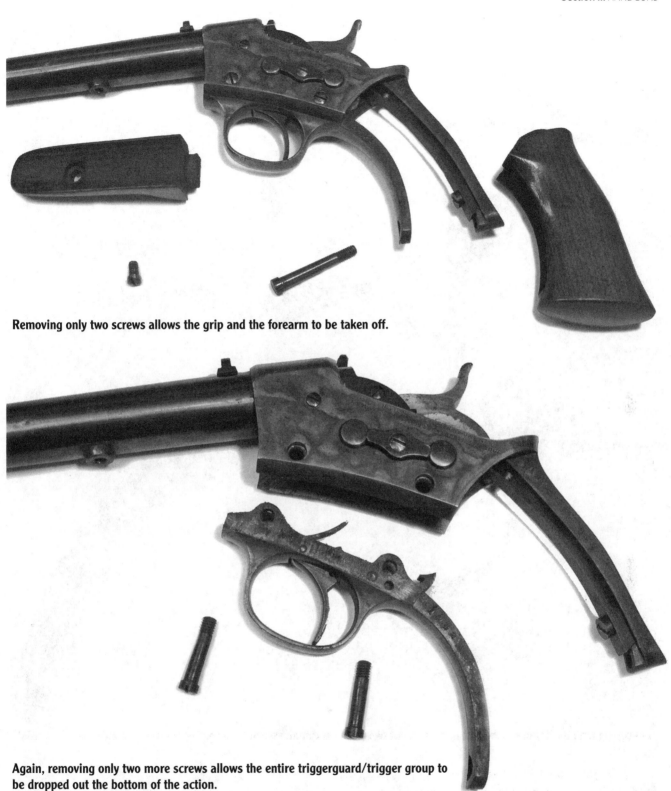

Removing only two screws allows the grip and the forearm to be taken off.

Again, removing only two more screws allows the entire triggerguard/trigger group to be dropped out the bottom of the action.

2 To remove the wood: Unscrew and remove the tang screw (#63) at the base of the front grip-strap. The grip (#11) may be pulled straight down and off the frame. Unscrew and remove the forend screw (#183); the forend (#68) can now be removed by pulling it forward and down.

3 To remove the triggerguard group: Unscrew and remove the two triggerguard screws (#167) from the lower left side of the frame. The triggerguard assembly (#26) may be pulled straight down and out the bottom of the frame.

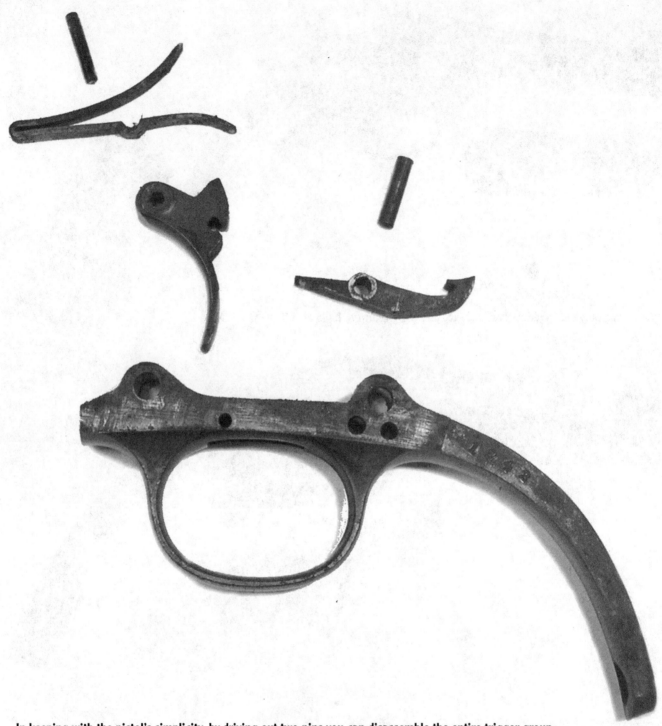

In keeping with the pistol's simplicity, by driving out two pins you can disassemble the entire trigger group.

4 To remove the mainspring and major action parts: Use your thumb to press the center of the mainspring in toward the inside of the rear frame strap and hold pressure while you loosen and then remove the mainspring screw (#36) from the bottom of the spring. The mainspring (#20) may be pulled straight out through the bottom. Note for later reassembly how its top attaches to the hammer stirrup. Loosen and remove the plate screw (#185) and lift off the pin plate (#180). Push out the hammer pin (#177-rear)

toward the left side of the frame and pull the hammer (#2) straight down, out through the bottom of the frame. Push out the block pin (#177-front) and then lift the breechblock (#170) out through the top of the frame. The extractor nose (#176) will come off with the breechblock; note its position for reassembly. (Original .22 rimfire Remington pistols do not use [#176]). On .22 rimfire caliber models, remove the extractor retaining screw from the left side of the frame and slide the extractor (#79) out through the back of the barrel.

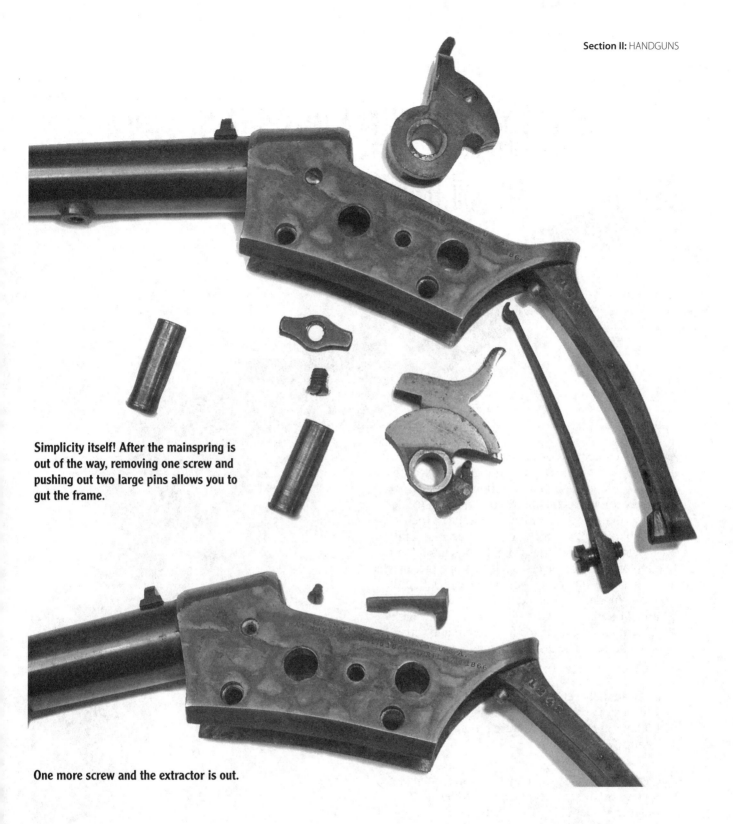

Simplicity itself! After the mainspring is out of the way, removing one screw and pushing out two large pins allows you to gut the frame.

One more screw and the extractor is out.

5 To disassemble the trigger group and breechblock: Drift out the trigger pin (#99) and the sear pin (#179) through the sides of the triggerguard. The trigger (#10), sear (#174) and sear spring (#175) may be lifted out of the triggerguard; note their relationships for correct reassembly. To remove the firing pin (#98) on some models, drift out the firing pin retaining pin (#173) or remove the firing pin screw from the left side of the breechblock. The firing pin can be withdrawn toward the rear of the breechblock.

REASSEMBLY

Reassemble the pistol in the reverse order of above.

Remington and Remington-Type
1875 and 1890 Revolvers and Replicas

A contemporary of and Remington's answer to the Colt Single Action Army was their Model 1875 Single Action Army, also known as the Improved Army or Frontier Army. Virtually the same size and shape as the Colt, the old Ilion, N.Y. gunmaking firm re-used several of its own reliable features from the percussion era Remington-Beals revolvers, such as a one-piece frame and grip straps and one fewer action screw than the Colt. The model was offered in 45 Colt (scarce), 44-40 and 44 Remington CF calibers and mainly with 7-1/2-inch barrels, though a few were made with 5-3/4-inch barrels. The distinctive features of the 1875 were its web-shaped ejector housing and the fact that the ejector rod was mostly outside the weapon, the housing actually serving as a support and container for the ejector spring. Somewhere between 25,000 and 30,000 of the 1875 Models were produced between 1875 and 1889.

In 1890, the Remington company, having gone through receivership and now under the management of Hartley & Graham, replaced the 1875 with a new model, the Model 1890. The Model 1890 was almost an identical revolver to the earlier 1875, except that the mass of the web which formed the ejector housing was greatly reduced, thus serving to streamline the gun's overall appearance. Only about 2,000 Model 1890s were produced; they were offered in both 5-1/2- and 7-1/2-inch barrel lengths and chambered in caliber 44-40 only. Even though comparatively few Remington 1875 and 1890 Model Single Action Army revolvers were manufactured, they were nevertheless excellent-quality guns, every bit as good as their Connecticut competition. They remain well thought of today.

Remington's 1875 was competition for the Colt SAA. This fine replica made in Italy by Uberti is a very shootable modern copy of the 1875. Revolver courtesy of EMF Company. Author photos.

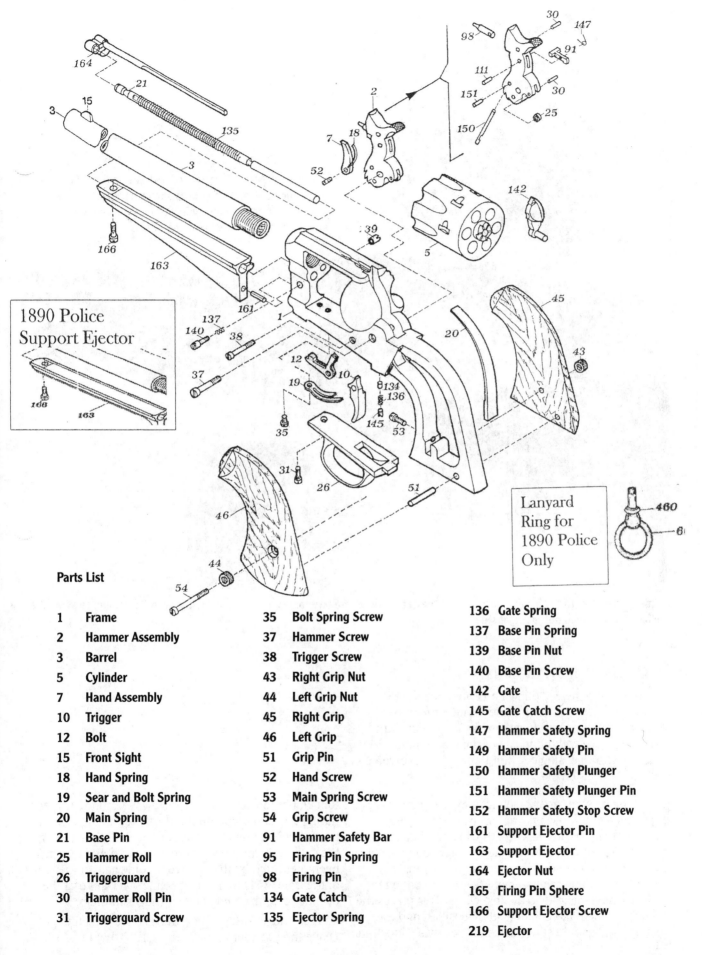

1890 Police
Support Ejector

Lanyard
Ring for
1890 Police
Only

Parts List

1	Frame	35	Bolt Spring Screw	136	Gate Spring
2	Hammer Assembly	37	Hammer Screw	137	Base Pin Spring
3	Barrel	38	Trigger Screw	139	Base Pin Nut
5	Cylinder	43	Right Grip Nut	140	Base Pin Screw
7	Hand Assembly	44	Left Grip Nut	142	Gate
10	Trigger	45	Right Grip	145	Gate Catch Screw
12	Bolt	46	Left Grip	147	Hammer Safety Spring
15	Front Sight	51	Grip Pin	149	Hammer Safety Pin
18	Hand Spring	52	Hand Screw	150	Hammer Safety Plunger
19	Sear and Bolt Spring	53	Main Spring Screw	151	Hammer Safety Plunger Pin
20	Main Spring	54	Grip Screw	152	Hammer Safety Stop Screw
21	Base Pin	91	Hammer Safety Bar	161	Support Ejector Pin
25	Hammer Roll	95	Firing Pin Spring	163	Support Ejector
26	Triggerguard	98	Firing Pin	164	Ejector Nut
30	Hammer Roll Pin	134	Gate Catch	165	Firing Pin Sphere
31	Triggerguard Screw	135	Ejector Spring	166	Support Ejector Screw
				219	Ejector

To be sure the 1875 is unloaded, pull the hammer back two clicks, open the loading gate as shown here and use your other hand to revolve the cylinder to visibly check if any cartridges are in the cylinder chambers.

With the hammer in the loading position and the gate opened, the base pin is unlocked and withdrawn far enough to allow the cylinder to be rolled out the right side.

DISASSEMBLY INSTRUCTIONS

Note: Uberti 1875 Outlaw parts nomenclature is used within the text. With some minor variations, as covered in the text, the following instructions are suitable for use with nearly all of the large-frame, metallic-cartridge, single action Remington revolvers as well as copies thereof.

1 First be sure the weapon is unloaded. Grasp the revolver around the grip firmly, keeping your finger away from the trigger (#10) while holding the muzzle pointed in a safe direction. Check to make sure the weapon is unloaded by opening the loading gate (#142) and pulling the hammer (#2) slowly to the rear until you have heard two audible clicks. This places the hammer in the half-cock or loading position and the cylinder (#5) should spin freely in a clockwise direction.

Remember to keep your fingers away from the trigger during this entire operation. Slowly rotate the cylinder two full revolutions by hand, all the while examining the cylinder's chambers through the opening that has been presented by the opened loading gate at the rear of the frame (#1) to make absolutely certain that the cylinder chambers have no cartridges in them.

If cartridges are present, this is a loaded gun. Leave the hammer right where it is, in the half-cock

The grips, mainspring and trigger guard are all very simple to remove. Notice that the strain screw at the bottom front of the butt has been loosened.

or loading position, and with the loading gate opened. Using your left hand to maintain your secure grip on the weapon and still keeping your fingers away from the trigger, tilt the revolver so that the barrel's muzzle is facing away from you and upwards, in a safe direction. Use your right hand to rotate that cylinder slowly, one chamber at a time, pausing at each audible click to allow each successive cartridge to fall out of its chamber and onto your workbench. If any cartridge will not fall out of its own weight; manually operate the ejector by pushing the ejector rod head (#164) located under the front right side of the barrel to the rear with your right hand until the ejector rod has forced the cartridge out of the chamber. When you are absolutely certain that there are no more cartridges left in the cylinder chambers, the revolver may now be safely disassembled. Be sure you move any live ammunition to a separate location.

2 To remove the cylinder: With the hammer (#2) still in the loading position so that the cylinder (#5) will spin freely, open the loading gate (#142). Note: The Uberti replicas use a push-button base pin retainer system that is very much like the one used in the Colt SAA; this is actually an improvement over the more fragile original system. Push in on the base pin screw (#140), which is located on the left-front of the frame, just under the barrel. Withdraw the base pin (#21) to the front far enough so that the cylinder is free

to be taken out the right side of the frame. The cylinder assembly may now be removed from the frame by rolling it out the right side of the frame (#1). Original Remington: Depress the base pin catch, located out at the front end of the base pin, and withdraw the base pin from the front far enough so the cylinder may be rolled out to the right side of the frame.

3 To remove the grips, mainspring and trigger guard: Unscrew and remove the grip screw (#54) from the center of the left hand grip (#46) and then lift off the two grips (#45) and (#46). Loosen the mainspring screw (#53). The bottom of the mainspring #20 may then be tapped sideways out of its slot in the grip frame in either direction by using a small hammer and straight punch. Lift the spring out of the frame. Unscrew and remove the trigger guard screw (#31) from the front of the guard bow. The trigger guard (#26) may now be tilted down from the front and pulled forward and down, off the frame. Note: To reinstall the mainspring, hold its top up against the bottom of the roller (#25) at the lower-rear side of the hammer. Grasp the spring by its bottom side with a strong pair of pliers and push upwards, causing the spring to bend just far enough for you to reseat it within its slot in the frame. Once you have the mainspring started into the slot, you can release your grip with the pliers and then use the small punch and hammer to reseat the spring fully into the frame slot).

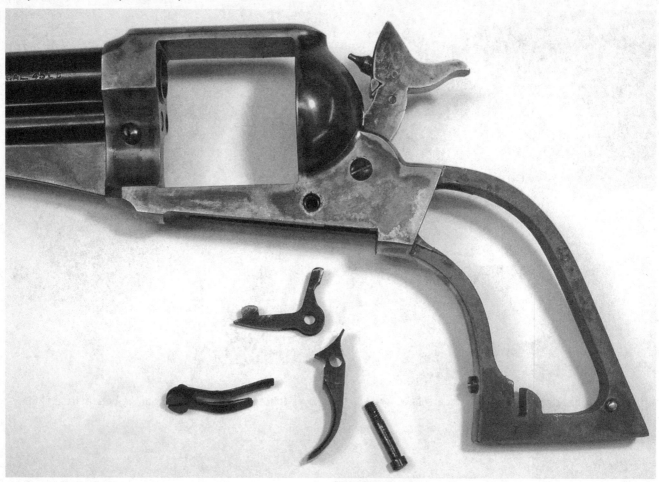

Removing just two screws allows the sear/bolt spring, the trigger and the bolt to be dropped out the bottom of the frame.

The first step in removing the hammer is to take out the hammer screw and push the hammer down into the frame so the hand screw and hand can be removed from the bottom. The hammer is then pulled out through the top of the frame.

In this view the hand and the hammer have been taken out and the gate has been removed. Notice the gate screw, spring and plunger just in front of the hand at the lower left.

4 To disassemble the action: Unscrew and remove the trigger bolt spring screw (#35), the only screw inside the action that is facing straight up, from the underside of the frame. The trigger bolt spring (#19) will fall out the bottom of the frame. Next, remove the forwardmost of the two screws on the left side of the frame. (This is also the smaller of the two screws and is called the trigger screw [#38]; it holds the bolt [#12] and the trigger [#10] in place.) The trigger and the bolt may now be removed through the bottom of the frame.

The hammer screw (#37) can now be unscrewed and removed, after which the hammer assembly (#2) should be pushed down far enough so that the hand screw (#52) becomes fully exposed through the trigger guard opening at the frame bottom. Remove the hand screw (#52). The hand assembly (#7) and (#18) can now be withdrawn out the bottom of the frame. To remove the hammer, push the hammer back up through the frame and remove it through the hammer opening at the top of the frame.

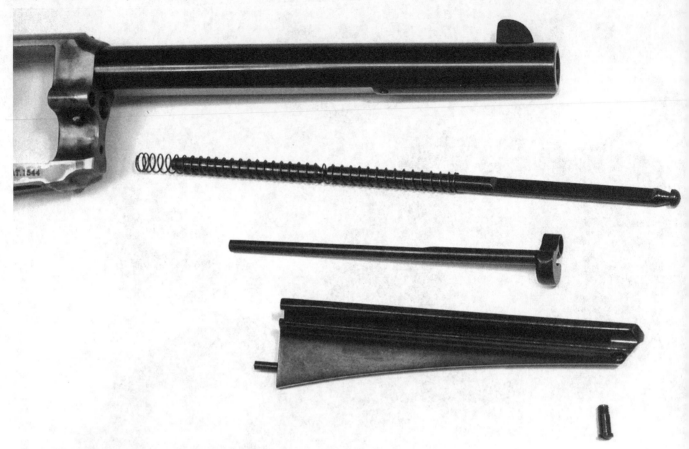

The removal of just one screw allows the entire ejector assembly to be pulled off from the front.

5 To disassemble the peripherals: The support ejector (163) may be removed by first removing the support ejector screw (#166) from the bottom/front of the barrel (#3) and pulling the support ejector down slightly and along with the ejector and base pin assemblies, then forward and out the front of the frame. Once the support ejector is out of the frame, the base pin (#21) can be fully withdrawn from the front, and the ejector assembly (#219) along with the ejector spring (#135) may be withdrawn out the rear of the support ejector. Replica: It is not recommended that the hammer safety components be disassembled except by factory-trained personnel. To remove the gate (#142): Unscrew and remove the gate catch screw (#145) from the underside of the frame. The gate catch spring (#136) and gate catch (#134) will fall out through this same screw hole. The gate is now free and may be pulled forward out of the frame.

REASSEMBLY

Reassemble the revolver in the reverse order.

Remington Double Derringer

R emington produced this popular and neat-looking superposed, two-shot derringer designed by William H. Elliot from about 1866 until 1935. These little derringers were available in blue or nickel finishes and with hard rubber, rosewood or walnut grips. Each barrel was fired individually by means of a pivoting firing pin that was operated by a ratchet, so each time the hammer was cocked the firing pin would contact a shell in either the upper or lower barrel. In all, the company manufactured more than 150,000 of these simple and very reliable 41 Rimfire caliber pistols. Be aware that because of the delicate size of the frame hinge, Remington derringers that have been roughly handled are commonly encountered with cracked frame hinge ears.

Remington's little two-shot derringer was a very popular gun, remaining in production for almost 70 years. This one has been given some gold touches along with a set of modern plastic grips. From the Duff Armfield collection. Author photos.

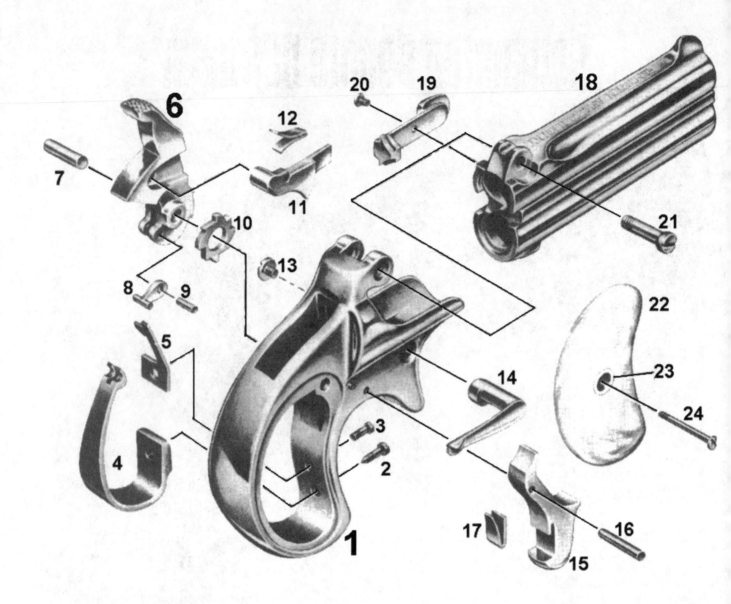

Remington Double Derringer Parts

1	Frame	9	Stirrup Pin	18	Barrels
2	Mainspring Screw	10	Firing Pin Ratchet	19	Ejector
3	Firing Pin Ratchet Spring Screw	11	Firing Pin	20	Ejector Screw
4	Main Spring	12	Firing Pin Spring	21	Barrel Hinge Screw
5	Firing Pin Ratchet Spring	13	Barrel Lock Screw	22	Grips (2)
6	Hammer	14	Barrel Lock	23	Grip Escutcheon
7	Hammer Pin	15	Trigger	24	Grip Screw
8	Stirrup	16	Trigger Pin		
		17	Trigger Spring		

Illustration by James Triggs, from *NRA Illustrated Firearms Assembly Handbook,* 6th printing, edited and renumbered by the author.

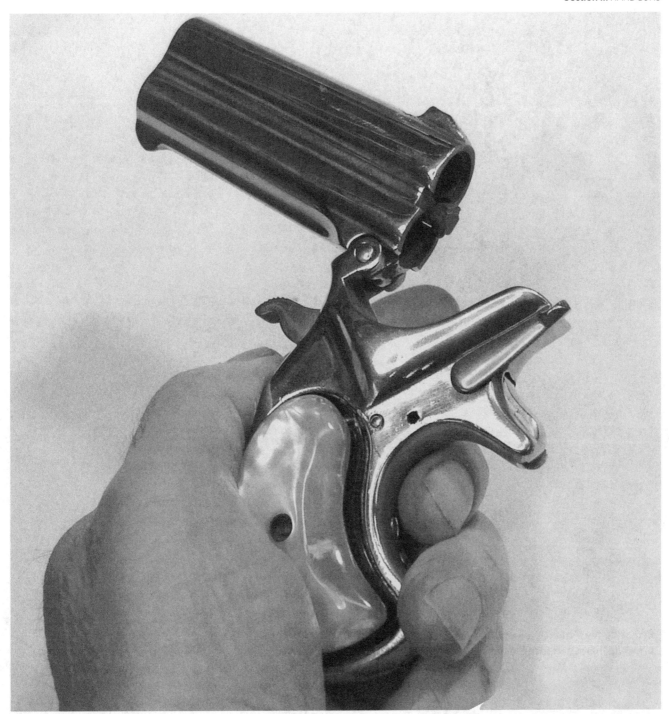

To check the derringer to make sure that it's unloaded, simply rotate the barrel lock and pivot the barrels upward. Author photos.

DISASSEMBLY INSTRUCTIONS

1 First be sure that the weapon is unloaded. Grasp the pistol around the grips (#22) while pointing the muzzle in a safe direction and being very careful to keep your fingers away from the trigger (#15) at all times. Pull the hammer (#6) back just slightly until you hear one click; this should be the half-cock or loading position. On the right hand side of the frame you will find the barrel lock, which looks like a little lever. Rotate the barrel lock foreward (#14) to unlock the barrels (#18) and tilt the barrels up. Check the chambers at the rear of the barrels to be sure there are no cartridges in them. If cartridges are present remove them and take any live ammunition to a separate location before attempting any disassembly.

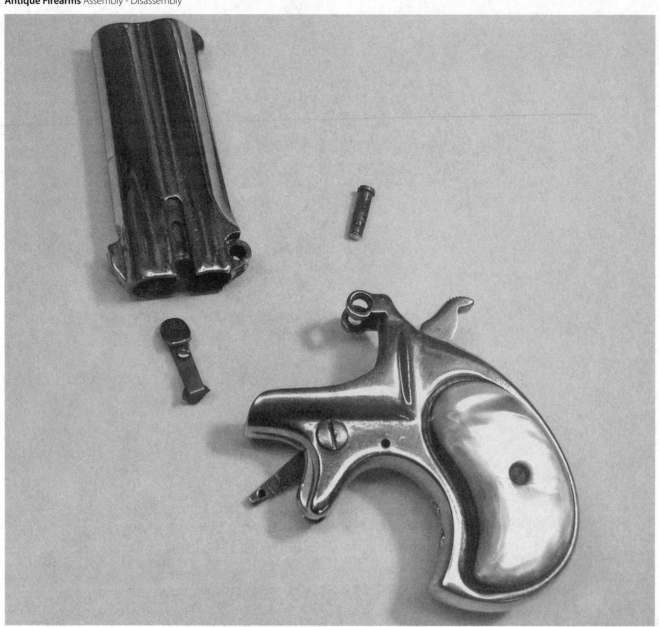

Removing the Remington barrel is as simple as taking out the hinge screw; we have also removed the extractor, shown just below the barrels. Notice the tiny crack in the lower side of the hinge, a common malady in this model.

After the grips are removed, the mainspring and ratchet spring can also be removed.

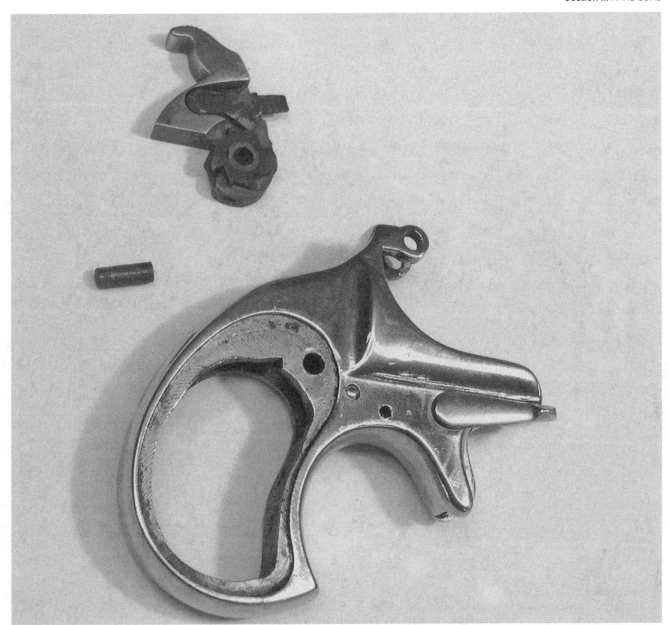

Driving out the hammer pin allows the hammer to be removed through the top of the frame. Notice the firing pin and its ratchet.

2 To remove the barrel: With the barrel still in the open position, unscrew and remove the barrel hinge screw (#21) and lift the barrels (#18) out of the frame (#1). The ejector (#19) can be removed by first unscrewing the ejector screw (#20). The ejector can now be slid to the rear and out of its mortise in the left side of the barrel.

3 To disassemble the frame: Unscrew and remove the grip screw (#24) from the center of the grips and then lift off both grip panels (#22). Bring the hammer to the half-cock position and pry the top of the mainspring (#4) forward with a small screwdriver blade while shaking or tapping the frame lightly on a wooden bench top to disengage the top of the mainspring from the ears of the hammer stirrup (#8). When the stirrup

is disengaged, allow the hammer to fall forward gently and then release the mainspring. Unscrew and remove the mainspring screw (#2), the lower of the two screws in the front grip frame, and the firing pin ratchet spring screw (#3), the upper of the two screws in the front grip frame. Remove the mainspring (#4) and the firing pin ratchet spring (#5) from the frame. Use a pin punch and hammer to drive out the hammer pin (#1). The hammer can now be pulled out through the top of the frame along with the firing pin ratchet (#10), firing pin (#11) and firing pin spring (#12) as an assembly. These three parts – (#10), (#11) and (#12) – may be removed from the hammer by pulling them free with your fingers. Note the positions of each part for reassembly later.

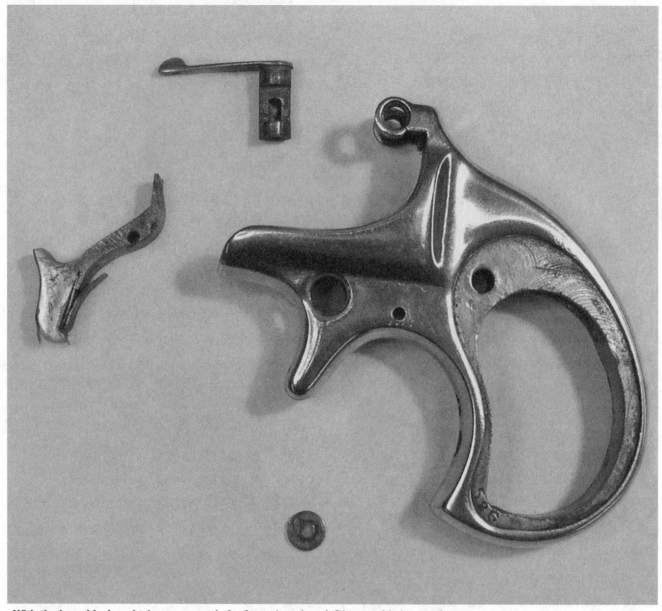

With the barrel lock and trigger removed, the frame is stripped. Disassembly is complete.

4 To disassemble the lower frame: Unscrew and remove the barrel lock screw (#13) from the left side of the frame. The barrel lock (#14) may be pulled out of the frame from the right side. Use a small pin punch to drift out the trigger pin (#16). The trigger (#15), along with the trigger spring (#17), can be withdrawn through the inside top of the frame.

REASSEMBLY

Reassemble the pistol in the reverse order of above.

Robbins & Lawrence Pepperbox
Percussion Pistol

The Robbins & Lawrence Pepperbox was loaded with innovative features. This one is a larger-framed .31-caliber version. From the John Watts collection. Author photos.

During the 1850s, the Robbins & Lawrence Armory at Windsor, Vermont, on the Connecticut River, was the largest private armory in the world. The company gained their success by manufacturing high-quality Model 1842 rifles for the U.S. Army and by doing this ahead of time and on budget.

An innovative gun-maker, Robbins & Lawrence played a key role in developing the precision machinery required for true interchangeable parts. Ably headed by firearms genius Richard Lawrence, R&L was also the primary manufacturer of the famed Sharps rifle, a design that Lawrence played a large part in perfecting. During the early 1850s, the superintendent of the armory was none other than B. Tyler Henry, later of Henry rifle fame.

From 1851 through 1854 R&L manufactured a unique pepperbox pistol designed by George Leonard Jr. The shop foreman at the Leonard Pistol Works (that portion of the R&L Armory devoted to this project) was Daniel B. Wesson and, at the same time, Horace Smith was employed on a separate repeating rifle project. Both soon left R&L to form Smith & Wesson.

Unlike the commonly-seen Allen pepperbox that used rotating barrels, the Leonard used a fixed barrel set with an internal rotating hammer so it had the appearance of being a hammerless weapon. The barrels also broke open like a shotgun to give access to the percussion nipples. Furthermore, the barrels themselves unscrewed and pulled forward from the breech, which allowed them to be charged from the breech.

The Leonard also used a unique split-ring trigger which served a dual purpose as trigger and decocking mechanism. . .yes, in 1851! The ring trigger is actually used to cock the striker; the lever forward of the ring is the trigger that fires the gun. There is a decocking button at the rear of the grip. To decock a cocked pistol, the ring is held back and the button depressed, allowing the ring to be eased forward, independently of the trigger.

The Leonard's innovations included a clean, simple hammerless design that shielded the shooter from the exploding caps, a top-break breech, and a quick-opening barrel set that allowed breech loading. The design was so novel and the guns were so popular that were it not for Sam Colt's even more popular revolver, it could easily have been the Leonard Pepperbox that won the west! A total of about 7,000 of these Leonard-designed pepperbox pistols were made by R&L. They were offered in .28 and .31 caliber and all were five-shots. As you will note from the photos, had the gun been around long enough, the design would have lent itself readily to firing metallic cartridges. The pistol illustrated here is in .28 caliber. There are many minor engineering differences among various models.

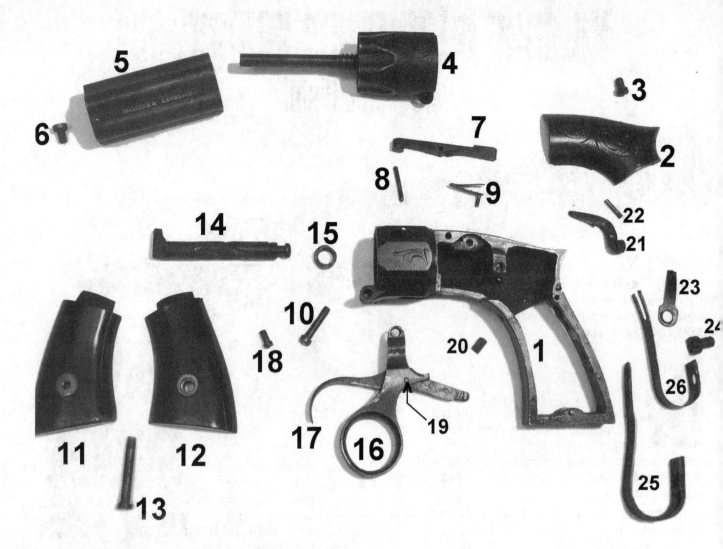

Robbins & Lawrence Pepperbox
Parts List

1	Frame	14	Ratchet-Hammer
2	Sideplate	15	Ratchet Nut
3	Sideplate Screw	16	Cocking Piece
4	Breech Plate Assembly	17	Trigger
5	Barrel	18	Cocking Piece Screw
6	Barrel Screw	19	Trigger Pin
7	Barrel Latch	20	Strain Screw
8	Barrel Latch Pin	21	Decocker
9	Barrel Latch Spring-Ratchet Cam	22	Decocker Pin
10	Barrel Pivot Screw	23	Decocker Spring
11	Right Grip	24	Mainspring Screw
12	Left Grip	25	Mainspring
13	Grip Screw	26	Trigger Spring

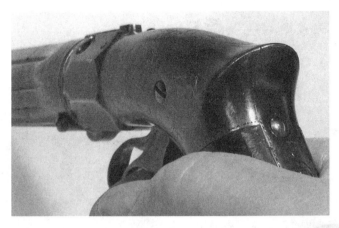

The decock button can be seen in the rear of the grip frame, just above the shooter's hand.

Opened for loading, the R-L pepperboxes exposed the nipples and the rear of the barrels.

DISASSEMBLY INSTRUCTIONS

1 First, before doing any work, be certain the weapon is unloaded. Grasp the pistol around the grips (#11) and (#12), being careful to keep your finger off the trigger (#17) and to keep the muzzles pointed in a safe direction. Depress the barrel latch (#7) to allow the barrels (#4) and (#5) to break open. Examine the nipples at the rear of the breech plate (#5) to be sure no percussion caps are present.

If caps are present on the nipples, you may very well have a loaded gun. You can check further to see if the barrels are loaded by unscrewing the barrels (#4) in a clockwise direction (viewed from the rear) to open their breech ends. If you find the breech plate is loaded, proceed at once to step 2 and remove the barrels/breech plate from the frame. Once the barrels and breech plate are off the frame, it may be disassembled safely.

Shown here are the two different types of hinges you may encounter on R-L pepperboxes; there are others but they are all variations of these. The top pistol is a .28-caliber with a conventional-type hinge while the bottom is a .31-caliber with the machined one-piece hinge. Both pistols are from the John Watts collection.

2 To remove the barrels: Unlatch the barrel and unscrew and remove the barrel pivot screw (#10). The barrel and breech plate assembly will lift off the frame (#1). To disassemble the barrels: Unscrew and remove the barrel screw (#6) from the front of the barrels and unscrew the barrels (#5) from the breech plate (#4) by turning them counterclockwise. Slide the barrels forward, off the center pin on the breech plate.

3 To disassemble the frame: Unscrew and remove the grip screw (#13) and lift off the grips (#11) and (#12). Unscrew and remove the sideplate screw (#3) and lift off the sideplate (#2) to expose the action. Loosen the strain screw (#20) at the front of the grip frame. Insert a tapered punch between the inside of the

frame and the bottom front of the mainspring (#25) and use an off-set screwdriver to loosen and then remove the mainspring screw (#24.) Lift out the decocker spring (#23). Remove the tapered punch and carefully lift out the trigger spring (#26) from the bottom, taking careful note of where the spring fits at the top end.

Next, remove the mainspring (#25), also from the bottom, being sure to note its position for reassembly. To reassemble these springs, assemble them into the grip frame and compress them using the tapered punch as you did earlier. Use a line-up punch to align the trigger and mainsprings with their hole in the rear of the grip frame, and install the decocker spring with the mainspring screw.

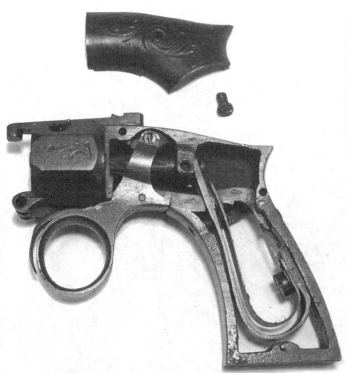

The pepperbox sideplate has been removed, giving the gunsmith excellent access to the internal mechanism. This and the following photos are of the .28-caliber version.

Here the spring package has been removed. Only one screw holds this bundle of springs in the gun.

A tapered punch has been wedged between the grip frame and the mainspring to hold the springs in place while the screw is being removed (or installed).

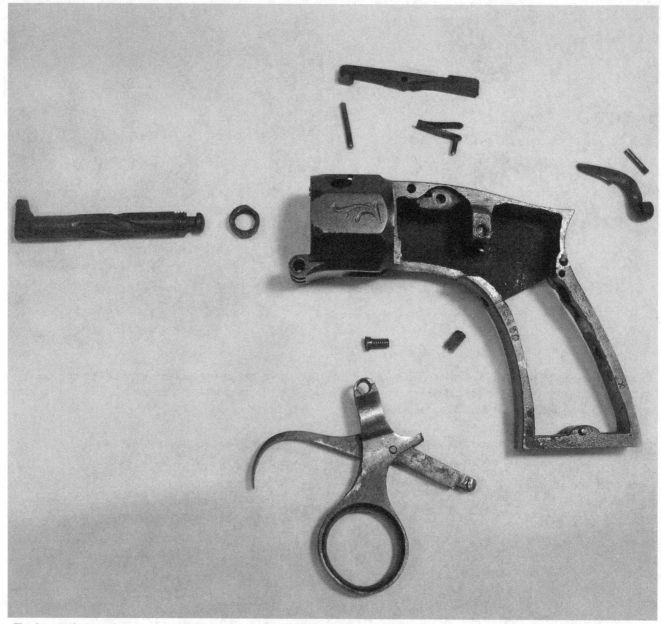

The Leonard pepperbox is a very simple pistol. In this view the remainder of the parts have been removed from the frame.

4 Further disassembly: Unscrew and remove the cocking piece screw (#18) at the top inside area of the frame and lift out the cocking piece/trigger assembly (#16) and (#17). Use a cup-tipped pin punch and hammer to drive out the barrel latch pin (#8) and lift out the barrel latch (#7) and the barrel latch spring (#9). Notice that the bottom leg of the barrel latch spring has a long pin attached; this acts as the stationary cam for the ratchet-hammer (#14). Use a pin punch and hammer to drive out the decocker pin (#22) and lift out the de-cocker (#21).

Carefully unscrew the ratchet nut (#15) from the ratchet-hammer (#14), turning the nut in a counterclockwise direction. The ratchet-hammer may now be withdrawn from the front.

REASSEMBLY

The pistol may be reassembled in the reverse order of above.

Ruger's New Model
Single Action Revolvers

Ruger's New Model Vaquero, shown with a 5-1/2-inch barrel in .45 Colt, is a very popular revolver in Cowboy action events. revolver courtesy of Sturm-Ruger & Company. Author photos.

William B. Ruger completely replaced the actions in his entire line of single action revolvers in 1973 with a radically new single action design. This was probably at least partially motivated by a desire to remove any potential for frivolous lawsuits that might grow out of the basic single action design (which was as old as the Colt Paterson revolver of 1836). What Ruger did would never win any popularity contests with the single action "purists," but he had managed to produce the safest single action revolver that the world had ever seen and the only single action that was safe to carry with all six chambers loaded.

These "New Models," as they are universally called, were equipped with a transfer bar to remove the possibility of an accidental discharge should the revolver ever be dropped on its hammer. The old "three clicker" hammer was gone forever from the New Models; in fact these hammers do not have to be touched during the loading or the unloading process. New Model Ruger single actions are loaded by simply opening the loading gate, which depresses the bolt, thus allowing the cylinder to rotate freely for loading and unloading.

The hammer may only make contact with the firing pin when the trigger has been pulled to the rear, the action of which pushes the transfer bar up so it is in between the hammer and the firing pin, where it will transfer the hammer blow to the firing pin. A conversion is available for owners of "old model" (three-clicker) Ruger single action revolvers who desire greater safety. This conversion replaces some of the old internal parts with re-designed parts and adds a transfer bar ignition, similar to the ones used on New Model Blackhawk and Vaquero models.

The hammer face on Ruger's New Model single action is stepped to accommodate the transfer bar ignition system.

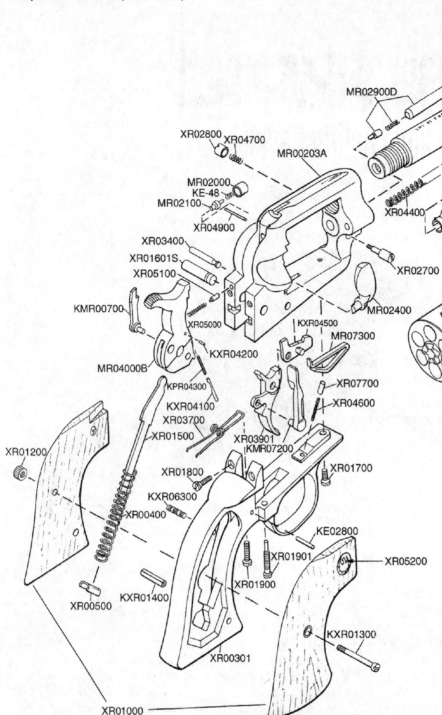

Grip frame screw, and pivot lock,
XR01901
Grip Panel Dowel, KXR01400
Grip Panel Ferrule - Left, XR01200
Grip Panel Ferrule – Right, XR01100
Panel Screw, KXR01300
Grip Panels, Sold in Pairs Only,
XR01000
Hammer Assembly, MR04000B
Hammer Pivot Pin, XR01601S
Hammer PlungerKXR04100
Hammer Plunger Cross Pin,
KXR04200
Hammer Plunger Spring, KXR04300
Hammer Strut, XR01500
Mainspring, XR00400
Mainspring Seat, XR00500
Medallion, 2 Req'd., XR05200
Pawl, KMR00700
Pawl Spring, XR05000
Pawl Spring Plunger, XR05100
Recoil Plate, MR02000
Recoil Plate Cross Pin, XR04900
Transfer Bar, KMR07200
Trigger, XR03901
Trigger Pivot Pin, XR03400
Trigger Spring, XR03700
Trigger Spring Pivot Pin, KE02800
Trigger Spring Retaining Pin,
KXR06300

*** PARTS SO MARKED MUST BE
FACTORY FITTED**

Illustrations reprinted with permission
from Sturm, Ruger & Co.

Parts List (Vaquero)

Part Name and Number
* Barrel, MR20604
Base Pin Assembly, MR02900D
Base Pin Latch Body, XR02700
Base Pin Latch Nut, XR02800
Base Pin Latch Spring, XR04700
* Cylinder, MR-1
Cylinder Latch Assembly, KXR04500
Cylinder Latch Spring, XR04600
**Cylinder Latch Spring Plunger,
XR07700**
Ejector Housing, MR02208

Ejector Housing Screw, XR03300
Ejector Housing Spring, XR04400
Ejector Rod Assembly, XR-55
Firing Pin, MR02100
Firing Pin Rebound Spring, KE-48
Front sight Blade, MR03617
Gate, MR02400
Gate Detent Spring, MR07300
Grip Frame, BR00300
Grip Frame Screw Front, XR01700
**Back (2 Req'd.) Grip Frame Screw,
BR01801**
**Grip frame screw, rear, bottom,
XR01900**

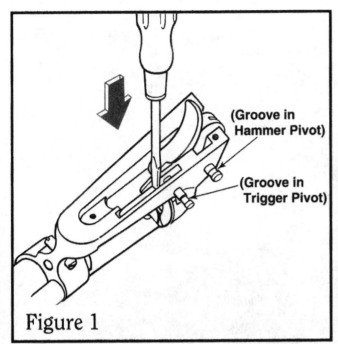

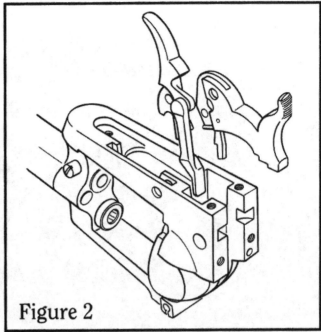

Figure 1

The factory method for depressing the gate detent spring. Illustration courtesy Sturm, Ruger & Co.

Figure 2

The relationship of the hammer-hand, trigger-transfer bar for reassembly. Illustration courtesy Sturm, Ruger & Co.

DISASSEMBLY INSTRUCTIONS

These instructions will also work for the New Model Blackhawk, Super Blackhawk and New Model Single Six (not illustrated).

Note: Ruger New Model single actions are the only single actions that can be considered safe to carry with all six chambers loaded and the hammer down. Old style or old model single actions of any make are only safe to carry loaded when only five chambers loaded and the hammer is down, resting on the empty chamber

1 Make sure the weapon is unloaded. Ruger New Model single action revolvers were the first really safe single actions, but the method used to determine if the revolver is loaded is different from that of other single action designs. You may check to make absolutely sure this weapon is unloaded by holding the revolver around its grip with your left hand, taking precautions to keep the muzzle pointed in a safe direction and to keep your fingers away from the trigger (#XR03901).

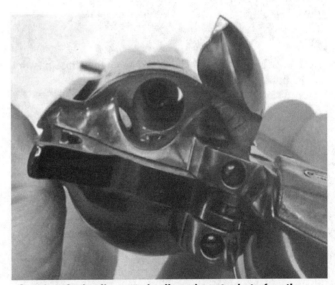

Opening the loading gate is all you have to do to free the cylinder so you can check to be sure the weapon is empty. Notice that the hammer remains down.

Next, open the gate (#MR02400). This enables the cylinder (#MR1) to spin freely in a clockwise direction. Use your right hand to slowly rotate the cylinder two full revolutions by hand while examining the cylinder chambers through the opening that has been presented by the opened gate at the rear of the frame (#MR00203A). Make absolutely certain that the cylinder chambers have no cartridges in them.

If cartridges are present in the chambers this is a loaded gun! Leave the gate open. Still using your

By depressing the base pin latch and pulling the base pin forward, the cylinder is released and may be rolled out the right side of the frame.

left hand to hold the revolver securely by the grip, remembering to keep your fingers away from the trigger (#XR03901); tilt the revolver so that the barrel muzzle (front) is facing away from you and upwards, in a direction that you determine is safe (so that if the gun did accidentally fire no one would be injured). Now, use your right hand to rotate that cylinder slowly, one chamber at a time; pausing at each chamber to allow each successive cartridge to fall out of its chamber and onto your workbench. If any cartridge will not fall out of its own weight; manually operate the ejector by pushing the ejector rod head (#XR-55) located under the front of the barrel (#MR10603) to the rear with your right hand, until the ejector rod has forced that cartridge out of the chamber. When you are absolutely certain that there are no more cartridges left in the cylinder chambers, the revolver may be safely disassembled.

2 To remove the cylinder: The gate should still be open for this operation. The Ruger New Model single action cylinder rotates on a part called the base pin (#MR02900D), which must first be removed through the front of the frame before the cylinder can be taken out. The base pin is removed by first depressing the base pin latch (#XR02700) from left to right and then pulling the base pin straight out the front of the frame.

The cylinder (#MR1) may now be carefully rolled out sideways from the right side of the frame.

3 To remove the grips and the grip frame: Close the gate. Unscrew and remove the grip panel screw (#XR01300) and lift off both grip panels (#XR01000). Pull the hammer (#MR04000) all the way to the rear until it locks at the full cock position. Insert a small nail about an inch long or a heavy duty paper clip through the hole which has presented itself at the lower end of the hammer strut (#XR01500); this will be used to hold the spring assembly captive later. Maintain rearward thumb pressure against the hammer and squeeze the trigger, and then ease the hammer all the way forward. Once it is forward, release the trigger. Unscrew and remove the five screws that hold the grip frame to the frame. Pull the grip frame (#XR00301) to the rear and down to separate it from the frame while you pull the hammer to the rear just slightly. You may now remove the mainspring assembly through the side of the grip frame. Notice its relationship to the hammer and to the grip frame for later reassembly. Notice that the pawl spring (#XR05000) and its plunger (XR05100) are now sticking out of a hole at the rear of the frame. You may pull these parts out to the rear, noting their positions.

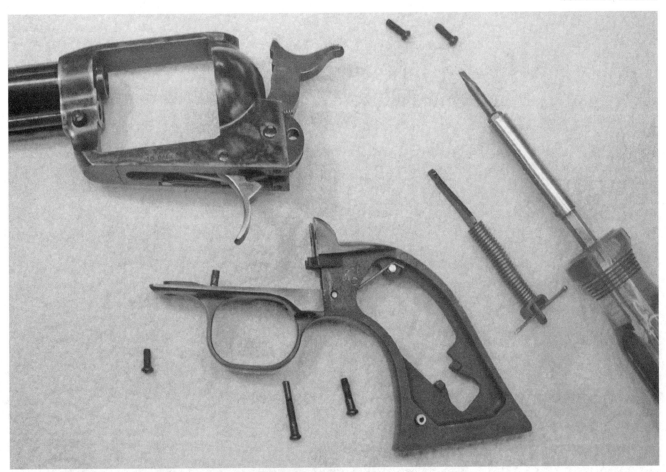

Here is what the New Model Vaquero looks like with its grip frame removed.

This is the Brownells gate detent clamp in use on the Vaquero, a neat little tool that compresses the gate detent spring so the hammer and trigger pivot pins can be easily removed.

The gate, gate detent spring, trigger pivot pin and cylinder latch are shown removed from the frame.

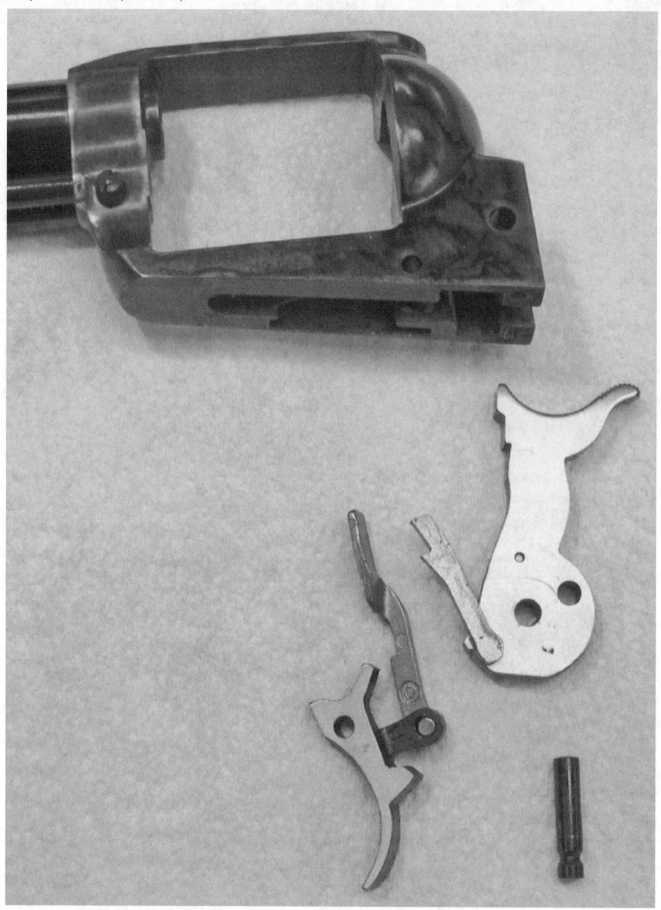

This view shows the relationship of the hammer-to-hand, trigger-transfer bar when removed from the frame. The pin below the hammer is the hammer pivot pin.

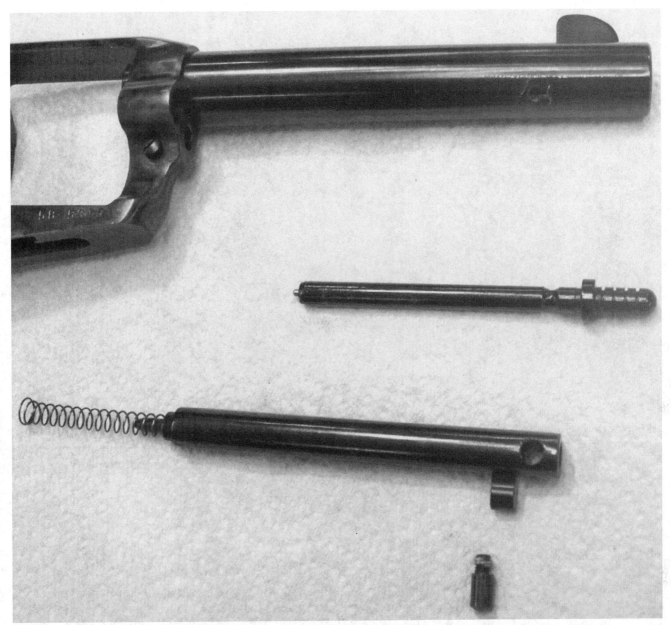

The ejector assembly is fastened to the barrel by one screw. Once the ejector is off the barrel, the base pin can be fully withdrawn from the frame.

4 To remove the trigger and hammer: Turn the frame so the bottom is facing up on your bench and use a small screwdriver to depress the gate detent spring (#MR07300) so that the end of this spring, which sits in the groove of the trigger pin (#XR03400), is freed from that groove. Now use a drift punch and hammer to push the trigger pin out of the frame from either direction. You may now lift out the cylinder catch (#XRO4500) and the gate detent spring. The gate (#MRO2400) may be removed toward the front of the frame. Use a flat punch and hammer to drift out the hammer pin (#XR01601). The hammer (#MRO4000) and the pawl (#KMR00700) assembly, as well as the trigger (#XR03901) and the transfer bar assembly (#KMR07200), may be removed straight out the bottom of the frame. Carefully notice for later reassembly how the pawl is attached to the hammer and how the transfer bar is connected to the trigger.

Using the Brownells base pin nut spanner to disassemble the base pin catch.

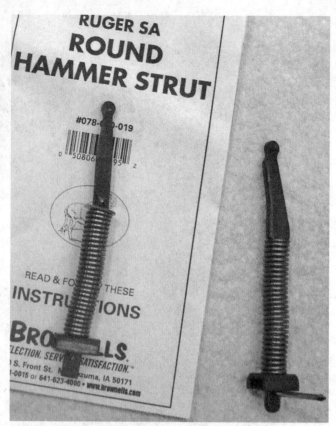

There are many aftermarket parts available for the New Model Ruger such as this solid, round hammer strut, which offers smoother and quieter mainspring operation.

TO DISASSEMBLE PERIPHERALS:

5 Ejector housing: Holding the ejector housing (#MR02208) into the barrel, unscrew and remove the ejector housing screw (#XR03300) from the front of the ejector housing. Pull the ejector housing assembly forward and away from the barrel. The ejector rod (#XR-55) and ejector spring (#XR04400) can now be pulled out from the rear of the ejector housing.

Base pin latch assembly: Holding the base pin latch nut (#XR02800) with a special tool such as the one from Brownells shown in the illustration, use a screwdriver to unscrew the base pin latch (#XR02700) from it, pull the parts out their respective sides. The base pin latch spring (#XR04700) can be withdrawn along with the base pin latch nut.

REASSEMBLY

Reassemble the revolver in reverse order of above.

Ruger Old Army

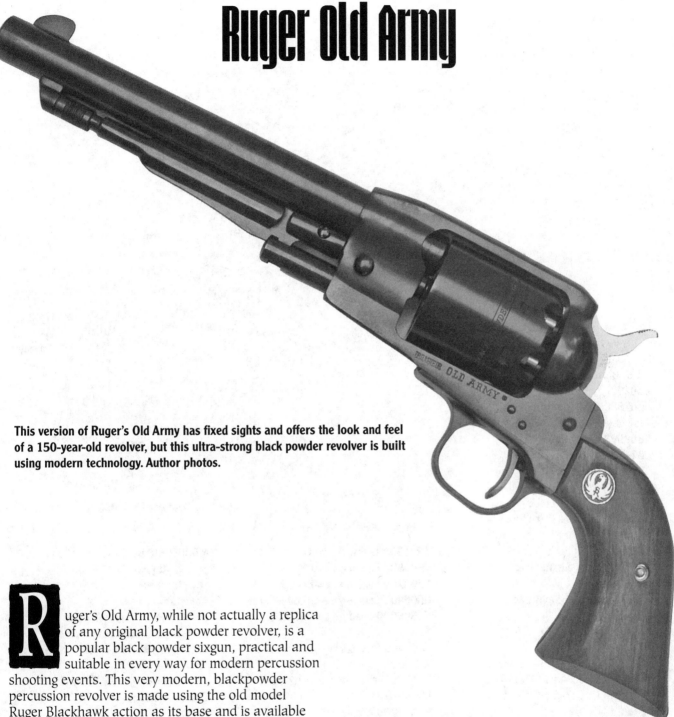

This version of Ruger's Old Army has fixed sights and offers the look and feel of a 150-year-old revolver, but this ultra-strong black powder revolver is built using modern technology. Author photos.

R uger's Old Army, while not actually a replica of any original black powder revolver, is a popular black powder sixgun, practical and suitable in every way for modern percussion shooting events. This very modern, blackpowder percussion revolver is made using the old model Ruger Blackhawk action as its base and is available either with or without adjustable target sights and in blue carbon steel or all-stainless steel versions. The Old Army comes with the Vaquero size and shape grip, meaning that it has the feel of a Colt grip but is just a bit stouter. In a departure from the Colt style percussion revolvers, the Ruger has a strong, solid topstrap over the cylinder frame, not unlike the 1858 Remington revolvers. Also similar to the Remingtons, the Ruger uses a removable base pin, but in this case the head of the base pin also serves as the fulcrum for the loading lever.

From the mechanical aspect, Ruger has put some thought into making this an extremely practical revolver. They added a gas ring to the face of the cylinder to help keep hot powder gases from fouling the cylinder axis pin and they have set the rear of the barrel well back into the cylinder opening in the frame. By doing this they have located the barrel-to-cylinder gap behind and away from the front of the gas ring, a trick Colt and S&W learned early in the days of black powder cartridge revolvers and one that aids greatly in keeping black powder fouling out of the base pin area.

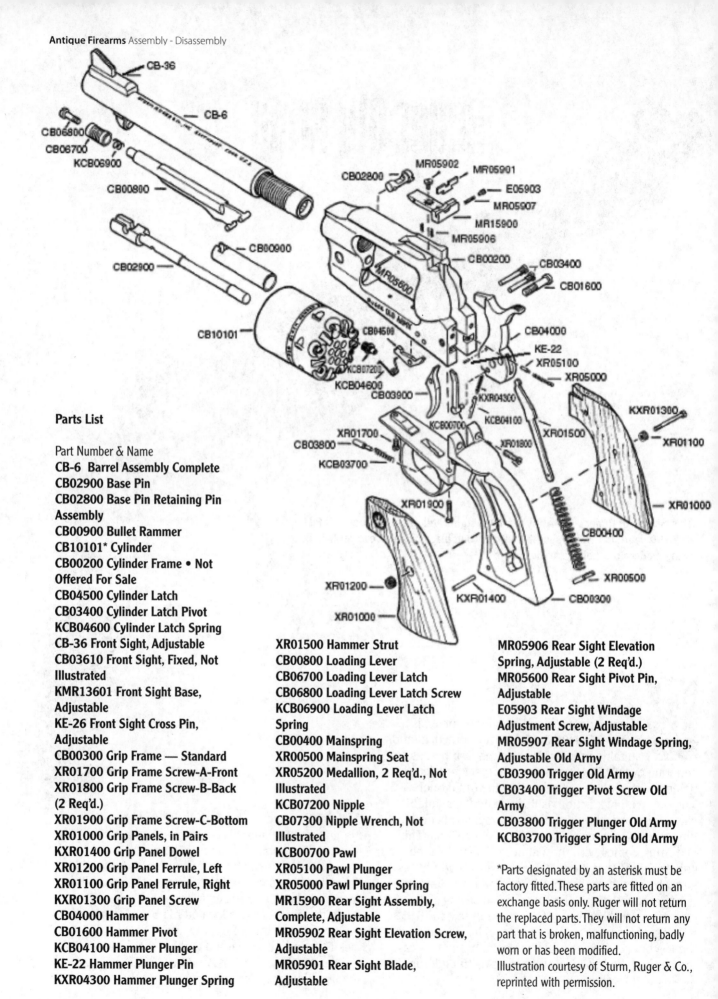

Parts List

Part Number & Name

CB-6 Barrel Assembly Complete
CB02900 Base Pin
CB02800 Base Pin Retaining Pin Assembly
CB00900 Bullet Rammer
CB10101* Cylinder
CB00200 Cylinder Frame • Not Offered For Sale
CB04500 Cylinder Latch
CB03400 Cylinder Latch Pivot
KCB04600 Cylinder Latch Spring
CB-36 Front Sight, Adjustable
CB03610 Front Sight, Fixed, Not Illustrated
KMR13601 Front Sight Base, Adjustable
KE-26 Front Sight Cross Pin, Adjustable
CB00300 Grip Frame — Standard
XR01700 Grip Frame Screw-A-Front
XR01800 Grip Frame Screw-B-Back (2 Req'd.)
XR01900 Grip Frame Screw-C-Bottom
XR01000 Grip Panels, in Pairs
KXR01400 Grip Panel Dowel
XR01200 Grip Panel Ferrule, Left
XR01100 Grip Panel Ferrule, Right
KXR01300 Grip Panel Screw
CB04000 Hammer
CB01600 Hammer Pivot
KCB04100 Hammer Plunger
KE-22 Hammer Plunger Pin
KXR04300 Hammer Plunger Spring

XR01500 Hammer Strut
CB00800 Loading Lever
CB06700 Loading Lever Latch
CB06800 Loading Lever Latch Screw
KCB06900 Loading Lever Latch Spring
CB00400 Mainspring
XR00500 Mainspring Seat
XR05200 Medallion, 2 Req'd., Not Illustrated
KCB07200 Nipple
CB07300 Nipple Wrench, Not Illustrated
KCB00700 Pawl
XR05100 Pawl Plunger
XR05000 Pawl Plunger Spring
MR15900 Rear Sight Assembly, Complete, Adjustable
MR05902 Rear Sight Elevation Screw, Adjustable
MR05901 Rear Sight Blade, Adjustable

MR05906 Rear Sight Elevation Spring, Adjustable (2 Req'd.)
MR05600 Rear Sight Pivot Pin, Adjustable
E05903 Rear Sight Windage Adjustment Screw, Adjustable
MR05907 Rear Sight Windage Spring, Adjustable Old Army
CB03900 Trigger Old Army
CB03400 Trigger Pivot Screw Old Army
CB03800 Trigger Plunger Old Army
KCB03700 Trigger Spring Old Army

*Parts designated by an asterisk must be factory fitted. These parts are fitted on an exchange basis only. Ruger will not return the replaced parts. They will not return any part that is broken, malfunctioning, badly worn or has been modified.
Illustration courtesy of Sturm, Ruger & Co., reprinted with permission.

Here we are using the tool supplied by Ruger to turn the base pin retaining pin. Note that the base pin is partially withdrawn.

DISASSEMBLY INSTRUCTIONS

1 Always begin by making absolutely sure the revolver is not loaded. Start by holding the revolver firmly by its grip, being conscious to keep your fingers away from the trigger (#CB03900). Point and hold the barrel muzzle in a safe direction, that is, facing away from any person, pet, vehicle or dwelling. Now, place the hammer (#CB04000) in the loading position by pulling it to the rear until one audible click is heard; at that point you can check to be certain that the revolver's cylinder (#CB10101) is unloaded before attempting any disassembly or before handling the revolver. This check is performed by carefully examining the rear of the cylinder at each chamber to be certain that there are no percussion caps on any of the nipples (#KCB07200). If percussion caps are present on the nipples, then you should consider this a loaded firearm. Do not attempt any further disassembly.

You should always look at the front of the cylinder to make sure that there are no charges in the cylinder chambers. (A good indication that a chamber is most likely loaded is the presence of bullets or balls showing at the front end of the chamber.) Never look directly into the barrel or chambers, but instead view the chambers by looking down into them from the side. A loaded cylinder may be emptied by taking the gun to a range and firing it until it is empty, or the loaded cylinder may be carefully removed in order to render the weapon safe without firing the revolver by carefully following the instructions to remove the cylinder, below at 2). Note: Once the loaded cylinder has been removed from the revolver, set it aside, away from the remainder of the firearm.

2 To remove the cylinder: With the hammer still in the loading position, use the screwdriver portion of the combination tool supplied with the revolver to turn the base pin retaining pin (#CB2800) one-quarter turn counterclockwise. Unlatch the loading lever (#CB0800) by pulling the loading lever latch (#CB06700) to the rear. The loading lever is then pulled down to an angle of about 90 degrees to the barrel, then pulled forward, which will withdraw the base pin (#CB02900) and the bullet rammer (#CB00900) from the frame. The cylinder assembly (#CB10101) is now free, allowing it to be rolled out through the right side of the cylinder frame (#CB00200).

Here the base pin and loading lever are removed and the cylinder has been taken out. The loading lever/base pin design is very similar to, but much stronger than, the one used on the Civil War era Rogers & Spencer .44 percussion revolver.

After the grips are removed, the hammer is cocked to compress the mainspring. This reveals a hole in the strut where you may insert a pin or, as shown here, a small finishing nail. When the hammer is dropped, the pin holds the mainspring assembly captive, allowing it to be removed either with or without the grip frame.

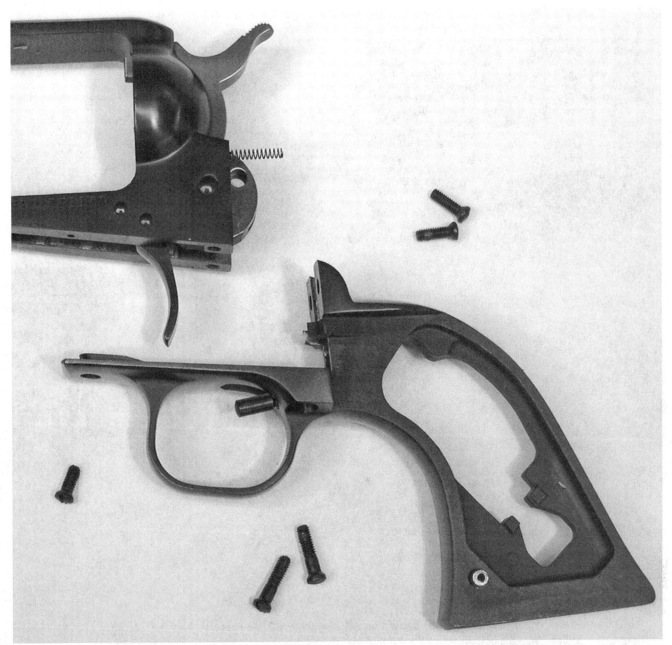

After the five screws that retain the grip frame have been removed, the grip frame is moved rearward and down to remove it from the cylinder frame. Notice the small spring just under the hammer spur? That is the hand spring. It and its plunger can now be pulled out.

3 To remove the grips and grip frame: Remove the grip screw (#KXRO1300) from the center of the grip and then remove the two grips (#XR01000). Bring the hammer (#CB04000) to the fully cocked position and slip a small steel pin or nail through the exposed hole at the bottom of the hammer strut (#XR01500). This will confine the mainspring when the hammer is released from full cock. Now, pull the trigger and allow the hammer to ease forward gently. Remove the five screws (see illustration) that hold the grip frame (#CB00300) to the cylinder frame. As the grip frame is separated from the frame, note the pawl

spring (#XRO5100) and plunger (#XRO500), which are sandwiched between the rear of the frame and the top of the grip frame. These may be pulled out to the rear. The grip frame may be removed by pulling it slightly to the rear and then down, using care to hold the pawl spring and plunger captive. The mainspring/strut assembly may be removed through the opening from side of the grip frame, and the trigger spring (#KCB03700) with its plunger (#CB03800) may be withdrawn out of their hole located at the inside rear of the trigger guard.

The next step is to use a small tool to turn the frame leg of the bolt spring loose.

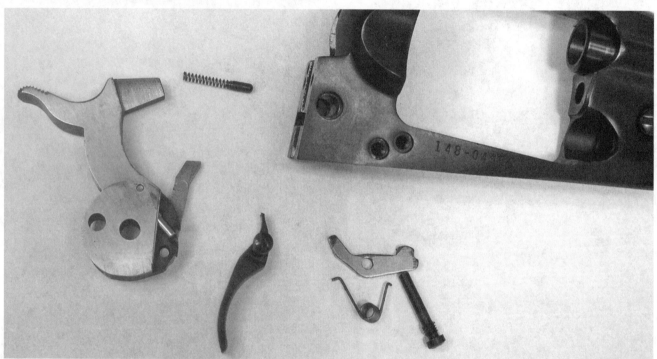

Removing the screws from the right side of the frame allows the hammer with the hand, the bolt and its spring, along with the trigger, to be removed from the bottom.

4 To disassemble the action: The hammer screw (#CB01600) – this is the rearmost screw in the right side of the frame – may now be removed, after which the hammer assembly may be rotated slightly to the rear and pulled down and out of the frame. The pawl (#KCB00700) is connected to the hammer and will withdraw with it. Once the hammer assembly is out, the pawl may be removed by lifting it up out of its socket hole on the left side of the hammer. Remove the trigger screw (#CB03400), the center screw in the right side of the frame). The trigger (#CB03900) will fall out the bottom of the frame. Use a small pick or screwdriver blade and carefully lift the fixed arm of the cylinder latch spring (#KCB04600) to free it, removing its tension from the cylinder latch. Remove the cylinder latch screw (#CB03400), the forward-most screw in the right side of the frame. The cylinder latch (#CB04500) and its spring (#CB04600) may be taken out from the bottom of the frame. Before your remove this spring, make note of the position of it and the cylinder latch for reassembly later.

5 To disassemble the hammer: The hammer plunger (#KCB04100) and plunger spring (#KXR04300) can, if required, be disassembled from the hammer by drifting out the hammer plunger retaining pin (#KE-22).

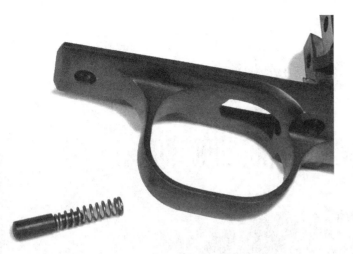

0a-trigspring.tif: The trigger spring and plunger are removed by simply pulling them forward. They fit into a hole drilled at the inside back of the trigger guard.

0a-nipple.tif: Removing the nipples from the cylinder using Ruger's excellent combination tool.

6 To disassemble the peripherals: Once the loading lever is off the revolver, it simply lifts out of its seat and, along with the base pin and the bullet rammer (#CB00900), is removed from its seat with the loading lever by sliding it off. To remove the loading lever latch (#CB06700) from the loading lever, unscrew and remove the loading lever latch screw (#CB06800) from the front-center of the loading lever (#CB00800) and slide off the loading lever latch and the loading lever latch spring (#KCB06900).

If the cylinder is unloaded, the nipples may be unscrewed using the combination wrench supplied by the factory. Never attempt to disassemble a loaded cylinder.

The adjustable rear sight (if so equipped) may be removed by first unscrewing the rear sight elevation screw (#MR-05902) and then drifting out the rear sight pivot pin (#MR-05600). Once the sight is free, use caution: there are two tiny compressed rear sight elevation springs (#MR-05906) located directly under the rear sight. The rear sight blade (#MR-05901) may be removed by removing the rear sight leaf windage screw (#EO5903). Push the sight leaf to one side and tilt it up so it can be pulled out the top. The rear sight windage spring (#MR-05907) can now be removed through the screw hole in the sight of the sight.

REASSEMBLY

Reassemble the revolver in reverse order of above.

The Ruger Old Model Revolver
(Single Six, Blackhawk & Super Blackhawk)

The late William B. Ruger and Alexander Sturm started Sturm, Ruger & Company in 1949 with an ingenious design for a little semi-automatic .22 pistol that became known as the Ruger Standard Model. After the death of Alex Sturm in 1951, Bill Ruger turned his attention to his ideas for the manufacture of a modern single action revolver. Always keeping his partner's contributions to the company in the forefront, to this day the company retains the original Sturm, Ruger and Co. name. The first Ruger single action, which was also the first truly modern single action, was introduced in 1953 as the .22-caliber, six-shot Single Six. The Single Six was based on the appearance of the Colt Single Action Army, only smaller, and it used a lock mechanism powered by music wire coil springs in place of the leaf springs used in the original Colts. This innovative new revolver used a grip frame that was made of aluminum and cast in one piece and featured a modern, frame-mounted, floating firing pin. Ruger was also one of the great pioneers in the process of modern investment casting.

Bill Ruger expanded his original single action idea in 1955 with the release of the Blackhawk, a full-sized 357 Magnum revolver, followed in 1956 by the 44 Magnum caliber Blackhawk. Both revolvers are known today by collectors as the "Flat-top Blackhawk" because their topstraps were perfectly flat and factory machined to accept the Micro adjustable rear sight. These original Blackhawk revolvers were manufactured up until 1962-63. For a great many single action lovers, myself included, these early Blackhawks were the most beautiful and practical sixguns Ruger ever built. They were just the same size as a Colt Single Action Army and their grip angles were identical to the Colt's, so they were very well balanced, the .44-caliber version especially so. Roughly 42,000 of the .357-caliber Blackhawk and some 28,000 .44-caliber Blackhawk revolvers were manufactured.

Ruger saw a need for a more robust revolver to hold the powerful 44 Magnum cartridge so in 1959, a stronger version of the Blackhawk with a larger frame, known as the "Super Blackhawk" was released. The Super frame was larger and thicker and a new

The first Ruger single actions were the .22 caliber Single Six like this one, an early fixed-sight model. All old style Ruger Single Six, Blackhawk or Super Blackhawk single actions, regardless of caliber, share this disassembly procedure. Note that the revolver has three screws that pass through the frame like the Colt single action, but the Ruger's enter from the right side instead of the left as do the Colt's. Author photos.

Ruger-designed adjustable rear sight was added. The receiver's topstrap around the sight was also beefed up, providing more protection for the sight. Standard Blackhawks in 44 Magnum were dropped from the Ruger line in 1963, and for years the Super Blackhawk was the only 44 Magnum available from Ruger. In 1962, William Ruger took the strong points from the Super Blackhawk's design and scaled it down to create a new family of Blackhawk, one that eventually included chamberings in 30 US Carbine, 357 Magnum, 41 Magnum and 45 Colt. Some of these redesigned Blackhawk revolvers were offered as convertible revolvers with interchangeable cylinders in 9mm/357 Magnum and 45 Colt/45 ACP calibers.

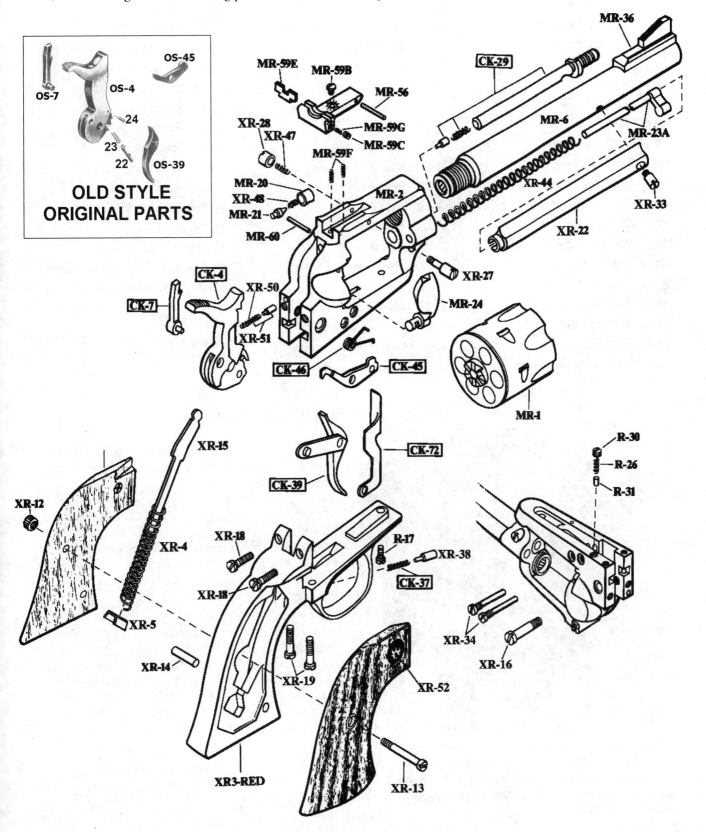

Parts List
(shown with conversion parts, old style
parts in inset)

Part Number & Name

Mr-1	**Cylinder**		
Mr-2	**Cylinder Frame**	Xr-18 **Top Grip Frame Screw**	Os-39 **Trigger, Old Style**
Xr-3-	**Red Grip Frame**	Xr-19 **Lower Grip Frame Screw**	Xr-44 **Ejector Spring**
Ck-4	**Hammer, New Style**	Mr-20 **Recoil Plate**	Ck-45 **Cylinder Latch, Conversion**
Os-4	**Hammer, Old Style**	Mr-21 **Firing Pin**	Os-45 **Cylinder Latch, Old Style**
Xr-4	**Mainspring**	Xr-22 **Ejector Housing**	Ck-46 **Cylinder Latch Spring**
Xr-5	**Mainspring Seat**	Mr-23a **Ejector Rod Assembly**	Xr-47 **Base Pin Latch Spring**
Mr-6	**Barrel**	Mr-24 **Gate**	Xr-48 **Firing Pin Spring**
Ck-7	**Hand, Conversion**	R-26 **Gate Spring**	Xr-50 **Handspring**
Os-7	**Hand, Old Style**	Xr-27 **Base Pin Latch**	Xr-51 **Handspring Plunger**
22.	**Hammer Plunger, Old Style**	Xr-28 **Base Pin Nut**	Mr-56 **Rear Sight Pivot Pin**
23.	**Hammer Plunger Spring, Old Style**	Ck-29 **Base Pin**	Mr-59b **Elevation Screw**
24.	**Hammer Plunger Pin, Old Style**	R-30 **Gate Detent Screw**	Mr-59c **Windage Screw**
Xr-12	**Grip Escutcheon**	R-31 **Gate Detent**	Mr-59e **Rear Sight Blade**
Xr-13	**Grip Screw**	Xr-33 **Ejector Housing Screw**	Mr-59f **Rear Sight Elevation Springs**
Xr-14	**Grip Pin**	Xr-34 **Pivot Screws**	Mr-59g **Rear Sight Windage Spring**
Xr-15	**Hammer Strut**	Mr-36 **Front Sight**	Ck-72 **Transfer Bar, Conversion**
Xr-16	**Hammer Screw**	Ck-37 **Trigger Spring**	
R-17	**Front Grip Frame Screw**	Xr-38 **Trigger Spring Plunger**	
		Ck-39 **Trigger, Conversion**	

Illustration courtesy of Sturm, Ruger & Co.,
reprinted with permission.

**Checking to see if the Ruger is loaded involves bringing
the hammer back two clicks and opening the loading gate.
This is what an empty chamber should look like. Notice the
gunsmith's trigger finger is pointing straight ahead, not
touching the trigger.**

DISASSEMBLY INSTRUCTIONS

Note: "Old style" single actions – usually those
with the firing pin mounted in the hammer – of any
manufacture are not safe to carry with all six chambers
loaded. The only safe way to carry an old style or
old model single action is with five chambers loaded
and with the hammer down, resting on an empty
chamber. The only single action revolvers that may be
considered safe to carry with all chambers loaded and
the hammer down are the Ruger New Models, Vaquero
and Ruger Bisley Model.

This illustration shows a Ruger Old Model single
action fitted with the Ruger factory safety conversion
parts. Original old style parts, which are removed
during the conversion, are shown in the inset. Owners
of original Old Model Ruger single actions may receive
a free factory safety conversion by writing to Sturm,
Ruger & Co., Dept. KC, Lacey Place, Southport, CT
06890 and requesting details.

The Single Six shown with its base pin and cylinder removed.

1 Always be sure the revolver is unloaded by opening the loading gate (#MR-24). Pull the hammer (#OS-4) slowly to the rear until you hear two audible clicks; this should place the hammer in the half-cock or loading position and the cylinder (#MR-1) should spin freely in a clockwise direction. Keep your fingers away from the trigger during this entire operation! Slowly rotate the cylinder (#MR-1) two full revolutions by hand while examining the cylinder chambers through the opening that has been presented by the opened loading gate at the rear of the frame (#MR-2). Make absolutely certain that the cylinder chambers have no cartridges in them.

If cartridges are present, this is a loaded gun. Leave the hammer where it is, in the half-cock or loading position and with the loading gate opened. Using your left hand to hold the revolver securely by the grip, remembering to keep your fingers away from the trigger (#OS-39), tilt the revolver so that the muzzle is facing away from you and upwards in a direction that you determine is safe. Next, use your right hand to rotate the cylinder slowly, one chamber at a time, pausing as each chamber comes

into alignment with the open loading port to allow each successive cartridge to fall out of its chamber and onto your workbench. If a cartridge will not fall out of its own weight, manually operate the ejector by pushing the ejector rod head (#MR-23A) located under the front of the barrel (#MR-6) to the rear with your right hand until the ejector rod has forced that cartridge out of the chamber. When you are absolutely certain that there are no more cartridges left in the cylinder chambers, the revolver may now be safely disassembled.

2 To remove the cylinder: The hammer should still be resting in the loading or half-cocked position and the loading gate should still be open. The Ruger single action Blackhawk cylinder rotates on a part called the base pin (#29), which must first be removed through the front of the frame before the cylinder can be taken out. The base pin is removed by first depressing this cross bolt, which Ruger calls the base pin latch (#XR-27) and (XR-28) from left to right and then pulling the base pin straight out the front of the frame (#MR-2). The cylinder (#MR-1) may now be carefully slid out sideways from the right side of the frame.

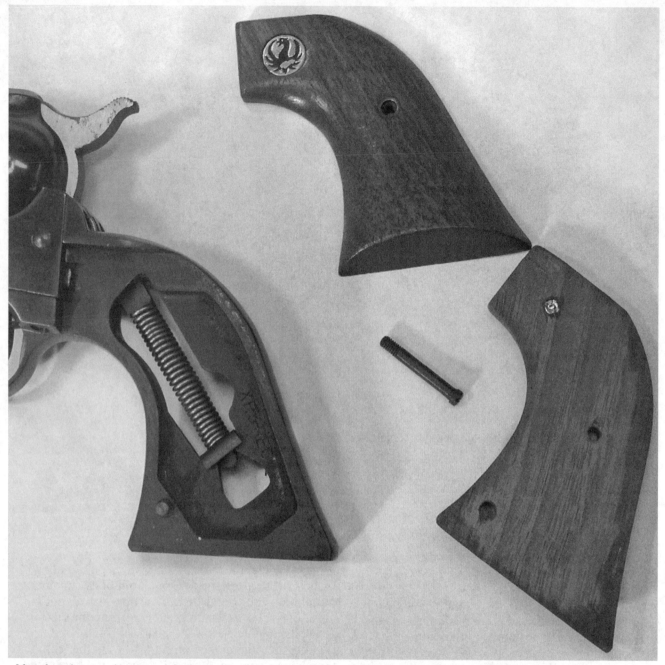

After the grip screw is removed, both grip panels are removed. Here the Ruger coil mainspring is clearly visible.

3 To remove the grips and grip frame: Remove the grip screw (#XR-13) from the center of the grip and then remove the two grips (#XR-52). Bring the hammer (#OS-4) to the cocked position and slip a small steel pin or nail through the exposed hole at the bottom of the hammer strut (#XR-15), which will confine the mainspring when the hammer is released from full cock. Now pull the trigger and gently release the hammer. Remove the five screws – (#XR18), (#XR19) and (#R17) – that hold the grip frame (#XR3-ED) to the cylinder frame. As the grip frame is separated from the frame, note the position of the pawl spring (#XR50) and plunger (#XR51), which are sandwiched between the rear of the frame and the top of the grip frame. The grip frame may be removed by pulling it slightly to the rear and then down, using care to hold the pawl spring and plunger captive. The mainspring/strut assembly (#s XR-15, XR-4 & 5) may be removed from the side of the grip frame and the trigger spring (#XR-37) with its plunger (#XR-38) may be withdrawn out of their hole at the inside rear of the trigger guard.

A finishing nail has been inserted into the hole in the mainspring strut to hold the spring captive for removal.

After you have removed the five screws that hold the grip frame on, the grip frame assembly is pulled off the frame. Notice the coil spring sticking out of the rear of the frame next to the hammer? This is the hand spring, which can now be removed along with its plunger (not yet visible).

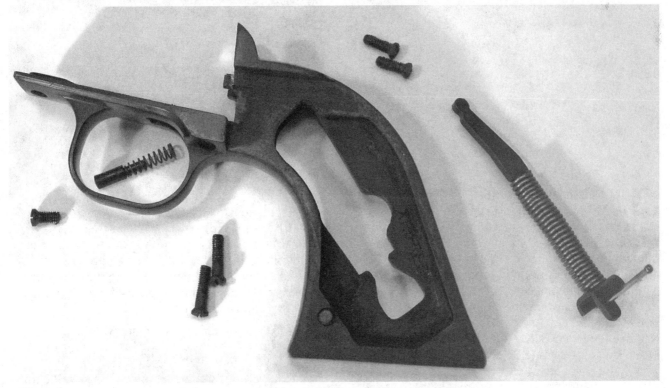

This shows the trigger spring and plunger removed along with the mainspring assembly.

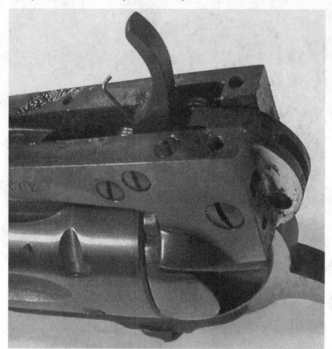

The cylinder latch spring with one leg unfastened from the frame.

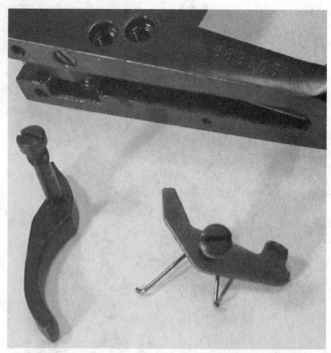

The trigger and cylinder latch (bolt) along with its spring are removed from the frame.

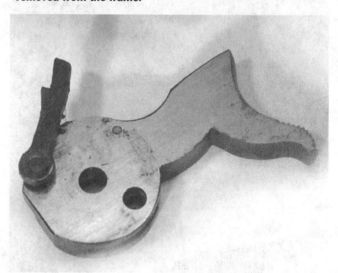

The hammer and hand out.

4 To disassemble the action: The hammer screw (#XR-16), the rearmost screw in the side of the frame, may now be removed, after which the hammer assembly (inset #0S-4) may be rotated slightly to the rear and pulled down and out of the frame. The pawl (#OS-7) is connected to the hammer and will withdraw with it. Once the hammer assembly is out, the pawl may be removed by lifting it up out of its socket hole on the left side of the hammer. Remove the trigger screw (#XR-34), the center screw in the side of the frame. The trigger (inset #0S-39) will fall out the bottom of the frame. Use a small pick or screwdriver blade and carefully lift the fixed

arm of the cylinder latch spring (#CK-46) to free it, removing its tension from the cylinder latch (inset #OS-45). Remove the cylinder latch screw (#XR-34), the forwardmost screw in the side of the frame. The cylinder latch (inset #OS-45), along with its spring (#CK-46), may be taken out the bottom of the frame. Before you remove it, make note of the positioning of this spring for reassembly.

4a To disassemble the hammer: The hammer plunger (inset #22) and plunger spring (inset #23) can, if required, be disassembled from the hammer by drifting out the hammer plunger retaining pin (inset #24).

Only one screw holds the entire ejector assembly on the barrel.

The gate and its component parts removed from the frame.

This special tool from Brownells, along with a screwdriver, enables you to easily disassemble the base pin latch screw and its nut.

5 To disassemble the peripherals: The ejector housing screw (#XR-33) is removed from the front of the ejector housing (#XR-22). The entire ejector housing assembly may be pulled to the side by its front until it moves slightly away from the barrel. In this position the assembly may be drawn forward and off the barrel. The ejector rod (#MR-23A) and its spring (#XR-44) are removed by pulling them both straight back and out of the ejector housing.

The gate (#MR-24): Under the frame in the right side frame rail you will notice a small screw that faces up. This is the gate spring screw (#R-30). Remove it and its plunger – (#R-31) and spring (#R-26) – out through the screw hole. The gate (#MR-24) itself may now be removed by pulling it out toward the front of the frame.

The adjustable rear sight may be removed by first unscrewing the rear sight elevation screw (#MR-59B) and then drifting out the rear sight pivot pin (#MR-56). Once the sight is free, use caution: there are two tiny rear sight elevation springs (#MR-59F) located directly under the rear sight. The rear sight leaf (#MR-59E) may be removed by removing the rear sight leaf windage screw (#MR-59C). Push the sight leaf to one side and tilt it up so it can be pulled out the top. The rear sight leaf spring (#MR-59G) can now be removed.

REASSEMBLY

Reassemble the revolver in reverse order of above.

Sharps Four-Barrel Derringer

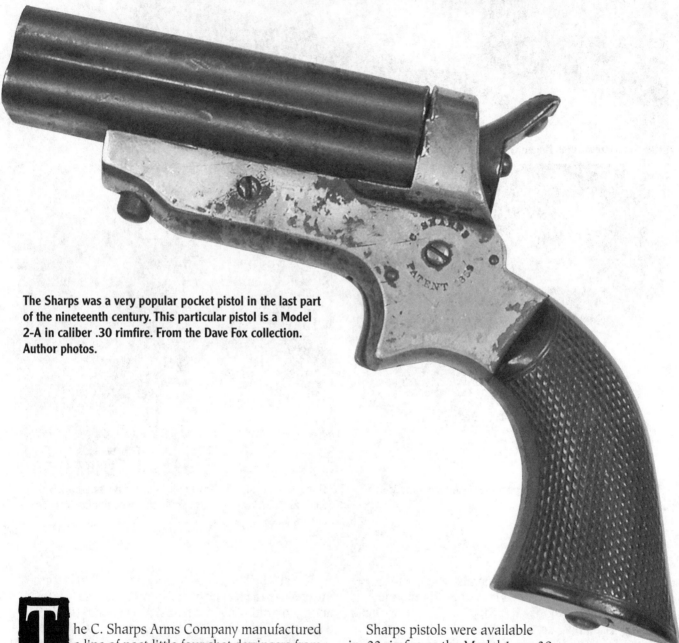

The Sharps was a very popular pocket pistol in the last part of the nineteenth century. This particular pistol is a Model 2-A in caliber .30 rimfire. From the Dave Fox collection. Author photos.

The C. Sharps Arms Company manufactured a line of neat little four-shot derringers from 1859 though about 1874. These unique pistols, officially called "Sharps & Hankins Breech Loading 4-shot Pepperbox Pistols," used a one-piece, four-shot barrel set that slid forward on the frame for loading and unloading. Many people have the misconception that these guns fire all the barrels at once but that is not the case. A ratchet-powered, rotating firing pin is mounted in the hammer and automatically advances to fire the next chamber each time the hammer is pulled to the rear.

Sharps pistols were available in .22 rimfire as the Model 1, or .30 or .32 rimfire as the Models #2 through #4. The Sharps was one of the simplest pistols ever built and was very reliable, mainly because it had few moving parts. While there were quite a few small mechanical differences between the models of the gun, the basic design remained the same. All were single action with a safety or half-cock notch. The pistols were not equipped with an ejector or extraction mechanism and all were four-shots.

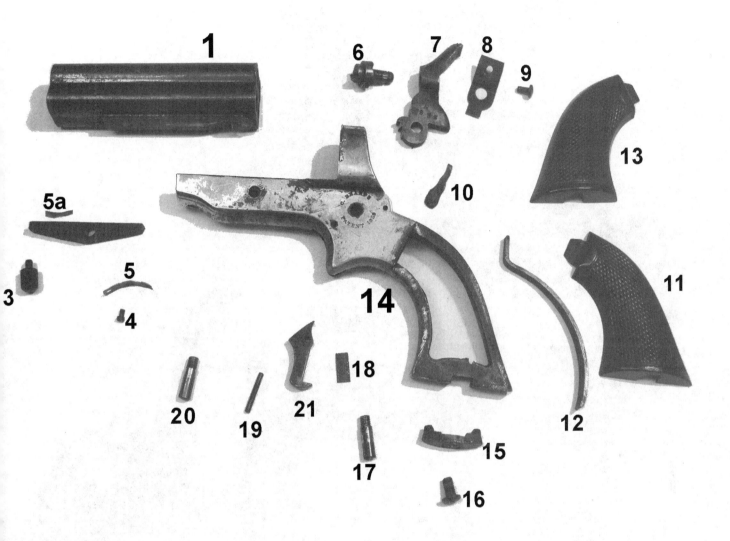

Parts List

1	Barrel	8	Hand Spring	16	Grip Retainer Screw
2	Barrel Lock	9	Hand Spring Screw	17	Hammer Screw
3	Barrel Lock Button	10	Hand	18	Trigger Spring
4	Barrel Lock Spring Screw	11	Grip, Left	19	Trigger Pin
5	Barrel Lock Spring	12	Mainspring	20	Barrel Lock Screw
5a	Barrel Retainer	13	Grip, Right	21	Trigger
6	Firing Pin	14	Frame		
7	Hammer	15	Grip Retainer		

Here is what the Sharps looks like with its barrel set opened. The entire breech area is very accessible.

The barrels have been removed and the barrel latch assembly lifted up out of the frame. Notice the latch button has also been unscrewed. If the barrels do not readily slide off after removing the barrel catch screw, do not try and force them off. It may be time for a gunsmith!

DISASSEMBLY INSTRUCTIONS

1 First be sure the weapon is unloaded. Grasp the pistol around its grips, being careful to keep your fingers away from the trigger (#21) and to keep the muzzle pointed in a safe direction. Pull the hammer (#7) back one audible click to the safety position. Push up on the barrel lock button (#3) and slide the barrel set (#1) forward. This exposes the chamber area of all four barrels. If any cartridges are present in the chambers, remove them now and take any live ammunition to a separate location.

2 To remove the barrels: With the barrels still open, unscrew and remove the barrel latch screw (#20) and pull down slightly on the barrel latch button. This should free the barrel set to be pulled forward off the frame (#14). The barrel latch assembly – (#2), (#3), (#4), (#5) and (#5a) may now be lifted up out of the frame.

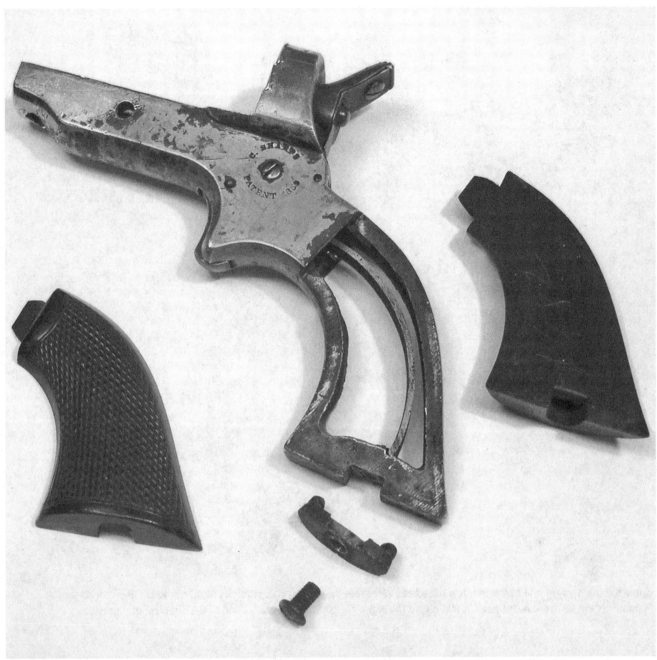

The Sharps grips are held on by a retainer plate at the butt.

Note 1: If the barrel will not remove easily and appears to be jammed on the frame, do not proceed any further, but instead take the gun to a competent gunsmith. Never try to force off the barrel set as you may permanently damage the pistol. Over the years, the author has seen Sharps barrel locks altered in many different ways after the barrel retainer has broken or become lost. If the lock or retainer has been altered, the barrel set may not want to come off in the normal fashion.

Note 2: Some barrel locks have the barrel retainer screwed in place, while on others it is riveted on. The barrel latch button is threaded into the barrel latch. Some are equipped with screw slots; some are not. The barrel lock spring (#5) is fastened onto the barrel lock with a screw (#4).

3 To remove the grips: Unscrew and remove the grip retainer screw (#16) from the bottom of the frame. Lift out the grip retainer (#15); always set this aside in the exact position it came off as the part is often hand fitted to the grips. Lift off each grip, (#11) right and (#13) left.

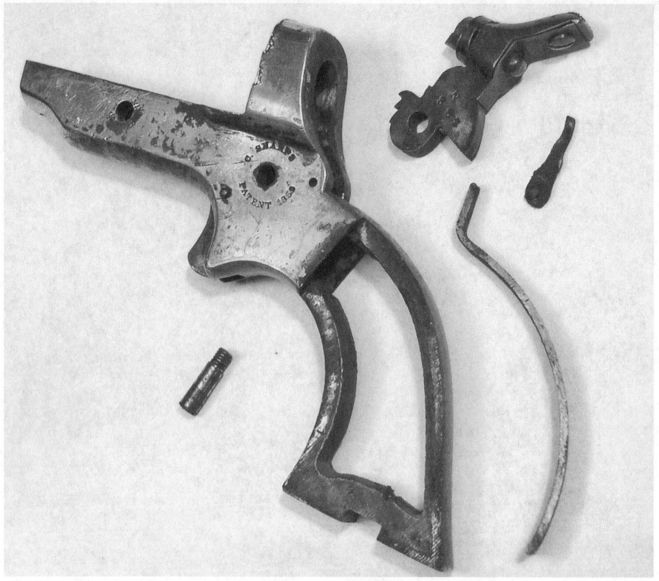

After the mainspring and hammer screw have been removed, the hammer assembly is lifted out to the top rear. Once the hammer is out of the way, the hand is slid out to the right. The Sharps 4-barrel is one of the simplest of all pistols.

4 To remove the hammer, mainspring, hand and trigger: Grasp the bottom of the mainspring (#12) with a strong pair of needle nosed pliers and pull the bottom of the spring sideways, out of its seat with the frame, the spring is now pulled down and out of the frame. Pull the trigger (#21) and hold it to the rear. Unscrew and remove the hammer screw (#17) and slowly lift the hammer (#7) to the rear and up out of the frame. Take notice as you pull the hammer out how it fits together with the hand (#10). The hand may now be slid to the right slightly and removed from the frame. Use a cup-tipped pin punch and hammer to drive out the trigger pin (#19). The trigger is now loose and will pull out toward the bottom-front of the frame. The trigger spring (#18) is actually crimped into two small slots within the frame and unless it requires replacement, it may be left right where it is. Note: Some Sharps pistols used a V-shaped trigger spring that will come out with the trigger. Others may have been altered over time to use a coil trigger spring.

5 To disassemble the hammer: Unscrew and remove the hand spring screw (#9) from the rear of the hammer. The hand spring (#8) is pried out very slightly at the bottom and pushed down just a small amount. This will place the rear of the firing pin (#6) in the enlarged, oval portion of the hole in the hand spring and allow the spring to be removed. The firing pin may now be pushed out to the front of the hammer.

REASSEMBLY

Reassemble the revolver in reverse order of above.

Smith & Wesson Tip-Up
.22 and .32 Rimfire Models 1, 1-1/2 & 2

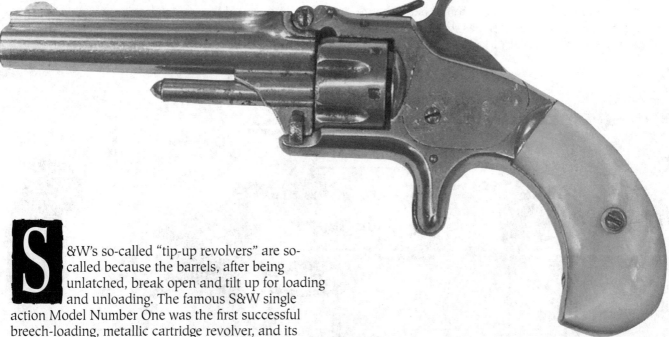

The Model 1 was a very small seven-shot, single action revolver chambered in .22 rimfire. The revolver shown is a Model 1 - Third Issue built about 1872.

S&W's so-called "tip-up revolvers" are so-called because the barrels, after being unlatched, break open and tilt up for loading and unloading. The famous S&W single action Model Number One was the first successful breech-loading, metallic cartridge revolver, and its tiny .22 caliber cartridge, today called the .22 Short, was also the first metallic cartridge to be a commercial success. These pistols used a weak and very unconventional design, especially when viewed from a modern perspective, but they quickly became popular as pocket guns before the Civil War. In an era of muzzle loading revolvers, the new S&W with its ability to be loaded so quickly was considered something very special. The basic concept of this invention would eventually cause the demise of the cap-n-ball revolver. S&W had secured the rights to the very important Rollin White patent before they started production. White's patent was on the idea of a revolver cylinder with bored-through chambers to allow rimmed, metallic cartridges to be inserted from behind. The protection it gave Smith & Wesson enabled them to hold a monopoly on cartridge revolver manufacture, at least until the patent expired in 1869.

S&W's tiny seven-shot, .22-caliber Model 1 revolver went though a series of mechanical improvements and before long it was joined by two other revolvers built on bigger frame sizes and of larger caliber. In 1861 the Model 2, a.k.a. the Model Two Army, appeared and it was, comparatively, only a medium-sized revolver but still much larger than the Model 1. The Model 2's cylinder held six shots in 32 Long rimfire caliber.

Next, in 1865, S&W introduced the Model 1-1/2. This revolver fell in between the Model 1 and the Model 2 in size and its cylinder held five .32 rimfire cartridges. Each of these larger pistols was single action only and built around the same kind of tip-up barrel arrangement. All of the tip-up revolvers made by S&W were chambered for rimfire calibers only.

Smith & Wesson's cartridge revolvers were so heavily sought after during the Civil War that the factory had trouble filling all the orders it received. Even after that, tip-up revolvers stayed surprisingly popular through the 1860s and 1870s and were kept in production seemingly well beyond the point of being obsolete by many of the new metallic cartridge revolver designs. The final version of the Model 1 .22, an advanced tip-up known to collectors as the Model 1 Third Issue, left the factory in 1868. By then, Smith & Wesson had sold more than 257,000 of the .22-caliber Model 1 revolvers alone. Total production of all tip-ups in all chamberings by the time manufacture ceased in 1881 was just over 461,000.

Identification details of the S&W Tip-Up revolvers:

Model 1: .22 rimfire caliber, manufactured 1857 to 1881 (cylinder stop on top of frame)

Model 1 - 1st Issue: seven shots, octagon barrel, square butt grip, bronze frame with circular sideplate. Made 1857 to 1860. Serial #1 to #11,671.

Model 1 - 2nd Issue: seven shots, octagon barrel, square butt grip, bronze frame with irregular shaped sideplate. Made 1860 to 1868. Serial #11,672 to #126,361.

Model 1 - 3rd Issue: seven shots, round barrel, round butt grip, steel frame with irregular shaped sideplate. Made 1868 to 1881. Serial #1 to #131,163.

Model 1-1/2: .32 rimfire caliber, manufactured 1865 to 1875

Model 1-1/2, Old Model: five shots, octagon barrel, square butt grip; the only tip-up with a cylinder stop mounted on the bottom of the frame. Made 1865 to 1868. Serial #1 to #26,300.

Model 1-1/2, New Model: five shots, round barrel, round butt grip, cylinder stop mounted on top of frame. Made 1868 to 1875. Serial #26,301 to #127,100.

Model 2: .32 caliber rf, manufactured 1861-1872, 6 shots, octagon barrel, square butt grip, cylinder stop on top of frame. Serial #1 to #77,155.

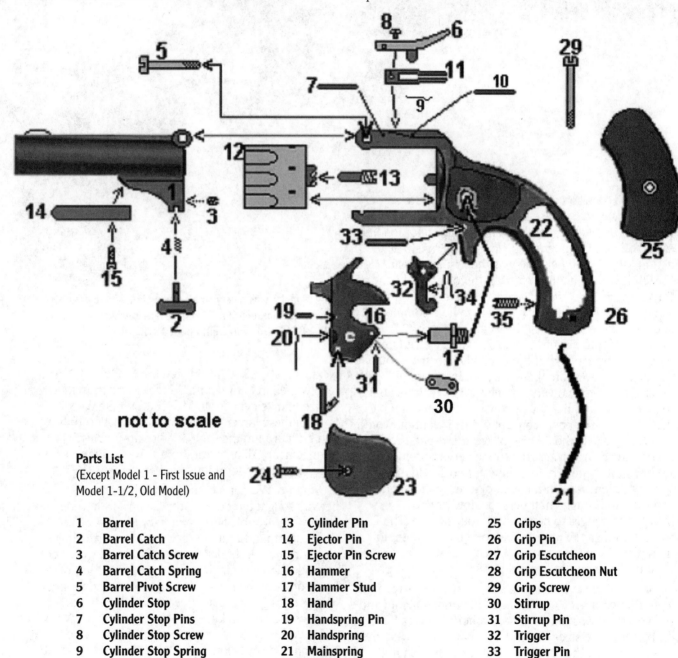

not to scale

Parts List
(Except Model 1 - First Issue and Model 1-1/2, Old Model)

1	Barrel	13	Cylinder Pin	25	Grips
2	Barrel Catch	14	Ejector Pin	26	Grip Pin
3	Barrel Catch Screw	15	Ejector Pin Screw	27	Grip Escutcheon
4	Barrel Catch Spring	16	Hammer	28	Grip Escutcheon Nut
5	Barrel Pivot Screw	17	Hammer Stud	29	Grip Screw
6	Cylinder Stop	18	Hand	30	Stirrup
7	Cylinder Stop Pins	19	Handspring Pin	31	Stirrup Pin
8	Cylinder Stop Screw	20	Handspring	32	Trigger
9	Cylinder Stop Spring	21	Mainspring	33	Trigger Pin
10	Cylinder Stop Spring Pin	22	Frame	34	Trigger Spring
11	Striker	23	Sideplate	35	Strain Screw
12	Cylinder	24	Plate Screw		

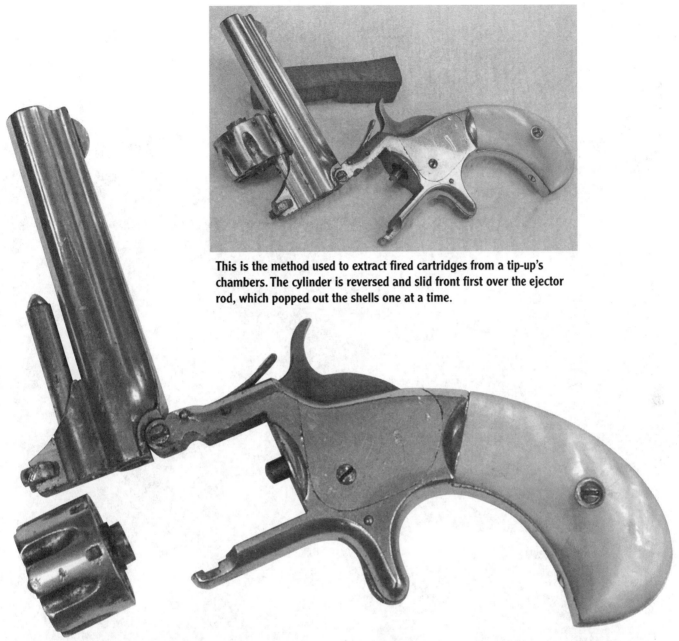

This is the method used to extract fired cartridges from a tip-up's chambers. The cylinder is reversed and slid front first over the ejector rod, which popped out the shells one at a time.

Tipping the barrel up and pulling the hammer just slightly to the rear allows the cylinder to be removed from the front. Built long before the days of what we call product liability, these revolvers had no half-cock or safety positions on their hammers.

DISASSEMBLY INSTRUCTIONS

Disassembly procedures for all Smith & Wesson tip-up Models, except the Model 1 - First Issue and Model 1-1/2, Old Model, are similar.

1 First, make sure the revolver is unloaded. Grasp the revolver around the grip, being careful to keep your fingers away from the trigger (#32). Keep the muzzle pointed in a safe direction until you have the cylinder exposed and can make absolutely certain that the chambers are not loaded.

Initial disassembly and cylinder removal: Lift up on the barrel catch (#2) and tilt the revolver barrel all the way up to open the action and expose the cylinder. Pull the hammer (#16) to the rear slightly, just enough to operate the cylinder stop so the cylinder will spin freely, then withdraw the cylinder straight out through the front of the frame opening. If any cartridges remain in the chambers, remove them now and place them in a location apart from the revolver.

· 173 ·

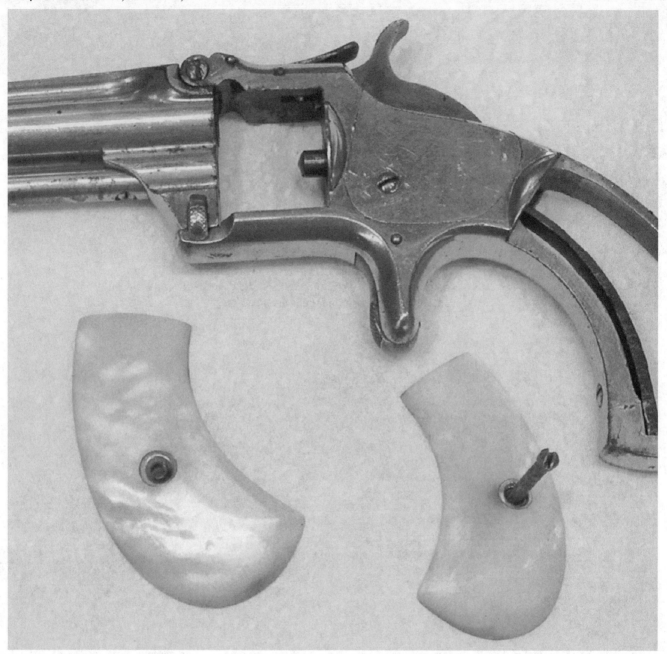

Here the grips have been removed.

2 Barrel removal and disassembly: Unscrew and remove the barrel pivot screw (#5) from the left side of the hinge on the frame (#22). The barrel (#1) may now be lifted out of the hinge in the frame.

On Model 1 - 3rd Issue, Model 1-1/2 and Model 2 the ejector pin screw (#15) may be removed and the ejector pin (#14) may be withdrawn from the barrel. On Model 1 - 2nd Issue revolvers the ejector pin is fixed in place. Unscrew and remove the barrel catch screw (#3) from the rear face of the barrel. The barrel catch (#2) and its spring (#4) may be taken out from the bottom of the barrel. Notice the relationship of the barrel catch and its parts to the barrel for reassembly.

3 Grip and sideplate removal: Remove the grip screw (#29) and lift off the grips (#25). Unscrew and remove the sideplate screw (#24). Turn the frame on its side, holding it by its front end with the sideplate (#23) facing up over a padded surface. Strike the grip frame one or more quick, sharp blows using a plastic or hardwood mallet. This will cause the sideplate (#23) to jump up out of its seat in the frame for removal. Never attempt to pry off the sideplate as you may cause damage to the frame and sideplate.

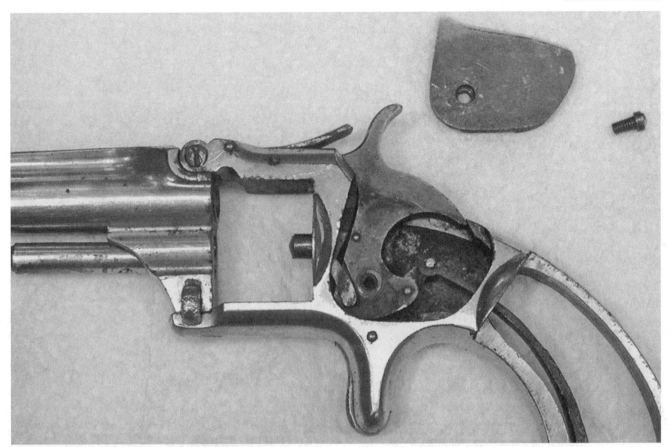

A wooden mallet is used after the sideplate screw is removed to strike the grip frame, shocking the plate up out of its seat in the frame.

Compress the mainspring with spreader-pliers. After you have removed the mainspring and hammer, always check to be sure the hammer stud is still tightly screwed into the frame.

4 Mainspring and action disassembly: Use a pair of spreader-type pliers to compress the top of the mainspring (#21) so that the stirrup (#30) on the rear of the hammer may be rotated forward and out of its seat between the ears at the top of the mainspring. Loosen the strain screw (#35), which is located in the bottom front of the front grip strap on the frame, and withdraw the mainspring (#21), bottom first, from the frame side. Carefully rotate the top of the hand (#18) to the rear using a small screwdriver as a tool, and while holding the hand to the rear, pull the trigger (#32) and hold it to the rear. The hammer (#16) may now be rotated about one-half way back and then carefully pulled upwards, off its hammer stud (#17) and out of the frame through the sideplate opening. Examine the hammer stud to be sure it is screwed in tightly; these have a habit of loosening over time, especially in bronze-frame revolvers.

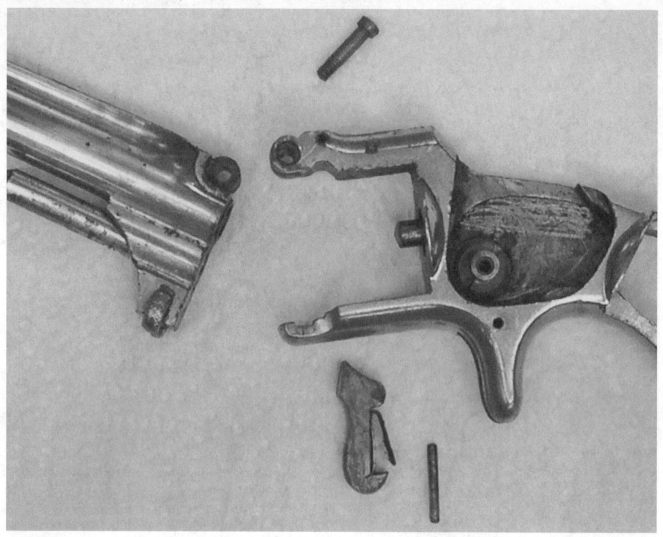

In the final stages of disassembly, the trigger and its spring have been removed and the barrel is lifted out of its hinge in the frame.

5 Trigger removal: Drift out the trigger pin (#33) with a suitable cup-tipped pin punch and hammer. The trigger (#32) and its trigger spring (#34) may be removed through the bottom front of the trigger opening in the frame. Notice that the trigger spring (#34) is a press fit within the trigger.

6 Cylinder stop disassembly: On Model 1 revolvers, drift out the cylinder stop pin (#7) – this is the forwardmost of the pins that pass through the frame's topstrap from side to side). On Model 1-1/2 and Model 2 revolvers, also remove the rearmost pin that passes from side to side in the frame topstrap. Pull the cylinder stop (#6) as an assembly straight up and off the frame.

The cylinder stop spring (#9) is wedged under the cylinder stop spring (#10). The spring may be withdrawn by lifting it up and forward. Except to clean under it, there is usually no need to remove the pin (#10). The cylinder stop itself may be disassembled

by simply unscrewing and removing the cylinder stop screw (#8) from its top; this frees the cylinder stop striker, split spring, (#11) for removal.

7 Hammer disassembly: Rotate the hand (#18) about 180 degrees forward and pull it out of the left side of the hammer (#16). Drift out the handspring pin (#19), which is located at the center front of the hammer and holds in the handspring (#20). The handspring now may be slid out of its recess in the front of the hammer. The stirrup (#30) may be removed by drifting out its pin (#31) at the rear of the hammer. Be sure to support the hammer from below while driving the pin. Take note of the position of the stirrup for reassembly.

REASSEMBLY

Reassemble the revolver in reverse order of above.

Smith & Wesson Top Break
.32 Single Action Model 1-1/2

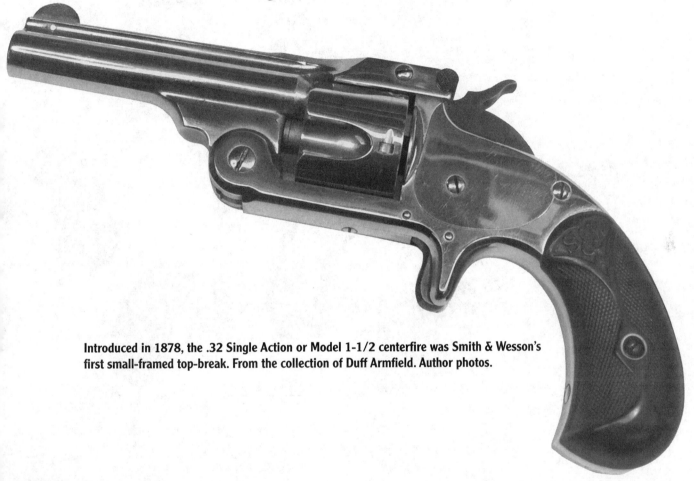

Introduced in 1878, the .32 Single Action or Model 1-1/2 centerfire was Smith & Wesson's first small-framed top-break. From the collection of Duff Armfield. Author photos.

S mith & Wesson's small-frame top-break series, which was also known as the Model 1-1/2 frame, began in 1878 with the introduction of the .32 Single Action Model 1-1/2. The design of this revolver followed the general lines of the earlier and popular tip-up revolver, the New Model 1-1/2 in .32 rimfire. Retaining the earlier rimfire revolver's basic size, appearance and birdshead grip, this new .32 centerfire was built with the hinged-frame, top-break design originally introduced by S&W in 1870. The .32 Single Action was offered only in 32 Smith & Wesson centerfire and had a cylinder with five-shot capacity. This smallest top-break was offered with the same simultaneous, automatic cartridge extraction of all the other revolvers in S&W's famous top-break line-up. The .32 S.A. also sported a new rebounding hammer,

an important engineering feature shared with the much larger .44 New Model 3 single action, also introduced in 1878.

The .32 Single Action was a revolver design that you could say "hit the ground on its feet," meaning that the initial design was so completely functional it required no major improvements. S&W made use of design features taken from previous top-break single action experience and already incorporated into the .38 Single Action - Second Model. Thus, the company made only minor engineering changes throughout the .32 Single Action's entire production from 1878 to 1892. This revolver was the only small-framed, .32-caliber single action top break revolver ever offered by Smith & Wesson, who produced 97,574 of them, usually with 3- or 3-1/2-inch barrels although 6-, 8- and even a few 10-inch barrels were produced.

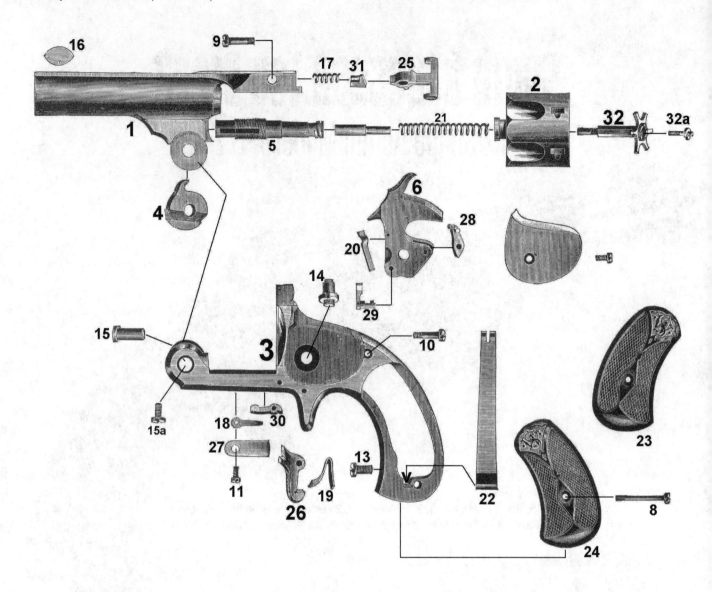

Parts List

1	**Barrel**	12	**Sideplate Screw, Long**	23	**Stock, Left Hand**
2	**Cylinder**	13	**Strain Screw**	24	**Stock, Right Hand**
3	**Frame**	14	**Hammer Stud**	25	**Barrel Catch**
4	**Extractor Cam Assembly**	15	**Joint Pivot And Screw**	26	**Trigger**
5	**Base Pin**	16	**Front Sight**	27	**Stop Plate**
6	**Hammer**	17	**Barrel Catch Cam Spring**	28	**Hammer Stirrup**
7	**Sideplate**	18	**Cylinder Stop Spring**	29	**Hand**
8	**Stock Screw**	19	**Trigger Spring**	30	**Cylinder Stop**
9	**Barrel Catch Screw**	20	**Handspring**	31	**Barrel Catch Cam**
10	**Sideplate Screw, Short**	21	**Extractor Spring**	32	**Extractor**
11	**Stop Plate Screw**	22	**Mainspring**	33	**Extractor Post**

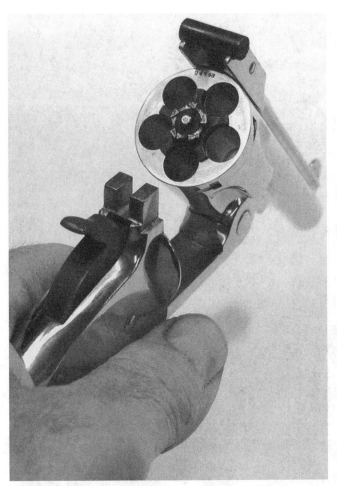

Always make sure the revolver is empty before attempting to handle it for any reason.

Like all later model S&W top-break revolvers, to remove the .32 SA cylinder, the barrel catch is held up and the cylinder is pulled back, while rotating it counterclockwise.

DISASSEMBLY INSTRUCTIONS

1 Grasp the revolver firmly by its grip, being careful not to put your finger on the trigger (#26) and making certain to keep the barrel muzzle pointed in a safe direction. With your other hand, lift up on the barrel catch (#25), and tilt the revolver barrel all the way down to open the action. This exposes the entire rear of the cylinder (#2). Check to be certain the cylinder is unloaded and if cartridges are present, remove them now and place them in a location separate from the gun.

2 To remove the cylinder: With the barrel still in the open position, lift up on the barrel catch and pull the cylinder to the rear while at the same time turning it in a counterclockwise direction. The cylinder will withdraw from the base pin (#5) toward the rear of the gun.

3 To remove the barrel: Unscrew and remove the joint pivot screw (#15a) from the left side of the hinge on the frame (#3) and then use an appropriate-size straight punch to drive the joint pivot (#15) out of the frame toward the right side. Note the witness mark on the joint pivot and its corresponding mark on the frame for reassembly. The barrel (#1) is now loose and may be lifted up and out of its joint with the frame. The extractor cam (#4) is located between the ears of the barrel hinge and it may now be pulled down and out of the barrel. Make note of the extractor cam's position for reassembly. Most extractor cams, especially in early revolvers, have a separate bushing at the center (not shown in the illustration).

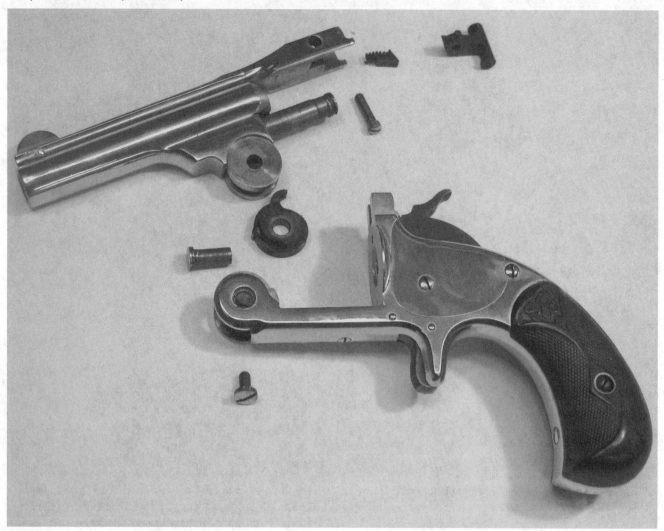

Removing the joint pivot (hinge pin) allows the barrel to be lifted right off the frame. The extractor cam lies just above the frame hinge. This is an early example with a bushing and a pivoting pawl; the parts drawing shows the later type with a sliding pawl.

4 To remove the grips and the sideplate: Remove the stock screw (#8) and lift off the stocks (#23) and (#24). Unscrew and remove the two sideplate screws (#10) and (#12). Turn the frame on its side, holding it by the hinge with the sideplate facing up over a padded surface. Strike the grip frame a sharp blow or two using a plastic or hardwood mallet. This will cause the sideplate (#7) to jump up out of its seat in the frame for removal. Never attempt to pry off the sideplate.

5 To remove the mainspring and hammer: Use a pair of spreader-type pliers to compress the top of the mainspring (#22) so the hammer stirrup (#28) may be rotated forward, and out of its seat between the ears at the top of the mainspring. Loosen the strain screw (#13) located in the bottom front of the front grip strap on the frame and withdraw the mainspring from the frame side. Using a small screwdriver as a lever, carefully rotate the top of the hand (#28) to the rear, and while holding the hand to the rear pull the trigger (#26) and hold it to the rear. The hammer (#6) may be pulled about halfway to the rear and carefully pulled upward, off its hammer stud (#14) and out of the frame.

Note: Some early production revolvers used an eccentric cam instead of a strain screw to tension the mainspring (see photo). This cam is located under the mainspring and passes transversely through the lower grip frame opening.

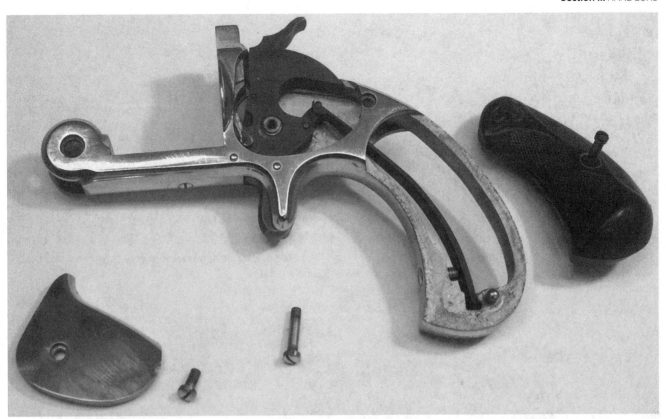

Access to the internals is gained by removing the grips and sideplate.

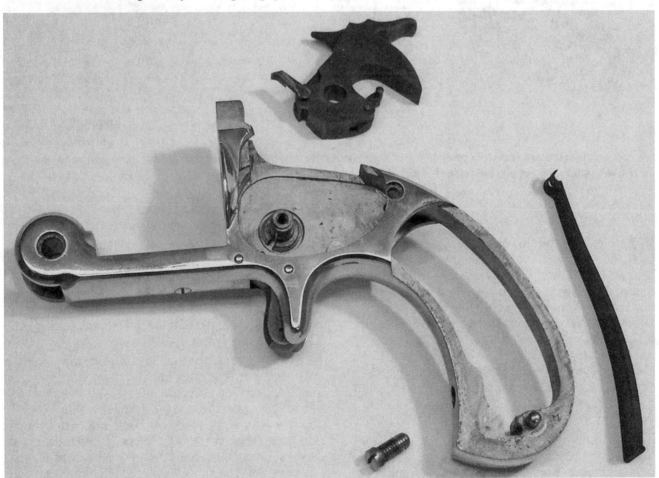

After the mainspring is removed, it's a simple matter to take out the hammer. This revolver uses the later type of strain screw that threads into the front grip strap.

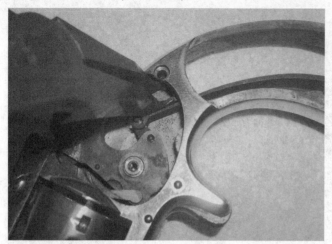

Compressing the top of the mainspring so it can be disengaged from the stirrup.

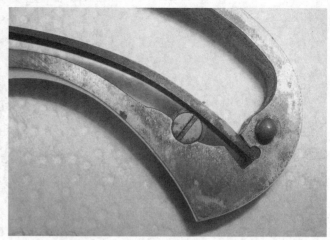

The eccentric strain screw used in very early production .32 Single Actions.

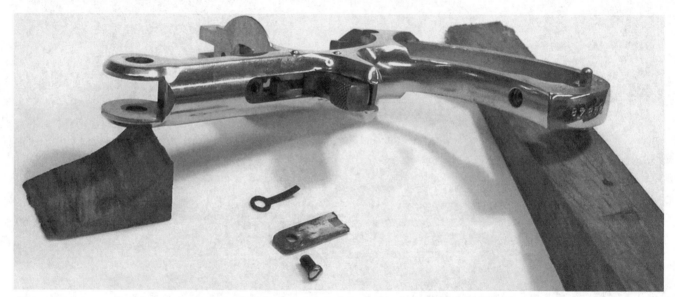

The stop plate screw and stop plate come off the bottom front of the frame. The cylinder stop spring (shown just above the plate) will usually fall out with the plate. This provides access to the trigger and cylinder stop.

6 To remove the stop plate: Unscrew and remove the stop plate screw (#11). (This tiny screw is located on the frame bottom between the trigger and hinge joint.) Hold the frame upside down by the grip, and while holding the trigger to the rear, strike the frame just behind the hinge joint several short, sharp blows with a plastic mallet. This impact will cause the stop plate (#27) to jump up out of its seat with the frame. Never attempt to pry off the stop plate. Once the stop plate has jumped loose, remove it and the cylinder stop spring (#18), making note of their positions for reassembly.

7 To remove the cylinder stop and trigger: Using an appropriate-sized cup-tipped pin punch, drift out the cylinder stop pin. This is the forwardmost of the two pins that pass through the frame from side to side. Next, push the cylinder stop (#30) out toward the bottom, using a small punch through its window in the frame, under the area where the cylinder rotates. Use the same punch and hammer to drift out the trigger pin, which is the rearmost of the two pins that pass through the frame from side to side. The trigger may now be pulled out the bottom of the frame along with its attached trigger spring (#19).

8 To disassemble the cylinder: Insert five fired cartridge cases into the chambers for support. Grasp the extractor post (#33) in the jaws of a drill chuck and rotate the cylinder (#2) in a counterclockwise direction to unscrew the extractor post from the extractor (#32). Notice the witness mark "dot" on one of the rear facing legs of the extractor star; this dot should be aligned with the serial numbers on the cylinder for reassembly. Note: To prevent damaging the extractor spring during reassembly of the cylinder,

· 182 ·

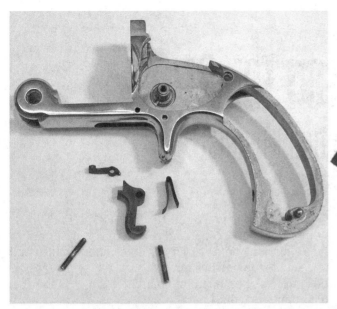

Removing the cylinder stop and trigger pins allows these parts to be dropped out the bottom.

Driving out the handspring pin allows the handspring to be lifted out of the hammer face.

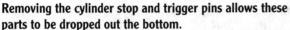

start the post on the extractor only about one-half turn, then grasp the first ¼ inch of the post in a drill chuck and push the cylinder forward, compressing the extractor spring. Tighten the cylinder (clockwise) while the spring is compressed, every so often releasing and then recompressing the spring before continuing. In this manner you will prevent binding the spring coils and ruining the spring.

9 To disassemble the hammer: Rotate the hand (#29) forward about 180 degrees and pull it out of the hammer. Drift out the pin in the center-front of the hammer that holds in the handspring (#20). The handspring can now be slid out of its recess in the hammer. The hammer stirrup (#28) may be removed by drifting out its pin at the rear of the hammer. Be sure you make careful note of the position of the stirrup (#28) for reassembly later. Its position is critical to rebound operation.

10 To disassemble the barrel: Remove the barrel catch screw (#9) from the left side of the barrel topstrap. The barrel catch (#25) may now be withdrawn to the rear. Holding the barrel in a muzzle-up position and tapping the rear of the barrel topstrap directly, straight down on a wooden bench-top, will cause the barrel catch cam (#31) and barrel catch cam spring (#17) to fall out of their recess in the topstrap. Notice their positions for reassembly.

REASSEMBLY

Reassemble the revolver in reverse order of above.

Smith & Wesson Top Break
.32 Double Action Models

Smith & Wesson's top-break .32 Double Action was introduced in 1880. From the start it proved to be a very popular pocket revolver and it was kept in production until 1919 with a total of 327,641 revolvers being manufactured. Like the .32 Single Action before it, the double action was built on the same Model 1-1/2 frame and was offered in 32 Smith & Wesson caliber with a five-shot cylinder with simultaneous automatic cartridge extraction. The .32 double action went through five separate engineering changes during the period of manufacture, forming five unique models as S&W perfected this well-liked design:

1st Model: manufactured 1880, serial numbers 1 to 30. Features straight-sided sideplate; rocker-type cylinder stop; short cylinder flutes with double stop notches and free cuts on cylinder; reverse curved trigger guard bow; front sight pinned into barrel. 3-inch barrel only.

2nd Model: manufactured 1880 to 1882, serial numbers 31 to 22,172. Features irregular-shaped sideplate; rocker-type cylinder stop; short cylinder flutes with double stop notches and free cuts on cylinder; reverse curved trigger guard bow; front sight pinned into barrel. Three-inch barrel only.

3rd Model: manufactured 1882 to 1883, serial numbers 22,173 to 43,405. Features pivoting spring-type cylinder stop; cylinder has conventional flutes and one set of stop notches; reverse curved trigger guard bow; front sight pinned into barrel. 3-, 3-1/2-, and 6-inch barrel lengths.

4th Model: manufactured 1883-1909, serial numbers 43,406 to 282,999 (approximate). Features pivoting spring-type cylinder stop; cylinder has conventional flutes and only one set of stop notches, rounded trigger guard bow, front sight pinned into barrel. 3-, 3-1/2-, 6-, 8- and 10-inch barrel lengths.

5th Model: manufactured 1909 to 1919, serial numbers 283,000 (approximate) to 327,641. Features pivoting spring type cylinder stop; cylinder has conventional flutes and only one set of stop notches; rounded trigger guard bow; front sight forged as one piece with barrel. S&W name and address only on barrel rib without patent markings. 3-, 3-1/2- and 6-inch barrel lengths.

The illustration that follows is a representative .32 Double Action 4th Model. .32 D.A. 3rd and 5th models are nearly identical to the illustration. .32 D.A. 1st and 2nd models are different externally as noted above and internally as noted in the disassembly instructions later.

Note: Readers can refer to the sections listed under Smith & Wesson .38 Double Action Models for photographic guidance; these photos will work for .32 or .38 caliber double action models.

DISASSEMBLY INSTRUCTIONS

1 Grasp the revolver firmly by its grip, being careful not to put your finger on the trigger (#44) and making certain to keep the barrel muzzle pointed in a safe direction. Pull the hammer back slightly until you hear one click. This should be the half-cock position. With your other hand, lift up on the barrel catch (#42) and tilt the revolver barrel all the way down to open the action. This exposes the entire rear of the cylinder (#37). Check to be certain the cylinder is unloaded and if cartridges are present, remove them now and place them in a separate location from the gun.

2 To remove the cylinder: Hold the barrel catch (#42) in the up position and pull the cylinder toward the rear while at the same time turning it in a counterclockwise direction. The cylinder will withdraw off the base pin (#40), toward the rear.

3 To remove the barrel (#33): Unscrew and remove the joint pivot screw (#52a) from the left side of the hinge on the frame (#34) and use an appropriate-size straight punch to drive the joint pivot (#52) out of the frame toward the right side. Take note of the witness mark on the joint pivot and of its corresponding mark on the frame for correct reassembly. The barrel is now loose and may be lifted up out of its joint with the frame. The extractor cam (#41) is located between the ears of the barrel hinge and can now be pulled down and out of the barrel. Make note of the extractor cam's position for reassembly.

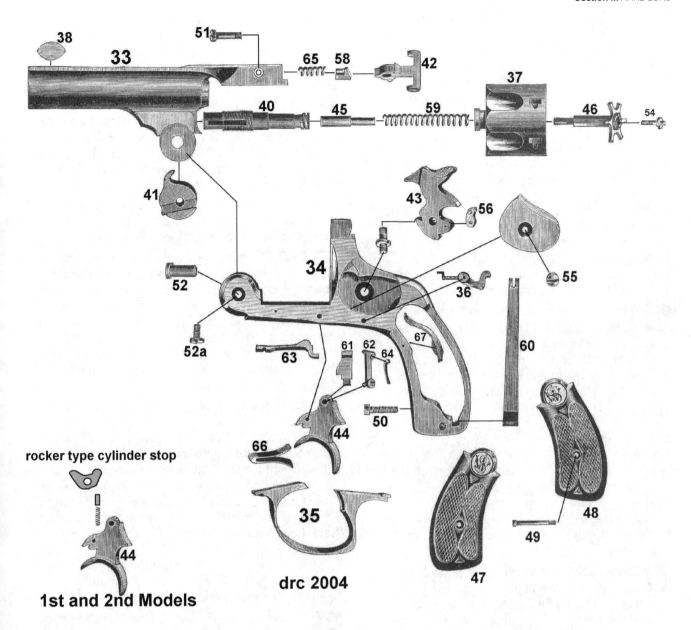

rocker type cylinder stop

1st and 2nd Models

drc 2004

Parts List

33	Barrel	48	Grip	63	Cylinder Stop		
34	Frame	49	Grip Screw		3rd - 5th Model		
35	Triggerguard	50	Strain Screw	64	Hand spring		
36	Rear Sear	51	Barrel Catch Screw	65	Barrel Catch Cam Spring		
37	Cylinder	52	Joint Pivot	66	Trigger Spring		
38	Front Sight	52A	Joint Pivot Screw	67	Rear Sear Spring		
39	Sideplate	53	Hammer Stud	67A	Trigger or Sear Pin		
40	Base Pin	54	Extractor Stud	67B	Stop Plunger,		
41	Extractor Cam	55	Hammer Stud Nut		1st & 2nd Model		
42	Barrel Catch	56	Stirrup	67C	Stop Spring,		
43	Hammer	58	Barrel Catch Cam		1st & 2nd Model		
44	Trigger	59	Extractor Spring	67D	Cylinder Stop, 1st & 2nd		
45	Extractor Rod	60	Mainspring	67E	Stop Pin, 1st & 2nd Model		
46	Extractor	61	Front Sear	67F	Stirrup Pin		
47	Grip	62	Hand	67G	Sear Spring Pin		

4 To remove the grips and sideplate: Unscrew and remove the stock screw (#49) and lift off the stocks (#47) and (48). Unscrew and remove the hammer stud nut (#55) from the center of the sideplate (#39) (this part acts as the sideplate screw). Turn the frame on its side, holding it by the hinge with the sideplate facing up over a padded surface. Strike the grip frame a sharp blow or two using a plastic or hardwood mallet. This will cause the sideplate to jump up out of its seat in the frame for removal. Never attempt to pry off the sideplate. Use a pair of spreader pliers to compress the top of the mainspring (#60) so the hammer stirrup (#56) may be rotated forward and out of its seat between the ears at the top of the mainspring. Loosen the strain screw (#50) to relieve tension on the mainspring (located in the bottom front of the front grip strap on the frame) and withdraw the mainspring through the frame side.

5 To remove the triggerguard and trigger spring: The triggerguard (#35) is itself a spring; it has no fastening screws and is held in place by machined tabs at its front and rear tops which mate with machined mortise cuts in the frame. Hold the frame upside down by the grip, and tap the rear-lower face of the triggerguard with a plastic mallet, causing the rear of the triggerguard to jump out of its seat in the frame. Next, pull the trigger (#44) all the way to the rear. The triggerguard may now be moved rearward slightly to disengage its front tab from the frame, continue by tilting the front of the triggerguard down and push forward to remove. The trigger spring (#66) is now loose and may be lifted out of the frame forward of the trigger. Be sure to make note of its position for reassembly.

6 To disassemble the action, 3rd through 5th models: Use a small pin punch to drift out the retaining pin (#67G) for the rear sear spring (#67) and remove the spring. Pull the trigger to the rear and hold it all the way back. The hammer (#43) may now be carefully worked up off its hammer stud (#53) and out of the frame. As you release the trigger, make note of the position of the rear sear (#36). Next, use a cup-tipped pin punch to drift out the rear sear pin (this is the rearmost of the two large pins [#67A] that pass through the frame) and remove the rear sear, noting its position for reassembly. Again, use the cup-tipped punch and hammer to drift out the trigger pin (this is the forward most of the two large pins). Push the trigger assembly up and to the rear slightly, enough so that the entire face of the hand (#62) is exposed in the sideplate opening. Grasp the hand along with its spring (#64) with a small pair of needlenosed pliers and pull the assembly straight up and out of the frame. The trigger (#44) may be removed through the bottom of the frame while the front sear (#61) may be removed through the sideplate opening.

For 1st and 2nd Models, make careful note of the relationship of the trigger assembly – trigger (#44), front sear (#61), and hand (#62) – for reassembly later (see below).

7 Trigger and cylinder stop, 1st and 2nd Models: The cylinder stop (#67D) is mounted in the top center of the trigger. Under the cylinder stop is a small plunger and coil spring that power the stop. The spring and plunger will be under tension during trigger removal, so use care when removing the trigger that these two tiny parts are not lost.

For 3rd through 5th Models, the cylinder stop (#63) is held into the frame by a cross pin (#67E) and may be removed by carefully drifting out this pin.

8 To disassemble the cylinder: Insert five fired cartridge cases into the chambers for support. Grasp the extractor rod (#45) by its head in the jaws of a drill chuck and rotate the cylinder in a counterclockwise direction to unscrew the extractor rod from the extractor (#46). Note the witness mark dot on one of the rear facing legs of the extractor star. This mark should be aligned with the serial numbers on the cylinder for reassembly.

Note: To prevent damage to the extractor spring during reassembly, grasp the front 1/4 inch of the extractor rod by its head in the jaws of a drill chuck. Assemble the spring onto the extractor rod. Place the cylinder with the extractor over the rear end of the rod and push the cylinder forward, thus compressing the extractor spring as much as possible, while turning the cylinder in a clockwise direction until the threads have started by about one-half turn. Stop turning about every one half turn and allow the extractor to return by spring tension, and then push the cylinder in again to re-compress the spring. Continue tightening in one-half-turn increments until the rod is tight.

9 To disassemble the barrel: Unscrew and remove the barrel catch screw (#51) from the left side of the barrel topstrap. The barrel catch (#42) may now be withdrawn to the rear. By holding the barrel (#33) in a muzzle-up position and tapping the rear of the barrel topstrap on a soft wooden bench-top, the barrel catch cam (#58) and barrel catch cam spring (#65) will fall out of their recess in the topstrap. Note their positions for reassembly.

REASSEMBLY

Reassemble the action in reverse of the order given above.

Smith & Wesson .32
New Departure / Safety Hammerless

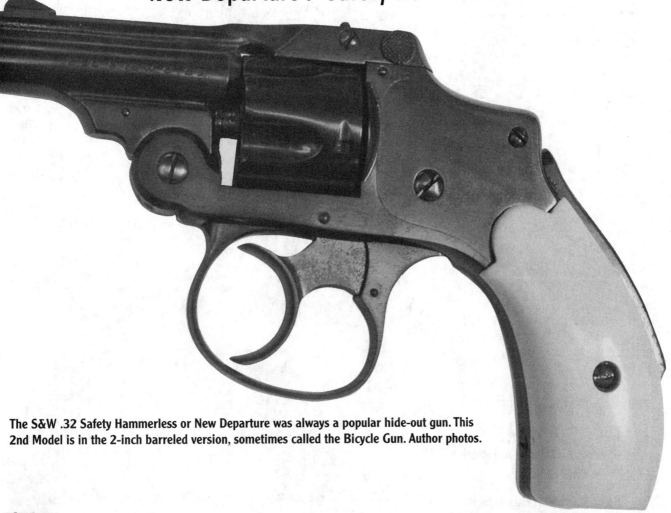

The S&W .32 Safety Hammerless or New Departure was always a popular hide-out gun. This 2nd Model is in the 2-inch barreled version, sometimes called the Bicycle Gun. Author photos.

The Smith & Wesson .32 Safety Hammerless was first introduced in 1888. Also called the "New Departure," this hammerless model actually had a hammer, but it was concealed within the frame. Chambered for the 32 S&W cartridge, the novel 5-shot revolver was double action-only and equipped with a rebounding hammer, frame-mounted rebounding firing pin and a manual grip safety that had to be squeezed before the gun could be fired.

In its 49 years of manufacture, S&W's .32 New Departure did undergo some engineering changes, mostly in the method of unlatching the barrel. Internally, the design remained the same from 1888 to 1937 with a total production of 242,981 revolvers. The following variations were produced:

1st Model: manufactured 1888 to 1902, serial numbers 1 to 91,417. Front sight pinned into barrel. 2- (scarce), 3- and 3-1/2-inch barrel. Barrel catch pushes down to open barrel.

2nd Model: manufactured 1902 to 1909, serial numbers 91,418 to around 170,000. Front sight pinned into barrel. 2- (scarce), 3-, 3-1/2- and 6-inch (scarce) barrel. T-shaped barrel catch lifts up to open barrel.

3rd Model: manufactured 1909 to 1937, serial numbers around 170,000 to 242,981. Front sight forged integral with barrel rib. 2- (scarce), 3-, and 3-1/2-inch barrel lengths. T-shaped barrel catch lifts up to open barrel.

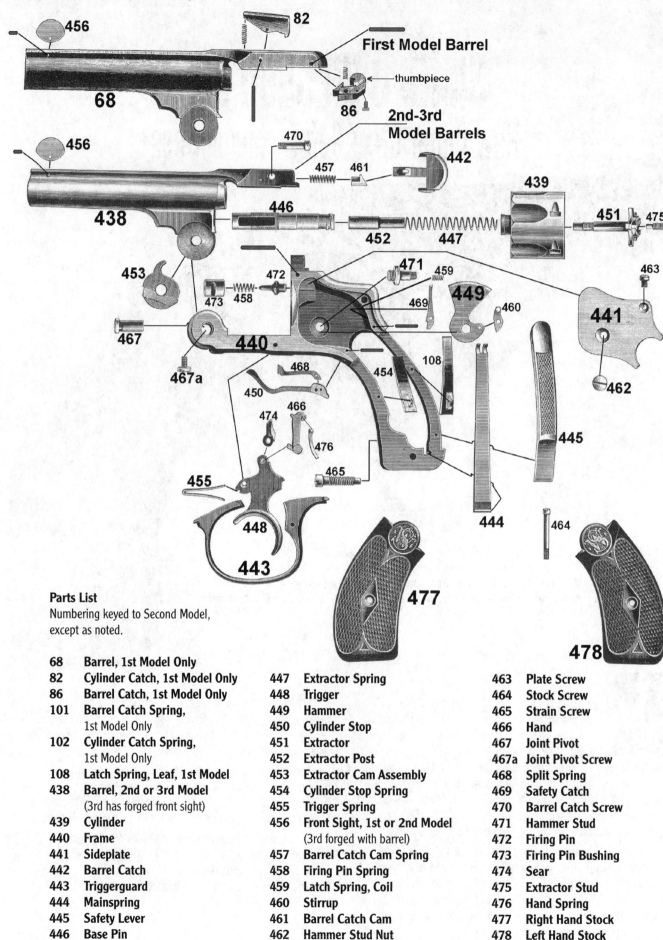

First Model Barrel

thumbpiece

2nd-3rd
Model Barrels

Parts List
Numbering keyed to Second Model,
except as noted.

68	**Barrel, 1st Model Only**	447	**Extractor Spring**	463	**Plate Screw**
82	**Cylinder Catch, 1st Model Only**	448	**Trigger**	464	**Stock Screw**
86	**Barrel Catch, 1st Model Only**	449	**Hammer**	465	**Strain Screw**
101	**Barrel Catch Spring,** 1st Model Only	450	**Cylinder Stop**	466	**Hand**
102	**Cylinder Catch Spring,** 1st Model Only	451	**Extractor**	467	**Joint Pivot**
		452	**Extractor Post**	467a	**Joint Pivot Screw**
108	**Latch Spring, Leaf, 1st Model**	453	**Extractor Cam Assembly**	468	**Split Spring**
438	**Barrel, 2nd or 3rd Model** (3rd has forged front sight)	454	**Cylinder Stop Spring**	469	**Safety Catch**
		455	**Trigger Spring**	470	**Barrel Catch Screw**
439	**Cylinder**	456	**Front Sight, 1st or 2nd Model** (3rd forged with barrel)	471	**Hammer Stud**
440	**Frame**			472	**Firing Pin**
441	**Sideplate**	457	**Barrel Catch Cam Spring**	473	**Firing Pin Bushing**
442	**Barrel Catch**	458	**Firing Pin Spring**	474	**Sear**
443	**Triggerguard**	459	**Latch Spring, Coil**	475	**Extractor Stud**
444	**Mainspring**	460	**Stirrup**	476	**Hand Spring**
445	**Safety Lever**	461	**Barrel Catch Cam**	477	**Right Hand Stock**
446	**Base Pin**	462	**Hammer Stud Nut**	478	**Left Hand Stock**

In order to remove the cylinder, the barrel catch has to be held up while the cylinder is rotated in a counterclockwise direction.

DISASSEMBLY INSTRUCTIONS

1 Check first to be certain the revolver is unloaded. Grasp the revolver around the grip with your right hand, being cautious to keep your finger off the trigger. Push down (1st Model) or lift up (2nd or 3rd models) on the barrel catch (#86) or (#442) respectively. This will unlock the barrel from the frame. Next, tilt the revolver barrel all the way down to open the action. Look at the rear of the cylinder to be certain the cylinder is unloaded.

2 To remove the cylinder (#439): Push down (1st Model) on the front of the cylinder hook (#82) or hold the barrel catch (#442) in the up position (2nd or 3rd models) and pull the cylinder to the rear while turning it in a counterclockwise direction. The cylinder will withdraw from the base pin (#446) toward the rear.

After the grips have been removed, the next step is to remove the sideplate, exposing the action.

3 To remove the barrel: Remove the joint pivot screw (#467a) from the left side of the hinge on the frame (#440) and use an appropriate straight pin punch to drive the joint pivot (#467) out of the frame toward the right side. Make note of the witness mark on the joint pivot and its corresponding mark on the frame for reassembly. The barrel (#68) (1st model) or (#438) (later models) is now loose and may be lifted up out of its joint with the frame. The extractor cam (#453) is located between the "ears" of the barrel hinge and may be pulled down and out of the barrel. Make note of its position for reassembly.

4 To remove the grips and sideplate: Unscrew and remove the stock screw (#464) and the stocks (#477) and (#478). Remove the hammer stud nut (#462) from the center of the sideplate (#441) and the sideplate screw (#463) from the rear of the sideplate. Turn the frame on its side. Holding it by the hinge, sideplate facing up, over a padded surface. Strike the grip frame a sharp blow or two using a plastic mallet. The blow will cause the sideplate (#441) to jump up out of its seat in the frame for removal. Never attempt to pry off the sideplate.

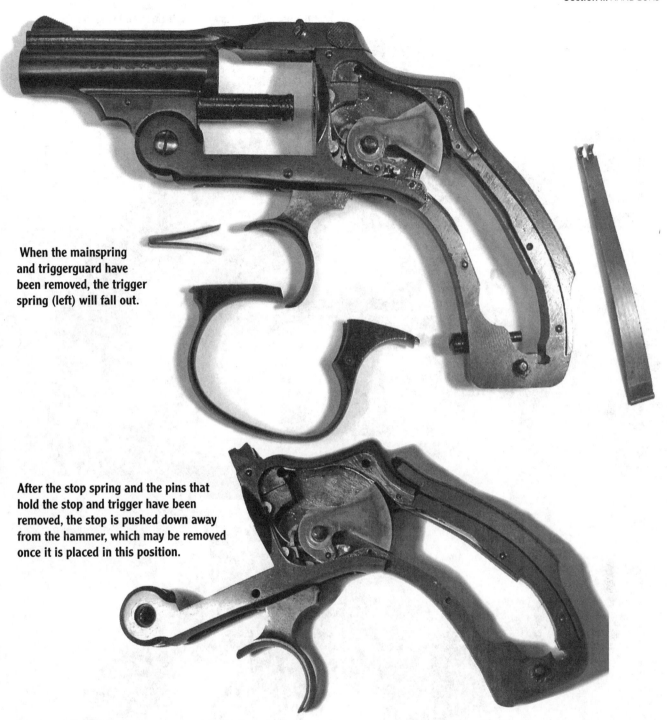

When the mainspring and triggerguard have been removed, the trigger spring (left) will fall out.

After the stop spring and the pins that hold the stop and trigger have been removed, the stop is pushed down away from the hammer, which may be removed once it is placed in this position.

5 To disassemble the action: Use a pair of spreader pliers to compress the top of the mainspring (#444) so the hammer stirrup (#460) may be rotated forward and out of its seat between the "ears" at the top of the mainspring. Loosen the strain screw (#465) located in the bottom front of the front grip strap on the frame and withdraw the mainspring (#444) from the grip frame side opening. Using a straight pin punch, drift out the pin in the front strap of the grip frame that holds the cylinder stop spring (#454) in place and remove the cylinder stop spring by withdrawing it to the rear.

Using a wooden hammer handle or a small plastic mallet, strike the rear of the triggerguard (#443) bow a mild blow on the bow's backside. This will cause the rear of the triggerguard (which is a compressed spring itself) to unhook itself from the frame and to drop down slightly. Depress the safety lever (#440) and pull the trigger (#448) all the way to the rear. The triggerguard (#443) may now be removed by first pulling it toward the rear to unhook its front lip from the frame and then by pivoting it down at the front and pushing forward on the bow. The V-shaped trigger spring (#455) may now be removed from the triggerguard opening in the bottom of the frame. Note the position of the trigger spring for reassembly.

Once the hammer is out, the trigger and stop can be removed. Here the action components are shown out of the revolver.

Before removing the cylinder stop pin to access the hammer, remove the stop spring.

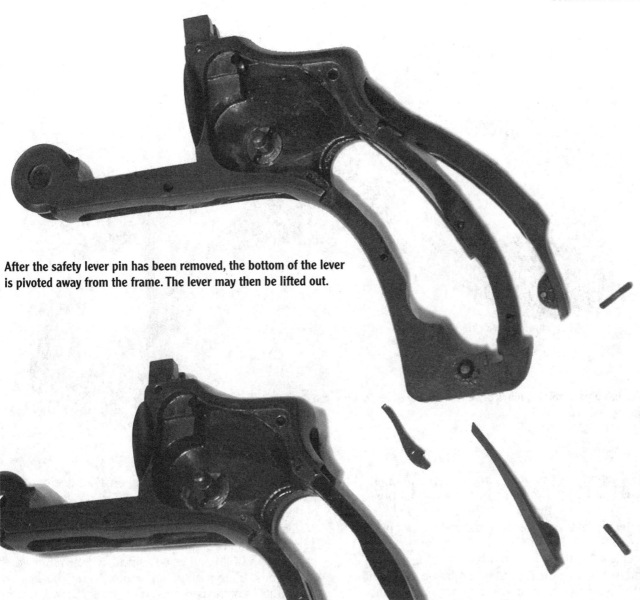

After the safety lever pin has been removed, the bottom of the lever is pivoted away from the frame. The lever may then be lifted out.

With the safety lever removed, the safety spring and safety can be removed from the frame.

6 Disassembling the action further: Push both the trigger (#448) and the hammer (#449) to their forward positions. Drift out the cylinder stop pin from the frame and push the entire cylinder stop (#450) down slightly so the stop moves out of the way of the hammer. Depress the safety lever (#445) again and pull the trigger (#448), causing the hammer (#449) to rotate to the rear. With the stirrup (#460) in the rearmost position, the hammer is gently worked up off the hammer stud (#471) and out of the frame. The trigger pin (this is the large pin that passes through the frame from side to side) is now drifted out of the frame. The assembly consisting of the trigger (#449), hand (#466) and sear (#474) is moved up and to the rear so that the entire hand (#466) is visible through the sideplate opening in the frame. Note the position of these three parts for reassembly.

The hand and its spring (#476) may be grasped with a pair of needlenosed pliers and pulled upward out of its seat with the trigger and sear. The trigger (#448) can be withdrawn from the bottom of the frame and the cylinder stop assembly (#450) and the sear (#474) can be taken out through the sideplate opening of the frame.

7 The safety lever (#445) may be removed by first drifting out its retaining pin from the lower-rear of the rear grip strap. Pivot the bottom of the safety lever to the rear and pull down. The safety catch or latch (#469) may be powered by a coil spring (1st models and later 3rd models) or a leaf spring (#108). The leaf spring will be located on the inside of the rear grip strap and is held by a cross pin. The coil type spring is located in the safety catch recess in the frame, directly behind the top portion of the safety catch.

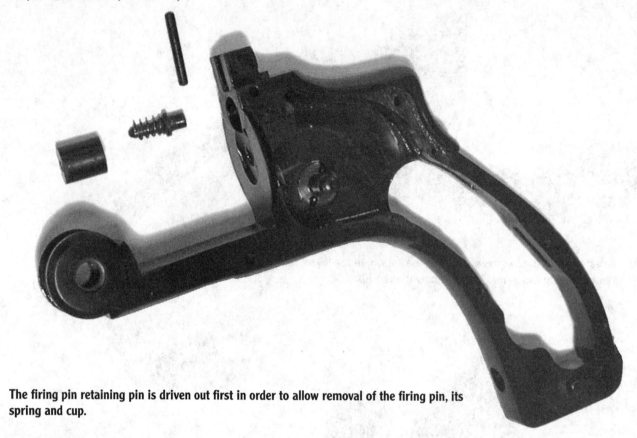

The firing pin retaining pin is driven out first in order to allow removal of the firing pin, its spring and cup.

8 Removing the firing pin: The firing pin (#472) is retained in the frame by the firing pin bushing (#473), which is in turn held by a cross pin located at the top of the frame. To remove the firing pin, the cross pin is first drifted out of the frame. A small pin punch is then used to drive the firing pin (#472) and its bushing (#473) out of the frame from rear to front. A small coil spring at the front of the firing pin shoulder acts to retract the firing pin after firing. Note the positions of these parts for reassembly. These revolvers are equipped with rebounding hammers, the action of which is controlled by mainspring tension on the stirrup.

9 To disassemble the cylinder: Insert five fired cartridge cases into the chambers for support. Grasp the extractor rod (#452) in the jaws of a drill chuck and rotate the cylinder (#439) in a counterclockwise direction to unscrew the extractor rod (#452) from the extractor (#451). Note the witness mark "dot" on one of the rear facing legs of the extractor star, which should be aligned with the serial numbers on the cylinder for reassembly. To prevent damage to the extractor spring (#447) during reassembly, start the extractor rod into the threads on the extractor by only one turn. Now, hold the front 1/4 inch of the extractor rod tightly in a padded vise and push the cylinder forward, compressing the extractor spring as you tighten the extractor rod by turning the cylinder in a clockwise direction.

10 To disassemble the barrel on 1st models: Remove the tiny screw from the bottom rear of the thumb piece (#86). The thumb piece can be removed by lifting it straight up. Drift out the rearmost of the two pins in the barrel's top strap. The barrel catch (#86) and its coil spring can be removed through the bottom of the top strap. Drifting out the forwardmost of the two pins in the barrel's top strap will free the cylinder hook (#82) and its coil spring for removal through the top.

10a To disassemble the barrel on 2nd and 3rd models: Remove the barrel catch screw (#470) from the left side of the barrel topstrap. The barrel catch (#442) may be withdrawn to the rear. Hold the barrel (#438) in a muzzle-up position and tap the rear of the barrel topstrap on a wooden benchtop. The barrel catch cam (#461) and barrel catch cam spring (#457) will fall out of their recess in the topstrap. Note their positions for reassembly.

REASSEMBLY

Reassemble the revolver in exact reverse order of above.

Smith & Wesson Top Break
.38 Single Action, Model No. 2, First Model;
(Model 2 - First Model; "Baby Russian")

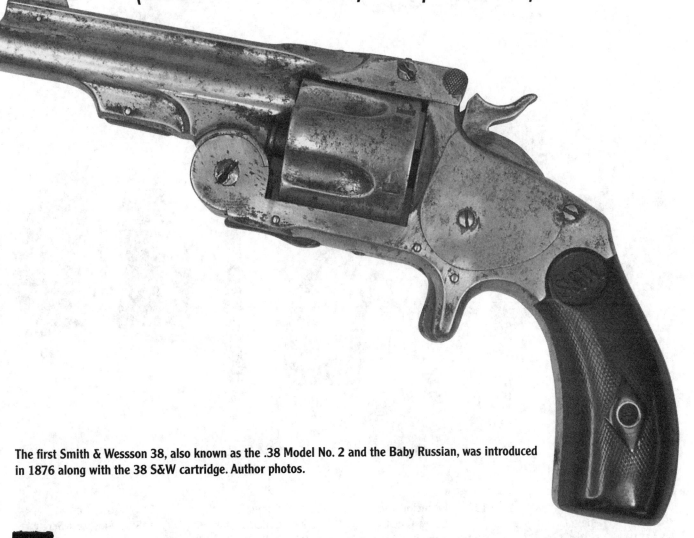

The first Smith & Wesson 38, also known as the .38 Model No. 2 and the Baby Russian, was introduced in 1876 along with the 38 S&W cartridge. Author photos.

Introduced in 1876, the .38 Single Action First Model is a spur trigger, single action only revolver with a round butt grip shape. The revolver uses a "T" shaped barrel catch that is lifted-up to open the revolver, allowing the barrel to tilt downward. On opening, this revolver features simultaneous, automatic ejection of the spent cases.

This was Smith & Wesson's first medium framed, top-break revolver and was quickly nick-named "Baby Russian" because of the similarities between it and its larger .44-caliber cousin made in the same time period.

The 38 Smith & Wesson cartridge was introduced along with this revolver. Like the large, Model No. 3, .44 New Model Russian, the .38 Single Action First Model used a separate cylinder catch mounted in the barrel top strap, as well as a rack and gear extraction system with a square extractor shank.

Manufactured 1876 to 1877; serial numbers 1 to 25,548; chambered in 38 S&W; five-shot cylinder; spur trigger sheathed in the frame; long extractor housing under barrel; geared extraction mechanism with squared extractor shank.

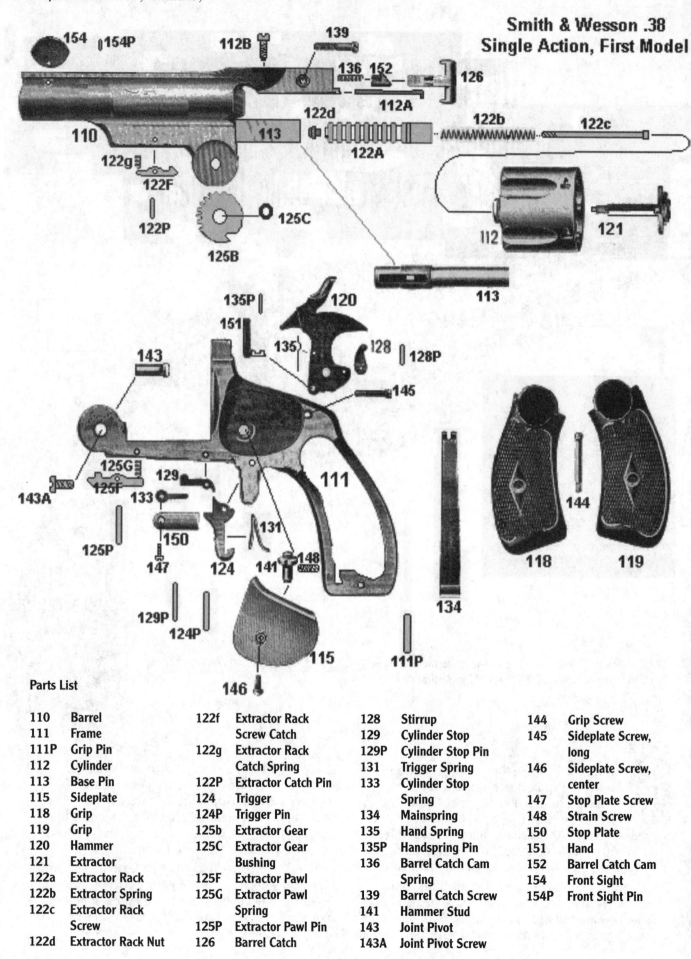

**Smith & Wesson .38
Single Action, First Model**

Parts List

110	Barrel	122f	Extractor Rack Screw Catch	128	Stirrup	144	Grip Screw
111	Frame			129	Cylinder Stop	145	Sideplate Screw, long
111P	Grip Pin	122g	Extractor Rack Catch Spring	129P	Cylinder Stop Pin		
112	Cylinder			131	Trigger Spring	146	Sideplate Screw, center
113	Base Pin	122P	Extractor Catch Pin	133	Cylinder Stop Spring		
115	Sideplate	124	Trigger			147	Stop Plate Screw
118	Grip	124P	Trigger Pin	134	Mainspring	148	Strain Screw
119	Grip	125b	Extractor Gear	135	Hand Spring	150	Stop Plate
120	Hammer	125C	Extractor Gear Bushing	135P	Handspring Pin	151	Hand
121	Extractor			136	Barrel Catch Cam Spring	152	Barrel Catch Cam
122a	Extractor Rack	125F	Extractor Pawl			154	Front Sight
122b	Extractor Spring	125G	Extractor Pawl Spring	139	Barrel Catch Screw	154P	Front Sight Pin
122c	Extractor Rack Screw			141	Hammer Stud		
		125P	Extractor Pawl Pin	143	Joint Pivot		
122d	Extractor Rack Nut	126	Barrel Catch	143A	Joint Pivot Screw		

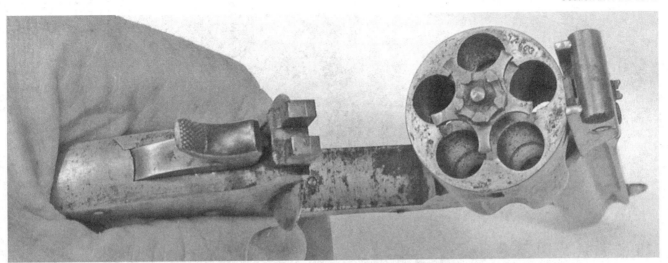

Always check to be certain the cylinder chambers are unloaded. They should look like this.

With the cylinder assembly out, you can clearly see the gear teeth on the extractor rack. The small flat plate just over the barrel is the cylinder catch.

DISASSEMBLY INSTRUCTIONS

1 Always begin by checking to be certain the cylinder is unloaded. Grasp the revolver around the grips, being careful to keep your fingers away from the trigger (#124). Use caution and be sure the barrel muzzle is pointed in a safe direction. Pull the hammer back slightly until one click is heard to place it in the loading position. Lift up on the barrel catch (#126) and tilt the revolver barrel all the way down to open the action. Examine the cylinder to be sure no cartridges are present and if there are, lift them out with your fingers and place them in a separate location.

2 To remove the cylinder (#112): With the barrel opened all the way, loosen the cylinder catch screw (#112B) located in the barrel top strap. Depress the front of the extractor rack screw catch (#122F) and pull the cylinder (#112) to the rear. The cylinder will withdraw from the base pin (#113) toward the rear. Note: The cylinder catch (#112A) will come out along with the cylinder. Note the location of this part so that it may be reinstalled properly.

Once the joint pivot is removed from the hinge, the barrel can be lifted out of the frame. Notice the extractor gear that fits up into the barrel hinge.

This is the correct position for reinstalling the extractor gear into the barrel hinge after the cylinder assembly has been installed on the barrel.

3 To remove the barrel: Unscrew and remove the joint pivot screw (#143a) from the left side of the hinge on the frame (#111). Use an appropriate-size straight punch to drive the joint pivot (#143) out of the frame toward the right side. Make note of the witness mark on the joint pivot and its corresponding mark on the frame for reassembly. The barrel (#110) is now loose and can be lifted up out of its joint with the frame. The extractor gear (#125B) is located between the ears of the barrel hinge and may be pulled down and out of the barrel. Make note of its position for reassembly.

4 To remove the grips and sideplate: Unscrew and remove the stock screw (#144) and lift off the stocks (#118 and #119). Unscrew and remove the two sideplate screws (#145) and (#146). (Note: Early guns below serial #2616 use only one sideplate screw.) Holding the gun by the hinge, turn the frame on its side, sideplate facing up, over a padded surface. Strike the grip frame a sharp blow or two using a plastic or hardwood mallet. This will cause the sideplate (#115) to jump up out of its seat in the frame for removal. Never attempt to pry off the sideplate.

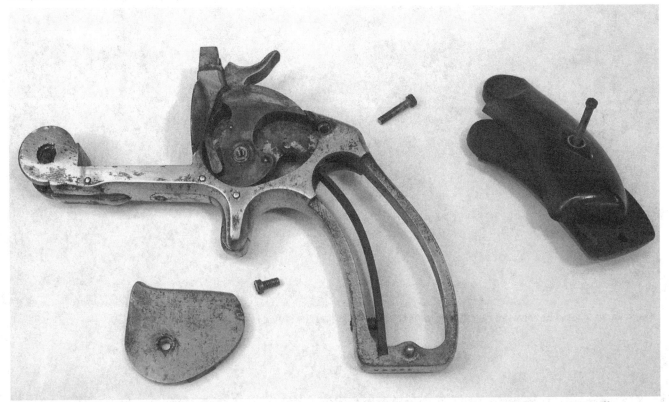

Here the grips and sideplate have been removed. Always use inertial shock to remove a sideplate. Trying to pry one off can badly damage the frame and sideplate.

The mainspring is compressed slightly using a spreader-type pliers, and then its ears are disengaged from the hammer stirrup.

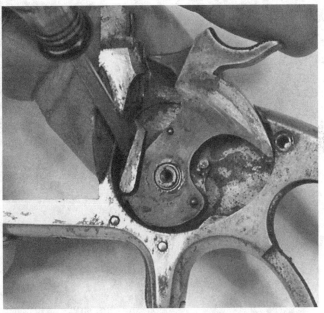

The hammer is in the correct position to be removed, with the hand held back by a small screwdriver.

5 To remove the mainspring and hammer: Use a pair of spreader-type pliers to compress the top of the mainspring (#134) so the hammer stirrup (#128) may be rotated forward and out of its seat between the ears at the top of the mainspring. Loosen the strain screw (#148); this is located in the bottom front of the front grip strap on the frame. Withdraw the mainspring (#134) from the frame side. Carefully rotate the top of the hand (#151) to the rear, using a small screwdriver as a lever. While holding the hand to the rear, pull the trigger (#124) and hold it to the rear. The hammer (#120) may now be rotated about halfway back and carefully pulled upward off its hammer stud (#141) and out of the frame.

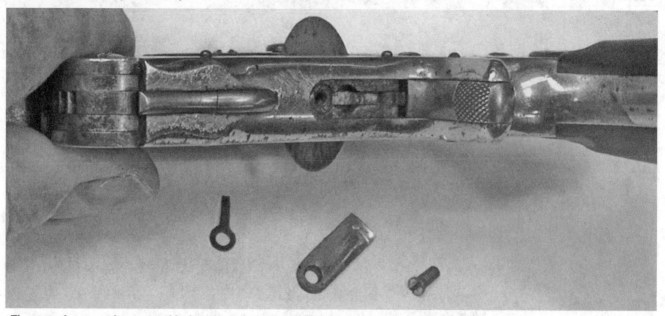

The stop plate must be removed before the cylinder stop spring and the stop can be taken out.

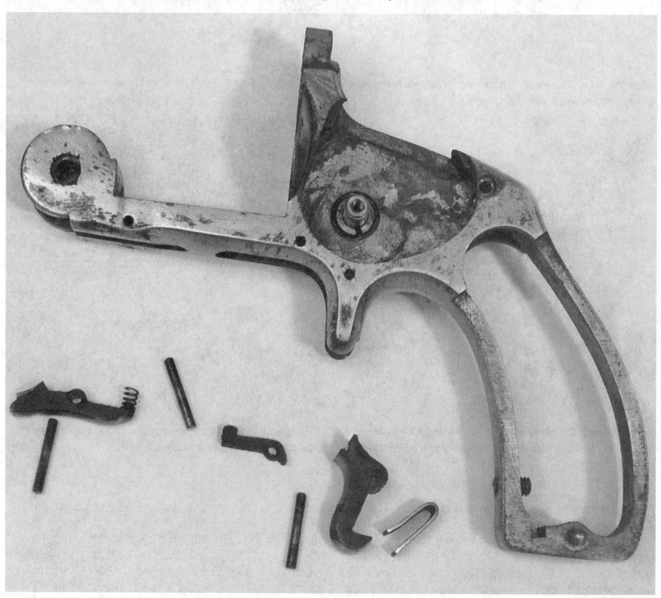

The remainder of the action parts are removed from the bottom after the three pins in the frame side have been removed.

Here is the cylinder apart. The extractor rack screw, nut and spring are contained within the extractor rack. The screw and nut are threaded together but the factory riveted them, so disassembly is not suggested.

The witness dot on the extractor leg should line up with the serial number on the rear face of the cylinder for reassembly.

Removing the extractor rack from the extractor using fired cartridge cases and a small open-end wrench.

6 To remove the stop plate and spring: Unscrew and remove the stop plate screw (#147) (located on the frame bottom, between the trigger and the hinge joint). Hold the frame upside-down by the grip. While holding the trigger (#124) to the rear, strike the frame several short, sharp blows just behind the hinge joint with a plastic or hardwood mallet. This will case the stop plate (#150) to jump up and out of its seat with the frame. Never attempt to pry off the stop plate. Once the stop plate has jumped loose, remove it and the cylinder stop spring (#133), making sure to note their position for reassembly.

7 To remove the stop, pawl and trigger: Use cup-tipped pin punches for the following steps in order to avoid damaging the pins or the surrounding area on the frame. Drift out the cylinder stop pin (this is the center of the three pins that pass through the side of the frame) and push the cylinder stop (#129) out toward the bottom by using a small punch through the window in the frame (under the area where the cylinder rotates). Drift out the trigger pin (the rearmost

of the three pins that pass through the frame from side to side). The trigger (#124) can now pulled out the bottom of the frame along with its attached trigger spring (#131). Drift out the extractor pawl pin (#125P) – the front pin of the three pins that pass through the side of the frame – and pull out the extractor pawl (#125F) and its spring (#125G).

8 To disassemble the cylinder: Insert five fired cartridge cases into the chambers for support. Grasp the extractor ratchet (#122A) on its flats with a suitable open-ended wrench and rotate the cylinder (#112) in a counterclockwise direction to unscrew the extractor ratchet (#122A) from the extractor (#121). Notice the witness mark dot on one of the rear facing legs of the extractor star (this dot should be aligned with the serial numbers on the cylinder for reassembly). The extractor rack screw (#122C) and its nut (#122D) are threaded together, but the factory riveted them so they and their spring would remain as a single assembly inside the rack. Further disassembly is not suggested.

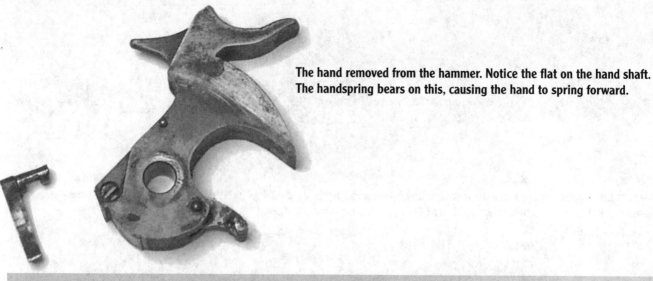

The hand removed from the hammer. Notice the flat on the hand shaft. The handspring bears on this, causing the hand to spring forward.

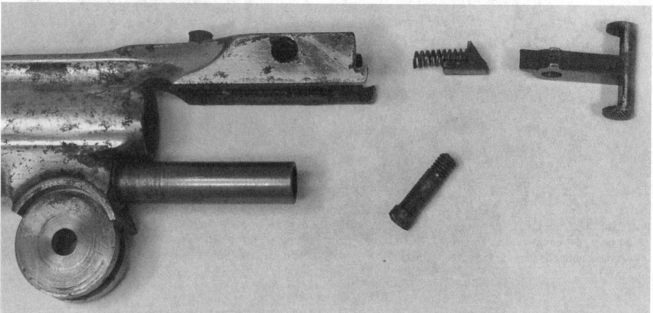

Removing the barrel catch screw allows the barrel catch, barrel catch cam and spring to be removed from the back. The screw you see sticking up on top of the barrel is the cylinder catch screw.

9 To disassemble the hammer: Rotate the hand (#151) 180 degrees forward and pull it out of the hammer. Drift out the pin in the center front of the hammer. This pin holds in the handspring (#135). The handspring now may be slid out of its recess in the hammer. The hammer stirrup (#128) may be removed by drifting out its pin at the rear of the hammer. Note the positioning of the stirrup for reassembly.

10 To disassemble the barrel: Unscrew and remove the barrel catch screw (#139) from the left side of the barrel topstrap. The barrel catch (#126) may now be withdrawn to the rear. By holding the barrel (#110) in a muzzle-up position and tapping the rear of the barrel topstrap on a wooden bench-top, the barrel catch cam (#152) and barrel catch cam spring (#136) will fall out of their recess in the top-strap. Note

their positions for reassembly. The extractor rack screw catch (#122F) and its spring (#122G) may be removed by drifting out the pin (#122P) that passes through the extractor housing under the barrel.

REASSEMBLY

Reassemble the revolver in reverse order of above, paying special attention to the relationships of the gear teeth on the extractor rack and the extractor gear. One easy way is to assemble the cylinder onto the barrel before the barrel is assembled to the frame. Next, install the gear into the barrel hinge with the large tooth facing straight up, and then assemble the barrel to the frame.

Smith & Wesson Top Break
.38 Single Action Model No. 2, Second and Third Models

Introduced in 1877, the .38 Single Action 2nd Model is, like the 1st Model, a spur trigger, single action-only revolver with a round-butt grip. All these revolvers were five-shots and were chambered for the 38 S&W cartridge. The revolver uses a T-shaped barrel catch that is lifted up to open the revolver by tilting the barrel downward. On opening, this revolver features simultaneous, automatic ejection of the spent cases. The 2nd Model .38 S.A. was simpler in many areas compared to the .38 S.A. 1st Model. The extraction system was changed from the early rack and gear to a less complicated, and easier to manufacture, hook and pivoting pawl system mounted on the extractor cam. The new system was not only less expensive to manufacture, but it was faster to make, used fewer parts and was considerably more reliable.

Later in production (about 1880) the extractor cam was simplified further still to the final sliding bar type. The extractor shank was changed from square to a pentagon shape, and the barrel extractor housing was shortened to what would be its final form. The separate cylinder catch, which had been mounted in the barrel topstrap, was eliminated in favor of a machined cylinder catch point on the bottom side of the barrel catch. This allowed a lower profile to be machined at the barrel's topstrap and frame ears. An interrupted thread was provided on the base pin, with a corresponding thread inside the cylinder axis, to help hold the cylinder in place during extraction. At about this same period, a hardened steel recoil plate was added to the front of the frame around the firing pin hole.

The 3-1/4-, 4- and 5-inch barrels are by far the most commonly found on this model, with the 6-inch being somewhat rare. The 8- and 10-inch barrel lengths (introduced about 1888), being extremely scarce, are truly desirable collector finds. The .38 S.A. 2nd Model was a best-seller; from serial #1 in 1877, it remained in production until 1891 with 108,255 guns manufactured over its 14-year lifespan.

.38 Single Action, 3rd Model
(Model No.2, 3rd Model, Model of 1891)

This model was the final design for the .38 Single Action No. 2 frame series. The 3rd Model incorporated the engineering changes and improvements (except the hammer/barrel catch interlock feature) taken from the current New Model No. 3 .44 Single Action revolver. Like the New Model No. 3, the .38 S. A. 3rd Model used a conventional trigger with a removable, bow-shaped triggerguard along with a rebounding hammer (a feature that had been in use in the .32 Single Action and the New Model No. 3 revolvers since 1878) that had a checkered, oversized spur. The trigger spring was changed from a small V-type mounted in the rear of the trigger in previous models to a heavy leaf type that was pinned into the front gripstrap of the frame. The separate cylinder stop plate used on 1st and 2nd models was omitted since this area was now covered by the triggerguard, and a new stop spring was used that fitted into a dovetail on the inside of the guard. Other than the lack of the hammer interlock feature, the .38 S.A. Third Model looks remarkably like a New Model No. 3 made in miniature.

This model was available as a combination set with extra single shot barrels in .22, .32 or .38 chamberings in 6- 8- and 10-inch lengths. Extension hard rubber target grips would have been included with such a set. Target sights were available for the first time on a .38 revolver with this model. A standard Paine blade was provided (though the factory offered many optional target front sights) along with a special barrel catch/target rear sight adjustable for both windage and elevation.

Another variation on the 1891 frame was the so-called Mexican Model, a .38 Single Action 3rd Model fitted with a removable sheath triggerguard and spur trigger as well as a different hammer with a small, checkered spur. The changes made the revolver appear to be a .38 Single Action 2nd Model. The half-cock notch was omitted on the Mexican model, which used only the rebounding position and full-cock notches. For a time, a spur trigger kit was available from S&W consisting only of a triggerguard and trigger that allowed a person to convert an 1891 into a spur-trigger gun. Such a piece would not be a true Mexican Model since it would still have the wide spur hammer with a half-cock position. The total of true Mexican Models made is very small, estimated to be around 2000 revolvers, with the majority of them being shipped to Mexico, South America and Russia.

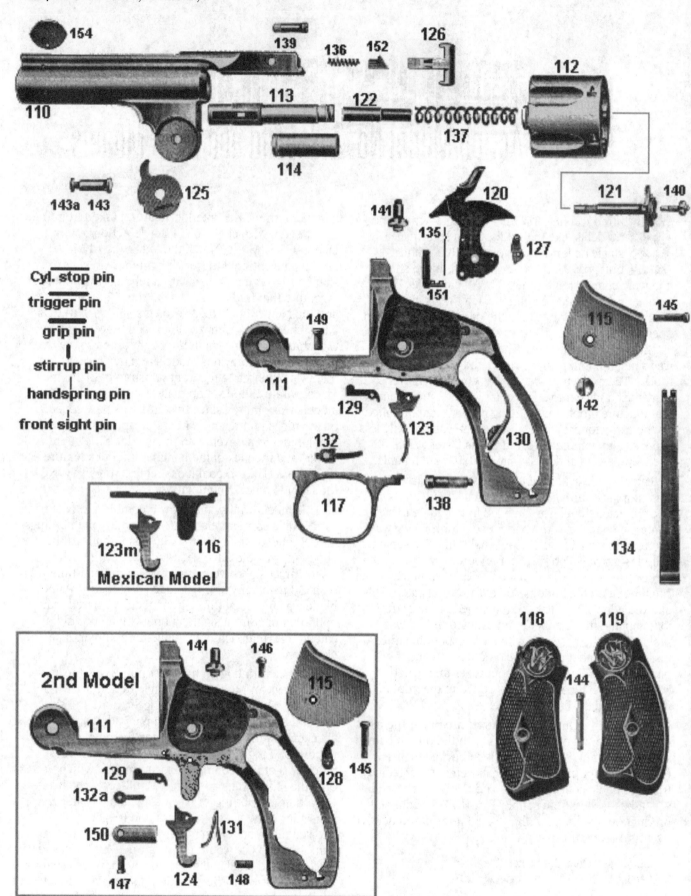

154

139

136 152 126

112

110

113

122

137

114

143a 143

125

141 120

135 127

Cyl. stop pin

trigger pin

grip pin

stirrup pin

handspring pin

front sight pin

151

149

115 145

111

142

129

123

132 130

117 138

134

123m 116

Mexican Model

118 119

2nd Model

141 146

115

111

144

129

132a

128 145

150 131

147 124 148

Parts List
(1891 3rd Model Illustrated,
2nd model inset)

Note: See the sections listed under Smith & Wesson .38 Double Action Models for photographic guidance in disassembling external parts and the extraction mechanism; see instructions for the .38 SA 1st Model for guidance with internal action parts.

111	Frame	127	Stirrup, 1891 3rd Model	142	Hammer Stud Nut, 3rd Model	
112	Cylinder	128	Stirrup, 2nd Model	143	Joint Pivot	
113	Base Pin	129	Cylinder Stop	143A	Joint Pivot Screw	
114	Gas Ring	130	Trigger Spring, 3rd Model	144	Grip Screw	
115	Sideplate	131	Trigger Spring, 2nd Model	145	Sideplate Screw, long	
116	Triggerguard, Mexican	132	Cylinder Stop Spring	146	Sideplate Screw, short	
117	Triggerguard, 3rd Model	132A	Cylinder Stop Spring, 2nd Model	147	Stop Plate Screw	
118	Grip	133	Mainspring	148	Strain Screw, 2nd Model	
119	Grip	135	Hand Spring	149	Triggerguard Screw, 3rd Model	
120	Hammer	136	Barrel Catch Cam Spring	150	Stop Plate	
121	Extractor	137	Extractor Spring	151	Hand	
122	Extractor Rod	138	Strain Screw, 3rd Model	152	Barrel Catch Cam	
123	Trigger, 3rd Model, 1891	139	Barrel Catch Screw	154	Front Sight	
124	Trigger, 2nd Model	140	Extractor Stud			
125	Extractor Cam	141	Hammer Stud			
126	Barrel Catch					

Note: Readers may refer to the sections listed under Smith & Wesson .38 Double Action Models for photographic guidance in disassembling external parts and the extraction mechanism; see instructions for the .38 SA 1st Model for guidance with internal action parts.

DISASSEMBLY INSTRUCTIONS

1 Check first to be sure the revolver is not loaded. Grasp the revolver firmly by its grip, being careful not to put your finger on the trigger (#123) or (#124) and making certain to keep the barrel muzzle pointed in a safe direction. With your other hand, lift up on the barrel catch (#126) and tilt the revolver barrel all the way down to open the action. This exposes the entire rear of the cylinder (#112). Check to be certain the cylinder is unloaded and if cartridges are present, remove them and place them in a separate location from the gun.

2 To remove the cylinder: Hold the barrel catch (#126) in the up position and pull the cylinder (#112) to the rear while at the same time turning it in a counterclockwise direction. The cylinder will withdraw from the base pin (#114), toward the rear.

3 To remove the barrel: Unscrew and remove the joint pivot screw (#143A) from the left side of the hinge on the frame (#111) and use an appropriate straight punch to drive the joint pivot (#143) out of the frame toward the right side. Notice the witness mark on the joint pivot and its corresponding mark on the frame. These must be aligned for reassembly. The barrel (#110) is now loose and may be lifted straight up out of its joint with the frame. The extractor cam (#125) is located between the ears of the barrel hinge and may be pulled down and out of the barrel. Note the extractor cam's position for reassembly.

4 To remove the grips and sideplate: Unscrew and remove the stock screw (#144) and lift off the stocks (#118) and (#119). Unscrew and remove the two sideplate screws (#145) and (#146) on 2nd

Models. (On 3rd models the hammer stud nut [#142] takes the place of the center or short sideplate screw.) Turn the frame on its side holding it by the hinge, sideplate facing up, over a padded surface. Strike the grip frame a sharp blow or two using a plastic mallet. This will cause the sideplate (#115) to jump up out of its seat in the frame for removal. Never attempt to pry off the sideplate.

5 Remove the mainspring and hammer: Use a pair of spreader-type pliers to compress the top of the mainspring (#134) so the hammer stirrup (#127) or (#128) may be rotated forward and out of its seat between the ears at the top of the mainspring. Loosen the strain screw (#138) or (#148) located in the bottom front of the front grip strap on the frame and withdraw the mainspring from the frame side. Using a small screwdriver as a lever, carefully rotate the top of the hand (#151) to the rear; while holding the hand to the rear, pull the trigger (#123) or (#124) and hold it to the rear. The hammer (#120) may be rotated about half way to the rear and carefully pulled upward, off of its hammer stud (#141) and out of the frame.

6 To remove the stop plate or triggerguard, 2nd Models only: Remove the stop plate screw (#147), the small screw located on the frame bottom between the trigger and hinge joint. Hold the frame upside down by the grip, and while holding the trigger to the rear, strike the frame just behind the hinge joint several short, sharp blows with a plastic or hardwood mallet. This will cause the stop plate (#150) to be shocked out of its seat with the frame. Never attempt to pry off the stop plate. Once the stop plate has jumped loose, remove it and the cylinder stop spring (#133), noting their position for reassembly. 3rd Models only: Remove the guard screw (#149) and remove the guard (#117) or (#116) by pulling down on its front. The cylinder stop spring (#132) is fitted into, and held captive by, a small dovetail slot inside the guard.

7 To remove the cylinder stop and trigger: Use a cup-tipped pin punch to drift out the cylinder stop pin (this is the forwardmost of the two pins that pass through the frame from side to side). Next, push the cylinder stop (#129) out toward the bottom, using a small punch through its window in the frame, under the area where the cylinder rotates. Again using the cup-tipped pin punch and hammer, drift out the trigger pin (this is the rearmost of the two pins that pass through the frame from side to side). On 2nd Models only, the trigger may now be pulled out the bottom of the frame along with its attached trigger spring (#131). The 3rd Model trigger spring (#130) is mounted inside the front grip strap and is held in place by a cross pin running through the grip frame.

8 To disassemble the cylinder: Insert five-fired cartridge cases into the chambers for support. Grasp the extractor post (#122) in the jaws of a drill press or lathe chuck and rotate the cylinder (#112) in a counterclockwise direction to unscrew the extractor post from the extractor (#121). Note the witness mark "dot" on one of the rear facing legs of the extractor star. This should be aligned with the serial numbers on the cylinder for reassembly.

9 To disassemble the hammer: Rotate the hand (#151) about 180 degrees forward and pull it out of the hammer. Drift out the pin in the center front of the hammer that holds in the handspring (#135). The handspring is now free to be slid out of its recess in the hammer. The hammer stirrup (#127) or (#128) may be removed by drifting out its pin at the rear of the hammer. Note the position of the stirrup for reassembly.

10 To disassemble the barrel: Remove the barrel catch screw (#139) from the left side of the barrel topstrap. The barrel catch (#126) may now be withdrawn to the rear. By holding the barrel (#110) in a muzzle-up position and tapping the rear of the barrel top-strap on a wooden bench-top, the barrel catch cam (#152) and barrel catch cam spring (#136) will fall out of their recess in the top-strap. Note their positions for reassembly.

REASSEMBLY

Reassemble the revolver in reverse order of above.

Smith & Wesson .38
Double Action Models

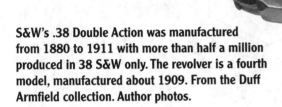

S&W's .38 Double Action was manufactured from 1880 to 1911 with more than half a million produced in 38 S&W only. The revolver is a fourth model, manufactured about 1909. From the Duff Armfield collection. Author photos.

S mith & Wesson's top-break .38 Double Action, like the smaller .32, was introduced in 1880. This design proved itself a very popular pocket revolver and it was kept in production until 1911 with a total of 554,077 revolvers being manufactured. In common with the .38 Single Action before it, the double action was the same Model 2 frame size and was offered in 38 Smith & Wesson chambering with a five-shot cylinder featuring the same simultaneous, automatic cartridge extraction the S&W top-break was famous for. The .38 double action went through five separate engineering changes during the period of manufacture, forming five unique models as outlined below as the company was always perfecting this popular design:

1st Model: manufactured 1880, serial numbers 1 to around 4000. (Note: Ending serial number data is approximate; the exact transitional serial number from 1st to 2nd model is unknown.) Features straight-sided sideplate, rocker type cylinder stop, short cylinder flutes with double stop notches and free cuts on cylinder, reverse curved triggerguard bow, front sight pinned into barrel. 3-1/4- and 4-inch barrels.

2nd Model: manufactured 1880 to 1884, serial numbers around 4001 to 119,000. (Note: Beginning serial number data is approximate; the exact

transitional serial number from 1st to 2nd model is unknown.) Features irregular shaped sideplate, rocker type cylinder stop, short flutes with double stop notches and free cuts on cylinder, reverse curved triggerguard bow, front sight pinned into barrel, addition of hammer fly. 3-1/4-, 4-, 5- and 6-inch barrels.

3rd Model: manufactured 1884 to 1895, serial numbers 119,001 to 322,700. Features pivoting spring type cylinder stop, reverse curved triggerguard bow, front sight pinned into barrel; cylinder has conventional flutes and stop notches. 3-1/4-, 4-, 5-, 6-, 8- and 10-inch barrel lengths.

4th Model: manufactured 1895 to 1909, serial numbers 322,701 to 539,000. Features pivoting spring type cylinder stop, reverse curved triggerguard bow, front sight pinned into barrel; cylinder has conventional flutes and stop notches. Barrel lengths same as for 3rd Model.

5th Model: manufactured 1909 to 1911, serial numbers 539,001 to 554,077. Features pivoting spring-type cylinder stop and reverse curved triggerguard bow; front sight now forged as one piece with barrel; cylinder has conventional flutes and stop notches; S&W name and address only on barrel rib without patent markings. 3-1/4-, 4-, 5- and 6-inch barrel lengths.

The illustration that follows is a representative .38 Double Action 4th Model. Third and 5th models are nearly identical to the illustration. .38 D.A. 1st and 2nd models are different externally as noted above and internally as noted in the following disassembly instructions.

The photos used in the disassembly process below may also be used as guides when disassembling .32 Double Action S&Ws.

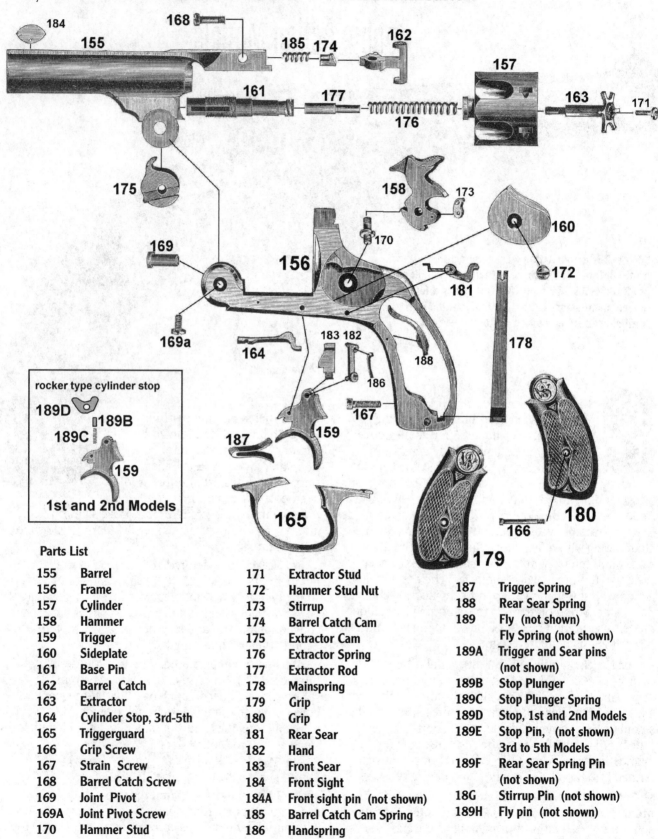

Parts List

155	Barrel	171	Extractor Stud	187	Trigger Spring		
156	Frame	172	Hammer Stud Nut	188	Rear Sear Spring		
157	Cylinder	173	Stirrup	189	Fly (not shown)		
158	Hammer	174	Barrel Catch Cam		Fly Spring (not shown)		
159	Trigger	175	Extractor Cam	189A	Trigger and Sear pins		
160	Sideplate	176	Extractor Spring		(not shown)		
161	Base Pin	177	Extractor Rod	189B	Stop Plunger		
162	Barrel Catch	178	Mainspring	189C	Stop Plunger Spring		
163	Extractor	179	Grip	189D	Stop, 1st and 2nd Models		
164	Cylinder Stop, 3rd-5th	180	Grip	189E	Stop Pin, (not shown)		
165	Triggerguard	181	Rear Sear		3rd to 5th Models		
166	Grip Screw	182	Hand	189F	Rear Sear Spring Pin		
167	Strain Screw	183	Front Sear		(not shown)		
168	Barrel Catch Screw	184	Front Sight	18G	Stirrup Pin (not shown)		
169	Joint Pivot	184A	Front sight pin (not shown)	189H	Fly pin (not shown)		
169A	Joint Pivot Screw	185	Barrel Catch Cam Spring				
170	Hammer Stud	186	Handspring				

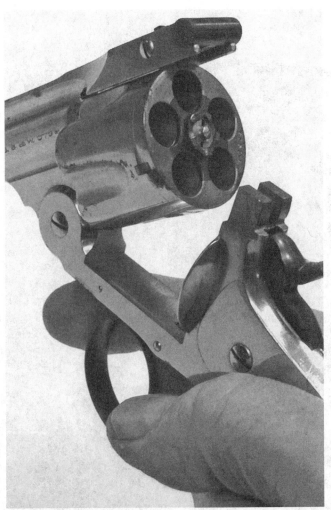

Pull the hammer back to the half-cock position as shown here and lift up on the barrel catch to break open the revolver.

To remove the cylinder from all models of double action S&Ws, lift up and hold the barrel catch, then turn the cylinder counterclockwise while pulling rearward.

DISASSEMBLY INSTRUCTIONS

1 Grasp the revolver firmly by its grip, being careful not to put your finger on the trigger (#159) and making certain to keep the muzzle pointed in a safe direction. Pull the hammer back slightly until you hear one click; this is the half-cock position. With your other hand, lift up on the barrel catch (#162) and tilt the revolver barrel all the way down to open the action. This exposes the entire rear of the cylinder (#157). Check to be certain the cylinder is unloaded and if cartridges are present, remove them now and place them in a separate location from the gun.

2 To remove the cylinder: Hold the barrel catch (#162) in the up position and pull the cylinder (#37) to the rear while at the same time turning it in a counterclockwise direction. The cylinder can now be withdrawn from the base pin (#161), toward the rear.

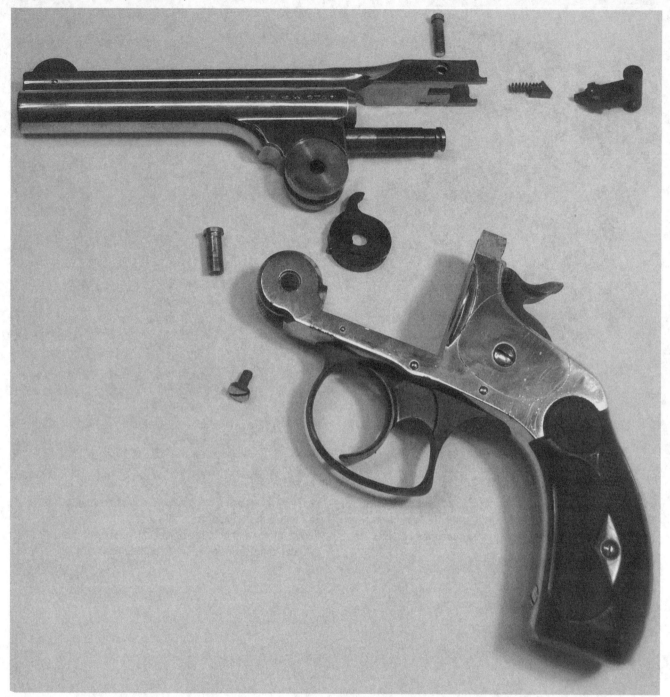

All double action S&W barrels come off the same way: remove the joint pivot (hinge pin) and lift the barrel off the frame. The rounded piece below the hinge is the extractor cam. We have also disassembled the barrel catch to illustrate how its components go together.

3 To remove the barrel: Unscrew and remove the joint pivot screw (#169A) from the left side of the hinge on the frame (#156) and use an appropriate straight punch to drive the joint pivot (#169) out of the frame toward the right side. Make a note of the witness mark on the joint pivot and its corresponding mark on the frame. (These must be aligned for reassembly.) The barrel (#155) is now loose and can be lifted up out of its joint with the frame. The extractor cam (#175) is located between the ears of the barrel hinge and can now be pulled down and out of the barrel. Make note of the extractor cam's position for reassembly.

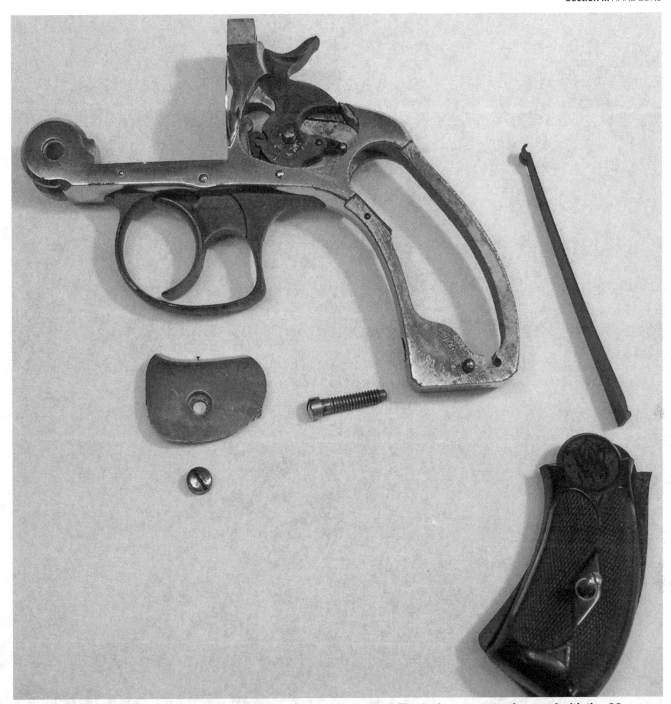

After the grips and sideplate are removed, the mainspring is also removed. This is the same procedure used with the .32 double action models.

4 To remove the grips, sideplate and mainspring: Unscrew and remove the stock screw (#166) and lift off the stocks (#179) and (#180). Remove the hammer stud nut (#172), which acts as the sideplate screw. Turn the frame on its side holding it by the hinge, the sideplate facing up over a padded surface. Strike the grip frame a sharp blow or two using a plastic or hardwood mallet. This will cause the sideplate (#160) to jump up out of its seat in the frame for removal. Never attempt to pry off the sideplate. Use a pair of spreader-type pliers to compress the top of the mainspring (#178) so the hammer stirrup (#173) may be rotated forward and out of its seat between the ears at the top of the mainspring. Loosen the strain screw (#167) located in the bottom front of the front grip strap on the frame and withdraw the mainspring from the frame side.

Tapping the rear of the triggerguard causes it to jump forward and out of its seat in the frame.

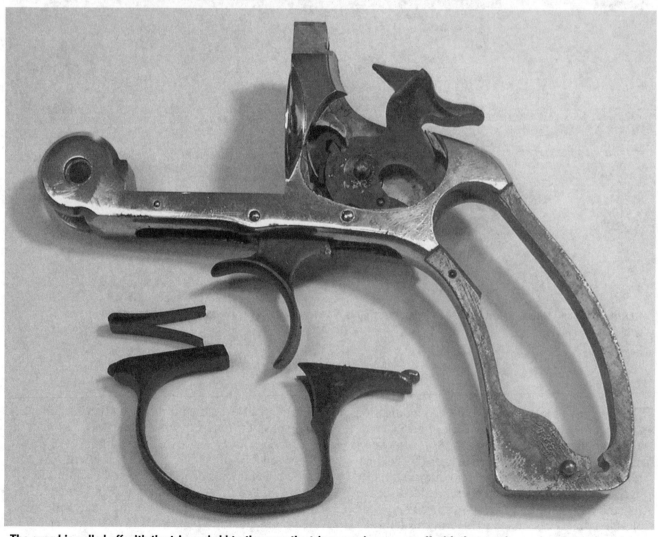

The guard is pulled off with the trigger held to the rear; the trigger spring comes off with the guard.

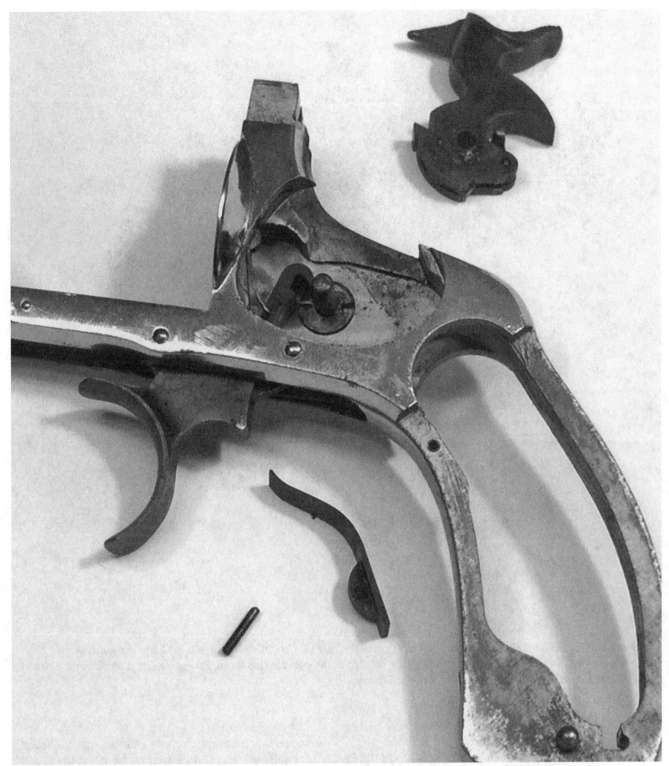

Here the rear sear spring and hammer are removed from the frame; .32 double actions come apart the same way.

5 To remove the triggerguard: The triggerguard (#165) is a spring; it has no fastening screws and it is held in place by machined tabs at its front and rear tops that mate with machined mortise cuts in the frame. Hold the frame upside down by the grip and tap the lower rear edge of the triggerguard forward with a plastic or hardwood mallet, causing the rear of the guard to jump out of its seat in the frame. Pull the trigger (#159) all the way to the rear. The triggerguard may now be moved rearward slightly to disengage its front tab from the frame. Tilt the front of the triggerguard down and push forward to remove. The trigger spring (#187) is now free and can be removed with the triggerguard. Make note of its position for reassembly.

All the remaining action parts as they came out of the gun. The rear sear (right) rocks up into the half-cock notch of the hammer, causing its front to pivot down and push the rear leg of the cylinder stop down. Except for size, this design is virtually identical in .32 and .38 double actions, 3rd through 5th models.

6 To disassemble the action: Use a small pin punch and hammer to drift out the retaining pin (#189F) for the rear sear spring (#188) and remove the spring. Pull the trigger to the rear and hold it all the way back. The hammer (#158) may now be carefully worked up off its stud (#170) and out of the frame. As you release the trigger, make note of position of the rear sear (#181). Use a cup-tipped pin punch and hammer to drift out the rear sear pin, the rearmost of the two large pins (#189A) that pass through the frame, and remove the rear sear, noting its position for reassembly. Use the same cup-tipped punch and hammer to drift out the trigger pin, the forwardmost of these two large

pins (#189A). Push the trigger assembly up and to the rear slightly until the entire face of the hand (#182) is exposed in the sideplate opening. Grasp the hand along with its spring (#186) with a small pair of needle nosed pliers and pull the assembly straight up and out of the frame. The trigger (#159) may be removed through the bottom of the frame while the front sear (#183) may be removed through the sideplate opening.

Note: In 1st and 2nd Models, make careful note of the relationship of the trigger assembly – consisting of the trigger (#159), front sear (#183), and hand (#182) – for reassembly.

The double action cylinder disassembled.

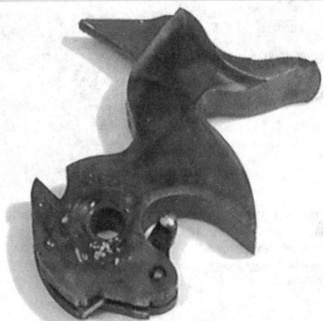

If you look closely at the half-cock notch you can see the fly. This tiny pivoting piece was introduced in later production .32 and .38 DAs to help prevent sear breakage.

7 Removing the cylinder stop: On 1st and 2nd Models, the rocker-type cylinder stop (#189D) is mounted in the top center of the trigger. It and its spring and plunger become accessible as soon as the trigger is removed. Under the cylinder stop is a small plunger and coil spring that power the stop. The spring and plunger will be under tension during trigger removal, so use care when removing the trigger that these two tiny parts are not lost.

For 3rd through 5th Models, the cylinder stop (#164) is held into the frame by a cross pin and may be removed by carefully drifting out this pin.

8 To disassemble the cylinder: Insert five fired cartridge cases or dummy cartridges into the chambers for support. Grasp the extractor rod (#177) by its head in the jaws of a drill chuck and rotate the cylinder (#157) in a counterclockwise direction to unscrew the extractor rod from the extractor (#163).

Notice the witness mark "dot" on one of the rear facing legs of the extractor star. This mark should be aligned with the serial numbers on the cylinder for reassembly.

Note: To prevent damage to the extractor spring during reassembly, grasp the front 1/4 inch of the extractor rod by its head in the jaws of a drill chuck. Assemble the spring onto the extractor rod, place the cylinder with the extractor over the rear end of the rod, and push the cylinder forward, compressing the extractor spring as much as possible while turning the cylinder in a clockwise direction until the threads

have started by about one-half turn. Stop turning every one-half turn and allow the extractor to return by spring tension, then push the cylinder in to recompress the spring and continue tightening in one-half turn increments until the rod is hand tight.

9 To disassemble the barrel: Remove the barrel catch screw (#168) from the left side of the barrel topstrap. The barrel catch (#162) may be withdrawn to the rear. By holding the barrel (#155) in a muzzle-up position and tapping the rear of the topstrap on a soft wooden bench-top, the barrel catch cam (#174) and barrel catch cam spring (#185) will fall out of their recess in the topstrap. Make careful note of their positions for reassembly.

REASSEMBLY

Reassemble the action in the reverse order of that given above.

Smith & Wesson .38
New Departure Safety Hammerless Models 1 through 5

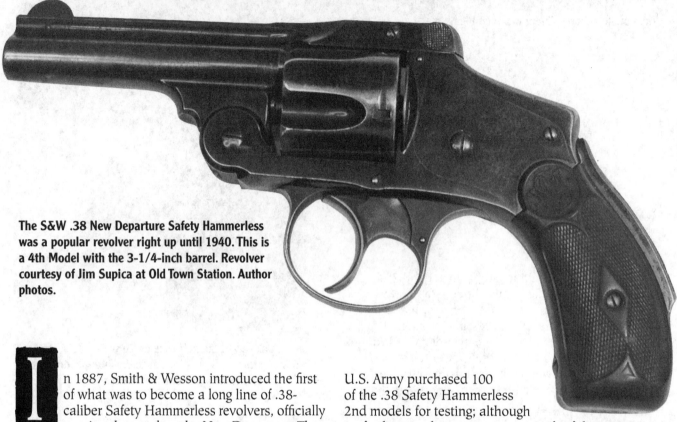

The S&W .38 New Departure Safety Hammerless was a popular revolver right up until 1940. This is a 4th Model with the 3-1/4-inch barrel. Revolver courtesy of Jim Supica at Old Town Station. Author photos.

In 1887, Smith & Wesson introduced the first of what was to become a long line of .38-caliber Safety Hammerless revolvers, officially naming the revolver the New Departure. The New Departure featured the automatic, simultaneous ejection of the fired cartridges as did all previous S&W top-break revolvers. This new model also carried other advanced characteristics that truly put it into the category of a departure from the old. These double-action only, safety hammerless revolvers actually had hammers, but the hammers were internal and the trigger could not be operated unless the grip safety were first squeezed. Once it had been squeezed, the grip safety lever pressed into the frame where it caused a steel bar called the safety latch to pivot out of contact with the hammer, allowing the gun to be fired. A truly novel design, the New Departure also used a rebounding hammer as well as a self-retracting, frame-mounted, floating firing pin.

Several barrel lengths were offered by S&W with the most common being the 3-1/4-, 4- and 5-inch, in that order. New Departures with 2-inch barrels are certainly the rarest of the .38 Safety Hammerless revolvers. Six-inch barrels are not quite so rare as the ultra-short barrels, but they are nevertheless unusual. In 1890, the U.S. Army purchased 100 of the .38 Safety Hammerless 2nd models for testing; although no further purchases came as a result of those tests, the results were generally favorable. Captain Hall of the US Army speaks in his writings of the S&W .38 Safety Hammerless revolver he examined prior to the 1890 tests: "The workmanship of the revolver leaves nothing to be desired and the accuracy of shooting is most satisfactory. Whether it will stand the rough usage of service is another question. . . ."

These five-shot revolvers were compact, about the size of a modern S&W J frame (actually, they were just a bit smaller than the J) and they were offered only in 38 Smith & Wesson. The .38 Safety was the last top-break revolver S&W carried in its line until the limited-production of the recent Schofield replica. They were manufactured up into 1940, when the last revolver (#261,493) was shipped. In 53 years of production, five distinct mechanical variations of the .38 Safety Hammerless were produced and four of those have at least minor mechanical differences from one another. The five variations are listed here below, with deviations in takedown procedure noted within the instructions:

1st Model: manufactured 1887, serial numbers 1 to 5,250 (approximate). Features irregular-shaped sideplate, rounded triggerguard bow, front sight pinned into barrel. 3-3/4-, 4-, 5- and 6-inch barrels. Barrel catch pushes to the side to open barrel.

2nd Model: manufactured 1887 to 1890, serial numbers 5,000 (approximately) to around 42,483. Features irregular-shaped sideplate, rounded triggerguard bow, front sight pinned into barrel. 3-3/4-, 4-, and 5-inch barrel lengths. Barrel catch pushes down to open barrel.

3rd Model: manufactured 1890 to 1898, serial numbers about 42,484 to 116,002. Features irregular-shaped sideplate, rounded triggerguard bow, front sight

pinned into barrel rib. Barrel lengths same as those for 1st Model. Barrel catch pushes down to open barrel.

4th Model: manufactured 1898 to 1907, serial numbers 116,002 to around 220,000. Features irregular-shaped sideplate, rounded triggerguard bow, front sight pinned into barrel rib. Barrel lengths same as those for 1st Model. Barrel catch lifts-up to open barrel.

5th Models: manufactured 1907 to 1940, serial numbers around 220,000 to 261,493. Features irregular-shaped sideplate, rounded triggerguard bow, front sight forged as integral part of barrel rib. 2-, 3-3/4-, 4-, 5- and 6-inch barrel lengths. Barrel catch lifts-up to open barrel.

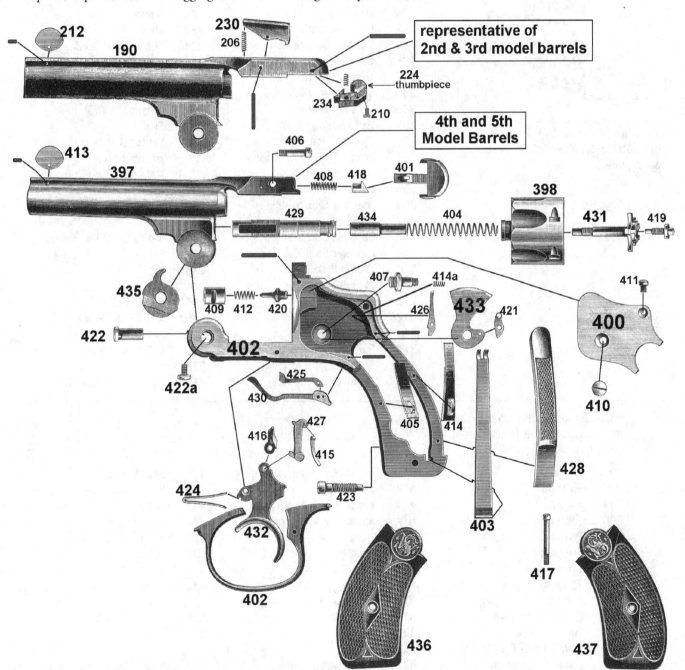

This drawing shows the components of the .38 New Departure, 4th and 5th Models, with the 2nd and 3rd Model differences shown (inset). 1st Model differences are shown separately.

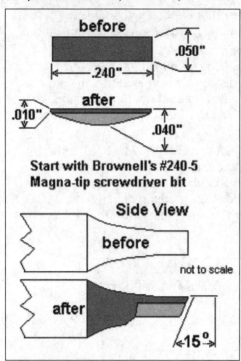

before

.050"

.240"

after

.010"

.040"

Start with Brownell's #240-5 Magna-tip screwdriver bit

Side View

before

not to scale

after

15°

You can easily make this special tool to drive off the 1st Model's barrel catch cover plate.

Parts List for Smith & Wesso .38 Safety Hammerless, 3rd Model
(Representative of 1st, 2nd, and 3rd Models with model differences outlined within the text.)

(NS) = Not Shown

190	Barrel	216	Base Pin
191	Frame	217	Joint Pivot
192	Cylinder	217A	Joint Pivot Screw
193	Sideplate	218	Cylinder Stop
194	Triggerguard	218A	Cylinder Stop Pin
194A	Trigger Stop Pin	219	Hammer Stud
195	Trigger	220	Extractor
195A	Trigger Pin (NS)	221	Extractor Stud
196	Mainspring	222	Hammer
197	Extractor Spring	223	Firing Pin
198	Cylinder Stop Spring	223A	Firing Pin Retaining Pin
198A	Cylinder Stop Spring Pin (NS)	224	Thumb Piece
199	Trigger Spring	225	Gas Ring
200	Split Spring (NS)	226	Stirrup
200A	Split Spring Pin	226A	Stirrup Pin (NS)
201	Hand Spring	227	Sear
202	Cylinder Hook Spring	228	Extractor Post
203	Spiral (Coil) Latch Spring	229	Hammer Stop (NS)
204	Firing Pin Spring	229A	Hammer Stop Pin (NS)
205	Barrel Catch Spring	230	Cylinder Hook
206	Hammer Stop Spring	230A	Cylinder Hook Pin
207	Firing Pin Bushing	231	Safety Latch
208	Base pin Bushing	231	Safety Latch Pin
209	Hammer Stud Nut	232	Extractor Cam Assembly
210	Thumb Piece Screw	233	Hand
211	Plate Screw	234	Barrel Catch
212	Sight	234A	Barrel Catch Pin
212A	Sight Pin	235	Right Hand Stock
213	Strain Screw	235A	Stock Pin (NS)
214	Stock Screw	236	Left Hand Stock
215	Safety Lever	237	Latch spring, Leaf
215A	Safety Lever Pin (NS)	237A	Latch Spring pin (NS)

Parts List for Smith & Wesson .38
New Departure/Safety Hammerless 4th and 5th Models

397	Barrel	412	Firing Pin Return Spring	425	Split Spring
398	Cylinder	413	Front Sight	426	Safety latch
399	Frame	414	Latch Spring, Leaf Type	427	Hand
400	Sideplate	41A	Same As Above, Coil	428	Safety Lever
401	Barrel Catch	415	Handspring	429	Base Pin
402	Triggerguard	416	Sear	430	Cylinder Stop
403	Mainspring	417	Grip Screw	431	Extractor
404	Extractor Spring	418	Barrel Catch Cam	432	Trigger
405	Cylinder Stop Spring	419	Extractor Stud	433	Hammer
406	Barrel Catch Screw	420	Firing Pin	434	Extractor Rod
407	Hammer Stud	421	Stirrup	435	Extractor Cam
408	Barrel Catch Cam Spring	422	Joint Pivot	436	Stock (Grip)
409	Firing Pin Bushing	422A	Joint Pivot Screw	437	Stock (Grip)
410	Hammer Stud Nut	423	Strain Screw		
411	Plate Screw	424	Trigger Spring		

The Safety Hammerless opened for loading. The gun shown here is a 1930s vintage 5th model. Notice the front sight forged as part of the barrel rib.

DISASSEMBLY INSTRUCTIONS

(Numbers in the text are keyed to 4th Model parts diagram except where noted; separate parts lists are shown for 1st through 3rd models and 4th through 5th models.)

1 Make certain the revolver is unloaded. Grasp the revolver firmly around the grip, being careful that the barrel muzzle is pointed in a safe direction and to keep your finger away from the trigger (#432). Depending on the model, there are three different methods of opening the barrel that you may encounter. With 1st Models, you open the barrel by pushing in on the side of the barrel catch from left to right. For 2nd or 3rd Models you unlatch the barrel by pushing down on the barrel catch thumb piece (#224). For the 4th and 5th models, you lift up on the barrel catch (#401). After doing this, for all models, tilt the revolver barrel all the way down to open the action. This enables you to view the entire rear of the cylinder. Check to be absolutely certain that all the cylinder chambers are unloaded. If cartridges are present, remove them and put them in a separate location from the revolver.

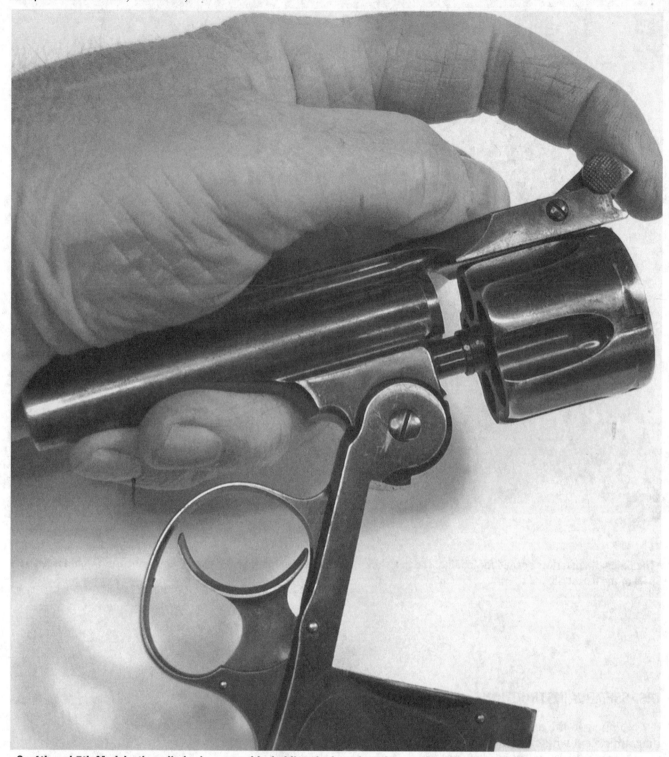

On 4th and 5th Models, the cylinder is removed by holding the barrel catch up and turning the cylinder in a counterclockwise direction while pulling it back.

1a To remove the cylinder, 1st models: Hold the barrel catch depressed. This will automatically operate the cylinder hook (cylinder catch). With 2nd or 3rd models: Notice the depressed area on the barrel top strap; push down on the front of the cylinder hook (#230) at this depression. For 4th and 5th models: Hold the barrel catch (#401) in the up position. Next,

for all models: Pull the cylinder (#398) to the rear while at the same time turning it in a counterclockwise direction. The cylinder is held captive by the large interrupted thread on the base pin, and these actions will allow it to be withdrawn to the rear and off the base pin (#429).

Removing the joint pivot allows the barrel to be lifted out of its hinge in the frame. The part under the hinge is the extractor cam. This is a 4th Model and the barrel catch has also been disassembled.

2 To remove the barrel: Unscrew and remove the joint pivot screw (#422A) from the left side of the hinge on the frame (#399). Use an appropriate-size straight pin punch to drive the joint pivot (#422) out of the frame to the right side. Notice the witness mark on the joint pivot and its corresponding witness mark on the frame. These must be aligned during reassembly.

The barrel (#397) can now be lifted straight up out of its joint with the frame. The extractor cam (#435) is located between the ears of the barrel hinge and now may be pulled down and out of the barrel. Be sure to make note of the extractor cam's position for reassembly later.

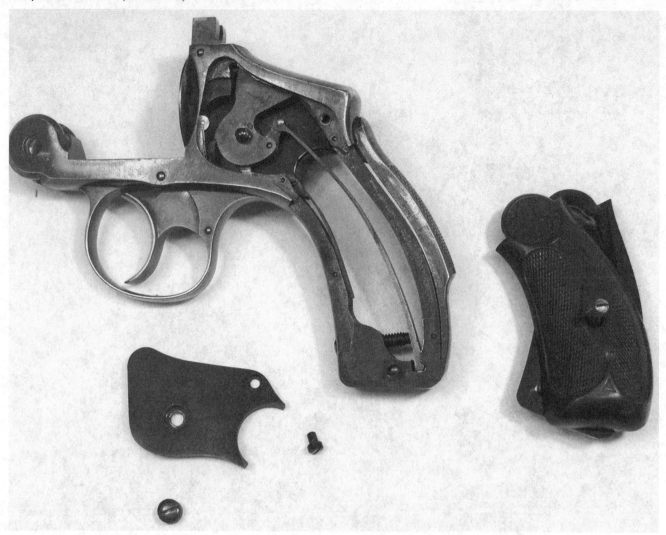

After the grips have been removed, the sideplate screw and hammer stud nut are unscrewed, leaving the sideplate ready to be removed.

3 To remove the grips and sideplate. Unscrew and remove the stock screw (#417) and lift off the stocks (#436) and (#437). Unscrew and remove the hammer stud nut (#410) from the center of the sideplate (#400) and the sideplate screw (#411) from the rear of the sideplate. Turn the frame over on its side, holding it in the area by the hinge with the sideplate facing up over a padded surface. Strike the grip frame a sharp blow or two with a plastic or hardwood mallet. This will shock the frame and cause the sideplate to jump up out of its seat in the frame for removal. Do not under any circumstances try to pry off the sideplate; you could easily cause serious damage to the sideplate and the frame.

4 To remove the mainspring and stop spring: These revolvers are equipped with rebounding hammers, and the rebound action is controlled by mainspring tension acting on the rebounding action stirrup. Taking careful note of the position of the hammer before any further disassembly is attempted will help you to understand how the rebound system functions. By placing a pair of spreader pliers between the inside of the frame and the mainspring, the top of the mainspring (#403) may be pressed forward so that the hammer stirrup (#421) can be pushed forward and out of its seat between the ears at the top of the mainspring. That disconnects the mainspring from the hammer. Loosen the strain screw (#423), which is located in the bottom front of the front grip strap on the frame. You may now withdraw the mainspring from the grip frame side opening. Using a straight pin punch, drift out the pin in the front strap of the grip frame, which holds the cylinder stop spring (#405) in place, and remove the cylinder stop spring by gently prying it out to the rear.

The strain screw and mainspring have been removed and the rear of the triggerguard is unlatched from its seat in the frame. Triggerguards in these revolvers are springs, so you must compress the rear leg to the front in order to unlock them from the frame.

Once the rear of the guard is unlatched, pull the trigger and slide the guard out toward the rear. The trigger spring will come out with the guard.

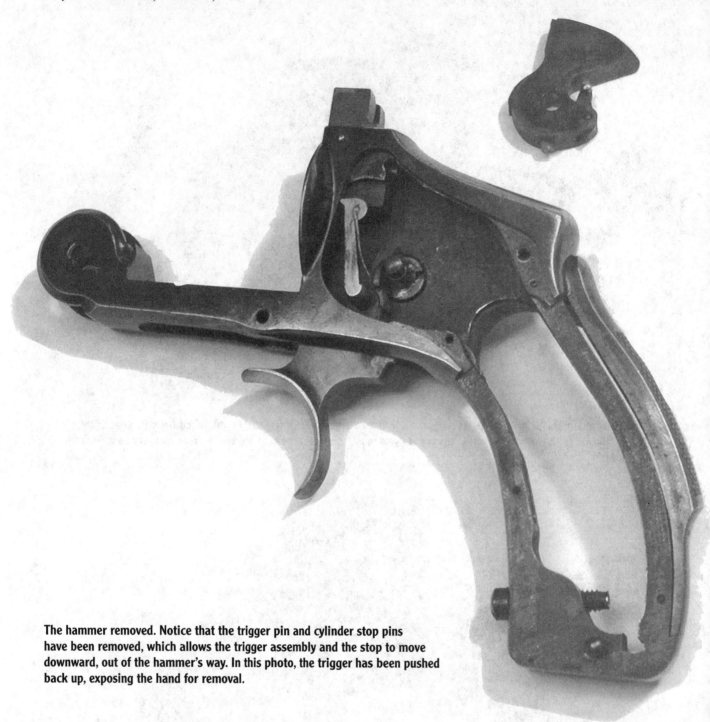

The hammer removed. Notice that the trigger pin and cylinder stop pins have been removed, which allows the trigger assembly and the stop to move downward, out of the hammer's way. In this photo, the trigger has been pushed back up, exposing the hand for removal.

4a To remove the triggerguard: Make use of a wooden hammer handle or a small plastic mallet to strike the lower rear edge of the triggerguard (#402) bow a sharp but light blow on the bow's backside (strike in such a way that you drive the rear leg of the guard toward the front). This will cause the rear leg of the triggerguard (the guard itself is a compressed spring) to jump forward and unhook itself from the frame and allow it to drop down slightly. Press in on the safety lever (#428) and pull the trigger (#432) all the way to the rear. The triggerguard is now removed by first pulling it toward the rear to unhook its front lip from the frame and then pivoting it down at the front and pushing forward on the bow. The V-shaped trigger spring (#424) may now be removed from the triggerguard opening in the frame (be sure to note the position of the trigger spring for reassembly).

5 To remove the action components: Push the trigger and the hammer (#433) back into their forward positions. Use a small pin punch to drift out the cylinder stop pin from the frame from the inside out. Push the entire cylinder stop (#430) down into the frame until it is out of the way of the hammer. Push in on the safety lever (#428) once again and pull the

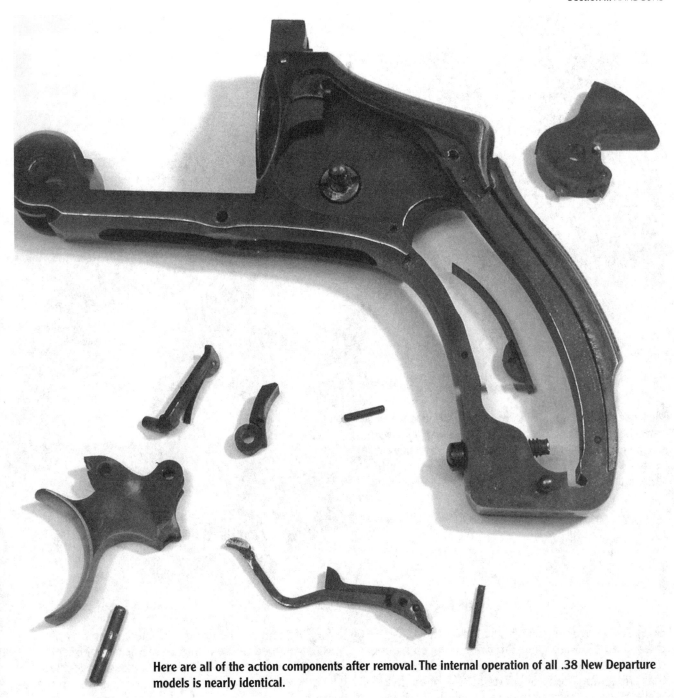

Here are all of the action components after removal. The internal operation of all .38 New Departure models is nearly identical.

trigger to cause the hammer to rotate to the rear. Now, with the stirrup (#421) held to the rearmost position, the hammer may be gently worked up and off of its hammer stud (#407) and thence out of the gun frame.

The trigger pin (the large pin that passes through the frame from side to side under the cylinder opening) is now drifted out of the frame using a cup-tipped pin punch. The assembly – consisting of the trigger (#432), the hand (#427) and sear (#416) – may now be pushed up and to the rear until it reaches a point where the entire hand is visible through the sideplate opening. Note the positioning of these three parts for later

reassembly. The hand and its handspring (#415) may be grasped with a pair of long, skinny needlenosed pliers and pulled upward out of its seat with the trigger and sear. The trigger may be pulled down from the bottom of the frame along with the cylinder stop assembly. The sear can be lifted out through the sideplate opening. The split spring (#425) can be disassembled from the cylinder stop, if required, by drifting out its retaining pin.

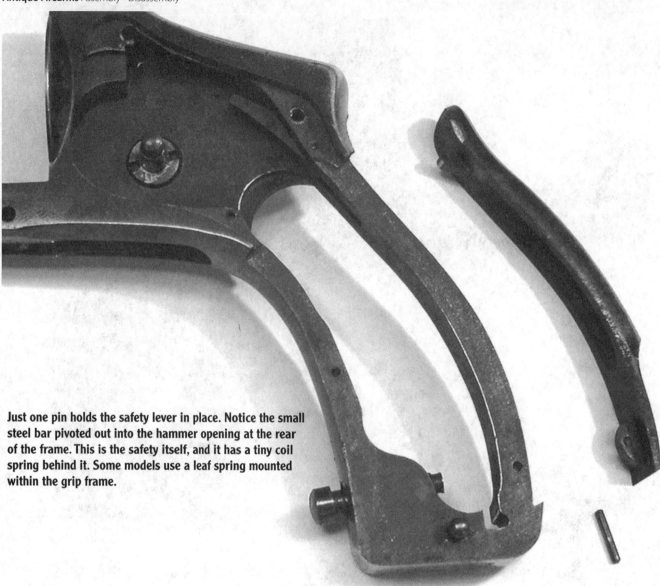

Just one pin holds the safety lever in place. Notice the small steel bar pivoted out into the hammer opening at the rear of the frame. This is the safety itself, and it has a tiny coil spring behind it. Some models use a leaf spring mounted within the grip frame.

6 To remove the safety: Located on the rear grip strap, the safety lever may be removed by first drifting out its retaining pin from the lower rear of the rear grip strap. Then hold in on the top of the lever while pivoting the bottom of the safety lever out to the rear and pull it down. The safety catch (#426) may be powered either by a coil spring or a leaf spring. The leaf-type spring will be located on the inside of the rear grip strap and is held in place by a cross pin. Coil-type springs (if equipped) are located within the safety catch recess in the frame, directly behind the top portion of the safety catch. On 2nd models only, the barrel catch is mounted at the top of the frame and can be removed by drifting out the pin located just behind the firing pin bushing cross pin. A small coil spring is located just under the barrel catch.

7 To remove the firing pin: The firing pin (#420) is retained in the frame by the firing pin bushing (#409), which is in turn held by a cross pin located near the top of the frame. To remove the firing pin, the cross pin must be drifted out of the frame. This should be done with a cup-tipped pin punch and a small hammer. (Be sure you solidly support the frame before trying to drive this pin out.) A small straight pin punch can be used to drive the firing pin and the firing pin bushing forward out of the frame. You will find a small coil spring (#412) at the front of the firing pin shoulder that retracts the firing pin after firing. Take note of the positions of these parts for reassembly.

.38 Safety Hammerless First Model
barrel catch components

barrel catch cover plate

bolt

bolt spring

cylinder catch

barrel catch

barrel

The barrel catch components of the 1st Model are unlike that of any other model.

8 To disassemble the cylinder: Insert five fired cartridge cases or dummy cartridges into the cylinder chambers for support. Grasp the extractor rod (#434) in the jaws of a drill chuck and rotate the cylinder (#398) in a counterclockwise direction to unscrew the extractor rod and its spring (#404) from the extractor (#431). Take note of the witness mark "dot" on one of the rear facing legs of the extractor. This dot should be aligned with the serial numbers on the rear face of the cylinder for reassembly.

To prevent damage to the extractor spring during its reassembly, start screwing the extractor rod into the threads on the extractor and stop after one turn. Hold the front 1/4-inch of the extractor rod tightly in a drill chuck or padded vise and then push the cylinder forward. This will compress the extractor spring while you tighten the extractor rod by turning the cylinder in a clockwise direction.

9 To disassemble the barrel, 1st Model only: (Note: This operation is recommended only for an experienced gunsmith.) Shape a screwdriver blade into a driving tool as shown in the illustration. With the barrel off the frame, support the bottom of the barrel topstrap by holding the bottom of the topstrap against a wooden bench top. Use the tool you just made and a small hammer to drive the barrel catch cover plate (see photo) toward the rear about 1/8 of an inch. The barrel catch cover plate may now be lifted straight up and off the barrel. Doing this exposes the bolt and spring, the Z-bar barrel catch and the cylinder hook (cylinder catch). With one finger, place a small amount of tension of the left side of the barrel catch. While you are holding the barrel catch there, use a small dental pick to lift the lock and its spring straight up out the top of the barrel topstrap. The Z-bar barrel catch can now be pushed out from either side of the topstrap and the cylinder hook lifted out the top. Pay close attention to the order in which these parts came out.

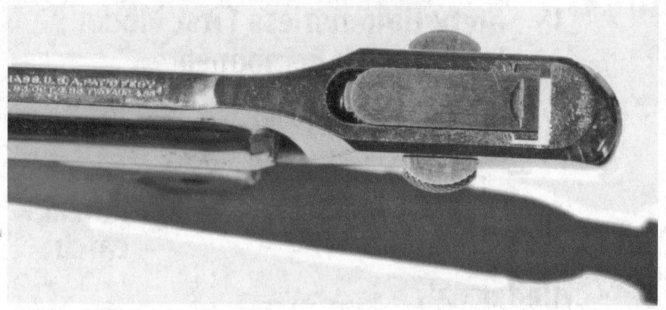

38nd1-bccover.tif: This photo shows the barrel catch cover being removed on the .38 New Departure 1st Model.

9a To disassemble the barrel, 2nd model: Drift out the rearmost of the two pins in the barrel top strap. The barrel catch (#234) and its coil spring will come out from the bottom of the top strap. Drifting out the foremost of the two pins in the barrel topstrap will free the cylinder hook (#230) and its spring for removal from the top.

9b To disassemble the barrel, 3rd Models: Unscrew and remove the tiny screw from the bottom rear of the thumb piece (#224). This allows you to remove the thumbpiece by lifting it straight up. 2nd and 3rd models: Drift out the rearmost of the two pins in the barrel topstrap and the barrel catch (#234) and its coil spring will come out from the bottom of the topstrap. Drifting out the foremost of the two pins in the barrel topstrap will free the cylinder hook (#230) and its coil spring for removal from the top.

9c To disassemble the barrel, 4th and 5th Models: Remove the barrel catch screw (#406) from the left side of the barrel topstrap. The barrel catch (#401) can now be withdrawn to the rear. Hold the barrel (#397) in a muzzle-up position and tap the rear of the barrel topstrap on a wooden bench-top. The barrel catch cam (#418) and barrel catch cam spring (#408) will fall out of their recess in the topstrap. Note the positions of the parts for reassembly.

REASSEMBLY

Reassemble the revolver in the exact reverse order of above.

Smith & Wesson .38
Double Action Perfected Model

Smith & Wesson's .38 Perfected was an unusual combination, using the top-break system on a modern, double action Hand Ejector frame. Author photos.

R he S&W .38 double action Perfected model was an unusual blending of the old and new. Introduced in 1909, it was the last "new" top-break revolver design the company would ever introduce. How it came to be in the first place is the subject of some speculation. An old story has it that a policeman was injured when a felon he was struggling with reached over to the policeman's .38 Double Action and unlatched the barrel, leaving the cop unarmed. The tale goes that when D.W. Wesson heard this, he combined the best of the top-break design with the best of the new Hand Ejector design to produce a top-break revolver that could not be opened so easily. Whether or not that story is true, the Perfected was a true hybrid, using the internal workings of the modern .32 Hand Ejector double action along with the fast reloading top-break barrel of the .38 Double Action. In order to open a Perfected, one must not only lift the conventional top-break barrel catch but also depress a thumb piece to release the center pin lock, just as on S&W revolvers with side-swing cylinders.

In 1909, revolvers using side-swing cylinders were really catching on and top-break revolvers were on their way out, so the Perfected was manufactured only up until 1920, with a total of just over 59,000 revolvers being produced. Like the earlier .38 Double Action designs, the Perfected Model held five shots in 38 S&W and was offered in 3-1/4-, 4-, 5- and 6-inch barrel lengths. The Perfected barrel and cylinder were the same physical size as the previous .38 top-break models and while the rear end of the revolver frame was borrowed from the .32 Hand Ejector, they all shared the same size of grip. Internally, the lockwork was the same as that of contemporary .32 Hand Ejectors, e.g., the 1903 - 3rd Change. The Perfected actions followed the rapid advances made in the .32 HE design until near the end of their production, by which time the last Perfected models used the same hammer block safety device as the .32 Hand Ejector Third Model.

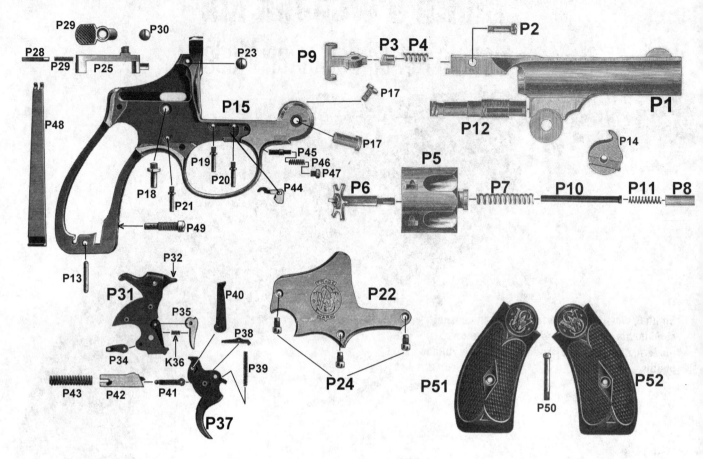

Parts List
NS - Not Shown

P1	Barrel	P18	Hammer Stud	P36	Sear Spring
P2	Barrel Catch Screw	P19	Trigger Stud	P37	Trigger
P3	Barrel Catch Cam	P20	Cylinder Stop Stud	P38	Hand Lever
P4	Barrel Catch Cam Spring	P21	Rebound Slide Stud	P39	Hand Lever Spring
P5	Cylinder	P22	Sideplate	P40	Hand
P6	Extractor	P23	Sideplate Screw, Large Head	P41	Trigger Lever
P7	Extractor Spring	P24	Sideplate Screw, Small Head	P42	Rebound Slide
P8	Extractor Rod	P25	Bolt	P43	Rebound Slide Spring
P9	Barrel Catch	P27	Bolt Plunger Spring	P44	Cylinder Stop
P10	Center Pin	P28	Bolt Plunger	P45	Cylinder Stop Plunger
P11	Center Pin Spring	P29	Thumb Piece	P46	Cylinder Stop Spring
P12	Base Pin	P30	Thumb Piece Nut	P47	Cylinder Stop Screw
P13	Grip Pin	P31	Hammer	P48	Mainspring
P14	Extractor Cam Assembly	P32	Hammer Nose (Firing Pin) (NS)	P49	Strain Screw
P15	Frame	P33	Hammer Nose Rivet	P50	Stock Screw
P16	Joint Pivot	P34	Stirrup	P51	Stock
P17	Joint Pivot Screw	P35	Sear	P52	Stock

Once the joint pivot screw is removed, and the joint pivot is driven out of the frame, the barrel assembly can be lifted clear of the frame.

DISASSEMBLY INSTRUCTIONS

1 First make sure the gun is unloaded. Grasp the revolver firmly by its grip, keeping your fingers away from the trigger (#P37) and being careful to keep the muzzle pointed in a safe direction. Push forward on the thumb-piece (#P29) while at the same time lifting up on the barrel catch (#P9). You may now tilt down the barrel, exposing the rear of the cylinder. At this point, check to be certain all the chambers are unloaded; if cartridges are present, remove them now and place them in a separate location from the gun.

2 To remove the cylinder (#P5): With the barrel still open, hold the barrel catch (#P9) in the up position and pull the cylinder to the rear while at the same time turning it in a counterclockwise direction. The cylinder will withdraw off the base pin (#P12), toward the rear.

3 To remove the barrel: Remove the joint pivot screw (#P17) from the left side of the hinge on the frame (#P15) and use an appropriate straight punch to drive the joint pivot (#P16) out of the frame toward the right side. Make a note of the witness mark on the joint pivot and its corresponding mark on the frame. These components must be aligned for reassembly. The barrel (#P1) is now loose and can be lifted up out of its joint with the frame. The extractor cam (#P14) is located between the ears of the barrel hinge and can now be pulled down and out of the barrel. Make note of the extractor cam's position for reassembly.

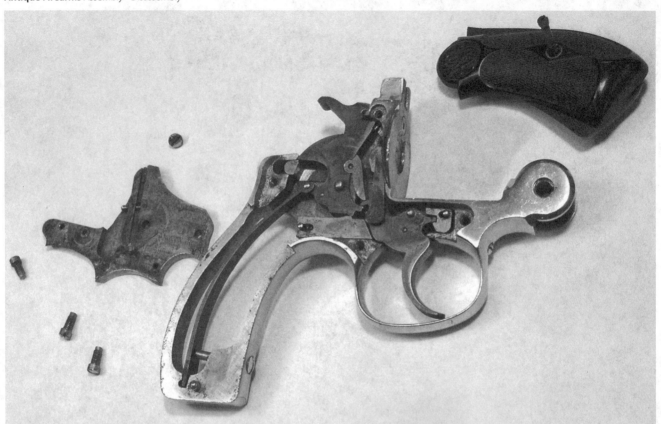

Viewed with the grips and sideplate removed, the Perfected action is identical to those of contemporary .32 Hand Ejector revolvers.

After the mainspring is removed, the hammer can be taken out. Notice that this one has a broken firing pin tip, the reason for its disassembly. S&W Hand Ejector firing pins are held in place by a hollow rivet.

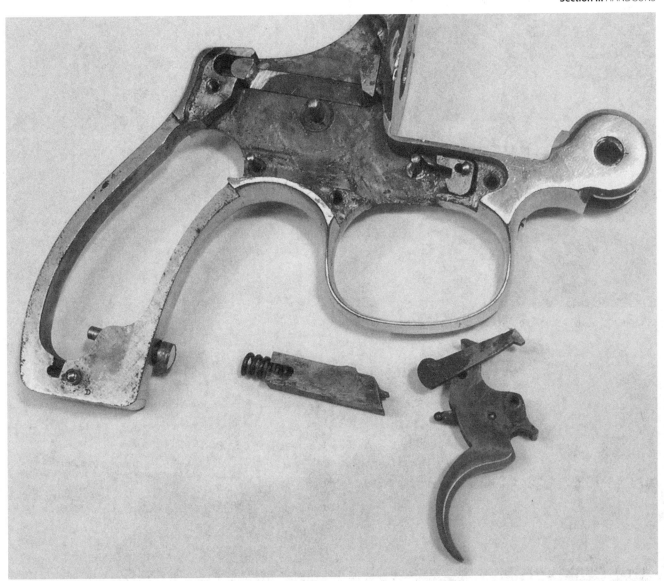

Here the rebound slide and its spring (which serves as the trigger spring) and the trigger are removed from the frame. The trigger and hand are the late type and the hand is shown out of its seat in the trigger. Tension for the hand is supplied by a spring and plunger in the sideplate.

4 To remove the grips and sideplate: Remove the stock screw (#P50) and lift off the stocks (#P51) and (#P52). Unscrew and remove the four sideplate screws (#P23) and (#P24). Turn the gun on its side with the sideplate facing up and hold the revolver by the barrel over a well-padded bench-top. Use a wooden or plastic mallet to strike the grip frame one or more sharp blows. This will cause the sideplate (#P22) to jump up and out of its seat with the frame. Never attempt to pry off the sideplate as you may damage it or the frame.

5 To remove the mainspring and hammer: Remove the strain screw (#P49) from the front of the grip frame. The mainspring (#P48) may now be disengaged from its seat at the lower grip frame and then disengaged from the hammer stirrup (#P34) at its top and withdrawn from the frame. While holding the thumb piece to the rear, pull the trigger all the way back. This will cause the hammer to rise. Pull the hammer straight up and off its stud (#P18) in the frame while the trigger is still pulled to the rear. Once the hammer is out, you can release the trigger.

6 To remove the trigger: Using a small screwdriver or suitable tool, pry up on the rear of the rebound slide (#P42) until it pivots up off its stud (#P21) in the frame. Use caution here: this action will free the coiled rebound slide spring (#P43), which is under heavy tension. Pull rearward to remove the rebound slide and its spring from the frame. With the trigger in the forward position, use a small tool to pivot the top of the hand (#P40) toward the rear until it is clear of the frame. While holding the hand to the rear, lift the trigger and hand assembly straight up and off its stud (#P19) on the frame.

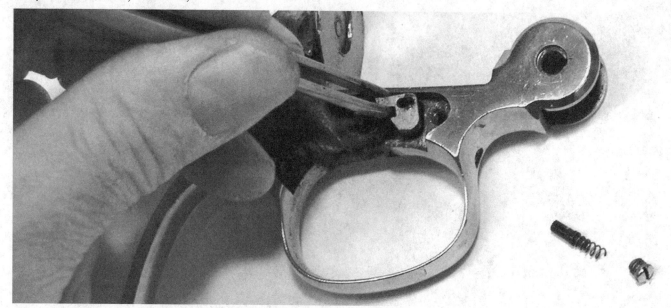

Perf-stopout.tif: Removing the Perfected cylinder stop.

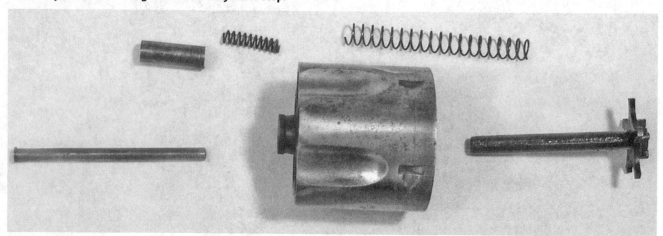

With the Perfected cylinder disassembled, you can see the hybridization of the top-break and the Hand Ejector designs.

7 To remove the cylinder stop: Unscrew and remove the cylinder stop screw (#P47) located at the front of the triggerguard. The cylinder stop plunger (#P45) and its spring (#P46) may now be withdrawn through the same screw hole. Push the ball-end of the cylinder stop (#P44) to its lowest position and then use a pair of shop tweezers to withdraw the cylinder stop straight up and off its stud (#P20) in the frame.

8 To disassemble the cylinder: Insert five fired cartridge cases into the chambers for support. Grasp the extractor rod (#P8) by its head in the jaws of a drill chuck and rotate the cylinder (#P5) in a counterclockwise direction to unscrew the extractor rod from the extractor (#P6). The extractor spring (#P7) and the center pin (#P1) may be pulled out from the front. The center pin spring (#P11) may be pulled out of the extractor rod. The extractor may be pushed out the back of the cylinder.

Note: To prevent damage to the extractor spring during reassembly, grasp the front 1/4 inch of the extractor rod by its head in the jaws of a drill chuck. Assemble the spring onto the extractor. Place the cylinder with the extractor over the rear end of the rod and push the cylinder forward, compressing the extractor spring as much as possible, all the while turning the cylinder in a clockwise direction until the threads have started by about one-half turn. Stop turning every one-half turn and allow the extractor to return by spring tension, and then push the cylinder in to recompress the spring and continue tightening in one-half turn increments until the rod is hand tight.

After the thumb piece nut and thumb piece are removed, the bolt is removed thus. Be mindful of the small spring and plunger that will come out its rear end when you remove it.

9 To disassemble the barrel: Remove the barrel catch screw (#P2) from the left side of the barrel topstrap. The barrel catch (#P9) can now be withdrawn to the rear. By holding the barrel in a muzzle-up position and tapping the rear of the barrel topstrap on a soft wooden bench-top, the barrel catch cam (#P3) and barrel catch cam spring (#P4) will fall out of their recess in the topstrap. Note their positions for reassembly.

10 To disassemble the trigger: Always support the trigger by laying it on its side on a flat steel block with holes drilled through it for the pins to be driven through. Pull the hand (#P40) straight out the right side of the trigger. Using a tiny pin punch, drift out the hand lever pin. (This is the only cross pin in the trigger.) Pull the hand lever (#P38) and its spring (#P3) out through the top of the trigger. For reassembly of the hand, the rear of the trigger lever must be held up while the hand is inserted back into the trigger to put it under spring pressure from the hand lever.

11 To disassemble the hammer: Always support the hammer by laying it on its side on a flat steel block with holes drilled through it for the pins to be driven through. Use a small pin punch and hammer to drive out the sear pin. The sear (#P35) and sear spring (#P36) are free and can be pulled off the front of the hammer. Driving out the stirrup pin frees the stirrup (#P34) for removal, but before doing so note the position of the stirrup before taking it off the hammer. It must be reassembled in this same position.

Further disassembly is not required for normal cleaning and maintenance of the revolver mechanism.

REASSEMBLY

Reverse the above procedures to reassemble the revolver.

Smith & Wesson Top Break
.44 Single Action Model No. 3
American Models and 1st & 2nd Russian Models

Smith & Wesson's .44 Model No. 3 of 1870 (1st Model American) was their first top-break. Subsequent American Models and the 1st Model Russian had a similar appearance and all had 8-inch barrels as standard. Notice that the hammer does not interlock with the barrel catch. Author photos.

S&W's Model Number 3 was a large-framed, six-shot revolver of top-break design, first introduced in 1870. The model No. 3 was manufactured in several variations that are today known commonly as the American, Russian, Schofield, New Model No. 3 and Double Action models.

The instructions below illustrate how to disassemble five mechanically similar variations of the Smith & Wesson Model No. 3 single action. They are the 1st, 2nd and 3rd Model American and 1st and 2nd Model Russian. The primary drawing illustrates basic component parts as applied to a 1st Model American; the inset shows some of the basic parts that differ in later models.

Produced from 1870 to 1874, the .44 Single Action American is a single action-only revolver with a square butt grip shape. This top-break revolver uses

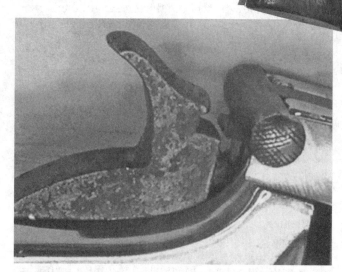

The 1st Model Russian and 2nd and 3rd Model American used an interlocking hammer and barrel catch that looked like this.

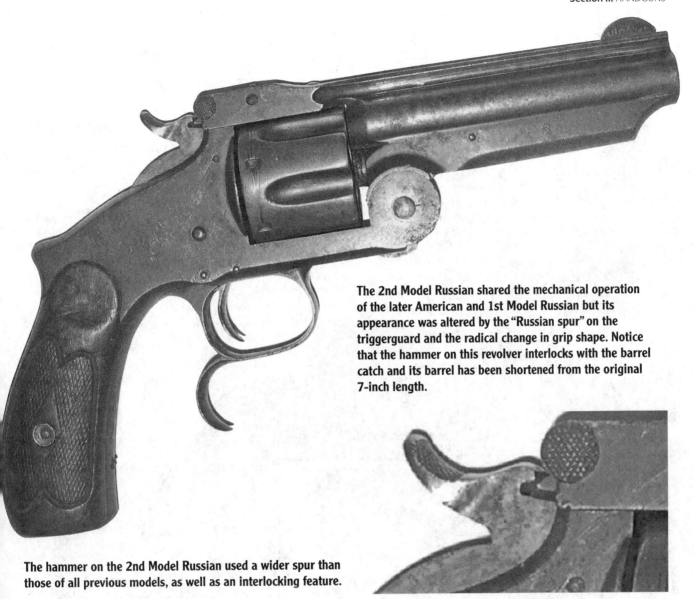

The 2nd Model Russian shared the mechanical operation of the later American and 1st Model Russian but its appearance was altered by the "Russian spur" on the triggerguard and the radical change in grip shape. Notice that the hammer on this revolver interlocks with the barrel catch and its barrel has been shortened from the original 7-inch length.

The hammer on the 2nd Model Russian used a wider spur than those of all previous models, as well as an interlocking feature.

a T-shaped barrel catch that is lifted up to unlock the revolver so the barrel and cylinder can be tilted downward. An advanced feature of the revolver was its top-break action with simultaneous, automatic ejection of the spent cases. The American Models were chambered in 44 S&W American centerfire cartridge. The First Model American lacked the barrel-hammer interlock feature of all later American and Russian model and was also the only Model No. 3 to use a one-piece joint pivot screw. The 2nd Model American sported the barrel-hammer interlock and several other mechanical improvements that were first introduced on the 1st Model Russian. Both 1st and 2nd model Americans used a hammer-actuated cylinder stop, while Russians and the 3rd, or last, Model American revolvers used a trigger-actuated cylinder stop.

Smith & Wesson's Russian Model was also built on the Model No. 3, .44 top-break frame. The 1st Model Russian was produced from 1871 to 1874 and its design features are essentially the same as the 2nd and 3rd Model American. Model No. 3 Russian Models are chambered in 44 S&W Russian centerfire. Both the American and the Russian models were also manufactured, though in lesser numbers, in 44 Rimfire. The 2nd Model Russian revolvers, introduced in 1873 and made until 1878, used a radically different rounded butt shape along with a "hook"-shaped spur at the bottom of the triggerguard, but they shared most of their internal mechanism with the 1st model Russian.

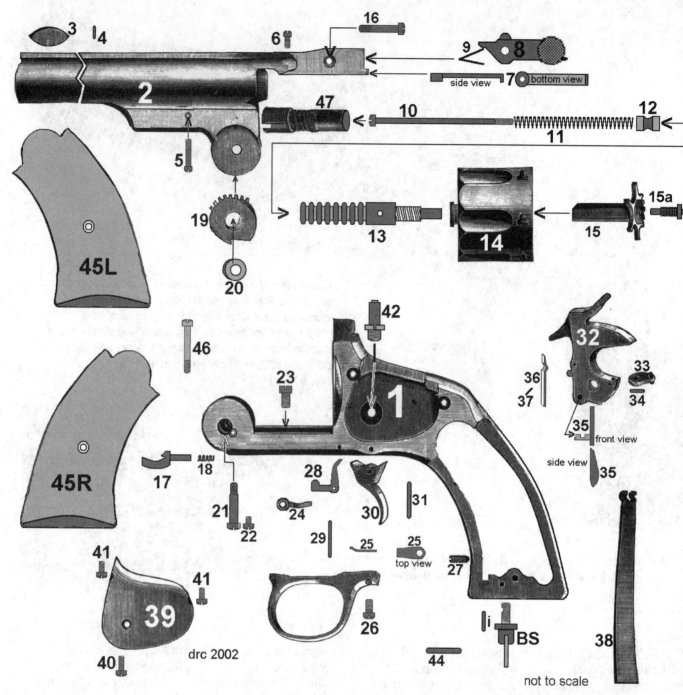

drc 2002

not to scale

Parts List

A1	Frame	A12	Extractor Collar	A23	Guard Screw, front	A36	Hand Spring
A2	Barrel	A13	Extractor Rack	A24	Cylinder Stop Spring	A37	Hand Spring Pin
A3	Front Sight	A14	Cylinder	A25	Trigger Spring	A38	Mainspring
A4	Front Sight Pin	A15	Extractor	A26	Guard Screw, rear	A39	Sideplate
A5	Cylinder Pin Screw	A16	Barrel Catch Screw	A27	Strain Screw	A40	Sideplate Screw, Center
A6	Cylinder Catch Screw (also see inset)	A17	Ratchet Pawl	A28	Cylinder Stop (also see inset)	A41	Sideplate Screw, Front or Rear
A7	Cylinder Catch (also see inset)	A18	Ratchet Pawl Spring	A29	Stop Pin	A42	Hammer Stud
A8	Barrel Catch (also see inset)	A19	Ratchet (gear)	A30	Trigger	A43	Triggerguard
		A20	Ratchet Bushing	A31	Trigger Pin	A44	Stock Pin
A9	Barrel Catch Spring	A21	Joint Pivot (also see inset)	A32	Hammer (also see inset)	A45	Stocks (grips)
A10	Rack Screw	A21A	Joint Pivot Screw (see inset)	A33	Hammer Stirrup	A46	Stock Screw
A11	Extractor Spring	A22	Joint Pivot Lock Screw (also see inset)	A34	Stirrup Pin	A47	Base Pin
				A35	Hand		

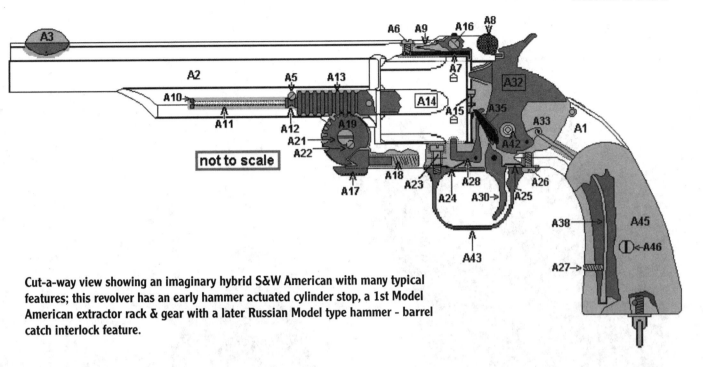

not to scale

Cut-a-way view showing an imaginary hybrid S&W American with many typical features; this revolver has an early hammer actuated cylinder stop, a 1st Model American extractor rack & gear with a later Russian Model type hammer - barrel catch interlock feature.

Distinguishing Features of the .44 Single Action American Models:

1) Chambered in 44 S&W American centerfire (standard) and 44 Henry rimfire, 6 shots.

2) Removable bowed triggerguard held on with two screws.

3) Long extractor housing under the barrel.

4) Gear-driven extraction mechanism with square (four-sided) extractor shank.

5) Square butt shape.

6) Hammer-actuated cylinder stop on 1st and 2nd models. Trigger-actuated stop on late 3rd models.

7) Flat-tipped trigger.

8) 1st model American has no barrel catch/ hammer interlock feature; all later models do.

9) 1st model American used a one-piece screw joint pivot, threaded into ear of frame. Later models used 2-piece joint pivot.

Distinguishing Features of the .44 Single Action Russian 1st and 2nd Models:

1) Chambered in 44 S&W Russian centerfire (standard) and 44 Henry rimfire, 6 shots.

2) Removable bowed triggerguard; 2nd model used a "spur" below the bow.

3) Long extractor housing under the barrel.

4) Gear-driven extraction with square (four-sided) extractor shank.

5) 1st Model uses square butt shape as the American and has an 8-inch barrel. 2nd Model uses rounded Russian plowhandle shape and 7-inch barrel.

6) Hammer-actuated cylinder stop on a very few 1st models. Trigger-actuated stop on all others.

7) Pointed tip trigger.

8) Russian models use barrel catch/hammer interlock feature.

9) 1st and early 2nd Russian models use two-piece joint pivot with lock screw; later 2nd Russian use a two-piece joint pivot with no lock screw.

Opening the barrel on the Model No. 3 S&W completely exposes all the cylinder chambers.

DISASSEMBLY INSTRUCTIONS

1 Make sure the revolver is unloaded. Grasp the revolver firmly by the grip with your right hand, being cautious to keep your finger away from the trigger (#A30). Pull the hammer (#A32) back to the loading position (one audible click). Lift up on the barrel catch (#A8) and tilt the revolver barrel all the way down to open the action. This exposes the rear of the cylinder chambers. Check to be certain the chambers are unloaded.

2 To remove the cylinder (#A14), 1st Model American: With the barrel remaining all the way open, unscrew the cylinder catch screw (#A6) several turns. You will note that this allows the rear "hook" of the cylinder catch (#A7) to pivot upward slightly, releasing the cylinder so it may move rearward. Remove the cylinder pin screw (#A5). The cylinder (#A14) may now be withdrawn back off the base pin (#A47), toward the rear and out of the gun. Note: If the cylinder is being removed only for simple cleaning, be sure you do not change the position of the

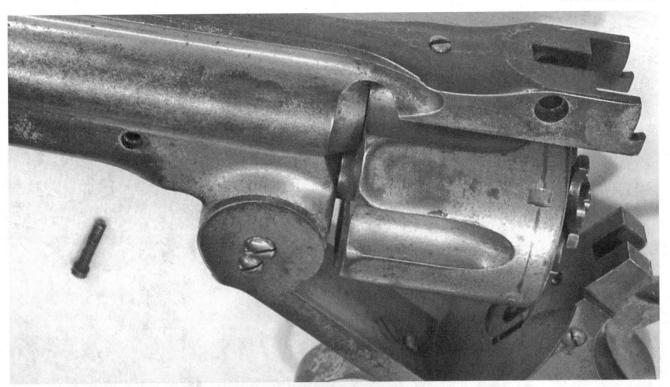

In the first photo, the cylinder catch screw has been loosened and the cylinder pin screw has been removed. The next photo shows the cylinder catch, the screw of which has been loosened, held up in the position that will permit the cylinder to be pulled off the barrel to the rear. The illustration is of a 1st Model American.

barrel, causing the ratchet gear (#A19) position to be disturbed; in this way the cylinder may be reinstalled in exactly the reverse order of the above procedure. 1st Model American extractor racks and ratchets have evenly-spaced gear teeth.

To remove the cylinder (#A14), 2nd and 3rd Models American and 1st and 2nd Models Russian: With the barrel remaining all the way open, unscrew the cylinder catch screw (#A6) several turns. Remove the cylinder pin screw (#A5) and pull the cylinder (#A14) slightly to the rear (about 1/4 inch) then push it back

forward. The cylinder catch (#A7) will move rearward 1/4 inch and may now be withdrawn by pulling it out the rear of the barrel. The cylinder (#A14) may now be withdrawn off the base pin (#A47) toward the rear and out of the gun. Note: If the cylinder is being removed only for simple cleaning, be sure you do not change the position of the barrel, causing the ratchet gear (#A19) position to be disturbed; in this way the cylinder may be reinstalled in exactly the reverse order of the above procedure. Later American and Russian model extractor racks and ratchets have evenly-spaced gear teeth with one double-spaced tooth.

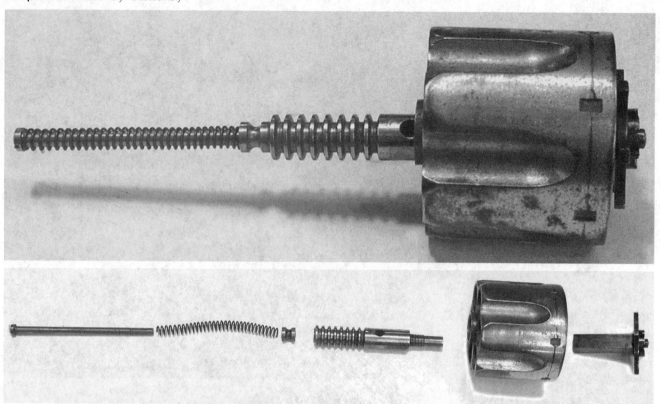

These two photos illustrate a 1st Model American cylinder before and after disassembly.

S&W extractors will have a small pip mark aligned with assembly markings on the cylinder.

The sideplate removed from the frame.

To disassemble the cylinder: Insert six fired cartridge cases or dummy cartridges into the chambers. Locate a strong, straight punch that will fit into the hole in the extractor rack (#A13) and unscrew the rack, using the punch as a wrench by turning it counterclockwise. The extractor (#A15) will push out to the rear of the cylinder. The extractor rack screw (#A10) may be unscrewed from the extractor using a screwdriver, and the extractor spring (#A11) and collar (#A12) will come free along with it.

Note: To assemble the cylinder, reverse the above procedure. To reinstall the cylinder in the weapon: Open the barrel all the way, noting the position of the gear teeth on the ratchet gear; to install the cylinder correctly with the barrel on the frame, the forwardmost tooth of the ratchet gear must be standing straight up. In other words, that tooth must be pointing exactly perpendicular to the bore so that as the cylinder is reinstalled, the forward tooth on the extractor rack will engage the forward tooth on the ratchet gear. While holding the extractor tightly into the cylinder with your thumb, slide the cylinder assembly forward all the way back into the rear of the base pin until it will not move any farther forward. Once the cylinder has been installed correctly, the cylinder catch screw (#A6) may be retightened (1st Model), or the cylinder catch (#A7) may be slid back into place on the barrel and the cylinder catch screw (#A6) may be retightened.

Reassembly tip: Install the assembled cylinder onto the barrel before installing the barrel on the frame. Next, install the ratchet gear so the rearmost tooth (the one large tooth on 2nd and 3rd Models) is standing straight up and perpendicular to the bore, so that as the gear is reinstalled, the rear tooth (or large tooth) on the extractor rack engages the rear tooth (or large tooth) on the ratchet gear. On both parts, all the remaining gear teeth should be forward of the engaged teeth. Now you can reinstall the barrel-cylinder assembly on the frame.

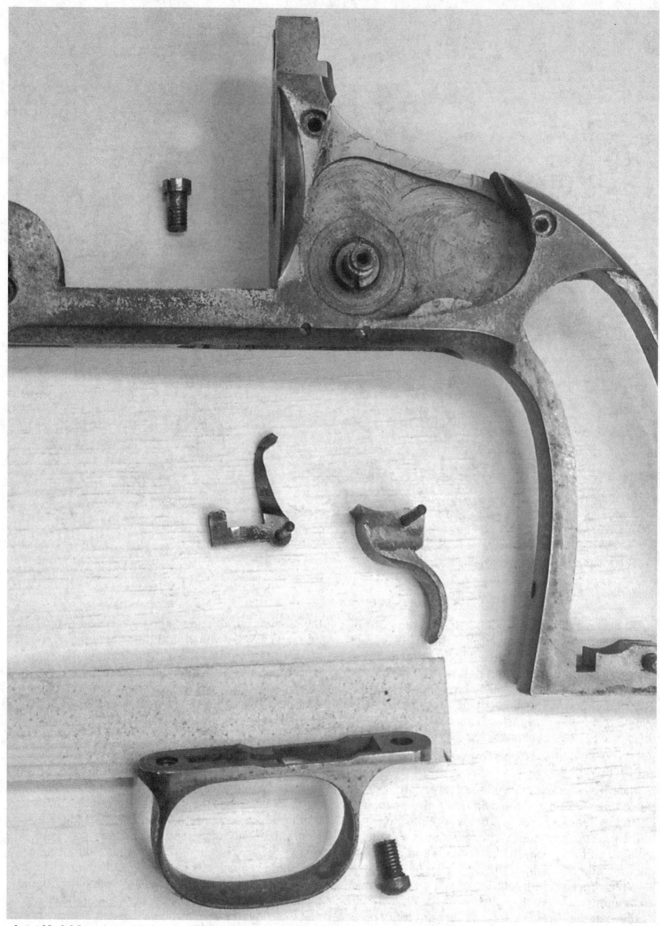

A 1st Model American .44 shown with its triggerguard and action components disassembled.

An American mainspring is shown being compressed with spreader pliers so that its top may be disengaged from the hammer stirrup.

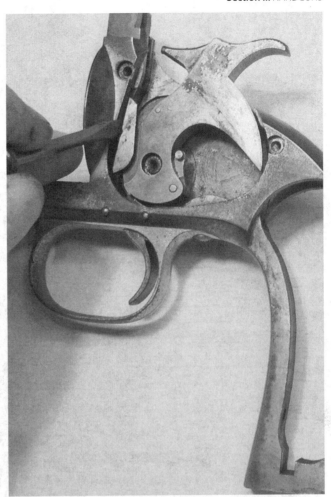

The hammer may be lifted out of the frame as the hand is held to the rear with a small tool.

3 Grips, sideplate and mainspring removal: Remove the stock screw (#47) and lift off the stocks (#45). Remove the three sideplate screws (#A40) and (#A41). Turn the frame on its side, holding it by the hinge with the sideplate facing up over a padded surface. Strike the grip frame a sharp blow or two using a plastic or hardwood mallet. This will cause the sideplate (#A39) to jump up out of its seat in the frame for removal. Never attempt to pry off the sideplate; you may cause permanent damage to the frame and the sideplate. Using a pair of spreader pliers, pry down on the top rear of the mainspring (#A3) and disengage it from the hammer stirrup (#A33). Loosen the mainspring strain screw (#A27). The mainspring (#A38) may be removed through the side of the grip frame (#A1).

4 Triggerguard and hammer removal: Remove the two guard screws (#A23) and (A26), and then the guard (#A43) may be pulled down and off the frame. Use care: the trigger spring (#A25) and cylinder stop spring (#A24) are held in place by the guard and its screws, and these springs are now loose, so notice their positions for reassembly later. Using a small screwdriver as a lever, pull back on the hand (#A35) so it pivots to the rear. While you are holding the hand back, rotate the hammer (#A32) into a position where it will clear the frame opening. Lift the hammer up off the hammer stud (#A42) and out of the frame. Now that the hammer is out of the gun, the hand (#A35) may be rotated forward one-half turn and pulled straight up and out of the hammer. (On later hands, notice the back end of the hand shaft is ground, making it a tool to enable you to reassemble the hand more easily.) The trigger (#A30) and cylinder stop (#A28) are held in place by cross pins which may be drifted out from either side of the frame using a suitable pin punch. On 1st Model Americans these pins are the same diameter; later guns use a larger diameter trigger pin.

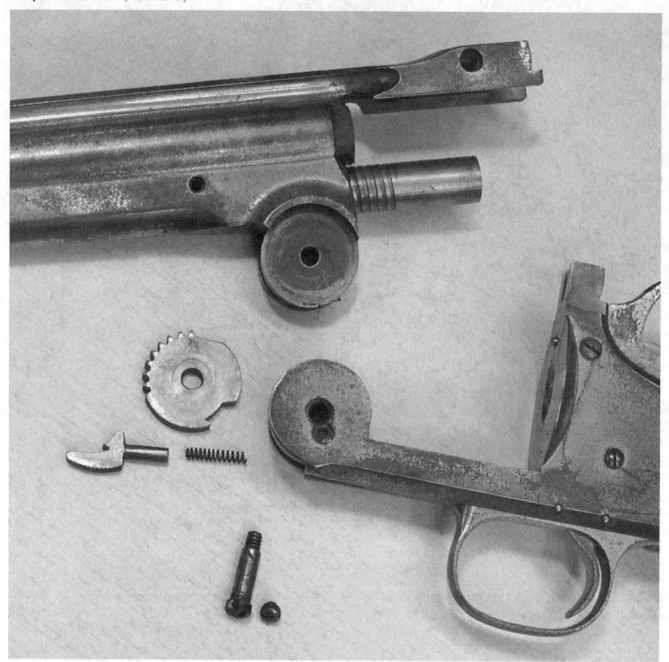

Here, the joint pivot has been removed, allowing the barrel to be lifted out of the frame hinge with the related parts. The illustration is of a 1st Model American.

5 To remove the barrel, 1st Model American: With the barrel opened just slightly, remove the joint pivot lock screw (#A22) from the left side of the frame joint. The joint pivot (#A21) may now be unscrewed and removed out of the left frame joint. Hold the ratchet pawl (#A17) to the rear with your thumb. The barrel (#A2) is now free to be lifted up and out of the frame joint.

For all later American, 1st and early 2nd Russian Models: With the barrel opened just slightly, remove the joint pivot screw (#A21A) from the right side of the frame joint. Next, remove the joint pivot lock screw from the left side of the frame joint. The joint pivot (#A21) may now be pushed out from right to left and removed out of the left frame joint. Hold the ratchet pawl (#A17) to the rear with your thumb. The barrel (#A2) is now free to be lifted up and out of the frame joint.

Once the barrel is removed, ease off on the ratchet pawl (#A17) with your thumb. The pawl can now be removed through the front of the frame joint, along with its spring (#A18). The ratchet (#A19) may be removed from the center of the barrel hinge joint by pulling it downward, making careful note of the ratchet gear's position for reassembly (see above). The ratchet bushing (#A20) (not shown) is at the center

Late American And Russian Parts Differences

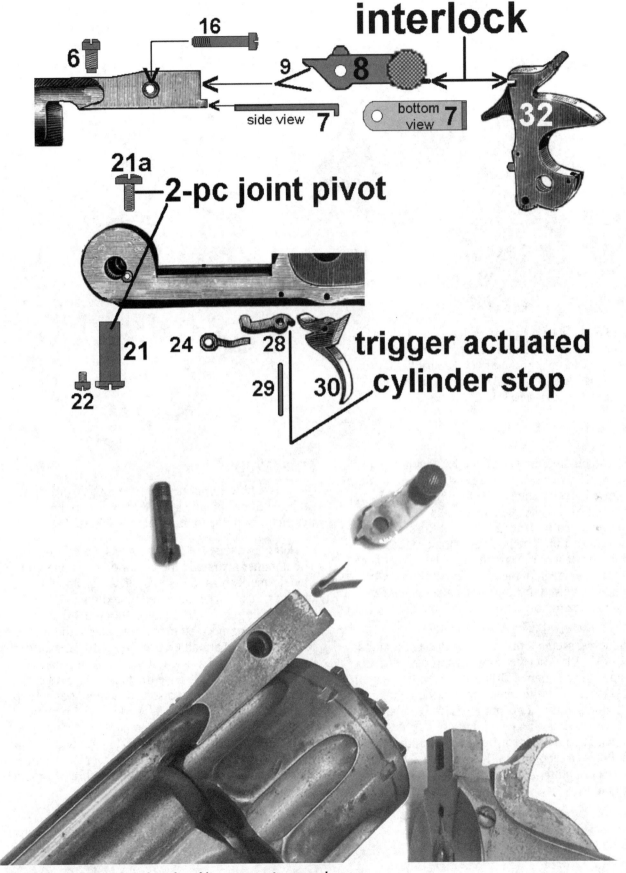

interlock

6

16

9

8

side view 7

bottom view 7

32

21a

2-pc joint pivot

21

24

28

trigger actuated

22

29

30

cylinder stop

This photos shows the barrel catch and its components removed.

The S&W Model No. 3 hammer with the hand installed. This one is from a 1st Model American. Notice it has no interlocking lip in front of the spur. The small "nub" to the right of the hand is the cylinder stop cam for the early hammer-actuated cylinder stop.

of the ratchet and may be pushed out with finger pressure. The barrel catch screw (#A16) can now be unscrewed, freeing the barrel catch (#A8) and barrel catch spring (#A9) for removal through the rear of the barrel topstrap. Later 2nd Model Russians used a different two-piece joint pivot without a lock screw; the joint pivot screw enters from the left. 1st Model Americans: If desired, the cylinder catch screw (#A6) may be unscrewed, freeing the cylinder catch (#A7), which may be removed from the bottom of the barrel topstrap.

6 To disassemble the hammer: Rotate the hand (#A35) 180 degrees forward and pull it out the left side of the hammer. Drift out the handspring pin ((#A37) located at the center front of the hammer, which holds in the handspring (#A36). The hand spring can now be slid forward out of its recess in the hammer. The hammer stirrup (#A33) can be removed by drifting out its pin (#A34) at the rear of the hammer. Note the orientation of the stirrup (#A33) for later reassembly.

REASSEMBLY

Reassemble components in the reverse order of disassembly, paying special attention to the instructions above to reinstall the cylinder.

Notes: Two types of cylinder stops may be found. The hammer-actuated type is found on 1st and 2nd model Americans and on a very few 1st Model Russian revolvers. The trigger-actuated type (illustrated in the inset drawing) is found on later 2nd and 3rd Model Americans, on most 1st model and all on 2nd model Russians. There are differences in the triggers used with both stop types. The latter type of stop has a shoulder on its front, above the finger piece, that actuates the stop, and it also uses a more pointed tip on the finger piece. The early models of stop do not have this shoulder on the trigger and have a squared tip on the finger piece. Also, the diameter of the trigger pin (#A31) was increased on all Model No. 3s made after the First Model American, and the frame around the trigger pin was reinforced.

Smith & Wesson Model No. 3 Russian
Third Model .44 Single Action

This well-worn 3rd Model Russian was produced in Berlin, Germany by Ludwig Lowe & Co. for the Russian military. It shares all the typical Third or New Model features with its S&W parent and the Russian copy made at Tula arsenal. Author photos.

The Third Model Russian, otherwise known as the New Model Russian, was the last, the most copied, and most refined model in the Russian contract series of Smith & Wesson's large frame top-break revolvers, known also as the Model No. 3 frame size. Third Model Russians, sometimes called the Cavalry Model, retained the size and appearance of the Second Model Russian but incorporated the following changes: a somewhat shortened extractor housing under the barrel contained a more simplified extraction mechanism, using a pivoted-pawl in place of the sliding-pawl. The barrel length was shortened to 6-1/2 inches and the front sight was forged in one piece with the barrel. A large knurled thumbscrew was added to the barrel topstrap in order to facilitate cylinder removal. Also, only one screw was used to retain the triggerguard at its front, the rear being fastened to the frame by means of a machined lip.

Between 1874 and 1878, some 60,638 of these revolvers were manufactured by Smith & Wesson, 41,138 of which were military contract arms manufactured for the Russian government. Five thousand were also made in 44 Rimfire for the Turkish government. Close copies of the Third Model Russian were also manufactured in large quantities in Germany by Ludwig Lowe of Berlin; in Russia at the Tula Arsenal and in both Spain and Belgium in unknown but probably large quantities. Smith & Wesson-made Russian contract revolvers carry Cyrillic markings on the barrel ribs with KO or HK inspectors markings next to the Tsarist Imperial Russian Eagle.

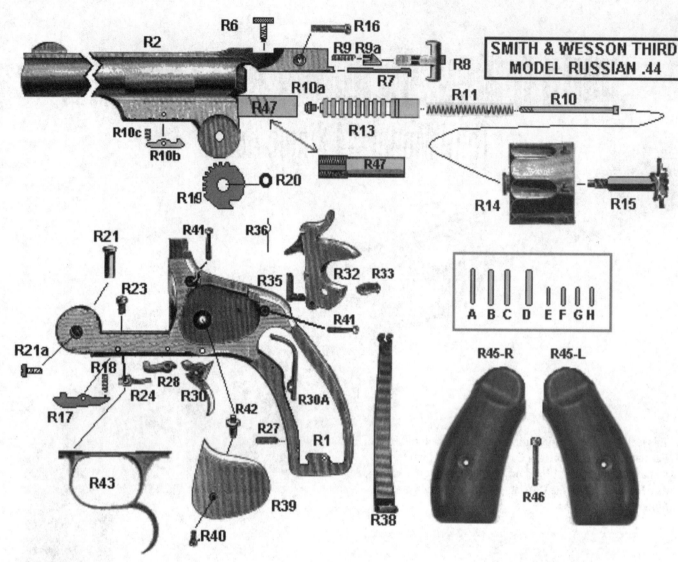

SMITH & WESSON THIRD
MODEL RUSSIAN .44

Parts List

R1	Frame	R17	Ratchet Pawl	R41	Sideplate Screw, front or rear
R2	Barrel	R18	Ratchet Pawl Spring	R42	Hammer Stud
R6	Cylinder Catch Screw	R19	Ratchet (Gear)	R43	Triggerguard
R7	Cylinder Catch	R20	Ratchet Bushing	R45	Stocks (Grips)
R8	Barrel Catch	R21	Joint Pivot	R46	Stock Screw
R9	Barrel Catch Spring	R21A	Joint Pivot Screw	R47	Base Pin
R9A	Barrel Catch Cam	R23	Guard Screw	A	Cylinder Stop Pin
R10	Extractor rack pin (S&W)	R24	Cylinder Stop Spring	B	Trigger Pin
R10	Extractor Rack Screw	R27	Strain Screw	C	Ratchet Pawl Pin
	(Russian and German only)	R28	Cylinder Stop	D	Stock Pin
R10A	Extractor Rack Screw Nut	R30	Trigger	E	Hand Spring Pin
	(Russian and German only)	R30A	Trigger Spring	F	Stirrup Pin
R10B	Extractor Catch	R32	Hammer	G	Trigger Spring Pin
R10C	Extractor Catch Spring	R33	Hammer Stirrup	H	Extractor Catch Pin, Smith &
R11	Extractor Spring	R35	Hand		Wesson Top Break .44 Single
R13	Extractor Rack	R36	Hand Spring		Action, Third or New Model
R14	Cylinder	R38	Mainspring		Russian
R15	Extractor	R39	Sideplate		
R16	Barrel Catch Screw	R40	Sideplate Screw, center		

After loosening the cylinder catch screw, the front of the extractor catch is pushed up. This frees the cylinder for removal. The cylinder catch will be pushed back slightly by the cylinder but stays in the barrel.

The Third Model Russian barrel viewed from the top. The large screw just forward of the barrel catch is the cylinder catch screw; it must be loosened for cylinder removal.

DISASSEMBLY INSTRUCTIONS

1 First, be sure the revolver is unloaded. Hold the revolver firmly in one hand by its grip, always keeping your fingers away from the trigger (#R30) and the muzzle in a safe direction. Pull the hammer very slightly to the rear, until you hear an audible click. With your other hand, lift up on the barrel catch (#R8) and tilt the revolver barrel all the way down toward the floor to open the barrel. This exposes the rear of the cylinder. Check to be certain all chambers in the cylinder are unloaded. If cartridges are present, remove them and place them in a location apart from the revolver. To remove the cylinder (#R14): with the barrel still opened all the way, unscrew the cylinder catch screw (#R6) several turns (this is the large

knurled screw located in the barrel topstrap). Depress the front of the extractor rack catch (#R10A) and pull the cylinder (#R14) to the rear. The cylinder can be withdrawn off the base pin (#R47) toward the rear.

Note: The cylinder catch (#R7) will be partially removed by the action of removing the cylinder. To completely remove the cylinder catch, simply pull it to the rear. Pay attention to this part so that it may be reinstalled properly after the cylinder is installed. Be aware that on most third model Russians the cylinder catch also acts as a floorplate for the barrel catch assembly (see below) and that these parts may fall out.

The barrel removed, showing the joint pivot, its screw and ratchet gear, which has been pulled down out of the barrel hinge. Notice that the gear has one large tooth – and remember this for reassembly.

2 To remove the barrel: Unscrew and remove the joint pivot screw (#R21A) from the left side of the hinge on the frame (#R1) and use an appropriate straight punch to drive the joint pivot (#R21) out of the frame toward the right side. Make note of the witness mark on the joint pivot and its corresponding mark on the frame; these have to be aligned for reassembly. The barrel (#R2) is now loose and may be lifted up out of its joint with the frame. The extractor gear (#R19) is located between the ears of the barrel hinge and may be pulled down and out of the barrel. Make careful note of the extractor gear's position for reassembly.

Reassembly tip: Install the assembled cylinder onto the barrel before installing the barrel on the frame. Next, install the ratchet gear so the one large tooth is standing straight up and perpendicular to the bore, so that as the gear is reinstalled, the large tooth on the extractor rack will engage with the large tooth on the ratchet gear. On both parts, all the small teeth should be forward of the large teeth. Now you may reinstall the barrel-cylinder assembly to the frame.

3 To remove the grips and sideplate: Remove the stock screw (#R46) and lift off the stocks (#R45-R) and (#R45-L). Unscrew and remove the two long sideplate screws (#R41) and the center sideplate screw (#R40). Holding it by the hinge, turn the frame on its side, sideplate facing up, over a padded surface. Strike the grip frame a sharp blow or two using a plastic or hardwood mallet. This will cause the sideplate (#R39) to jump up out of its seat in the frame for removal. Never attempt to pry off the sideplate.

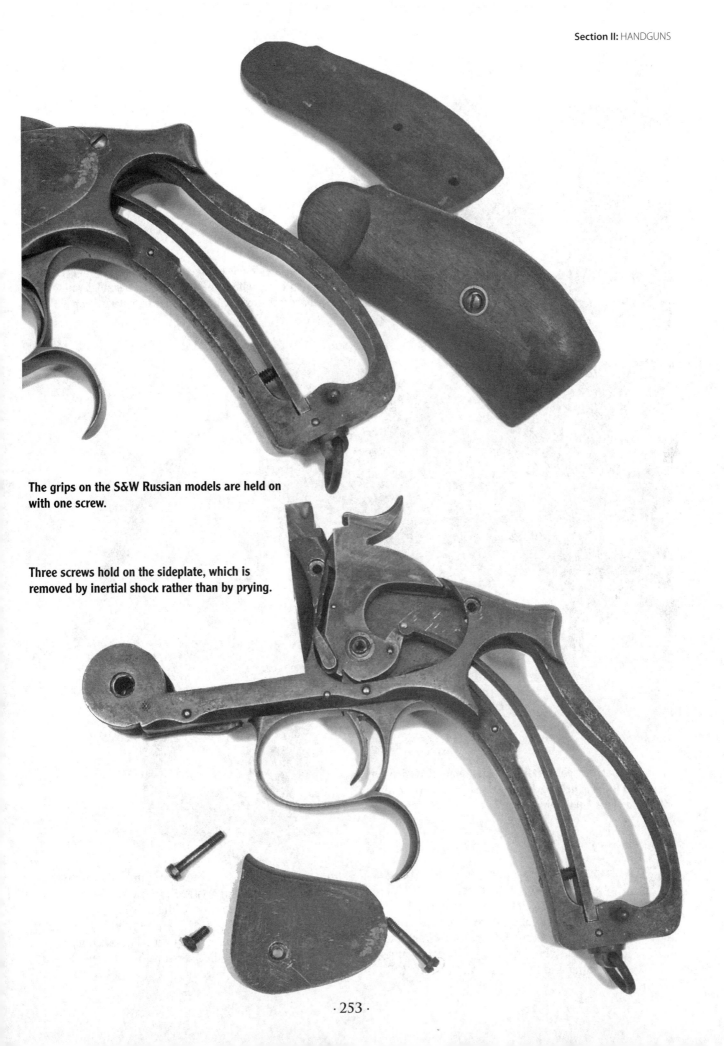

The grips on the S&W Russian models are held on with one screw.

Three screws hold on the sideplate, which is removed by inertial shock rather than by prying.

Once the sideplate is off, the rear of the mainspring can be compressed with spreader pliers. This enables you to disconnect the mainspring from the hammer stirrup.

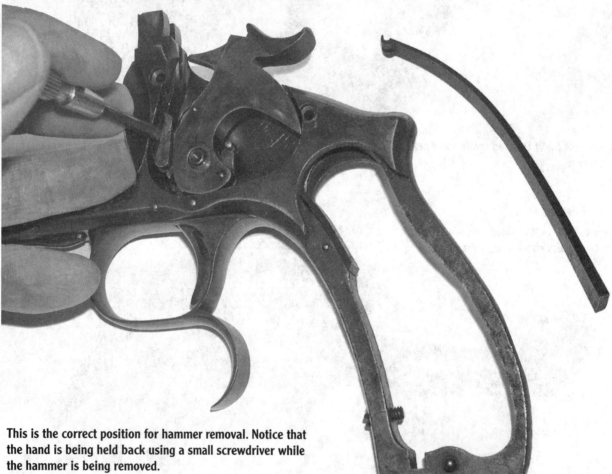

This is the correct position for hammer removal. Notice that the hand is being held back using a small screwdriver while the hammer is being removed.

4 To remove the mainspring and hammer: Use a pair of spreader pliers to compress the top of the mainspring (#R38) so the hammer stirrup (#R33) may be rotated forward and out of its seat between the ears at the top of the mainspring. Loosen the strain screw (#R27) located in the bottom front of the front grip strap on the frame and remove the mainspring (#R38) from the top of the frame side. Carefully rotate the hand (#R35) to the rear using a small screwdriver as a lever and while holding the hand to the rear, pull the trigger (#R30) and hold it to the rear. The hammer (#R32) may be rotated about half-way back and carefully pulled upward off its hammer stud (#R42) and out of the frame.

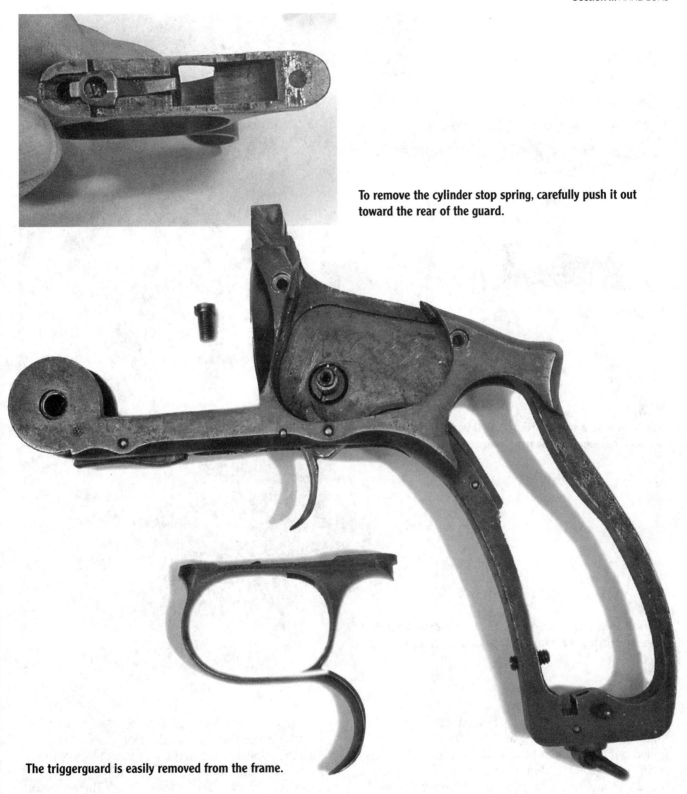

To remove the cylinder stop spring, carefully push it out toward the rear of the guard.

The triggerguard is easily removed from the frame.

5 To remove the triggerguard: Unscrew and remove the triggerguard screw (#R23) located inside the cylinder opening of the frame, on the bottom. Pull down on the front of the triggerguard (#R43) and then pull it forward to disengage the lip at the rear of the guard from the frame. Remove it and the cylinder stop spring (#R24) as an assembly, noting their position for reassembly.

6 To disassemble the action: Use a cup-tipped pin punch and hammer to drift out the cylinder stop pin (this is the center of the three pins that pass through the frame from side to side) and push the cylinder stop (#R28) out toward the bottom using a small punch through its window in the frame, under the area where the cylinder rotates. Use the same punch and hammer to drift out the trigger pin (this is

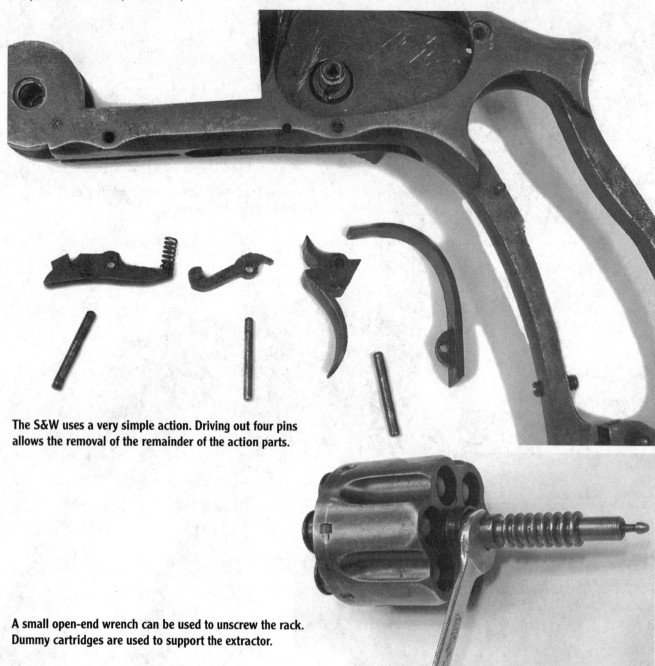

The S&W uses a very simple action. Driving out four pins allows the removal of the remainder of the action parts.

A small open-end wrench can be used to unscrew the rack. Dummy cartridges are used to support the extractor.

the rearmost of the three pins that pass through the frame from side to side). The trigger (#R30) may be pulled out through the bottom of the frame. The trigger spring (#R30A) is held into the frame by a pin that passes through the front grip strap. Remove this pin and the trigger spring (#R30A) will lift out of its seat in the frame. Use the same cup-tipped pin punch and hammer to drift out the front pin in the frame side; this is the ratchet pawl pin (C). The ratchet pawl (#R17) and its spring (#R18) may be pulled out to the bottom.

7 To disassemble the cylinder: Insert six fired cartridge cases into the chambers for support. Grasp the extractor ratchet (#R13) on its flats with a suitable spanner wrench and rotate the cylinder

(#R14) in a counterclockwise direction to unscrew the extractor ratchet (#R13) from the extractor (#R15). Notice the "dot" on one of the rear facing legs of the extractor star: this should be aligned with the serial numbers on the cylinder for reassembly. The extractor rack pin on S&W revolvers (#R10) is a one-piece component. The extractor rack screw (#R10) and its nut (#R10) are threaded together on many Tula- and Lowe-manufactured revolvers, but unless it has been taken apart previously, this is a riveted assembly (i.e., with the forward end of the screw thread riveted over the nut) held captive with the extractor rack spring (#R11) inside the extractor rack (#R13). Further disassembly is not recommended.

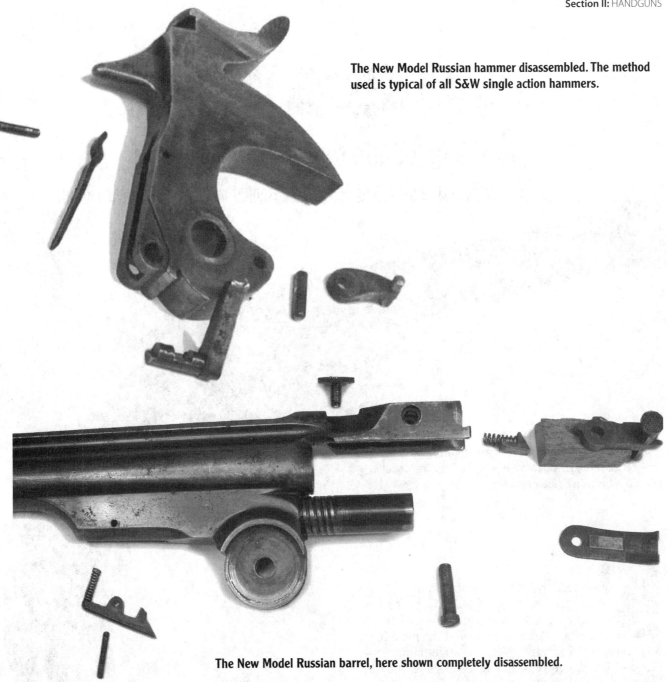

The New Model Russian hammer disassembled. The method used is typical of all S&W single action hammers.

The New Model Russian barrel, here shown completely disassembled.

8 To disassemble the hammer: Rotate the hand (#R35) 180 degrees forward and pull it up and out of the hammer. Use a small pin punch to drift out the pin in the center front of the hammer that holds in the handspring (#R36). The handspring now may be slid out of its recess in the hammer. The hammer stirrup (#R33) is removed by first drifting out its pin at the rear of the hammer. Be sure to make note of the position of the stirrup (#R33) for reassembly.

9 To disassemble the barrel: Unscrew and remove the barrel catch screw (#R16) from the left side of the barrel topstrap. The barrel catch (#R8) may be withdrawn to the rear. By holding the barrel (#R2) in a muzzle-up position and tapping the rear of the barrel topstrap on a wooden bench-top, the barrel catch cam (#R9A) and barrel catch cam spring (#R9) will fall out of their recess in the topstrap. Note their positions for reassembly. Using a small cup-tipped pin punch, drift out the extractor catch pin (located in the lower portion of the barrel extractor housing). Remove the extractor catch (#10C) and extractor catch spring (#10B) out the bottom of the barrel.

REASSEMBLY

Reassemble the revolver in reverse order of the above, paying special attention as you do to the relationships of the gear teeth on the extractor rack and the extractor gear (see the reassembly tip above).

Smith & Wesson Top-Break

.44 Single Action/New Model No. Three

(Including 32-44 and 38-44 Target & New Model No. 3 Frontier Model .320 Revolving Rifle)

Smith & Wesson's New Model No. 3 .44 was the last and most advanced in a long line of large-framed, top-break revolvers. This particular revolver is the Frontier Model in 44-40 Winchester. Author photos.

Introduced in 1878 and made until 1912, the commercial New Model No. 3 was a success with around 35,796 produced. The New Model No. 3 was the last and the most highly refined model in Smith & Wesson's large-frame, top-break series of revolvers. This revolver's size was also known as the Model No. 3 size, and as such it retained the basic size and appearance of the Model No. 3 Russian except with a shortened ejector housing under the barrel and a new and (for most) more comfortable rounded butt grip shape. The New Model was the first Model No. 3 that was cataloged with optional factory target sights. The standard caliber was 44 S&W Russian although an array of optional calibers was available including 32 S&W, 32/44 S&W, 320 Rifle, 38 S&W, 38/44 S&W, 38/40 Winchester, 41 S&W, 44 Rimfire, 44 American, 44/40 Winchester, 45 S&W, 450 Revolver, 45 Webley, 455 Mark I, 455 Mark II.

An inherently accurate revolver, as were most Models No. 3, it soon became a popular competition target revolver during the 1880s and 1890s. Annie Oakley and several other well-known, world-class target shooters of the day used them.

Standard New Model No. 3s were manufactured with a rebounding hammer, as was the smaller, S&W .32 Single Action of the same time. This feature was omitted on target-sighted models. New Model No. 3 revolvers chambered for the .38 and .44 Winchester calibers were known as the Frontier Model. These revolvers had specially lengthened frames, cylinders and topstraps that allowed them to accommodate the longer Winchester rifle cartridge. To help tell the difference between the two here is an identification tip: Standard length cylinders are 1-7/16 inches long; Frontier cylinders are 1-9/16 inches long. On account of slow sales in Winchester calibers, the S&W factory chambered some New Models with the longer frame configuration in 44 S&W Russian. Quite a few of these were later sold to the Japanese Navy.

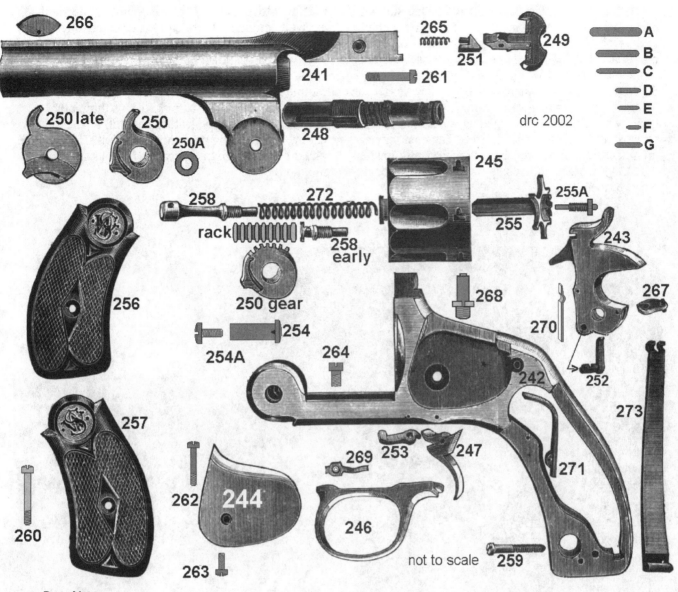

drc 2002

rack

not to scale

Parts List

241	Barrel	254	Joint Pivot	268	Hammer Stud
242	Frame	254A	Joint Pivot Screw	269	Cylinder Stop Spring
243	Hammer	255	Extractor	270	Hand Spring
244	Sideplate	256	Stock (Grip)	271	Trigger Spring
245	Cylinder	257	Stock (Grip)	272	Extractor Spring
246	Triggerguard	258	Extractor Rod	273	Mainspring
247	Trigger	259	Strain Screw	A	Stock (Grip) Pin
248	Base Pin	260	Stock Screw	B	Trigger Pin
249	Barrel Catch	261	Barrel Catch Screw	C	Cylinder Stop Pin
250	Extractor Cam (early pivoted pawl)	262	Sideplate Screw, Long	D	Stirrup Pin
		263	Sideplate Screw, Short	E	Handspring Pin
250A	Extractor Cam (late, slide bar)	264	Triggerguard Screw	F	Front Sight Pin
		265	Barrel Catch Cam Spring	G	Trigger Spring Pin
251	Barrel Catch Cam	266	Front Sight		
252	Hand	267	Stirrup, Rebounding		
253	Cylinder Stop	267A	Stirrup, Non-rebounding, Target		

The New Model No. 3 was offered with a standard 6-1/2-inch barrel with some as short as 3-1/2 inches and as long as 8 inches. Beginning in 1886, S&W also manufactured smaller-caliber target-specific versions of the New Model No. 3 in 32-44 S&W and 38-44 S&W target as a separately-cataloged New Model No. 3 Target. These smaller-caliber models were made in their own serial number range and were equipped with target sights and 6-1/2-inch barrels. The company also manufactured an odd revolver/rifle that was known as the .320 Revolving Rifle using the basic New Model No. 3 frame.

New Model No. 3 extractor operating mechanisms evolved gradually. The factory used three different types of mechanisms during the production of the revolver (parts shown in the illustration). The earliest or 1st type was a rack and gear with a pivoting pawl mounted on the gear (the barrels used with this early system had longer extractor housings than later barrels.) The 2nd type featured a hook-type extractor cam with a pivoting pawl mounted on it. The 3rd type had a hook-type extractor cam with a sliding pawl mounted on it.

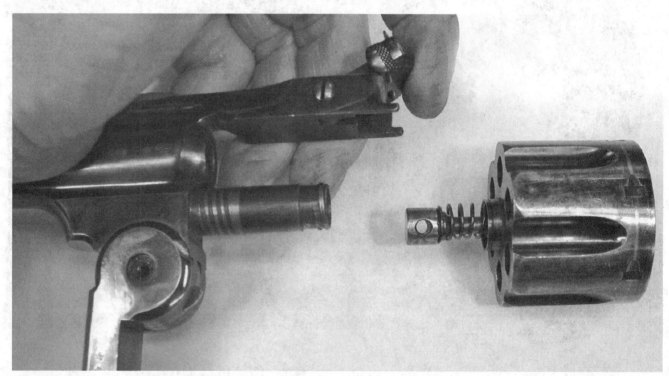

Holding the barrel catch up moves the cylinder catch out of the way so the cylinder may be unscrewed and pulled backward off the base pin.

DISASSEMBLY INSTRUCTIONS

1 First, be sure the revolver is unloaded. Hold the revolver firmly in one hand by its grip, always paying attention to keep your fingers away from the trigger and the muzzle pointed in a safe direction. It is necessary to pull the hammer very slightly to the rear until you hear an audible click before the barrel catch may be operated. With your other hand, lift up on the barrel catch (#249) and tilt the revolver barrel all the way down to open the barrel. This exposes the rear of the cylinder so you can check to be certain all chambers in the cylinder are unloaded. If cartridges are present, remove them and place them in a location apart from the revolver.

2 To remove the cylinder (#245): Hold the barrel catch (#249) in the up position and pull the cylinder (#245) to the rear while you are turning it in a counterclockwise direction. The cylinder may be withdrawn off the base pin (#248), toward the rear.

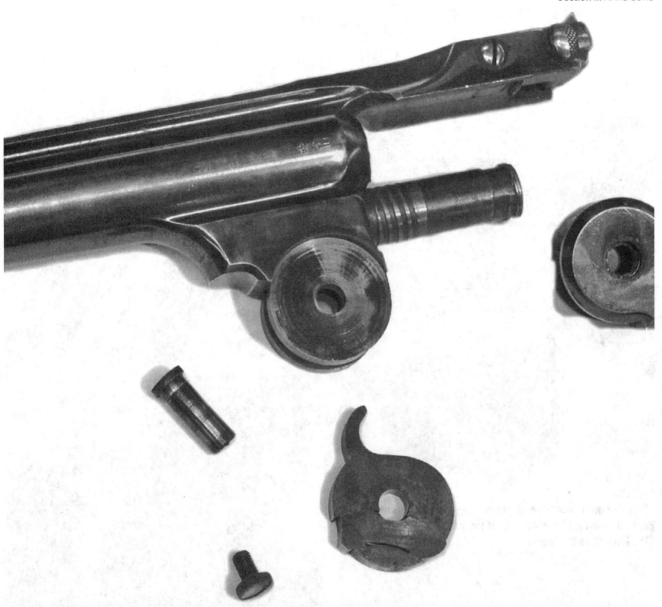

Removing the joint pivot enables the barrel to be removed. The disk-shaped small part under the barrel hinge is the extractor cam.

3 To remove the barrel: With the barrel still in the open position, unscrew and remove the joint pivot screw (#254A) from the left side of the hinge on the frame (#242) and use an appropriate straight punch to drive the joint pivot (#254) out of the frame toward the right side. Make note of the witness mark on the joint pivot and its corresponding mark on the frame. These must be aligned for reassembly. The barrel (#241) is now loose and may be lifted up out of its joint with the frame. The extractor cam (#250) is located between the ears of the barrel's hinge and is now loose and can now be pulled down and out of the barrel. Make note of the extractor cam's position for reassembly.

Note: For those early New Models that use the rack and gear extractor: The extractor cam on these revolvers has gear teeth. With these types, inside the base pin is a part called the rack. Once the cam or gear is removed, tilt the barrel to the rear and allow the rack to slide out of the base pin. Assembly tip for barrels with rack and gear extraction: Turn the barrel so its top rib faces away from you with the muzzle to the left. Insert the rack inside the base pin so that the large gear tooth is at the rear of the barrel. Use a punch to push the rack all the way into the base pin. Next, reinstall the extractor cam gear into the barrel hinge. (The large tooth faces straight up while the smaller gear teeth should face to the left of the large tooth.)

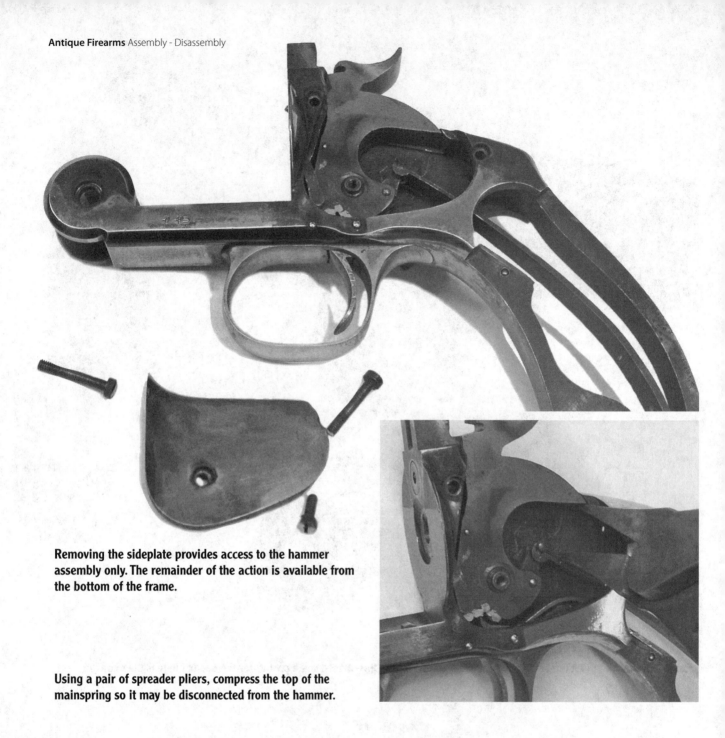

Removing the sideplate provides access to the hammer assembly only. The remainder of the action is available from the bottom of the frame.

Using a pair of spreader pliers, compress the top of the mainspring so it may be disconnected from the hammer.

4 To remove the grips and sideplate: Remove the stock screw (#260) and lift off the stocks (#256) and (#257). Unscrew and remove the three sideplate screws (#262) – one each – and (#263) – two each. Holding it by the hinge, turn the frame on its side, with the sideplate facing up over a padded surface. Strike the grip frame a sharp blow or two using a plastic or hardwood mallet. This will cause the sideplate (#244) to jump up out of its seat in the frame for removal. Never attempt to pry off the sideplate as you may damage it or the frame.

5 To remove the mainspring and hammer: Use a pair of spreader pliers to compress the top of the mainspring (#273) so the hammer stirrup (#267) may be rotated forward and out of its seat between the ears at the top of the mainspring. Loosen the strain screw (#259) located in the bottom front of the front gripstrap on the frame and withdraw the mainspring (#273) from the frame side. With the hammer down, carefully rotate the top of the hand (#252) to the rear using a small screwdriver as a lever, and while holding the hand to the rear, pull the trigger (#247) and hold it to the rear. The hammer (#243) may be rotated about halfway back and carefully pulled upward, off its hammer stud (#268) and out of the frame.

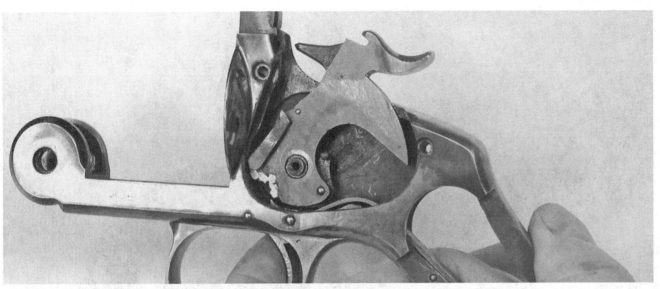

The hammer is being shown here in the correct position for removal from the frame. Notice this hammer has previously had some not-so-professional work performed in the notch area.

Once the triggerguard has been removed you have access to the cylinder stop and trigger. You also can see how the cylinder stop spring is placed in the guard.

6 To remove the triggerguard: Unscrew and remove the triggerguard screw (#264) located facing up on the frame, inside the bottom of the cylinder cut. Hold the frame upside down by the grip, and the triggerguard (#246 can be pulled down from the front out of its seat with the frame. Notice the machined lip at the rear of the triggerguard that fits up into a machined recess in the frame so that no rear guard screw is required. The cylinder stop spring (#269) is fitted into and held captive by a small dovetail slot inside the guard in front of the trigger hole. The spring may be slid toward the rear of the guard for removal.

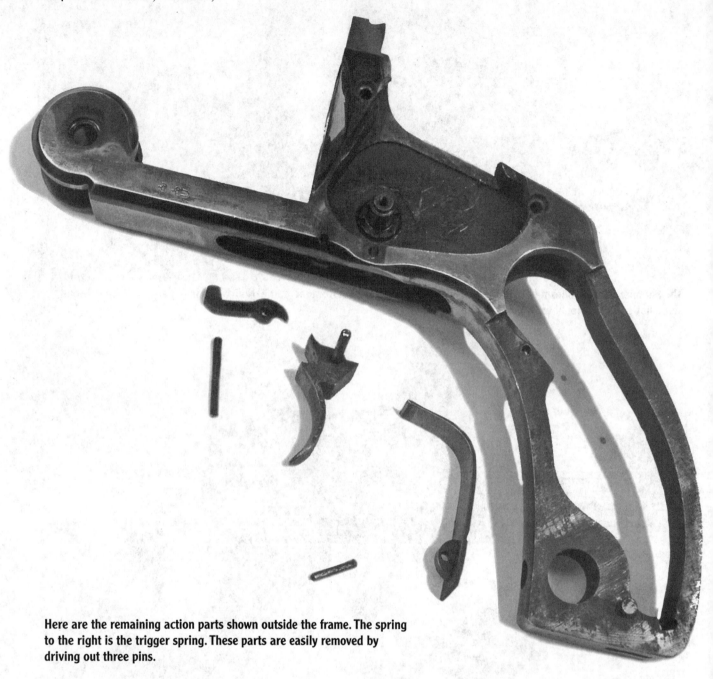

Here are the remaining action parts shown outside the frame. The spring to the right is the trigger spring. These parts are easily removed by driving out three pins.

7 To remove the cylinder stop and trigger: Use a cup-tipped pin punch and hammer to drive out the cylinder stop pin; this is the forwardmost of the two pins that pass through the frame from side to side. Push the cylinder stop (#253) out toward the bottom, using a small punch through its window in the frame, under the area where the cylinder rotates. Use the same cup-tipped punch and hammer to drift out the trigger pin, the rearmost of the two pins that pass through the frame from side to side. The trigger (#24) can be pulled out the bottom of the frame. The trigger spring (#271) is mounted inside the front grip strap and is held in place by a cross pin running through the grip frame. Once its pin is driven out, the trigger spring may be carefully pulled out of the frame to the rear.

8 To disassemble the cylinder: Insert six fired cartridge cases or dummy cartridges into the chambers for support. Grasp the extractor rod (#258) in the jaws of a drill chuck or pass a 1/8-inch pin punch through the hole in the extractor rod and rotate the cylinder (#245) in a counterclockwise direction to unscrew the extractor rod from the extractor (#255). Notice the witness mark dot on one of the rear facing legs of the extractor star. This dot should be aligned with the serial numbers on the cylinder for reassembly.

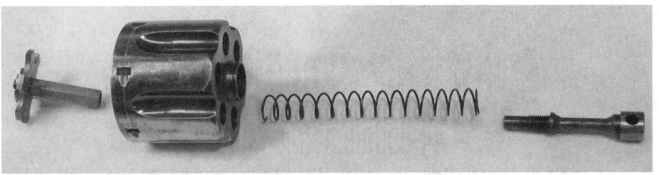

The disassembled cylinder. This one is from a 32-44 caliber New Model No. 3 Target.

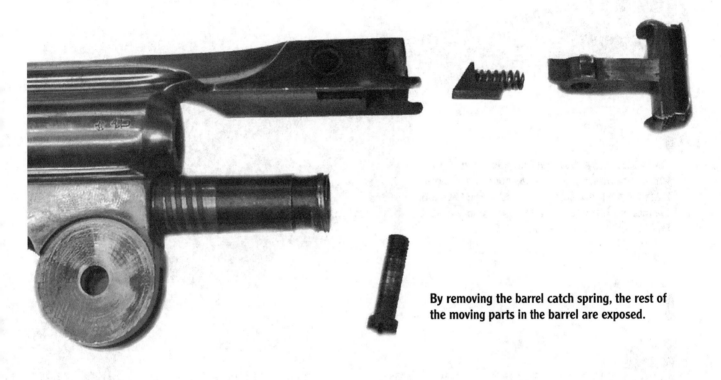

By removing the barrel catch spring, the rest of the moving parts in the barrel are exposed.

9 To disassemble the hammer: Rotate the hand (#252) 180 degrees forward and pull it out of the hammer. Drift out the pin in the center front of the hammer that holds in the handspring (#270). The handspring now may be slid out of its recess in the hammer. The hammer stirrup (#267) may be removed by drifting out its pin at the rear of the hammer. Note the position of the stirrup (#267) for correct reassembly.

10 To disassemble the barrel: Unscrew and remove the barrel catch screw (#261) from the left side of the barrel topstrap. The barrel catch (#249) can now be withdrawn to the rear. By holding the barrel (#241) in a muzzle-up position and tapping the rear of the barrel topstrap on a wooden bench-top, the barrel catch cam (#251) and barrel catch cam spring (#265) will fall out of their recess in the topstrap. Be sure to note the positions of these two parts for later reassembly.

REASSEMBLY

Reassemble the revolver in reverse order of above.

Smith & Wesson Model No. 3

.44 Double Action Models

(Including .44 Double Action First Model, .44 Double Action Frontier, 44 Wesson Favorite)

The .44 Double Action S&W introduced in 1881 was a very comfortable gun to shoot. It had a grip that is almost identical in size and shape to that of the modern K frame round butt. This one is a 44-40 Frontier model. Author photos.

Smith & Wesson's .44 Double Action was their first large-framed self-cocking revolver. It was introduced in 1881 and produced until 1913, by which time over 54,000 standard model revolvers had been sold. The revolvers were initially chambered in 44 S&W Russian caliber, the standard off-the-shelf caliber. This standard .44 DA, often called the .44 Double Action First Model by collectors, is identified quickly by its cylinder length of 1-7/16 inches. That contrasts with the 38-40 and 44-40, or so-called Frontier versions, that used a longer 1-9/16-inch cylinder with a correspondingly longer frame and barrel topstrap. On these variations the frames, barrels and cylinder were built longer because the standard length frame and cylinder would not accommodate the longer Winchester cartridges. Just about 15,300 of these Frontier models with the longer cylinders were manufactured and serial numbered within their own serial numbering sequence. A few late production guns used the long barrel-frame-cylinder but were chambered in 44 S&W Russian in the interest of using up spare parts.

One other variant of the .44 DA is the .44 Wesson Favorite. This revolver is worth mentioning here because one will turn up every now and again and to confuse things, Favorites were serial numbered within the standard .44 DA series. The Favorite had extra metal machined away both inside and externally to produce an extra-lightweight version of the .44 DA First Model. These guns were chambered only in 44 S&W Russian and were offered with the 5-inch barrel length only. The Wesson Favorite was originally manufactured at the request of the Russian government for potential sale there. The factory shipped samples to Russia as well as a few of their major distributors in 1882. However, the contract never materialized with the Russians, so the remaining revolvers were eventually assembled and sold from 1888 through 1892. The Wesson Favorite is a rare collector's find with only about 1000 ever manufactured.

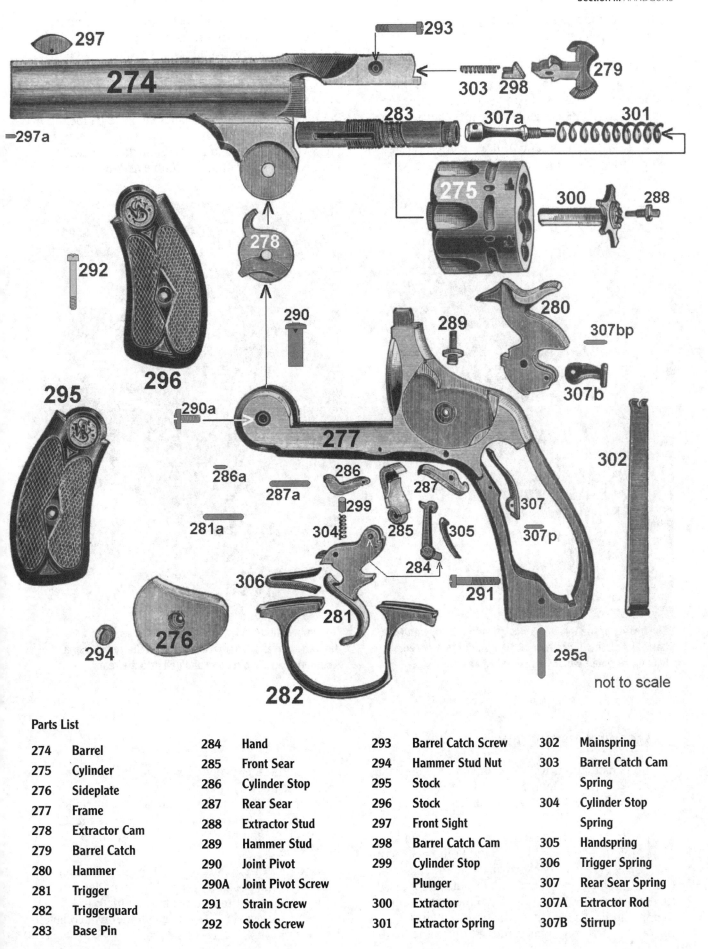

Parts List

274	Barrel	284	Hand	293	Barrel Catch Screw	302	Mainspring
275	Cylinder	285	Front Sear	294	Hammer Stud Nut	303	Barrel Catch Cam
276	Sideplate	286	Cylinder Stop	295	Stock		Spring
277	Frame	287	Rear Sear	296	Stock	304	Cylinder Stop
278	Extractor Cam	288	Extractor Stud	297	Front Sight		Spring
279	Barrel Catch	289	Hammer Stud	298	Barrel Catch Cam	305	Handspring
280	Hammer	290	Joint Pivot	299	Cylinder Stop	306	Trigger Spring
281	Trigger	290A	Joint Pivot Screw		Plunger	307	Rear Sear Spring
282	Triggerguard	291	Strain Screw	300	Extractor	307A	Extractor Rod
283	Base Pin	292	Stock Screw	301	Extractor Spring	307B	Stirrup

In appearance and mechanical operation, the .44 Double Action revolvers are in many ways an enlarged version of S&W's .38 DA - 2nd Model (1880 to 1884) and .32 DA - 2nd Model (1880-1882.) All of these guns used the same awkward-appearing cylinder with two sets of stop notches and free lead cuts (the oval-shaped cut leading into the cylinder stop notch) that dictated short, unattractive cylinder flutes. This design uses two cylinder stops, the rear being a trigger-mounted pivoting stop that locks the cylinder only during the cocking cycle. A separate fixed cylinder stop, made as part of the trigger itself, is used to hold the cylinder from rotating when the trigger is forward.

Perhaps because of the comparatively small sales numbers (compared to their smaller frame revolvers), Smith & Wesson never updated the large-caliber double action design to follow the cylinder stop and action improvements they made to the much better-selling small- and medium-framed double action revolvers.

The beauty of the top-break design is that by opening the barrel latch, the entire rear of the cylinder is exposed, leaving no doubt whether it is loaded or not.

To remove the cylinder, after the barrel is unlatched, hold the barrel catch up while you turn the cylinder in a counterclockwise direction and pull it to the rear.

DISASSEMBLY INSTRUCTIONS

These instructions will work for standard .44 Double Action, .44 Double Action Frontier and .44 Double Action Wesson Favorite models.

1 First, always be sure the revolver is unloaded. Hold the revolver in one hand firmly by its grip, always keeping your fingers away from the trigger (#281) and the muzzle pointed in a safe direction. Pull the hammer (#280) very slightly to the rear until you hear an audible click before the barrel catch (#279) is operated. With your other hand, lift up on the barrel catch and tilt the revolver barrel all the way down toward the floor. This exposes the rear of the cylinder and you may check to be certain all chambers in the cylinder are unloaded. If cartridges are present, remove them and place them in a location apart from the revolver.

To remove the cylinder (#275): Hold the barrel catch in the up position and pull the cylinder to the rear while at the same time turning it in a counterclockwise direction. The cylinder will come off the base pin (#283) toward the rear.

Removing the joint pivot allows the revolver to be pulled apart at the hinge. Here you see the result. The small disc is the extractor cam that fits up in between the ears of the barrel hinge.

2 To remove the barrel: Unscrew and remove the joint pivot screw (#290A) from the left side of the hinge on the frame (#242) and use an appropriate straight punch to drive the joint pivot (#290) out of the frame toward the right side. Make note of the witness mark on the joint pivot and its corresponding mark on the frame; these must be aligned for reassembly. The barrel (#274) is now loose and may be lifted up out of its joint with the frame. The extractor cam (#278) is located between the ears of the barrel hinge and may now be pulled down and out of the barrel. Make note of its position for reassembly.

· 269 ·

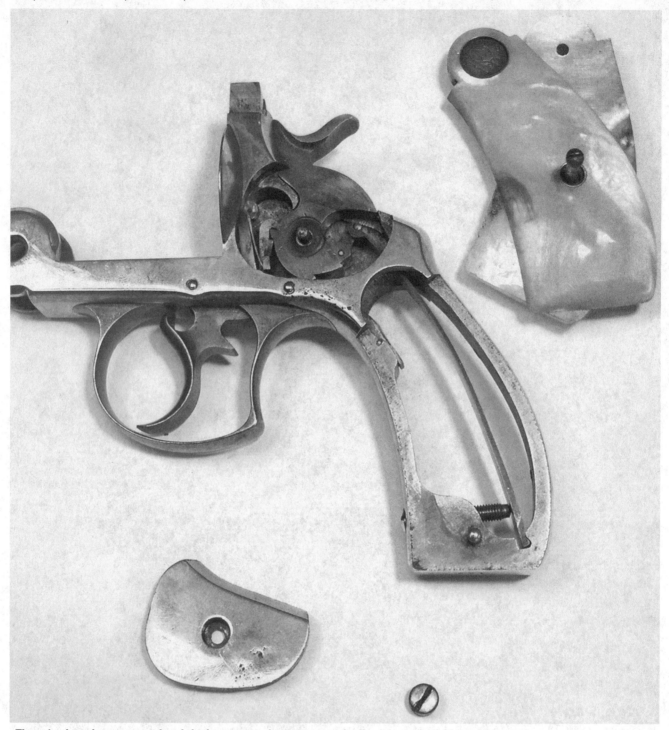

The grips have been removed and the hammer stud nut unscrewed, allowing removal of the sideplate.

3 To remove the grips, sideplate and mainspring: Remove the stock screw (#292) and carefully lift off the stocks (#295) and (#296). Unscrew and remove the hammer stud nut (#294), which acts as the sideplate screw. Holding it by the hinge, turn the frame on its side, sideplate facing up, over a padded surface. Strike the grip frame a sharp blow or two using a plastic or hardwood mallet. This will cause the sideplate (#276) to jump up out of its seat in the frame for removal.

Never attempt to pry off the sideplate. You can damage the plate and the frame. Use a pair of spreader pliers to compress the top of the mainspring (#302) so the hammer stirrup (#307B) may be rotated forward and out of its seat between the ears at the top of the mainspring. Note the position of the stirrup for reassembly. Loosen the strain screw (#291) located in the bottom front of the front grip strap on the frame and withdraw the mainspring (#302) from the frame side.

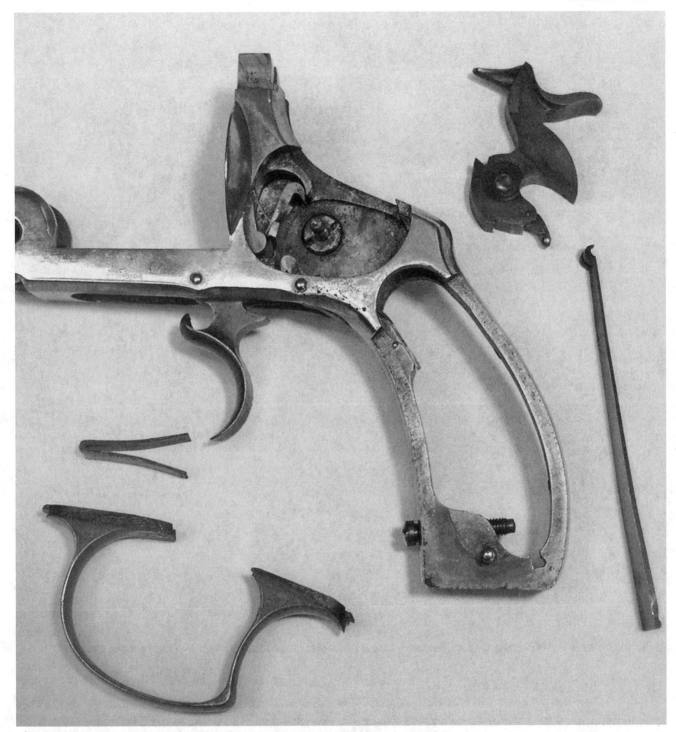

Here the mainspring, hammer, triggerguard and trigger spring have been removed.

4 To remove the triggerguard: The triggerguard (#282) is itself a spring; it has no fastening screws and is held in place by machined tabs at its front and rear tops that mate with machined mortise cuts in the frame. Hold the frame upside down by the grip and tap the rear face of the triggerguard toward the front with a plastic mallet. This will cause the rear of the guard to jump out of its seat in the frame. Pull the trigger (#281) all the way to the rear. The guard may now be

moved rearward slightly to disengage its front tab from the frame. Tilt the front of the guard down and push it forward to remove. The trigger spring (#306) will come off with the guard. Note its position for reassembly.

5 To disassemble the action: Pull the trigger to the rear and hold it all the way back. The hammer (#280) may now be carefully worked up off its stud (#289) and out of the frame. As you release the trigger, make note of the rear sear (#287): it is under spring

· 271 ·

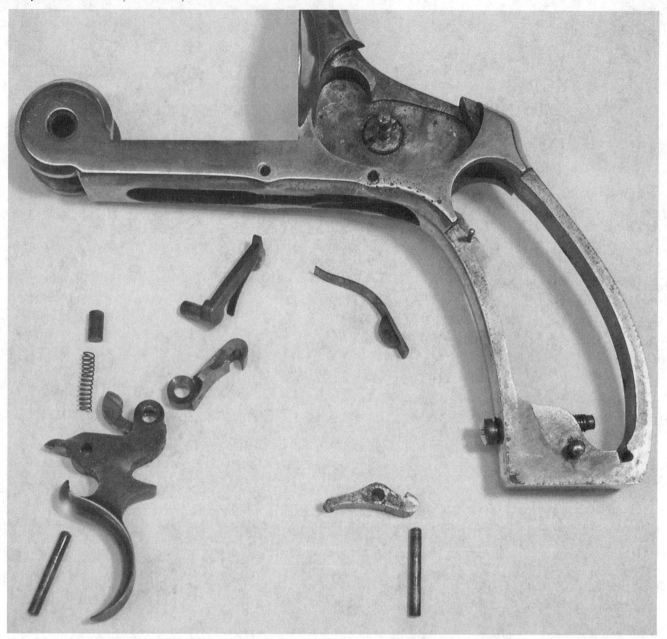

After the hammer and triggerguard have been removed, the remainder of the action parts shown here are disassembled.

tension and will rotate down on its own as the trigger moves forward. Use a pin punch and hammer to drift out the retaining pin for the rear sear spring (#307) and remove the spring. Next, use a cup-tipped pin punch and hammer to drift out the rear sear pin (the rearmost of the two large pins that pass through the frame) and remove the rear sear, noting its position for reassembly. Again, use the cup-tipped pin punch and hammer to drift out the trigger pin (the forwardmost of the two large pins). Push the trigger assembly up and to the rear slightly until the entire side face of the hand (#284) is exposed in the sideplate opening. Grasp the hand and the hand spring (#305) with a small pair of needlenosed pliers and pull the assembly

straight up and out of the frame. The trigger (#281) may be removed through the bottom of the frame while the front sear (#285) may be removed through the sideplate opening. Make a note of the relationship of the trigger assembly, consisting of the trigger, rear sear and hand, for reassembly later.

6 To disassemble the trigger and cylinder stop: The cylinder stop (#286) is mounted in the top center of the trigger (#281). Under the rear of the cylinder stop is a small plunger and coil spring that power the stop. The spring and plunger will be under tension during trigger removal, so use care when removing the trigger that these two tiny parts are not lost. To remove the stop, simply drift out its pin.

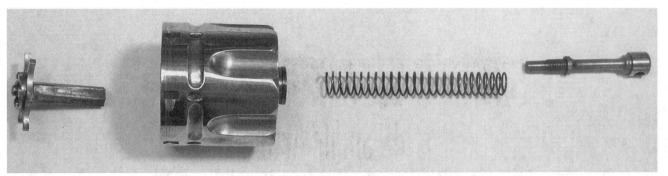

The cylinder is shown completely disassembled. Be sure you insert six dummy cartridges or fired cases into the chambers to support the extractor before you try to unscrew the extractor rod.

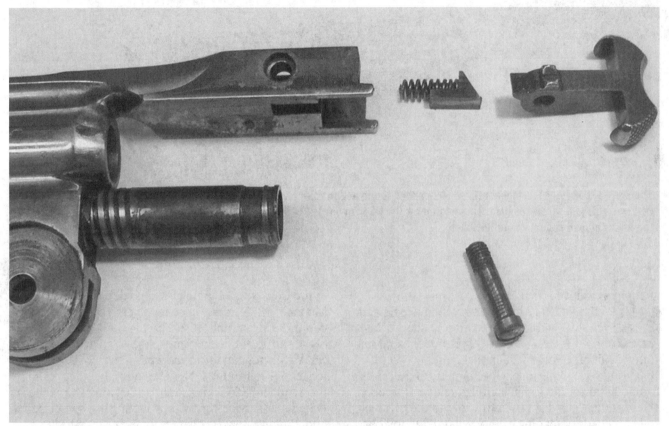

Disassembling the 44 DA barrel is a snap, requiring the removal of only one screw to free the barrel catch assembly.

7 To disassemble the cylinder: Insert six fired cartridge cases into the chambers for support. The extractor rod (#307A) has a small hole through its head. Insert and appropriate-sized pin punch through this hole or grasp the rod in the jaws of a drill chuck and rotate the cylinder (#275) in a counterclockwise direction. This will unscrew the extractor rod from the extractor (#300). Note the witness mark "dot" on one of the rear facing legs of the extractor star. This mark should be aligned with the serial numbers on the rear face of the cylinder for reassembly.

8 To disassemble the barrel: Unscrew and remove the barrel catch screw (#293) from the left side of the barrel topstrap. The barrel catch (#279) can now be withdrawn to the rear. By holding the barrel (#274) in a muzzle-up position and tapping the rear of the barrel topstrap on a soft wooden bench-top, the barrel catch cam (#298) and barrel catch cam spring (#303) will fall out of their recess in the topstrap. Remember the positions of these parts for reassembly.

REASSEMBLY

Reassemble the action in exactly the reverse of the order given above.

Smith & Wesson Top-Break
.45 Single Action
(Model No. 3 Schofield, 1st and 2nd Models)

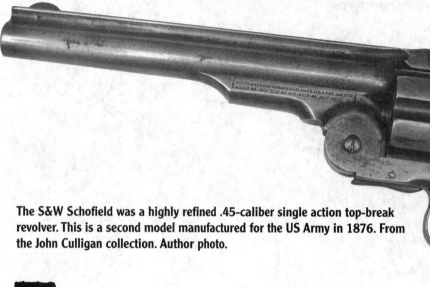

The S&W Schofield was a highly refined .45-caliber single action top-break revolver. This is a second model manufactured for the US Army in 1876. From the John Culligan collection. Author photo.

I ntroduced in 1875, the .45 Single Action Schofield 1st Model is a six-shot, single action revolver with a square butt grip shape. Based on a the designs of a U.S. Army officer, Major (later Colonel) George W. Schofield, the revolver is an alteration of the Model No. 3 American that uses a unique barrel catch that is pulled rearward to open the revolver. This distinct feature allows the revolver to be opened for loading with one hand, an obvious advantage for mounted cavalry troops. Like all Smith & Wesson top-break revolvers, on opening, this revolver features simultaneous, automatic ejection of the spent cases. The Schofield S&W was originally manufactured with uncheckered walnut stocks and a seven-inch, ribbed barrel with a full length V-shaped sighting rib. In addition to the automatic, simultaneous ejection, one outstanding feature of the Schofield that the Army liked was the extraction system, which was much simpler and markedly more dependable than the extraction mechanisms used on earlier S&W American and Russian models that had been previously tested by the Army.

Schofield revolvers were chambered for a centerfire cartridge now called the 45 S&W. The cartridge was just a bit shorter than the standard 45 Colt service cartridge of the day, and it also used a lighter bullet (230 grains as opposed to the 250-grain bullet used in the Colt) and 12 grains less powder. Model of 1873 Colt service revolvers could readily chamber and fire the S&W cartridge but the Schofield S&W was not capable of accepting the longer 45 Colt rounds. Not long after the adoption of the Schofield S&W into service, the Army shortened its .45-caliber service cartridge, adopting the lighter bullet and 28-grain powder charge of the S&W cartridge specifications.

Three thousand 1st Model S&W Schofield revolvers were made for the U.S. Army during 1875, with only 35 of these produced for civilian sale. In 1876 the 2nd Model Schofield was introduced and built through 1877. Schofields were, for a time, issued in conjunction with Colt revolvers in army service and saw service with units of the U.S. 9th and 10th Cavalry. The 2nd Model barrel catch differs from the 1st Models in that it has a flattened-checkered top and uses a larger diameter screw. Second Model frames are also made of forged steel whereas the 1st Models were forged from iron; they were also equipped with an improved, stronger base pin. Around 5,285 of the 2nd models were manufactured and sold to the U.S. Army and 649 were produced for commercial sale. To many collectors and shooters, the Schofield was the ultimate top-break single action revolver.

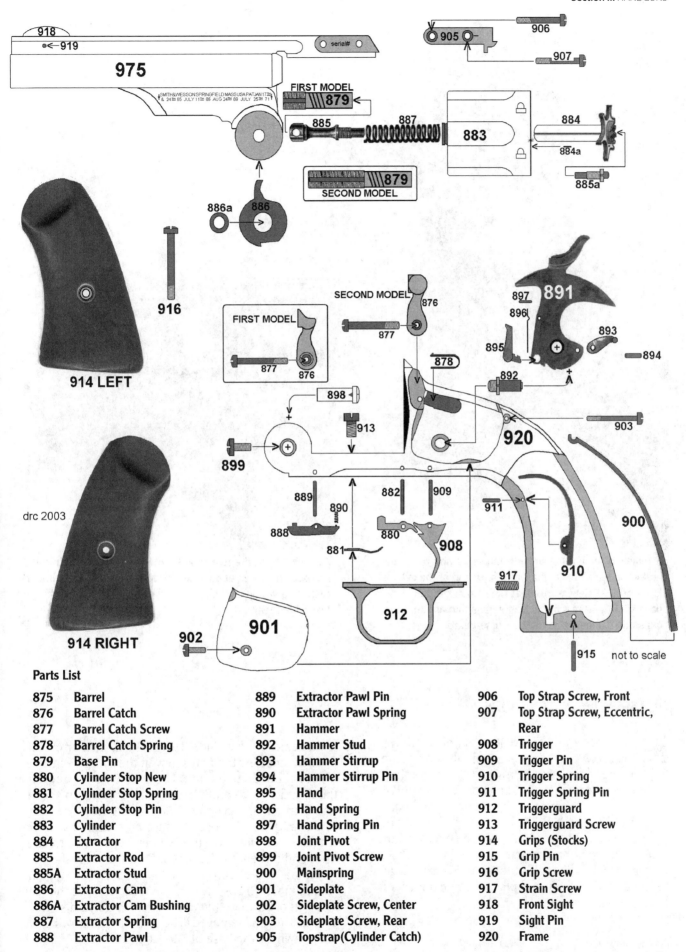

Parts List

875	Barrel	889	Extractor Pawl Pin	906	Top Strap Screw, Front	
876	Barrel Catch	890	Extractor Pawl Spring	907	Top Strap Screw, Eccentric,	
877	Barrel Catch Screw	891	Hammer		Rear	
878	Barrel Catch Spring	892	Hammer Stud	908	Trigger	
879	Base Pin	893	Hammer Stirrup	909	Trigger Pin	
880	Cylinder Stop New	894	Hammer Stirrup Pin	910	Trigger Spring	
881	Cylinder Stop Spring	895	Hand	911	Trigger Spring Pin	
882	Cylinder Stop Pin	896	Hand Spring	912	Triggerguard	
883	Cylinder	897	Hand Spring Pin	913	Triggerguard Screw	
884	Extractor	898	Joint Pivot	914	Grips (Stocks)	
885	Extractor Rod	899	Joint Pivot Screw	915	Grip Pin	
885A	Extractor Stud	900	Mainspring	916	Grip Screw	
886	Extractor Cam	901	Sideplate	917	Strain Screw	
886A	Extractor Cam Bushing	902	Sideplate Screw, Center	918	Front Sight	
887	Extractor Spring	903	Sideplate Screw, Rear	919	Sight Pin	
888	Extractor Pawl	905	Topstrap(Cylinder Catch)	920	Frame	

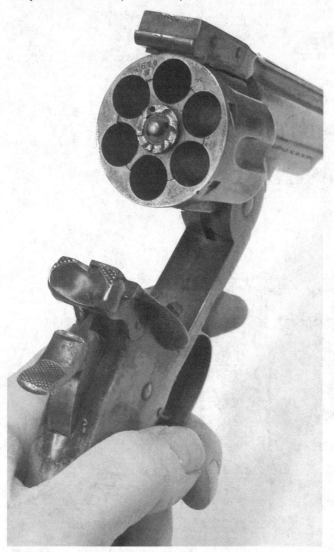

It's easy to see if a top-break is loaded or not: once you break the barrel open, the entire back end of the cylinder is exposed to view. Notice that the hammer is pulled back slightly to rest in the loading position and that the gunsmith's finger is not in the triggerguard.

As shown here, the rear cylinder catch screw is eccentric. It has been loosened about one-half turn, allowing the cylinder catch to pivot up enough for the cylinder to be pulled off toward the rear.

DISASSEMBLY INSTRUCTIONS

1 First, be certain the weapon is unloaded. Grasp the revolver around its grip firmly, being sure to keep your fingers off the trigger (#908), pointing the barrel muzzle in a safe direction. Gently pull the hammer (#891) to the rear slightly until you hear one click. Pull back on the barrel catch (#876) and tilt the revolver barrel all the way down to open the action. This exposes the rear of the cylinder. Check to be certain the cylinder is unloaded. If cartridges are present, remove them and place them in a location apart from the weapon.

To remove the cylinder (#883): With the barrel still opened, unscrew the rear screw in the cylinder catch (#905) about one-half turn. Loosen the front screw on the cylinder catch and tilt the cylinder catch up slightly and then pull the cylinder (#883) to the rear. The rear screw (#907) is supposed to have an eccentric screw-shank which will allow the cylinder catch to be tilted up slightly when it is loosened. Over the years the screw may have been changed for a screw with a plain shank, in which case you may have to remove the rear screw in order to tilt the cylinder catch upward so the cylinder may be removed. The cylinder can now be withdrawn off the base pin, toward the rear.

Once the joint pivot and its screw are removed, the barrel is lifted out of its hinge with the frame. The extractor cam is then taken down out of the barrel hinge.

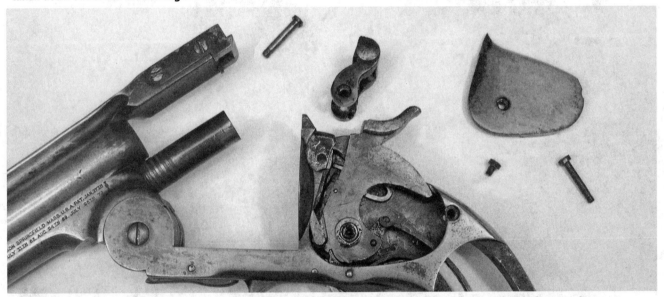

The barrel catch has to be removed before the sideplate can be tackled. After the barrel catch and with the two plate screws have been removed, the sideplate may be removed. Remember, never pry a sideplate off. Always use shock.

2 To remove the barrel: Unscrew and remove the joint pivot screw (#899) from the left side of the hinge on the frame (#920) and use an appropriate straight punch to drive the joint pivot (#898) out of the frame toward the right side. Make note of the witness mark on the joint pivot and its corresponding mark on the frame; these marks must be aligned for reassembly. The barrel (#875) is now free, and it can be lifted up out of its joint with the frame. The extractor cam (#886) is located between the ears of the barrel hinge and may be pulled down and out of the barrel. Make note of the extractor cam's position for reassembly.

3 To remove the grips, barrel catch and sideplate: Unscrew and remove the grip screw (#91) and lift off the grips (#914). Unscrew and remove the barrel catch screw (#877). With the hammer (#891) still in the loading position, withdraw the barrel catch (#876) from the top by pulling up and pivoting it slightly to the rear. Remove the two sideplate screws (#902) and (#903). Turn the frame on its side, holding it by the hinge with the sideplate facing up, over a padded bench surface. Strike the grip frame a sharp blow or two using a plastic or hardwood mallet. This will shock the sideplate (#901) and cause it to jump up out of its seat in the frame for removal. Never attempt to pry off the sideplate.

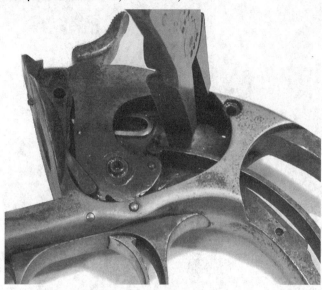

Compressing the top of the mainspring so it can be disengaged from the hammer stirrup.

After removing the mainspring, hold the hand to the rear, pull the trigger, move the hammer about halfway back and slowly work the hammer up and off its stud.

4 To remove the mainspring and hammer: Use a pair of spreader pliers to compress the top of the mainspring (#900) so the hammer stirrup (#893) may be rotated forward and out of its seat between the ears at the top of the mainspring. Loosen the strain screw (#917) located in the bottom front of the front grip strap on the frame and withdraw the mainspring from the frame side. Carefully rotate the top of the hand (#895) to the rear using a small screwdriver as a lever and while holding the hand to the rear, pull the trigger (#908) and also hold it to the rear. The hammer (#891) may now be rotated about halfway back and carefully pulled upward off its hammer stud (#892) and out of the frame.

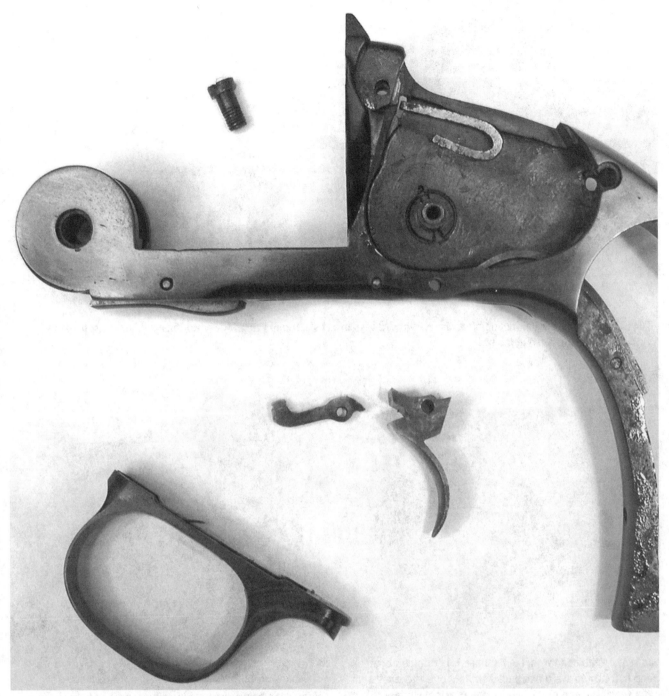

Once the triggerguard has dropped off, the trigger and cylinder stop are easily accessible for removal.

5 To remove the triggerguard: Unscrew and remove the triggerguard screw (#913) and remove the triggerguard (#912) by pulling down on its front. The cylinder stop spring (#88) is fitted into, and held captive by, a small dovetail slot inside the guard. It can be removed by sliding it to the rear.

6 To remove the remaining action parts: Use a cup-tipped pin punch and hammer to drift out the cylinder stop pin (the center of the three pins that pass through the frame from side to side) and push the cylinder stop (#880) out toward the bottom, using a

small punch through its window in the frame under the area where the cylinder rotates. Using the same punch and hammer, drift out the trigger pin (the rearmost of the three pins that pass through the frame from side to side). The trigger (#908) may be pulled out the bottom of the frame. The trigger spring (#910) is mounted inside the front grip strap and is held in place by a cross pin running through the grip frame. The same punch and hammer are now used to drive out the front pin in the frame (#889). Removing this pin frees the extractor pawl (#888) and its spring (#888).

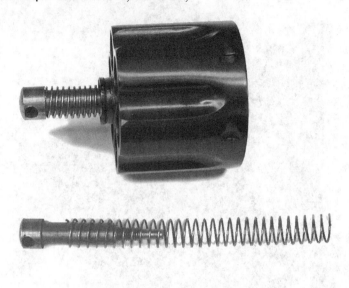

The Schofield cylinder before and after disassembly. Always insert six dummy cartridges into the chambers to support the extractor while unscrewing the rod.

To remove the hand from the hammer, it is rotated about one-half turn forward and pulled straight out. The small step you see at the end of the hand shank is actually a tool to aid in its assembly to the hammer.

Here is the barrel catch spring when removed from the frame.

7 To disassemble the cylinder: Insert six fired cartridge cases into the chambers for support. Push a straight punch through the hole in the ejector rod (#885) and rotate the cylinder (#883) in a counterclockwise direction to unscrew the ejector rod from the extractor (#884).

8 To disassemble the hammer: Rotate the hand (#895) about 180 degrees forward and pull it straight out of the side of the hammer. Use a small pin punch to drift out the pin in the center front of the hammer which holds in the hand spring (#896). The hand spring now may be slid out of its recess in the hammer. The hammer stirrup (#893) may be removed by drifting out its pin at the rear of the hammer. Be sure to notice the position of the stirrup for reassembly.

REASSEMBLY

Reassemble the revolver in reverse order of above.

Uberti Schofield
Replica

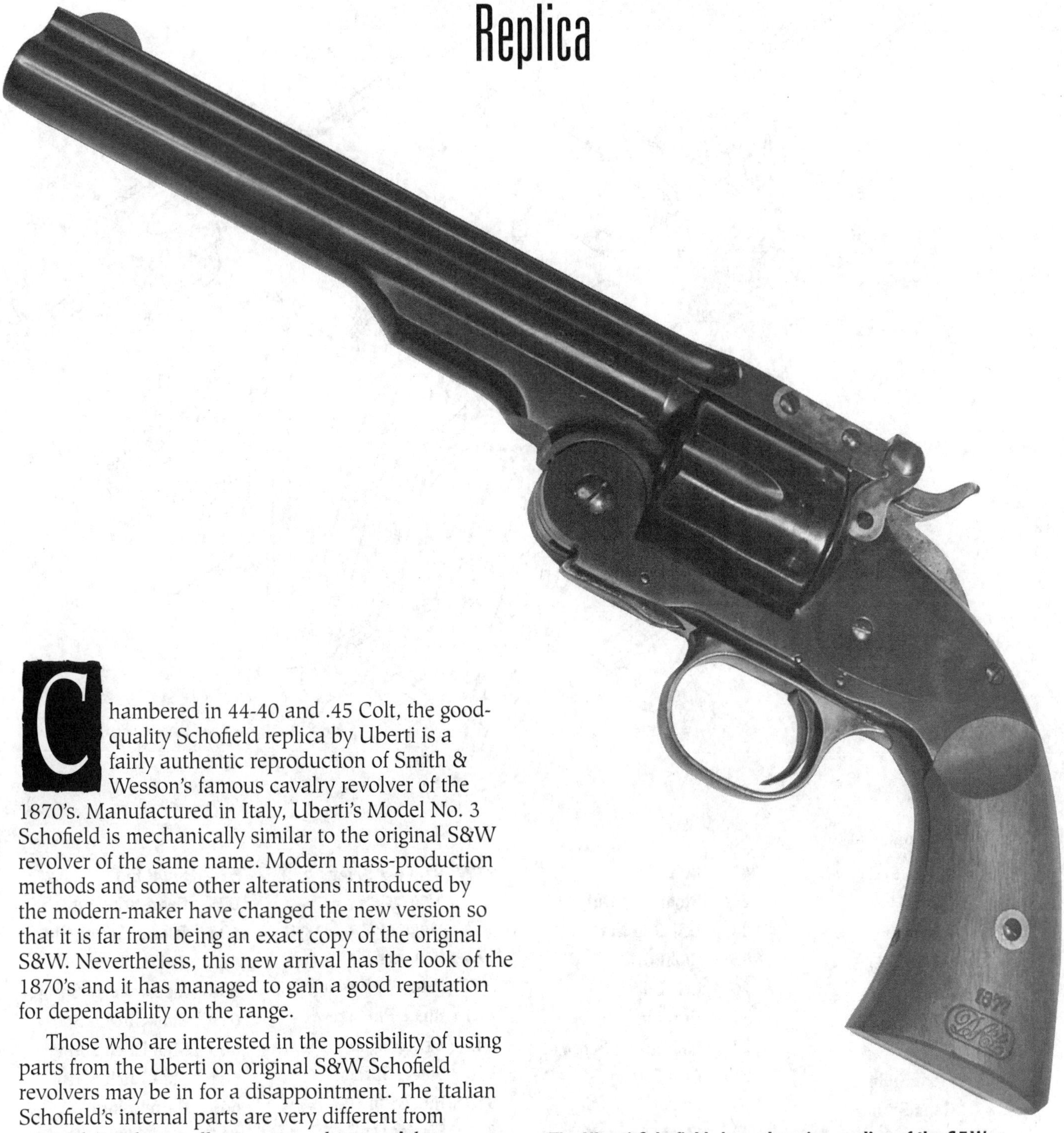

C hambered in 44-40 and .45 Colt, the good-quality Schofield replica by Uberti is a fairly authentic reproduction of Smith & Wesson's famous cavalry revolver of the 1870's. Manufactured in Italy, Uberti's Model No. 3 Schofield is mechanically similar to the original S&W revolver of the same name. Modern mass-production methods and some other alterations introduced by the modern-maker have changed the new version so that it is far from being an exact copy of the original S&W. Nevertheless, this new arrival has the look of the 1870's and it has managed to gain a good reputation for dependability on the range.

Those who are interested in the possibility of using parts from the Uberti on original S&W Schofield revolvers may be in for a disappointment. The Italian Schofield's internal parts are very different from originals in almost all respects and most of them cannot be made to work in an original S&W. There are a few exceptions to this; with alterations, the cylinder stop spring, the extractor spring, the barrel catch spring and the hand (this will require some welding) can be altered to work in an original Schofield.

The Uberti Schofield shown here is a replica of the S&W Second Model Schofield. While not an exact likeness of the original, the Uberti is popular in cowboy action matches. Revolver courtesy of Stoeger Industries. Author photos.

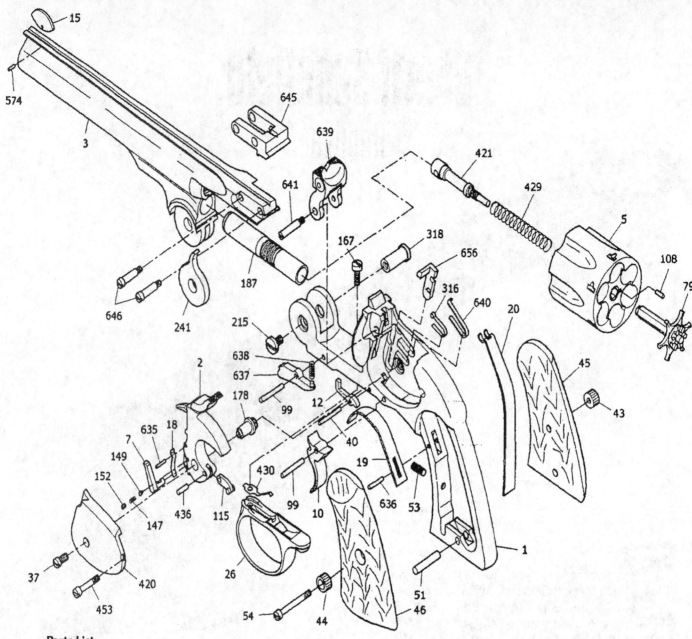

Parts List
(Uberti nomenclature)

1	Frame Assembly	40	Bolt Pin	152	Hammer Safety
2	Hammer	43	Right Grip Nut		Stop Screw
3	Barrel	44	Left Grip Nut	167	Triggerguard Screw
5	Cylinder (.45)	45	Right Grip	178	Hammer Pin
7	Hand	46	Left Grip	187	Base Pin Bushing
10	Trigger	51	Grip Pin	215	Hinge Pin Screw
12	Bolt	53	Mainspring Screw	241	Ejector Cam
15	Front Sight	54	Grip Screw	316	Safety Spring
18	Hand Spring	79	Ejector	318	Hinge Pin
19	Trigger Spring	99	Sight Pin	421	Ejector Rod
20	Mainspring	115	Stirrup	429	Ejector Spring
26	Triggerguard	147	Hammer Safety	430	Bolt Spring
37	Hammer Pin Screw		Spring	436	Stirrup Pin
	(Center Sideplate)	149	Hammer Safety Pin	453	Sideplate Screw

574	Sight Pin
635	Handspring Pin
636	Trigger Spring Pin
637	Ejector Lever
638	Ejector Lever Spring
639	Stud Latch
640	Stud Latch Spring
641	Stud Latch Screw
645	Barrel Block
646	Barrel Block Screw
656	Safety Bar

Below is a list of some differences you may spot if you closely compare an original S&W Schofield to the Uberti-made Schofield.

On the Uberti:

- The barrel catch screw is headless.

- The barrel's top-strap is longer, it extends farther forward on the rib and is higher than the S&W.

- The cylinder has been lengthened toward the front and the gas ring seal has been eliminated.

- The cylinder stop ball (the locking portion) is shorter.

- The extractor cam does not use a bushing.

- The ratchet teeth angles and shape differ from the S&W.

- The hand shape differs from original and may interfere with the ratchet teeth as the gun is closed.

- The extractor stem is hexagon instead of round and the extractor stud is not removable.

- The frame and hammer have been manufactured to accept a new hammer block safety.

- The front sight is a dark colored brass in stead of steel.

- The hammer stud is ground flush with the frame side and has no slots for a spanner wrench.

- The diameter of the joint pivot has been increased.

- The screw threads all differ from the original.

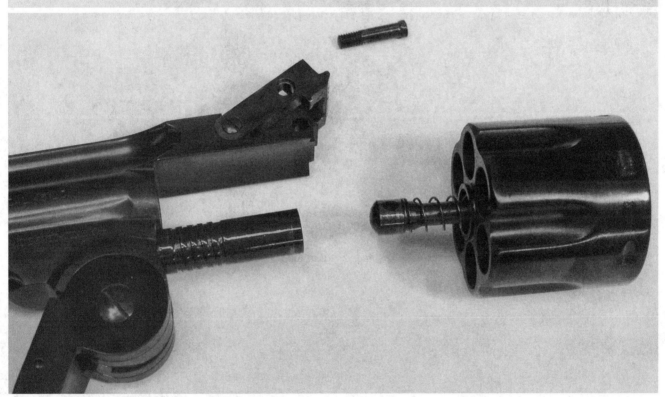

To remove the Uberti Schofield's cylinder, the rear barrel block screw must be removed so the rear of the barrel block, which retains the cylinder, may be lifted out of the way.

DISASSEMBLY INSTRUCTIONS

1 First, make sure the revolver is unloaded. Hold it by the grip, being careful to point the muzzle in a safe direction and to keep your fingers away from the trigger (#10) at all times. Pull back hammer (#2) until it reaches the loading position, i.e., the first audible click. Pull back on the stud latch (#639) and tilt the revolver barrel (#3) all the way down to open the action, thus exposing the rear of the cylinder (#5) chambers. If any cartridges are present in the chambers, remove them now and place them in a separate location.

2 To remove the cylinder (#5): With the revolver barrel still open, unscrew and remove the rear screw from the barrel block (#645). Loosen the front screw on the barrel block and tilt the barrel block up slightly, then pull the cylinder assembly to the rear. The cylinder can be withdrawn off the base pin (#187), toward the rear.

Removing the hinge pin allows the entire barrel to be lifted up out of the frame hinge.

3 To remove the barrel: Unscrew and remove the hinge pin screw (#215) from the left side of the hinge on the frame (#1) and then use an appropriate straight punch to drive the hinge pin (#318) out of the frame toward the right side. The barrel is now loose and may be lifted up out of its joint with the frame. The extractor cam (#241) is located between the ears of the barrel hinge and may be pulled down and out of the barrel. Make note of the position of the extractor cam for reassembly. The extractor pawl (#637) is located in the frame bottom, just to the rear of the hinge ears. To remove the extractor pawl, simply drive out its retaining pin (#99) and withdraw the extractor pawl along with its spring (#638) through the frame bottom.

Note: When reinstalling the barrel and extractor cam onto the frame, push up on the rear of the extractor pawl and hold it there until you have successfully reinstalled the hinge pin. Make note of the small lug on the hinge pin just under its head and its corresponding notch within its seat in the frame for reassembly. The lug and its seat must be aligned correctly.

In this view the grips, stud latch and sideplate have been removed to expose the hammer.

4 To remove the grips, barrel catch and sideplate: Unscrew and remove the grip screw (#54) and list off the grips (#45) and (#46.) Unscrew and remove the stud latch screw (#641). Bring the hammer back to the loading position and withdraw the stud latch (#639) by pulling it slightly to the rear and up. Unscrew and remove the two sideplate screws (#37) and (#453).

Holding it by the hinge over a padded surface, turn the frame on its side with the sideplate facing up. Strike the grip frame a sharp blow or two using a plastic or hardwood mallet. This will cause the sideplate (#420) to jump up and out of its seat in the frame for removal. Never attempt to pry off the sideplate; you may damage the frame and the sideplate.

Here the mainspring is being compressed so it can be disconnected from the hammer stirrup.

Here the mainspring, hammer and triggerguard have been removed. Notice the hammer block safety device inside the frame just above the trigger.

5 To remove the hammer and mainspring: Use a pair of spreader-type pliers to compress the top of the mainspring (#20) so the hammer stirrup (#115) may be rotated forward and out of its seat between the ears at the top of the mainspring. Loosen the mainspring screw (#53) located in the bottom front of the front grip strap on the frame and withdraw the mainspring from the frame side. Carefully rotate the top of the hand (#7) to the rear, using a small screwdriver as a lever and while holding the hand to the rear, pull the trigger (#10) and hold it to the rear. The hammer (#2) may be rotated about halfway back and carefully pulled upwards, off its hammer pin (#178) and up out of the frame.

This cylinder is about to be disassembled. The dummy cartridges in the chambers are there to support the extractor as the rod is unscrewed.

6 To disassemble the action: Unscrew and remove the triggerguard screw (#167). Remove the triggerguard (#26) by pulling down and forward on its front. The bolt spring (430) is fitted into and held captive by a small dovetail slot inside the guard. This spring may be removed by sliding it to the rear of the guard. Use a cup-tipped pin punch to drift out the bolt pin (#40), the centermost of the three pins that pass through the frame from side to side, and push the bolt out toward the bottom by using a small punch through its window in the frame, under the area where the cylinder rotates. Again using a cup-tipped pin punch and hammer, drive out the trigger pin (#99), the rearmost of the three pins that pass through the frame from side to side. The trigger (#10) can be pulled out the bottom of the frame. The trigger spring (#19) is mounted inside the front grip strap of the frame and is held in place by a cross pin (#636) running through the grip frame. The hammer block safety (#656) and its spring (#316) rest in a mortise cut within the lock frame forward of the hammer stud and are simply lifted up and out of the frame. Be sure to pay careful attention to their orientation for later reassembly. The stud latch spring (#640) is fitted into a machine cut within the lock frame and can be pried out of its mortise and lifted out of the frame.

7 To disassemble the barrel: The only part remaining on the barrel is the barrel block (#645). Unscrew and remove the front barrel block screw and pull the barrel block off the barrel toward the rear. Reinsert the front barrel block screw into the barrel block while the gun remains apart so the two screws do not become mixed up during assembly.

8 To disassemble the cylinder: Insert six fired cartridge cases or dummy cartridges into the cylinder chambers to support the ejector. Push a punch through the hole in the ejector rod (#421) and rotate the cylinder in a counterclockwise direction in order to unscrew the ejector rod from the ejector (#79).

9 To disassemble the hammer: Rotate the hand about 180 degrees forward and pull it out of the side of the hammer (#2). Use a small pin punch and hammer to drift out the pin in the center front of the hammer (#635) that holds in the hand spring (#18). The hand spring now may be slid out of its recess in the hammer. The hammer stirrup (#115) may be removed by using a pin punch and hammer to drive out its pin (#436) at the lower/rear of the hammer. Note the position of the stirrup for later reassembly. Do not remove the small screw located on the left side of the hammer (#152). This screw is factory staked in place and it retains the hammer block safety cam pin (#149).

REASSEMBLY

Reassemble the revolver in reverse order of above.

Navy Arms/ Uberti .44
New Model Russian

Uberti's New Model Russian is a replica of the Smith & Wesson 44 Russian single action, top-break revolver. Revolver courtesy of Stoeger Industries. Author photos.

The Uberti-manufactured New Model Russian is different mechanically from the original Smith & Wesson in several areas. In addition to a new hammer block safety, the extractor mechanism in the Uberti revolver uses a more simplified extractor cam, similar to the S&W Schofield instead of the rack and gear of the S&W 3rd Model Russian. Uberti's revolver also uses a hexagonal extractor shank in place of the squared original.

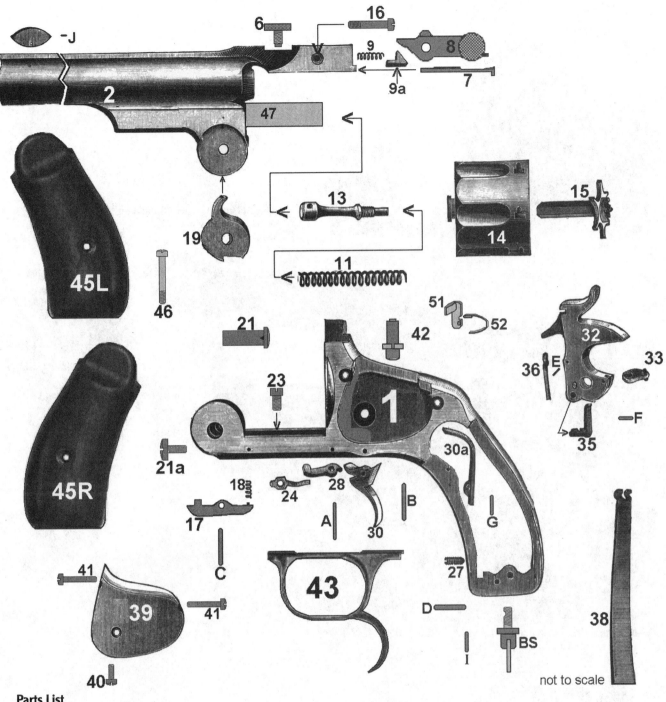

Parts List

1	Frame	13	Extractor Rod	24	Cylinder Stop Spring	E	Hand Spring Pin
2	Barrel	14	Cylinder	27	Strain Screw	38	Mainspring
3	Front Sight	15	Extractor	28	Cylinder Stop	39	Sideplate
F	Front Sight Pin	16	Barrel Catch Screw	A	Cylinder Stop Pin	40	Plate Screw, Center
6	Cylinder Catch	17	Extractor Pawl	30	Trigger	41	Plate Screw,
	Thumb Screw	B	Pawl Pin	30A	Trigger Spring		Front or Rear (2)
7	Cylinder Catch	18	Extractor	C	Trigger Pin	42	Hammer Stud
8	Barrel Catch		Pawl Spring	32	Hammer	43	Triggerguard
9	Barrel Catch	19	Extractor Cam	33	Stirrup	D	Grip Pin
	Cam Spring	21	Joint Pivot	H	Stirrup Pin	45L	Grip, Left
9A	Barrel Catch Cam	21A	Joint Pivot Screw	35	Hand	45R	Grip, Right
11	Extractor Spring	23	Triggerguard Screw	36	Hand Spring	46	Grip Screw
						47	Base Pin

A New Model Russian opened for loading and unloading.

The Uberti Russian cylinder removed.

DISASSEMBLY INSTRUCTIONS

1 Check to be certain the cylinder is unloaded. Grasp the revolver by its grip, being careful to keep the muzzle pointed in a safe direction and to keep your fingers away from the trigger. Pull the hammer back one click to the loading position. Lift up on the barrel catch (#8) and tilt the revolver barrel (#2) all the way down to open the action, thus exposing the rear of the cylinder chambers. If any cartridges are present, remove them now and place any live ammunition in a separate location from your work area.

2 To remove the cylinder: With the barrel opened, loosen the cylinder catch thumbscrew (#6) located on the barrel topstrap about two full turns. Pull the cylinder (#14) to the rear slightly. You will notice that the cylinder catch (#7) has withdrawn slightly to the rear and has moved up, freeing the cylinder to be pulled all the way off the revolver straight toward the rear. When reinstalling the cylinder, push the cylinder assembly all the way forward onto the barrel, then push in on the cylinder catch (#7). Push the catch all the way forward until you see that its lip has locked over the rear edge of the cylinder. Retighten the cylinder catch thumb screw.

Removing the hinge pin allows the barrel to be pulled out of the frame. The piece under the barrel is the extractor cam.

3 To remove the barrel: Remove the hinge pin screw (#21A) from the left side of the hinge on the frame (#1) and use an appropriate-size straight punch to drive the hinge pin (#21) out of the frame toward the right side. Make note of the witness mark on the joint pivot and its corresponding mark on the frame for reassembly. (Note: Not all Uberti Russian models use a witness mark.) The barrel (#2) is now loose and may be lifted up out of its joint with the frame. The extractor cam (#19) is located between the ears of the barrel hinge and can be pulled down and out of the barrel. Make note of its position for reassembly. If desired, the extractor pawl (#17) and its spring may be removed by using a cup-tipped pin punch and hammer to drive out its pin (#C), which located just behind the hinge (the forwardmost pin in the side of the frame).

Here are the tools required to remove the Russian sideplate.

Compress the mainspring with spreader pliers so it can be disconnected from the hammer stirrup.

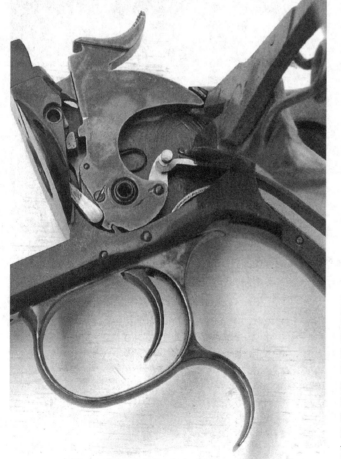

4 To remove the grips and sideplate: Unscrew and remove the grip screw (#46) and lift off the grips (#45L) and (#45R). Remove the three sideplate screws (#40) and (#41). Turn the frame on its side holding it by the hinge, sideplate facing up, over a padded surface. Strike the grip frame a sharp blow or two using a hardwood or plastic mallet. This will cause the sideplate (#39) to jump up out of its seat in the frame for removal. Never attempt to pry off the sideplate as you could damage the frame and the sideplate.

After the mainspring is removed, the hammer may be removed. Notice the hammer block safety device inside the frame, just in front of the hammer stud.

5 To remove the mainspring and hammer: Use a pair of spreader pliers to compress the top of the mainspring (#38) so the hammer stirrup (#33) can be rotated forward, out of its seat between the ears at the top of the mainspring. Loosen the strain screw (#27) located in the bottom front of the front grip strap on the frame and then withdraw the mainspring from the frame side. Carefully rotate the top of the hand (#35) to the rear using a small screwdriver as a lever and while holding the hand to the rear, pull the trigger (#30) and hold it to the rear. The hammer (#32) can be rotated about halfway back and carefully pulled upwards, off its hammer pin (#42) and out of the frame. Carefully note the positions of the hammer block safety and its spring within the frame mortise. Should these parts be removed for any reason, be certain to reinstall them in these exact positions.

Only one screw at the front holds the triggerguard in place. The rear of the guard locks up into a mortise cut in the frame.

6 To remove the triggerguard: Unscrew and remove the triggerguard screw (#23) and remove the triggerguard (#43) by pulling down on its front and then sliding the guard forward until the rear comes out of its machined slot in the frame. The bolt spring (#24) is fitted into and held captive by a small dovetail slot inside the triggerguard, and the spring is removed by sliding it out to the rear.

7 To disassemble the action: Use a cup-tipped pin punch and hammer to drift out the bolt pin (#A), the center of the three pins that pass through the frame from side to side. Using a small punch, push the bolt (#28) out toward the bottom, passing it through its window in the frame, under the area where the cylinder rotates. Use a cup-tipped pin punch and hammer to drive out the trigger pin (#B), the rearmost of the three pins that pass through the frame from side to side. The trigger (#30) may be pulled out the bottom of the frame. The trigger spring (#30A) is mounted inside the front grip strap and is held in place by a crosspin (#G) running through the grip frame.

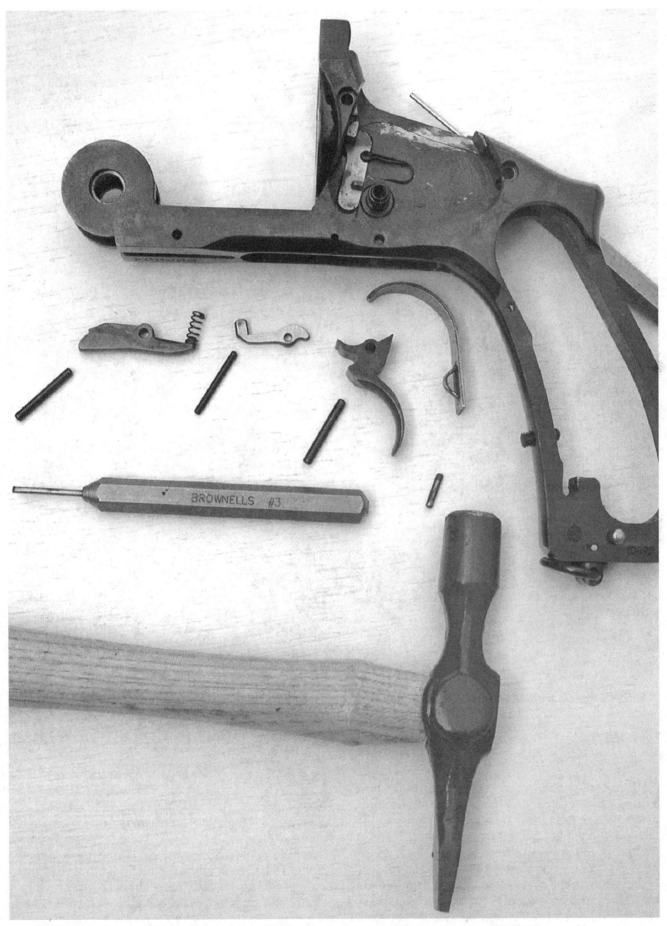

Here is the Russian action disassembled, shown with the cup-tipped pin punch and hammer used in its disassembly.

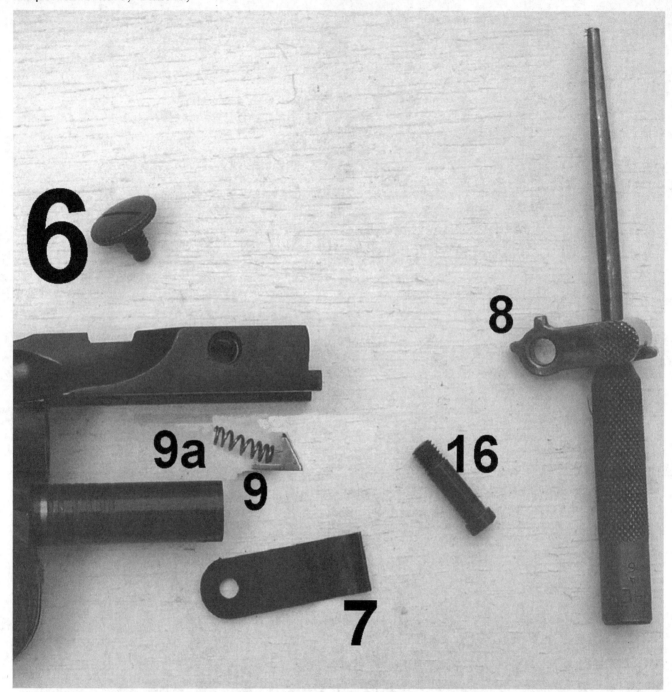

The Uberti Russian barrel shown disassembled. The punch in the photo is merely a prop to hold the barrel catch up.

8 To disassemble the barrel: Unscrew and remove the barrel catch screw (#16) and pull the barrel catch (#8) out from the rear of the barrel topstrap, along with the barrel catch cam (#9) and the barrel catch cam spring (#9A). Notice how the barrel catch parts come out so they may be reinstalled correctly. Remove the cylinder catch thumb screw (#6) from the top of the topstrap and pull the cylinder catch (#7) straight out the rear of the topstrap, noting carefully its position for later reassembly.

9 To disassemble the cylinder: Insert six fired cartridge cases or dummy cartridges into the chambers for support. Push a straight punch through the hole in the ejector rod (#13) and rotate the cylinder (#14) in a counterclockwise direction to unscrew the ejector rod (#13) from the ejector (#15). The ejector spring (#11) can be removed with the ejector rod. The ejector may be pulled out the rear of the cylinder.

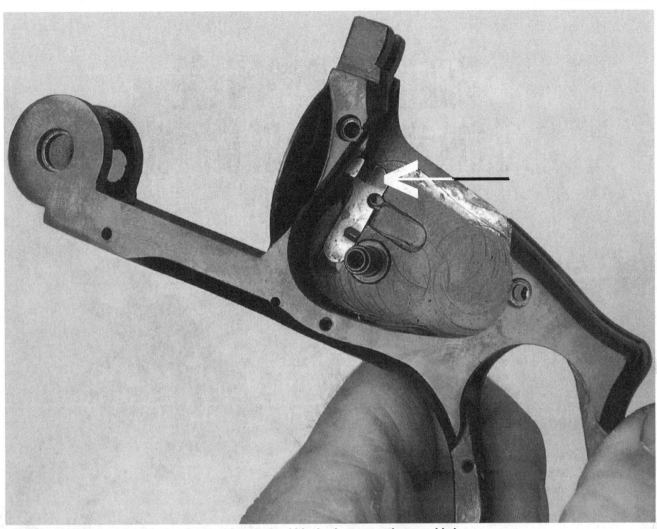

A close-up of the hammer block safety and how it should look when correctly assembled.

10 To disassemble the hammer: Rotate the hand (#35) about 180 degrees and pull it out the left side of the hammer. Use a small pin punch and hammer to drift out the pin (#E) in the center front of the hammer, which holds in the hand spring (#36). The handspring now may be slid out of its recess in the hammer. The hammer stirrup (#33) may be removed by using a pin punch and hammer to drive out its pin (#F) at the rear of the hammer. Note the position of the stirrup (#33) for reassembly. Pay attention to the small screw you see passing through the lower portion of the hammer just behind the hand. It's the actuator for the hammer block safety. This actuator screw is factory installed; it is staked in place and should not be removed.

REASSEMBLY

Reassemble the revolver in reverse order of above.

Smith & Wesson .32 Hand Ejector First Model
(Model of 1896)

The .32 Hand Ejector First Model or Model 1896 was one of only two centerfire revolvers ever made by S&W to have its maker's name, address and patent markings on the cylinder flutes. Revolver courtesy of Jim Supica at Old Town Station. Author photos.

The 1896 or .32 Hand Ejector Model "I" or "i" was the very first side-swing cylinder or Hand Ejector revolver to be produced by S&W. This model was manufactured from 1896 until 1903, at which time it was superseded by the familiar Model 1903 .32 Hand Ejector series. Smith & Wesson's 1896 Model I revolvers were unique compared to all later Hand Ejector revolvers in several areas. First, the cylinder stop was partly external and mounted on top of the lock frame. Actuated by an enlarged spur made as part of the hammer nose or firing pin, the cylinder stop worked in a similar fashion to those used by S&W's tip-up, rimfire revolvers manufactured many years before. In another deviation from their standard practice, the familiar S&W name, address and patent markings were stamped on the flat areas of the cylinder, in between the flutes, instead of on the top of the barrel rib. The Model 1896 and the .44 Wesson Favorite top-break were the only S&W centerfire revolvers to have their cylinders marked like this. Lastly, this model did not use a thumb piece that pushed forward to open the cylinder, as did all later S&W's side-swing revolvers. Instead, the cylinder could be opened by pulling forward on the extractor knob which, in turn, pulled the center pin out of the frame, unlocking the cylinder to be opened for loading and unloading.

The Model of 1896, .32 Hand Ejector First Model was designed around and chambered for the then-brand-new 32 S&W Long caliber. The cylinder held six shots and the revolver was numbered in its own separate serial number range from 1 through 19,712. These interesting little revolvers came with 3-1/4-, 4-1/4- or 6-inch barrels that, like their top-break predecessors, had full-length top ribs. Some examples of the 1896 will have three sideplate screws as illustrated in the photographs below while others will use four sideplate screws. The fourth screw is a short, large-headed screw and is located at the top of the sideplate in a manner similar to all later S&W Hand Ejector Models produced up until about 1962.

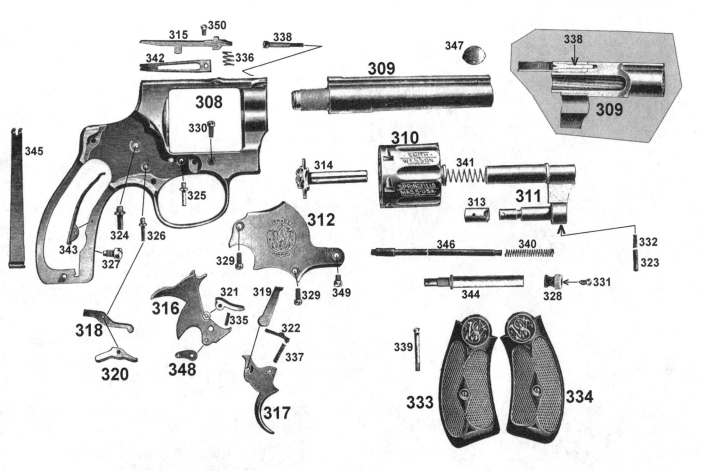

Parts List

309	Barrel		330	Yoke Screw
310	Cylinder		331	Check Screw
311	Yoke		332	Yoke Stop Spring
312	Sideplate		333	Grip
313	Trigger Stop		334	Grip
314	Extractor		335	Sear Spring
315	Cylinder Stop		336	Stop Spring
316	Hammer		337	Hand Spring
317	Trigger		338	Barrel Screw
318	Trigger Lever		339	Grip Screw
319	Hand		340	Center Pin Spring
320	Rebound Lever		341	Extractor Spring
321	Sear		342	Split Spring
322	Hand Lever		343	Trigger Spring
323	Yoke Stop		344	Extractor Rod
324	Hammer Stud		345	Mainspring
325	Trigger Stud		346	Center Pin
326	Trigger Lever Stud		347	Front Sight
327	Strain Screw		348	Hammer Stirrup
328	Extractor Rod Knob		350	Stop Screw
329	Plate Screw			

Unlike any other S&W, to open the cylinder on the 1896 you have to pull the extractor knob forward.

One feature the 1896 shares with other S&W Hand Ejectors is the single screw that holds the yoke and cylinder in the gun.

DISASSEMBLY INSTRUCTIONS

1 Grasp the revolver firmly by its grip, keeping your fingers away from the trigger (#317) and using care to keep the muzzle pointed in a safe direction. Pull forward on the enlarged knob (#328), located at the front of the ejector rod (#344) and push the cylinder (#310) open toward the left side of the revolver. At this point, check to be certain all the cylinder chambers are unloaded. If cartridges are present, tilt the revolver so the rear of the cylinder faces the bench top and push in on the front of the extractor rod knob. This will cause the extractor to eject the cartridges from the cylinder. Be sure you remove all live cartridges from the work area.

2 To remove the cylinder: Remove the yoke screw (#330), the forwardmost screw on the right frame side, located just forward of the sideplate (#312). Line up one of the cylinder flutes with the bottom front of the yoke (#311) and withdraw the cylinder-extractor-yoke assembly out toward the front of the frame (#308). Be aware that most of these models use a yoke stop (#323), a small spring-loaded plunger at the base of the yoke body that pops out when the yoke is withdrawn from the frame. Remove the yoke stop and its spring (#332) by pulling them out the bottom of the yoke.

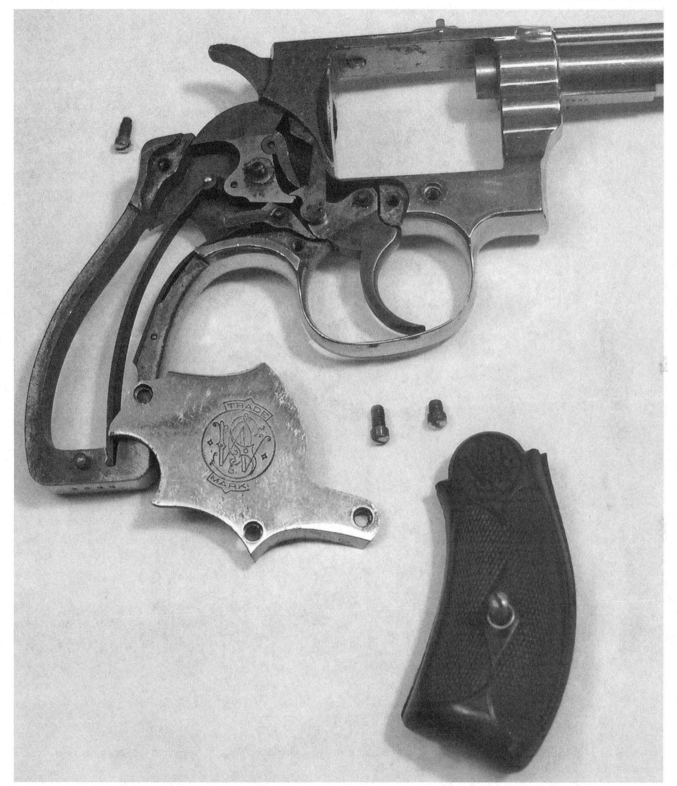

This 1896 has three sideplate screws; some use four. The screw hole forward of the sideplate opening is for the yoke screw.

3 To remove the grips and sideplate: Unscrew and remove the stock screw (#339) and lift off the stocks (#333) and (#334). Unscrew and remove the three (or four, see above) remaining sideplate screws (#329) and (#349). Turn the gun on its side, with the sideplate facing up, and hold the revolver by the barrel over a well-padded bench-top. Use a wooden or plastic mallet to strike the grip frame one or more sharp blows. This will cause the sideplate to jump up and out of its seat with the frame. Never attempt to pry off the sideplate; doing so may damage it or the frame.

Once the mainspring is removed, the hammer may be withdrawn by cocking it, holding the trigger to the rear and lifting the hammer out of the frame.

4 To remove the mainspring and hammer: Unscrew and remove the strain screw (#327) from the lower front of the grip frame. The mainspring (#345) can now be disengaged from its seat at the lower grip frame, then disengaged from the hammer stirrup (#348) at its top and withdrawn from the frame. Pull the trigger all the way to the rear. This will cause the hammer (#316) to rise. Withdraw the hammer straight up and off its stud (#324) in the frame while the trigger is still pulled to the rear. Once the hammer is out, release the trigger.

Here the trigger spring, trigger, rebound and trigger lever have been removed. Notice the positions of these parts and pay attention to how they fit together. The trigger, trigger lever and rebound are removed and installed as an assembly.

5 To remove the trigger components: Using a small pin punch, drive out the pin that holds in the trigger spring (#343). This is located in the front grip strap. For later reassembly, note how the trigger spring bears on the trigger lever (#318) and the rebound lever (#320). Remove the trigger spring from the gun. With the trigger in the forward position, use a small tool to pull the top of the hand (#319) toward the rear until it is clear of the frame. While holding the hand to the rear, withdraw the trigger and hand assembly, along with the attached trigger lever and rebound lever, straight up and off their studs on the frame. Stop here to make a careful note of the relationship of these assembled trigger components for later reassembly.

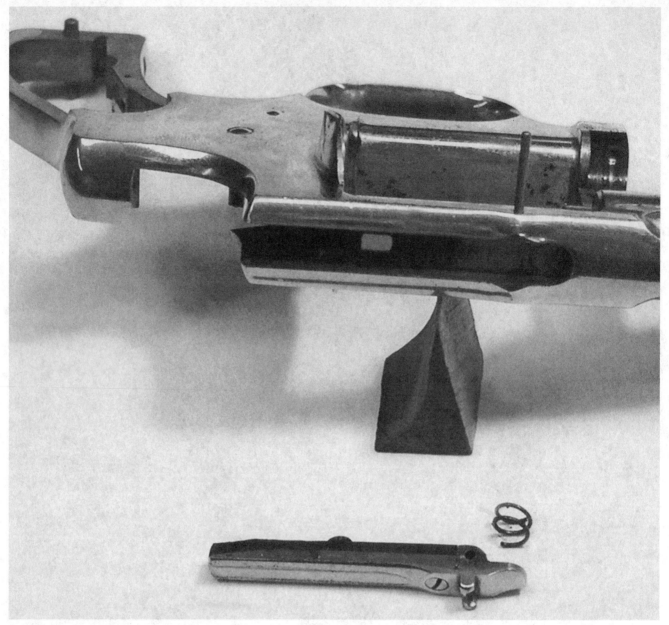

Removing the cylinder stop and its spring involves the removal of only one pin and it may be done, if needed, without disassembling any other area of the revolver.

6 To remove the cylinder stop: Use a cup-tipped pin punch and hammer to remove the cylinder stop retaining pin located at the frame topstrap. The cylinder stop (#315) and its spring (#336) may now be withdrawn through the top of the frame. The split spring (#342) is held onto the bottom of the cylinder stop by the stop screw (#350), which passes through the top of the cylinder stop. Note: Some examples of the Model 1896 have a barrel screw (#338-see inset) that passes through the top of the frame into the rear of the barrel rib to prevent the barrel from turning. Removal of this screw is not recommended.

7 To disassemble the cylinder: Insert six fired cartridge cases in the chambers to support the extractor. Hold the extractor knob (#326) in leather-padded vise jaws to keep it from turning and carefully unscrew and remove the check screw (#331) from the center front of the extractor knob. Hold the rear of the center pin (#346) tightly in a drill press chuck while unscrewing the extractor knob from the center pin in a counterclockwise direction. The center pin and its spring (#340) can now be pulled out through the rear of the extractor (#314). Withdraw the yoke (#311) toward the front, off the rod. Next, grasp the extractor rod (#344) in a drill press chuck or lathe chuck and turn the cylinder (#310) in a counterclockwise direction to unscrew the extractor from the extractor

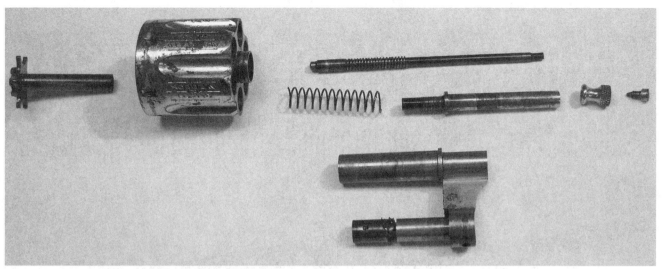

The pieces that make up the 1896 cylinder assembly.

The split spring is located under the cylinder stop and is held on by this screw.

rod. Then pull the extractor rod and extractor spring (#341) out the front of the cylinder. The extractor (#314) is now free and can be pulled out the rear of the cylinder.

If necessary, the trigger stop (#313) may be removed from the yoke by pulling the trigger stop all the way to the rear of the yoke stem and driving out its pin (not shown). Pay careful attention to the relationship of the trigger stop and yoke before removing the trigger stop. The trigger stop can then be slid off to the rear.

8 To disassemble the trigger: Pull the hand straight out the right side of the trigger. Using a tiny pin punch and hammer, drift out the hand lever pin, the only cross pin in the trigger, and pull the hand lever

(#322) and its spring (#337) out through the top of the trigger. For reassembly of the trigger and hand, the rear of the trigger lever must be held up while the hand is inserted back into the trigger to be sure it receives spring pressure from the hand lever.

Further disassembly is not required for normal cleaning and maintenance of the revolver mechanism.

REASSEMBLY

Reverse the above procedures to reassemble the revolver.

Smith & Wesson .32 Hand Ejector (H.E.)
Models 1903 2nd Change through 32 Hand Ejector Third Model

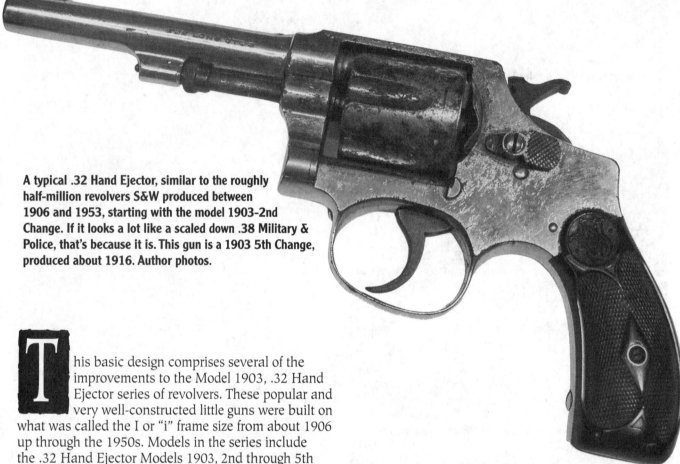

A typical .32 Hand Ejector, similar to the roughly half-million revolvers S&W produced between 1906 and 1953, starting with the model 1903-2nd Change. If it looks a lot like a scaled down .38 Military & Police, that's because it is. This gun is a 1903 5th Change, produced about 1916. Author photos.

This basic design comprises several of the improvements to the Model 1903, .32 Hand Ejector series of revolvers. These popular and very well-constructed little guns were built on what was called the I or "i" frame size from about 1906 up through the 1950s. Models in the series include the .32 Hand Ejector Models 1903, 2nd through 5th changes; the .32 Hand Ejector - 3rd Model; 22-32 Target and Kit Gun; .32 and .38 Regulation Police; and the .38 Terrier.

For ease of identification, the models are outlined below by serial number with their dates of manufacture. .32- and .22-caliber revolvers built on this frame had six-shot capacity while the .38 caliber revolvers held only five shots.

1903 2nd: manufactured 1906 to 1909, serial numbers 51,127 to 95,500.

1903 3rd: manufactured 1909 to 1910, serial numbers 95,501 to 96,125.

1903 4th: manufactured 1910, serial numbers 96,126 to 102,500.

1903 5th: manufactured 1910 to 1917, serial numbers 102,501 to around 263,000.

32 Hand Ejector 3rd Model: manufactured 1917 to 1942, serial numbers around 263,000-534,532.

22/32 Hand Ejector: manufactured 1911 to 1953, serial numbers start at around 160,000 within the .32 H.E. number series.

22/32 Kit Gun: manufactured 1935 to 1953. Serial numbers from 525,670 within .32 Hand Ejector series.

.32 Regulation Police: manufactured starting 1917. Serial numbers from about 263,000 within the .32 Hand Ejector numbering series.

.38 Regulation Police: starting 1917. Serial numbers in its own series beginning with 1.

.38 Terrier: starting 1936. Serial numbers within the .38 Regulation Police series from 38,796.

The illustration that follows is representative of a late-production Hand Ejector, 1903 - 5th change, circa

1917. Other models in this series are nearly identical to the illustration shown. There are differences between type and model. Early models have a separate ejector rod head or knob and a screw in the rear of the bolt to retain the bolt plunger. .32 Hand Ejector Third Models have a hammer block safety, and many of these have a spring and plunger mounted within the sideplate to supply tension to the hand, thereby taking the place of the hand lever and hand lever spring used in earlier and in later models.

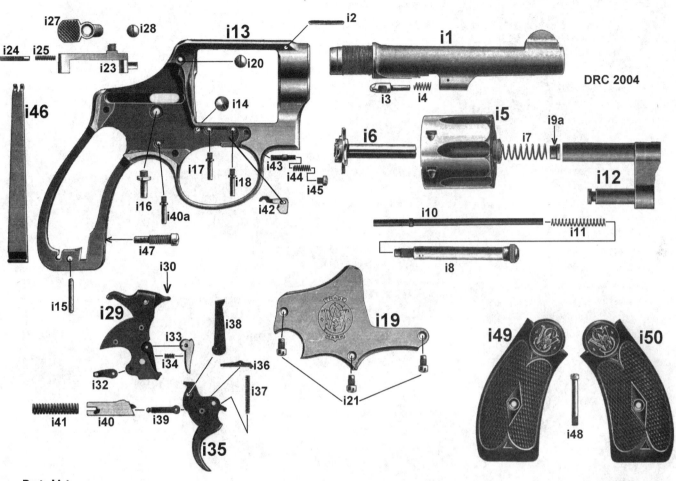

DRC 2004

Parts List

i1	Barrel	i17	Trigger Stud	i32	Hammer Stirrup	i48	Stock Screw
i2	Barrel Pin	i18	Cylinder Stop Stud	i33	Sear	i49	Stock
i3	Locking Bolt	i19	Sideplate	i34	Sear Spring	i50	Stock
i4	Locking Bolt Spring	i20	Sideplate Screw, large head	i35	Trigger	i53	Hammer Block, 1st type, not shown
i5	Cylinder	i21	Sideplate Screw, small head	i36	Hand Lever	i53A	Hammer Block Plunger, not shown
i6	Extractor			i37	Hand Lever Spring		
i7	Extractor Spring	i23	Bolt	i38	Hand	i53B	Hammer Block Spring, not shown
i8	Extractor Rod	i24	Bolt Plunger	i39	Trigger Lever		
i9	Extractor Knob (early models only)	i25	Bolt Plunger Spring	i40	Rebound Slide	i53C	Hammer Block, 2nd type, not shown
		i26	Bolt Plunger Screw, early	i41	Rebound Slide Spring		
i9A	Extractor Collar			i42	Cylinder Stop		
i10	Center Pin	i27	Thumb Piece	i43	Cylinder Stop Plunger		
i11	Center Pin Spring	i28	Thumb Piece Nut				
i12	Yoke	i29	Hammer	i44	Cylinder Stop Spring		
i13	Frame	i30	Hammer Nose (firing Pin)	i45	Cylinder Stop Screw		
i14	Frame Lug			i46	Mainspring		
i15	Grip Pin	i31	Hammer Nose Rivet	i47	Strain Screw		
i16	Hammer Stud						

Always check first to be sure the cylinder is unloaded.

In this photo, the cylinder assembly has been removed, as well as the grips and the sideplate.

DISASSEMBLY INSTRUCTIONS

1 Check first to be sure the revolver is unloaded. Grasp the revolver firmly by its grip, keeping your fingers away from the trigger (#i35) and being careful to keep the muzzle pointed in a safe direction. Push forward on the thumb piece (#i27) and push the cylinder (#i5) open toward the left side of the revolver. At this point, check to be certain all the chambers are unloaded. If cartridges are present, tilt the revolver so the rear of the cylinder faces the bench top and push in on the front of the extractor rod (#i8). This will cause the extractor to eject the cartridges from the cylinder. Be sure to remove all live cartridges from the work area.

2 To remove the cylinder: Remove the yoke screw (#i22), the forwardmost of the sideplate screws. Line up one of the cylinder flutes with the bottom front of the yoke (#i12) and withdraw the cylinder-extractor-yoke assembly out toward the front of the frame (#i13).

The mainspring and hammer are the next parts to be removed once the sideplate is off the frame. Please read the caution regarding sideplate removal in the text.

3 To remove the grips and sideplate: Remove the stock screw (#i48) and lift off the stocks (#i49) and (#i50). Unscrew and remove the three remaining sideplate screws (#i20) and (#i21). Turn the gun on its side with the sideplate facing up and hold the revolver by the barrel over a well-padded bench-top. Use a wooden or plastic mallet to strike the grip frame one or more sharp blows. This will cause the sideplate (#i19) to jump up and out of its seat with the frame. Never attempt to pry off the sideplate as you may damage it or the frame.

4 To remove the mainspring and hammer: Remove the strain screw (#i47) from the front of the grip frame. The mainspring (#i46) can now be disengaged from its seat at the lower grip frame and then disengaged from the hammer stirrup (#i32) at its top and withdrawn from the frame. While holding the thumb piece to the rear, pull the trigger all the way back. This will cause the hammer to rise. Withdraw the hammer straight up and off its stud (#i16) in the frame while the trigger is still pulled to the rear. Once the hammer is out, you may release the trigger.

The rebound slide, trigger assembly and cylinder stop shown out of the frame. The small plunger and spring to the right power the cylinder stop. They fit into a small hole in the frame at the front of the triggerguard.

5 To remove the trigger: Using a small screwdriver or suitable tool, pry up on the rear of the rebound slide (#i40) until it pivots up off its stud (#i40a) in the frame. Use caution here: this action will free the coiled rebound slide spring (#i41), which is under heavy tension. Pull rearward to remove the rebound slide and its spring from the frame. With the trigger in the forward position, use a small tool to pivot the top of the hand (#i38) toward the rear until it is clear of the frame. While holding the hand to the rear, withdraw the trigger and hand assembly straight up and off its stud (#i17) on the frame.

Beginning with the .32 Hand Ejector Third Model, S&W used a small plunger and spring mounted in the sideplate to supply tension to the rear of the hand. The plunger was tapered and controlled the action of the hammer block safety, also mounted within the plate.

The .32 Hand Ejector cylinder shown disassembled. These early models used a separate ejector rod head that had to be unscrewed first before the cylinder would come off the yoke. Always insert six fired cases or dummy cartridges into the chambers to support the extractor before trying to unscrew the rod.

6 To remove the cylinder stop: Unscrew and remove the cylinder stop screw (#i45) located at the front of the triggerguard. The cylinder stop plunger (#i43) and its spring (#i44) may now be withdrawn through the same screw hole. Push the ball-end of the cylinder stop (#i42) to its lowest position and then use a pair of tweezers to withdraw the cylinder stop straight up and off its stud (#i18) in the frame.

7 To disassemble the cylinder: Using an extractor rod removal tool or, alternatively, grasp the extractor rod (#i8) by the round area behind the head in a drill press chuck. Insert six-empty cartridges casings in the chambers to support the extractor. Unscrew the cylinder (#i5) from the extractor rod (#i8) in a counterclockwise direction. Remove the chuck or tool from the extractor rod and withdraw it from the front of the cylinder. The center pin (#i10) and its spring (#i11) can now be withdrawn from the front of the cylinder. Withdraw the yoke (#i12) from the front of the cylinder. The extractor collar (#i9A) and extractor spring (#i7) can now be removed from the front. The extractor (#i6) can be pushed out of the cylinder (#i5) toward the rear.

This trigger and hand are typical of all .32 H.E.s before the
32 Hand Ejector Third Model. Triggers have a coil spring
(shown) and lever within them to supply tension to the hand.

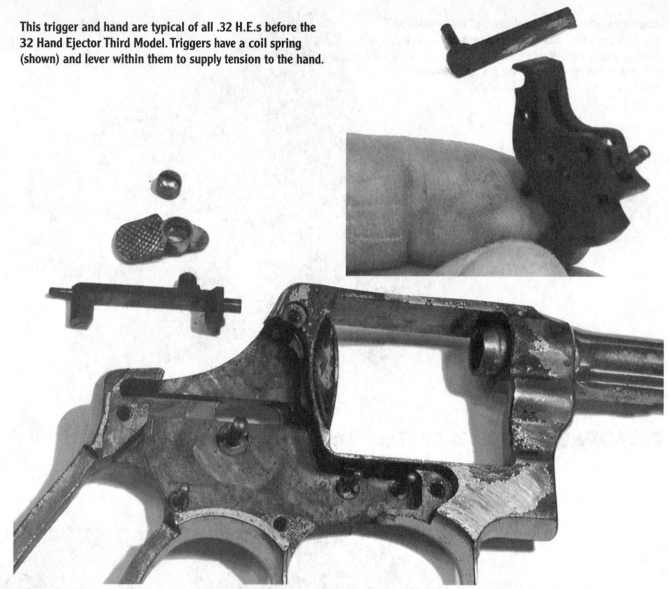

The thumb piece, its nut and the bolt shown out of the frame. This bolt is typical of early 32 H.E.'s. Notice the small screw at
the lower left leg that retains its plunger and spring. The screw was eliminated with the .32 H.E. Third Model.

8 To disassemble the trigger: Always support the
trigger by laying it on its side on a flat steel
block with holes drilled through it for the pins to be
driven through. Pull the hand (#i38) straight out the
right side of the trigger. Using a tiny pin punch, drift
out the hand lever pin (this is the only cross pin in
the trigger) and pull the hand lever (#i36) and its
spring (#i37) out through the top of the trigger. 32 HE
Third Models do not use a hand lever and hand lever
spring; instead, there is a spring and plunger mounted
within the sideplate that supply tension to the hand
as well as activate the hammer block safety. For
reassembly of the hand, the rear of the trigger lever
must be held up while the hand is inserted back into
the trigger to be sure it receives spring pressure from
the hand lever.

9 To disassemble the hammer: Always support
the hammer by laying it on its side on a flat
steel block with holes drilled through it for the pins
to be driven through. Use a small pin punch and
hammer to drive out the sear pin. The sear (#i33) and
sear spring (#i34) are now free and can be pulled off
the front of the hammer. Driving out the stirrup pin
frees the stirrup for removal. Note the position of the
stirrup before taking it off the hammer, for it must be
reassembled in this same position.

Further disassembly is not required for normal
cleaning and maintenance of the revolver mechanism.

REASSEMBLY

Reverse the above procedures to reassemble the
revolver.

Smith & Wesson "K" frame
.38 Hand Ejector (H.E.) 1st Model
(Model of 1899 Military & Police 38 & 32/20)

The first M&P or Military & Police was introduced in 1899 as the .38 (or 32-20) Hand Ejector First Model. Revolver courtesy of Jim Supica of Old Town Station. Author photos.

The Smith & Wesson 38 or 32/20 caliber Hand Ejector First Model, also known as the Model of 1899, was the first of what would become the world-famous "K"-frame S&W Hand Ejector series of revolvers. All these revolvers featured side-swing, six-shot cylinders and manual, simultaneous rod ejection of the spent cartridges. The 1899 was manufactured from 1899 until 1902 and is the only model in the long-lived M&P series of revolvers that does not use a barrel underlug to house the front locking bolt, by which feature it may be easily distinguished from all later models. This model was chambered in 38 S&W Special and 38 Long Colt as well as in 32-20. Available barrels lengths were 4, 5, 6 and 6-1/2 inches. The revolvers were furnished with a round butt. Beginning with this model and continuing into all later Military & Police models, target sights adjustable for windage and elevation were available. Target front sight blades were removable and were pinned into the barrel's sight base.

One thousand each of this model were purchased by the U.S. Army and the U.S. Navy, all of which were supplied with 6-inch barrels and blue finish. All military revolvers were chambered in caliber 38 Long Colt, the then standard U.S. service cartridge, and used walnut stocks. Army models are serial numbered in the S&W 13,001 to 14,000 number range. U.S. Navy models were stamped with their own separate serial numbers from 1 to 1,000 in addition to the factory serial number and occur within the S&W 5,001 to 6,000 serial range.

Serial Numbering: 32/20- and .38-chambered Military & Police Hand Ejectors were each numbered in their own individual number series. 32/20: serial number 1 to 5,311; .38: 1 to 20,975.

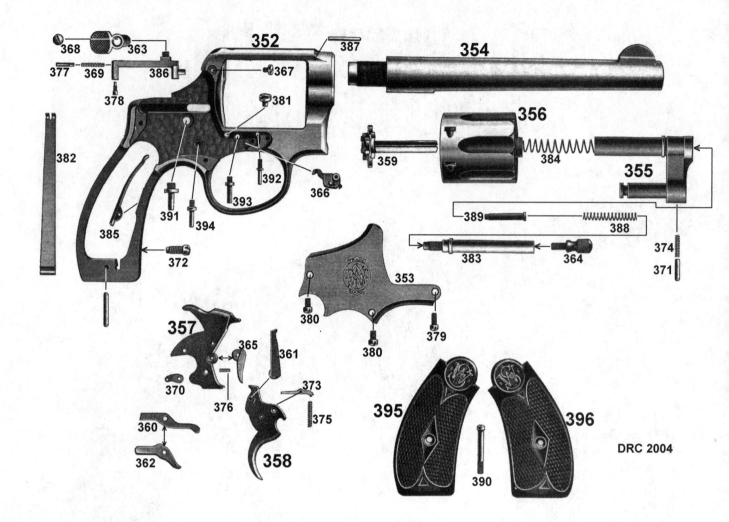

DRC 2004

Parts List

353	Sideplate	367	Sideplate Screw, Domed	382	Mainspring
354	Barrel	368	Thumb Piece Nut	383	Extractor Rod
355	Yoke	369	Bolt Plunger Spring	384	Extractor Spring
356	Cylinder	370	Stirrup	385	Trigger Spring
357	Hammer	371	Yoke Stop	386	Bolt
358	Trigger	372	Strain Screw	387	Barrel Pin
359	Extractor	373	Hand Lever	388	Center Pin Spring
360	Trigger Lever	374	Yoke Stop Spring	389	Center Pin
361	Hand	375	Hand Lever Spring	390	Stock Screw
362	Rebound Lever	376	Sear Spring	391	Hammer Stud
363	Thumb Piece	377	Bolt Plunger	392	Cylinder Stop Stud
364	Extractor Knob	378	Bolt Plunger Screw	393	Trigger Stud
365	Sear	379	Yoke Screw	394	Trigger Lever Stud
366	Cylinder Stop	380	Sideplate Screw, Large Head	395	Grip
		381	Frame Lug	396	Grip

Removing the front sideplate screw, called the yoke screw, enables the yoke-cylinder assembly to be removed from the front. Notice the small plunger protruding from the bottom of the yoke. This is the yoke stop and it is under spring tension, so hold it captive with your thumb as you withdraw the yoke.

DISASSEMBLY INSTRUCTIONS
(also see Model 1902)

1 First, make sure the revolver is unloaded. Grasp the revolver firmly by its grip, keeping your fingers away from the trigger (#358) and being careful to keep the muzzle pointed in a safe direction. Push forward on the thumb piece (#363) and push the cylinder (#356) open, toward the left side of the revolver. At this point, check to be certain all the cylinder chambers are unloaded. If cartridges are present, tilt the revolver so the rear of the cylinder faces the bench top and push in on the extractor rod knob (#364). This will cause the extractor to eject the cartridges from the cylinder. Remove all live cartridges from the work area.

2 To remove the cylinder: Remove the yoke screw (#379), which is the forwardmost sideplate screw. Line up one of the cylinder flutes with the bottom front of the yoke (#355) and withdraw the cylinder-extractor-yoke assembly through the front of the frame (#352). Take note of the yoke stop (#371) and yoke stop spring (#374) located in the lower yoke barrel. These parts are under spring tension and are now free to fall out upon removal of the yoke.

The sideplate comes off after removing its four retaining screws. Notice the front screw is the only one with a pilot at the end of the threads to fit into the yoke stem.

3 To remove the grips and sideplate: Remove the stock screw (#390) and lift off the stocks (#395) and (#396). Unscrew and remove the three remaining sideplate screws (#367) and (#380). Turn the gun on its side with the sideplate facing up and hold the revolver by the barrel over a well-padded bench-top. Use a wooden or plastic mallet to strike the grip frame one or more sharp blows. This will cause the sideplate (#353) to jump up and out of its seat with the frame. Never attempt to pry off the sideplate as damage to the frame or sideplate may result.

Once the mainspring is taken out, hold the thumb piece to the rear and pull the trigger to raise the hammer and lift it out of the frame.

4 To remove the mainspring and hammer: Remove the strain screw (#372) from the front of the grip frame. The mainspring (#382) may now be disengaged from its seat at the lower grip frame, then disengaged from the hammer stirrup at its top and withdrawn from the frame. While holding the thumb piece to the rear,

pull the trigger (#358) all the way back. This will cause the hammer (#357) to rise. Withdraw the hammer by lifting it straight up and off its stud (#391) in the frame while the trigger is still held to the rear. Once the hammer is out, release the trigger.

Here you can see that after the trigger spring is removed, the trigger with its attendant components can be lifted out as a unit. The parts are separated here to illustrate their correct relationship.

5 To remove the trigger and its component parts: Using an appropriate-sized pin punch, drive out the trigger spring pin located in the front grip strap. This will free the trigger spring (#385) for removal. Hold the hand (#361) to the rear far enough so it will clear the frame. At the same time pull the trigger (#358), the rebound (#362) and the trigger lever (#360) as an assembly straight up off their studs (#393) and (#394) in the frame and remove all of these components as a unit. Make careful note of the positioning of these parts for reassembly.

At reassembly: Reinstall the trigger with the hand, trigger lever and rebound as an assembly onto their studs in the frame. Place the trigger spring in place in its seat in the grip frame and compress the bottom of the spring into the frame by using a pair of spreader pliers until the pin holes align, and then reinstall the trigger spring pin.

The cylinder stop and bolt assemblies are removed and the frame is stripped as far as necessary for routine maintenance.

6 To remove the cylinder stop: Hold down on the locking bolt portion of the cylinder stop (#366) until its locking bolt is clear of the frame, and then pull the cylinder stop straight up off its stud (#392) and out of the frame.

7 To remove the bolt: Unscrew and remove the thumb piece nut (#368) and lift off the thumb piece (#363). The bolt (#386) may now be removed by pushing it all the way to the rear and pivoting its front end up clear of the frame. The bolt spring (#369) and plunger (#377) are held captive in the rear of the bolt by the bolt plunger screw (#378).

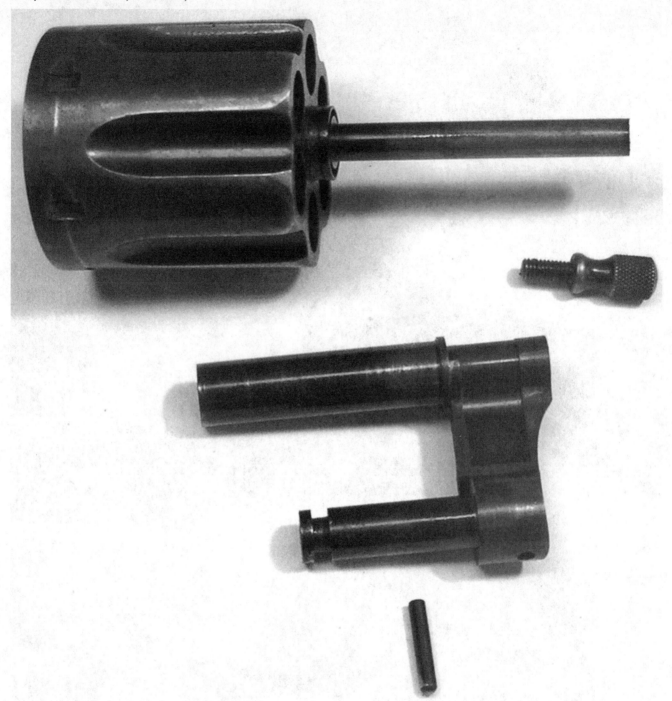

After the extractor knob has been unscrewed, the yoke may be slid out from the front of the cylinder. The plunger under the yoke is the yoke stop. Its spring is still inside the yoke bottom.

8 To disassemble the cylinder: Insert six empty cartridge casings or dummy cartridges into the cylinder chambers. Grasp the extractor knob (#364) in a padded vise and unscrew it from the extractor rod (#383) by turning in a counterclockwise direction. Note: It may be necessary to grasp and hold the round portion of the extractor rod with an extractor rod removal tool to keep it from turning along with the knob. Using an extractor rod removal tool or, alternatively, grasping the extractor rod (#383) by

the round area in a drill press chuck, unscrew the cylinder (#356) from the extractor rod by rotating it in a counterclockwise direction. Remove the chuck or tool from the extractor rod and withdraw the yoke (#355) from the front of the cylinder. The extractor rod and the extractor spring (#384) can also be removed from the front of the cylinder. The center pin (#389) and its spring (#388) are free and may now be withdrawn from the front of the extractor (#359) stem. The extractor is now pushed out of the cylinder, toward the rear.

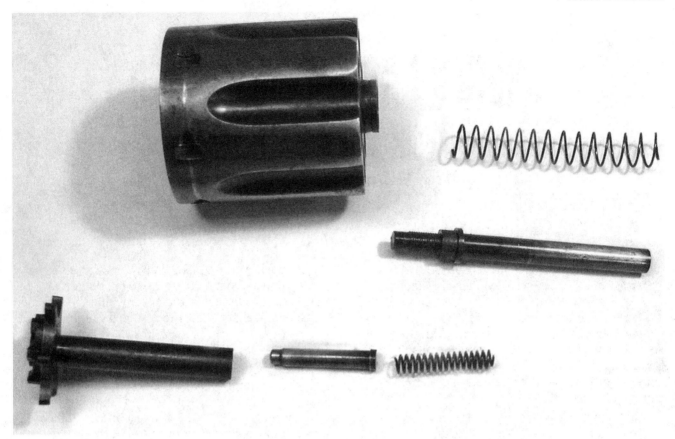

The 1899's cylinder all disassembled. Notice the short center pin, which is unique to this model Hand Ejector.

9 To disassemble the trigger: Pull the hand straight up, out of the right side of the trigger. Using a tiny pin punch, drift out the hand lever pin (this is the only cross pin in the trigger) and pull the hand lever (#373) and its spring (#375) out through the top of the trigger. For reassembly of the hand, the rear of the trigger lever must be held in the up position while the hand is inserted back into the trigger to be sure it receives spring pressure from the hand lever.

10 To disassemble the hammer: Use a cup-tipped pin punch and hammer to drive out the sear pin. This frees the sear (#365) and the sear spring

(#376) to be pulled off the front of the hammer. To remove the stirrup, drive out the stirrup pin and lift the stirrup (#370) off the rear. Take note of the position of the stirrup for later reassembly so that it is not installed upside down. The firing pin or hammer nose is riveted in place with a solid rivet and its removal is not required for normal maintenance.

Further disassembly is not required for normal cleaning and maintenance of the revolver mechanism.

REASSEMBLY

Reassemble in the reverse order of above.

Smith & Wesson "K" frame,
.38 Hand Ejector (H.E.) 2nd Model
(Models 1902 and 1902 1st Change, Military & Police 38 & 32/20)

The Smith & Wesson Model 1902, Military and Police Second Model, also known as the Model of 1902, was the second in what would become the long evolutionary chain of famous "K"-frame S&W Hand Ejector series of revolvers. 1902 Models were available in 38 S&W Special, 38 Long Colt and 32/20 and featured side-swing cylinders with six-shots and manual, simultaneous rod ejection.

Although it shared the same basic internal action as the earlier 1899 M&P, this was the first of the M&P series of revolvers to use a barrel underlug that housed the front locking bolt to lock the extractor rod when the cylinder was closed. The hammers on 1902s also used two pins inserted through the hammer sides that were intended to prevent them from chafing on the interior of the action. The 1902 was made from 1902 to 1903 with barrel lengths of 4, 5, 6 and 6-1/2 inches and with a rounded butt. One thousand of the 1902 model revolvers were purchased by the U.S. Navy with 6-inch barrels and blue finish. The Navy revolvers were chambered in 38 Long Colt, the then-standard U.S. service cartridge, and featured walnut stocks. U.S.

Navy models were stamped with their own separate serial numbers from 1,001 to 2,000 in addition to the factory serial numbering and occur within the Smith & Wesson .38-caliber 25,001 to 26,000 serial range.

The 1902, 1st Change was identical to the Model 1902 except for the following changes: the barrel's thread diameter was increased from .500" to .546" with slight alterations to the yoke and frame. Round or square butt shapes were offered, starting with serial number 58,000 (.38 caliber) on November 18, 1904. Built from 1903 through 1905, the 1902, 1st Change was available commercially with 4, 5, and 6-1/2-inch barrels.

Serial numbering: 32/20 and .38 S&W/S&W Special Hand Ejectors were numbered in their own separate serial number series.

1902: 32/20: 5,312 to 9,811

1902, 38 S&W/S&W Special: 20,976 to 33,803

1902 1st Change, 32/20 caliber: 9,812 to 18,125

1902 1st Change, 38 S&W/S&W Special: 33,804 to 62,449

Please refer to the photos in the Model 1899 section. The two revolvers are internally almost identical with the obvious differences being the 1899's lack of a barrel underlug as well as differences in extractor rods and center pins.

DISASSEMBLY INSTRUCTIONS

1 First, make sure the revolver is unloaded. Grasp the revolver firmly by its grip, keeping your fingers away from the trigger (#531) and being careful to keep the muzzle pointed in a safe direction. Push forward on the thumb piece (#536) and push the cylinder (#529) open toward the left side of the revolver. At this point, check to be certain all the chambers are unloaded. If cartridges are present, tilt the revolver so the rear of the cylinder faces the bench top and push in on the extractor rod knob (#538). This will cause the extractor to eject the cartridges from the cylinder. Remove all live cartridges from the work area.

2 To remove the cylinder: Remove the yoke screw (#551). This is the forwardmost sideplate screw. Line up one of the cylinder flutes with the bottom front of the yoke (#528) and withdraw the cylinder-extractor-yoke assembly through the front of the frame (#525). Note: be sure to watch out for the yoke stop (#568) and yoke stop spring located in the lower yoke barrel. These parts are under spring tension and are free to fall out on removal of the yoke.

3 To remove the grips and sideplate: Remove the stock screw (#566) and lift off the stocks (#570) and (#571). Unscrew and remove the three remaining sideplate screws (#550) (#552). Turn the gun on its

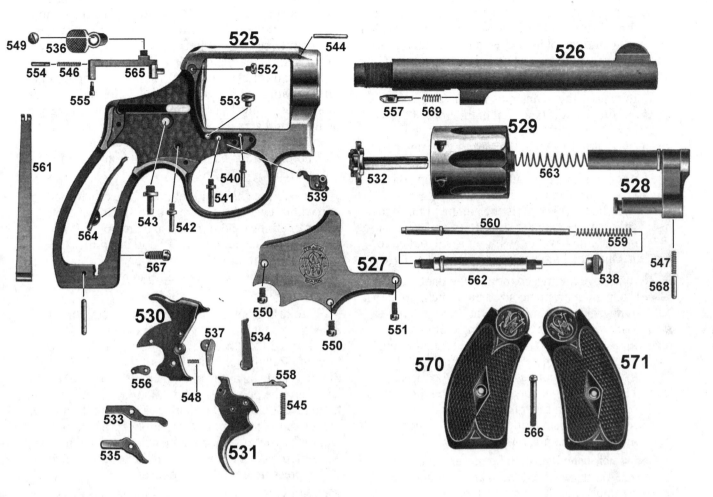

Parts List

525	Frame	541	Trigger Stud	557	Locking Bolt
526	Barrel	542	Trigger Lever Stud	558	Hand Lever
527	Sideplate	543	Hammer Stud	559	Center Pin Spring
528	Yoke	544	Barrel Pin	560	Center Pin
529	Cylinder	545	Hand Lever Spring	561	Mainspring
530	Hammer	546	Bolt Plunger Spring	562	Extractor Rod
531	Trigger	547	Yoke Stop Spring	563	Extractor Spring
532	Extractor	548	Sear Spring	564	Trigger Spring
533	Trigger Lever	549	Thumb Piece Nut	565	Bolt
534	Hand	550	Sideplate Screw, Domed	566	Stock Screw
535	Rebound Lever	551	Yoke Screw	567	Strain Screw
536	Thumb Piece	552	Sideplate Screw, Large Head	568	Yoke Stop
537	Sear	553	Frame Lug	569	Locking Bolt Spring
538	Extractor Knob	554	Bolt Plunger	570	Grip
539	Cylinder Stop	555	Bolt Plunger Screw	571	Grip
540	Cylinder Stop Stud	556	Stirrup		

side with the sideplate facing up and hold the revolver by the barrel over a well-padded bench-top. Use a wooden or plastic mallet to strike the grip frame one or more sharp blows. This will cause the sideplate (#527) to jump up and out of its seat with the frame. Never attempt to pry off the sideplate as damage to the frame or sideplate can result.

4 To remove the mainspring and hammer: Remove the strain screw (#567) from the front of the grip frame. The mainspring (#561) may now be disengaged from its seat at the lower grip frame and then disengaged from the hammer stirrup at its top and withdrawn from the frame. While holding the thumb piece (#536) to the rear, pull the trigger (#531) all the way back. This causes the hammer (#530) to rise. Withdraw the hammer straight up and off its stud (#543) in the frame while the trigger is still pulled to the rear. Once the hammer is out, release the trigger.

5 To remove the trigger and its attendant parts: Using an appropriate-sized pin punch, drive out the trigger spring pin (located in the front grip strap). This will free the trigger spring (#564) for removal. Hold the hand (#534) to the rear far enough so it will clear the frame. At the same time pull the trigger (#531), the rebound (#535) and the trigger lever (#533) as an assembly straight up off their studs (#541) and (#542) in the frame and remove all of these components as a unit. Take careful notice of the positioning of these parts for reassembly.

Reassembly note: Reinstall the trigger (#531) with the hand (#534), trigger lever (#533) and rebound (#535) as an assembly into the frame on their studs. Place the trigger spring (#564) in place at its seat and press the bottom of the spring down by using a pair of spreader-type pliers until the pin holes align. Then reinstall the trigger spring pin.

6 To remove the cylinder stop: Hold down on the bolt portion of the cylinder stop (#539) until its locking bolt is clear of the frame and then pull the cylinder stop straight up, off its stud (#540) and out of the frame.

7 To remove the bolt: Unscrew and remove the thumb piece nut (#549) and lift off the thumb piece (#536). Working now from the inside of the frame, you can remove the bolt (#565) by pushing it all the way to the rear and pivoting its front end up and out of the frame.

8 To disassemble the cylinder and yoke: Insert six empty cartridge cases in the cylinder chambers. Grasp the extractor knob (#538) in a padded vise and unscrew it from the extractor rod (#562) by turning it in a counterclockwise direction. It may be necessary to grasp and hold the round portion of the extractor rod with an extractor rod removal tool to keep it from turning with the knob. Using an extractor rod removal tool or, alternatively, grasping the extractor rod (#562) by the round area in a drill press chuck, unscrew the cylinder from the extractor rod in a counterclockwise direction. Withdraw the yoke (#528) from the front of the cylinder.

Remove the chuck or tool from the extractor rod and withdraw it from the front of the cylinder. The extractor spring (#563) may also be removed from the front. The center pin (#560) and its spring (#559) may now be withdrawn from the front of the extractor (#532) stem. The extractor (#532) may be pushed out of the cylinder toward the rear.

9 To disassemble the trigger: Always support the trigger by laying it on its side on a flat steel block with holes drilled through it for the pins to be driven through. Pull the hand straight out the right side of the trigger. Using a tiny pin punch, drift out the hand lever pin (the only cross pin in the trigger) and pull the hand lever (#558) and its spring (#545) out through the top of the trigger. For reassembly of the hand, the rear of the trigger lever must be held up while the hand is inserted back into the trigger to be sure it receives spring pressure from the hand lever.

10 To disassemble the hammer: Always support the hammer by laying it on its side on a flat steel block with holes drilled through it for the pins to be driven through. Use a small pin punch and hammer to drive out the sear pin. The sear (#537) and sear spring (#548) are free and can be pulled off the front of the hammer. Driving out the stirrup pin frees the stirrup (#55) for removal. Note the position of the stirrup before taking it off the hammer; it must be reassembled in this same position.

Further disassembly is not required for normal cleaning and maintenance of the revolver mechanism.

REASSEMBLY

Reassemble in reverse order of above.

Smith & Wesson "K" Frame,

38 and 32/20 Hand Ejector (H.E.)

Military & Police Models of 1905 (Includes Victory Model and K-22)

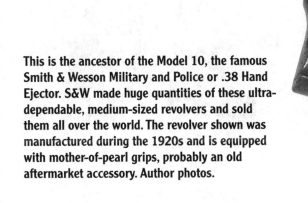

This is the ancestor of the Model 10, the famous Smith & Wesson Military and Police or .38 Hand Ejector. S&W made huge quantities of these ultra-dependable, medium-sized revolvers and sold them all over the world. The revolver shown was manufactured during the 1920s and is equipped with mother-of-pearl grips, probably an old aftermarket accessory. Author photos.

T he Smith & Wesson Military & Police Model of 1905 (built in 1905 and 1906) differed from previous M&P models by being the first to feature the now-common reciprocating cylinder stop, powered by a coiled spring and plunger inserted through the frame forward of the triggerguard. That change necessitated a new trigger. With the Model 1905, 1st Change, the leaf-type trigger return spring and the rebound lever assembly were replaced by the now common rebound slide and coil spring to return the trigger. The new system automatically provided a steel block under the hammer to prevent the firing pin from reaching the primer unless the trigger was pulled to the rear. From 1906 on, the Model 1905 went through to additional model changes, each having subtle internal mechanical improvements over the former, until the final variation, the Model 1904, 4th Change, emerged in 1914.

These Model 1905, 4th Change revolvers were changed and improved from the earlier Model 1905 versions in the following areas: chafing bushings were removed from the hammer and trigger and a new, plunger-operated leaf spring hammer block safety was introduced. This added safety device was intended to prevent accidental discharge should the revolver be dropped on its hammer. All Military and Police cylinders were heat-treated starting in 1919 with the serial number 316,648 in the .38 calibers and at serial number 81,287 in the 32/20 numbering series. Barrel lengths were also standardized to 4, 5 and 6 inches. The 2-inch barrel length was added to the .38-caliber series in 1933.

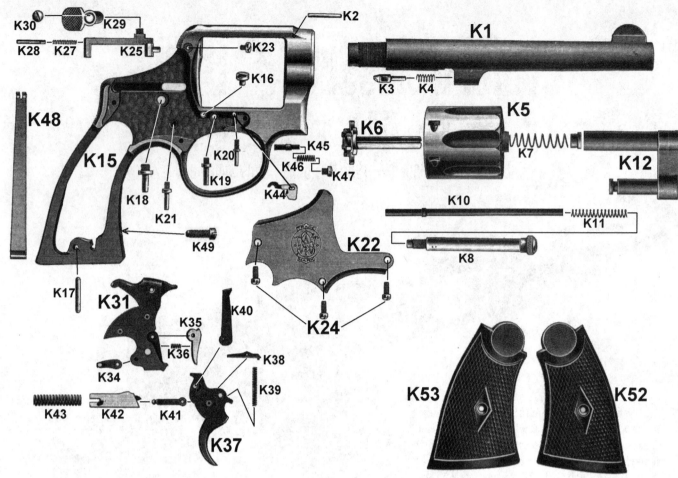

Parts List

(S&W .38 & 32/20 Hand Ejector
Models 1905 through 1945)

K1	Barrel	K20	Cylinder Stop Stud	K39	Hand Lever Spring
K2	Barrel Pin	K21	Rebound Slide Stud	K40	Hand
K3	Locking Bolt	K22	Sideplate	K41	Trigger Lever
K4	Locking Bolt Spring	K23	Sideplate Screw, Large Head	K42	Rebound Slide
K5	Cylinder	K24	Sideplate Screw, Small Head	K43	Rebound Slide Spring
K6	Extractor	K25	Bolt	K44	Cylinder Stop
K7	Extractor Spring	K26	Locking Bolt Pin	K45	Cylinder Stop Plunger
K8	Extractor Rod	K27	Bolt Plunger Spring	K46	Cylinder Stop Spring
K9	Extractor Collar	K28	Bolt Plunger	K47	Cylinder Stop Screw
K10	Center Pin	K29	Thumb Piece	K48	Mainspring
K11	Center Pin Spring	K30	Thumb Piece Nut	K49	Strain Screw
K12	Yoke	K31	Hammer	K50	Stock Screw
K13	Stirrup Pin	K32	Hammer Nose	K52	Left Stock
K14	Sear Pin	K33	Hammer Nose Rivet	K53	Right Stock
K15	Frame	K34	Hammer Stirrup	K54	Hammer Block, (not shown)
K16	Frame Lug	K35	Sear	K54A	Hammer Block Plunger, (not shown)
K17	Stock Pin	K36	Sear Spring	K54B	Hammer Block Spring, (not shown)
K18	Hammer Stud	K37	Trigger		
K19	Trigger Stud	K38	Hand Lever		

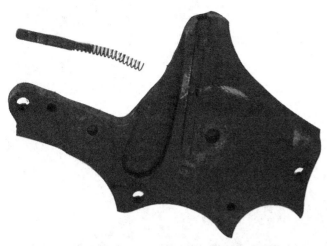

This is the sideplate from a 1905, 4th Change with the 1st Type hammer block safety, here shown with the hammer block safety plunger and spring removed. This plunger and spring also supply tension to the rear of the hand when the sideplate is on. Note that the plunger is beveled. It must be reassembled exactly as it came out.

In 1926, the first type hammer block safety was replaced by a leaf spring hammer block safety requiring fewer parts and operated by a cam on the hand. A patent marking was added to hammers and triggers at this time. During WWII in 1942, when serial number 1,000,000 was reached, a "V" prefix was added to the serial numbers. Huge quantities of the V or Victory model chambered in .38 S&W caliber were sold to the British commonwealth countries during WWII. Roughly another 300,000 Victory model revolvers with a parkerized finish and chambered in 38 S&W Special were produced for American military use. In 1944 at serial number V800,000, another new hammer block safety was used (thus making the 3rd type). This is identical to the hammer block safety used in modern K frames; serial numbers were changed to "VS" prefixes at that point to denote the change. Target-sighted models were equipped with serrated front and back straps on the grip frames and grooved triggers after August 14, 1923.

The K-22 Outdoorsman was introduced in 1930 and produced until 1940 when it was superseded by the K-22 Masterpiece. Chambered in 22 Long Rifle and built on the same "K" frame as the Military and Police, the K-22 Masterpiece was the first S&W revolver to be equipped with the new short-throw or short-action hammer and the now-common Smith & Wesson Micrometer Click rear target sight.

Serial numbers:

38 S&W/38 S&W Special: 241,704 (1915) to 1,000,000 (1941). In 1941 .38-caliber serial numbers began again with the V prefix (designating Victory Model) changed to VS at 850,000 (1945).

K-22) 1st Model Outdoorsman (1930 to 1940): 632,132 to 682,419; total production of 19,500 revolvers. 2nd Model Masterpiece (1940-1942): 682,404 to 696,952; total production of 1,067 revolvers. The K-22 serial numbers are all within the .38-caliber serial number ranges.

32-20: serial numbered in its own unique serial numbering series.

32/20 Hand Ejector Model 1905: (1905 to 1906) 18,126 to 22,426.

32/20 Hand Ejector Model 1905, 1st Change (1906 to 190?): 22,427 to 33,500.

32/20 Hand Ejector Model 1905 2nd Change (190? to 1909): 33,501 to 45,200.

32/20 Hand Ejector Model 1905 3rd Change (1909 to 1915): 45,201 to 65,700.

32/20 Hand Ejector Model 1905 4th Change (1915 to 1940): (#65,701 to 144,684.

38 S&W/38 S&W Special serial numbered in their own unique serial numbering series.

38 Hand Ejector First Model (1899 to 1902): 1 to 20,975.

38 Hand Ejector 2nd Model (1903 to 1905): 20,976 to 33,803.

38 Hand Ejector Model 1902 1st Change (1902 to 1903): 33,804 to 62,449.

38 Hand Ejector Model 1905 (1905 to 1906): 62,450 to 73,250.

38 Hand Ejector Model 1905 1st Change (1906 to 190?): 73,251 to ? (Factory records do not show exactly when 1905 1st Change ended and 2nd Change began.)

38 Hand Ejector Model 1905 2nd Change (190? to 1909): ? to 146,899.

38 Hand Ejector Model 1905 3rd Change (1909 to 1915): to 146,900-241,703.

38 Hand Ejector Model 1905 4th Change (1915 to 1942): 241,703 to ?

K-22s numbered as follows.

K-22 1st Model Outdoorsman (1930-1940): 632,132 to 682,419 in the .38 H.E. series.

K-22 2nd Model Masterpiece (1940-1942): 682,420 to 696,952 in the .38 H.E. series.

The first step before performing any work is to be certain the revolver cylinder is unloaded! The revolver pictured is the 32-20 version of the 1905, 4th Change but its internal workings are identical to the .38-caliber versions.

After removing the grips, the cylinder can be taken out by first removing the front sideplate screw, opening the cylinder and pulling it and the yoke assembly out through the front. Before you do, it's a good idea to line up one of the cylinder flutes with the bottom left area of the frame.

DISASSEMBLY INSTRUCTIONS

1 First, make sure the revolver is unloaded. Grasp the revolver firmly by its grip, keeping your fingers away from the trigger (#K37) and being careful to keep the muzzle pointed in a safe direction. Push forward on the thumb piece (#K29) and push the cylinder (#5K) open toward the left side of the revolver. At this point, check to be certain all the chambers are unloaded. If cartridges are present, tilt the revolver so the rear of the cylinder faces the bench top and push in on the front of the extractor rod (#K8). This will cause the extractor to eject the cartridges from the cylinder. Remove all live cartridges from the work area.

2 To remove the cylinder: Remove the yoke screw (#K24). This is the forwardmost sideplate screw. Line up one of the cylinder flutes with the bottom front of the yoke (#K12) and withdraw the cylinder-extractor-yoke assembly through the front of the frame (#K15). Note: On early models take note of the position of the yoke stop and yoke stop spring located in the lower yoke barrel.

Here is what a 1905 4th Change looks like with its sideplate removed. The plunger you see in the sideplate at the left is a 1st Type hammer block safety, which also supplies tension to the hand. Take note that the bolt has moved forward so it is now under the tail of the hammer. By doing this it prevents the hammer from being cocked. This happens as soon as you open the cylinder.

3 To remove the grips and sideplate. Remove the stock screw #K50 and lift off the stocks (#K52) and (#K53). Unscrew and remove the three remaining sideplate screws (#K23) and (#K24). Turn the gun on its side with the sideplate facing up, and hold the revolver by the barrel over a well padded bench-top. Use a wooden or plastic mallet to strike the grip frame one or more sharp blows, this will cause the sideplate (#K22) to jump up, and out of its seat with the frame. Never attempt to pry off the sideplate as you can easily damage the frame and sideplate in the process. On late 1905 - 4th change revolvers, lift the hammer block safety (#K54) - 3rd type, out of its seat in the frame and away from its lug on the rebound slide (#K42).

After the mainspring has been removed, the thumb piece is pulled back and the trigger is held to the rear, freeing the hammer to be lifted out of the action.

4 To remove the mainspring and hammer: Remove the strain screw (#K49) from the front of the grip frame. The mainspring (#K48) may now be disengaged from its seat at the lower grip frame and then disengaged from the hammer stirrup at its top and withdrawn from the frame. While holding the thumb piece (#K29) to the rear, pull the trigger (#K37) all the way back. This will cause the hammer (#K31) to rise. Lift the hammer straight up and off its stud (#K18) in the frame while the trigger is still pulled to the rear. Once the hammer is out, release the trigger.

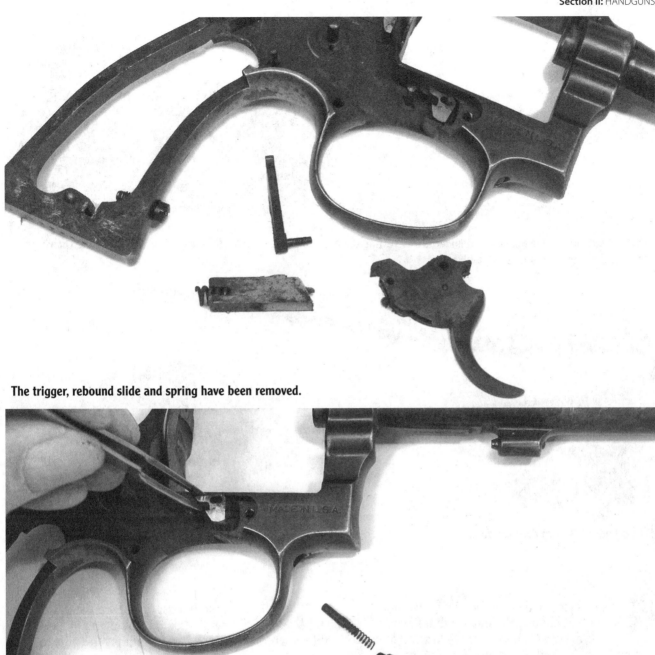

The trigger, rebound slide and spring have been removed.

The cylinder stop is shown being removed, but first we had to take out its screw, plunger and spring (lower right).

5 To remove the trigger and its attendant parts: Using a small screwdriver or a suitable tool, pry up on the rear of the rebound slide (#K42) until it pivots up and off its stud in the frame. Use caution: this action will free the coiled rebound slide spring (#K43), which is under heavy tension. Pull rearward and up to remove the rebound slide and its spring from the frame. With the trigger in the forward position, use a small tool to pry the hand (#K40) to the rear until it is clear of the frame. While holding the hand to the rear, withdraw the trigger and hand assembly straight up and off its stud (#K19) on the frame.

6 To remove the cylinder stop: Unscrew and remove the cylinder stop screw (#K47), which is located at the front of the triggerguard. The cylinder stop plunger (#K45) and cylinder stop plunger spring (#K46) may now be withdrawn through the same screw hole. Push the locking bolt portion of the cylinder stop (#K44) to its lowest position and using a pair of tweezers to grasp it, withdraw the cylinder stop straight up and off its stud in the frame.

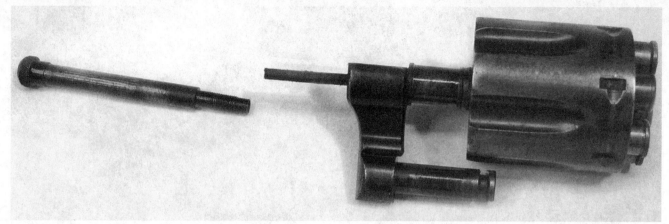

The first step in disassembling the cylinder is unscrewing the extractor rod. Note the fired cartridge casings in the chambers to support the extractor during assembly.

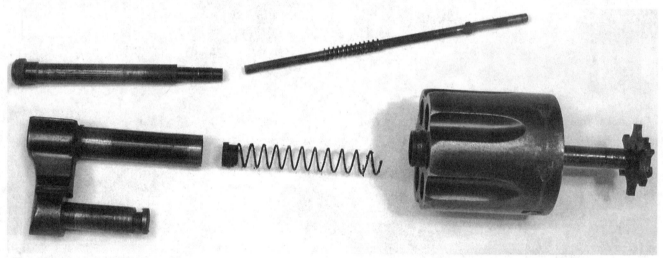

The cylinder is shown disassembled.

7 To disassemble the cylinder: For early models (1905, 3rd change and earlier) that have a separate extractor rod knob, grasp the extractor knob in a padded vise and unscrew it from the extractor rod (#K8) by turning it in a counterclockwise direction. It may be necessary to grasp and hold the round portion of the extractor rod with an extractor rod removal tool to keep it from turning with the knob. Using an extractor rod removal tool or, alternatively, grasping the extractor rod (#K80) by its round area in a drill press chuck, insert six empty cartridges cases in the chambers. Unscrew the cylinder (#K5) from the extractor rod (#K8) in a counterclockwise direction. Remove the chuck or tool from the extractor rod and withdraw the rod from the front of the cylinder (#K5). The center pin (#K10) and its spring (#K11) are now free. They may also be withdrawn from the front of the cylinder. Next, withdraw the yoke (#K12) from the front of the cylinder. The extractor collar (#K9) and extractor spring (#K7) can be removed now from the front of fhe cylinder. The extractor (#K6) is now pushed out of the cylinder toward the rear.

8 To disassemble the trigger: Always support the trigger by laying it on its side on a flat steel block with holes drilled through it for the pins to be driven through. Pull the hand straight out the right side of the trigger. Using a tiny pin punch, drift out the hand lever pin. This is the only cross pin in the trigger and pull the hand lever (#K38) and its spring (#K39) out through the top of the trigger. During the reassembly of the hand, the rear of the trigger lever must be held up while the hand is inserted back into the trigger to be sure it receives spring pressure from the hand lever. Note: Guns with the 1st Type hammer block safety do not use a hand lever or a hand lever spring; instead, hand tension is supplied by the hammer block safety plunger and spring (see step 10). Drive out the trigger lever pin (not listed; this is the larger of the two pins) and the trigger lever is free to be pulled out the rear.

Here the hammer is shown with the sear and sear spring removed; the stirrup is still in place.

Removing the thumb piece nut and the thumb piece frees up the bolt so it can be removed from the inside of the frame. Don't forget: there are a small spring and plunger at the rear of the bolt!

9 To disassemble the hammer: Always support the hammer by laying it on its side on a flat steel block with holes drilled through it for the pins to be driven through. Use a small pin punch and hammer to drive out the sear pin (#K14). The sear (#K35) and sear spring (#K36) are now free and can be pulled off the front of the hammer. Driving out the stirrup pin (#K13) frees the stirrup for removal. Be sure to note the position of the stirrup before taking it off the hammer; it must be reassembled in this same position.

10 To disassemble the hammer block safety: 1st type, illustrated in photo. Working from the inside of the sideplate (#K22), use a small punch to hold down on the hammer block safety (#K54) in by pushing down on the safety block itself to compress it back into its mortise in the sideplate, push in on the area just below the notch which you will see about half-way up the safety block. Pushing the safety block down into the side plate frees the hammer block plunger (#K54a) and hammer block plunger spring (#K54b) to come out through the opening in the sideplate at the slot. Notice the relationship of the plunger and spring as they emerge from the sideplate, so they will be reinstalled correctly. The safety block itself (#K54) – 1st type, is staked in place within the sideplate and is not intended to be removed. 2nd type hammer block safety devices are made in one-piece and are staked into place with in the sideplate, they are not intended for removal.

Further disassembly is not required for normal cleaning and maintenance of the revolver mechanism.

REASSEMBLY

Reverse the above procedures to reassemble the revolver.

Smith & Wesson .44 Hand Ejector (H.E.)
First Model (New Century or Triplelock)

The .44 Hand Ejector 1st Model or Triplelock was
Smith & Wesson's first large-framed Hand Ejector.
The 44 S&W Special was the standard chambering. The
Triplelock was intended to replace the double and single
action top-break revolvers the company built its fortunes on.
Author photos.

This big revolver was introduced by Smith &
Wesson in 1908 as the modern successor
to their large-bore, Model No. 3 top-break
revolvers. Known as the .44 Hand Ejector,
the revolver was the first large-frame revolver marketed
by S&W that used a side-swing cylinder and rod
ejection (hence the term Hand Ejector). This model
was the grandpa of the entire modern family of "N"-
framed double action revolvers that includes the
stainless steel 44 Magnum Model 629.

Notice the modern-looking
"magnum"-type extractor rod
housing under the barrel.
This housing appeared
here almost 30 years
before the 357 Magnum
cartridge did and it was
intended to house the
locking-bolt for the third or
"triple" lock. Unlike any revolver before

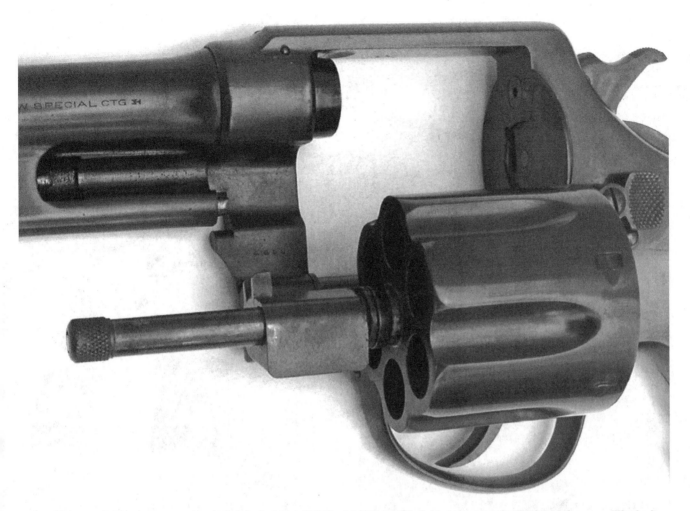

Noted for its excellent workmanship and tight lock-up, S&W's .44 H.E. 1st Model is known as the Triplelock because it locked the cylinder in three locations: in front and rear on the axis, as seen in conventional Smith & Wesson Hand Ejector revolvers, and at the front of the yoke with a strong steel bolt.

or since, the S&W .44 Hand Ejector First Model used a third lock to fasten the yoke to the barrel and frame. This lock was located in the rear of the barrel's ejector housing, where it locked into the front end of the yoke. This lock augmented the other two locks S&W used at the rear of the cylinder and the front of the ejector rod. Adjustable target sights were also available as an option on these models.

On account of the exceptional craftsmanship S&W put into in its manufacture and the rigid, accurate cylinder lock-up offered by the "Triplelock" system, many consider this revolver to be the hallmark of Smith & Wesson revolver production, indeed, of anyone's. The level of craftsmanship necessitated extra machining and handwork and served to make the First Model .44 a very expensive revolver to manufacture. In 1915, when the .44 Hand Ejector 2nd Model was introduced, the third lock with its extra labor requirements and the large extractor housing were dropped. The large barrel housing soon made a comeback in 1926 when the .44 Hand Ejector 3rd Model was introduced, only this time without the third lock. This style is still in use on modern S&W magnums. Over its lifetime, 15,375 .44 H.E. 1st Models were manufactured for commercial sale.

Another, separate batch of 5,000 of these revolvers was also manufactured specifically for the British commonwealth in .455 MK II caliber. The original caliber was the 44 S&W Special cartridge, which was also introduced for the first time in this revolver. Barrel lengths of 4, 5, 6-1/2, and 7-1/2 inches were available. Other calibers such as the 44-40 Winchester, 45 Colt and 455 MK II (at the time the current British service revolver cartridge) were made in lesser quantities.

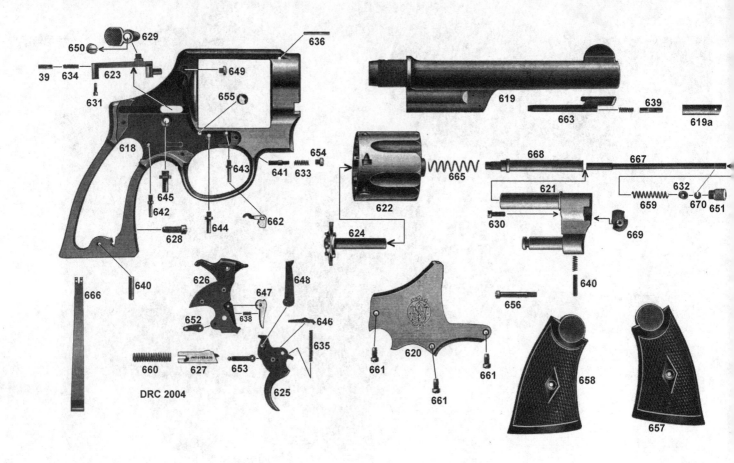

DRC 2004

Parts List

618	Frame	636	Barrel Pin	655	Frame Lug
619	Barrel	637	Stock Pin	656	Stock Screw
619A	Locking bolt cover	638	Sear Spring	657	Stock
620	Sideplate	639	Bolt Plunger	658	Stock
621	Yoke	640	Yoke Stop	659	Center Pin Spring
622	Cylinder	641	Stop Plunger	660	Rebound Slide Spring
623	Bolt	642	Rebound Slide Stud	661	Sideplate Screw, Small Head
624	Extractor	643	Stop Stud	662	Cylinder Stop
625	Trigger	644	Trigger Stud	663	Locking Bolt
626	Hammer	645	Hammer Stud	663	Locking Bolt Housing
627	Rebound Slide	646	Hand Lever	664	Locking Bolt Plunger
628	Strain Screw	647	Sear	665	Extractor Spring
629	Thumb Piece	648	Hand	666	Mainspring
630	Yoke Cam Screw	649	Plate Screw, Large Head	667	Center Pin
631	Bolt Screw	650	Thumb Piece Nut	668	Extractor Rod
632	Center Pin Collar	651	Extractor Rod Knob (Head)	669	Yoke Cam
633	Stop Spring	652	Hammer Stirrup	670	Center Pin Washer
634	Bolt Spring	653	Trigger Lever		
635	Hand Lever Spring	654	Cylinder Stop Screw		

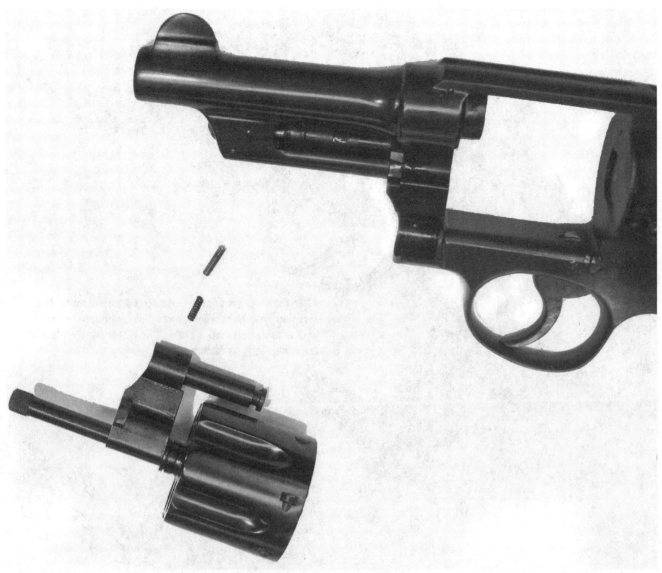

The cylinder-yoke assembly shown removed from the Triplelock S&W. Just as in modern Smith & Wesson revolvers, the cylinder-yoke will come out after you remove the front sideplate screw. Be sure to watch out for the yoke stop plunger and spring as the yoke is pulled forward.

DISASSEMBLY INSTRUCTIONS

1 First, make sure the revolver is unloaded. Grasp the revolver firmly by its grip, keeping your fingers away from the trigger (#625) and being careful to keep the muzzle pointed in a safe direction. Push forward on the thumb piece (#629) and push the cylinder (#622) open toward the left side of the revolver. At this point check to be certain all the chambers are unloaded. If cartridges are present, tilt the revolver so the rear of the cylinder faces the bench top and push in on the extractor rod knob (#651), causing the extractor to eject the cartridges from the cylinder. Remove any live cartridges from the work area.

2 To remove the cylinder: Remove the yoke screw (#661), the forwardmost sideplate screw. Open the cylinder once again and line up one of the cylinder flutes with the bottom front of the yoke (#621) and withdraw the cylinder-yoke assembly out toward the front of the frame (#618). Note: It is helpful to store the yoke screw (#661) separately from the two other small-headed sideplate screws so that it is always returned to its proper position. Use caution when withdrawing the yoke from the frame; on this model, the yoke is equipped with a yoke stop (#640) and a spring located at the bottom front of the yoke. Be careful so the yoke stop does not fall out and become lost. Disassembly to this point is all that is required for routine maintenance and cleaning.

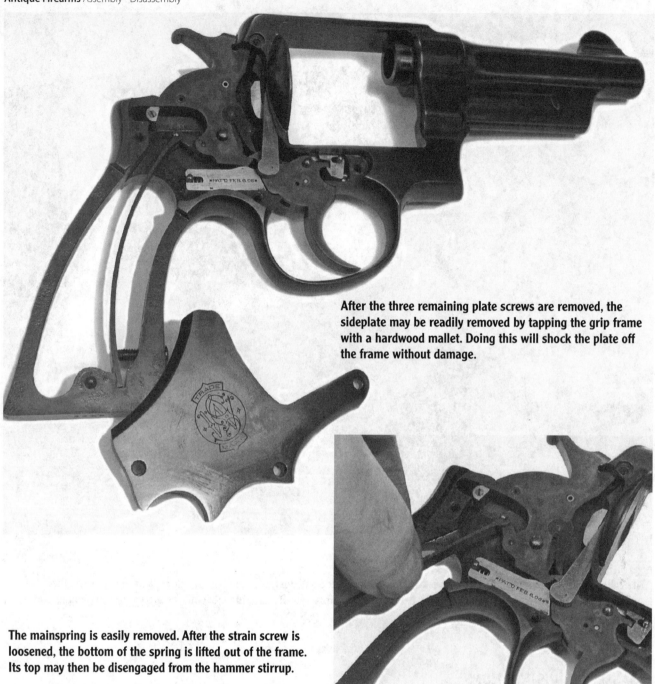

After the three remaining plate screws are removed, the sideplate may be readily removed by tapping the grip frame with a hardwood mallet. Doing this will shock the plate off the frame without damage.

The mainspring is easily removed. After the strain screw is loosened, the bottom of the spring is lifted out of the frame. Its top may then be disengaged from the hammer stirrup.

3 To remove the grips and sideplate: Unscrew and remove the stock screw (#656) and lift off the stocks (#657) and (#658). Remove the three remaining sideplate screws (#661) and (#649). Turn the gun on its side with the sideplate facing up and hold the revolver by the barrel over a well-padded bench-top. Use a wooden or plastic mallet to strike the grip frame one or more sharp blows. This will cause the sideplate (#620) to jump up and out of its seat with the frame. Never attempt to pry off the sideplate of any firearm.

4 To remove the mainspring and hammer: Remove the strain screw (#628) from the front of the grip frame. The mainspring (#666) may now be disengaged from its seat at the lower grip frame and then disengaged from the hammer stirrup at its top and withdrawn from the frame. While holding the thumb piece to the rear, pull the trigger all the way back. This will cause the hammer (#62) to pivot back toward the cocked position. From this point, you can now withdraw the hammer straight up and off its stud in the frame while the trigger is still pulled to the rear. Once the hammer is out, release the trigger and thumb piece.

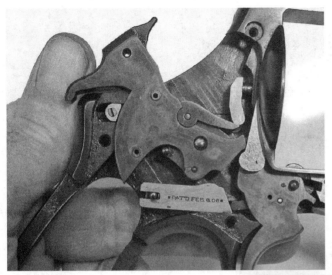

The hammer must be cocked and the trigger held all the way to the rear before the hammer can be lifted out. Notice the patent date on the side of the rebound slide, an indication that this is an early production gun.

After the rebound slide and spring have been removed, the hand is held to the rear as shown here. Then, in the forward position, the trigger is lifted straight up and out of the frame. Note that the cylinder stop is in the up position; if it were pulled down slightly, the trigger would not come out. The rectangular machine cut you see in the frame, just behind the trigger, is a keyway. Early rebound slides had a key to match this cut machined on the left side.

5 To remove the trigger: Using a small screwdriver, pry up on the rear of the rebound slide (#627) until it pivots up and off its stud in the frame. Use caution: doing this will free the coiled rebound slide spring (#660), which is under heavy tension. Pull rearward to remove the rebound slide and its spring from the frame. With the trigger in the forward position, use a small tool to pry the hand (#648) to the rear until it is clear of the frame. While holding the hand to the rear, withdraw the trigger (#625) straight up and off its stud on the frame.

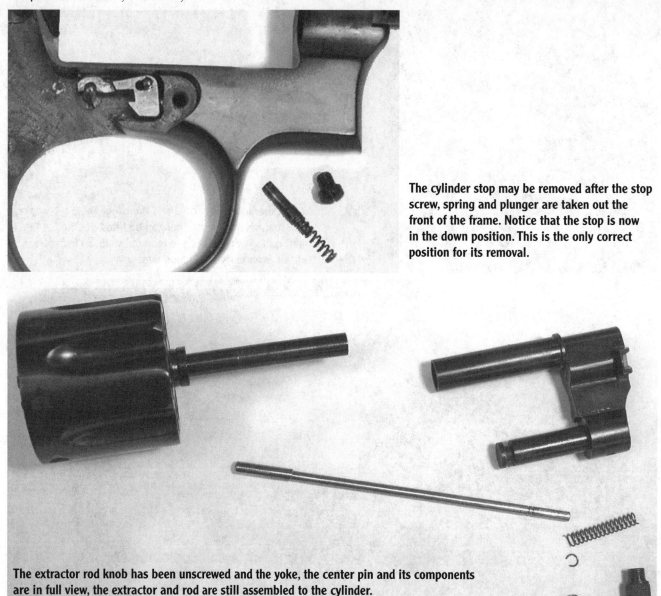

The cylinder stop may be removed after the stop screw, spring and plunger are taken out the front of the frame. Notice that the stop is now in the down position. This is the only correct position for its removal.

The extractor rod knob has been unscrewed and the yoke, the center pin and its components are in full view, the extractor and rod are still assembled to the cylinder.

6 To remove the cylinder stop: Unscrew and remove the cylinder stop screw (#654) located at the front of the trigger guard. The cylinder stop spring (#633) and plunger (#641) may now be withdrawn through the same screw hole. Push the cylinder stop (#662) to its lowest position and use a pair of tweezers to withdraw the cylinder stop straight up and off its stud in the frame.

7 To disassemble the cylinder: Grasp the body of the extractor rod (#668) in a suitable clamp. Insert six empty cartridge cases in the chambers and, using a pair of pliers padded with leather, unscrew the extractor rod knob (#651) in a counterclockwise direction. The yoke (#621) can now be withdrawn off the front of the extractor rod. From the rear of the

extractor, use a small pin punch to push the center pin (#667) forward so its front end protrudes from the front of the extractor rod (#668). Slide the center pin collar (#632) toward the rear and lift the small C-shaped center pin washer (#670) off the center pin. Slide the center pin collar and the center pin spring (#659) off the center pin. The center pin (#667) can now be withdrawn out the rear of the extractor (#624). Carefully chuck the extractor rod (#668) in the jaws of a drill press (be cautious not to crush the front of the rod) and unscrew the cylinder (#622) from the extractor rod in a counterclockwise direction. The extractor rod (#668) can now be withdrawn from the front. The extractor is removed by pulling it out to the rear of the cylinder.

To remove the bolt, the thumb piece nut and the thumb piece are first removed from the left side of the frame. The bolt is then pulled rearward and the back end lifted and tilted out of the frame.

8 To remove the thumb piece and bolt: Unscrew the thumb piece nut (#650) and pull the thumb piece (#629) off the frame. Working now from inside the frame, push the bolt (#623) slightly to the rear while tilting its rear end upwards and withdraw the bolt from the frame. Note: The bolt plunger (#639) and plunger spring are located at the rear of the bolt and are under spring tension; they are held in place by the bolt plunger screw (#631). If you remove this screw, be sure to hold your thumb over the rear of the bolt during disassembly to prevent the loss of these two small parts.

REASSEMBLY

Reverse the procedures to reassemble the revolver.

Smith & Wesson .44 Hand Ejector
2nd & 3rd Models

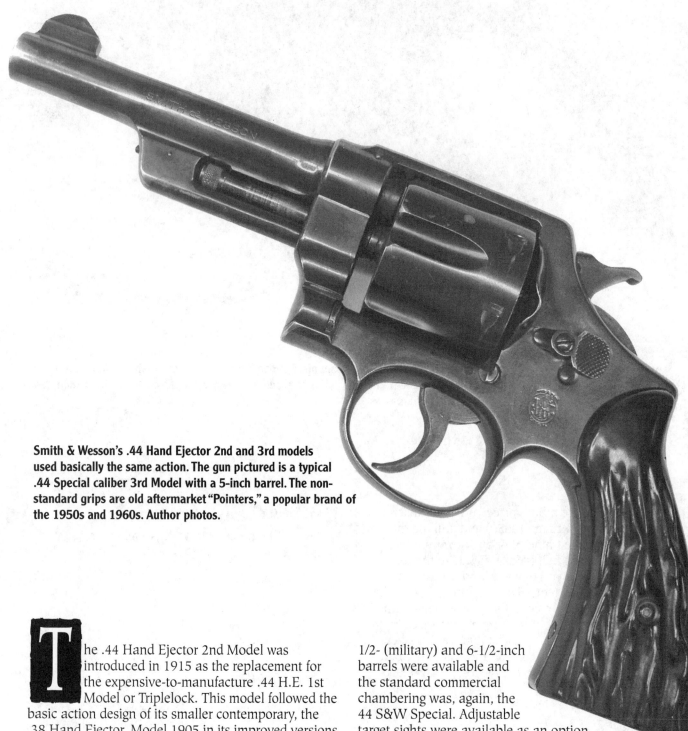

Smith & Wesson's .44 Hand Ejector 2nd and 3rd models used basically the same action. The gun pictured is a typical .44 Special caliber 3rd Model with a 5-inch barrel. The non-standard grips are old aftermarket "Pointers," a popular brand of the 1950s and 1960s. Author photos.

T he .44 Hand Ejector 2nd Model was introduced in 1915 as the replacement for the expensive-to-manufacture .44 H.E. 1st Model or Triplelock. This model followed the basic action design of its smaller contemporary, the .38 Hand Ejector, Model 1905 in its improved versions and was manufactured through 1937. Four-, 5-, 5-1/2- (military) and 6-1/2-inch barrels were available and the standard commercial chambering was, again, the 44 S&W Special. Adjustable target sights were available as an option on these models.

This photo shows the back side of a 3rd Model .44 Hand Ejector sideplate. The revolver is equipped with a 2nd Type hammer block safety, which is staked permanently in place within the sideplate.

A separate and important variation of the .44 H.E. 2nd Model was the U.S. Model 1917 chambered in 45 ACP and equipped with a 5-1/2-inch barrel. Around 175,000 of these were delivered to U.S. Army from April 6, 1917 through February 1, 1919. A further order of approximately 35,000 of this model was also delivered to Brazil in 1937. Still another, separate variation of the .44 H.E. 2nd Model was the .455 H.E. 2nd Models. These had 6-1/2-inch barrels and were serial numbered in their own series from 5,001 (starting where the British order for the .44 H.E. 1st Model left off) to 74,755. This order was delivered to British commonwealth nations from 1915 to 1917.

In 1926, S&W introduced the .44 Hand Ejector 3rd Model in the same serial number series as the 2nd Model. (Second Model serial numbers started at 15,376 and, transitioning to the 3rd Model, ran to around 60,000 in the commercial .44 Hand Ejector series.) Mechanically, the 3rd Model was essentially a .44 H.E. 2nd Model but with a large barrel underlug, similar to the one originally used on the Triplelock but without the third lock. Third Model Hand Ejectors were manufactured from 1926 to 1950 and include the .357 Magnum Hand Ejector made from 1935 to 1941 and the 38/44 Hand Ejector in 38 Special caliber manufactured from 1931 to 1941. The late .44 H.E. 2nd Models and the 3rd Models used a new sideplate-mounted, hammer block safety. Calibers offered were 38 Special, 357 Magnum, 44 S&W Special (the standard commercial chambering), 44/40, 45 ACP (the standard military chambering), 45 Colt, and 455 MK II.

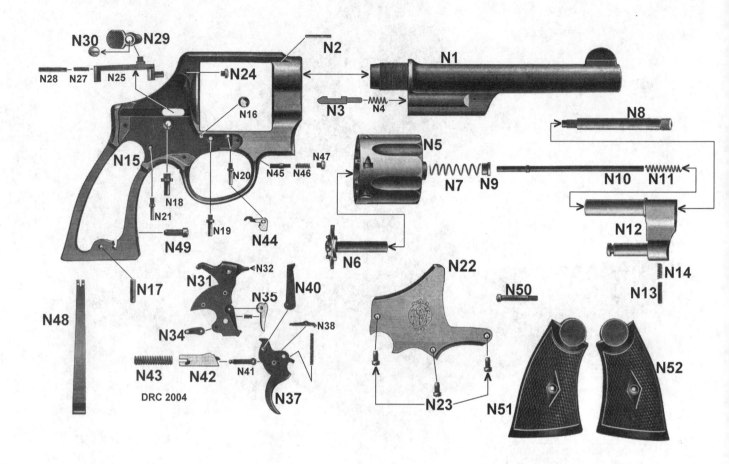

DRC 2004

Parts List

N1	Barrel	N19	Trigger Stud	N39	Hand Lever Spring
N2	Barrel Pin	N20	Rebound Slide Stud	N40	Hand
N3	Locking Bolt, 2nd Model	N22	Sideplate	N41	Trigger Lever
N4	Locking Bolt Spring	N23	Sideplate Screw, Small Head	N42	Rebound Slide
N5	Cylinder	N24	Sideplate Screw, Large Head	N43	Rebound Slide spring
N6	Extractor	N25	Bolt	N44	Cylinder Stop
N7	Extractor Spring	N26	Pin, Butt Swivel, not shown	N45	Cylinder Stop Plunger
N8	Extractor Rod	N27	Bolt Plunger Spring	N46	Cylinder Stop Spring
N9	Extractor Collar	N28	Bolt Plunger	N47	Cylinder Stop Screw
N10	Center Pin	N29	Thumb Piece	N48	Mainspring
N11	Center Pin Spring	N30	Thumb Piece Nut	N49	Strain Screw
N12	Yoke	N31	Hammer	N50	Stock Screw
N13	Yoke Stop	N32	Hammer Nose Rivet	N51	Stock, Right
N14	Yoke Stop Spring	N34	Stirrup	N52	Stock, Left
N15	Frame	N35	Sear	N53	Hammer Block, (not shown)
N16	Frame Lug	N36	Sear Spring	N54	Butt Swivel, (not shown)
N17	Stock Pin	N37	Trigger		
N18	Hammer Stud	N38	Hand Lever		

Removing the front sideplate screw and opening the cylinder frees the cylinder-yoke assembly for removal from the front. Caution: Some earlier models are equipped with a yoke stop (see [#N13] in the drawing) that is under spring tension and may drop out the bottom of the yoke as it is removed from the frame.

DISASSEMBLY INSTRUCTIONS

1 First, make sure the revolver is unloaded. Grasp the revolver firmly by its grip, keeping your fingers away from the trigger (#N37) and being careful to keep the muzzle pointed in a safe direction. Push forward on the thumb piece (#N29) and push the cylinder (#N5) open toward the left side of the revolver. At this point, check to be certain all the chambers are unloaded. If cartridges are present, tilt the revolver so the rear of the cylinder faces the bench top and push in on the extractor rod knob (#N8), causing the extractor to eject the cartridges from the cylinder. Remove any live cartridges from the work area.

2 To remove the cylinder: Unscrew and remove the yoke screw (#N23), the forwardmost sideplate screw. Line up one of the cylinder flutes with the bottom front of the yoke (#N12) and withdraw the cylinder-extractor-yoke assembly from the front of the frame (#N15). Note: It helps to store the yoke screw (#N2) separately from the two other small-headed sideplate screws so that it is always returned to its original location. On many of the earlier models, the yoke is equipped with a yoke stop (#N13) and spring (#N14) located at the bottom front of the yoke. Use caution when you are withdrawing the yoke from the frame so that the yoke stop doesn't fall out and become lost.

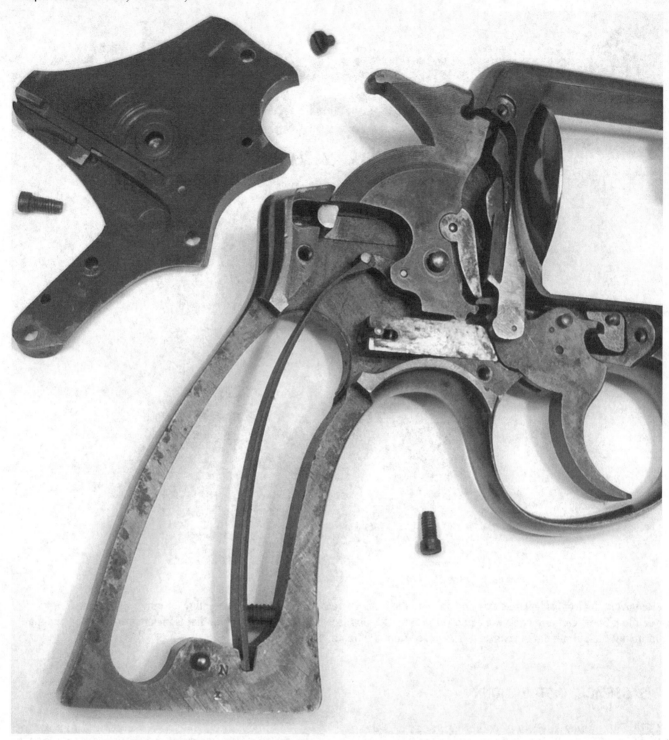

Removing the sideplate on an S&W Hand Ejector exposes the entire action to viewing. Notice that the rear of the bolt has moved under the tail of the hammer. This prevents the hammer from being cocked until either the cylinder is closed or the thumb piece is pulled back. The grooves on the hammer side indicate the hammer is probably from a 1930s vintage 357 Magnum, which was built on the same frame size.

3 To remove the grips and sideplate: Remove the stock screw (#N50) and lift off the stocks (#N51) and (#I52). Unscrew and remove the three remaining sideplate screws (#N23) and (#N24). Turn the gun on its side with the sideplate facing up and hold the revolver by the barrel over a well-padded bench-top.

Use a wooden or plastic mallet to strike the grip frame one or more sharp blows. The shock from the blows will cause the sideplate (#N22) to jump up and out of its seat with the frame. Never attempt to pry off the sideplate; you could cause damage to the frame and the sideplate.

After the mainspring is removed, it's a simple task to take the hammer out.

4 To remove the mainspring and hammer: Remove the strain screw (#N4) from the front of the grip frame. The mainspring (#N48) can now be disengaged from its seat at the lower grip frame and then it may be disengaged from the hammer stirrup at its top and withdrawn from the frame. While holding the thumb piece (#N29) to the rear, pull the trigger all the way back. This will cause the hammer to pivot back toward the cocked position. Lift the hammer straight up and off its stud in the frame while the trigger is still being pulled to the rear. Once the hammer is out, release the trigger.

Once the rebound slide spring is disengaged from the stud, the rebound slide and then the trigger/hand assembly may be removed. Notice the "ramp" on the backside of the hand, this operates the hammer block safety shown on page 346.

5 To remove the trigger: Using a small screwdriver or a suitable tool, pry up on the rear of the rebound slide (#N42) until it pivots up and off its stud in the frame. Use caution here: this action will free the coiled rebound slide spring (#N43), which is under heavy tension. Pull rearward to remove the rebound slide and its spring from the frame. With the trigger in the forward position, use a small tool to pry the hand (#N40) to the rear until it is clear of the frame. While holding the hand to the rear, lift the trigger (#N37) with the hand assembly straight up and off its stud on the frame.

6 To remove the cylinder stop: Unscrew and remove the cylinder stop screw (#N47). This is located at the front of the trigger guard. The cylinder stop plunger (#N45) and its spring (#N46) may now

Here, the cylinder stop screw, spring and plunger have been removed and the gunsmith is lifting out the cylinder stop, aided by a pair of shop tweezers.

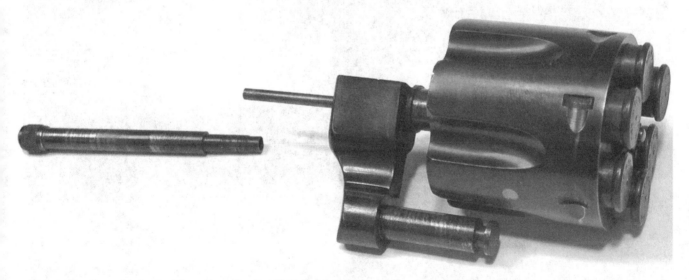

Unscrewing the extractor rod from the extractor. Note the dummy cartridges being used to provide support to the extractor during disassembly.

be withdrawn through the same screw hole. Push the cylinder stop (#N44) down until it reaches its lowest position and use a pair of tweezers to lift the cylinder stop straight up and off its stud in the frame.

7 To disassemble the cylinder: Grasp the body of the extractor rod (#N8) in a suitable clamp or in the jaws of a lathe chuck. Insert six empty cartridge cases in the chambers to support the extractor and unscrew the cylinder (#N5) in a counterclockwise direction. The extractor rod, the center pin (#N10) and the center pin spring (#N11) can now be withdrawn through the front of the yoke (#N12). The yoke may be pulled out the front of the cylinder. The extractor collar (#N9) and its spring (#N7) can also be pulled from the front of the cylinder. The extractor (#N6) can now be removed out the rear of the cylinder.

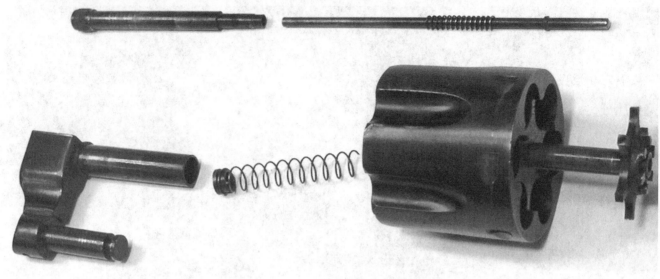

Here is the cylinder, completely disassembled.

The last parts to come out of the frame are the thumb piece, the bolt and their related components.

8 To disassemble the thumb piece/bolt: Unscrew the thumb piece nut (#N30) and pull the thumb piece (#N29) and its nut off the frame. Working from inside the frame, push the bolt (#N25) just slightly to the rear while tilting its rear end upwards and begin the withdrawal of the bolt from the frame, toward the rear. Note: Use caution here; the bolt plunger (#N28) and plunger spring (#N27) are located at the rear of the bolt and they are under spring tension, so be sure you hold your thumb over the rear of the bolt during disassembly to prevent their loss.

Further disassembly is not required for normal cleaning and maintenance of the revolver mechanism.

REASSEMBLY

Reverse the above procedures to reassemble the revolver.

SECTION III
RIFLES

Lightning Pump Rifle
U. S. Firearms Mfg. Co.

The USFA Mfg. Co. Lightning rifle.

An old factory patent drawing for the Lightning showing its workings.

The Lightning pump or slide action rifle was originally manufactured by Colt from 1884 until 1904. Lightnings were known for their fast, short-stroke slide action and compact size. The Lightning Magazine Rifle was an incredible gun for its day. Colt's Lightning magazine rifle was manufactured in three different sizes: small-frame, chambered for .22 rimfire; medium-frame, intended for pistol sized rounds such as the 32-20 and 44-40; and the large, express-frame size that used large, high-powered rifle cartridges of the late 1800s. These Colt pump guns were very high-quality products, very different perhaps from the Winchester pump rifles we are familiar with, but well-made with the kind of superb workmanship you would expect from the old Colt factory.

The U. S. Firearms Mfg. Co.'s Lightning rifle is currently being offered on the medium-sized frame and is available in 38 WCF, 44 WCF and 45 Colt. The rifle is offered in grades ranging from a 20-inch-barreled plain-Jane carbine to a 26-inch-barreled rifle in round, octagonal, or half-round, half-octagonal configuration. Stocks are available with straight or pistol-grip stocks with or without checkering. There are several grades of walnut available as well. The USFA Lightning is an excellent quality firearm that is a spittin'-image of the medium-framed Colt Lightning, and disassembly procedures for the two are identical.

DISASSEMBLY INSTRUCTIONS
USFA Lightning pictured, takedown drawing courtesy USFA Mfg. Co.

1 First, be certain the gun is empty. Pointing the muzzle in a safe direction, hold the rifle with your right hand by the grasping the stock at the wrist at the same time being careful to keep your finger away from the trigger (#17). Open the action by grasping the forend stock wood (#47) and (#48) with your left hand and sliding the forend all the way to the rear. The action is now open. Look into the chamber at the rear of the barrel and be sure there is no cartridge there. Also, examine the top of the carrier (#34). This is inside the open action and directly in front of the open bolt (#25). If there is a cartridge is present here, there may be more cartridges in the magazine tube; all cartridges must be removed to render the rifle safe. If you do not feel competent to continue, leave the rifle with the action open; this is a safe position for now, because the rifle cannot be fired unless the action is closed.

To unload a loaded rifle: Be extra-careful to keep the muzzle pointed in a safe direction and slowly slide the action closed. Doing this will chamber the cartridge. Be aware: The gun is now loaded and ready to fire. Using the right hand, which is holding the stock, use your thumb to hold the hammer back. Pull the trigger and release the hammer, slowly and carefully easing it all the way forward with your thumb. Now operate the slide action again and the cartridge you just chambered will be ejected from the rifle. Repeat this operation until the magazine is completely empty and no more cartridges appear in the carrier area.

Alternate method: Leave the action open and complete the second part of the disassembly operation in #2 below. This operation will disassemble the magazine components and allow you to dump the cartridges in the magazine out through the front of the magazine tube onto your workbench. After this, cycling the action as described above will remove the last cartridge (the one on the carrier) from the action.

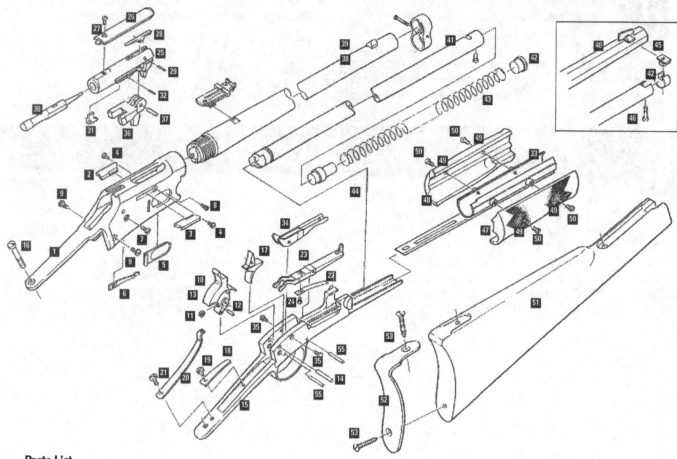

Parts List

1	Receiver	19	Trigger Spring Screw	37	Locking Brace Pin
2	Left Ejector	20	Main Spring	40	Barrel
3	Right Ejector	21	Main Spring Screw	41	Magazine Tube
4	Ejector Screws (2)	22	Magazine Stop Spring	42	Magazine Tube Spring
5	Loading Trap	23	Magazine Stop	43	Magazine Spring
6	Loading Trap Spring	24	Magazine Stop Spring Screw	44	Follower
7	Loading Trap Spring Screw	25	Bolt	45	Magazine Lug
8	Loading Trap Stop Screw	26	Top Cover	46	Rifle Tube Screw
9	Sideplate Screw	27	Top Cover Screw	47	Forend Stock Wood, Right
10	Hammer	28	Extractor	48	Forend Stock Wood, Left
11	Hammer Roller	29	Extractor Pin	49	Grip Escutcheon (4)
12	Hammer Roller Pin	30	Firing Pin	50	Grip Screw (4)
13	Hammer Safety Pin	31	Firing Pin Lever	51	Butt Stock
14	Hammer Pin	32	Firing Pin Lever Pin	52	Butt Plate
15	Tang	33	Slide	53	Buttplate Screw (2)
16	Tang Screw	34	Carrier	55	Trigger and Stop Pin (2)
17	Trigger	35	Carrier Screws (2)		
18	Trigger Spring	36	Locking Brace		

Here is how the magazine lug is removed. It fits in a circular dovetail so it may be slid out to either side of the barrel.

The first step in disassembly is removing the buttstock. This is accomplished by removing the tang screw.

2 Remove the butt stock and magazine assembly: Using the appropriate-size screwdriver, loosen and remove the tang screw (#16) and pull the buttstock assembly (#51) off toward the rear of the rifle. The butt plate may be removed by unscrewing and removing the two butt plate screws (#53) and lifting off the butt plate (#52).

To disassemble a rifle magazine: Loosen and remove the magazine tube screw (#46) from the front end of the magazine tube. Hold your thumb over the magazine plug (#42) and pull the front of the magazine tube (#41) down away from the barrel until the plug is released. Ease the magazine plug forward and withdraw the magazine spring (#43) and the follower (#44) out the front of the tube.

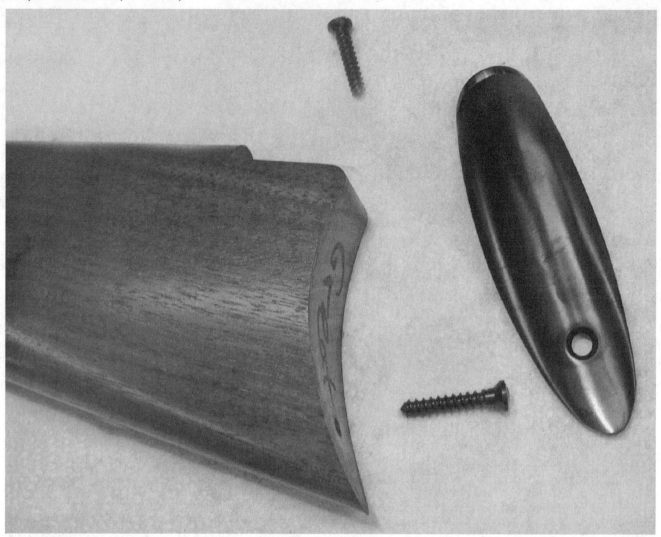

Removing the buttplate is easy; there are only two wood screws holding it on.

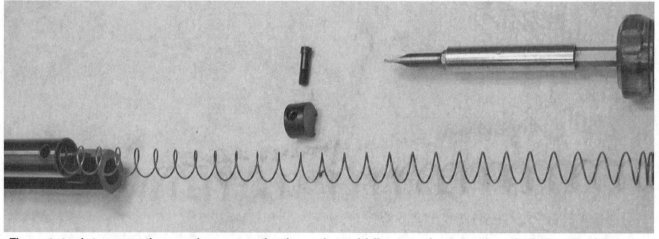

The next step is to remove the magazine screw so the plug, spring and follower can be removed out the front end and then pulling the tube itself forward and out of the rifle.

To disassemble a carbine magazine: Loosen and remove the magazine tube screw (#46) while holding your thumb over the magazine tube plug (#42.) The magazine plug (#42), magazine spring (#43) and follower (#44) can now be removed through the front of the tube. Unscrew and remove the magazine band screw and slide the band off the front.

Rifle and carbine: Pull the magazine tube (#41) straight forward and out of the rifle, noting its position for later reassembly.

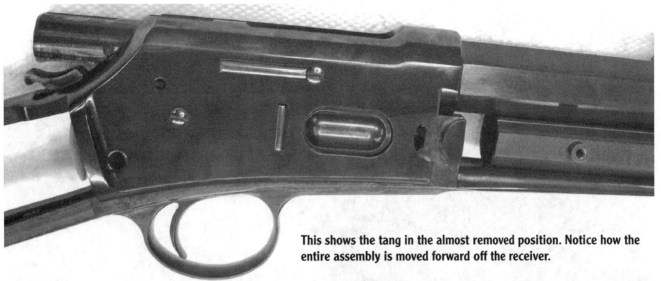

This shows the tang in the almost removed position. Notice how the entire assembly is moved forward off the receiver.

Here the locking brace pin (#37) is being driven out.

After the bolt brace pin is removed, the brace itself (#36) can be lifted out the bottom of the receiver.

3 Break the action apart: Open the action by moving the forend to the rear, leaving the hammer cocked. Move the forend forward slightly so the action remains about halfway open. Remove the two side plate screws (#9) from either side of the receiver (#1), the rearmost screws on each side of the receiver). The trigger plate assembly, which is called the tang (#15), may be withdrawn by pushing it forward and down, out of the receiver.

4 Disassemble the receiver: Slide the bolt assembly (#25) all the way to the rear and use an appropriate-size pin punch to drift out the locking brace pin (#37) from left to right through the holes provided at the rear of the receiver. Withdraw the bolt out the rear of the receiver and lift the locking brace (#36) out through the receiver bottom. Remove the loading trap spring screw (#7) and the loading trap spring (#6). The loading trap (#5) will fall into the receiver for removal. Make careful note of the position of the spring for reassembly. Remove the two ejector screws (#4), one on either side of the receiver, then lift out the ejectors (#2) and (#3), noting their positions so that the ejectors are reassembled into the correct sides later. The magazine lug (#45) can be removed from the barrel by pushing it out either side.

· 357 ·

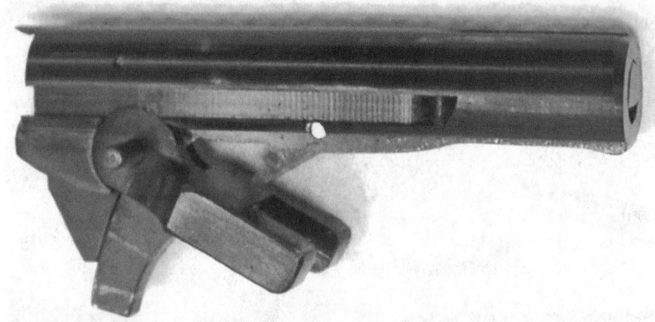

This is what the assembled bolt (#10) and locking brace (#36) look like after disassembly. They have been assembled outside the receiver for reference only.

Here is what the entire lower end looks like assembled.

5 Disassemble the bolt: Unscrew and remove the top cover screw (#27) and lift off the top cover (#26). Using a pin punch and hammer, drift out the firing pin lever pin (#32) and remove the firing pin lever (#31) through the bottom of the bolt (#25). Note of the position of this part. The firing pin (#30) may be withdrawn out through the rear of the bolt. Note the position of the slot in the bolt for reassembly. Drift out and remove the extractor pin (#29). The extractor (#28) can now be lifted off the bolt.

6 Disassemble the tang-trigger group: Slide the forearm forward and pull the trigger (#17), allowing the hammer (#10) to go forward. Unscrew and remove the 4 grip screws (#50) from the forend wood and lift off the left (#48) and right (#49) forend stocks. Unscrew and remove the mainspring screw (#21) and the mainspring (#20). Unscrew and remove the trigger spring screw (#19) and lift out the trigger spring (#18). Drift out the hammer pin (#14) and lift out the hammer (#10). Unscrew and remove the two carrier screws (#35)

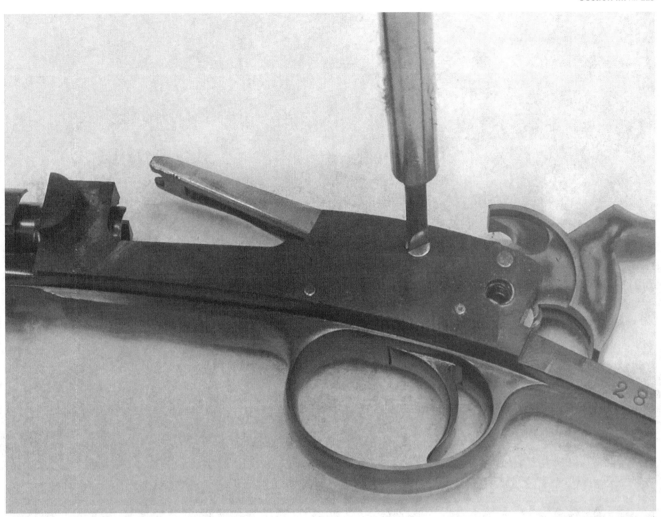

Removing the carrier screws.

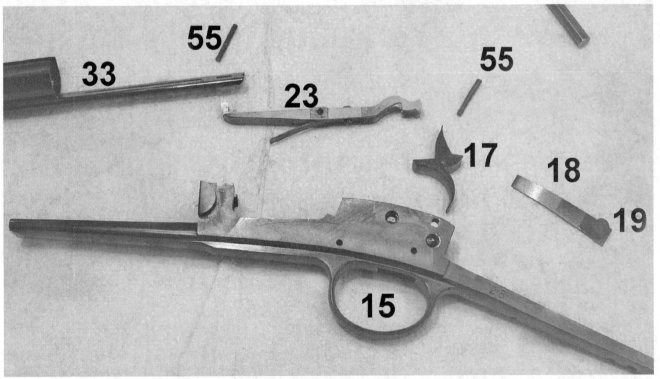

Final disassembly of the lower end involves removing the slide (#33), magazine stop and trigger pins (#55), magazine stop assembly (23), trigger (#17), trigger spring (#18) and its screw (#19).

Mainspring, hammer pin and hammer have been removed from the tang.

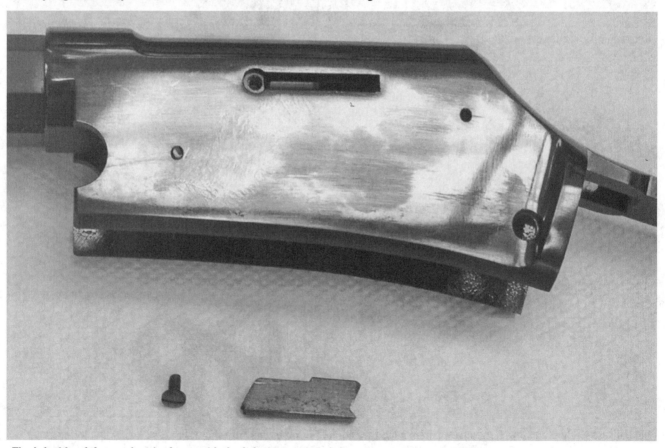

The left side of the receiver is shown with the left ejector removed.

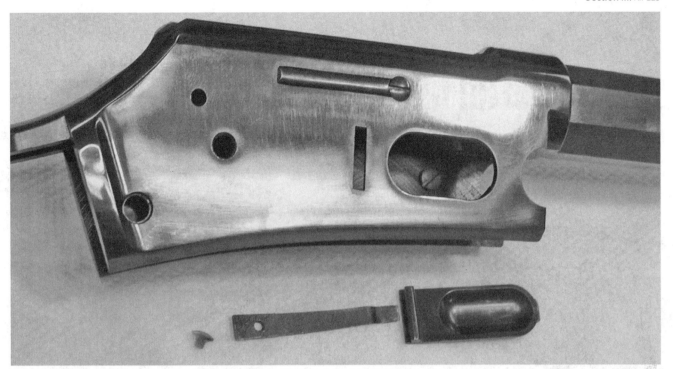

Here, the right side of the receiver is shown with the loading trap (right), the loading trap spring-center, and its screw (left).

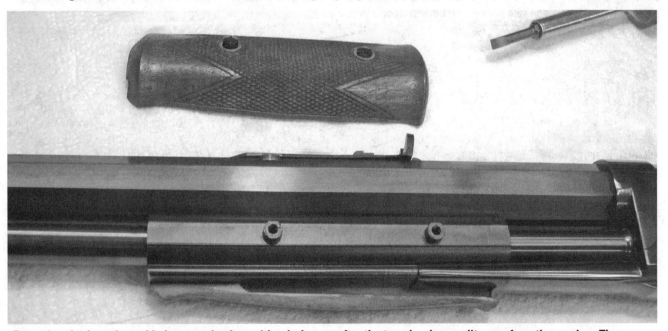

Removing the forend wood halves may be done either before or after the tang has been split away from the receiver. The author prefers to remove them before.

from each side of the tang and lift out the carrier (#34). Drift out the trigger pin and the magazine stop pin (#55). Move the slide (#33) to the rear slightly and tilt the rear of the magazine stop up enough to allow you to lift out and remove the trigger (#17). Once the trigger is out, move the slide farther rearward and continue to tilt up the rear of the magazine stop assembly (#23), at the same time pushing the front of the magazine stop down until it becomes disengaged with the slide (#33). Remove the magazine stop from the tang, being careful to make note of its position within the slide for later reassembly. Move the slide (#33) forward and out of the tang (#15). Remove the magazine stop spring screw (#24) from the bottom of the magazine stop and lift off the magazine stop spring (#22).

REASSEMBLY

Reassemble the rifle in the reverse order of above.

marlin models 1891 and 1892

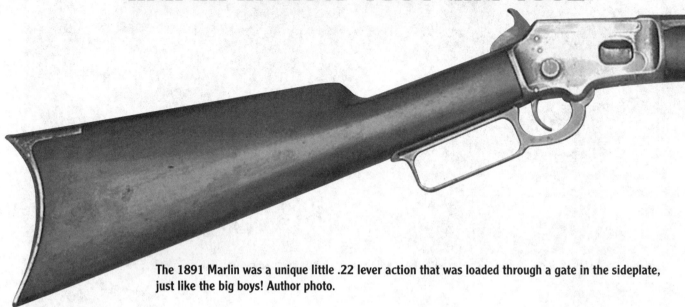

The 1891 Marlin was a unique little .22 lever action that was loaded through a gate in the sideplate, just like the big boys! Author photo.

Marlin's Model 1891 lever action was offered in .22 and .32 rimfire and was manufactured from 1891 through about 1897, with approximately 18,600 rifles manufactured. The 1891 was unique in that it was the only Marlin lever action .22 to use a loading port or gate in the sideplate. A very few of the late-manufacture Model 1891s used tube loading, just as the later 1892 did. The wonderfully simple 1891 design was carried over into the Model 1892 introduced in 1895, which used a two-piece magazine tube that was loaded through the front end. The 1892 was made until about 1916 with a total of something over 45,000 guns manufactured. The 1892 was further improved and introduced as the 1897, a neat little takedown .22 and essentially the rifle we now know as the Model 39.

These instructions will work with the Model 1891 and the later Model 1892, the differences between the two being the 1892 did not use a loading gate in the sideplate and it made use of an inner and outer magazine tube that is loaded from the front. The basic workings and internal parts remain essentially the same between the two models.

DISASSEMBLY INSTRUCTIONS

1 First, make sure the rifle is unloaded. Point the muzzle in a safe direction, holding the rifle around the wooden forearm and barrel with your left hand. Open the action by pulling the finger lever (#27) all the way down with your right hand. Use care to keep your finger away from the trigger (#65) at all times. Check now to be absolutely certain there is no cartridge in the barrel's chamber, and look through the bolt opening into the action to make sure there is no cartridge lying in the carrier (#7) within the action.

If there is a cartridge in the carrier, when you close the lever the rifle will be loaded. To safely unload a rifle with a loaded magazine, always be sure the muzzle stays pointed in a safe direction so that if there were an accidental discharge no one would be injured. Keep your finger away from the trigger while you operate the lever to the fully open and fully closed positions to expel the cartridges in the magazine. Repeat this operation until no more cartridges are expelled from the action.

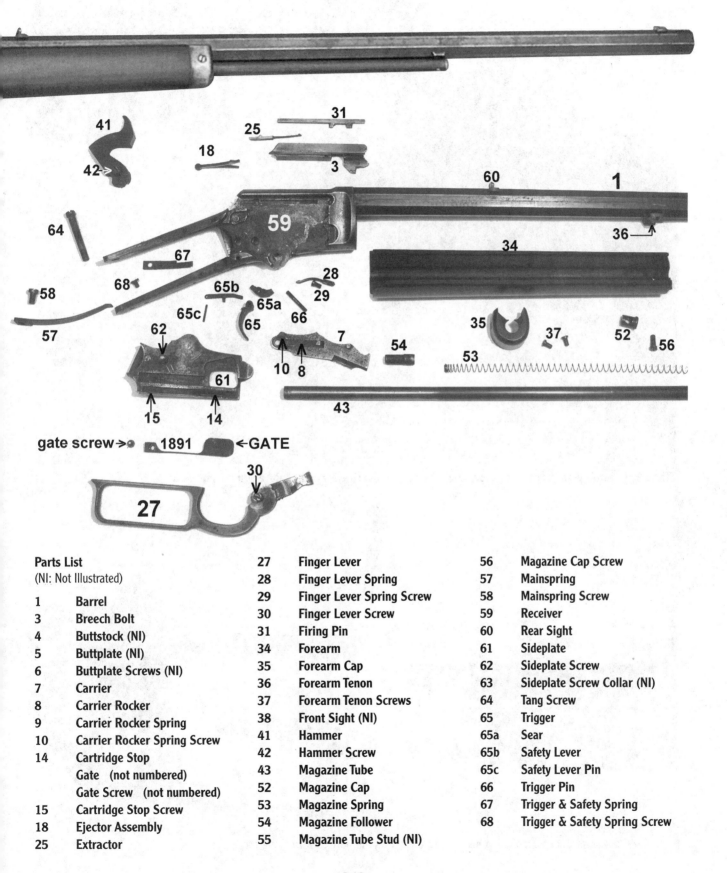

gate screw→ 1891 ←GATE

Parts List
(NI: Not Illustrated)

1	Barrel
3	Breech Bolt
4	Buttstock (NI)
5	Buttplate (NI)
6	Buttplate Screws (NI)
7	Carrier
8	Carrier Rocker
9	Carrier Rocker Spring
10	Carrier Rocker Spring Screw
14	Cartridge Stop
	Gate (not numbered)
	Gate Screw (not numbered)
15	Cartridge Stop Screw
18	Ejector Assembly
25	Extractor
27	Finger Lever
28	Finger Lever Spring
29	Finger Lever Spring Screw
30	Finger Lever Screw
31	Firing Pin
34	Forearm
35	Forearm Cap
36	Forearm Tenon
37	Forearm Tenon Screws
38	Front Sight (NI)
41	Hammer
42	Hammer Screw
43	Magazine Tube
52	Magazine Cap
53	Magazine Spring
54	Magazine Follower
55	Magazine Tube Stud (NI)
56	Magazine Cap Screw
57	Mainspring
58	Mainspring Screw
59	Receiver
60	Rear Sight
61	Sideplate
62	Sideplate Screw
63	Sideplate Screw Collar (NI)
64	Tang Screw
65	Trigger
65a	Sear
65b	Safety Lever
65c	Safety Lever Pin
66	Trigger Pin
67	Trigger & Safety Spring
68	Trigger & Safety Spring Screw

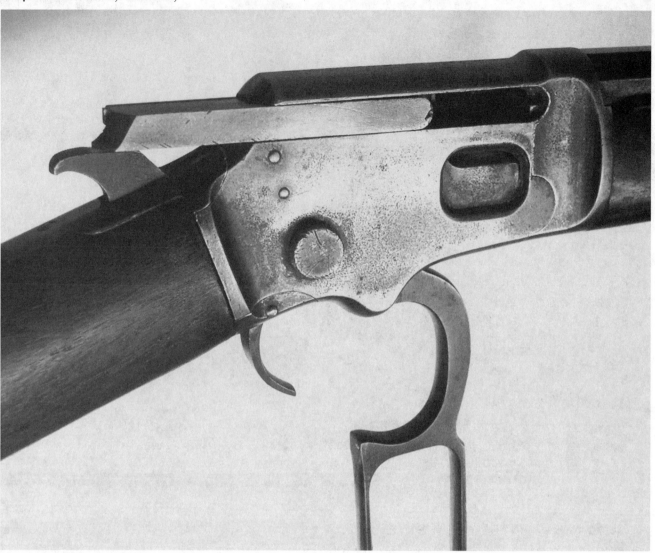

The 1891 Marlin with its action opened. Check to be sure the rifle is empty before you do any work!

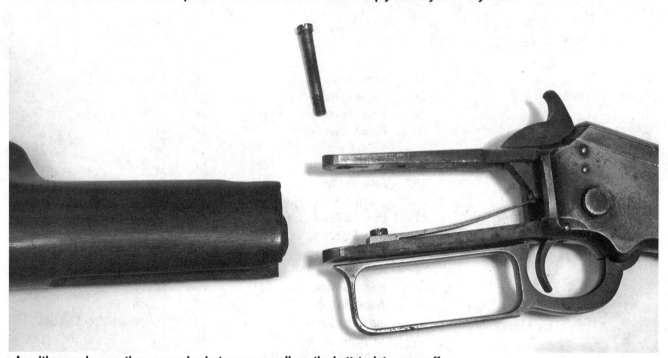

As with many lever actions, removing just one screw allows the buttstock to come off.

You get almost instant access to the whole action by simply removing the sideplate.

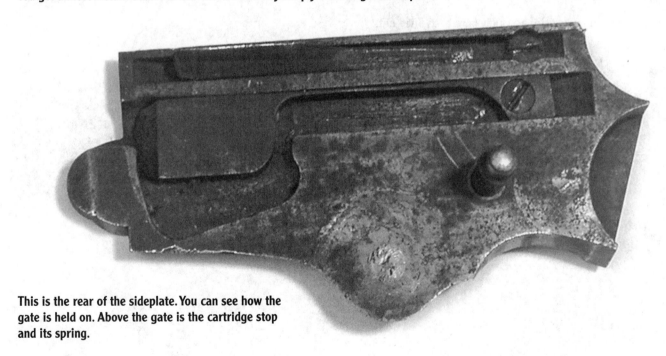

This is the rear of the sideplate. You can see how the gate is held on. Above the gate is the cartridge stop and its spring.

2 To remove the sideplate, lever, breech bolt, carrier and buttstock: Close the finger lever and unscrew the sideplate screw (#62). Lift the sideplate off from the left side, rear end first.

Pull the hammer (#41) all the way back until it stays cocked. Open the finger lever about halfway down. Lift the breech bolt (#3) all the way to the rear and out of the receiver then lift out the ejector (#18). Remove the tang screw (#64) from the upper receiver tang and pull the buttstock (#4) straight off to the rear. Lift out the cartridge carrier assembly (#7).

Here the bolt and ejector assembly have been lifted out.

With the hammer, lever and carrier out, the action is nearly bare. All this took only seconds to accomplish!

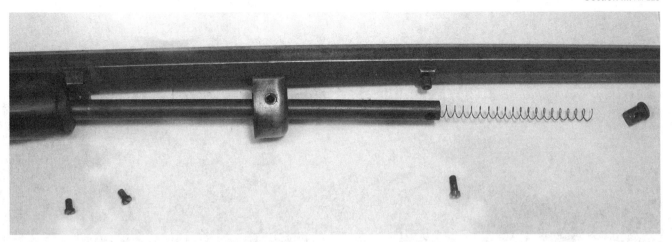

Here, the magazine and forearm are being disassembled.

3 To remove the finger lever, hammer, trigger and safety: Unscrew the mainspring screw (#58) and lift out the mainspring (#58). Unscrew the finger lever spring screw (#29) and lift out the finger lever spring (#29) from the bottom of the receiver. The finger lever (#27) can be lifted straight up off its screw (#30); if desired, the screw may also be removed. Unscrew and remove the hammer screw (#42) and lift the hammer out through the hammer opening in the receiver top tang. Remove the trigger spring screw (#68) and lift off the trigger and safety spring (#67). Use a cup-tipped pin punch and hammer to drift out the trigger pin (#66). The trigger (#65) and sear (#65a) can be pulled out through the bottom of the receiver. Note their correct positions for later reassembly. Use a small pin punch and hammer to drive out the safety lever pin (#65c) and lift out the safety lever (#65b) from the lower receiver tang.

4 To remove the forearm, magazine assembly and buttplate: Unscrew and remove the two forearm tenon screws (#37) and slide the forearm cap (#35) forward slightly until it is away from the forearm tenon (#36). Now unscrew and remove the magazine cap screw (#56) and pull the magazine tube (#43) down slightly. The magazine cap is free and can now be pulled off to the front. The magazine spring (#53) will now come out. Note: The magazine tube spring is under tension. The magazine tube can be pulled out of the forearm along with the forearm tip (#35) and the forearm can also be pulled off the barrel. If the magazine tube is tilted forward, the magazine follower (#54) will fall out. Note its position for correct reassembly. The buttplate (#5) is removed simply by unscrewing the two buttplate screws (#6) and lifting the buttplate off the buttstock (#4).

REASSEMBLY

Reassemble the rifle in the reverse order of the above procedure.

Marlin Model 1894

Marlin's new Model 1894 Cowboy in 45 Colt is very much like the original 1894 with the addition of a hammer block safety. Rifle courtesy Marlin Firearms. Author photos.

Marlin Firearms first introduced a lever action rifle that was built to accept revolver-sized cartridges in the Model 1888. Marlin made only about 4,800 Model 1888 rifles until the next year when the Model 1888 was improved and continued as the Model 1889. The 1889 was manufactured until about 1899, with about 55,000 rifles produced. The last and most successful version of this medium framed rifle series was the Model 1894 made from 1894 to 1935.

The 1888 and 1889 were chambered for 32-20, 38-40 and 44-40 Winchester cartridges while for the 1894, Marlin added 25-20 to the chambering lineup. About 250,000 of these first production 1894s were produced in many variations, both as carbines and as rifles, with round and octagon barrels ranging from 20 to 32 inches. Like all of Marlin's early rifles, the 1894 used a square breech bolt and incorporated more safety features than any of their competition. The 1894 was reintroduced by Marlin in the latter part of the twentieth century and is currently still being manufactured in 44 Magnum, 45 Colt, 357 Magnum and 41 Magnum.

DISASSEMBLY INSTRUCTIONS,

Illustration from Marlin Firearms Co., reprinted with permission.

These instructions apply to new Marlin 1894 models. The procedures in these instructions may be applied to older model 1894 models with the exception that those earlier rifles are not equipped with a hammer block safety, and use a leaf-type mainspring.

This is the new Marlin crossbolt hammer block safety, shown here in the off position.

The 1894 action wide open. Look inside and make sure there is not a cartridge in the carrier or in the barrel.

1 First, make sure the weapon is unloaded. Hold the rifle around the barrel and wooden forearm with your left hand and point the muzzle in a safe direction. With your thumb, pull the hammer (#35) back until you hear one audible click, then press the hammer block safety on SAFE by pushing it from left to right (rifle viewed from the rear). Open the action by pulling the finger lever (#15) all the way down with your right hand. Check now to be certain there is no cartridge in the barrel's chamber. Also check to be sure there is not a cartridge lying in the carrier (#7) within the action. If there is a cartridge in the carrier block, when you close the lever, the rifle will be loaded. To safely unload a rifle with a loaded magazine, always be sure the muzzle stays pointed in a safe direction, keep your finger away from the trigger, and operate the lever to the fully open and fully closed positions several times to expel the cartridges in the magazine until no more cartridges are expelled from the action.

Marlin ®
CENTERFIRE
Lever Action Rifles
Model 1894

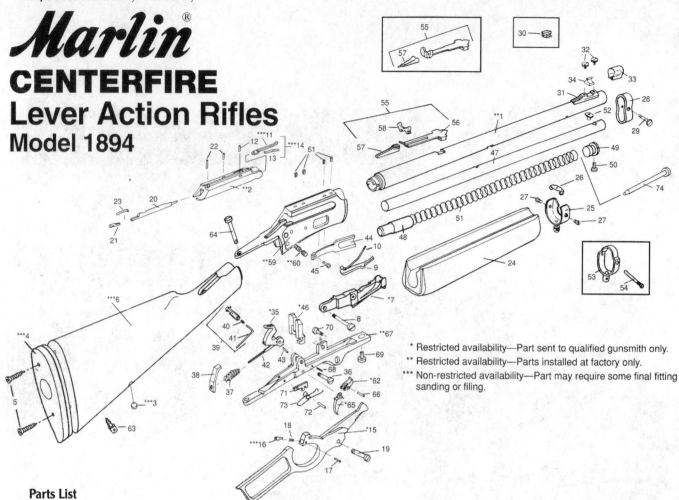

* Restricted availability—Part sent to qualified gunsmith only.
** Restricted availability—Parts installed at factory only.
*** Non-restricted availability—Part may require some final fitting sanding or filing.

Parts List

1	Barrel	27	Forearm Tip Tenon Screw (2)	52	Magazine Tube Stud
2	Breech Bolt	28	Front Band	53	Rear Band
3	Bullseye	29	Front Band Screw	54	Rear Band Screw
4	Buttplate / Buttpad	30	Front Sight	55	Rear Sight Assembly
5	Buttplate / Buttpad Screw (2)	31	Front Sight Base	56	Rear Sight Base
6	Buttstock	32	Front Sight Base Screw (2)	57	Rear Sight Elevator
7	Carrier Assembly	33	Front Sight Hood	58	Rear Sight Folding Leaf
8	Carrier Screw	34	Front Sight Insert	59	Receiver
9	Ejector W/Spring	35	Hammer	60	Safety Button Assembly
10	Ejector Spring	36	Hammer Screw	61	Scope Mount Dummy Screw (4)
11	Extractor	37	Hammer Spring (Mainspring)	62	Sear
12	Extractor Retaining Pin	38	Hammer Spring Plate	63	Swivel Stud, Rear
13	Extractor Spring	39	Hammer Spur Complete	64	Tang Screw
14	Extractor W/Spring		(Includes Parts 40 And 41)	65	Trigger
15	Finger Lever	40	Hammer Spur Screw	66	Trigger And Sear Pin
16	Finger Lever Plunger	41	Hammer Spur Wrench	67	Triggerguard Plate
17	Finger Lever Plunger Pin	42	Hammer Strut	68	Triggerguard Plate Latch Pin
18	Finger Lever Plunger Spring	43	Hammer Strut Pin	69	Triggerguard Plate Screw
19	Finger Lever Screw	44	Loading Spring	70	Triggerguard Plate
20	Firing Pin, Front	45	Loading Spring Screw		Support Screw
21	Firing Pin, Rear	46	Locking Bolt	71	Trigger Safety Block
22	Firing Pin Retaining Pin (2)	47	Magazine Tube	72	Trigger Safety Block Pin
23	Firing Pin Spring	48	Magazine Tube Follower	73	Trigger Safety Block Spring
24	Forearm	49	Magazine Tube Plug	74	10-Shot Plug
25	Forearm Tip	50	Magazine Tube Plug Screw		
26	Forearm Tip Tenon	51	Magazine Tube Spring		

Removing the lever screw allows the lever, breech bolt and ejector to be removed, making barrel cleanup a snap.

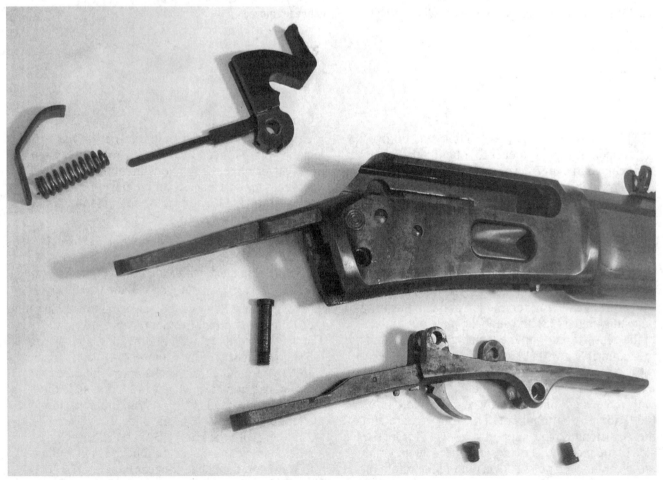

Here most of the action is removed, the result of removing only three more screws.

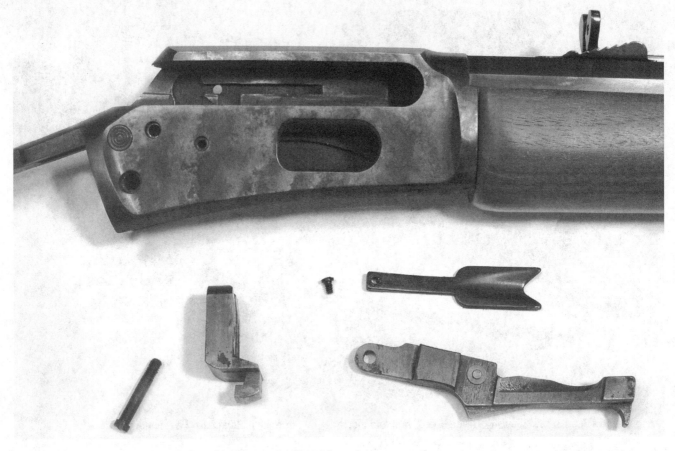

In this shot the carrier, locking bolt and loading spring (gate) have been removed.

2 To remove the lever, breech bolt and buttstock: Open the finger lever (#15) about half-way down and remove the finger lever screw (#19). Pull the finger lever down and out of the receiver (#59). Push the breech bolt (#2) all the way to the rear and out of the receiver and then lift out the ejector (#9). Remove the tang screw (#64) from the upper receiver tang and pull the buttstock (#6) straight off to the rear.

3 To disassemble the receiver: Push the safety off. Lower the hammer (#35) so it is all the way down. Push down on the top of the mainspring adjusting plate (#38) and slide the plate out to the side of the action along with the mainspring (#37). Remove the hammer screw (#36) and after depressing the trigger safety block (#71), hold the trigger (#65) to the rear and lift the hammer assembly (#35) up out the top of the receiver. Remove the triggerguard plate screw (#69) from the bottom-front of the triggerguard and the triggerguard plate support screw (#70) from the left side of the receiver. The triggerguard plate assembly (#67) can now be pulled down out of the bottom of the receiver. By removing the carrier screw (#8) from

the right side of the receiver, the carrier (#7) and the locking bolt (#46) can be removed from the bottom of the receiver. Note the relationship of these parts for later reassembly. Unscrew and remove the loading spring screw (#45). The loading spring (#44) can now be lifted out of the receiver.

4 To disassemble the forearm and magazine: Marlin has used several different methods of securing the magazine and forearm on different models over the years, so you may note some variances.

For carbines: Remove the magazine tube plug screw (#50) from the bottom front of the magazine tube. The magazine tube plug (#49), the magazine spring (#51) and magazine tube follower (#48) can now be withdrawn from the front of the magazine tube (#47). Unscrew the front band screw (#29) and slide the front magazine band (#28) off from the front. Remove the rear band screw (#54) and slide the forearm wood (#24) along with the band (#53) up the barrel just a little. Remove the magazine tube (#47) by pulling it forward and then slide the rear band off. Tilt the forearm down and remove it.

The magazine and forearm disassembled.

For rifles (illustrated): Unscrew and remove the magazine tube plug screw (#50) from the bottom-front of the magazine tube. Unscrew and remove the two forearm cap screws (#27) and slide the forearm cap (#25) forward so it disengages the tenon (#26). Hold your thumb tightly over the magazine tube plug while you pull the magazine tube down away from the barrel slightly. Once the tube is clear of the magazine stud (#52) on the barrel, the magazine tube plug (#49) is loose and may be removed out the front, along with the magazine spring (#51) and its follower (#48). The magazine tube (#47) can be withdrawn and then the forearm wood (#24) may be removed from the barrel.

5 To disassemble the triggerguard plate: Make note of the relative positions of these parts before disassembly. Drive out the trigger and sear pin (#66). The trigger (#65) and sear (#62) can now be removed from the triggerguard plate. To remove the trigger safety, first drift out the trigger safety block pin (#72). The trigger safety block (#71) and its spring (#73) can now be lifted out the top.

6 To disassemble the breech bolt and lever: The extractor (#11) may be removed from the breech bolt (#2) by carefully driving out the extractor retaining pin (#12). The extractor (#11) and the extractor spring (#13) can now be withdrawn out the front of the bolt. Remove the rear firing pin retaining pin (#22) by drifting it out from top to bottom. The rear firing pin (#21) and the firing pin spring (#23) can now be removed. The front firing pin (#20) is removed by first driving out the front firing pin retaining pin (#22). The firing pin will now slide out to the rear of the breech bolt.

Finger lever disassembly: The finger lever plunger (#16) and its spring (#18) can be removed by drifting out the finger lever plunger pin (#17).

Further disassembly is not required for normal maintenance.

REASSEMBLY

Reassemble the rifle in the reverse order of the above procedure.

· 373 ·

New Marlin Model 336 Series Rifles
(Including 444 and Post-1972 Model 1895)

The new Model 1895 Marlin shares the same basic, very strong action design with the Model 336. Disassembly is identical. Author photos.

The period of the 1880s to the turn of the century were Marlin's glory days. During it they produced a full line of excellent lever action rifles and carbines in various chamberings. These lever actions were offered in a plethora of different sizes ranging from large, handling big-game cartridges, to medium for the familiar pistol calibers such as 44-40 Winchester, to the small .22 and .32 rrimfire versions. Those original Marlin designs were beautiful, every bit as nice as their competition and generally much simpler internally. These nineteenth-century models gradually evolved into the modern versions of these classic rifles that we know today as the 336, the 444 and the 1895 models, all built around the sound concepts originally laid out by John Marlin.

Marlin rifles are considered by some shooters as the "other lever action." In this light they have in many ways played second-fiddle to Winchester's better-known lever guns. Rather than paying a lot of attention to high polish blueing or fancy woodwork, the modern Marlin Firearms Company has been making good, meat-and-potatoes hunting rifles for as long as most of us can remember. The basic Marlin design is robust and very simple, making for a very dependable lever action repeater that can be expected to last a lifetime. Modern Marlin lever actions also offer a sound basis for people wanting to build themselves great custom lever gun.

Marlin's 336 series of rifles is a continuation of, and an improvement of, the Model 36, which was

The Model 336 Cowboy in 38-55 caliber. The cross-bolt safety, located at the rear of the action, is in the off position.

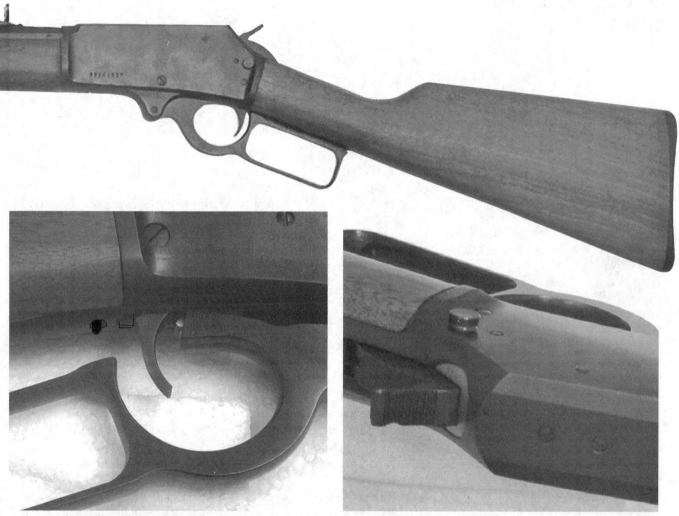

This is one more of Marlin's safety devices: the lever safety. The finger lever has to be held closed or the trigger cannot be pulled to fire the rifle.

All new Marlin lever actions have a cross-bolt safety button as shown here on a new Model 1895.

first introduced in 1936. The Model 36 in turn, had even earlier origins that can be traced back to the Model 1893. The designation 336 came about after an alteration to the Model 36 in 1948 that left the rifle with a round bolt that enabled Marlin to provide more strength in the receiver around the bolt. Rifles in the 336 series are primarily used for hunting. For this reason they are chambered for cartridges such as the 30-30, 32 Winchester Special and 35 Remington, although over the years they have also been chambered for the 44 Magnum, the 307, 356 and 375 Winchester, and the 444 Marlin. In 1972, the Model of 1895 was

"reintroduced" by Marlin in 45-70 caliber, but this time, in place of the original 1895's flat-bolt shape, the new Model 1895 was built on the stronger, round-bolt concept, just like the one used in the 336 action.

In recent years, Marlin has been closely following the public demands with their emphasis turning decidedly toward the needs of the Cowboy Action Shooter. Marlin now manufactures a Cowboy version of the 336 in 1999, offering it in 30-30 or 38-55 Winchester as well as a Cowboy Model 1895 chambered in 45-70.

Marlin®

CENTERFIRE
Lever Action Rifles
Models 336, 444
and 1895

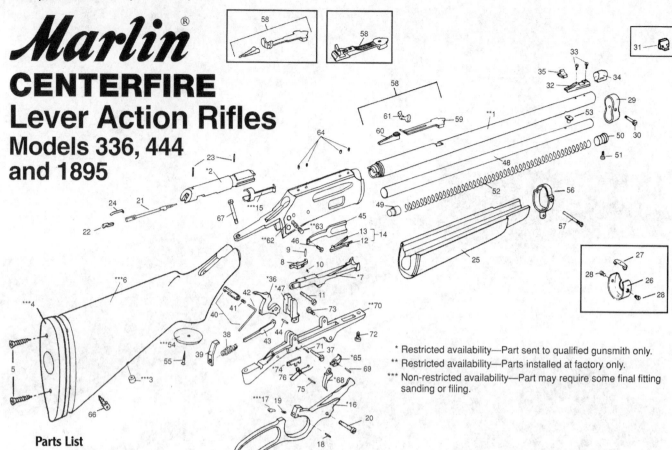

* Restricted availability—Part sent to qualified gunsmith only.

** Restricted availability—Parts installed at factory only.

*** Non-restricted availability—Part may require some final fitting sanding or filing.

Parts List

1	Barrel	27	Forearm Tip Tenon	52	Magazine Tube Spring
2	Breech Bolt	28	Forearm Tip Tenon Screw (2)	53	Magazine Tube Stud
3	Bullseye	29	Front Band	54	Pistol Grip Cap
4	Buttplate / Butt pad	30	Front Band Screw	55	Pistol Grip Cap Screw
5	Buttplate Screw (2)	31	Front Sight	56	Rear Band
6	Buttstock	32	Front Sight Base	57	Rear Band Screw
7	Carrier	33	Front Sight Base Screw (2)	58	Rear Sight Assembly
8	Carrier Rocker	34	Front Sight Hood	59	Rear Sight Base
9	Carrier Rocker Pin	35	Front Sight Insert	60	Rear Sight Elevator
10	Carrier Rocker Spring	36	Hammer	61	Rear Sight Folding Leaf
	Carrier Assembly	37	Hammer Screw	62	Receiver
	(consists of 7, 8, 9, &10 above)	38	Hammer Spring	63	Safety Button Assembly
11	Carrier Screw		(Mainspring)	64	Scope Mount Dummy Screw (4)
12	Ejector	39	Hammer Spring	65	Sear
13	Ejector Spring		Adjusting Plate	66	Swivel Stud, Rear
14	Ejector w/Spring	40	Hammer Spur Complete	67	Tang Screw
15	Extractor		(Includes 41 & 42)	68	Trigger
16	Finger Lever	41	Hammer Spur Screw	69	Trigger and Sear Pin
17	Finger Lever Plunger	42	Hammer Spur Wrench	70	Triggerguard Plate
18	Finger Lever Plunger Pin	43	Hammer Strut	71	Triggerguard Plate
19	Finger Lever Plunger Spring	44	Hammer Strut Pin		Latch Pin
20	Finger Lever Screw	45	Loading Spring	72	Triggerguard Plate Screw
21	Firing Pin, Front	46	Loading Spring Screw	73	Triggerguard Plate
22	Firing Pin, Rear	47	Locking Bolt		Support Screw
23	Firing Pin Retaining Pin (2)	48	Magazine Tube	74	Trigger Safety Block
24	Firing Pin Spring	49	Magazine Tube Follower	75	Trigger Safety Block Pin
25	Forearm	50	Magazine Tube Plug	76	Trigger Safety Block Spring
26	Forearm Tip	51	Magazine Tube Plug Screw		

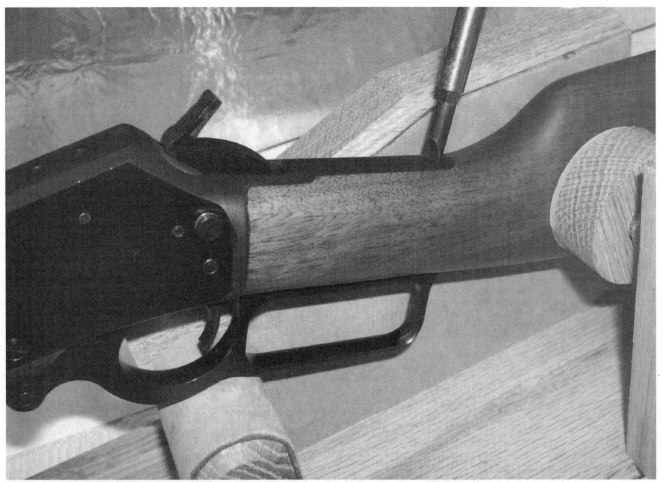

The first disassembly step is to remove the tang screw so the buttstock can be removed. Here, an 1895 is held captive in the oak gun cradle from Brownells made by Mountain Meadow Enterprises. Devices such as this are an excellent investment; they provide you with a secure means of holding a long gun while it is being worked on.

DISASSEMBLY INSTRUCTIONS
Illustration courtesy of Marlin Firearms Co.; reprinted with permission.

These instructions apply to new-manufacture Marlin Models 336, 444 and post-1972 Model 1895. The procedures in these instructions may be used with older model 336, 444 and 1895 models, with the exception that those rifles are not equipped with a hammer block safety.

1 First, make sure the gun is unloaded. Point the muzzle in a safe direction and hold the rifle around the wooden forearm and barrel with your left hand. With your right thumb, pull the hammer (#36) back until you hear one audible click, then press the hammer block safety to the SAFE position by pushing it from left to right (with the rifle viewed from the rear). Open the action by pulling the finger lever (#16) all the way down with your right hand. Check now to be absolutely certain there is no cartridge in the barrel's chamber and look in through the bolt opening into the action to make sure there is no cartridge lying in the carrier (#7) inside the action.

Note: If there is a cartridge in the carrier block, when you close the lever the rifle will be loaded. To safely unload a rifle with a loaded magazine, always be sure the muzzle stays pointed in a safe direction. Keep your finger away from the trigger while you operate the lever to the fully open and fully closed positions several times to expel the cartridges in the magazine. Repeat this operation until no more cartridges are expelled from the action.

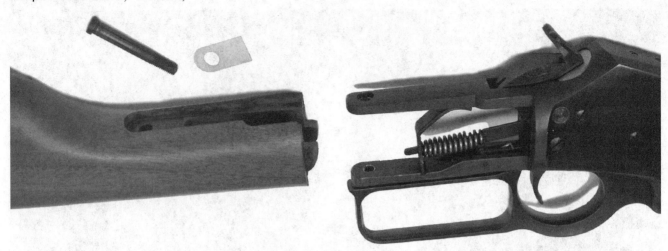

The buttstock removed. That plastic shim you see just below the screw gets sandwiched between the wood and the rear tang.

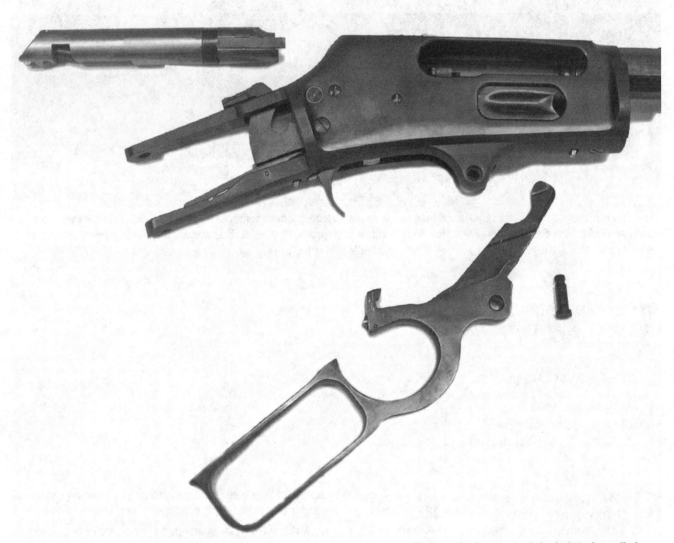

Opening the lever and removing the lever screw allows the finger lever to be pulled out the bottom and the bolt to be pulled out the rear of the receiver.

2 To remove the lever, breech bolt and buttstock: Open the finger lever (#16) about halfway down and remove the finger lever screw (#20). Pull the finger lever down and out of the receiver (#62). Push the breech bolt (#2) all the way to the rear and out of the receiver and then lift out the ejector (#14). Remove the tang screw (#67) from the upper receiver tang and pull the butt-stock (#6) straight off to the rear.

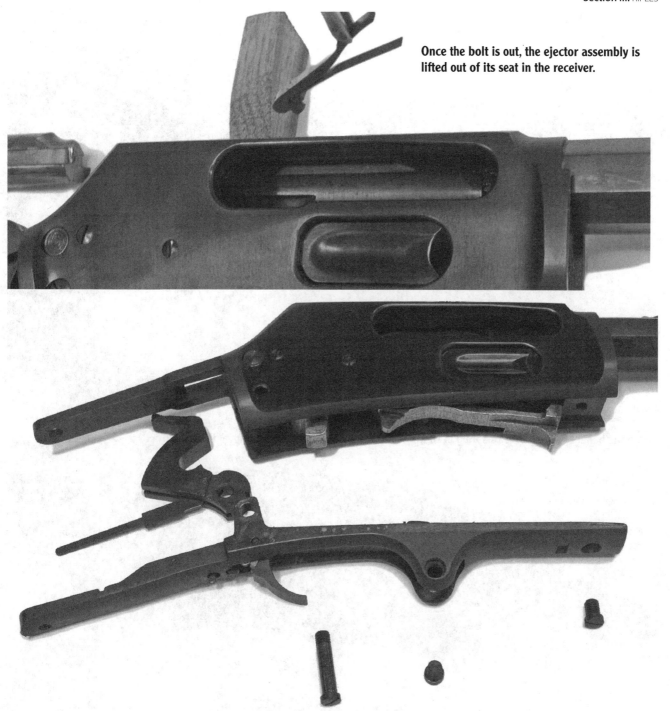

Once the bolt is out, the ejector assembly is lifted out of its seat in the receiver.

Removing the triggerguard plate exposes the entire Marlin action for disassembly.

3 To disassemble the receiver: Lower the hammer (#36) so it is all the way down. Push down on the top of the mainspring adjusting plate (#39) and slide the plate out to the side of the action along with the mainspring (#38). Remove the hammer screw (#37) and after depressing the trigger safety block (#74), hold the trigger (#68) to the rear and lift the hammer assembly (#36) up out of the top of the receiver. Remove the triggerguard plate screw (#72) from the bottom front of the triggerguard and the triggerguard plate support screw (#73) from the left side of the receiver. The triggerguard plate assembly (#70) can now be pulled down out of the bottom of the receiver. By removing the carrier screw (#11) from the right side of the receiver you can remove the carrier (#7) and the locking bolt (#47) from the bottom of the receiver. Make careful note of the relationship of these parts for later reassembly. Unscrew and remove the loading spring screw (#46). The loading spring (#45) can now be lifted out of the receiver.

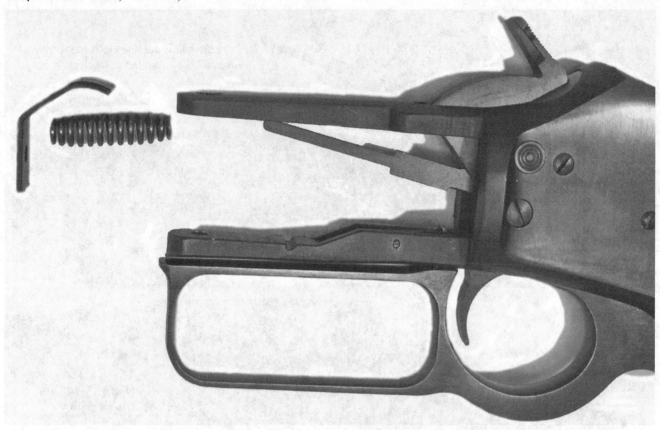

Here the hammer spring or mainspring is shown with its adjusting plate after removal from the rifle.

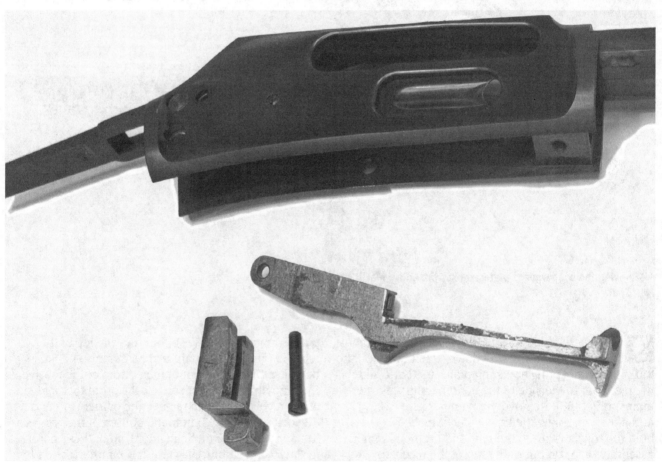

After the triggerguard plate is down, the locking bolt is removed from the receiver by pulling it straight down. Removing the carrier screw from the right side of the receiver lets the carrier fall out the bottom.

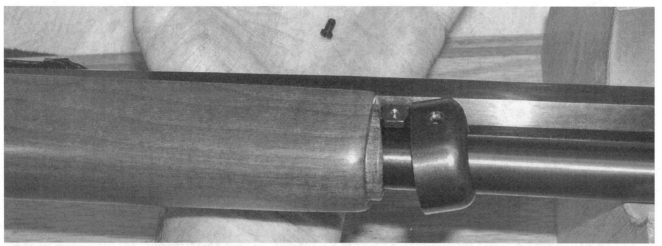

To get the magazine and forearm out, first you have to remove the two forearm tip tenon screws. This lets you slide the forend tip forward.

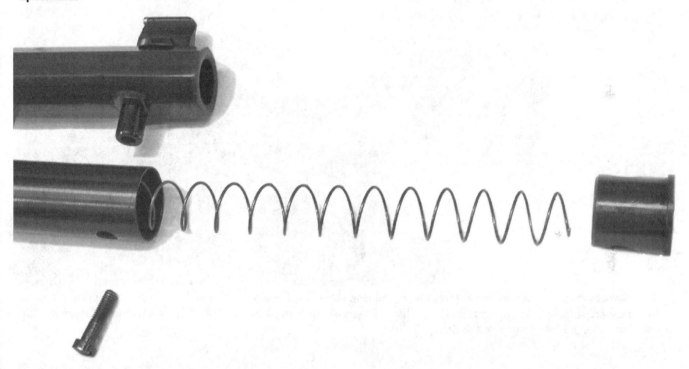

Next, remove the magazine tube plug screw and remove the plug, spring and follower. Use caution: the plug is under considerable spring tension.

4 To remove the forearm and magazine tube: Marlin has used several different methods of securing the magazine and forearm over the years, so you may note some variances.

For carbines: Unscrew and remove the magazine tube plug screw (#51) from the bottom front of the magazine tube. The magazine tube plug (#50) along with the magazine spring (#52) and magazine tube follower (#49) can now be withdrawn from the front of the magazine tube (#48). Unscrew the front band screw (#30) and slide the front magazine band (#29) off from the front. Remove the rear band screw (#57) and slide the forearm wood (#25) along with the band (#56) up the barrel just a little. Remove the magazine tube (#48)

by pulling it forward and then slide the rear band off and tilt the forearm down and remove it.

For rifles: Unscrew and remove the two forearm tip tenon screws (#28) and slide the forearm tip forward slightly. Remove the magazine tube plug screw (#51). Hold your thumb over the magazine tube plug and pull down on the front of the magazine tube. The magazine tube cap will come free and can be removed out the front of the magazine tube along with the magazine tube spring and magazine tube follower (#49). Pull the magazine tube along with the forearm wood and forearm tip forward, off the rifle. The forearm tip and forearm may be slid forward, off the magazine tube.

The loading spring (gate) comes off with only one screw.

This view of the rear of the breech bolt gives you a good look at the rear firing pin, which is down, in the bolt-open position. When the finger lever is closed, it pushes the locking bolt up, which in turn pushes the rear firing pin back into alignment with the front firing pin, allowing the gun to fire.

5 To disassemble the triggerguard plate: Make careful note of the relative positions of these parts as you disassemble them for ease of reassembly later. Drive out the trigger and sear pin (#69). The trigger (#68) and sear (#65) can now be removed from the triggerguard plate. To remove the trigger safety, first drift out the trigger safety block pin (#75). The trigger safety block (#74) and its spring (#76) may be lifted out the top.

6 To disassemble the breech bolt and finger lever: The extractor (#25) may be removed from the breech bolt (#2) by carefully prying it out of its slot and to the side, using a small screwdriver for leverage. Remove the rear firing pin retaining pin (#23) by using a suitable pin punch and hammer to drift it out from top to bottom. The rear firing pin (#22) and the firing pin spring (#24) can now be removed. The front firing

pin (#21) is removed by first driving out the front firing pin retaining pin (#23). The firing pin will now slide out to the rear of the breech bolt.

To disassemble the finger lever: The finger lever plunger (#17) and its spring (#19) can be removed by using a suitable pin punch and hammer to drift out the finger lever plunger pin (#18).

Further disassembly is not required for normal maintenance.

REASSEMBLY

Reassemble the rifle in the reverse order of the above procedure.

Remington Rolling Block Rifle

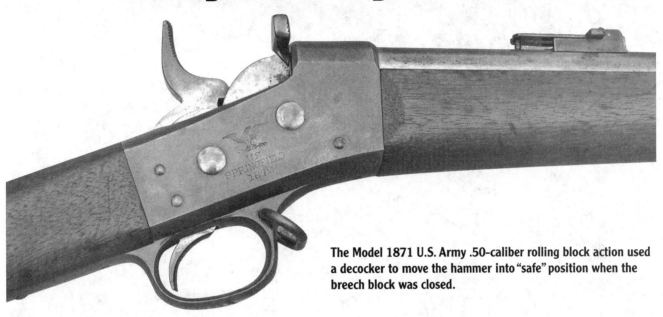

The Model 1871 U.S. Army .50-caliber rolling block action used a decocker to move the hammer into "safe" position when the breech block was closed.

One of the most recognizable and popular of all the nineteenth-century rifle designs was the Remington Rolling Block. This rifle was produced in many forms from 1864 up to as late as about 1934. The highly successful design was probably best known for its simplicity and for its incredible reliability. Exact quantities of the rolling blocks manufactured are not known, but the number is certainly huge. As far as military rifles and carbines go, from 1867 through 1902 more than a million arms were manufactured. As you might expect, the list of countries who bought the rifle is also impressive and includes Argentina, Chile, China, Columbia, Cuba, Denmark, Egypt, France, Honduras, Mexico, Norway, Spain, Sweden, the United States and others. Remington literally covered the globe with rolling block rifles.

Remington manufactured the rolling block action as a rifle, carbine, shotgun and even a single-shot pistol, and it was produced in both military and sporting configurations. During its long and colorful life, the ever-faithful rolling block was chambered in virtually every black powder cartridge known. It even offered an early version of the smokeless 7x57mm Mauser cartridge in the No.5 action for the Spanish and in 8mm Lebel for the French. The rolling block's action design, where the massive hammer rolls in front of the breech block and serves to effectively lock the breech block closed, was originally patented by Leonard

Geiger in 1863. Joseph Rider, the genius of Remington's Ilion, New York factory, improved Geiger's action and developed the split-breech carbine. Geiger and Rider worked together to perfect the design into the Remington Rolling Block in 1866 and further improved it by patent in August of 1867 and again in November of 1871.

There are four basic rolling block frame sizes, as follows:

No. 1 action: 1.250″ wide. The largest of the rolling block actions; intended for military use, it was used for the largest and most powerful cartridges. Also used on the Model No. 1-1/2 rifle.

No. 2 action: 1.125″ wide. Used for smaller, less powerful cartridges. Identified by the curved contour at the rear where it joins to the stock.

No. 3 action: Not actually a rolling block at all but rather a falling block, this was the Remington-Hepburn action.

No. 4 action: A short, lightweight action used for rimfire cartridges. Its forward end is much narrower than the larger actions.

No. 5 action: The No.1 size action, made starting in 1898 for use with smokeless powder cartridges, it was equipped with a rimless cartridge case extractor and was the last of the large military rolling block actions.

The famous Remington Rolling Block is most prolific in its military form; perhaps more than 1,000,000 were manufactured by Remington alone! The one was built at Springfield Army. It's an 1871 US Army model in 50-70. From the Ed Wade collection. Author photos.

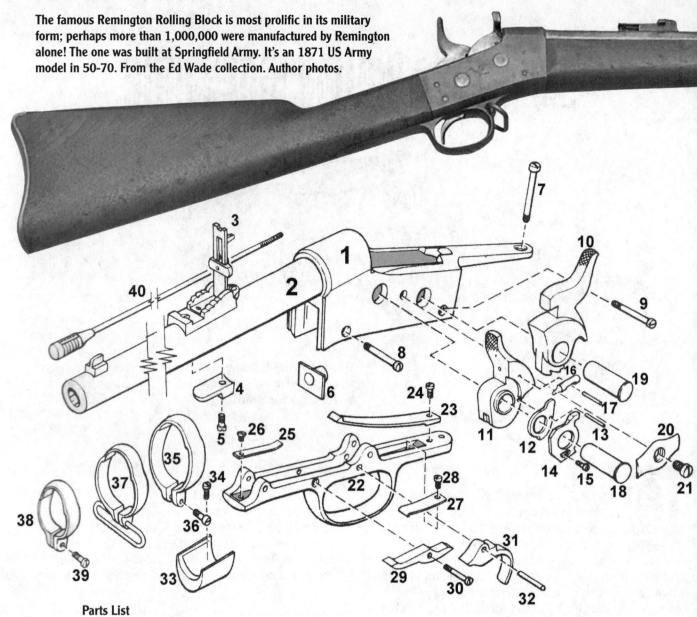

Parts List

1	Receiver	15	Extractor Screw	29	Locking Lever
2	Barrel	16	Firing Pin	30	Locking Lever Screw
3	Rear Sight	17	Firing Pin Limit Pin	31	Trigger
4	Recoil Stud	18	Breech Block Pin	32	Trigger Pin
5	Recoil Stud Screw	19	Hammer Pin	33	Stock Tip
6	Ramrod Stop	20	Button	34	Stock Tip Screw
7	Tang Screw	21	Button Screw	35	Rear Band
8	Front Guard Plate Screw	22	Guard Plate	36	Rear Band Screw
9	Rear Guard Plate Screw	23	Mainspring	37	Middle Band & Screw
10	Hammer	24	Mainspring Screw	38	Front Band
11	Breech Block	25	Lever Spring	39	Front Band Screw
12	Firing Pin Retractor	26	Lever Spring Screw	40	Ramrod
13	Retractor Pin	27	Trigger Spring		
14	Extractor	28	Trigger Spring Screw		

The rolling block is one of the easiest of all actions in which to check whether the chamber is loaded or not.

DISASSEMBLY INSTRUCTIONS

Illustration from *The Gun Digest Book of Exploded Firearms Drawings*, 2nd edition, edited by Harold A. Murtz, DBI Books Inc., 1977 Printed with permission of the publisher: Krause Publications, 700 E. State Street, Iola, WI 54990-0001 Phone 800 258-0929 (renumbered and retouched by the author).

These instructions are applicable to almost all large-frame Remington rolling block rifles and copies thereof, excepting the Model 1869 US Navy rifle. Note: As shown in the photos, the US Army Model 1871 rolling block rifle built by Springfield Armory uses several parts not found on conventional Remington rolling block actions.

1 First, unload the rifle. Keep your fingers away from the trigger at all times. Hold the rifle around the barrel and wooden forearm with your left hand. Point the muzzle in a safe direction and open the action by pulling the hammer (#10) all the way to the rear and then pulling back the breech-block (#11) lever all the way in order to roll the breech open. Look into the barrel and check to be certain there is no cartridge in the barrel chamber. If there is a cartridge present, reach in and remove it by pulling the cartridge straight out of the rear of the barrel. Remove any live ammunition to a separate location.

Getting the breech block out is a simple matter of removing one huge pin, as shown in this photo.

After the "other" huge pin has been removed, the massive hammer is lifted right out the top.

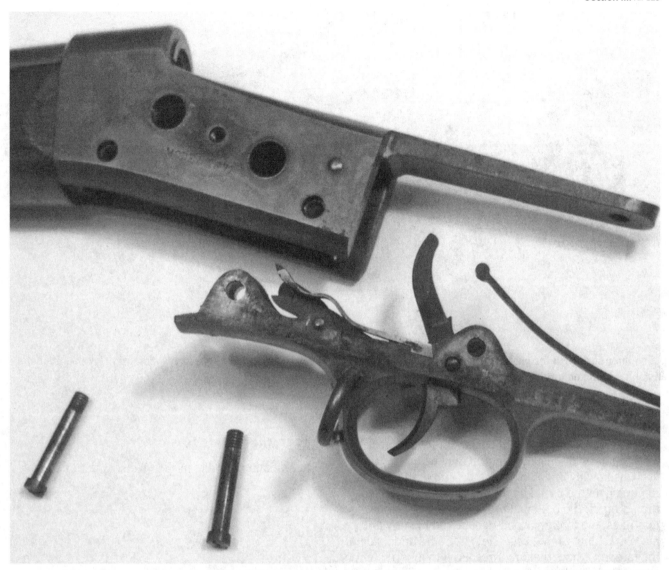

Removing the two side screws allows the entire trigger "group" to be removed out the bottom, leaving the action totally stripped. The one remaining pin you see in the action is a limiting pin for the mainspring. This feature is unique to the US Army M1871.

2 To disassemble the action: Unscrew and remove the button screw (#21) and lift the button (#20) off the left receiver side. Cock the hammer (#10) all the way back and then push the breech block pin (#18) out of the receiver (#1) from right to left. The breech block (#11) and the extractor (#14) can be lifted straight up out from the top. Hold the hammer (#10) with your thumb and pull the trigger (#31), allowing the hammer to ease all the way forward. Remove the hammer pin (#19) to lift the hammer up out of the receiver.

To disassemble the breech block: By drifting out the firing pin retaining pin (#17) from the breech block, the firing pin (#16) may be pulled out the rear of the breech block.

3 To remove the buttstock and guard plate and for further disassembly: Unscrew and remove the tang screw (#7). The buttstock can then be pulled straight off to the rear. Use an angle-head screwdriver to loosen the mainspring screw (#24) several turns. Unscrew and remove the front (#8) and rear (#9) guard plate screws and the guard plate (#22) can be pulled down to the rear and out of the receiver. The mainspring (#23) can now be removed after removing its screw (#24), and then the trigger spring screw (#28) can be removed and the trigger spring (#27) lifted out. Unscrew and remove the lever spring screw (#26). The lever spring (#25) can be lifted out of the front of the guard plate. Use a pin punch and hammer to drive out the trigger pin (#32) so the trigger (#31) may be removed. The locking lever (#29) may be withdrawn after removing the locking lever screw (#30- sometimes this is a pin) from the left side of the guard plate.

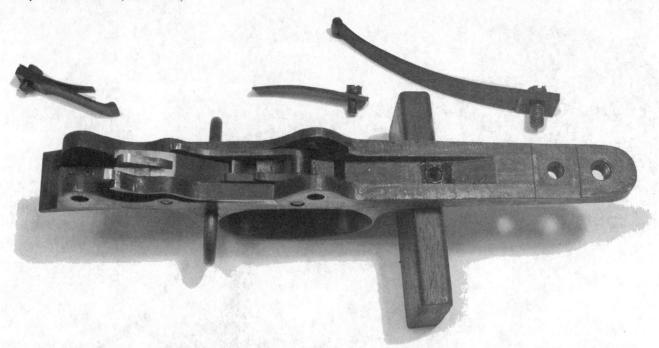

The three springs in the guard are removed next. This is the M1871 Springfield Armory guard. It's more complex than that of a standard Remington.

4 To remove the forearm wood: On rolling block military models the forearm may be removed by first unscrewing and removing the ramrod and then removing all the barrel bands. The forearm wood will then drop off the bottom. On some sporting carbines and rifles, the forearm wood may be retained by one or more machine screws, accessible from the underside of the forearm wood, that are threaded into a barrel tenon or tenons.

REASSEMBLY

Reassemble the rifle in the reverse order of above.

Remington-Keene
Magazine Bolt Action Rifle

The Remington-Keene was Remington's first real commercial-production, bolt action rifle. They were manufactured from 1880 through 1888; the total quantity of weapons produced is estimated to be about 5,000. The Keene had an external, manually-cocked hammer and, similar to contemporary lever action rifles, a tubular magazine mounted under the barrel. Showing U.S. military influence, the magazine is equipped with a manual cut-off, to allow the rifle to be used as a single shot if the shooter desires. The Keene's hammer is automatically placed in the half-cocked position as the bolt is closed and the hammer must be manually pulled back into the cocked position to be fired or to re-open the bolt. The bolt will remain locked closed while the hammer is in the half-cocked position.

Remington made the Keene available as a Hunter's Rifle (sporting rifle) with a 24-1/2-inch round barrel, but half round-half octagon barrels were available on special order. Carbines were made with 20- and 22-inch round barrels. The Navy model rifle used a 29-1/4-inch barrel while the Army model rifle came equipped with a 32-1/2-inch round barrel. Both military versions were stocked almost to the muzzle. In 1881 the U.S. Army purchased a few Remington-Keene rifles for trials but made no further purchases. Two hundred and fifty Remington-Keene Navy rifles were purchased by the U.S. Navy and issued to the Marines for field testing. A Frontier Model with a 24-inch round barrel was made for the U.S. Department of the Interior, in 1881 or 1882, and it is estimated some 620 to 800 were purchased and issued to Indian Police.

This classic early bolt action was chambered in 45-70 Government (by far, the most popular chambering), .40 caliber, and .43 caliber. Standard finish was blued with a casehardened hammer and rear band. Straight grip walnut stocks were standard, while pistol grip stocks, checkering and higher-grade walnut stocks were optional.

The Remington-Keene is an early American bolt action with loads of class! This one is a 20-inch-barreled carbine in 45-70. From the Ed wade collection. Author photos.

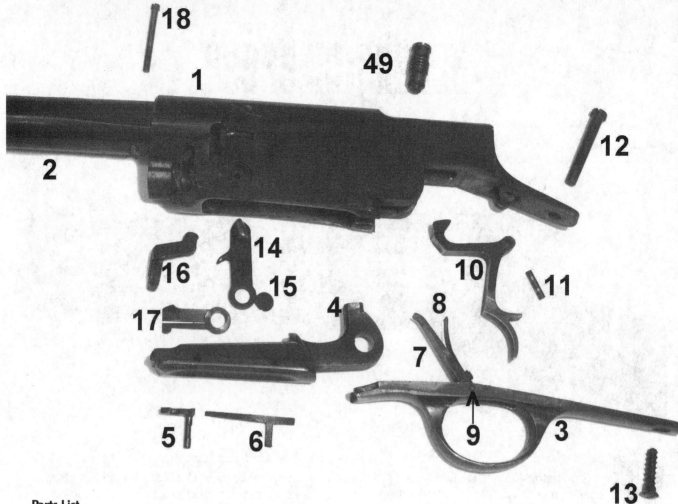

Parts List

1	Receiver	18	Draw Screw	38	Striker	
2	Barrel	19	Magazine Tube	39	Striker Spring	
3	Triggerguard	20	Magazine Follower	40	Fly	
4	Carrier	21	Magazine Spring	41	Sear	
5	Carrier Catch	22	Rear Band	42	Sear Link	
5A	Carrier Catch Lock (Not Shown)	23	Lock-Rib	43	Bolt Sleeve	
		24	Front Band	44	Striker Spring	
6	Carrier Catch Spring	25	Front Band Screw	45	Hammer	
7	Trigger Lever	26	Front Sight	46	Link Screw	
8	Trigger Lever Spring	27	Rear Sight Assembly	47	Hammer Screw	
8A	Trigger Lever Spring Screw	28	Rear Sight Base Screws	48	Stock (Not Shown)	
9	Trigger Lever Pin	29	Bolt	49	Carrier Screw	
10	Trigger	30	Ejector	50	Buttplate (Not Shown)	
11	Trigger Pin	31	Ejector Screw	51	Buttplate Screws (Not Shown)	
12	Upper Tang Screw	32	Extractor	52	Rear Swivel (Not Shown)	
13	Lower Tang Screw	33	Extractor Plunger	53	Rear Swivel Base Screws (Not Shown)	
14	Cut-Off Lever	34	Extractor Spring			
15	Cut-Off Lever Screw	35	Striker Lock	54	Front Swivel	
16	Cut-Off	36	Striker Lock Spring			
17	Cut-Off Spring	37	Striker Lock Screw			

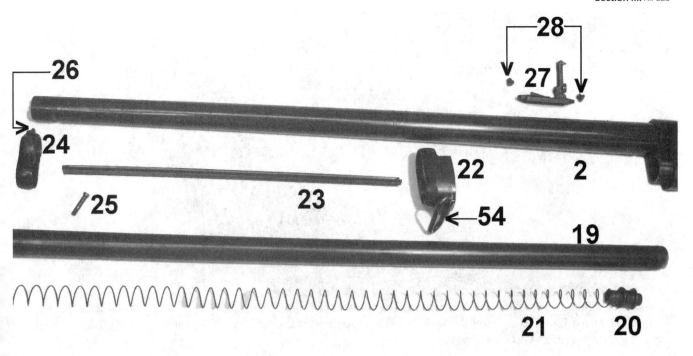

Look down into the carrier as well as into the chamber to be sure the rifle is unloaded.

DISASSEMBLY INSTRUCTIONS

1 First, be sure the rifle is unloaded before handling it. Grasp the rifle around the wood, forward of the triggerguard, always being mindful to keep your fingers away from the trigger (#10) and to keep the muzzle pointed in a safe direction. With your other hand, open the bolt (#29) by pulling up on its handle and the pulling the handle all the way to the rear. If the bolt will not open, pull the hammer to the rear and then open the bolt. If a cartridge is present in the action, resting on the carrier (#4), reach in and remove it.

Pull the magazine cut-off lever to the rear position. This allows the magazine to feed cartridges.

Check to see if more cartridges are present by opening and closing the bolt. Do not turn the bolt handle down, which would lock the bolt. Instead, simply push the bolt all the way forward and then pull it all the way back several times. If no cartridges come up into the carrier, flip the cut-off lever (#14) in the opposite direction and try cycling the bolt a few more times until no more cartridges present themselves.

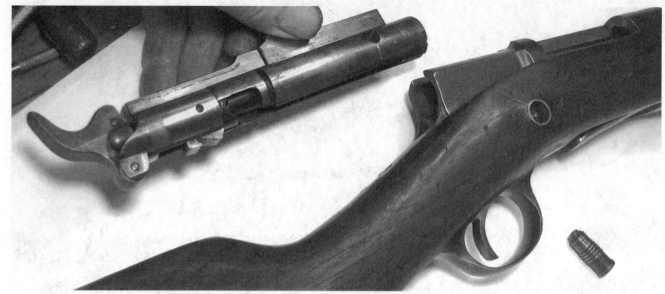

Removing the Keene bolt has proved to be a dilemma for some but once you understand how, it's a snap. Notice how the rear edge of the carrier is protruding below the stock line. That happens when the carrier screw is removed so the carrier can drop down far enough to allow the bolt to pass by.

The first step in removing the magazine is to get the front band off.

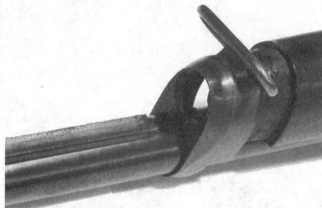

The magazine tube is simply unscrewed and the lock-rib lifted off, thus allowing the rear band to slide off to the front.

2 To remove the bolt: Close the bolt and unscrew the carrier screw (#49); this is the large screw located on the right side of the stock, just above and forward of the trigger. The carrier screw is a left-handed thread so it must be turned clockwise. Its thread is a large, square or Acme thread. As the carrier screw comes out, lift it off the rifle and you will notice that the carrier itself has dropped down slightly below the level of the stock. Open the bolt and pull it straight out to the rear. When reassembling the bolt into the receiver (#1), insert the bolt and push it forward to within about an inch of it being closed, and then grasp the carrier on its top and bottom sides by reaching into the top and bottom of the action opening with your thumb and forefinger. Move the carrier around until you see the pivot hole in the carrier align with the carrier screw hole in the stock. Reinstall and tighten the carrier screw.

3 To remove the bands and magazine tube: Unscrew and remove the front band screw (#25) and then slide the front band (#24) forward and off the barrel. Notice the band screw head is on the same side as the bolt handle. The lock-rib (#23) is now loose and may be slid out to the front. The rear band (#22) is also loose and may be slid forward and off the barrel. Take note of what is up and down on the lock-rib (try marking the top side of the lock-rib with a brightly colored marker) and of how the rear end of the lock-rib locks into the rear band for later reassembly. Insert a large screwdriver into the slot at the end of the magazine tube (#19) and unscrew the tube in a counterclockwise direction. Withdraw the magazine tube along with the magazine spring (#21) and follower (#20) out through the front of the stock (#48). The rear sight (#27) is retained by two screws (#28) located on top of the barrel.

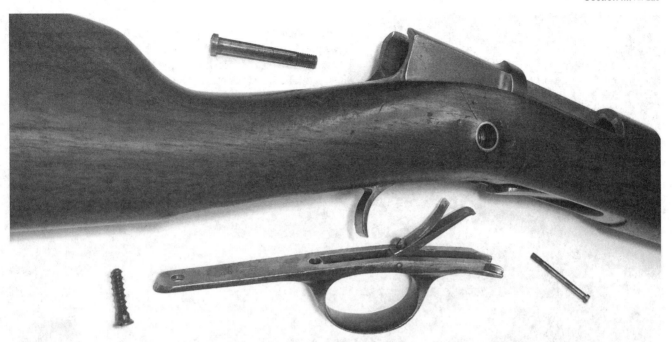

Removing the two tang screws allows the triggerguard to be dropped out the bottom. Notice the trigger lever assembly sticking up just above the guard bow. That lever and spring go in between the trigger and the carrier on assembly, acting on both parts.

The barreled action has been lifted out of the stock, leaving the carrier (center) free to drop out the bottom of the receiver.

4 To remove the triggerguard and buttstock: Unscrew and remove the upper (#12) and lower (#13) tang screws. Pull down on the rear of the triggerguard (#3) to remove it from the stock. Hold the barreled action (#1) and (#2) assembly and lift the stock straight off the bottom of the receiver. The carrier (#4) is now loose and can be lifted out of the receiver. Notice the carrier catch lock (#5A) on the right side of the receiver. This part is now loose and may be lifted out of its hole in the receiver. The buttplate (#50) may be removed by unscrewing and removing the two buttplate screws (#51).

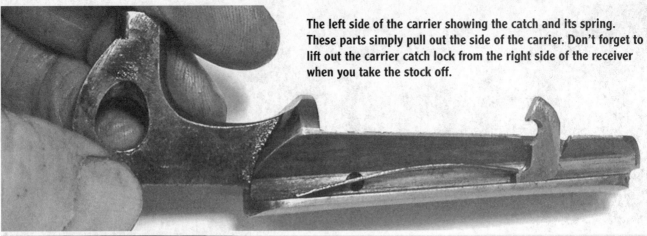

The left side of the carrier showing the catch and its spring. These parts simply pull out the side of the carrier. Don't forget to lift out the carrier catch lock from the right side of the receiver when you take the stock off.

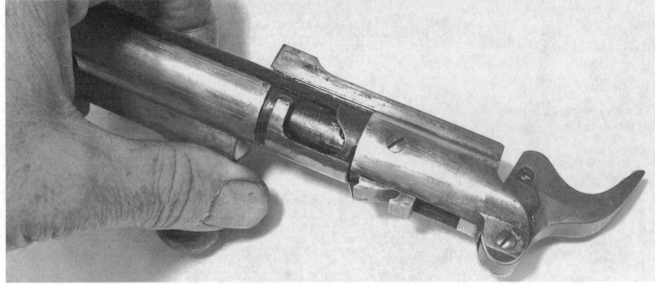

Here is the bolt with the bolt sleeve turned almost to the position where the sleeve can be separated from the bolt body.

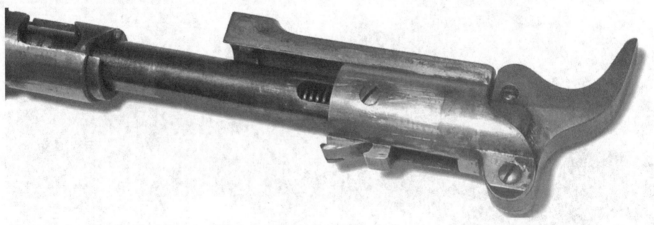

The correct position for the striker assembly to be pulled back out of the bolt.

5 To disassemble the carrier receiver and triggerguard: The carrier catch (#5) and its spring (#6) can simply be pulled out the right side of the carrier. Use a pin punch and hammer to drive out the trigger pin (#11). The trigger (#10) can be lifted out the bottom. Unscrew and remove the cut-off lever screw (#15) and lift off the cut-off lever (#14), cut-off spring (#17) and cut-off (#16) from the left side of the receiver. Be careful to note their positions for later reassembly. Use a pin punch and hammer to drift out the trigger lever pin (#9) from the triggerguard and lift out the trigger lever (#7) assembly. Unscrew and remove the trigger lever spring screw (#8A) and remove the trigger lever spring (#8).

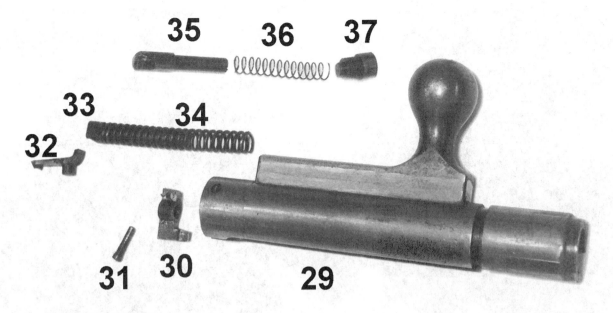

The Keene Bolt body, disassembled.

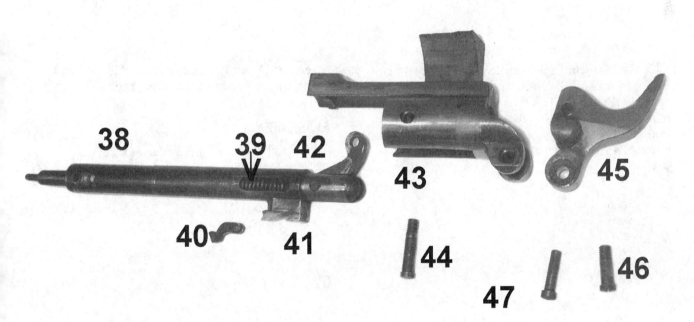

The rear of the Keene bolt or striker assembly, disassembled.

6 To disassemble the bolt: Hold the hammer (#45) back slightly and twist the bolt sleeve (#43) to the left (counterclockwise) about one-half turn until the tooth on the sleeve leg comes out of the slot on the bolt (#29). Pull the entire striker assembly out to the rear of the bolt. Unscrew the ejector screw (#31) and then use a small screwdriver blade to push up on the extractor slightly and lift out the ejector (#30) from the front of the bolt face. Notice the ejector also acts as a hardened firing pin bushing. Mount the bolt in a padded vise and use a stiff punch to depress the extractor plunger (#33). Carefully pry the extractor (#32) straight up until it comes off the bolt head and gently release tension on the extractor plunger and remove it and the extractor spring (#34) from the front of the bolt lug. Unscrew and remove the striker lock screw (#37) from the bolt knob and lift out the striker lock spring (#36) and striker lock (#35) from the bolt handle. Pay careful attention to the direction the striker lock faces for later reassembly; if you replace it backwards, the rifle will work but bolt operation will be stiff.

The ejector screw retains the ejector, which also acts as a hardened bushing for the firing pin.

Depressing the ejector plunger with a punch to release the ejector.

7 To disassemble the striker: Loosen the striker screw (#44). Unscrew and remove the hammer screw (#47) and the link screw (#46) and lift the hammer (#45) off to the rear of the bolt sleeve (#43). Pull the striker (#38) assembly out the front of the bolt sleeve. The fly (#40) may be lifted off the left side of

the sear (#41). Further disassembly of the striker is not recommended for normal maintenance.

REASSEMBLY

Reassemble the rifle in reverse order of above.

Savage Model 1899 rifle

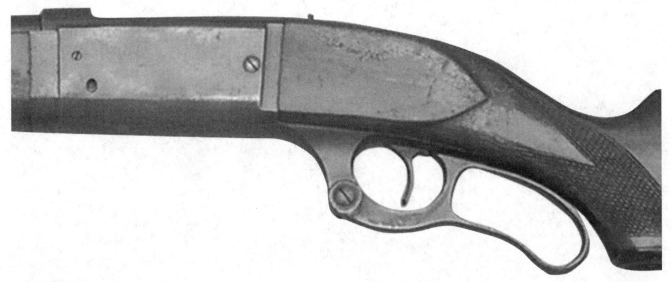

The Savage Model 1899 lever action rifle was introduced in that same year by the Savage Arms Company. It was based on the invention of Arthur W. Savage of Utica, N.Y. Savage had invented earlier lever action models, one for military trials in 1892 and another, a commercial version in 1895, produced for Savage by the Marlin Firearms Company in New Haven, Connecticut. The Savage Arms Company was formed in 1897 and began producing the rifles itself in 1899. In many ways a unique rifle, the Model 1899 offered a rotary magazine that held five shots; a strong, simple lever action operation; and an unusual but thoughtful cartridge counter feature by which you could see the number of cartridges remaining by viewing the counter through a small window on the left side of the receiver. The 1899 also had a hammer-cocked indicator on top of the receiver and it used a sliding safety that locked the trigger in place while at the same time locking the lever closed.

The Model 1899, or '99 as it was later called, has been a very popular rifle with hunters ever since it was introduced. Both solid frame and takedown versions have been available over the years. The 1899 was the first commercially-available rifle to be chambered for a high-velocity .22 cartridge, the 22 Savage Hi-Power of 1912. The following year Savage introduced their now-famous 250-3000, which pushed its little 87-grain bullet to velocities just over 3000 feet per second, a truly remarkable feat in 1913! Savage has changed many aspects of the 1899 through its long production life but the basic design remains the same. Because of its simple, versatile action, the 1899 has been chambered in 25-35, 30-30, 32-40, 38-55, 22 Hi-Power, 250-3000, 300 Savage, and 243, 308 and 358 Winchester. At one time a .410 shotgun barrel was available as an auxiliary barrel on takedown models; because the .410 shells would not feed through the rotary magazine, the gun functioned as a single shot.

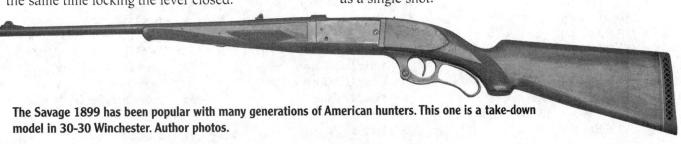

The Savage 1899 has been popular with many generations of American hunters. This one is a take-down model in 30-30 Winchester. Author photos.

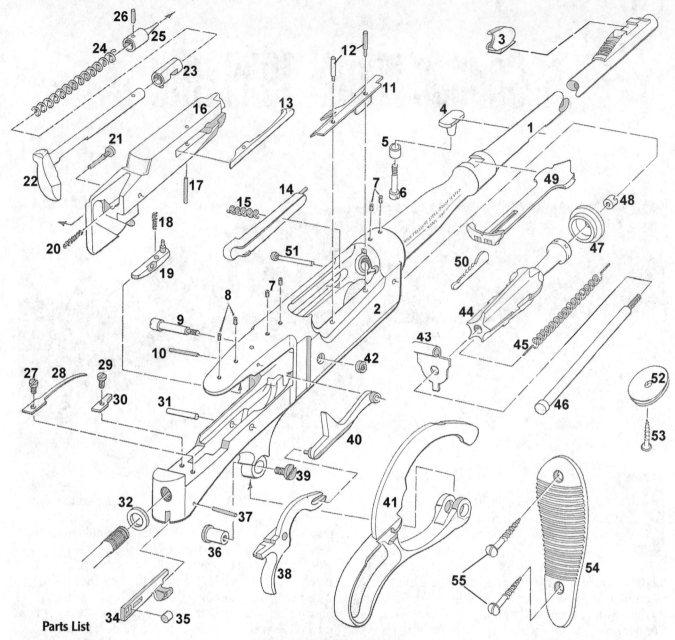

Parts List

1	Barrel	20	Hammer Retractor Spring	39	Lever Bushing Screw
2	Receiver	21	Hammer Bushing Screw	40	Sear
3	Front Sight	22	Hammer	41	Lever
4	Barrel Stud	23	Hammer Bushing	42	Sear Screw Nut
5	Fore-End Escutcheon	24	Mainspring	43	Carrier Spindle Support
6	Fore-End Screw	25	Firing Pin	44	Carrier
7	Dummy Screw-Telescope (4)	26	Firing Pin Securing Pin	45	Carrier Spring
8	Dummy Screw-Tang (2)	27	Trigger Spring Screw	46	Carrier Spindle
9	Sear Screw	28	Trigger Spring	47	Carrier Spindle Head
10	Hammer Indicator Pin	29	Breech Bolt Stop Screw	48	Carrier Spindle Nut
11	Cartridge Guide	30	Breech Bolt Stop	49	Rear Sight
12	Cartridge Guide Pin (2)	31	Trigger Pin	50	Rear Sight Step
13	Extractor	32	Stock Bolt Washer	51	Carrier Spindle Head Screw
14	Automatic Cutoff	33	Stock Bolt	52	Pistol Grip Cap
15	Automatic Cutoff Spring	34	Lever Lock-Safety	53	Pistol Grip Cap Screw
16	Breech Bolt	35	Lever Lock Tension Spring	54	Buttplate
17	Extractor Pin	36	Lever Bushing	55	Buttplate Screw (2)
18	Hammer Indicator Spring	37	Lever Lock Pin		
19	Hammer Indicator	38	Trigger		

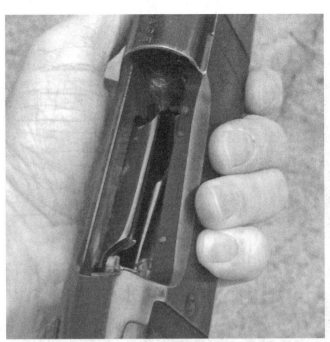

The 1899 action opened to be sure it is unloaded. Follow the procedures in the text to safely unload a loaded rifle.

It's a simple procedure to remove the 1899's buttstock and expose the action parts for disassembly.

DISASSEMBLY INSTRUCTIONS

1 First, be sure the rifle is unloaded before you attempt any work. Grasp the rifle around the forearm and barrel. Pull the safety lock (#34) to the off position and open the lever (#41), being careful to keep your fingers away from the trigger (#38). Look into the chamber to be sure it is empty and look into the cartridge carrier (#44) in the action to be sure no cartridges are present in the magazine spool. You can also view the cartridge counter through the little window on the left side of the receiver (#2). The counter should read -0-; if cartridges are present in the magazine, partially close the lever, about half-way,

just enough to push the cartridge in the carrier forward slightly and allow it to engage the bolt face. Now open the lever to expel the cartridge. Repeat as many times as is required until there are no more cartridges and the counter reads -0-. Remove any live ammunition to a separate location.

2 To remove the buttstock and forend: Remove the buttplate screws (#55) and lift off the buttplate (#54). Use a long, straight-bladed screwdriver to reach into the hole in the buttstock (not shown) and unscrew the stock bolt (#33). Once unscrewed, the buttstock may be pulled off the rear of the receiver (#2). Unscrew

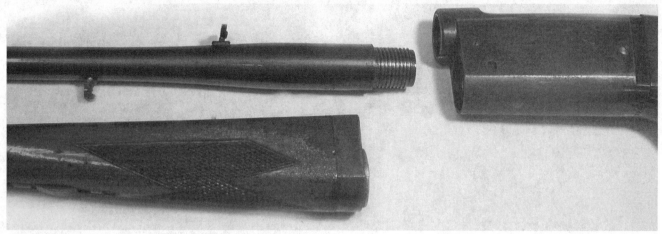

The 1899 takedown with the fore-end and barrel removed.

Notice the steel lug at the rear of the takedown fore-end. This fits into the groove (above) in the barrel and receiver to prevent the barrel from turning loose.

The Model 1899 breech bolt in the process of being removed.

and remove the forend screw (#6) and the forend (not shown) may be pulled down off the barrel. Takedown models: Push the takedown latch on the bottom of the forend to the rear and tilt the forend assembly down off the barrel. Open the lever and unscrew the barrel in a clockwise direction (looking from the rear).

3 To remove the breech bolt: Unscrew and remove the breech bolt stop screw (#29) and lift off the breech bolt stop (#30). Unscrew the trigger spring screw (#27) and lift off the trigger spring (#28). By opening the lever (#41) all the way down, the rear of the breech bolt (#16) may be pushed to the left side of the receiver and pulled back and out of the receiver.

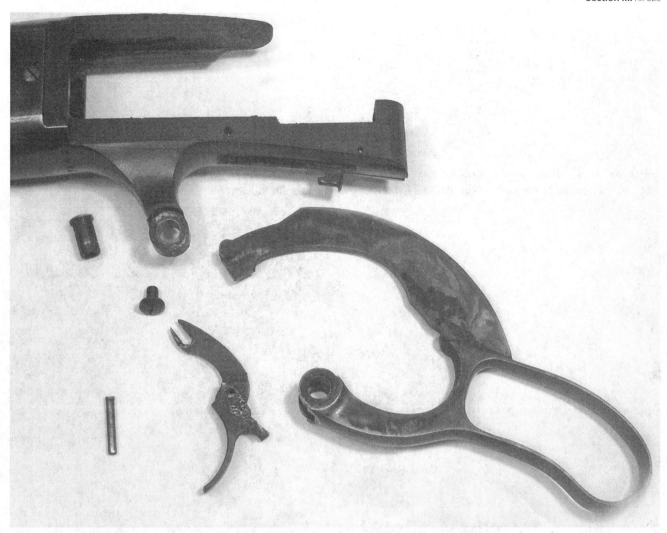

The trigger and lever are removed after the breech bolt. Both are very simple to remove.

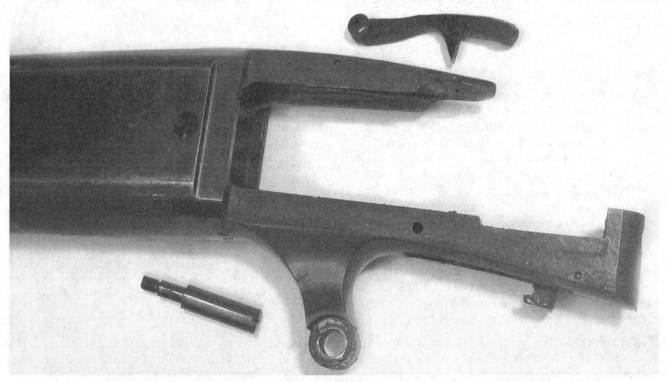

The sear is shown removed from the action along with the sear screw. The sear screw nut is not shown in this photo.

After the hammer bushing screw is removed, the entire hammer assembly may be pulled out the rear of the breech bolt. Note the retractor spring below the hammer; this will fall out as you withdraw the hammer.

When it is viewed from the right with the stock removed, you can see the hammer is cocked. Notice how it is held to the rear by the sear.

4 To remove the trigger, lever and sear: Use a 1/8-inch pin punch and hammer to drive out the trigger pin (#31). The trigger (#38) can now be removed. Unscrew the lever bushing screw (#39) and push out the lever bushing (#36). Notice the small "dog" or tooth under the head of the bushing; it must line up with the notch in the receiver for reassembly. The lever (#41) may be removed out the bottom of the action. Using a special spanner to hold the sear screw nut (#42), unscrew and remove the sear screw (#9) and lift out the sear (#40). Be careful that the carrier spindle support (#43) does not move out of alignment while the sear screw is out. Note: Because of the precise adjustment required to reinstall the carrier assembly, it is not recommended that any of the carrier parts be removed except by a skilled gunsmith.

5 To disassemble the breech bolt: Unscrew and remove the hammer bushing screw (#21) from the left rear of the breech bolt (#16). The hammer assembly may be slowly withdrawn to the rear. Note:

The hammer retractor spring fits under the tail of the hammer and it will fall out as you pull the hammer out of the breech bolt. Note its position carefully for reassembly later.

The hammer may be disassembled by first clamping the firing pin in a padded vise. Then, holding pressure on the hammer in a forward direction, use a small pin punch and hammer to drive out the firing pin securing pin and ease off pressure on the hammer. The firing pin (#25), mainspring (#24) and the hammer bushing (#23) are free and can now be withdrawn off the front of the hammer (#22). The extractor may be removed by using a small pin punch and hammer to drive out the extractor pin (#17). The extractor (#13) may be lifted out of the side of the breech bolt.

REASSEMBLY

Reverse the above procedures for reassembly.

Sharps Model 1874
and Replicas

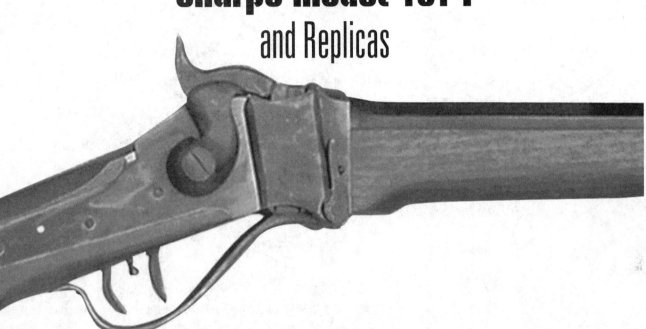

C hristian Sharps is among the most famous of all firearms inventors and the rifles he designed have gone down in history as some of the all time great firearms. From the 1850s when Christian designed the falling block, breechloading Sharps single shot rifle, Sharps rifles have played a part in the building of America. First designed as a breechloading percussion rifle, the system was markedly improved by Richard Lawrence of the Robbins & Lawrence Armory in Vermont during the mid-1850s and it went on to play an important role in the American Civil War, serving both sides in that long conflict equally well and gaining a reputation for utter dependability in the process. Indeed, the well-known Sharps nickname "Old Reliable," which the company later used in its advertising, is said to have come from very satisfied civil war troopers who, after living with the Sharps for years, had come to trust its operation.

Because it was a breechloader to start with, these Sharps rifles easily made the transition into the new metallic cartridges in the 1870s and quickly became popular with hunters and long-range shooters. Another advantage of the Sharps was its action's great strength and its ability to handle, in the days before the turn of the twentieth century, virtually any metallic cartridge known to man. The Sharps developed yet another reputation across the American plains in the 1870s and 1880s as it became very popular with buffalo hunters. The handwriting was on the wall for single shot rifles as the age of the repeating rifle continued to unfold, but the Sharps company refused to move into this new field, trying instead a new hammerless, single shot action designed by Hugo Borchardt. As the single shot fell from favor, regrettably in spite of the modern Borchardt design, the Sharps Rifle Company followed suit, passing into oblivion in 1881 but not before leaving behind an indelible legacy through their remarkable rifles.

The venerable Sharps rifle gained a well-deserved reputation for both accuracy and dependability back in the day when the single shot rifle was king. This faithful 1874 Sharps replica called the "silhouette" model is built in Italy by Pedersoli. Rifle courtesy of Cimarron Firearms. Author photos.

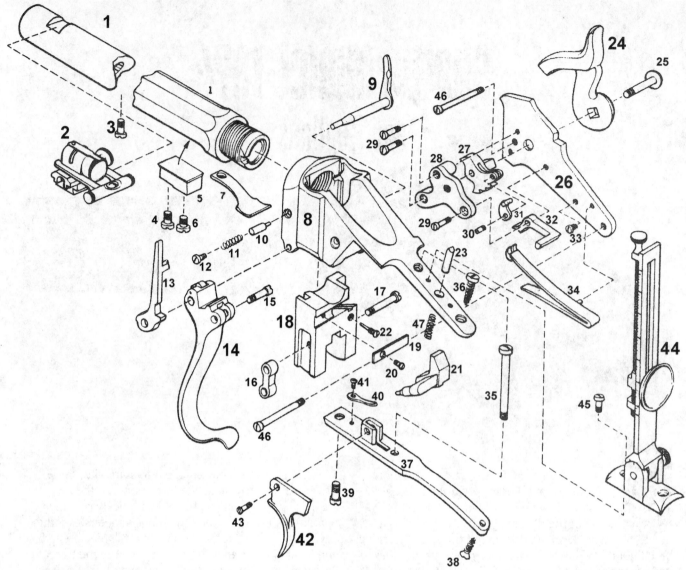

Parts List

1	Barrel	16	Lever Toggle Link	33	Mainspring Screw
2	Front Sight	17	Upper Toggle Link Screw	34	Mainspring
3	Front Fore-End Screw	18	Breechblock	35	Front Guard Plate Screw
4	Rear Fore-End Screw	19	Firing Pin Plate	36	Rear Guard Plate Screw
5	Barrel Stud	20	Firing Pin Plate Screw	37	Guard Plate
6	Lever Spring Screw	21	Firing Pin	38	Guard Plate Stock Screw
7	Lever Spring	22	Firing Pin Screw	39	Guard Plate Receiver Screw
8	Receiver	23	Rear Sight Detent	40	Trigger Spring
9	Lever Pin	24	Hammer	41	Trigger Spring Screw
10	Lever Pin Retainer Plunger	25	Tumbler Screw	42	Trigger
11	Lever Pin Retainer Plunger	26	Lock Plate	43	Trigger Screw
	Spring	27	Tumbler	44	Rear Sight Assembly
12	Lever Pin Retainer Plunger	28	Bridle	45	Rear Sight Mounting Screws
	Spring Screw	29	Bridle Screw	46	Lock Plate Screws
13	Extractor	30	Stirrup Screw	47)	Rear Sight Detent Spring
14	Lever	31	Stirrup		
15	Lever Toggle Link Screw	32	Sear		

The Sharps action opens wide for loading and unloading.

DISASSEMBLY INSTRUCTIONS

Illustration from *The Gun Digest Book of Exploded Firearms Drawings,* 2nd edition, edited by Harold A. Murtz, DBI Books Inc., 1977 Printed with permission of the publisher: K-P Publications, 700 E. State Street, Iola, WI 54990-0001.

Note: The following disassembly procedures apply to most of the earlier side-hammer Sharps rifles and carbines manufactured from 1851 on, including percussion models and most modern replicas.

1 Before handling any weapon, be sure it is unloaded. Hold the rifle around the barrel and wooden forearm with your left hand, point the muzzle in a safe direction, and pull back the hammer one "click" and open the action by pulling the lever (#14) all the way down with your right hand. Look into the barrel and check to be certain there is no cartridge in the chamber. If there is a cartridge present, reach in and manually remove it by pulling the cartridge straight out of the rear of the barrel. Remove any live ammunition to a separate location.

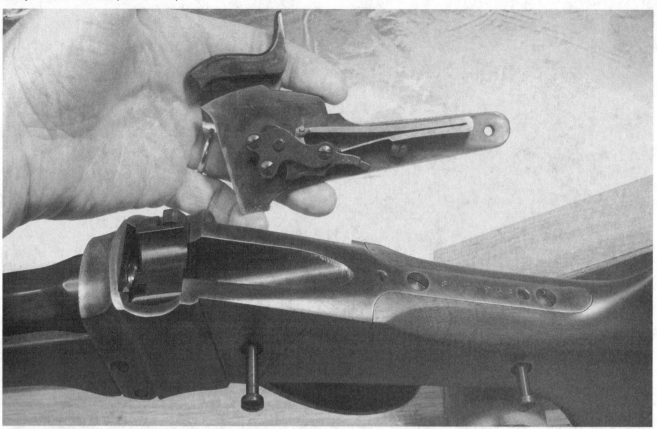

Simply taking out two screws allows the entire lock assembly to be removed from the stock.

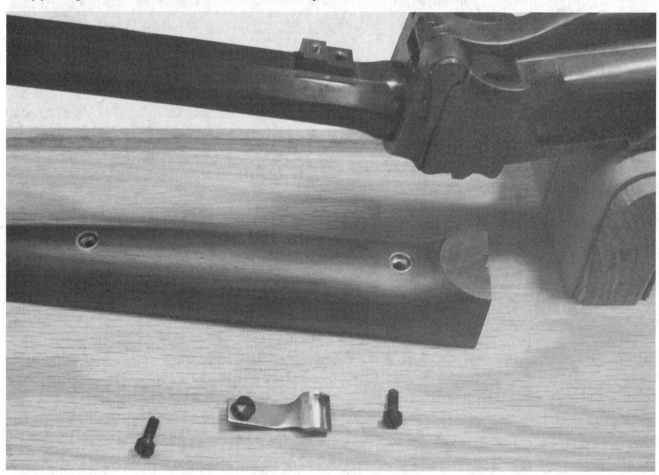

Breech bolt removal is made easier by taking off the forearm and removing the lever spring, shown here at front center.

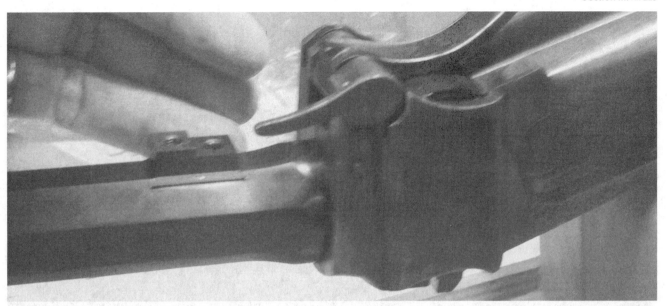

After the lever lock plunger is depressed, the lever lock pin is rotated forward, allowing it to come unlocked from its mortise in the frame.

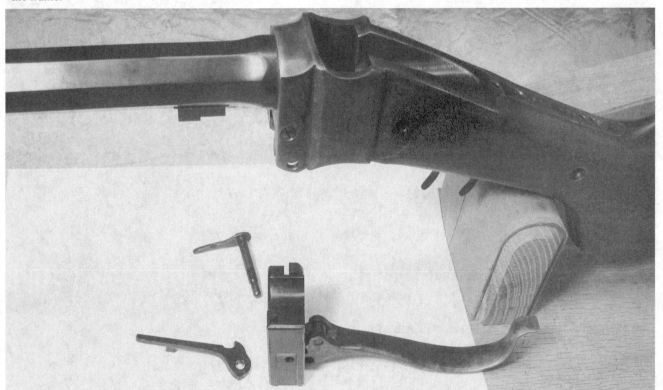

After the lever pin is removed, the bolt assembly and extractor (in cartridge rifles) drop right out the bottom.

2 To disassemble the action: Unscrew and remove the two lock plate screws (#46) from the left side of the receiver (#8) and slowly pull the lock plate assembly (#26) out the right side. Unscrew and remove the fore-end screws (#3) and (#4) and pull the fore-end down and off the barrel. On military models: depress the band spring(s) and slide the band(s) forward off the barrel. The fore-end may now be removed. Unscrew and remove the lever spring screw (#6) and lift off the lever spring (#7). Push in the lever pin retainer plunger (#10) located on the forward end of the right side of the receiver and rotate the handle of the lever pin (#9) forward until the lever pin unlocks from its mortise in the receiver. Open the lever and remove the lever pin (#9). The lever and breechblock (#18) assembly can now be pulled down and out the bottom of the receiver. In metallic cartridge models, the extractor (#13) can be lifted out the receiver bottom.

The Sharps with its buttstock and trigger plate removed.

3 Removing the stock: Remove the guard plate stock screw (#38) and the guard plate receiver screw (#39) from the guard plate. Now remove the front (#35) and rear (#36) guard plate screws from the top receiver tang. Carefully pull the buttstock toward the rear until it and the guard plate (#37) come loose and can be removed. The guard plate may be pulled straight down, out of the buttstock.

4 Lock plate disassembly: The hammer (#24) should be all the way forward. Use a mainspring vise, a machinist's clamp, or a small C-clamp to compress the mainspring (#34) enough so the stirrup (#31) can be rotated out of the mainspring's "ears," remove the mainspring screw (#33). The mainspring can now be pulled off the rear of the lock plate. Remove the tumbler screw (#25) from the center of the hammer (#24) and pull off the hammer. Next remove the three bridle screws (#29). The bridle (#28), the tumbler (#27) and the sear (#32) can all be lifted off the rear face of the lock plate. Make note of their positions for reassembly.

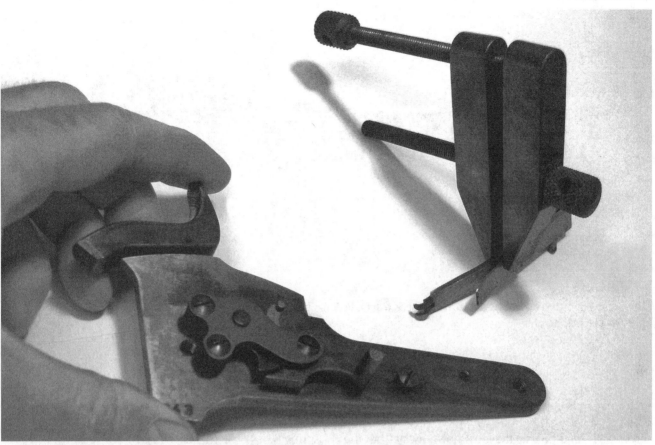

After the mainspring is compressed with a machinist's clamp, it is easily lifted off the lockplate.

The Sharps lockplate disassembled. Note how wonderfully simple this mechanism is and how much carry-over there is from muzzleloading actions.

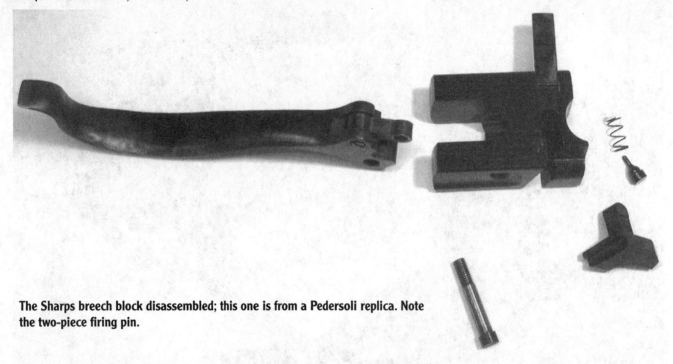

The Sharps breech block disassembled; this one is from a Pedersoli replica. Note the two-piece firing pin.

5 Breech bolt disassembly: The lever (#14) can be removed by unscrewing the lever toggle link screw (#15) and pulling the lever down away from the breechblock (#18). The lever toggle link (#16) can be removed by first removing the upper toggle link screw (#17). On cartridge models, the firing pin screw (#22) and the firing pin plate screw (#20) are now removed; the firing pin plate (#19) can be slid off the breechblock and the firing pin (#21) lifted out from the rear.

Pedersoli-made Sharps: Firing pin disassembly differs from American-made Sharps rifles; the Pedersoli uses no firing pin plate screw and the firing pin is two-piece. Hold forward on the firing pin and slide the firing pin stop plate to the left. The firing pin, firing pin nose and firing pin spring can be withdrawn out the rear of the breech block.

6 Peripheral disassembly. The guard plate: remove the trigger spring screw (#41) and the trigger spring (#40). The trigger (#42) is removed by first removing the trigger screw (#43); the trigger will drop out from the bottom. The buttplate may be removed by unscrewing the two buttplate screws and lifting off the buttplate.

REASSEMBLY

Reassemble in the reverse order of above.

U.S. Springfield Trap-Door
Single Shot Rifles

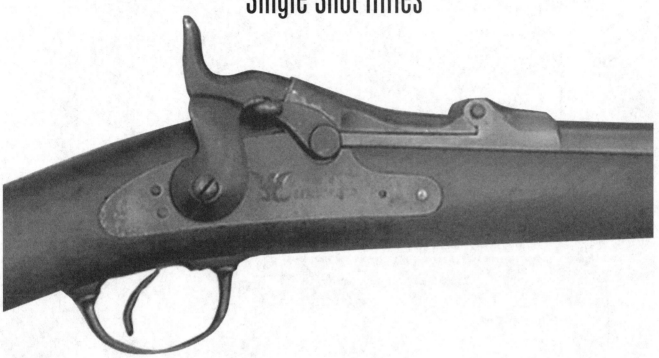

The so-called trap-door rifle was originally designed by Erskine S. Allin, Master Armorer at Springfield Armory, as a breech-loading conversion for the 1861 Springfield percussion rifle. The first 5000 of these built at Springfield Armory were designated the Model 1865 and were chambered for a .58-caliber rimfire cartridge. Allin's system cut away the top section of the barrel at the breech and used a hinged breech block attached to the barrel top that latched into the rear of the barrel. In 1866, 25,000 Model 1863 rifles were converted to .50-caliber centerfire by lining the barrels to the new caliber.

This basic design was continually improved, the Army in 1873 settling on a .45-caliber using 70 grains of black powder. The U.S. Army successfully used the trap-door action in regular service until it was officially replaced by the Krag bolt action repeater in 1892. By the mid-1870s, the trap-door Springfield was becoming quickly outdated by world military standards. Even commercially available repeaters like the Winchester left the single shot trap-door looking like a poor cousin. However, our Army liked their Springfield rifle and the Armory produced over half a million of them. Even after its official obsolescence, the trap-door was actively used by our military. Many trap-door rifles and carbines were taken into the Spanish American war and used by volunteers and guard units in Cuba. When pitted against the Spanish who were armed with state-of-the-art Mauser bolt-action repeaters and smokeless ammunition, the old single shot rifles clearly showed they were ready to be retired.

This beautiful example of an original trap-door Springfield Carbine is an 1873 model from the Ed Wade collection. Author photos.

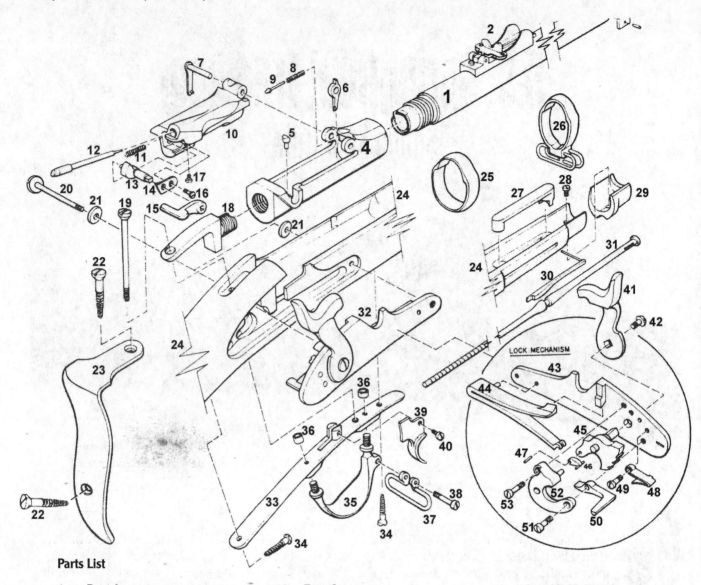

Parts List

1	Barrel	19	Tang Screw	37	Guard Bow Swivel
2	Rear Sight	20	Side Screws	38	Guard Bow Swivel Screw
3	Front Sight And Pin	21	Side Screw Washers	39	Trigger
4	Breech	22	Butt Plate Screws	40	Trigger Screw
5	Ejector Stud	23	Buttplate	41	Hammer
6	Extractor	24	Stock	42	Tumbler Screw
7	Hinge Pin	25	Lower Band	43	Lock Plate
8	Ejector Spring	26	Upper Band	44	Mainspring
9	Spindle	27	Ramrod Stop	45	Tumbler
10	Breech Block	28	Stock Tip	46	Mainspring Swivel
11	Cam Latch Spring	29	Stock Tip Screw	47	Mainspring Swivel Pin
12	Firing Pin	30	Band Springs	48	Sear Spring
13	Cam Latch	31	Ramrod	49	Sear Spring Screw
14	Breech Block Cap	32	Lock, Complete	50	Sear
15	Thumb Piece	33	Guard Plate	51	Sear Screw
16	Breech Block Cap Screw	34	Guard Screws	52	Bridle
17	Firing Pin Screw	35	Guard Bow	53	Bridle Screw
18	Breech Screw	36	Guard Bow Nuts		

Opening the trap-door action exposes the entire chamber area to close scrutiny.

DISASSEMBLY INSTRUCTIONS

Illustration from *The Gun Digest Book of Exploded Firearms Drawings,* 2nd edition, edited by Harold A. Murtz, DBI Books Inc., 1977 Printed with permission of the publisher: K-P Books, 700 E. State Street, Iola, WI 54990-0001.

Note: The following disassembly procedures, with minor variances, will work for all of the U.S. Springfield rifles and carbines using the trap-door system, as well as most modern reproductions of the Springfield.

1 First, always check to be sure the rifle is unloaded. Hold the rifle around the barrel and the wooden forearm with your left hand. Be sure that you point the muzzle in a safe direction. Pull back on the hammer (#41) to place it in the loading position (two audible clicks) and open the action by lifting up on the thumb piece (#15) to unlatch the breech block (#10), which is then tilted all the way up and open with your right hand. Look into the barrel and check to be certain there is no cartridge in the barrel's chamber. If there is a cartridge present in the chamber, reach in and manually remove it by pulling the cartridge straight out of the rear of the barrel. Remove any live ammunition to a separate location away from the area.

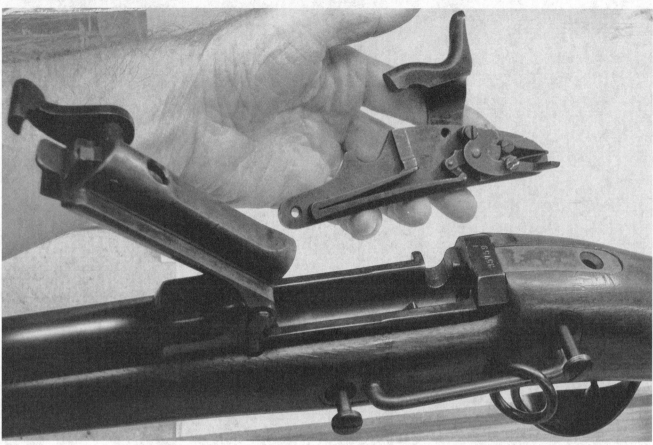

Just like its parent the Model 1861 Springfield percussion rifle, the trap-door's lock assembly is held to the stock by only two screws. Use care when removing the lock so as not to split the edges of the wood. Note the saddle ring bar on the left side of the stock. This is a carbine and the two lock screws pass through the bar's tangs.

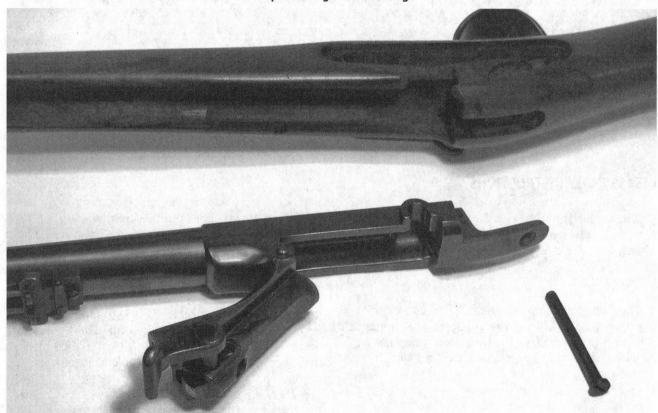

To remove the barreled action from the wood, remove the tang screw (front right) and bands. The metal is simply lifted out of the wood.

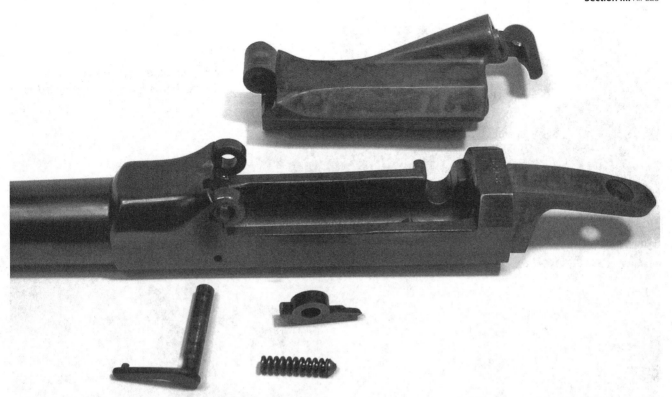

The wood holds the hinge pin in place, but once the barreled action is out of the stock, the hinge pin can be removed, freeing the bolt, extractor and the ejector parts.

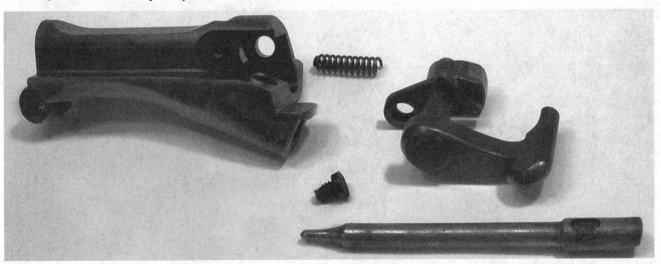

The trap-door bolt shown upside down and disassembled. Careful observation will reveal there is a missing screw in this picture: the breech-block cap screw (#16).

2 To remove the lock and the stock: If the weapon is a rifle, remove the ramrod (#31) first. With the hammer still at half-cock, remove the two side (lock plate) screws (#20) from the left side of the stock (#24). The lock (#32) assembly may now be gently pulled out from the right side of the stock. Unscrew and remove the tang screw (#19). Depress the band springs (#30) and slide the band or bands (#25) and (#26) off from the front of the barrel. The barrel and the breech assembly (#1) and (#4) are now loose and may be lifted straight up and out of the stock.

3 To disassemble the breech and the breech bolt: This next operation will free the extractor, which is powered by a strong coil spring, so hold your hand over the hinge area to prevent the loss of parts while performing this operation. With the breech bolt still open, remove the hinge pin (#7) and lift the breech bolt out of its hinge with the breech (#4). The extractor (#6), ejector spring (#8) and spindle (#9) can now be lifted out of the hinge. Take note of the relationship of these parts for reassembly later. The point of the ejector spindle must engage the detent on the rear of

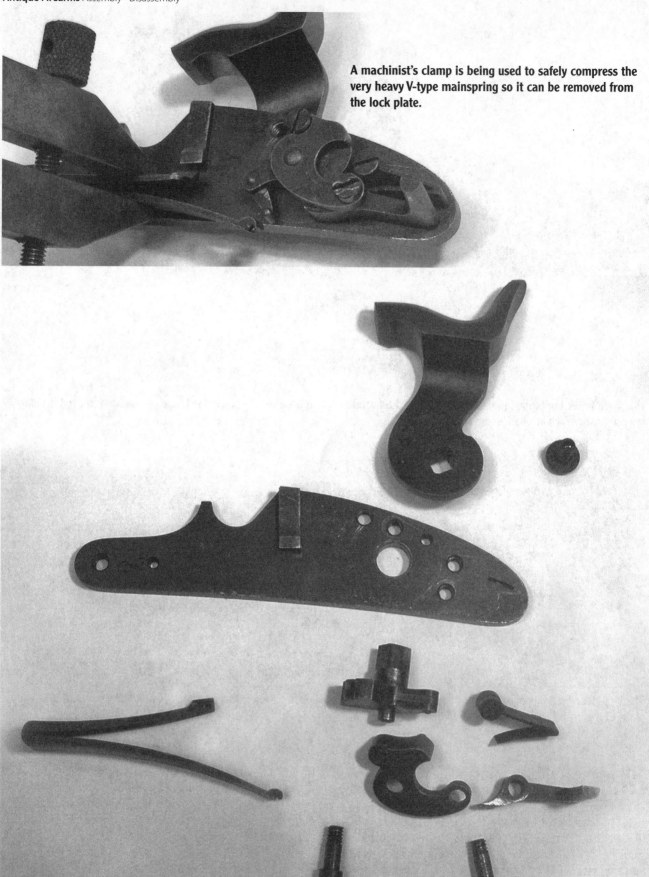

A machinist's clamp is being used to safely compress the very heavy V-type mainspring so it can be removed from the lock plate.

The disassembled Model 1873 Springfield lock. If these internal parts look a lot like 1861 Musket parts, that's because most of them are!

Trapdoor Springfields are very easy to understand. Only two large wood screws hold the lock plate to the stock.

the extractor during reassembly. It helps to have a long, tapered punch as an aid to keep the extractor and breech block holes aligned during reassembly of the breech-block to the receiver.

To disassemble the breech bolt: Unscrew and remove the breech block cap screw (#16) and remove these parts together: cam latch (#13), thumb piece (#15) and breech block cap (#14). These parts lift out to the side. Now, the cam latch spring (#11) can be lifted out of the breech block. By unscrewing the firing pin screw (#17) from the bottom side of the breech bolt, withdraw the firing pin (#12) through the rear. Some modern copies use a two-piece firing pin with a return spring.

4 To disassemble the lock and the guard plate: The hammer (#41) should be all the way forward for this operation. Use a mainspring vise, a machinists clamp, or a small C-clamp to compress the mainspring (#44). Disengage it from the mainspring swivel (#46) and tilt it out to the side, removing it from the lock plate (#43). Unscrew the sear spring screw (#49) and lift the sear spring (#48) out. Unscrew the sear screw (#51). The sear (#50) can be pulled off the lock plate. Remove the bridle screw (#53) and lift out the bridle

(#52). Unscrew and remove the tumbler screw (#42) from the center of the hammer. Insert a straight punch into the hole in the tumbler and tap the head of the punch until the hammer (#41) loosens. The hammer can now be pulled off. Now lift away the tumbler (#45). When you reassemble the lock assembly into the stock, be sure the hammer is set at the loading position. It helps to hold forward on the trigger as the lock plate is being inserted back into the stock.

Unscrew and remove the two guard screws (#34) from the guard plate (#33) and carefully ese the guard plate down and out of the stock. After unscrewing the two guard bow nuts (#36), pull the guard bow (#35) out of the guard plate. Unscrew and remove the trigger screw (#40). The trigger (#39) can now be dropped down out the bottom of the guard plate. The rear sight can be removed from the barrel by removing the two screws that fasten the sight base to the barrel.

REASSEMBLY

Reverse this procedure for reassembly.

The Henry Rifle

This beautiful modern copy of the model 1860 Henry in 44-40 is produced by A. Uberti. Rifle courtesy of Dixie Gun Works. Author photos.

The Henry repeating rifle was named after Benjamin Tyler Henry, a brilliant gunsmith, inventor and firearms designer who improved the rifle from a design originally developed by his former employers, Smith & Wesson. The Henry's parent, the S&W Magazine Pistol or Volcanic as it is commonly called, fired a caseless cartridge, that is, a bullet whose hollow base contained the priming and a small propellant charge. S&W's venture ended up failing financially but not because the ideas or the weapon were at fault. Their pistol used a lever-operated toggle action and a tubular magazine under the barrel to hold the cartridges, which were fed upward into the action by a moving carrier. The quick operation of the finger lever cocked the hammer, raised up a new cartridge and fed it into the barrel chamber. That was pretty exciting stuff in 1854 when most weapons were muzzleloading single shots that had to be loaded in several slow steps. S&W's financial backing came from a consortium of local businessmen, chief among whom was a fellow named Oliver Winchester.

B. T. Henry was S&W's shop foreman on the Magazine Pistol. After the financial buyout of his friends Horace Smith and Daniel Wesson, Henry moved from Norwich, Conn., to New Haven with the new owners, who started the Volcanic Repeating Arms Co. (1855 to 1856), which continued to produce the Magazine Pistols until early 1857 when the New Haven Arms Co. was formed, a company in which Winchester played an even larger role. New Haven expanded the Volcanic line to include rifles. The S&W Volcanic cartridge, as innovative as it was in its day, was underpowered and the volatile mixture of fulminate used as its powder charge was highly corrosive. Henry set to work to alter the design so the toggle action could be used to fire a more powerful, self-contained metallic cartridge. Henry's cartridge, the famous 44 Henry Flat rimfire (so named because of its flat-nosed bullet, which was designed to prevent the bullet nose from setting off the cartridge in front of it in the magazine) was essentially a scaled-up version of S&W's .22 rimfire No. 1 cartridge. Introduced in 1860 under Henry's name, the rifle used the same essential mechanical ingredients of the S&W magazine rifle, with an elongated action to hold the new metallic cartridge. Other additions to the S&W action included a redesigned firing pin or striker that could dent the hollow cartridge rim and explode the priming compound, as well as the addition of an extractor, mounted on the bolt, that would remove the fired cartridge cases from the chamber.

Henry's repeating rifle was an instant success. Some were even used in the Civil War, where this 15-shot repeater gained the nickname of "that damned Yankee rifle you could load on Sunday and shoot all week." Like that of the S&W Magazine Rifle, the Henry rifle's magazine tube was machined along with the barrel and it was loaded by pivoting a barrel extension and literally pouring cartridges, base down, into the front of the magazine. A brass, spring-loaded cartridge follower with a handle that stuck out through a slot in the bottom of the tube pushed the cartridges back into the action. That this follower handle could run into the shooter's hand and stop the cartridges from feeding was one serious flaw in the Henry rifle. Another was the lack of a wooden forearm so when the barrel got hot after a few shots, the Henry would quickly became too hot to handle! Henry's invention was the first in a long line of toggle-action repeaters. After Winchester took over the company from Henry in 1866, that old S&W design formed the foundation upon which fortunes were built, but that would happen under what is now the famous name of the Winchester Repeating Arms Co.

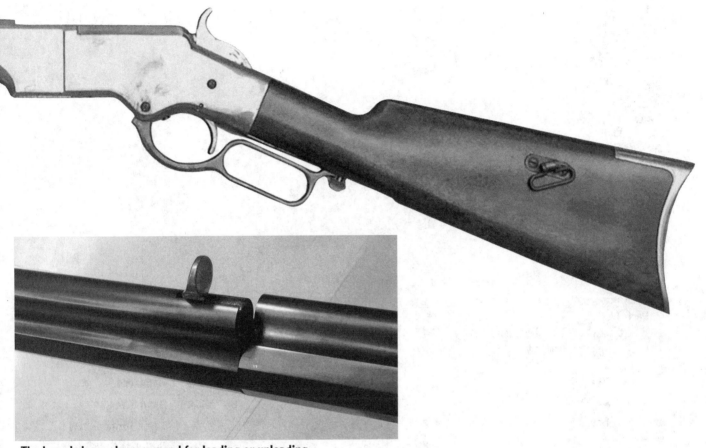

The barrel sleeve shown opened for loading or unloading.

DISASSEMBLY INSTRUCTIONS
(Uberti Replica Nomenclature)

These basic instruction steps work for Uberti-made modern replicas and original Henry rifles. Original rifles differ slightly, most especially in the firing pin and mainspring areas.

1 First be certain the rifle is unloaded. Holding the rifle around the barrel with your left hand, point the muzzle in a safe direction and turn the lever hook (some times called a lever lock) (#542) until it is pointing sideways; this unlocks the lever. Open the action by pulling the lever (#89) all the way down with your right hand. Check now to be absolutely certain there is no cartridge in the barrel's chamber and look down into the opened action to be sure that there is not a cartridge lying within the action, in the cartridge carrier (#7). If there is a cartridge in the carrier, when you close the lever, the rifle will be loaded.

To safely unload a Henry rifle with a loaded magazine, always be sure the muzzle stays pointed in a safe. Then with the lever *still in the open position*, push the magazine follower (#113) all the way forward and hold it there. Now twist the sleeve (#223) as far as it will turn clockwise (when viewed from the muzzle). Hold the rifle over a wooden bench or table top. The rifle can now be tipped so the muzzle is facing down and all cartridges in the magazine should be free to slide forward and out of the magazine. Now you can twist the sleeve back to its original position and ease the magazine follower back into place. Check one last time after unloading to be sure that no cartridges remain in the magazine. Keeping your fingers away from the trigger altogether, operate the lever all the way closed and then back all the way open. There should now be no cartridge in the cartridge carrier (#7).

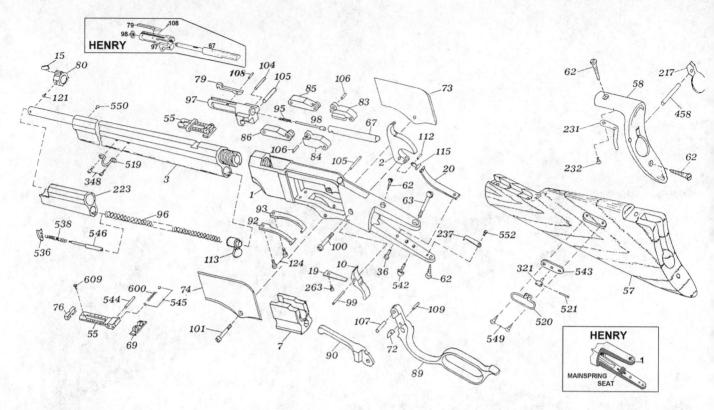

Parts List

(Uberti drawing, altered by author to illustrate original Henry rifle parts.)

1	Receiver	84	Left Rear Link	115	Hammer Link
2	Hammer	85	Right Front Link	121	Band Screw
3	Barrel	86	Left Front Link	124	Lever Spring Screw
7	Carrier Block	89	Lever	217	Buttplate Gate
15	Sight	90	Lifter Arm	223	Sleeve
19	Trigger Spring	92	Right Lever Spring	233	Protection Running Screw
20	Mainspring	93	Left Lever Spring	234	Protection Running Spring
36	Mainspring Screw	95	Firing Pin Spring	237	Lever Hook Spring
55	Rear Sight	96	Magazine Spring	263	Trigger Spring Screw
57	Buttstock	97	Breech Block	458	Buttplate Gate Pin
58	Buttplate	98	Firing Pin	536	Sleeve Latch
62	Buttplate Screw	99	Trigger Pin	538	Sleeve Latch Rod Spring
63	Tang Screw	100	Hammer Pin Screw	542	Lever Hook
67	Firing Pin Extension	101	Lever Screw	544	Rear Sight Pin
69	Rear Base	104	Firing Pin Stop	546	Sleeve Latch Rod
72	Cam Lever	105	Rear Link Pin	550	Magazine Follower Screw
73	Right Sideplate	106	Link Pin	552	Lever Hook Spring Screw
74	Left Sideplate	107	Lever Pin	600	Rear Sight Spring
76	Rear Running	108	Extractor Pin	609	Rear Running Stop Screw
79	Extractor	109	Cam Lever Pin		
80	Front Band	112	Hammer Link Pin		
83	Right Rear Link	113	Magazine Follower		

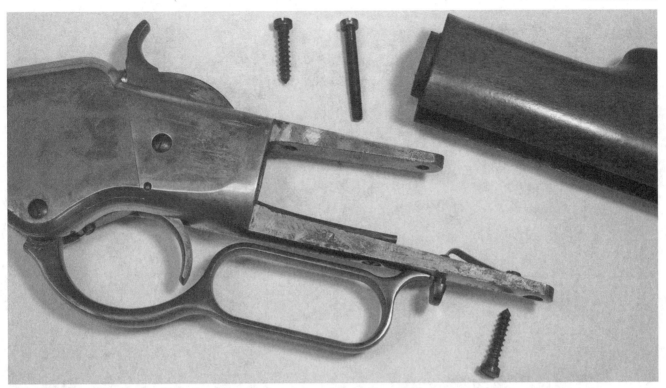

To remove the Henry buttstock, first remove both the upper and lower tang wood screws and the tang screw.

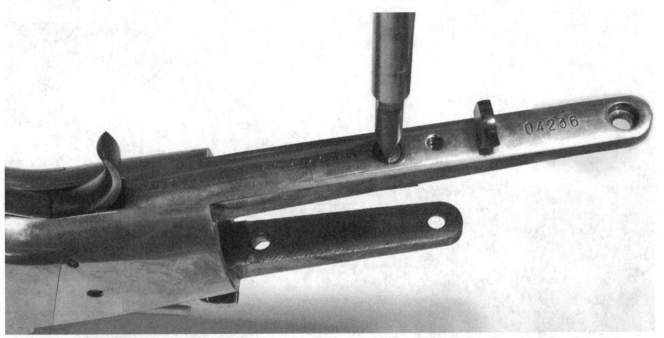

Removing the mainspring screw.

2 To remove the buttstock and mainspring: Remove both screws on the upper tang screw (#62 and #63). The buttstock (#57) is now loose and can be removed from the action (#1) by pulling it straight off to the rear. For Uberti replicas: Open the lever slightly and remove the mainspring screw (#36) from the lower tang. The mainspring (#20) can now be removed through the back of the action. Make note of the mainspring's position; during reassembly, the hooks at the front of the mainspring have to be manually engaged with the ears on the hammer link (#115). For original Henry rifles: With the hammer all the way forward, use a pair of spreader-type pliers to compress the top of the mainspring enough to disengage the spring from the stirrup. Release the tension on the spring and using a small drift punch and hammer, drive the mainspring sideways out of its seat in the lower tang.

Here, the sideplates and the lever and carrier springs have been removed. The sideplates are vertically dovetailed into the receiver.

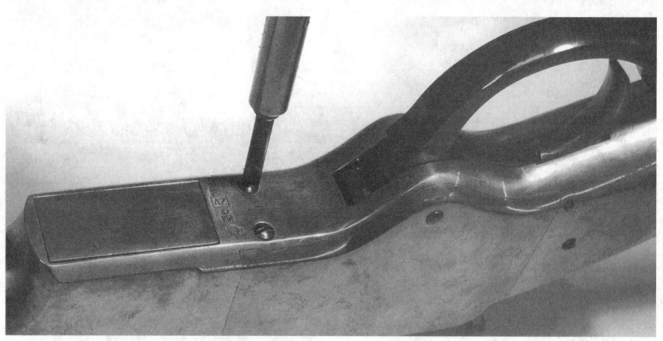

Loosen the lever springs about two turns before removing the lever screw and sideplates.

3 To remove the sideplates and lever spring: Loosen the two lever spring screws (#124) on the bottom of the receiver, located just in front of the lever, about two full turns each. Remove the lever screw (#101). The sideplates (#73-R) and (#74-L) are dovetailed into the receiver sides and they slide out from bottom to top. Using a small block of hard maple approximately 2" X 3/4" as a drift punch and a small hammer, carefully drive the sideplates down from the top, alternating blows between front and rear until both plates are freed from the receiver. Now remove the two lever spring screws (#124) and the left (#93) and right (#92) lever springs, noting their positions for later reassembly.

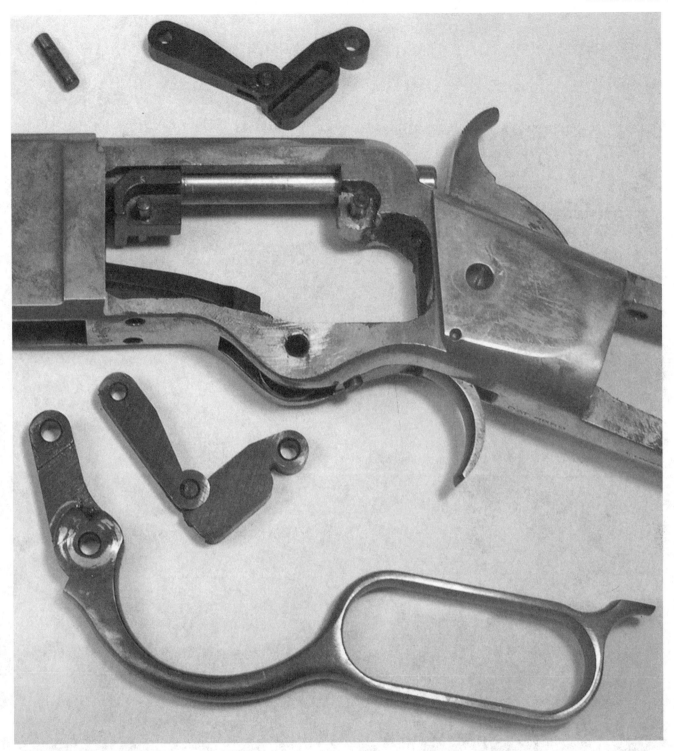

The lever and links removed.

4 To disassemble the action: Lift the left (#84 and #86) and right (#83 and #85) link assemblies out from their respective sides of the frame. Remove the lever pin (#107) from the top of the lever (#89). Lift up slightly on the lifter arm (#90) and pull the lever (#89) straight out through the bottom of the receiver. Push up on the carrier block (#7) and then withdraw the lifter arm (#90) down and rearwards until it can removed through the lever opening in the receiver bottom. Remove the trigger spring screw (#263) and the trigger spring (#19) from the front of the trigger (#10). Remove the hammer pin screw (#100) and the hammer (#2) can be withdrawn straight out through its opening in the receiver top. Push down on the carrier block (#7) and remove it through the bottom of its opening in the bottom of the receiver.

Next remove the hammer, trigger spring, carrier and lifter.

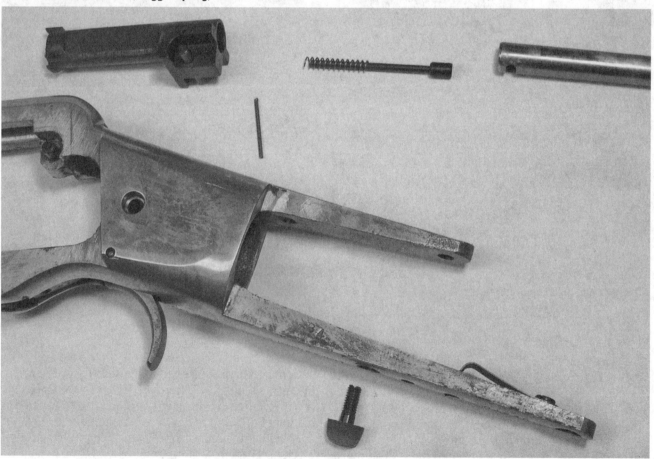

The modern, Uberti-made Henry bolt, disassembled outside the action.

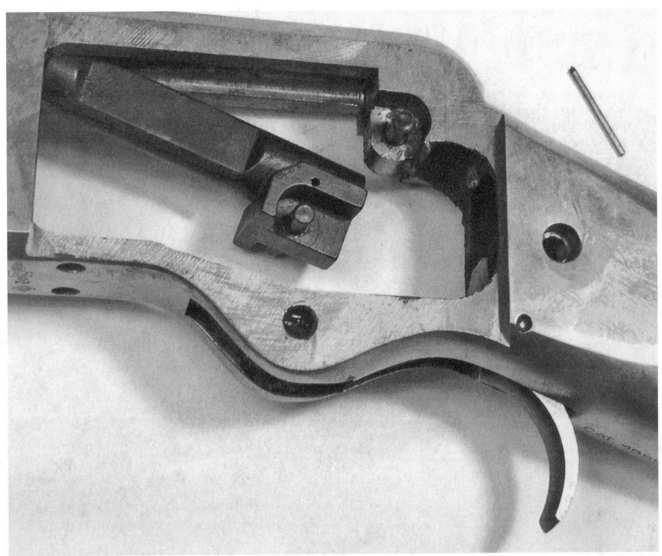

After the firing pin parts have been removed, this is what the bolt looks like in the correct position for removal.

TO REMOVE THE FIRING PIN, TRIGGER AND LEVER HOOK:

5 **For Uberti:** Using a small pin punch, drive the firing pin stop (#104) out through the side of the breech block (#97). The firing pin extension (#67), firing pin (#98) and firing pin spring can be withdrawn through the rear of the receiver. The breech block (#97) can be removed by tilting it all the way down as it is withdrawn toward the rear. Use a pin punch to drift the trigger pin (#99) out from either side of the receiver; the trigger can now be pulled out the bottom. The lever hook (#542) can be removed by unscrewing it through its hole the lower frame tang. The lever hook spring (#237) is removed by removing the lever hook spring screw (#552) located on the inside of the lower frame tang.

For Henry: Move the breech bolt assembly toward the rear until the extractor pin in the bolt is aligned with the notch in the receiver. Drive out the extractor pin using a long pin punch. The firing pin extension can now be unscrewed from the rear. Pull the firing pin straight out through the back of the receiver. The firing pin or bolt face can be lifted off the front of the breech block. When the bolt is moved forward, the extractor can now be lifted off the top. Withdraw the breech block by tilting it all the way down as it is withdrawn toward the rear.

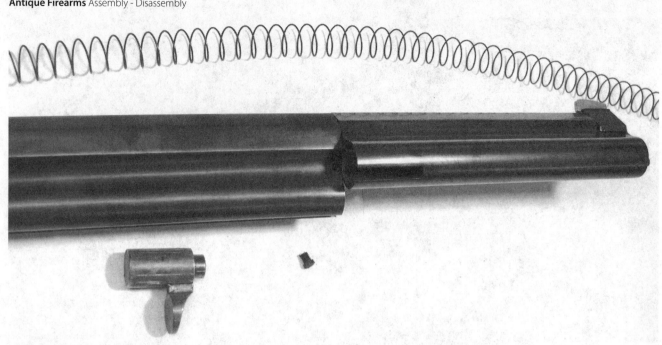

After the magazine follower screw is removed, the follower and its spring are free to be removed.

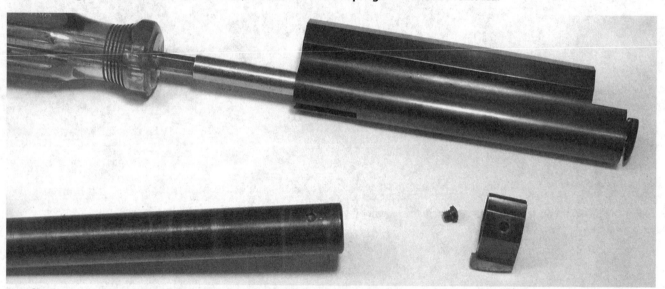

The front band and barrel sleeve removed. The gunsmith is inserting a screwdriver into the rear of the sleeve to unscrew the sleeve latch rod, which will enable the sleeve latch assembly to be taken apart.

6 To disassemble the magazine: Remove the magazine follower screw (#550) from the right barrel side. Push the magazine follower (#113) all the way forward and hold it there while you twist the sleeve (#223) clockwise (viewed from the front) as far as it will turn. The magazine follower (#113) can now be carefully eased back out of the sleeve, but use caution and both hands to control and contain the magazine spring (#96), which is very long and compressed under full tension. Remove the band screw (#121) from the left side of the barrel muzzle. The front band (#80) and the sleeve assembly (#223) can now be slid forward off the barrel. The sleeve can be further disassembled by unscrewing the sleeve latch rod and removing it and the sleeve latch

rod spring (#538) from the inside rear of the magazine portion of the sleeve. The sleeve latch (#536) is now free at the front of the sleeve.

7 To disassemble the buttstock: To remove the buttplate, remove the two buttplate screws, (#62) one at the top and one at the rear of the buttplate (#58). The buttplate gate spring (#231) can be removed by removing the buttplate gate spring screw (#232).

REASSEMBLY

Reassemble the rifle in the reverse order of above.

Winchester Model 1866

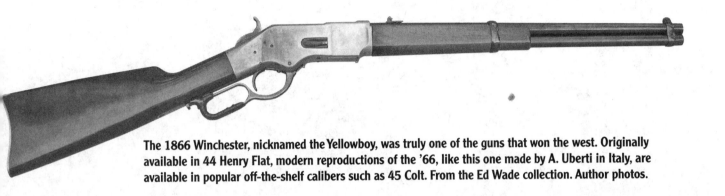

The 1866 Winchester, nicknamed the Yellowboy, was truly one of the guns that won the west. Originally available in 44 Henry Flat, modern reproductions of the '66, like this one made by A. Uberti in Italy, are available in popular off-the-shelf calibers such as 45 Colt. From the Ed Wade collection. Author photos.

The Henry repeating rifle was a remarkable firearm and it gained quite a reputation during the Civil War and shortly thereafter. But as good as the Henry was, it did have some drawbacks. Its lack of a wooden forearm meant the shooter had to grasp the rifle around the steel barrel, which got hot very quickly, making for an uncomfortable if not impossible grip. Henry's rifle did not use a forearm because it retained the external follower knob of the original Volcanic. The follower knob protruded through a slot that ran the full length of the bottom of the magazine. As this knob followed the cartridges rearward, it ran into the shooter's hand and stopped the cartridges from feeding.

As Oliver Winchester took control of the Henry company, he enlisted the efforts of some talented firearms designers to remove these faults. Among those was Nelson King, who devised a clever method of loading using a loading gate, or spring cover as Winchester called it. The spring cover fitted into a slot machined in the right sideplate, allowing the magazine to be charged from the side of the rifle. This feature not only did away with the need for an external follower knob, but it also allowed a proper forearm to be fitted. Some other areas of the Henry were also simplified: the sideplates, which were formerly dovetailed front and rear, were now dovetailed on the front ends only, thus removing one more needless and expensive machining operation.

For Winchester, the new loading method was a tremendous boon in many ways. From a manufacturing efficiency standpoint, the new loading method did away with the complicated machine operations that were required to manufacture the Henry barrel, which was made in one piece with the magazine. Still making use of the original, dependable, basic Henry toggle action, Oliver now had a really dependable and sensible repeating rifle that he could and did offer to the public as the Winchester Model 1866.

Winchester's new rifle was an instant success. An eager public bought as many of the new repeaters as his factory could produce. With its brass receiver, it was soon nicknamed "Yellowboy" by the general public, while native Americans sometimes referred to it as the "heap firing gun" or, appropriately, "many shots." The lion's share of 1866s were made in the standard Henry caliber, 44 Henry Flat rimfire but a few were produced in a .44-caliber centerfire that was quite similar to the 44 S&W American. About 170,000 Winchester 1866s were manufactured from 1866 through 1898 in carbine, rifle and musket configurations. Today, Uberti produces a very dependable replica of the 1866 that is available in easy to obtain calibers including 32 WCF, 38 Special, 38 WCF, 44 S&W Special, 44-40 and 45 Colt. Uberti's shooting replicas are imported into the USA by several companies including Cimarron Firearms, Dixie Gun Works, EMF, Navy Arms and Stoeger Industries.

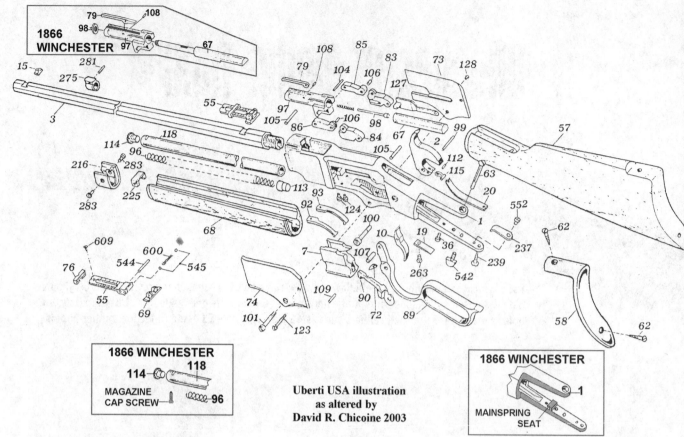

Uberti USA illustration
as altered by
David R. Chicoine 2003

Parts List (Uberti Replica Nomenclature)

1	Frame	83	Right Rear Link	118	Magazine Tube
2	Hammer	84	Left Rear Link	119	Rear Sight Screw
3	Barrel	85	Right Front Link	122	Rear Band Screw Carbine
7	Carrier Block	86	Left Front Link	123	Sideplate Screw
10	Trigger	89	Lever (Finger Lever)	124	Lever Spring Screw
15	Sight	90	Lifter Arm	127	Ladle (Spring Cover)
19	Trigger Spring	92	Right Lever Spring	128	Ladle Screw
20	Mainspring	93	Left Lever Spring		(Spring Cover Screw)
21	Front Band Screw, Carbine, (NI)	95	Firing Pin Spring	216	Fore-End Protection, Rifle
36	Mainspring Screw	96	Magazine Spring		(Forearm Cap)
53	Mainspring Adjusting Screw	97	Breech Block	225	Fore-End Protection Bearing,
55	Rear Sight	98	Firing Pin		Rifle (Forearm Hanger)
57	Buttstock	99	Trigger Pin	237	Lever Hook Spring
58	Buttplate	101	Lever Screw	238	Lever Hook Pin
62	Buttplate Screw	104	Firing Pin Stop	239	Lower Tang Screw
63	Tang Screw	105	Rear Link Pin	275	Magazine Tube Bearing, Rifle
67	Firing Pin Extension	106	Link Pin		(Front Magazine Band)
68	Fore-End Wood	107	Lever Pin	281	Magazine Tube Bearing Pin, Rifle
69	Rear Sight Base	108	Extractor Pin	283	Fore-End Protection Screw, Rifle
72	Cam, Lever	109	Cam Lever Pin		(Forearm Cap Screw)
73	Right Sideplate	111	Safety Spring Pin	542	Lever Hook
74	Left Sideplate	112	Hammer Link Pin	552	Lever Hook Spring Screw
79	Extractor	113	Magazine Follower		
80	Front Band, Carbine, (NI)	114	Magazine Tube Plug	(NI)	Not Illustrated
81	Rear Band, Carbine, (NI)	115	Hammer Link		

Before handling any firearm, you should always make sure it is unloaded.

DISASSEMBLY INSTRUCTIONS

These basic instructional steps work with the modern Uberti-made 1866 replicas as well as original Model 1866 Winchesters. The two rifles are of the same basic design, though differing slightly, especially in the firing pin, the mainspring seat and magazine tube areas. The differences between the two are outlined in the instructions below and in the accompanying photos.

1 First, make sure the rifle is unloaded. Pointing the muzzle in a safe direction, hold the rifle around the barrel with your left hand and turn the lever hook (#542) until it is pointing sideways to unlock the lever (#89). Pull the lever all the way down with your right hand to open the action. Check to be absolutely sure there is no cartridge in the barrel chamber and that there is not a cartridge lying in the cartridge carrier (#7) within the action. Understand that if there is a cartridge in the carrier, when you close the lever the rifle will be loaded.

To safely unload an 1866 with a loaded magazine, keep the muzzle pointing in a safe direction. While the lever is still in the open position, taking care to keep your fingers away from the trigger, operate the lever all the way closed and then back until it is all the way open again. As the lever is operated, any cartridges in the magazine will be fed out of the magazine and through the barrel chamber and then ejected from the rifle as the lever is opened. Perform this operation over and again as many times as it takes until there are no more cartridges in the magazine. Make one last check after unloading, just to be sure that no cartridges remain in the magazine. When the lever is opened there should not be a cartridge in the cartridge carrier (#7).

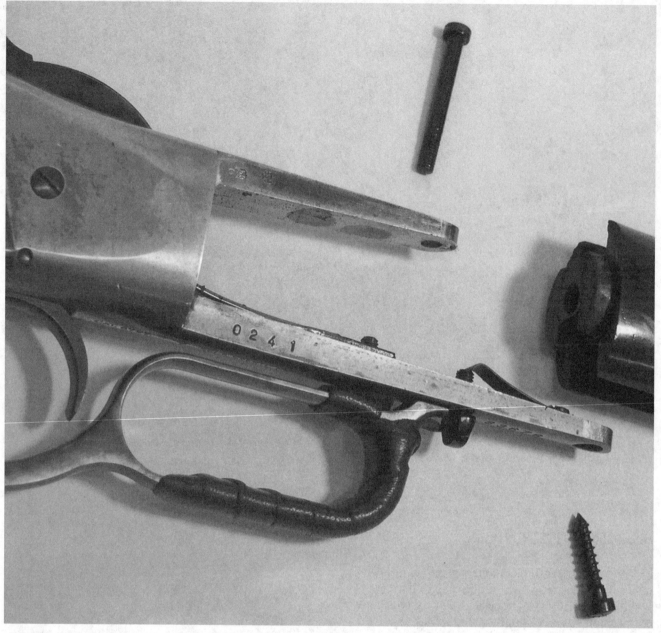

Whether original or replica (a replica is shown), this is how the buttstock is removed on the 1866.

2 Removing the buttstock and mainspring: Unscrew and remove the upper tang screw (#63) from the upper tang. This is the rearmost of the screws located behind the hammer. Unscrew and remove the lower tang wood screw (#62). Some of the early production Winchesters use another wood screw in the upper tang, which must be removed as well, a carry-over from the earlier Henry rifle. The buttstock (#57) is now loose and can be removed from the action (#1) by pulling it straight off to the rear. Use a pair of spreader-type pliers to compress the top of the mainspring to disengage the spring from the stirrup. You can now pivot the mainspring stirrup forward out of the mainspring hooks.

For Uberti: Open the lever slightly and remove the mainspring screw (#36) from the lower tang. The mainspring (#20) can now be lifted out through the back of the action.

For Winchester: Use a plastic or wooden punch and a hammer to drive the rear of the mainspring toward either side of the lower tang until it comes out of its seat in the lower tang. For reassembly you may have to compress the rear of the mainspring down far enough to get it started back into the mainspring seat.

For either rifle: Make note of the mainspring's position. During reassembly the hooks at the front of the mainspring have to be manually engaged with the ears on the hammer link (#115).

· 430 ·

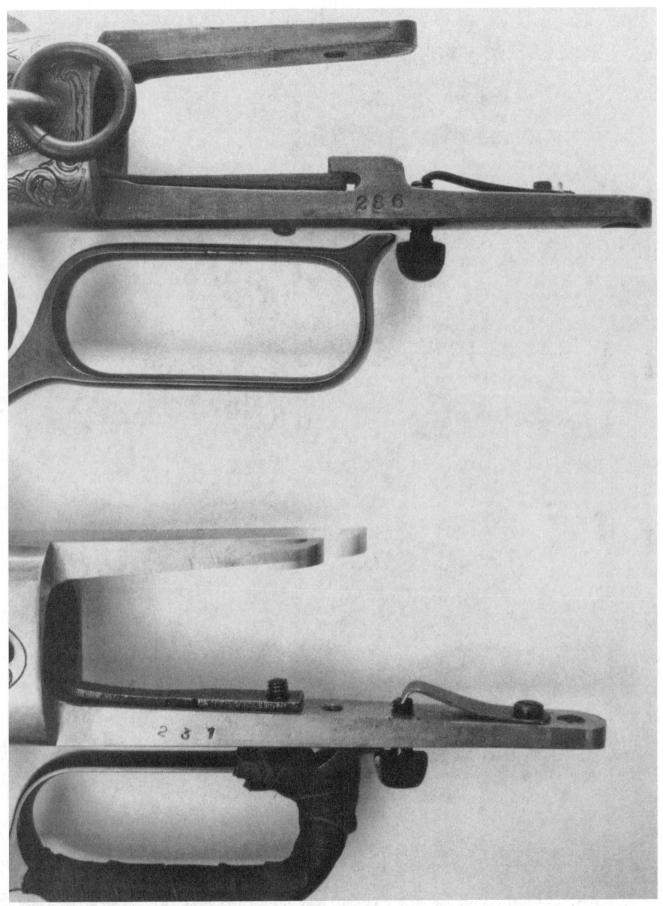

In the original 1866 Winchester (top), the mainspring was fitted into a machined lip in the lower tang. With modern Uberti-made 1866 (bottom), a screw is used to fasten the mainspring to the lower tang. Author photo.

The 1866 carbine made by Uberti, shown with its sideplates off and both the lever springs removed. These Italian-made, replica 1866s are proving themselves to be extraordinarily dependable rifles.

3 Removing the sideplate and lever spring: Loosen the two lever spring screws (#124), which are located on the bottom of the receiver just in front of the lever, about two full turns each. Remove the lever screw (#101). The sideplates (#73-R) and (74-L) are dovetailed into the front of the receiver sides. Remove the sideplate screw (#123) and both sideplates can be removed by tilting them out, rear end first. Unscrew and remove the two lever spring screws (#124) and the left (#93) and right (#92) side lever springs. Note their positions for later reassembly.

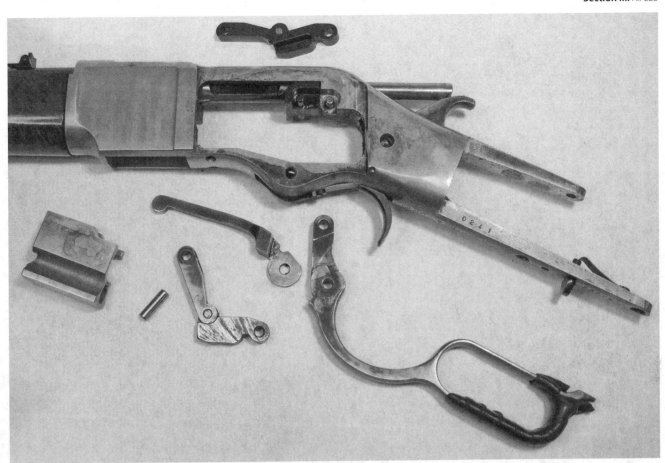

Once the plates and lever springs are out, it's a simple matter to remove the toggle links, lifter and carrier.

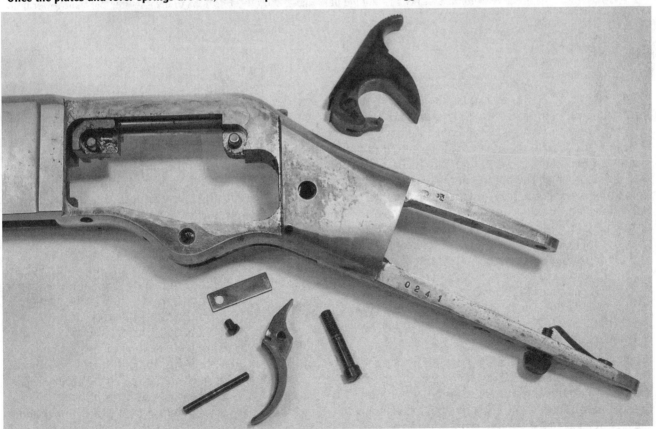

Original or repro, there isn't much that is complicated about the hammer and trigger. The parts look like this. Notice the lever-lock and its spring to the right of the photo.

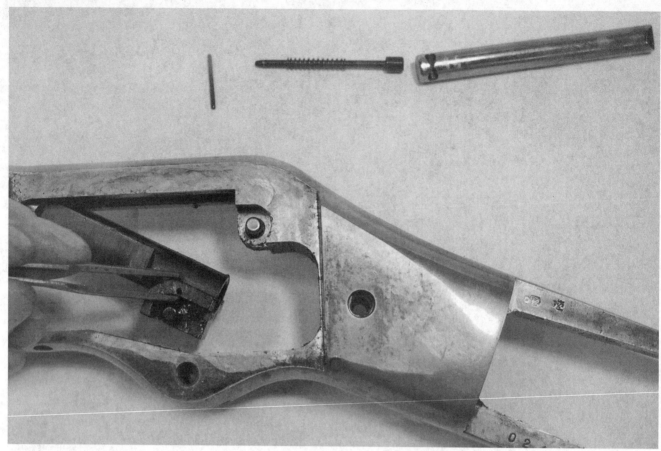

In the replica by Uberti, the removal of one pin allows the bolt to be taken apart. The bolt is shown here in the correct position for removal from the frame. Refer to the instructions and the parts illustration for directions to disassemble the Winchester bolt.

4 Disassembling the action: Lift the left (#84 and #86) and right (#83 and 85) link assemblies out from their respective sides of the frame. Remove the lever pin (#107) from the top of the lever (#89). Lift up slightly on the lifter arm (#90) and pull the lever (#89) straight out through the bottom of the receiver. Push up on the carrier block (#7) and then pull the lifter arm (#90) down and to the rear until it can be removed through the lever opening in the frame bottom. Unscrew and remove the trigger spring screw (#263) and the trigger spring (#19) from the front of the trigger (#10). Unscrew and remove the hammer pin screw (#100). The hammer (#2) can be withdrawn straight out through its opening in the receiver top. Push down the carrier block (#7) and remove it through the bottom of its opening in the frame.

5 Disassembly of the firing pin, bolt, trigger and lever hook, Uberti: Use a small pin punch to drive the firing pin stop (#104) out through the side of the breech block (#97). The firing pin extension (#67), firing pin (#98) and firing pin spring can now be withdrawn through the rear of the receiver. The breech block (#97) can be removed by tilting it all the

way down as it is withdrawn toward the rear. Use a pin punch to drift the trigger pin (#99) out from either side of the receiver so trigger can be pulled out through the bottom. The lever hook (#542) can be removed by unscrewing it from its hole in the lower frame tang. The lever hook spring (#237) can be removed by removing the lever hook spring screw (#552), located on the inside of the lower frame tang.

5a Firing pin and bolt disassembly, Winchester: Withdraw the bolt-firing pin assembly to the rear as far as it will move, place a pin punch through the hole in the receiver top-strap and drive out the extractor pin. Now push the bolt forward until it is almost all the way closed. The extractor can be lifted straight up out of the top of the bolt. Push the bolt back toward the rear of the action and unscrew the firing pin extension in a counterclockwise direction. When it is fully unscrewed, withdraw the extension out the rear of the receiver. The breech bolt can now be removed by tilting it down as it is withdrawn toward the rear. Note the firing pin at the face of the breech bolt; the firing pin extension screws into this part, which is now loose and can be lifted out to the front of the bolt.

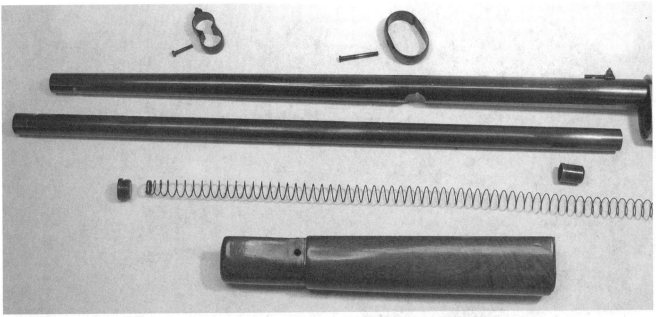

The carbine magazine and fore-end disassembled. This Uberti has an unusually large cutout for the rear band screw.

MAGAZINE TUBE AND FORE-END REMOVAL; RIFLES:

6 **For Uberti:** Unscrew the magazine tube plug (#214) at the front of the magazine tube (#118). The magazine spring (#96) and magazine follower (#113) can be removed through the front of the tube. Unscrew and remove the two fore-end protection (cap) screws (#283), one on each side of the fore-end cap, and then slide the fore-end cap forward slightly. With a pin punch, drive out the magazine tube bearing pin (#281) from the magazine tube bearing (#275) and pull the magazine tube (#118) out toward the front. Once the tube magazine is clear of the fore-end wood, the fore-end wood (#68) is tilted down and pulled forward off the rifle. The pivot the magazine tube toward either side of the rifle 1/4 turn. This frees the magazine tube bearing (#275) from its dovetail cut in the bottom of the barrel (#3).

For Winchester: Remove the magazine plug screw from the very bottom front of the magazine tube. The magazine tube cap is now loose and can be pulled out the front of the magazine tube along with the magazine spring and the magazine follower. Unscrew and remove the two fore-end cap screws, one on each side of the fore-end cap, and slide the fore-end cap forward slightly. Use a pin punch to drive out the magazine ring pin from the magazine ring and pull the magazine tube out toward the front. When the magazine tube is clear of the fore-end wood, the fore-end wood can be tilted down and pulled forward off the rifle. The magazine is then pivoted to either side of the rifle 1/4 turn, freeing the magazine ring from its dovetail cut in the bottom of the barrel.

DISASSEMBLE THE MAGAZINE TUBE AND FORE-END, CARBINES:

6a **For Uberti:** Unscrew the magazine tube plug (#214) from the front of the magazine tube (#118). The magazine spring (#96) and magazine follower (#113) can be removed through the front of the tube. Unscrew and remove the screws (#21) and (#122) from the front band (#80) and the fore-end (#81) band. Remove the magazine tube (#118) by pulling it straight out to the front. Slide the fore-end band (#81) forward. The fore-end (#68) can be pulled forward and off the gun. The front band (#80) is slid forward, off the barrel, followed by the fore-end band (#81).

For Winchester: Remove the magazine cap plug screw from the bottom front of the magazine tube. The magazine tube cap is now loose and can be pulled out the front of the magazine tube along with the magazine spring and the follower. Remove the band screws from the front and rear magazine bands. The magazine tube is pulled straight out to the front and off the weapon. Slide the rear magazine band forward off the fore-end wood. The fore-end wood can be tilted down and pulled off to the front. The forward magazine band can now be slid off to the front, as is the rear magazine band.

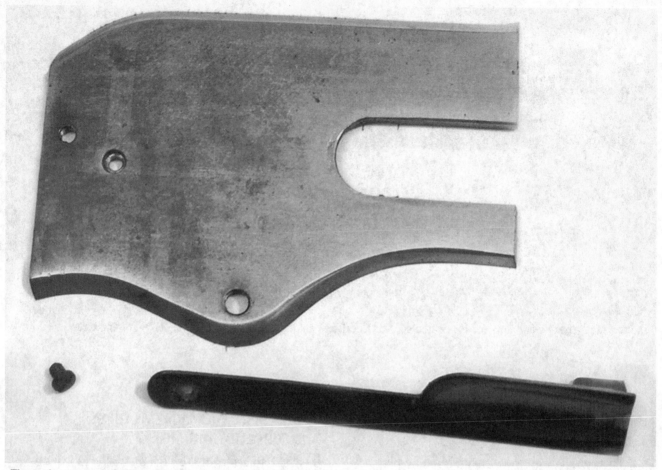

The spring cover, or ladle as Uberti calls it, is held onto the right sideplate with one screw. This is just about the only part in the replica '66 that has given some shooters trouble, but not often.

7 Disassembly of the buttstock: To remove the buttplate, remove the two buttplate screws (#62), one at the top and one at the rear of the buttplate (#58). On models that have a trap-door in the buttplate: The buttplate gate spring (#231) is removed by unscrewing and removing the buttplate gate spring screw (#232).

REASSEMBLY

Reassemble the weapon in reverse order of above.

Winchester Models 1873 and 1876
and Replicas

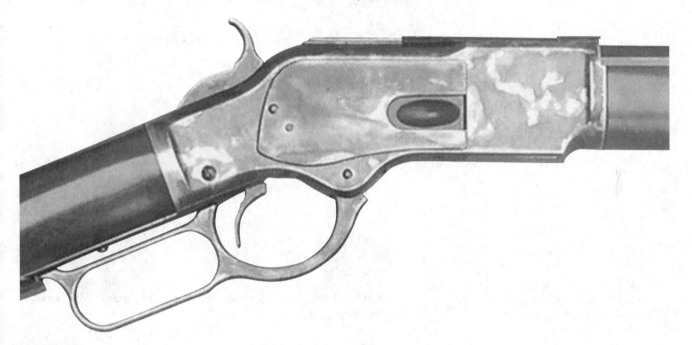

The Model 1873 was an instant success when it was introduced. This was their improvement to the world-standard lever action, the Model 1866 Yellowboy. The 1873 was offered with an iron frame and was initially chambered in the powerful new 44-40 centerfire caliber. Winchester manufactured the 1873 Model from 1873 through 1919 with a total of about 720,000 weapons produced. Model 1873 Winchesters were chambered to fire the 44-40 Winchester and, later, the 38-40 Winchester and 32-20 Winchester centerfire (WCF) cartridges. Although very rare, about 19,000 Models 1873 were also chambered in .22 rimfire. Most standard production 1873s were supplied in full blue finish with the lever, hammer, firearm cap and butt plate color case hardened. Some early guns and a few made on special order were supplied with color case-hardened receivers while the barrel and magazine tube were blued or browned. The Model 1873 was offered as a carbine with a lightweight 20-inch round barrel, a musket with a 30-inch barrel, and most popularly as a 24-inch barreled rifle in both octagon and round configurations.

Winchester's Model 1876 or Centennial model was essentially an oversized, elongated Model 1873. The big repeating rifle was introduced to fill the need for a more powerful rifle than the 1873. 1876 Models were chambered for big game cartridges of the day such as 40-60, 45-60, 45-75 and 50-95 Winchester cartridges. The 1876 was manufactured from 1876 through 1897 with a total of 63,871 manufactured in carbine, rifle (the most popular) and musket variations.

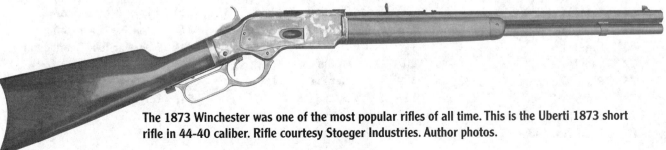

The 1873 Winchester was one of the most popular rifles of all time. This is the Uberti 1873 short rifle in 44-40 caliber. Rifle courtesy Stoeger Industries. Author photos.

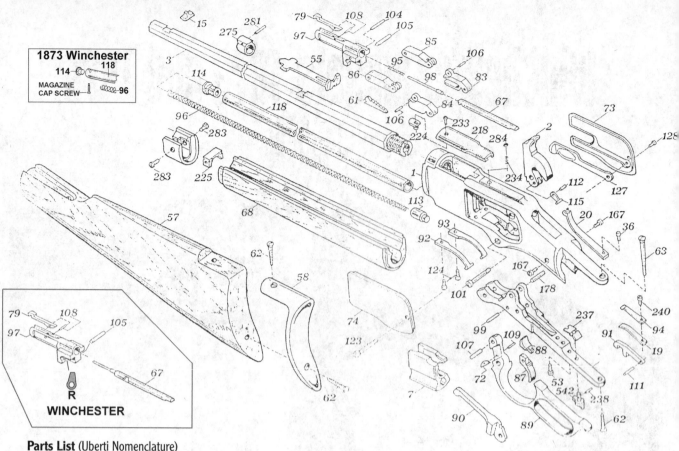

1873 Winchester

MAGAZINE CAP SCREW

WINCHESTER

R

Parts List (Uberti Nomenclature)
Illustration altered by the author to include Winchester differences. 1876 parts are similar but larger.

Uberti 1873 parts drawing, altered by the author to include Winchester differences.

1	Frame	84	Left Rear Link	114	Magazine Tube Plug
2	Hammer	85	Right Front Link	115	Hammer Link
3	Barrel	86	Left Front Link	118	Magazine Tube
7	Carrier Block	87	Trigger Lower Portion	123	Side Plate Screw
15	Sight	88	Trigger Upper Portion	124	Lever Spring Screw
19	Trigger Spring	89	Lever	127	Ladle
20	Mainspring	90	Lifter Arm	128	Ladle Screw
26	Triggerguard	91	Safety Bar	167	Triggerguard Screw
36	Mainspring Screw	92	Right Lever Spring	178	Hammer Pin
53	Mainspring Adjusting Screw	93	Left Lever Spring	216	Fore-End Protection
55	Rear	94	Safety Spring	218	Protection Running
57	Buttstock	95	Firing Pin Spring	224	Protection Running Guide
58	Buttplate	96	Magazine Spring	225	Protection Running Bearing
61	Rear Sight	97	Breech Block	233	Protection Running Screw
62	Buttplate Screw	98	Firing Pin	234	Protection Running Spring
63	Tang Screw	99	Trigger Pin	237	Lever Hook Spring
67	Firing Pin Extension	101	Lever Screw	238	Lever Hook Pin
67	Firing Pin (Win)	104	Firing Pin Stop	240	Trigger & Lever Screw
R	Firing Pin Retractor (Win)	105	Rear Link Pin	275	Magazine Tube Bearing
68	Fore-End	106	Link Pin	281	Magazine Tube Bearing Pin
72	Cam Lever	107	Extractor Pin	283	Fore-End Protection Screw
73	Right Side Plate	109	Cam Lever Pin	284	Protection Running Sphere
74	Left Side Plate	111	Safety Spring Pin	542	Lever Hook
79	Extractor	112	Hammer Link Pin		
83	Right Rear Link	113	Magazine Follower		

Removing two screws allows the buttstock to be pulled off from the rear.

DISASSEMBLY INSTRUCTIONS

These basic instruction steps will work for Uberti-made modern replicas and similar firearms. Original Winchester rifles will differ slightly as per notes within the text below, most especially in the firing pin and magazine-tube cap areas.

1 First, make sure the rifle is unloaded. Hold the rifle around the barrel and wooden forearm with your left hand. Point the muzzle in a safe direction and twist the lever lock (#542) located behind the lever loop on the lower tang so it faces side to side, thus allowing the lever to be opened. Open the action by pulling the lever (#89) all the way down with your right hand. Check now to be absolutely certain there is no cartridge in the barrel chamber and look closely to be sure there is no cartridge lying in the carrier block (#7) within the action. If there is a cartridge in the carrier, then when you close the lever, the rifle will be loaded. To unload a rifle with a loaded magazine, always be sure the muzzle stays pointed in a safe direction. Keep your fingers away from the trigger at all times while you operate the lever to the fully open and fully closed positions several times to expel the cartridges in the magazine. Remove any live cartridges to another location.

2 To remove the buttstock and mainspring: Remove the upper tang screw (#63) from the upper tang; this is the rearmost of the two screws located behind the hammer. Remove the lower tang wood screw (#62). The buttstock (#57) is now loose and may be removed from the action (#1) by pulling it straight off to the rear. Open the lever (#89) slightly and loosen the mainspring adjustment screw (#53), the forwardmost screw on the lower tang. Now remove the mainspring screw (#36) directly behind the mainspring adjustment screw. The mainspring can now be withdrawn through the rear of the tangs. Make note of the mainspring position; during reassembly the hooks at the front of the mainspring must be manually engaged with the ears on the hammer link (#115).

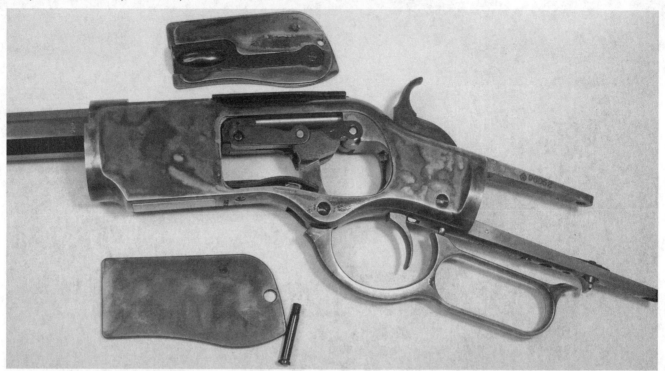

The action is quickly exposed by simply removing the side plates. Once the side plates are off, the links may be lifted out either side of the action.

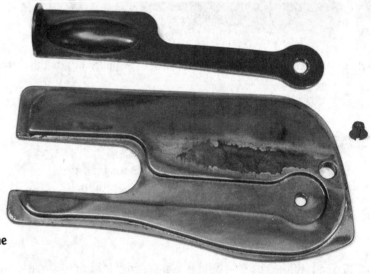

The ladle or loading cover is secured to the inside of the right sideplate with one small screw.

3 To remove and disassemble the sideplate and mortise cover: Unscrew the sideplate screw (#123) and tap the screw head with a soft plastic screwdriver handle. This will push the rear of the right sideplate (#73) away from the frame so it now can be pulled completely off. Reach back through the opening where the sideplate removed with a 1/4-inch hardwood dowel and tap the inside rear of the left sideplate (#74) and remove it in the same manner as the right sideplate. The ladle (#127) is located in the right hand sideplate and can be removed by taking out the ladle screw (#128). In Winchester terminology, the mortise cover is the sliding plate that keeps dirt out of the top of the action.

Uberti calls the mortise cover a protection running (#218). Remove the protection running screw (#233) and slide the protection running all the way back off its rails and off the receiver to the rear. Be careful: there are a small coil spring and ball detent (#234) and protection running spring and sphere (284) under the protection running! Lift the protection running guide (#224) out of the receiver top.

For Winchester rifles and carbines, remove the mortise cover screw and slide the mortise cover all the way back off its rails. Lift the mortise cover stop out of the recess in the receiver top. Remove the mortise cover spring screw and the mortise cover spring will lift off.

Removing the dust cover on the Uberti 1873. Notice the tiny ball and spring in the receiver top, just to the left of the cover. Be careful not to let this get away when you slide the cover back! Winchester uses a leaf spring held on with a screw.

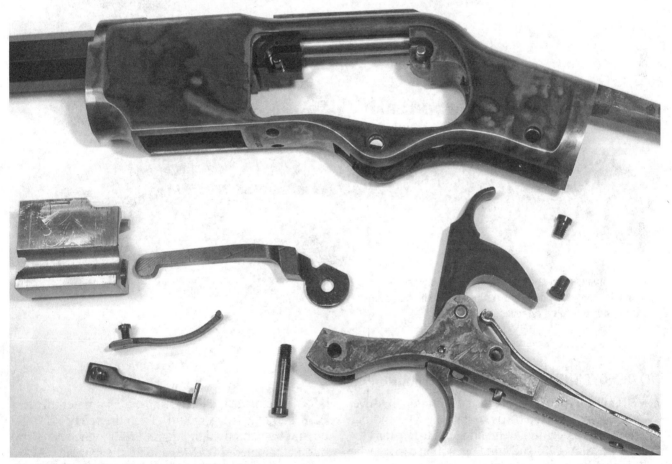

The lower tang assembly, carrier and lifter removed.

4 To remove and disassemble the links and the lower tang: Lift the left (#84) and (#86) and right (#83) and (#85) link assemblies out from their respective sides of the frame. Remove the two triggerguard screws (#167) from the sides of the receiver. Tilt the triggerguard (#26) and pull it out of the receiver from the bottom. Lift up slightly on the lifter arm (#90) and pull the finger lever (#89) straight out through the bottom of the receiver. Push up on the carrier block (#7) and withdraw the lifter arm (#90) down and rearward until it can removed through the lever opening in the receiver bottom. Push the carrier block (#7) down and out of the receiver.

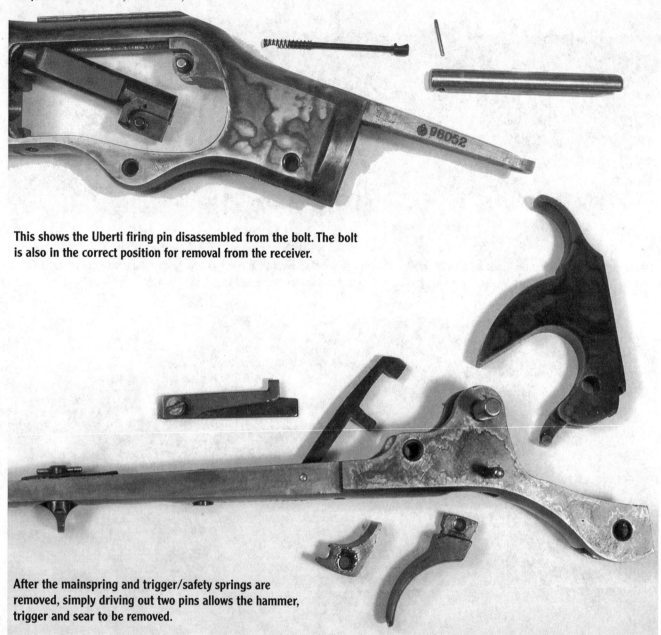

This shows the Uberti firing pin disassembled from the bolt. The bolt is also in the correct position for removal from the receiver.

After the mainspring and trigger/safety springs are removed, simply driving out two pins allows the hammer, trigger and sear to be removed.

TO REMOVE THE BREECH BLOCK AND FIRING PIN:

5 **For Uberti replicas:** Using a small pin punch, drive the firing pin stop (#104) out through the side of the breech block (#97). The firing pin extension (#67), firing pin (#98) and firing pin spring can now be withdrawn through the rear of the receiver. The breech block (#97) can be removed by tilting it all the way down as it is withdrawn toward the rear.

For Winchesters: Using a small pin punch and hammer, drive out the front link pin and pull the firing pin retractor (#R) down and out of the breech bolt. Be sure you make note of the firing pin retractor's position for later reassembly. The firing pin can now be pulled directly out through the rear of the receiver. The breech bolt can be removed by tilting it all the way down as it is withdrawn toward the rear.

6 To remove and disassemble the hammer-trigger and tang (triggerguard): Push the safety bar (#91) up and pull and hold the trigger (#87) to the rear. Drive out the hammer pin (#178) and lift the hammer (#2) out of its recess in the triggerguard (#26), the lower tang). Remove the trigger and lever screw. This will free the trigger spring (#19) and the safety spring (#94) to be lifted out of their recess behind the trigger. Drive out the trigger pin (#99) and lift the trigger (#87) and the trigger upper portion (#88). The safety bar (#91) is removed by driving out its pin (#111). The lever lock can be disassembled by driving out the lever lock pin (#238), which allows the lever lock (#542) to be pulled out from the bottom and the lever lock spring (#237) to be lifted off the top.

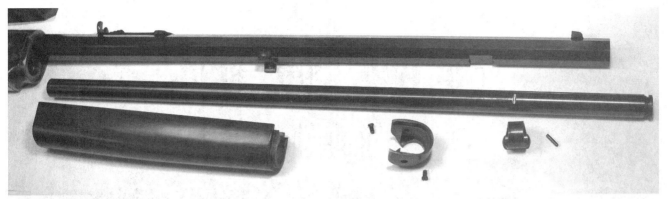

The entire Uberti 1873 magazine tube and fore-end are shown disassembled. Except for the method of securing the magazine cap, this is identical to a Winchester rifle.

Unscrewing the magazine cap from an Uberti 1873. Winchester magazine caps are held on with one screw through the bottom of the tube.

TO REMOVE THE MAGAZINE TUBE AND FOREARM, RIFLES:

7 **Uberti:** Unscrew the magazine tube plug (#114) from the front of the magazine tube (#118). The magazine spring (#96) and magazine follower (#113) can now be removed out through the front of the tube. Remove the two forend protection (cap) screws (#283), one on each side of the fore-end cap, and slide the forend cap forward slightly. Drift out the magazine tube bearing pin (#281) from the magazine tube bearing (#275) and pull the magazine tube (#118) out toward the front. Once the tube is clear of the forearm wood, the fore-end wood (#68) can be tilted down and pulled forward off the rifle. The magazine tube is then turned toward either side of the rifle 1/4 turn. This frees the magazine tube bearing (#275) from its dovetail cut in the bottom of the barrel (#3).

Winchester: Remove the magazine plug screw from the very bottom front of the magazine tube. The magazine tube cap is now loose and can be pulled out the front of the magazine tube along with the magazine spring and the magazine follower. Remove the two fore-end tip (cap) screws, one on each side of the fore-end cap, and slide the fore-end cap forward slightly. Drift out the magazine ring pin from the magazine ring and pull the magazine tube out toward the front. Once the tube is clear of the fore-end wood, the fore-end wood can be tilted down and pulled forward off the rifle. The magazine is then turned toward either side of the rifle 1/4 turn, thus freeing the magazine ring from its dovetail cut in the bottom of the barrel.

TO REMOVE THE MAGAZINE TUBE AND FOREARM, CARBINES:

7a **Uberti:** Unscrew the magazine tube plug (#114) from the front of the magazine tube (#118). The magazine spring (#96) and magazine follower (#113) can be removed out through the front of the tube. Remove both band screws (#121) and (#122) from the front band (#80) and the fore-end (#81) band. Remove the magazine tube (#118) by pulling it straight out the front. Slide the fore-end band (#121) forward. The fore-end (#68) can now be pulled forward and off the gun. The front band (#80) can be rotated 180 degrees and slid forward off the barrel, followed by the fore-end band (#81).

Winchester: Remove the magazine plug screw from the very bottom front of the magazine tube. The magazine tube cap is now loose and may be pulled out the front of the magazine tube along with the magazine spring and the magazine follower. Remove the front and rear band screws from the front and rear magazine bands. The magazine tube is pulled straight out the front and off the weapon. Slide the rear magazine band forward off the forearm wood and the fore-end wood may be tilted down and pulled off to the front. The forward magazine band is now rotated one half turn and slid off over the sight base, as is the rear magazine band.

REASSEMBLY

Reassemble rifle in the reverse order of above.

The 1885 Winchester
Single Shot

Uberti's version of the Winchester 1885 High-Wall single shot in 45-70. Author photos.

The 1885 Model was the first single shot rifle to be produced by the Winchester company. Up until that time they had been world famous for their lever action repeating rifles. Winchester's introduction of this rifle also marked the company's first use of the designs of firearms genius John M. Browning, thus beginning a long and fruitful relationship for both parties. The Browning brothers of Ogden, Utah, had been making John Browning's 1878-patented single shot rifles for several years before the manufacturing rights were purchased by Winchester in 1883. Browning's single shot was a much simpler and more efficient falling block action than the common standard, the Sharps. Browning's design was not only simple but lightweight, compact and utterly dependable.

Winchester introduced the Model 1885 in that year and continued its production through 1920, along the way offering an incredible array of options and variants. The rifle's action was made in "High Wall" (for large, powerful cartridges) and "Low Wall" (small cartridges of medium to low pressure) sizes and was offered in a large selection of calibers ranging from 22 Short rimfire up to a huge .50-caliber centerfire cartridge, and they even made one as a 20-gauge shotgun. Just over 100,000 Model 1885s were made by Winchester. These excellent Winchester 1885 actions, especially the High Wall variant, have long been a favorite of single shot rifle builders.

The modern Browning Arms company sold a Japanese-manufactured replica of the 1885 single shot from 1973 though 1983 in several calibers, including modern cartridges such as the 22-250, along with the 45-70. Beginning in 1985, the company introduced their new Model 1885, which is still being manufactured in several variations including a black powder cartridge rifle called the BPCR. Model 1885s are available in Low Wall or High Wall configurations and come in a variety of modern cartridges as well as some of the classic cartridges of the old west such as 45 Colt, 38-55, 40-60 and the workhorse 45-70. The modern Browning-made replicas are very well made, look good, shoot well and in my experience have proven to be very dependable. Of course Browning and Winchester are now part of the same organization.

The famous Italian arms maker Aldo Uberti also manufactures their own version of the Model 1885 High Wall as well as Low Wall rifles and I have been fortunate enough to have had several examples to test over the few years. Uberti's 1885s are available in several popular calibers from the .22 rimfire up through the 45/120. All the rifles I have shot were, by pure coincidence, all in 45-70 caliber. The rifles are being furnished with color case-hardened receiver, breech block, hammer, trigger, and finger lever that are forged from super-tough 8620 steel alloy, with the barrel, sights and buttplate blued. On all of the rifles I have handled, the metal shows very careful and professional

Parts drawing courtesy A. Uberti.

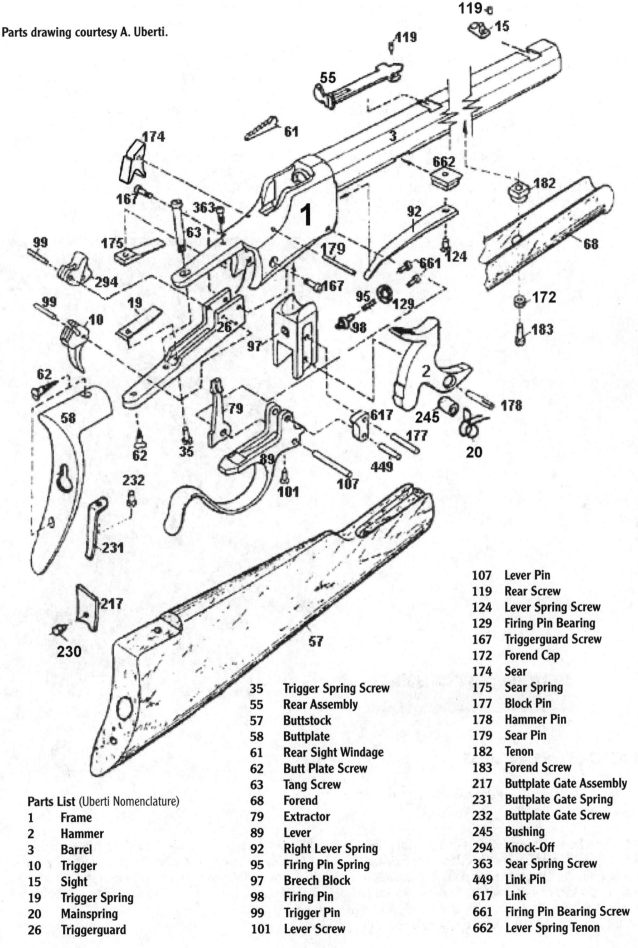

Parts List (Uberti Nomenclature)

1	Frame
2	Hammer
3	Barrel
10	Trigger
15	Sight
19	Trigger Spring
20	Mainspring
26	Triggerguard
35	Trigger Spring Screw
55	Rear Assembly
57	Buttstock
58	Buttplate
61	Rear Sight Windage
62	Butt Plate Screw
63	Tang Screw
68	Forend
79	Extractor
89	Lever
92	Right Lever Spring
95	Firing Pin Spring
97	Breech Block
98	Firing Pin
99	Trigger Pin
101	Lever Screw
107	Lever Pin
119	Rear Screw
124	Lever Spring Screw
129	Firing Pin Bearing
167	Triggerguard Screw
172	Forend Cap
174	Sear
175	Sear Spring
177	Block Pin
178	Hammer Pin
179	Sear Pin
182	Tenon
183	Forend Screw
217	Buttplate Gate Assembly
231	Buttplate Gate Spring
232	Buttplate Gate Screw
245	Bushing
294	Knock-Off
363	Sear Spring Screw
449	Link Pin
617	Link
661	Firing Pin Bearing Screw
662	Lever Spring Tenon

polishing before the blue and case coloring is applied, resulting in metal finishes of very high quality.

When the Uberti's action is disassembled, you will notice the firing pin has been altered to a modern, small-diameter, spring-loaded, free-floating type. Winchester's firing pin retractor on the link is still there, although the only remaining function it has is to lift the hammer slightly up off the firing pin as the action is opened. The breech block's face has been fitted with a removable firing pin bushing that contains the new firing pin and its spring. The only real objection I have to the Uberti is that it places the hammer at the half cock position, rather than

fully cocking the arm. This won't bother hunters; in fact it is a nice safety feature, but it slows down target shooters who would appreciate having the self-cocking feature.

Like its external appearance, the internal parts of the Uberti replica (other than the alterations noted) look as if Winchester could have made them and I don't know of a better compliment. In another variation from Winchester, Uberti uses the later High Wall coil-type main spring to power the hammer; however, they have retained the early Model 1885 under-barrel leaf spring as a lever tension spring. An odd combination, but it works.

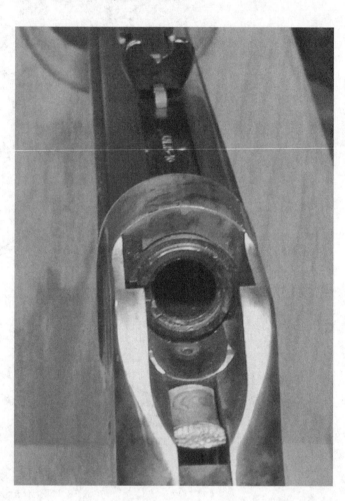

The 1885 Uberti High-Wall with its action opened.

DISASSEMBLY INSTRUCTIONS

These basic instruction steps will also work for the Winchester Model 1885 High-Wall and Low-Wall.

1 First, be sure the rifle is unloaded. Hold the rifle around the barrel and wooden forearm with your left hand, being careful to point the muzzle in a safe direction, and then open the action by pulling the finger lever (#89) all the way down with your right hand. Look into the barrel and check to be certain

there is no cartridge in the barrel's chamber. If there is a cartridge present, reach in and remove it by pulling the cartridge straight out of the rear of the barrel. Remove any live ammunition to a different location.

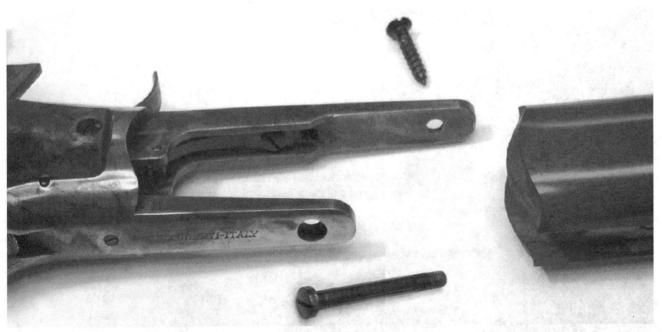

Two screws are all the hold the buttstock on the action; after they are removed, the wood can be pulled off to the rear.

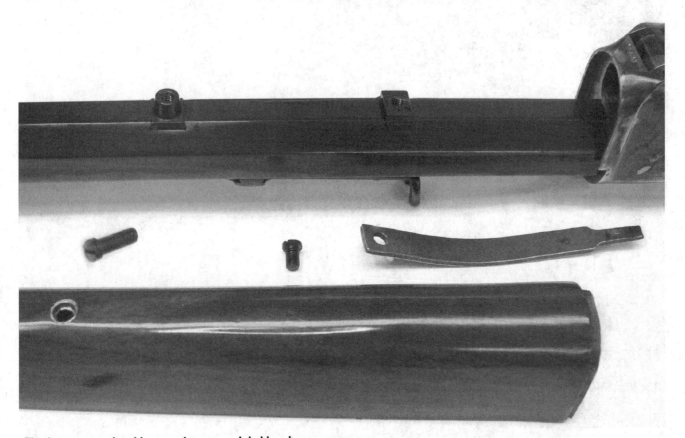

The forearm wood and lever spring are each held on by one screw.

2 To remove the buttstock, forearm and lever spring: Unscrew and remove the upper (#63) and lower (#62) tang screws and pull the buttstock (#97) off to the rear. Unscrew and remove the forearm screw (#183) and remove the forearm (68) by pulling it down first from the front and then towards the muzzle. Remove the lever spring screw (#124) from the underside of the barrel (#3). The right lever spring (#92) is now loose. Note: Early Winchester Models 1885 made before about 1910 used a leaf mainspring mounted under the barrel in the same fashion as Uberti uses its lever spring.

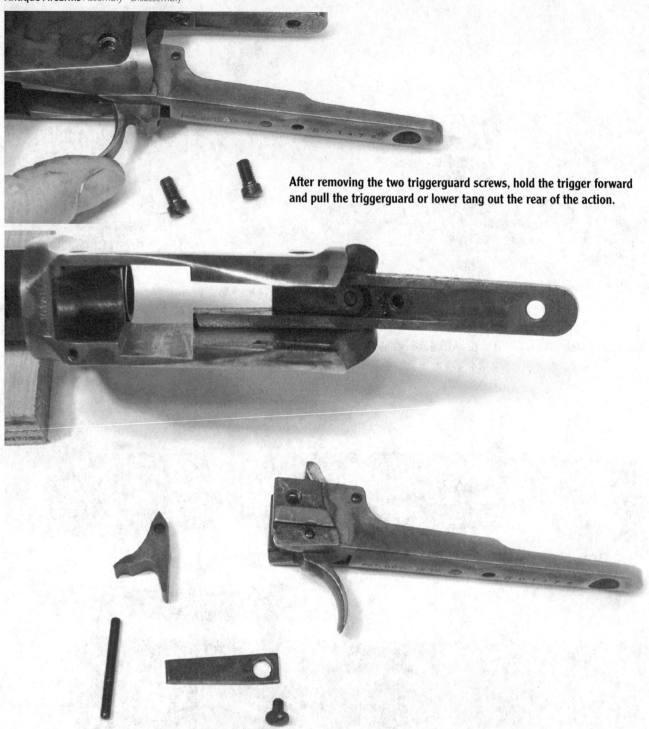

After removing the two triggerguard screws, hold the trigger forward and pull the triggerguard or lower tang out the rear of the action.

The triggerguard, sear and its spring disassembled.

3 To disassemble the action: Unscrew and remove the two trigger guard screws (#167) and pull the trigger guard (#26) off the receiver to the rear. Unscrew and remove the lever screw (#101) and drift out the lever pin (#107). Pull down on the finger lever while manually holding the sear (#174) to the rear and remove the breechblock/hammer/lever assembly through the bottom of the breech block opening in the receiver (#1). The extractor (#79) is now loose and will fall out the bottom of the receiver. Pay attention to how these parts fit together for later reassembly.

To disassemble the breech block (#97): The hammer (#2) and finger lever (#89) assembly can be disassembled by removing the two large axle pins. Uberti has made use of a coiled mainspring that is very similar, although slightly simpler in design, than the coiled mainspring used on later (post-1910 manufacture) Winchester single shots.

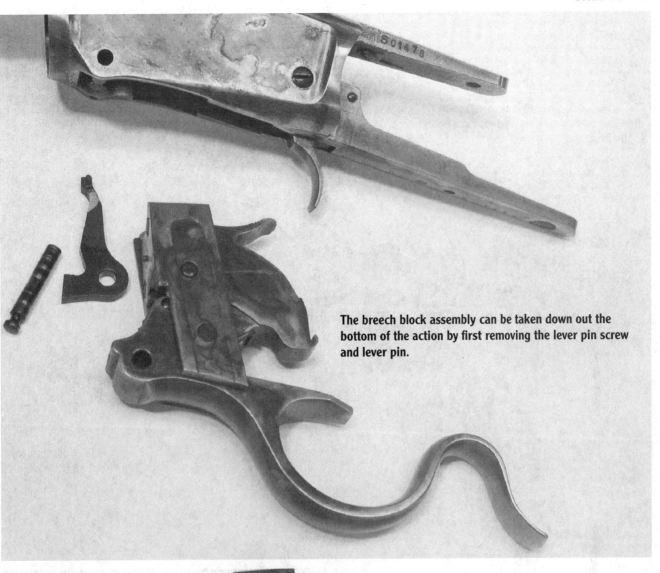

The breech block assembly can be taken down out the bottom of the action by first removing the lever pin screw and lever pin.

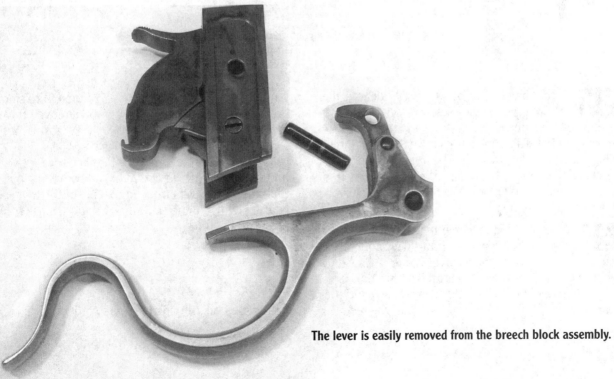

The lever is easily removed from the breech block assembly.

The breech face (firing pin bearing) comes off after two screws are removed to allow access to the firing pin.

The triggerguard or lower tang shown disassembled.

3a Further breech bolt disassembly: Remove the two firing pin bearing screws (#661) from the front face of the breech block (#97) and the firing pin bearing (#129). The firing pin spring (#95) and firing pin (#98) may be withdrawn from the front of the breech block. Note: Remove the firing pin retainer screw from the top of the breech block. The firing pin may now be removed through the rear of the breech block.

4 To disassemble the trigger mechanism: The sear portion of the trigger mechanism is mounted in the upper rear area of the receiver-frame (#1) itself, while the trigger portion is mounted within the trigger guard. Remove the sear spring screw (#363) and the sear spring (#175) from the underside of the receiver

tang. Drift out the sear pin (#179) from either side of the receiver. The sear (#174) can be removed through the bottom; pay careful attention to its positioning for reassembly. Remove the trigger spring screw (#35) and the trigger spring (#19). The trigger (#10) and the knock-off may be removed by driving out their respective pins from either side of the trigger guard, paying attention to their relationships for later reassembly.

REASSEMBLY

Reassemble the rifle in reverse order of the above.

Winchester Model 1886

The right side of the massive 1886 Winchester rifle action. The spring cover or loading gate is actually a hinged door mounted on a plate, unlike other Winchester spring covers, which are one-piece construction.

The famous Model 1886 Winchester was originally designed by John M. and Matthew S. Browning. Winchester purchased the Browning patent rights to the rifle in 1885 and, after some alterations, brought the rifle out in 1886 to replace the large-framed 1876 rifle. The '86 was a large rifle with a particularly strong action; it was popular from its introduction with hunters who could order it in just about any imaginable caliber from 33 WCF up to the huge 50-110 Express. Winchester made the 1886 in sporting rifle, carbine and musket variations and, for much of its early production, a take-down feature was also optional.

This classic Model 1886 Winchester was manufactured from 1886 until 1935 with nearly 160,000 produced. Even after the model was officially dropped in 1935, a modernized variation of the '86 with a coiled mainspring called the Model 71 was manufactured in 348 Winchester all the way up until 1957. Today the 1886 is still popular with collectors and with shooters who eagerly seek out the rifles in 45-70 and 45-90 calibers.

The 1886 is today being reproduced by Browning (Winchester) although these new rifles are actually being made in Japan. Winchester later greatly simplified and reduced the 1886 action in size to suit pistol sized cartridges and brought it out as the Model 1892, their replacement for the well-liked 1873. The 1892 had the distinct advantage a strong, double-locking bolt Browning action over the somewhat weak toggle link action of the 1873. Other advantages of the 1892, from a manufacturing point of view, were fewer and simpler parts and an action that could be made so compactly that Winchester was able to offer the public a much lighter and smaller rifle.

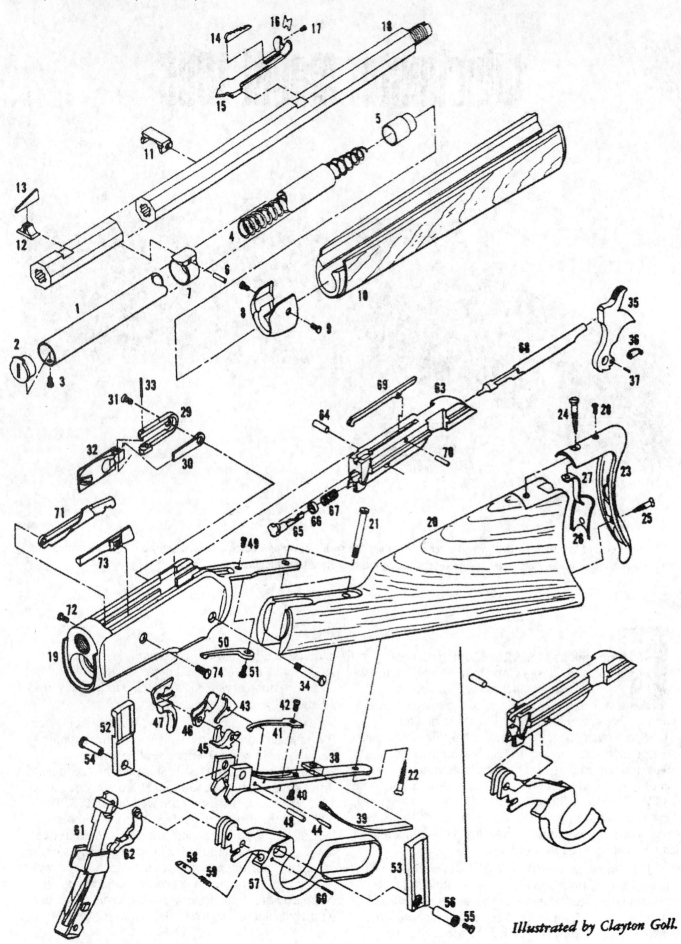

Illustrated by Clayton Goll.

Parts List

1	Magazine Tube	26	Buttplate Slide	51	Carrier Stop Screw
2	Magazine Plug	27	Buttplate Slide Spring	52	Locking Bolt, Right
3	Magazine Plug Screw	28	Buttplate Slide Screw	53	Locking Bolt, Left
4	Magazine Spring	29	Spring Cover Base	54	Finger Lever Pin
5	Magazine Follower	30	Spring Cover Spring	55	Bushing & Pin Screw
6	Magazine Ring Pin	31	Spring Cover Screw	56	Finger Lever Pin Bushing
7	Magazine Ring	32	Spring Cover Leaf	57	Finger Lever
8	Forearm Tip	33	Spring Cover Leaf Pin	58	Friction Stud
9	Forearm Tip Screws (2)	34	Receiver Screw	59	Friction Stud Spring
10	Fore-End	35	Hammer	60	Friction Stud Pin
11	Fore-End Tip Tenon	36	Stirrup	61	Carrier
12	Front Sight Base	37	Stirrup Pin	62	Carrier Hook
13	Front Sight	38	Lower Tang	63	Breech Bolt
14	Rear Sight Elevator	39	Mainspring	64	Lever & Breech Bolt Pin
15	Rear Sight Assembly	40	Mainspring Tension Screw	65	Ejector
16	Elevation Leaf	41	Sear & Trigger Spring	66	Ejector Collar
17	Elevation Leaf Screw	42	Sear & Trigger Spring Screw	67	Ejector Spring
18	Barrel	43	Sear Catch	68	Firing Pin
19	Receiver	44	Sear Catch Pin	69	Extractor
20	Stock	45	Sear	70	Extractor Pin
21	Upper Tang Screw	46	Kick-Off for Set Trigger	71	Cartridge Guide
22	Lower Tang Screw	47	Trigger	72	Cartridge Guide Screw
23	Buttplate	48	Trigger, Sear & KO Pin	73	Cartridge Stop
24	Upper Buttplate Screw	49	Carrier Stop Tension Screw	74	Cartridge Stop Screw
25	Lower Buttplate Screw	50	Carrier Stop		

DISASSEMBLY INSTRUCTIONS

Illustration from *The Gun Digest Book of Exploded Firearms Drawings,* 2nd edition, edited by Harold A. Murtz ©DBI Books Inc., 1977 Printed with permission of the publisher: K-P Publications, 700 E. State Street, Iola, WI 54990-0001.

This is what an empty 1886 rifle should look like.

1 First be sure the rifle is unloaded. Hold the rifle around the barrel and wooden forearm with your left hand. Be sure to point the muzzle in a safe direction and then open the action by pulling the finger lever (#57) all the way down with your right hand. Look into the opened action to be absolutely certain there is no cartridge in the barrel's chamber or lying in the cartridge carrier (#61) within the action. If there is

a cartridge in the carrier then when you close the lever, the rifle will be loaded. To safely unload a rifle with a loaded magazine, be sure the muzzle stays pointed in a safe direction. Keep your finger away from the trigger while you operate the lever to the fully open and fully closed positions several times to expel the cartridges in the magazine until no more cartridges remain. Remove any live ammunition to a separate location.

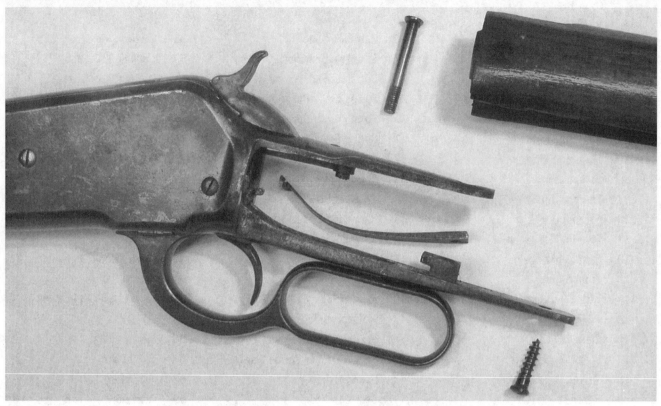

You have to remove the upper and lower tang screws in order to pull the buttstock off to the rear.

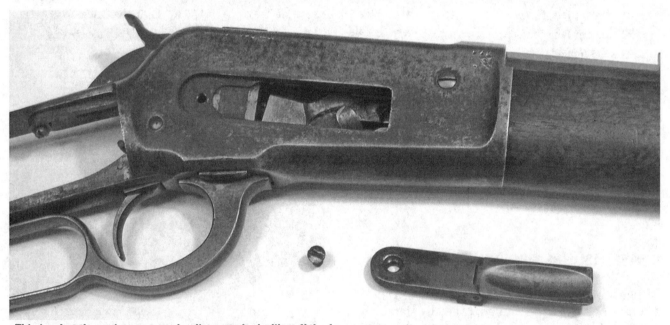

This is what the spring cover or loading gate looks like off the frame.

2 To remove the buttstock and mainspring: Unscrew and remove the upper tang screw (#21) from the upper tang; this is the rearmost of the two screws located behind the hammer and then remove the lower tang screw (#22), which is a wood screw. The buttstock (#20) is now loose and may be removed from the receiver (#19) by pulling it straight off to the rear. Unscrew and remove the spring cover screw (#31) from the right side of the receiver and lift the spring cover assembly (#29) and (32) from the receiver. With the hammer all the way forward and the lever closed, the rear tail of the mainspring (#39) may be driven out of its seat with the tang left to right. The ears of the mainspring (#39) are now lifted out of the hammer stirrup (#36) and the spring taken out of the frame.

The hammer and lower tang are shown removed from the action. Only one screw retains both.

3 To remove the hammer and lower tang and disassemble the lower tang: Close the lever and while holding the trigger (#47) to the rear, unscrew and remove the receiver (hammer) screw (#34). The hammer (#35) may now be removed by pulling it upward and to the rear out of the action. Open the lever and pull back on the lower tang (#38), which will come off by pulling it straight out the rear of the receiver (#19). The lower tang contains the trigger and its spring. Remove the trigger and sear spring screw (#42) from inside the lower tang and lift out the trigger and sear spring (#41). The trigger is removed through the bottom of the lower tang by first using a pin punch and hammer to drift out the trigger pin (#48) from the side of the lower tang.

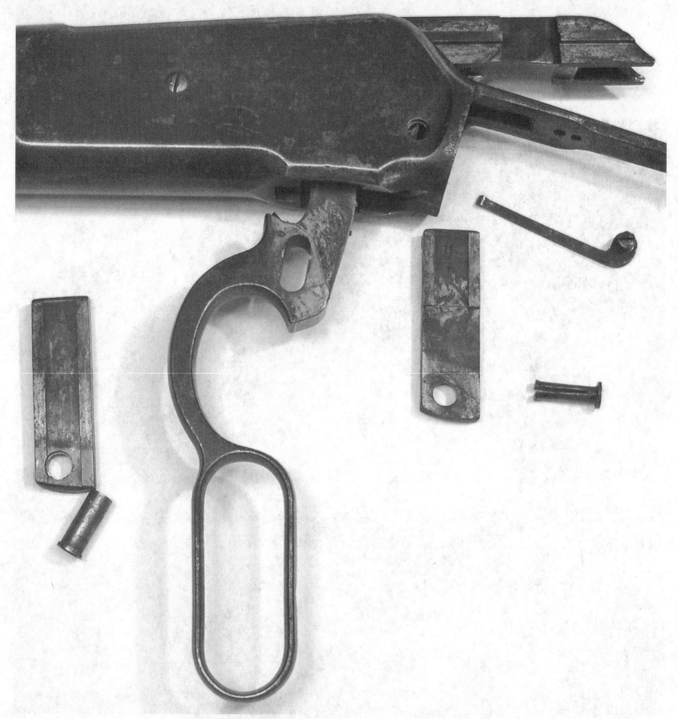

Here the finger lever bushing has been removed and as you can see, the locking bolts have been pulled down. The parts shown just below the upper tang are the carrier stop and its screw. These attach under the upper tang.

4 To disassemble the action: Remove the carrier stop screw (#51). The carrier stop (#50) can now be removed from behind the underside of the upper tang. Use a pin punch and hammer to drift out (from left to right) the finger lever bushing pin (#54) and remove the finger lever bushing (#56). This pin appears to be a slotted screw but it is actually a split pin. Remove the locking bolts (#53 Left) and (#52 Right) by

pulling them down and out of the receiver. Lower the finger lever and slide the breech bolt (#63) to the rear far enough to expose the lever and breechblock pin (#64). Use a hammer and pin punch to drift out the lever and breechblock pin (#64). This will disconnect the finger lever from the breech bolt (#63). The breech bolt assembly may be withdrawn through the rear of the receiver. Notice that the ejector (#65) is loose

The bolt has been mostly withdrawn, and the lever and breech bolt pin are about to be driven out of the bolt. Note the large pin punch is still in place. The parts to the left of the lever are the carrier and carrier hook.

now at the front of the breech bolt and can be pulled out the front of the breech bolt along with the ejector spring (#67) and ejector collar (#66). Pay careful attention to these parts for later assembly. The lever, along with the carrier #(61) and the carrier hook (#62), may be removed through the bottom of the receiver; pay attention to the relationships of these parts as you separate them. Remove the cartridge stop screw (#74) from the left side of the receiver and lift the cartridge stop (#73) out from inside of the receiver.

5 To disassemble the lever and breech bolt: Using a pin punch of appropriate size, drift the friction stud pin (#60) out of the finger lever (#57). This will free the friction stud (#58) and its spring (#59) so they can be pulled out of the hole in the finger lever. The extractor (#69) may be removed from the breech bolt by using a pin punch and hammer to drift out the extractor pin (#70). The extractor can now be removed by pulling it forward and up until it comes free of its seat in the breech bolt. The firing pin (#68) is removed by pulling it out the rear of the breech bolt.

The bolt and lever have been separated and the bolt is shown partially disassembled. Not shown is the ejector collar, which fits over the rear of the ejector shank.

TO DISASSEMBLE THE MAGAZINE TUBE AND FOREARM, RIFLES:

6 Remove the magazine plug screw (#3) from the very bottom front of the magazine tube (#1). The magazine tube cap (#2) is now loose and can be turned 1/4 turn with a screwdriver and then pulled out the front of the magazine tube along with the magazine spring (#4) and the magazine follower (#5). The plug will be under spring tension. Unscrew and remove the two fore-end tip (cap) screws (#9), one on each side of the forearm cap (#8), and slide the forearm cap forward slightly. Use a pin punch and hammer to drift out the magazine ring pin (#6) from the magazine ring (#7) and pull the magazine tube (#1) out toward the front. Once the tube is clear of the forearm wood, the forearm wood may be tilted down and pulled forward off the rifle. The magazine is then turned toward either side of the rifle 1/4 turn, which will free the magazine ring from its dovetail cut in the bottom of the barrel.

TO DISASSEMBLE THE MAGAZINE TUBE AND FOREARM, CARBINES:

6a Remove the magazine plug screw (#3) from the very bottom front of the magazine tube (#1). The magazine tube cap (#2) is now loose and can be pulled out the front of the magazine tube along with the magazine spring (#4) and the magazine follower (#5). Use caution: the plug will be under spring tension. Remove the front and rear band screws from the front and rear magazine bands. The magazine tube is pulled straight out the front and off the weapon. Slide the rear magazine band forward off the forearm wood so the forearm wood may be tilted down and pulled off to the front. The forward magazine band is now rotated one half-turn and slid off over the sight base, as is the rear magazine band.

REASSEMBLY

Reverse the above procedures for reassembly.

Model 1892 Winchester
Lever Action Rifle and Replicas

The EMF Hartford stainless steel '92 is a Rossi-built replica of the original Winchester. It's a surprisingly faithful copy but uses a coil mainspring in place of the original leaf spring. Author photos.

Many people have long held great admiration for Winchester's lever guns. Certainly they have long been a source of fascination for me, and the Model 1892 continues as one of my all-time favorites. The 1892 is yet another of those awesome John M. Browning designs that will always be hard to improve on although Winchester indeed managed to, since the 1892 is actually a simplified and somewhat smaller version of the 1886. Winchester intended the Model of 1892 to be the replacement for the venerable Model 1873, which was known worldwide as being both popular and dependable. The famous Winchester '73 evolved from the earlier Model 1866, the Henry, and Volcanic; its parentage derived from an 1850s Smith & Wesson design that was never known for the strength of its action. In addition, the 1873 was complicated and expensive for the company to manufacture. The altered

Browning design used in the 1892, on the other hand, was very strong, lightweight and much simplified, so it corrected all the '73's shortcomings in one tidy little package. Like the 1873 before it, the '92 was originally built to handle revolver cartridges, meaning a person could own a sixgun and rifle in the same caliber. Again, like the '73, the '92 was made in 44, 38 and 32 Winchester centerfire (WCF), the cartridges we have come to know as 44/40, 38/40 and 32/20.

So it was that Winchester's 1892 answered well for everything that the 1873 model lacked, and on top of that it weighed less than a comparable 1873. The famous Connecticut rifle company now had a truly dependable and brutally tough little lever action to take them into the new century. Folks who enjoy Winchesters will recognize right away that the 1892 looks like it might be a scaled down Model 1886 and that's what it essentially is. Actually, the 1892 is

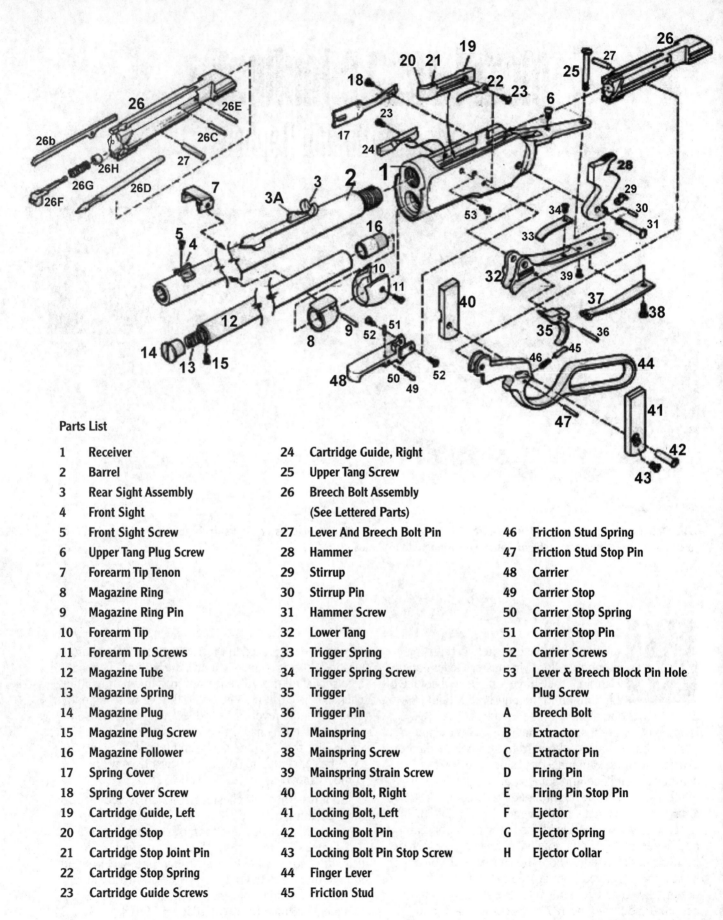

Parts List

1	Receiver	24	Cartridge Guide, Right
2	Barrel	25	Upper Tang Screw
3	Rear Sight Assembly	26	Breech Bolt Assembly
4	Front Sight		(See Lettered Parts)
5	Front Sight Screw	27	Lever And Breech Bolt Pin
6	Upper Tang Plug Screw	28	Hammer
7	Forearm Tip Tenon	29	Stirrup
8	Magazine Ring	30	Stirrup Pin
9	Magazine Ring Pin	31	Hammer Screw
10	Forearm Tip	32	Lower Tang
11	Forearm Tip Screws	33	Trigger Spring
12	Magazine Tube	34	Trigger Spring Screw
13	Magazine Spring	35	Trigger
14	Magazine Plug	36	Trigger Pin
15	Magazine Plug Screw	37	Mainspring
16	Magazine Follower	38	Mainspring Screw
17	Spring Cover	39	Mainspring Strain Screw
18	Spring Cover Screw	40	Locking Bolt, Right
19	Cartridge Guide, Left	41	Locking Bolt, Left
20	Cartridge Stop	42	Locking Bolt Pin
21	Cartridge Stop Joint Pin	43	Locking Bolt Pin Stop Screw
22	Cartridge Stop Spring	44	Finger Lever
23	Cartridge Guide Screws	45	Friction Stud

46	Friction Stud Spring
47	Friction Stud Stop Pin
48	Carrier
49	Carrier Stop
50	Carrier Stop Spring
51	Carrier Stop Pin
52	Carrier Screws
53	Lever & Breech Block Pin Hole
	Plug Screw
A	Breech Bolt
B	Extractor
C	Extractor Pin
D	Firing Pin
E	Firing Pin Stop Pin
F	Ejector
G	Ejector Spring
H	Ejector Collar

Rossi Lower Tang Assembly

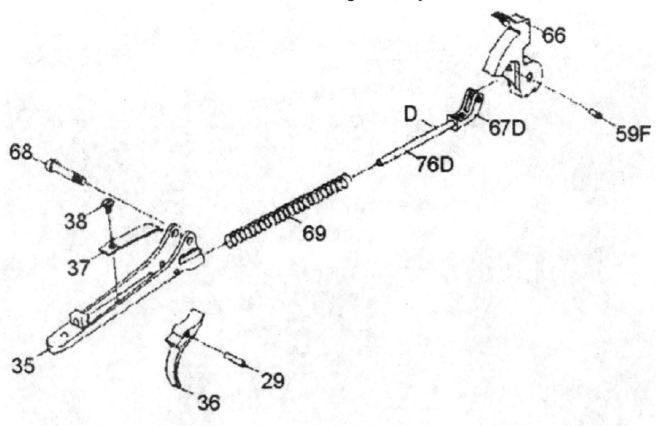

simpler than the 1886 was. It uses fewer internal parts but shares the rugged John Browning breech design. In addition, it has a firing pin retractor that will not let the gun fire until the bolt is locked.

Over a million 1892s were sold from the first in May of 1892 until the last Winchester Model 65 (which was an 1892 variant) sold in 1947: the design was in production for 55 years. There are few firearms designs that stand out as being exceptionally well engineered and built, but Winchester's 1892 is up near the top of that list for this author. Having handled hundreds of 1892s, the pattern I have seen is that this is one of those weapons that just doesn't quit. Aside from an occasional broken firing pin, a broken spring here and there, these are unusually dependable firearms.

The most popular caliber used in the 1892 was the 44/40, with almost 600,000 manufactured. Surprisingly, 25/20 was the next most popular with nearly 170,000 produced; the .32/20 was third with just a tad under 130,000 manufactured. The 38/40 brings up the rear with around 110,000 sold. Something on the order of about 640,000 rifles and 360,000 carbines were made, with Winchester's customers preferring the longer-barreled rifle over the carbine by a large percentage. The muskets were the scarcest Model 1892, with fewer than 600 of these weapons ever made. Always popular, the Winchester 1892 design has been revived in modern times by Rossi and Browning.

The EMF Hartford '92 in stainless, this one is chambered in 45 Colt. Photo courtesy of EMF Company.

Making sure the rifle is empty is your first chore. Never attempt any work on any firearm until you have done this.

DISASSEMBLY INSTRUCTIONS
(with additions for Rossi)

These basic instruction steps will also work for the following similar firearms: Winchester Models 53 and 65, Browning B92, Rossi manufacture M92 and Spanish "El Tigre."

1 Check first to be sure the weapon is unloaded. Point and hold the muzzle in a safe direction. Hold the rifle around the barrel and wooden forearm with your left hand and open the action by pulling the finger lever (#44) all the way down with your right hand. Check now to be absolutely certain there is no cartridge in the barrels chamber or lying in the cartridge carrier (#48) within the action. If there is a cartridge present in the carrier, when you close the lever the rifle will become loaded, and there may be more cartridges in the magazine. To safely unload a rifle with a loaded magazine, always be sure the muzzle stays pointed in a safe direction so that if there were an accidental discharge no one would be injured. Always keep your finger away from the trigger as you operate the lever to the fully open and fully closed positions several times to expel all the cartridges in the magazine.

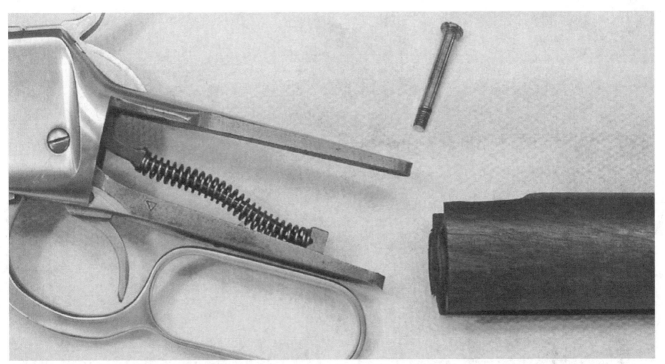

As is true of most Winchesters, removing the upper tang screw allows the buttstock to be pulled off to the rear. The rifle illustrated is the EMF stainless Hartford.

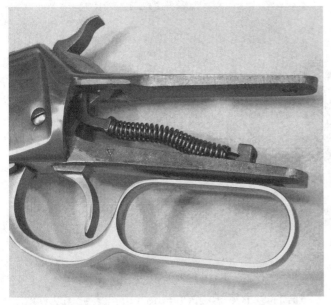

The Rossi 92. Notice the small pin we have inserted into the hole in the mainspring strut. This will hold the spring captive during disassembly.

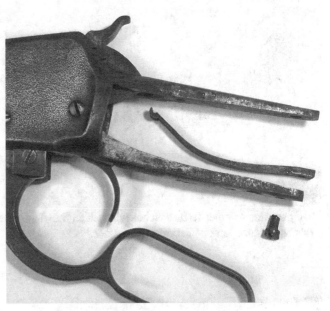

The Winchester with its mainspring removed.

2 Buttstock and mainspring removal, **Winchester:** Remove the upper tang screw (#25) from the upper tang. This is the rearmost of the two screws located behind the hammer. The buttstock is now loose and may be removed from the action (#1) by pulling it straight to the rear. Open the lever only far enough to give you access to the mainspring screw (#38), which is the rearmost screw on the lower action tang. Loosen and remove the mainspring screw. The mainspring (#37) can now be lifted out of its seat with the hammer stirrup (#29) and out of the frame.

Buttstock removal, Rossi (see inset): Remove the tang screw (#73) and pull off the buttstock (#70E) toward the rear.

Removing the hammer screw then holding back on the trigger allows the lower tang to be pulled off and the hammer to be removed. This photo shows an original Winchester 1892.

3 Hammer and lower tang removal and disassembly:

Winchester: Close the lever and while holding the trigger to the rear, remove the hammer screw (#31). The hammer (#28) can be removed by pulling it upward and to the rear. Open the lever and pull back on the lower tang (#39), which removes straight out through the rear of the action (#1). The lower tang contains the trigger and its spring. Remove the trigger spring screw (#34) from inside the lower tang and lift out the trigger spring (#33); note its position for reassembly. The trigger (#35) is removed through the bottom of the lower tang by first driving out the trigger pin (#36) from the side of the lower tang.

Rossi M92 (see inset): Pull the hammer (#66) toward the rear until the hole in the mainspring strut (#76D) becomes visible at the rear end of the mainspring (#69). Place a small pin or paper clip into the hole and allow the hammer to go down. Unscrew and remove the hammer screw (#68). Pull the trigger (#36) and slightly open the lever and slowly slide the tang assembly (#35) toward the rear and remove it. Close the lever to move the bolt all the way forward. The hammer assembly (#66, etc.) can be dropped out the bottom of the action. The lower tang contains the trigger and its spring. Remove the trigger spring screw (#38) from inside the lower tang and lift out the trigger spring (#37). The trigger (#36) is removed through the bottom of the lower tang by first drifting out the trigger pin (#29) from the side of the lower tang.

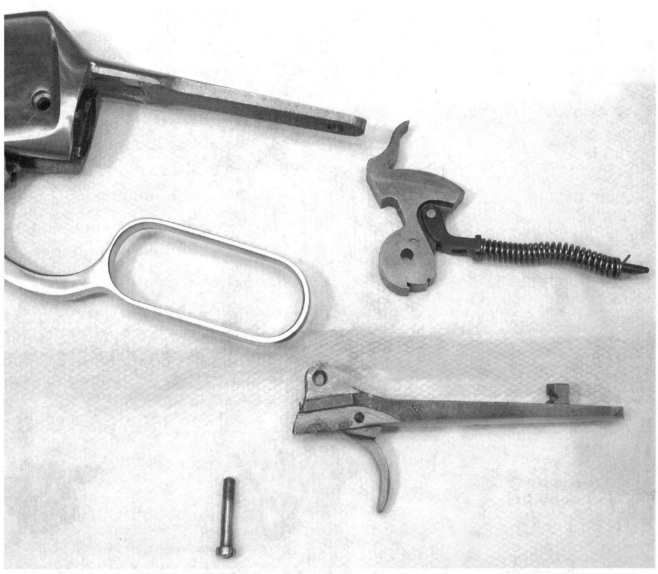

The same procedure allows the removal of the Rossi tang and hammer assembly. Note the mainspring is pinned so it stays captive.

The lower tang of either the Winchester or the Rossi (shown) has very few parts and is an easy disassembly.

Removing the locking bolt pin stop screw allows the locking bolt pin and locking bolts to be pulled out the bottom.

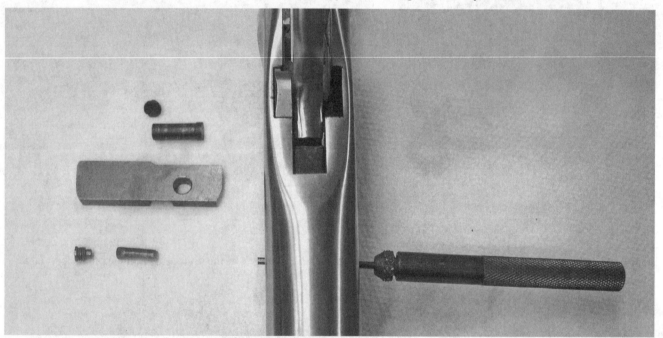

With one locking bolt installed to hold the bolt fully forward, the lever and breech block pin hole plug screw is removed and the lever and breech bolt pin is driven out from right to left with a long pin punch.

4 Action disassembly: Open the lever and remove the locking bolt pin screw (#43) from the left locking bolt. You can push out the locking bolt pin (#42) from right to left. The locking bolts (#40) and (#41) can be removed by sliding them out the bottom of the action. Note the positions of the locking bolts for reassembly: there is a right (#40) and a left (#41) side. Close the breech bolt (#26) by hand and slide one of the locking bolts back in place temporarily to hold the bolt closed in place. Remove the lever pin cover screw (#53), the front screw on the left side of the action.

Exactly opposite the locking bolt pin screw on the right side of the action you will see a small hole. Place a pin punch through this hole and drive out the lever and breech bolt pin (#27) from right to left. Remove the lever by pulling it straight out the bottom of the action and remove the temporarily installed locking bolt. The breech bolt (#26) can now be withdrawn out the rear of the action. Notice that the ejector (#26F) is now loose now at the front of the breech bolt and can be pulled out the front of the breech bolt along with the ejector spring (#26G) and ejector collar (#26H). Pay careful attention to these parts for later assembly.

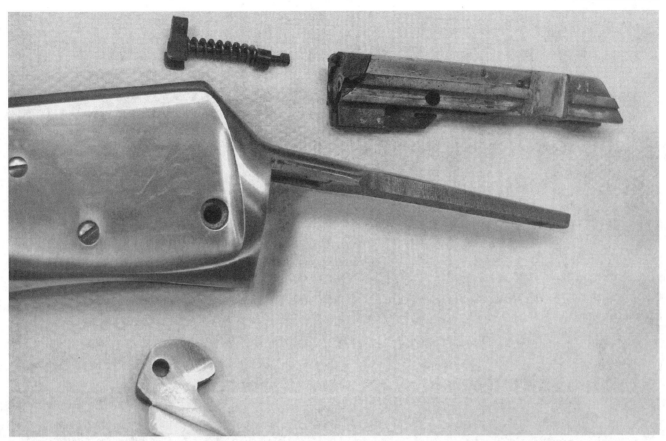

Once the lever and breech bolt pin is out, removing the locking bolt allows the breech bolt to be pulled to the rear and the lever dropped out the bottom. Pay attention to the ejector parts in the face of the breech bolt for later assembly.

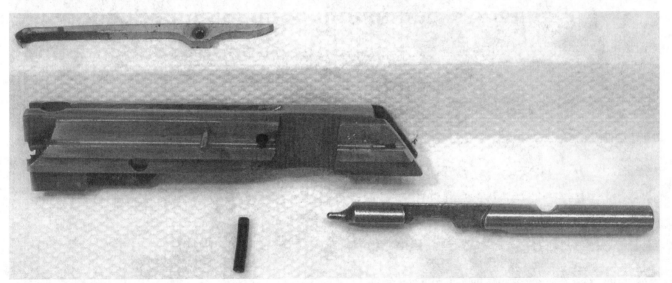

Model 1892 breech bolts also have very few parts. This Rossi bolt is shown completely disassembled.

5 Lever and breech bolt disassembly: Using a pin punch of appropriate size, drift out the friction stud stop pin (#47) from the side of the finger lever (#44). This will free the friction stop stud (#45) and its spring (#46) so they can be pulled out of the hole in the finger lever. The extractor (#26B) can be removed from the breech bolt by first drifting out the extractor pin (#26C). The extractor can be removed by pulling it forward and up until it comes free of its seat in the breech bolt. Drift out the firing pin stop pin (#26E) through the side of the breech bolt so the firing pin (#26D) can be removed by pulling it out the rear of the breech bolt.

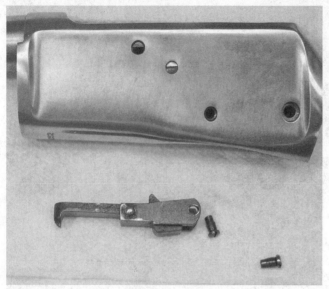

Removing the two carrier screws allows the carrier to be taken out.

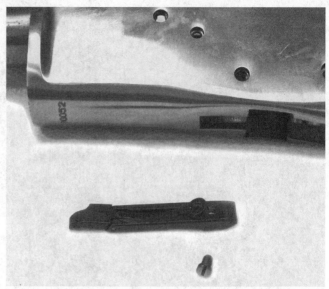

This is the left side cartridge guide. Notice the location of the leaf spring.

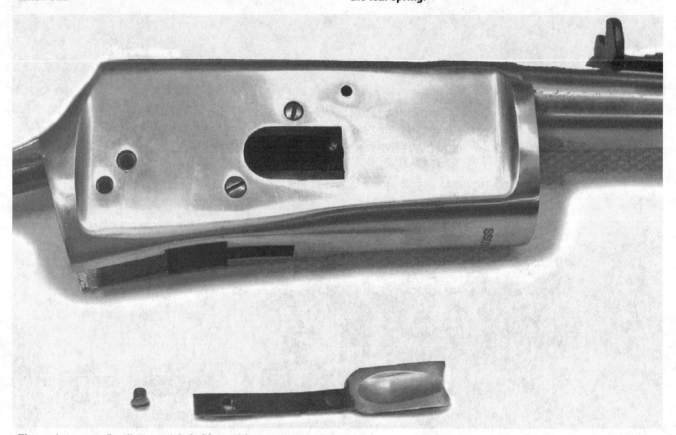

The spring cover (loading gate) is held on with one screw.

6 Further action disassembly: Remove the two carrier screws (#52), one from each side of the action. Move the carrier (#48) to the rear and pull it out the bottom of the action. The spring cover (#17) can now be removed by unscrewing and removing its screw (#18); this is the rearmost screw on the right side of the action. The spring cover (#17) will now fall loose and can be pulled out of the action. The last two screws in the action sides are called cartridge guide screws (#23). There is one on each side of the action and they hold the cartridge guides in place. Remove the screws one at a time and then the cartridge guides (#19) and (#24). Note the position of the cartridge stop spring (#22), which will remove along with the left side cartridge guide (#19).

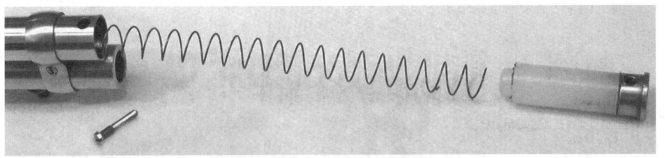

The Rossi carbine's magazine plug screw is removed and the plug, the spring and the follower all come out the front.

Removing the two barrel bands screws on a carbine frees up everything forward of the receiver (except the barrel) for quick removal.

MAGAZINE TUBE AND FOREARM DISASSEMBLY, RIFLES:

Remove the magazine plug screw (#15) from the very bottom front of the magazine tube (#12). The magazine tube cap (#14) is now loose and can be pulled out the front of the magazine tube along with the magazine spring (#13) and the magazine follower (#16). Remove the two fore-end tip (cap) screws (#11), one on each side of the forearm cap (#10), and slide the forearm cap forward slightly. Drift out the magazine ring pin (#9) from the magazine ring (#8) and pull the magazine tube (#12) out toward the front. Once the tube is clear of the forearm wood, the forearm wood can be tilted down and pulled forward off the rifle. The magazine is then turned toward either side of the rifle 1/4 turn, thus freeing the magazine ring from its dovetail cut in the bottom of the barrel.

MAGAZINE TUBE AND FOREARM DISASSEMBLY, CARBINES:

Remove the magazine plug screw (#15) from the very bottom front of the magazine tube (#12). The magazine tube cap (#14) is now loose and can be pulled out the front of the magazine tube along with the magazine spring (#13) and the magazine follower (#16). Remove the front and rear band screws from the front and rear magazine bands. The magazine tube can be pulled straight out the front and off the weapon. Slide the rear magazine band forward off the forearm wood so the forearm wood can be tilted down and pulled off to the front. The forward magazine band is now rotated one-half turn and slid off over the sight base, as is the rear magazine band.

8 Special reassembly notes: When you replace the breech bolt, be sure to assemble the ejector with its spring and collar into the bolt and then install the bolt with one of the locking bolts to hold it in the forwardmost position. This will hold the ejector components in place while you reinstall the lever and the lever and breech bolt pin. Remember also that we mentioned earlier to make note of the position of the cartridge stop spring (#22), which you will reinstall with the left side cartridge guide so the front of the spring fits in behind the cartridge stop.

REASSEMBLY

Reassemble the rifle in the reverse order of above.

Winchester Model 94

ere is a gun that literally needs no introduction (but we'll give it one anyway). The most successful, most popular lever action rifle of all time, the Winchester 94 has accounted for more deer, and probably everything else, than any other gun in history. It has also been in continuous production (except for the World War years) longer than any other American rifle. Few rifles – in fact, few guns of any type – reach a production total of 2,500,000, but the Model 94 reached that number – in 1961!

The brainchild of John M. Browning, the Model 94 has been made in innumerable variations, from the very early takedown models to carbines to muskets to commemoratives to the Big Bores to the Angle-Ejects to the 94/22 to the Models 55 and 64 (both of which were dandified 94s). The first rifle to chamber the first American smokeless cartridge, the equally-famous 30-30 Winchester, the 94 has also been chambered in 32-40, 38-55, 25-35, 32 Winchester Special, 7-30 Waters, 44 Magnum, 307 Winchester, 356 Winchester, 375 Winchester, 444 Marlin, .410 shotshell, and other cartridges. Various barrel lengths and wood options have been available over the years, making the 94 the collector's darling or his headache, depending on how you look at it.

It's difficult to overstate the influence the Model 94 has had on generations of American hunters over the years, and it is with a true sense of affection that we offer the following disassembly instructions, which are primarily applicable to pre-1964 models of the mighty Winchester Model 94.

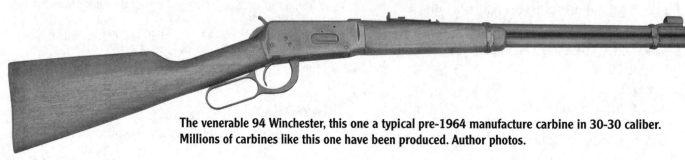

The venerable 94 Winchester, this one a typical pre-1964 manufacture carbine in 30-30 caliber. Millions of carbines like this one have been produced. Author photos.

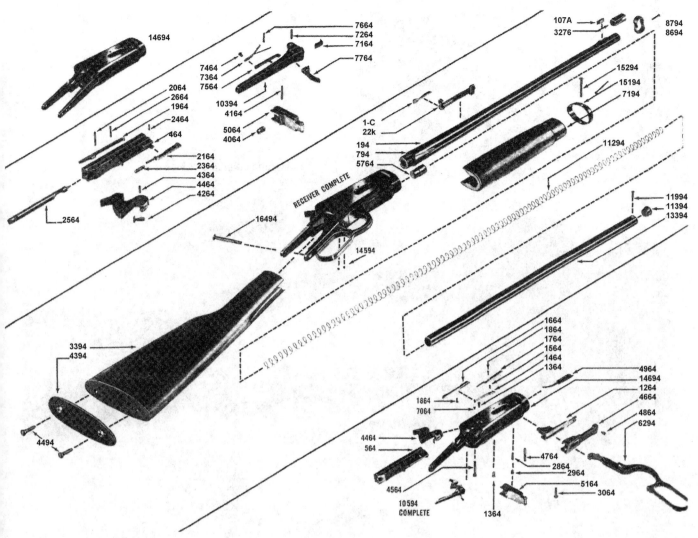

RECEIVER COMPLETE

10594 COMPLETE

Parts List (Representative)

194	Barrel	6294	Finger Lever	5664	Mainspring Strain Screw
464	Breech Bolt	2864	Finger Lever Pin	5764	Magazine Follower
3394	Buttstock	2964	Finger Lever Pin Stop Screw	11294	Magazine Spring
4394	Buttplate	3064	Finger Lever Link Screw	11394	Magazine Plug
4494	Buttplate Screws	7194	Forearm	11994	Magazine Plug Screw
1264	Carrier	8694	Front Band, Carbine	13393	Magazine Tube
1364	Carrier Screw	8794	Front Band Screw, Carbine	14594	Peep Sight Plug Screw
1464	Carrier Spring	3764	Friction Stud	14694	Receiver
1564	Carrier Spring Screw	3864	Friction Stud Spring	15194	Rear Band, Carbine
1664	Cartridge Guide, Right Hand	3964	Friction Stud Stop Pin	15294	Rear Band Screw, Carbine
1764	Cartridge Guide, Left Hand	4264	Hammer Stirrup	6964	Spring Cover
1864	Cartridge Guide Screw	4364	Hammer Stirrup Pin	7064	Spring Cover Screw
1964	Extractor	4464	Hammer	7164	Sear
2064	Extractor Pin	4564	Hammer Screw	7264	Sear Pin
2164	Ejector	4664	Link	7364	Sear & Safety Catch Spring
2364	Ejector Spring	4764	Link Pin	7464	Sear & Safety Catch Spring
2464	Ejector Stop Pin	4864	Link Pin Stop Screw		Screw
2564	Firing Pin	5064	Locking Bolt	7564	Safety Catch
4064	Firing Pin Striker	10394	Lower Tang	7664	Safety Catch Pin
4164	Firing Pin Striker Stop Pin	10694	Mainspring	7764	Trigger
2664	Firing Pin Stop Pin	5564	Mainspring Screw	16494	Upper Tang Screw

The 1894 action open and unloaded.

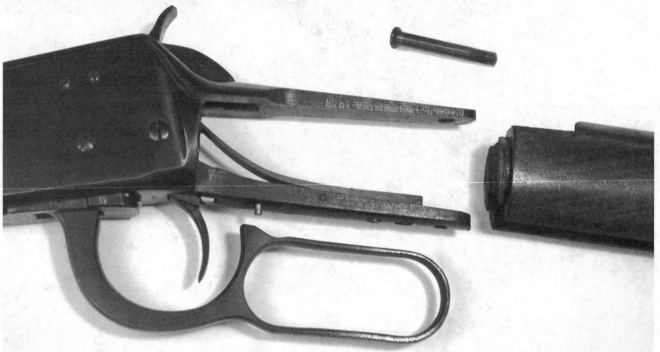

Removing the buttstock is a simple matter and begins to expose the interior of the rifle.

DISASSEMBLY INSTRUCTIONS
(pre-1964 Winchester parts nomenclature)

1 First, be sure the rifle is unloaded. Hold the rifle around the barrel and wooden forearm with your left hand, point the muzzle in a safe direction, and then open the action by pulling the finger lever (#6294) all the way down with your right hand. Check to be absolutely certain there is no cartridge in the barrel's chamber, and also look to be sure there is no cartridge lying in the cartridge carrier (#1294) within the action. If there is a cartridge in the carrier then when you close the lever, the rifle will be loaded. To safely unload a rifle with a loaded magazine: Always be sure the muzzle stays pointed in a safe direction. Keep your finger away from the trigger while you operate the lever to the fully open and fully closed positions several times to expel all the cartridges in the magazine.

2 To remove the buttstock and mainspring: Remove the upper tang screw (#16494) from the upper tang (this is the rearmost of the two screws located behind the hammer). The buttstock assembly (#3394) is now loose and can be removed from the receiver (#14694) by pulling it straight to the rear. Open the lever only far enough to give you access to the mainspring screw (#5564), which is the rearmost screw on the lower action tang. Loosen and remove the mainspring screw so the mainspring (#10694) can be lifted out of its seat with the hammer stirrup (#4264) and out of the frame.

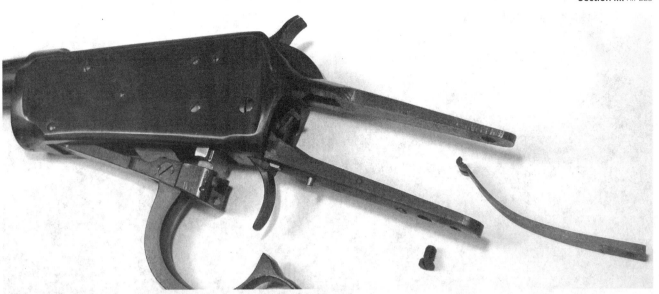

Next, the mainspring is removed. Be sure to have the hammer down.

Removing the hammer screw allows the hammer and lower tang assembly to be removed.

3 To remove and disassemble the hammer and lower tang: Close the finger lever and while holding the trigger to the rear, remove the hammer screw (#4564). The hammer (#4464) can be removed by pulling it upward and to the rear out of the action. Open the finger lever and pull back on the lower tang (#10394), which can be removed straight out the rear of the receiver (#14694). The lower tang contains the trigger and its spring. Remove the trigger stop spring screw (#7494) from inside the lower tang and lift out the trigger stop spring (#7394). The trigger (#7764) is removed through the bottom of the lower tang by first drifting out the trigger pin from the side of the lower tang and then the trigger and the sear (#7164) can be lifted out of the lower tang. Note their positions for reassembly.

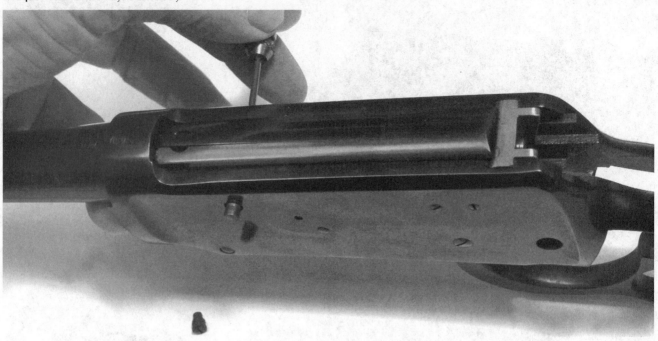

After the finger lever pin screw has been removed, the finger lever pin is driven out from right to left, using a long 1/8-inch pin punch.

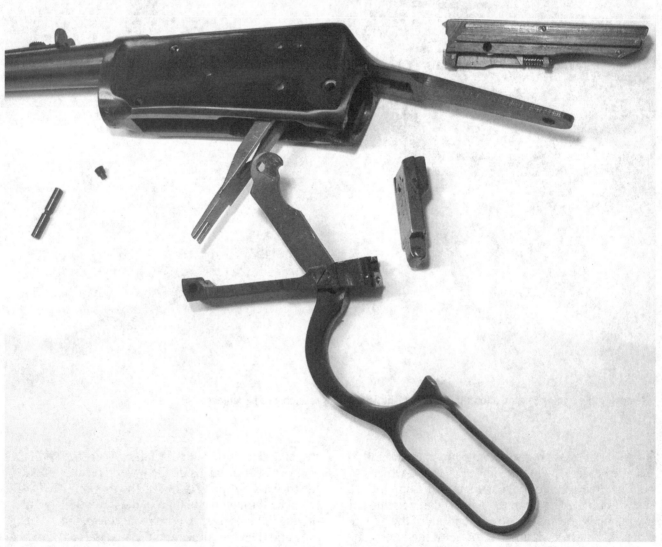

Once the finger lever pin screw is removed and the link pin taken out, the majority of the action can be removed from the receiver as shown here.

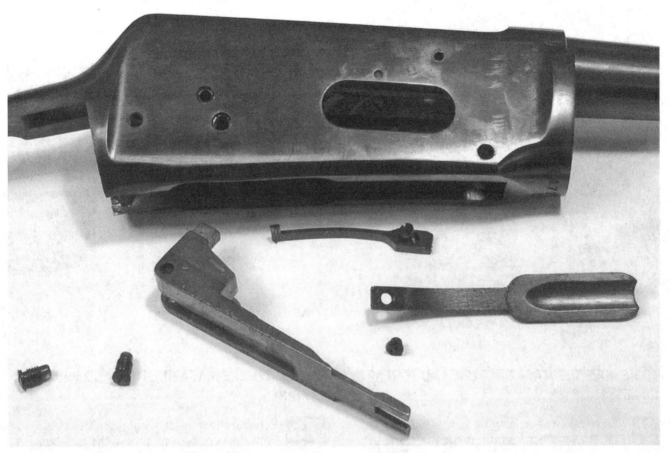

In this shot the spring cover (loading gate), the carrier and its screws have been removed.

4 To disassemble the action: With the finger lever (#6294) closed, remove the finger lever pin stop screw (#2964), the front screw on the left side of the action. Exactly opposite from this finger lever pin stop screw on the right side of the action, you will see a small hole. Use a pin punch through this hole to drive out the finger lever pin (#2864) from right to left. Remove the link pin stop screw (#4864) from the center of the link (#4664) and push out the link pin (#4764) from either side. Pull back and down slightly on the link to disengage it from the receiver. You can now remove the finger lever, link and locking bolt (#5064) as an assembly by pulling them straight down out of the receiver. Pay attention to how these parts fit together for later reassembly. Reach down into the receiver from the top and push the carrier (#1264) until its front is hanging out through the bottom of the receiver. The breech bolt (#464) can now be slid out through the rear of the receiver.

5 To disassemble the lever and link: The locking bolt is removed from the link by simply pulling it rearward. Unscrew and remove the finger lever link screw (#3064) and pull the finger lever down out through the link. The extractor (#1964) can be removed from the breech bolt (#494) by first drifting out the extractor pin (#2064). The extractor can

now be removed by pulling it forward and up until it comes free of its seat in the breech bolt. Drift out the firing pin stop pin (#2094) through the side of the breech bolt. The firing pin (#2564) can be removed by pulling it out the rear of the breech bolt. The ejector (#2164) and its spring (#2364) can be removed from the lower front of the breech bolt by driving out the ejector stop pin (#2464).

6 Further action disassembly: Remove the spring cover screw #7064) from the right action side and lift out the spring cover (#6964). Reach through the spring cover opening with a small screwdriver and remove the carrier spring screw (#1564). The carrier spring (#1464) can now be carefully pried up out of its mortise in the frame. Remove the two carrier screws (#1364) one from each side of the action. Remove the carrier (#1264) by pulling it out the bottom of the action. The last two screws are called cartridge guide screws (#1864). There is one on each side of the action; they are accessible only from the inside and they hold the cartridge guides in place. Remove the screws one at a time and then the cartridge guides (#1964 Right) and (#1764 Left). Note their positions for reassembly. For normal cleaning, it is not necessary to remove the cartridge guides.

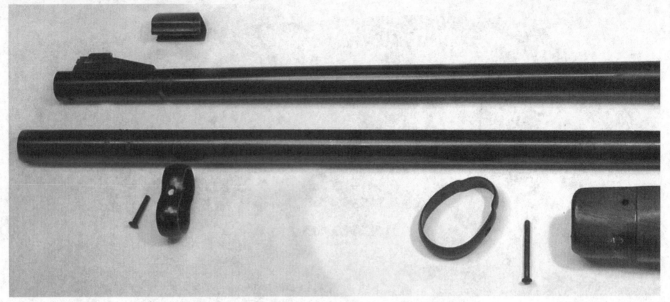

The magazine, bands and forearm shown disassembled from the barrel.

TO REMOVE THE MAGAZINE TUBE AND FOREARM, RIFLES:

7 Remove the magazine plug screw (#11994) from the very bottom front of the magazine tube (#13394). The magazine tube cap (#11394) is now loose and can be pulled out the front of the magazine tube along with the magazine spring (#11294) and the magazine follower (#5764). Remove the two forearm tip (cap) screws (not illustrated) one on each side of the forearm cap (not illustrated) and slide the forearm cap forward slightly. Drift out the magazine ring pin (not illustrated) from the magazine ring (not illustrated) and pull the magazine tube (#13394) out toward the front. Once the tube is clear of the forearm wood (#7194), the forearm wood can be tilted down and pulled forward off the rifle. The magazine is then turned toward either side of the rifle one-quarter turn, thus freeing the magazine ring from its dovetail cut in the bottom of the barrel.

TO REMOVE THE MAGAZINE TUBE AND FOREARM, CARBINES:

7a Remove the magazine plug screw (#11994) from the very bottom front of the magazine tube (#13394). The magazine tube cap (#11364) is now loose and can be pulled out the front of the magazine tube along with the magazine spring (#11294) and the magazine follower (#5764). Remove the front (#8794) and rear (#15294) band screws from the front (#18694) and rear (#15194) magazine bands. The magazine tube is pulled straight out the front and off the weapon. Slide the rear magazine band forward off the forearm wood. The forearm wood can be tilted down and pulled off to the front. The forward magazine band is now rotated one half-turn and slid off over the sight base, as is the rear magazine band.

REASSEMBLY

Reassemble rifle in the reverse order of above.

SECTION IV
SHOTGUNS

Colt Model 1883
Hammerless Shotgun

The Colt 1883 hammerless double shotgun was a very high-quality shotgun. Its workmanship was every bit as good as a Parker. Author photos.

When we think about the year 1883 and shotguns, a picture of a double barrel with outside hammers comes quickly to mind, but that was not necessarily the whole picture. The Colt Model 1883 hammerless double shotgun was produced at Colt's factory in Hartford, Conn., from 1883 to about 1895, during which time they manufactured a total of 7,366 guns. These were excellent-quality double-barreled shotguns, hammerless and were sold in both 10 and 12 gauge with barrel lengths of 28, 30 and 32 inches. As with any high grade gun, other barrel lengths and special

features were available on special order. Damascus barrels were standard, with optional "finest Damascus barrels" available for those who were willing to pay a bit more for a more handsome pattern.

Although Colt's Model 1883 shotgun was produced in limited numbers, these hammerless doubles were truly as good as such guns got. Probably their greatest competition, which would have been stiff, came from other high-quality double-barreled shotguns such as the American-made Parker and L.C. Smith as well as the finer British shotguns.

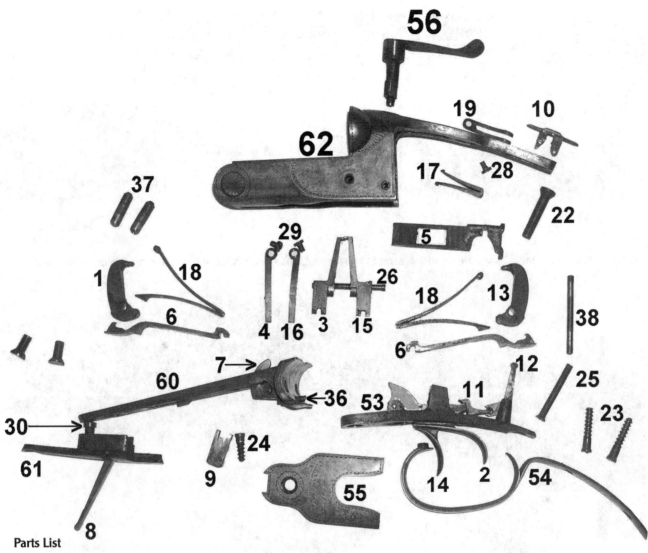

Parts List

(NI) = not illustrated

1	Left Hammer	22	Tang Screw	44	Extractor Cam Pin
2	Left Trigger	23	Guard Bow Screws	45	Hammer Roll (NI)
3	Left Sear	24	Fore End Strap Screws	46	Hammer Roll Pin (NI)
4	Left Sear Spring	25	Small Tang Screw	47	Draw Bore Pin (NI)
5	Action Bolt or Locking Bolt	26	Sear Screw	48	Mainspring Roll (NI)
6	Draw Bar	27	Extractor Screw	49	Fore End Lever Spring (NI)
7	Extractor Cam or Ejector Hook	28	Safety Spring Screw	50	Joint Pin or cocking Hinge (NI)
8	Forend Lever	29	Sear Spring Screw	51	Extractor (NI)
9	Forend Lever Bolt	30	Fore End Lever Plate Screw	52	Extractor Screws (NI)
10	Safety Slide or Safety Lever	31	Lock Cover Plate Screw	53	Trigger Plate
11	Safety Catch or Safety Bar Cam	32	Trigger Screw	54	Triggerguard bow
12	Safety Lever	33	Safety Lever Screw	55	Lock Cover Plate or Floorplate
13	Right Hammer	34	Fore End Lever Spring Screw	56	Top Lever
14	Right Trigger	35	Trigger Spring Screw	57	Buttplate (NI)
15	Right Sear	36	Extractor Push Pin	58	Forend Wood (NI)
16	Right Sear Spring	37	Cocking Hinge Screw Pin	59	Buttstock (NI)
17	Action Spring	38	Hammer Pin	60	Forend Iron
18	Mainspring	39	Safety Slide Pin	61	Forend Release Assembly
19	Safety Spring	40	Safety Catch Pin	62	Receiver
20	Trigger Spring	41	Extractor Cam Stop Pin	63	Barrel Set
21	Buttplate Screw	42	Forend Lever Pin		
		43	Forend Lever Step		

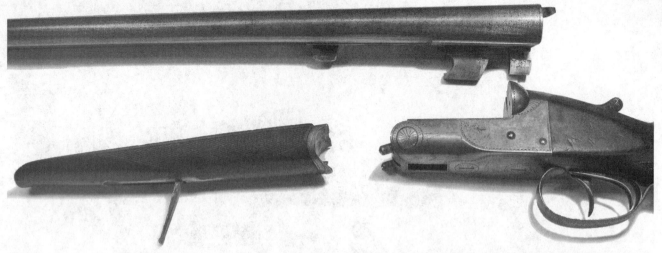

Pulling down on the forend lever allows the forearm to be removed, and then it is a simple matter to remove the barrels.

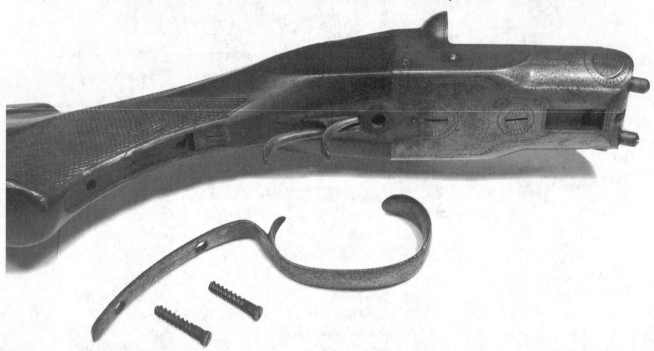

Remove the two guard screws and spin the guard about two turns counterclockwise to remove it from the action.

DISASSEMBLY INSTRUCTIONS

First, make sure the gun is unloaded. Hold the shotgun around the wrist of the grip and be sure you keep your fingers away from the triggers (#2) and (#14). Always keep the muzzles pointing in a safe direction. Open the shotgun by pushing the rear of the top lever (#56) toward the right and swing or break open the barrels (#63) downward, so they pivot away from the receiver (#62). Check the chambers to be certain there are no shells in them. If there are shells present in the chambers, lift them out and remove them to a safe location.

When working with any side-by-side double, it is a very good idea to have three parts containers on the bench: one marked right, one left, and one for universal parts, such as the safety. In this way it is easy to keep the left and right parts straight for reassembly later.

1 To remove the forend and the barrels: Close the barrels and turn the gun so its bottom is facing up. Operate the forend lever (#8) by pulling it up by its front end; the forend assembly can now be removed from the gun by pulling it up away from the barrels and forward. Now pick up the gun and turn it right side up. Operate the top lever once again and break open the barrels as before. When they are open, lift them up and slightly to the rear to remove them from the receiver.

After the three screws shown have been removed, the trigger plate assembly can be pulled out the bottom and the action lifted up slightly and slid forward out of the wood.

2 To remove the trigger assembly and the buttstock: Unscrew and remove the two screws (#23) at the rear of the triggerguard bow (#54). Pull the rear of the guard bow away from its inletting in the buttstock and rotate the entire guard bow about two full turns in a counterclockwise direction until it falls off the bottom of the trigger plate (#53). Unscrew and remove the small tang screw (#25) from the rear of the lower tang and the large tang screw (#22) from the upper tang, the latter being located under the top lever so you will have to hold the top lever to the right. Remove the screw from the front of the trigger plate (no part number given; this is the rearmost of the two large screws facing up on the bottom of the receiver, just in front of the trigger guard). Use a small wooden mallet or hammer handle to tap the side of the receiver in order to cause the trigger plate to be shocked up out of its seat, and then lift the trigger plate assembly off from the bottom of the receiver. Tilt the buttstock (#59) down, and gently ease it off the receiver by moving it to the rear and down.

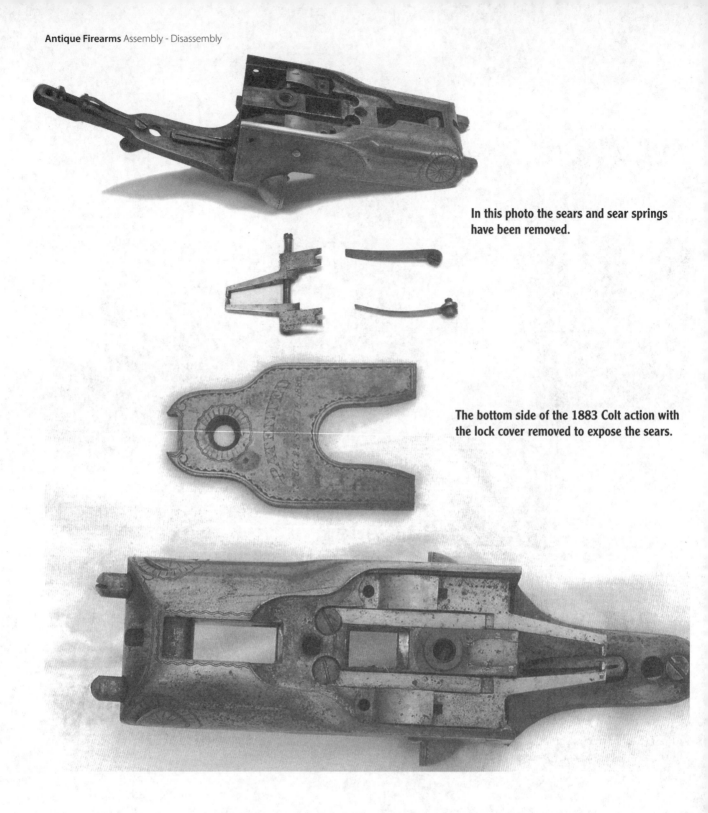

In this photo the sears and sear springs have been removed.

The bottom side of the 1883 Colt action with the lock cover removed to expose the sears.

3 To open the action and remove the sears: Remove the lock cover plate screw (#31), the forwardmost of the two large screws facing up on the bottom of the receiver, in front of the trigger guard. Use a small wooden mallet or plastic hammer to tap the side of the receiver, which will cause the lock cover plate (#55) to be shocked up out of its seat with the receiver. Lift off the lock cover plate to expose the action. Push on the rear of both the left (#3) and right (#15) sears to allow the hammers to fall. From the bottom of the action, loosen and remove the two trigger spring screws (#35) and lift out the trigger springs (#20). Note: Pay close attention to which spring is left and right so they can be reassembled correctly.

Now unscrew and remove the sear screw (#26). This is the screw located at the lower rear of the right side of the receiver) and lift out both the left (#3) and the right (#15) sears, paying attention to which sear is from which side so they can be reassembled correctly.

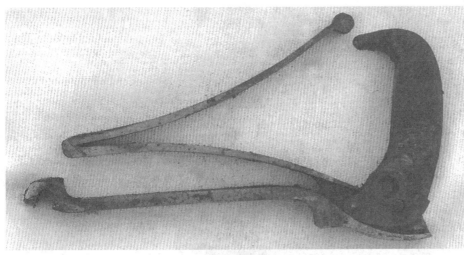

This photo illustrates what the components of the hammer-mainspring-drawbar assembly should look like for reassembly. Illustrated are the right side parts.

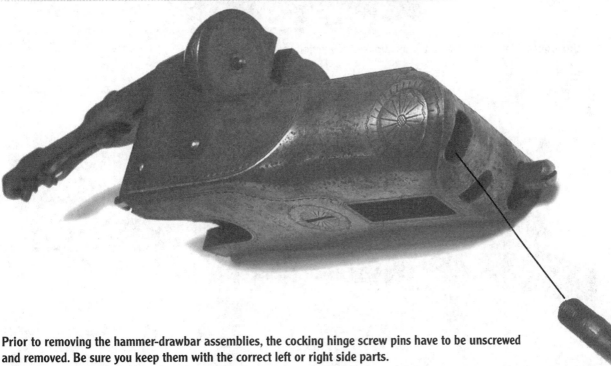

Prior to removing the hammer-drawbar assemblies, the cocking hinge screw pins have to be unscrewed and removed. Be sure you keep them with the correct left or right side parts.

4 Removing the hammers, mainsprings and draw bars: This next operation sounds tricky, and it is just a bit, but once you have done it you will understand how truly simple it is. Carefully clamp the receiver, bottom facing up, in a padded vise. Unscrew and remove the two cocking hinge screw pins (#37) from the front. Be sure you place these in separate left and right marked containers to avoid confusion later.

Now use a cup-tipped pin punch and hammer to drive out the hammer pin (#38). Use a screwdriver blade to push the tips of both firing pins into the receiver and push rearward on the left hammer-drawbar (#1) and (#6) assembly from the bottom. Use restraint and keep your thumb over the rear of the hammer because as the assembly slides to the rear, the mainspring (#18) will become decompressed. Carefully slide the hammer (#1), the drawbar (#6)

and the mainspring (#18) to the rear and lift them out of the receiver, being very cautious as you do this to note their relative positions for reassembly. Place the parts in your container marked "left." Before you do anything else, note the exact position of the hinge pin, which is the large, (often) engraved round pin at the front of the action on which that the barrels pivot, and mark its position on the outside of the action with a black marker. The reason for this is that the draw bars must hook back onto the cams on the hinge pin during reassembly, so the position of this pin is critical.

At this point you can remove the right side hammer (#13), drawbar (#6) and mainspring #18) exactly as you did with the left side, placing them in the container marked "right." The hinge pin can be removed from the side, but make sure you have marked its correct position (see above) for reassembly.

The 1883 action upside down, illustrating the locations of the action spring and bolt.

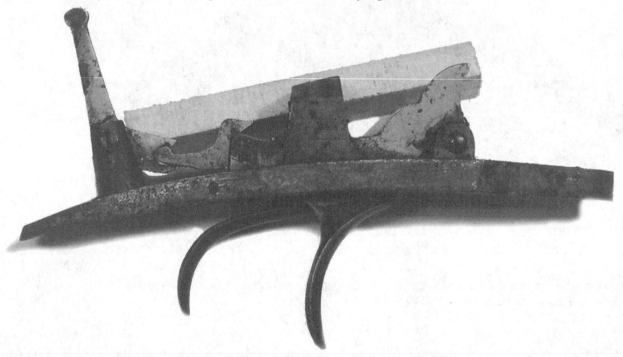

The 1883 trigger and safety assembly. In this photo the safety is on.

5 Further action disassembly: Looking up into the bottom of the upper tang, pry out and carefully remove the action spring (#17). Use caution to keep this captive while you are removing it; this spring supplies tension to the top lever. Rotate the top lever about 90 degrees to the right and lift it straight up and out of the receiver. The locking bolt (#5) can now be withdrawn to the rear and removed from the receiver. Unscrew and remove the safety spring screw (#28) from the underside of the upper tang and drive out the two safety slide pins #39) from the underside of safety slide (#10). The safety slide can now be pulled out from the top.

6 To disassemble the trigger plate: Unscrew and remove the safety lever screw (#33) and lift off the safety lever (#12). Drive out the safety catch pin (#40) and lift out the safety catch (#11). Unscrew and remove the trigger spring screw (#35) and lift out the trigger spring (#20). Unscrew and remove the trigger screw (#32) and pull both triggers (#2 Left) and (#14 Right) out the bottom of the trigger plate (#53). Carefully place each trigger in the proper (left or right) container.

To disassemble the forearm: Open the forend release lever (#61) and unscrew and remove the forend lever plate screw (#30), the larger-headed screw in the

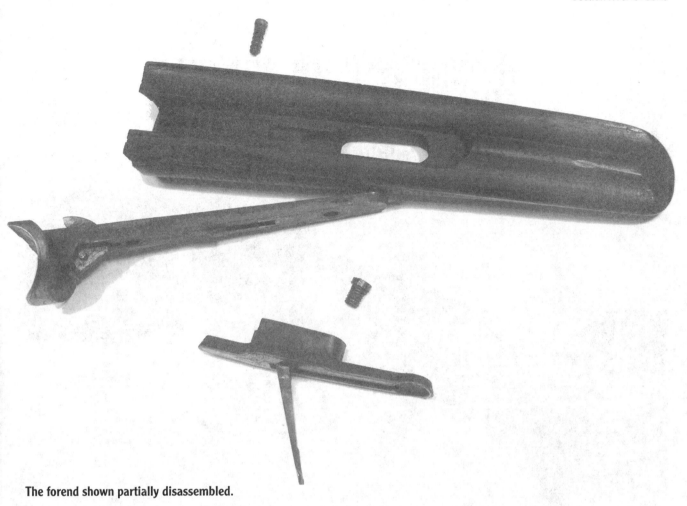

The forend shown partially disassembled.

top of the forend iron). The forend release assembly will drop out the bottom. Use caution: the forend lever bolt (#9) is now loose and can be lifted off the top of the forend release assembly. Use a pin punch and hammer to drift out the forend lever pin (#42) from the side of the forend release assembly. This will free the forend lever (#8), the forend lever spring (#49) and forend lever step (#43) for removal. Unscrew and remove the remaining screw in the top of the forend iron; this is the forend strap screw (#24). The forend

iron can now be lifted up and to the rear for removal from the wood (#58). Use a pin punch and hammer to drive out the extractor cam pin (#44) from the side of the forend iron and lift out the extractor cam (#7). The extractor push pin (#36) can now be lifted out toward the front of the forend iron.

REASSEMBLY

Reverse the procedure for reassembly.

Parker 10 Bore Hammer
Double Shotgun

P arker Brothers, of Meriden, Conn., was founded around 1866 by Charles Parker in partnership with his sons Wilbur and Dexter. In 1934, the firm was acquired by Remington Arms Company, which continued to manufacture Parker-labeled shotguns until 1938. Parker hammer-fired shotguns were available in 14 grades, ranging from the relatively plain-Jane "U" utility-grade gun to the "AA Pigeon Gun." The 10- and 12-gauge guns are the most commonly encountered, with other gauges being rarities.

The name "Parker" has become synonymous with excellence in the sphere of American-made shotguns.

All Parkers – of any grade or vintage – are prized collector's pieces, even the early Damascus barrel models that should never be fired, though some may argue this point. Parker manufactured hammer-fired shotguns from the company's founding until around 1920, so much of the production of this type occurred well before the introduction of high-pressure smokeless powders.

Early Parker hammerguns used a breech locking mechanism called the "lifter action"; however, the following instructions apply to the later top-lever designs.

The venerable Parker Brothers shotguns are an American legend. The gun we are working with here is a hammer double in 10 gauge made in the late 1870's. Author photos.

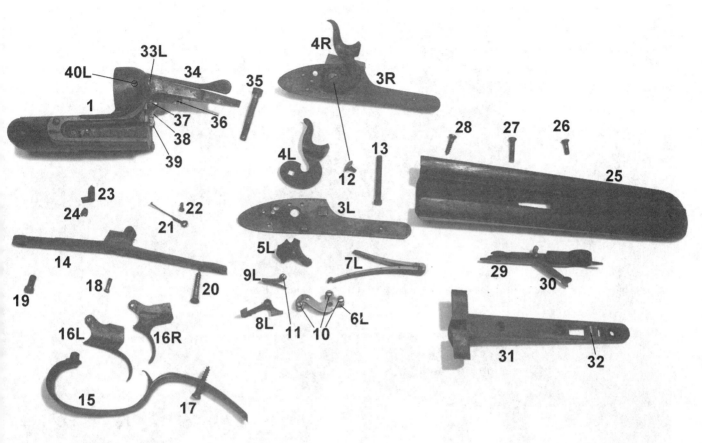

Parts List

1	Frame	16	Trigger	31	Forend Iron
2	Barrel Set	17	Triggerguard Screw	32	Forend Lock
3	Lock Plate	18	Trigger Screw	33	Firing Pin
4	Hammer	19	Front Trigger Plate Screw	34	Top Lever
5	Tumbler	20	Rear Trigger Plate Screw	35	Receiver Main Screw
6	Bridle	21	Trigger Spring	36	Top Lever Spring
7	Mainspring	22	Trigger Spring Screw	37	Top Lever Screw
8	Sear	23	Top Lever Stop	38	Top Lever Link
9	Sear Spring	24	Top Lever Stop Spring	39	Bolt
10	Bridle Screws	25	Forend Wood	40	Firing Pin Retaining Screw
11	Sear Spring Screw	26	Forend Iron Screw, Front	41	Extractor (Not Shown)
12	Hammer Screw	27	Forend Iron Screw, Middle	42	Extractor Screw (Not Shown)
13	Lock Plate Screw	28	Forend Iron Screw, Rear	43	Buttstock (Not Shown)
14	Trigger Plate	29	Opening Lever Frame	44	Buttplate (Not Shown)
15	Triggerguard	30	Opening Lever	45	Buttplate Screws (Not Shown)

Always open up the gun and check the chambers to be sure you are working with an empty firearm.

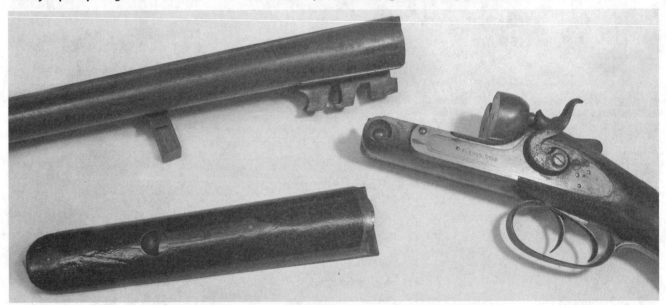

Removing the barrel set on most doubles is a very simple task.

DISASSEMBLY INSTRUCTIONS

1 First, always check first to be sure the weapon is empty before performing any work. Hold the shotgun around the forearm (#25) and barrels (#2), being careful to keep your fingers away from the triggers (#16L) and (#16R). Use your other hand to push the top lever (#34) to the right and open the barrels; they will tilt toward the floor, exposing the chambers. If any shells are present in the chambers, lift them out. Remove any live ammunition to a separate location.

2 To remove the forearm and barrel set: Close the barrels. Turn the shotgun over and pull down on the opening lever (#30), thus freeing the forearm assembly to be pulled down at the front and removed from the barrels. Operate the top lever again and this time, when the barrels have opened, push them slightly to the rear and lift them up and out of the frame (#1).

One screw at the rear holds both locks firmly on the gun. The front of each lock has a machined lip that fits tightly into a mortise in the frame.

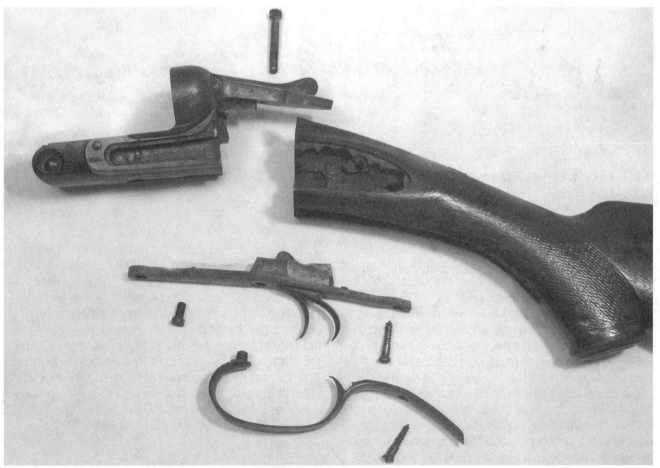

Removing the wood on the Parker takes some effort but it's actually easy.

The left side Parker lock, disassembled. The right is a reversed twin.

3 To remove the locks and triggerguard: Unscrew the lock plate screw (#13) and gently tap its head; this will cause the right hand lock (#3R) assembly to move away from the frame and stock at the rear. Pull the right lock to the rear and off the frame. Use a long punch to reach through an opening in the right side of the stock and tap the rear of the left lock plate (#3L) until it can be removed from the frame, exactly as the right lock plate was. Unscrew and remove the triggerguard screw (#17) and tap the rear of the trigger uard (#15) with a plastic mallet to break it free. Pull the rear of the guard tang out slightly, away from its seat in the buttstock, and then rotate the triggerguard several turns in a counterclockwise direction to unscrew its bow from the trigger plate (#14).

4 To remove the action from the stock: Unscrew and remove the front (#19) and rear (#20) trigger plate screws. Hold the top lever to the right and unscrew the main action screw (#35) from the top. Gently tap the head of the main action screw downward to cause the trigger plate to loosen from its fit in the buttstock. Lift off the trigger plate (#14) from the buttstock (#43) and carefully separate the buttstock from the frame. Take careful note of the top lever stop (#23) and the top lever stop spring (#24), which are now loose, for correct reassembly.

This close-up shows the top lever and bolt mechanism.

5 To disassemble a lock: Use a machinist's clamp or mainspring vise to compress the mainspring (#7) and disengage it from the stirrup (not illustrated) on the tumbler. Lift the mainspring off the lock plate (#3). Unscrew and remove the three bridle screws (#10) and lift off the bridle (#6). Loosen the hammer screw (#12) and, holding the lock in your hand, gently tap the head of the hammer screw to break the hammer (#4) loose from the tumbler (#5). Remove the hammer screw and lift off the hammer, and then lift out the tumbler (#5) from the inside of the lock plate. Unscrew the sear spring screw (#9) and lift off the sear spring (#9). The sear (#8) can be lifted off its pin on the lock plate.

6 To disassemble the frame: Use a small machinist's clamp to compress the top lever spring (#36) and pull it off the bottom of the frame.

Unscrew the top lever lock screw (not shown; it is on the inside of the left side of the frame, just under the top-lever). Unscrew the two screws from the top lever link and lift the top lever (#34) out the top of the action and the link (#38) out the rear. The bolt (#39) can now be pulled out the rear. The firing pins can be removed by first unscrewing the firing pin screws (#40) and pulling the firing pins (#33) out to the rear, along with their coil springs (not shown). Further disassembly of the lock frame is not normally required.

7 To disassemble the trigger plate (#14): Unscrew and remove the trigger spring screw (#22) and lift out the trigger spring (#21), noting as you do how it engages the triggers. Remove the trigger screw (#18) and pull first the left (#16L) and then the right (16R) trigger out the bottom of the trigger plate.

The Parker is similar to many double shotguns in that removing the extractor requires the removal of only one screw.

To remove the firing pins, the retaining screw for each pin, shown here, must be unscrewed first, not always an easy task on an old, rusty shotgun!

8 To disassemble the forearm: Unscrew the forend iron screw, front (#26) and the forend iron screw, middle (#27). Gently tap the head of each screw, alternating between the two to push the opening lever frame (#29) out the bottom of the forearm wood (#25). Unscrew and remove the forend iron screw, rear (#28) and gently slide the forend iron to the rear and out of the wood. Further disassembly is not normally required.

9 To remove the extractor: Unscrew and remove the extractor screw (#42) from the bottom of the barrels (#2) near the rear and withdraw the extractor (#41) out through the rear of the barrel set.

REASSEMBLY

Reverse the procedures to reassemble the shotgun.

The L.C. Smith Double-Barreled Shotgun

The famous L.C. Smith hammerless double. This basic design remained nearly unchanged from 1886 through about 1950. Author photos.

These good-quality, double-barreled shotguns were based on shotguns made starting about 1880 by the L. C. Smith Company of Syracuse, New York. The name L.C. Smith was first applied in 1884 to a line of hammer shotguns; the hammerless L.C. Smith was introduced about 1886. Beginning around 1889, L. C. Smith shotguns were manufactured by the Hunter Arms Co., Inc., of Fulton, New York. Hunter Arms Company also made the Fulton, Hunter and other brands of shotguns, including some private-brand shotguns in addition to the L. C. Smith line.

L. C. Smith double-barrel shotguns are unique among American doubles because of their side-lock construction in which the lock parts are contained on side-plates that are partly inletted into the steel

of the action and partly into the walnut buttstock. Hunter Arms adopted the Baker top-bolt for holding the barrels closed. This bolt was a rotating cylinder slotted to engage an extension of the top rib between the barrels, with a sloped locking surface that tightened automatically. This system was used later by Fox and Ithaca.

L. C. Smith shotguns were manufactured in a wide variety of grades, all using the same basic design but offered with different accessory features and in varying qualities of wood, finish and engraving. Marlin Firearms Co. bought Hunter Arms after World War II and, operating under the name L. C. Smith Gun Co., manufactured L. C. Smith guns on a limited basis up to about 1950, when production ceased.

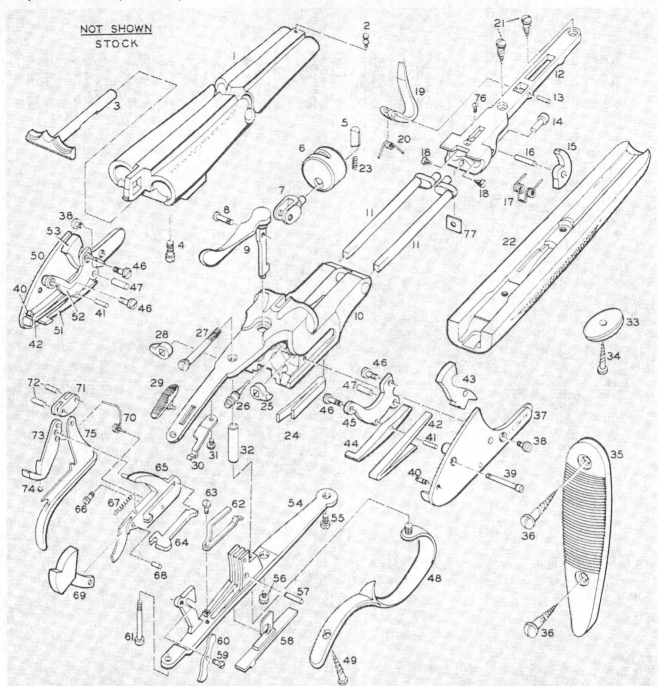

Parts List

1	Barrels	14	Extractor Actuator Bar	27	Trigger Plate Screw
2	Front Sight	15	Extractor Actuator	28	Left Lifter
3	Extractor	16	Extractor Actuator Pin	29	Safety Button And Pin
4	Extractor Screw	17	Extractor Actuator Spring	30	Safety Spring
5	Trip	18	Rear Fore-End Screw (2)	31	Safety Spring Screw
6	Bolt	19	Fore-End Spring	32	Trigger Plate Screw Bushing
7	Coupler	20	Fore-End Spring	33	Grip Cap
8	Coupler Screw		Retracting Spring	34	Grip Cap Screw
9	Top-Lever	21	Fore-End Screw (2)	35	Buttplate
10	Frame	22	Fore-End	36	Buttplate Screw (2)
11	Cocking Rod (2)	23	Trip Spring	37	Lockplate, Right
12	Fore-End Iron	24	Bolt Spring	38	Lockplate Retaining Screw (2)
13	Fore-End Spring Pin	25	Right Lifter	39	Lockplate Connector Screw
		26	Firing Pin (2)	40	Mainspring Retaining Screw (2)

41	Sear Pin	54	Trigger Plate	65	Firing Plate
42	Mainspring (2)	55	Trigger Plate Retaining Screw, Front	66	Spur Spring Screw
43	Hammer, Right			67	Recoil Weight Spring
44	Sear, Right	56	Top-Lever Screw	68	Recoil Weight Pin
45	Bridle, Right	57	Trigger Pin	69	Recoil Weight
46	Bridle Screw (4)	58	Selector	70	Spur Spring
47	Hammer Pin (2)	59	Safety Stud Screw	71	Spur Link
48	Triggerguard	60	Safety Stud	72	Spur Link Pin (2)
49	Trigger Guard Screw	61	Trigger Plate Retaining Screw, Rear	73	Spur
50	Lockplate, Left			74	Spur Ball
51	Sear, Left	62	Selector Spring	75	Trigger
52	Bridle, Left	63	Selector Spring Screw	76	Cocking Plate Screw
53	Hammer, Left	64	Sear Plate	77	Cocking Plate

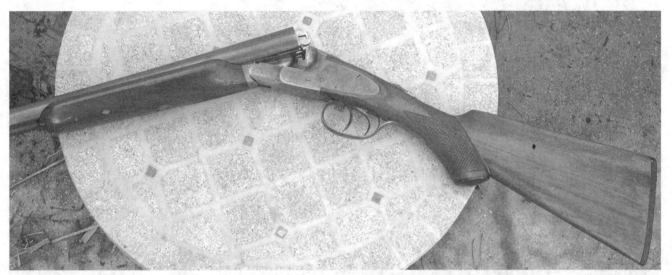

The L.C. Smith is an American classic.

As with all firearms, be sure the shotgun is unloaded before handling or attempting any work.

DISASSEMBLY INSTRUCTIONS

1 Start by making sure the gun is unloaded. Grasp the gun around the buttstock at the wrist, being careful to keep your fingers away from the triggers (#75) and to keep the muzzles pointed in a safe direction. Open the action by pushing the top-lever (#9) to the right and allowing the barrels (#1) to open. If any cartridges are present, remove them and take any live ammunition to a separate location.

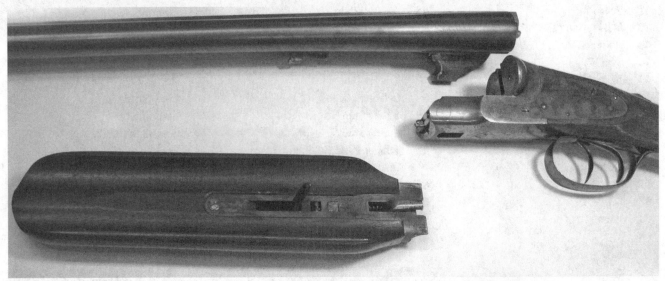

The barrel and fore-end are easy to remove. This phase of disassembly is typical of most double guns.

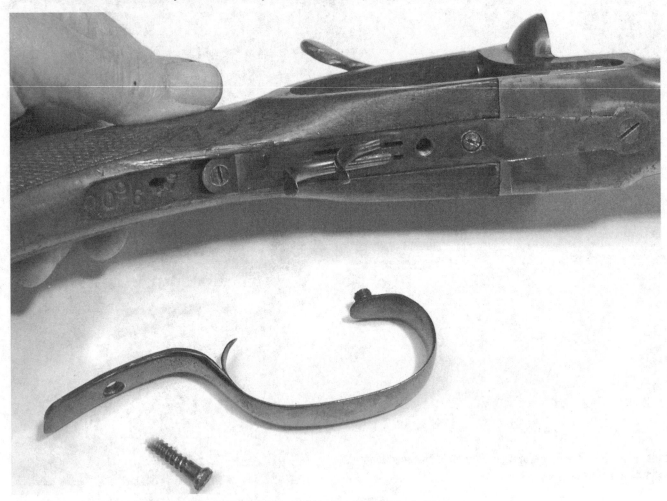

The Smith trigger guard unscrews in a fashion similar to that of many double shotguns.

2 To remove the barrels, fore-end and guard: With barrels closed, remove the fore-end by pulling the front end away from the barrels or by pushing the fore-end latch and pulling the fore-end away from the barrels. Press the top-lever to the right, open the barrels and lift the barrels off the action. Be careful not to pull the triggers and leave the hammers cocked. Unscrew and remove the triggerguard screw (#49) and unscrew the trigger guard (#48) in a counterclockwise direction.

Three screws secure the sideplates, which are neatly inletted into both wood and metal.

3 To remove the locks: Unscrew and remove the lockplate retaining screws (#38) from the right and left sides of the gun. Unscrew the lockplate connector screw (#39) from the right side of the gun.

Both locks can now be removed hinging them out to the rear by lightly tapping the frame (#10) with a hardwood or plastic mallet to loosen them. Be careful you do not trip the sears (#44) and (#51).

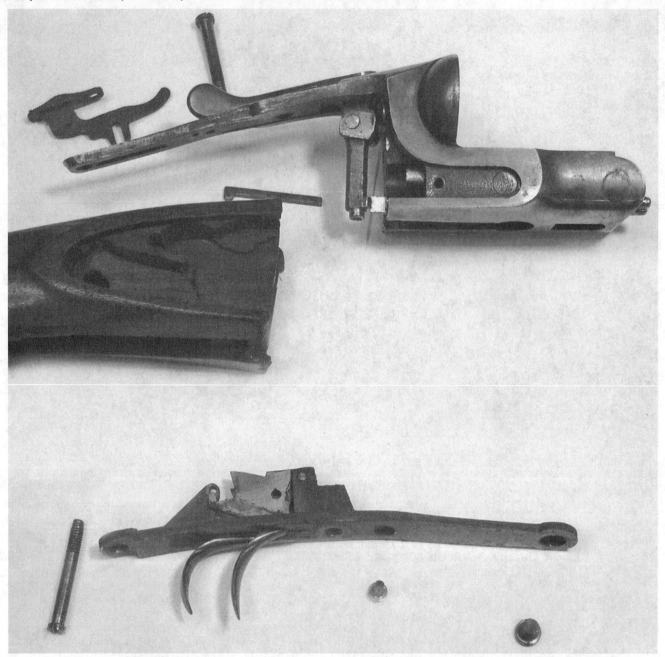

Four screws fasten the trigger plate onto the action. Once they are removed and the trigger plate dropped out, the stock is lifted away from the frame.

4 To remove the stock: With the top-lever (#9) still to the right, unscrew and remove the trigger plate screw (#27). Now turn the action over and unscrew and remove the trigger plate retaining screws (#55) and (#61). Unscrew and remove the top-lever screw (#56). The trigger plate (#54) containing the trigger mechanism may now be lifted off the frame. During reassembly of the trigger plate to the stock and frame, it may be necessary to insert a strong, tapered punch into the bottom of the top-lever to pull it back into alignment with the screw hole so it can drop into the hole in the trigger plate.

Further action disassembly: The firing pins (26) can be pulled straight out the rear of the frame. Place a punch against the long end of the bolt spring (#24) and a padded steel bar against frame on the opposite side. Use a C-clamp to take up the tension on the bolt spring and with the clamp still in place, remove the coupler screw (#8) and the coupler (#7). Then pull out the top-lever (#9). Release the tension on the bolt spring; it is not necessary or desirable to remove the bolt spring unless it is broken. The bolt (#6) can be pushed out to the rear of the action, and the trip (#5) and trip spring (#23) may now be lifted out the top of the action.

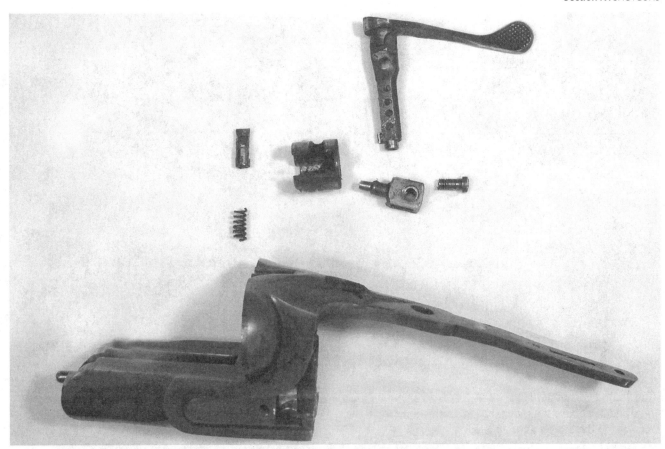

The top-lever components shown apart. Be careful of the trip (top, far left) when you push the bolt out toward the rear: it is spring-loaded and will sometimes pop out, so hold your hand over the top of the action.

The L.C. Smith lock all apart: very simple, very effective.

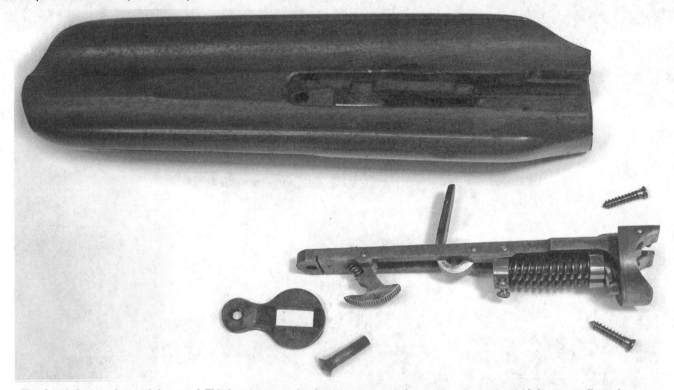

The Smith fore-end out of the wood. This is an automatic ejector gun; normal extractor guns are much less complicated up here and don't have the spring-loaded hammers shown at the right of the fore-end iron. Also, they don't use a latch to lock the fore-end to the barrels as this one does.

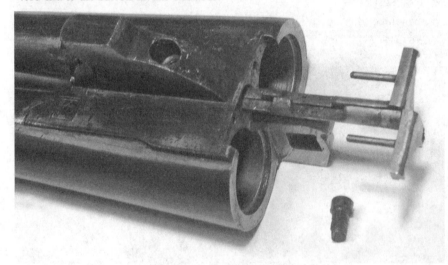

The extractors are easy to remove and are held with one large screw. This is an ejector gun; note the two-piece extractors.

5 To disassemble a lock assembly: Use a mainspring vise to compress the mainspring (#42) and take the tension off the hammer (#43) or (#53). Unscrew and remove the bridle screws (#46). Lift off the bridle (#45) or (#52), the mainspring and vise, the sear (#44 or #51), and the hammer together.

6 To disassemble the barrels and fore-end: Unscrew the extractor screw (#4) and withdraw the extractor(s) to the rear. Remove the two rear fore-end screws (#18) and the front fore-end screws (#21) or the lower fore-end screw (ejector guns). Further disassembly is not normally required for routine maintenance.

REASSEMBLY

Reassemble the gun in the reverse order of above.

Stevens Single-Barrel
Hammerless Shotgun

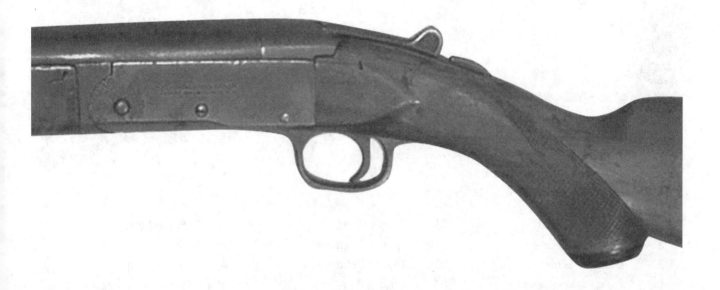

Overlooked by most collectors, the Stevens Single-Barrel Hammerless Shotgun was typical of the hundreds of different models of single shot "farmers' guns" that were so popular in the late nineteenth and early twentieth centuries (and remain so today). These guns were marketed under a variety of trade names, and some, such as the Winchester Model 37, have even gained a measure of respectability over time.

A surprising number of these old guns are still found in the field today. Though their value is generally limited, these shotguns exhibit surprising durability. The following disassembly procedures also pertain, at least in part, to other, similar Stevens single-barrel shotguns such as the Models 182, 185, 190, and 195.

The single-barreled, hammerless shotgun as made by the J. Stevens Arms and Tool Co. after the turn of the twentieth century was surprisingly well-designed and well-made. Author photos.

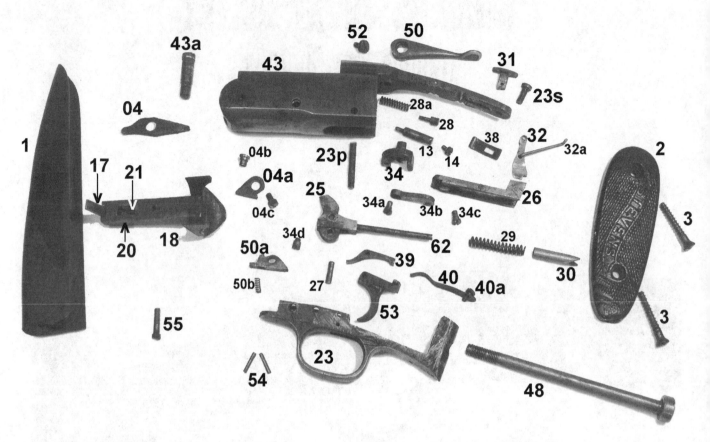

Parts List

1	Forearm Wood	23	Trigger Guard	38	Safety Spring
2	Buttplate	23P	Trigger Guard Pin	39	Sear
3	Buttplate Screw	23S	Trigger Guard Screw	40	Sear Spring
04	Front Cocking Lever	26	Locking Bolt	40A	Sear Spring Screw
04A	Rear Cocking Lever	27	Hammer Pin	43	Frame
04B	Rear Cocking Lever Nut	28	Locking Bolt Plunger	43A	Hinge Screw
04C	Rear Cocking Lever Screw	28A	Locking Bolt Spring	48	Stock Bolt
5	Cocking Plunger	29	Mainspring	50	Top Lever
6	Ejector Trigger	30	Mainspring Seat	52	Top Lever Screw
7	Ejector Spring	31	Safety Button	53	Trigger
9	Extractor	32	Safety Lever	54	Trigger And Sear Pins
13	Firing Pin	32A	Safety Lever Link	55	Forend Screw
14	Firing Pin Screw	34	Bell-Crank	61	Buttstock
17	Forend Spring	34A	Top Lever Arm Screw	62	Mainspring Plunger
18	Forend Iron	34B	Bolt Lever	63	Barrel
20	Forend Spring Pin	34C	Locking Bolt Screw		
21	Forend Spring-Spring	34D	Guide Screw		

For safety's sake, as always, open the weapon and make certain the chamber is empty before you attempt to handle or disassemble it.

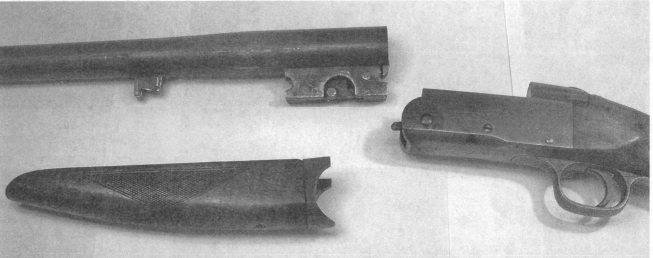

The first step in disassembling the Stevens single shotgun is to remove the forearm and barrel from the frame. This portion of the disassembly process is common to many single- and double-barreled shotguns.

DISASSEMBLY INSTRUCTIONS

1 First, always check first to be sure the weapon is empty before performing any work. Hold the shotgun around the forearm (#1) and barrel (#63), being careful to keep your fingers away from the trigger (#53) and using your other hand to push the top lever (#50) to the right and open the barrel. The barrel will tilt toward the floor exposing the chamber. If a shell is present in the chamber, lift it out. Remove any live ammunition to a separate location.

2 To remove the forearm and barrel: Close the barrel. Turn the shotgun over and pull down on the front of the forearm (#1). This frees the forearm assembly to be pulled down at the front and removed from the barrel. Operate the top lever again and this time, when the barrel has opened, push them slight to the rear and lift it up and out of the frame (#43).

3 To remove the action from the stock: Unscrew and remove the buttplate screws (#3) and lift off the buttplate (#2). Insert a large straight-blade screwdriver into the hole in the buttstock (#61) and unscrew the stock bolt (#48). The stock is now loose and may be pulled straight off the rear of the frame.

After the buttstock is removed, it's a fairly simple matter to remove the triggerguard assembly: one pin and two screws.

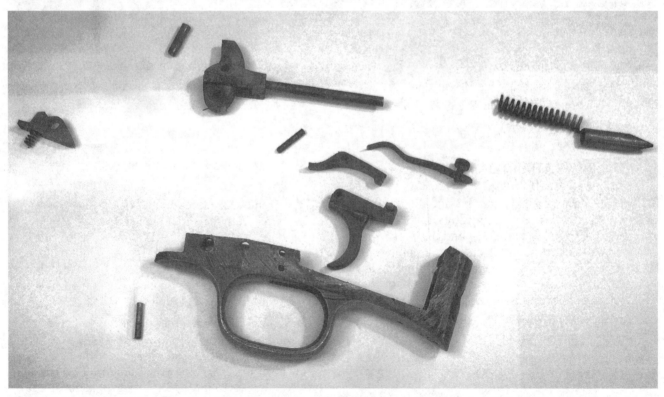

The triggerguard shown apart. The reassembly of the guard into the frame requires a slave pin to hold the top lever release in place.

Removing the bolt involves prying or pushing the safety lever off the receiver. The lever pin is riveted over the lever; however, in practice, once the buttstock is installed the lever can't fall off.

4 To remove the triggerguard assembly: Use a screwdriver blade to push down on the top-lever release (#50A), allowing the top lever (#50) to return to center. Slide the safety button (#31) forward to the off position and pull the trigger to allow the hammer to fall. Unscrew and remove the guide screw (#34D) from the side of the mainspring strut (#62). Unscrew and remove the tang screw (#23S) and use a large pin punch and hammer to drive out the guard pin (#23P), the large pin at the lower rear of the receiver. The guard assembly (#23) can now be slid carefully off toward the rear of the frame, being careful as you do to note the position of the top lever release (#50A) and spring (#50B), which are now loose at the top front of the guard. Note: For reassembly, a 3/16-inch steel pin about ½-inch long is used as a slave pin to hold the top lever release assembly into the guard. The slave pin will be driven out by and replaced with the guard pin as it is reinstalled.

5 To disassemble the triggerguard: Lift out the top lever release and its spring. Push the mainspring seat (#30) over to one side until it clears the frame. Ease the mainspring (#29) and its seat off the mainspring strut. Use a pin punch and hammer to drive out the hammer pin (#27) and lift the hammer assembly (#25) out the top. Unscrew and remove the trigger spring screw (#40A) and lift out the trigger spring (#40). Use a pin punch and hammer to drive out the sear pin and trigger pin (both #54) and lift the sear (#39) and trigger (#53) out from the top.

6 To disassemble the action: Use a punch and hammer to drive the safety lever (#32) off the lug on the frame and pivot it down and to the rear. The safety lever link (#32A) may be slid out of the safety button to the side. The safety spring (#38) is now loose and can be removed out the bottom; the safety button (#31) is lifted out from the top. Unscrew and remove the locking bolt screw (#34C) and withdraw the locking bolt through the rear of the frame. Pull the cocking lever plunger (#5, not shown) out the rear of the frame. Unscrew and remove the top lever screw (#52) and lift off the top lever (#50). The bell-crank (#34) may now be pushed down from the top. As it is sliding down, be sure to hold the bolt plunger (#28) and spring (#28A) captive so they are not lost. The bolt lever screw (#34A) can be unscrewed and removed and the bolt lever (34B) may be lifted off the bell-crank.

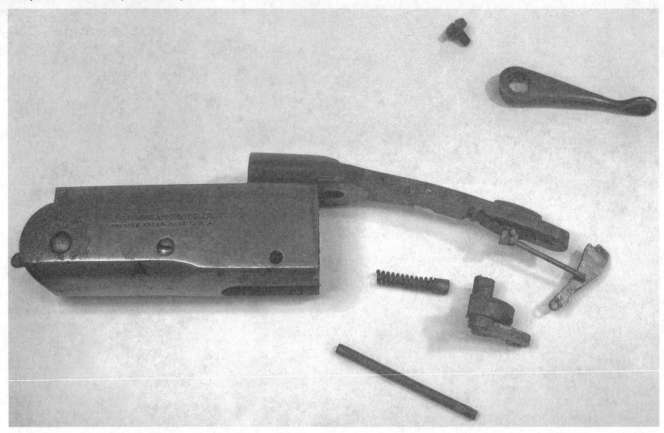

Here, the top lever and bell-crank have been removed. The round rod at the bottom of the picture is the cocking lever plunger.

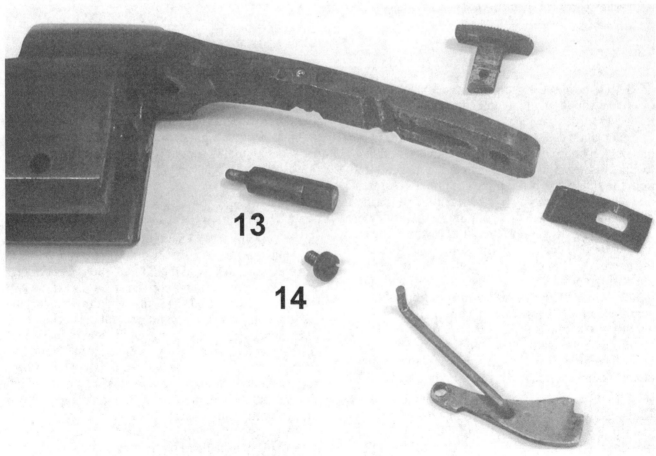

13

14

The firing pin has been removed and the safety disassembled.

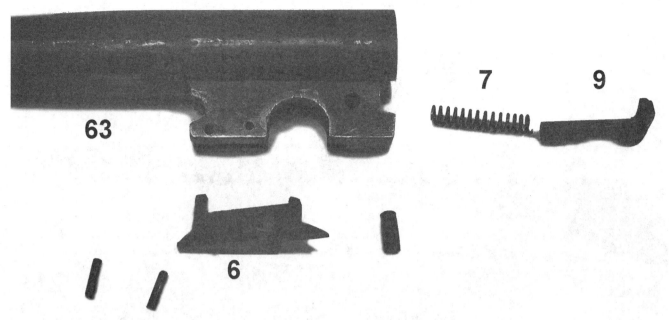

These nicely-made single barrel shotguns were equipped with a very simple automatic ejection system.

7 To disassemble the frame: A special tool is required. You will need a small offset screwdriver, made in the shape of a spanner, in order to hold the rear cocking lever nut (#04B) on the inside of the frame. Unscrew and remove the rear cocking lever screw (#04C) and the rear cocking lever (#04A). Its nut may be removed from the inside. The hinge screw (#43A) is unscrewed and removed, and the front cocking lever (#04) can now be removed. Be sure to note the positions of these parts for reassembly.

8 To disassemble the forearm: Unscrew the forend iron screw (#55) and gently slide the forend iron (#18) to the rear and out of the forend wood. The forend spring (#17) is held in place by a pin (#20). Inside the spring is another small clothespin-type

spring (#21). Make careful note of their positions for reassembly.

9 To disassemble the barrel: Pull down on the ejector trigger (#6) to allow the extractor (#9) to pop rearward. Drive out the extractor pin (the large pin) from the bottom of the barrel and withdraw the extractor and its spring (#7) out through the rear of the barrel. Use a pin punch and hammer to drive out the two remaining pins in the barrel lug and lift out the ejector trigger

REASSEMBLY

Reverse the procedures to reassemble the shotgun.

model 1897 Winchester

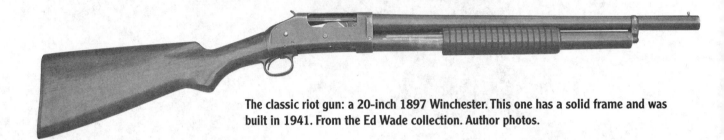

The classic riot gun: a 20-inch 1897 Winchester. This one has a solid frame and was built in 1941. From the Ed Wade collection. Author photos.

The famous Winchester Model 1897 pump shotgun was introduced in 1897 as an improvement to the John M. Browning-designed Model 1893. Model 1897s were manufactured beginning at serial #32,151 in the earlier Model 1893 numbering series. This shotgun design used a unique, heavy machined steel cartridge carrier that doubled as the locking bolt. Even though the operation of the 1893 and the 1897 models is similar, the '97 used a beefed-up receiver with material added so the spent shell was thrown out to one side. An action slide lock was also added to the design so that the shooter had to make a slight forward motion with the slide handle before the action would unlock. That seemingly insignificant change was actually a very important one for safety reasons, for it removed a very objectionable trait of the 1893 that the action might unlock too soon after firing.

The original 1897 was made only with solid frames (in other words, with the barrel permanently screwed to the frame) but in October of 1898, a takedown model was introduced. 1897s were equipped with a tubular 5-shot magazine and were available in either 12 or 16 gauge. Their standard barrel lengths ranged from 26 through 32 inches in 12 gauge, although shorter-barreled variants were available in the form of a 20-inch Riot Gun or so-called Trench Gun. Those special Model 1897 Trench guns with their short barrels and bayonet lugs were introduced for and used in the First World War. Trench guns were equipped with a perforated steel hand-guard that wrapped over the barrel to protect soldiers' hands from being burned by a hot barrel. Winchester continued to sell the Trench Gun until 1945.

This extremely rugged and successful slide action shotgun was the last Winchester pump shotgun to make use of an outside hammer and was manufactured continuously for sixty years, up through 1957, with a total of over one million weapons produced. Today, a copy of the ol' '97 is being imported from China.

Parts List (12 gauge)

297	Action Slide
1597	Action Slide Handle
2597	Action Slide Sleeve Screw Cap
2697	Action Slide Lock
2797	Action Slide Lock Joint Pin
2897	Action Slide Lock Joint Pin Stop Screw
2997	Action Slide Lock Spring
3097	Action Slide Lock Spring Screw
3197	Action Slide Lock Release Plunger
3297	Action Slide Lock Release Plunger Pin
3397	Action Slide Lock Release Plunger Pin Spring
3497	Action Slide Spring
3597	Action Slide Hook
3697	Action Slide Hook Screw
3797	Action Slide Complete
3312	Adjusting Sleeve, Takedown
3897	Adjusting Sleeve Lock, Takedown
3997	Adjusting Sleeve Lock Screw, Takedown
4197	Barrel
4597	Barrel Chamber Ring, Takedown
4797	Barrel Chamber Ring Retaining Screw, Takedown
5497	Breech Bolt
5897	Breech Bolt, Complete
6297	Buttstock
7097	Buttstock Bolt & Washer
7397	Buttplate
9112	Buttplate Screw
7797	Cartridge Guide
7997	Cartridge Guide Friction Spring
8097	Cartridge Guide Rivet
8197	Cartridge Guide Stop Screw
8297	Cartridge Stop & Spring, Right
8397	Cartridge Stop & Spring, Left

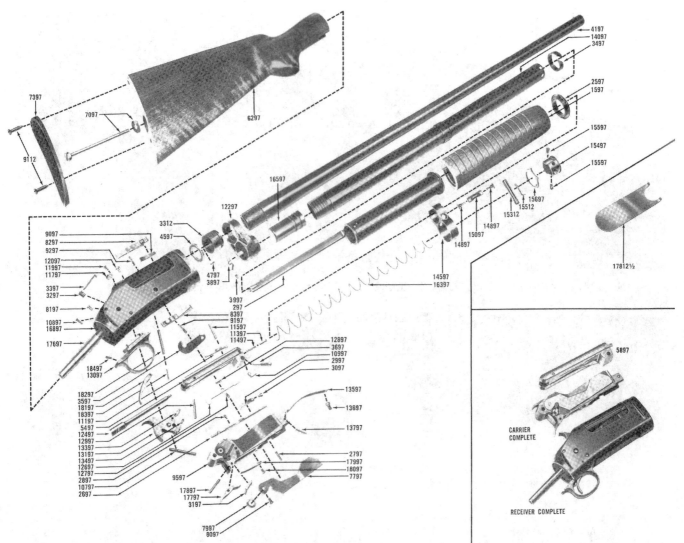

9097	Cartridge Stop Spring	12897	Firing Pin Lock Spring	15697	Magazine Plug Stop, Takedown
9197	Cartridge Stop Screw, Right	12997	Firing Pin Stop Pin	15897	Magazine Stop, Takedown
9297	Cartridge Stop Screw, Left	13097	Guard Bow	15312	Magazine Locking Pin & Spring TD
9597	Carrier	13197	Hammer	15512	Magazine Locking Pin Spring
10797	Carrier Pin	13297	Hammer Pin	16397	Magazine Spring
10897	Carrier Pin Stop Screw	13397	Hammer Stirrup	16597	Magazine Follower
10997	Extractor, Right	13497	Hammer Stirrup Pin	16897	Receiver, Takedown
11197	Extractor, Left	13597	Mainspring	17697	Receiver Shank
11397	Extractor Plunger, Right	13697	Mainspring Strain Screw	17797	Sear
11497	Extractor Plunger Spring, Right	13797	Mainspring Pin	17897	Sear Pin
11597	Extractor Pin, Left	14097	Magazine Tube, Takedown	17997	Sear Spring
11797	Ejector Spring	14297	Magazine Tube Complete, Takedown	18097	Sear Spring Screw
11997	Ejector Spring Screw	14597	Magazine Band, Takedown	18197	Trigger
12097	Ejector Pin	14897	Magazine Band Bushing Screw, TD	18297	Trigger Pin
12297	Extension, Takedown	15097	Magazine Band Bushing, Takedown	18397	Trigger Spring
12397	Extension Stop Screw, Takedown	15497	Magazine Plug, Takedown	18497	Trigger Stop Screw
12497	Firing Pin	15597	Magazine Plug Screw, Takedown	17812 1/2	Spanner Wrench
12697	Firing Pin Lock				
12797	Firing Pin Lock Screw				

Open the 1897 action and you are left with no doubt whether it is loaded or not. Everything is exposed!

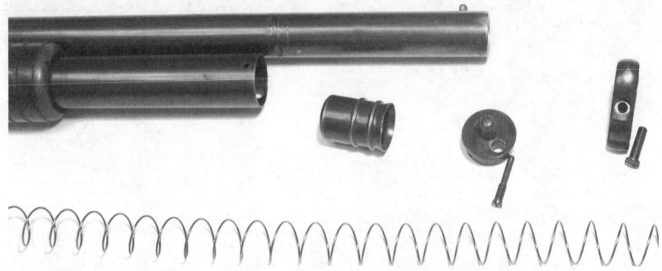

Here is the front of the magazine tube disassembled on the solid-framed gun.

DISASSEMBLY INSTRUCTIONS
(Winchester Parts Nomenclature)

Note: There are two basic versions of the Model 1897: a solid-frame model in which the barrel is permanently screwed into the receiver, and a take-down model in which the barrel is quickly detachable from the receiver. The weapon shown in the photographs is a solid frame. A dummy or slave pin will be required to reassemble the trigger group into the receiver.

1 First, make certain this weapon is empty before proceeding. Hold the shotgun by the grip area of the stock, being careful to keep your fingers away from the trigger and keeping the muzzle pointed in a safe direction. Press in on the action slide lock release plunger pin (#3297), the button or buttons on one or both sides of the receiver. This will allow any shells in the magazine to be pushed out the bottom of the receiver under spring pressure. Move the action slide handle (# 1597; the wooden forearm) all the way to the rear and look through the loading port in the side of the receiver (#16897) to be sure there is no cartridge in the barrel's chamber or in the carrier (#9567). When you are sure the weapon is empty, return the action slide to the forward position, hold back on the hammer (#13197) with your thumb, pull the trigger, and then ease the hammer all the way forward with your thumb.

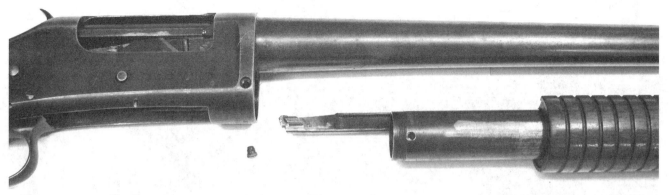

The solid-frame magazine tube unscrewed and the action slide removed.

This is the carrier pin stop screw. Remove it first.

2 Solid frame guns: (pictured) Remove the magazine band screw and slide the magazine band (#14597) forward off the barrel (#4197). Remove the magazine plug screw (#15597) from the front side of the magazine tube (#14297). Use caution: the magazine spring is pushing forward on the magazine plug, so hold the plug in place with your thumb as you take the screw out. Ease the magazine plug (#15497) forward out of the tube. The magazine spring (#16397) and magazine follower (#16597) can be removed out the front of the tube. Remove the magazine retaining screw (not shown) from the side of the receiver and unscrew the magazine tube in a counterclockwise direction. Once the magazine tube is unscrewed,

pull forward on the action slide handle (#1597) so the magazine tube and action slide assembly can be withdrawn forward off the gun. Further disassembly of this component group is not normally required.

2a Take-down guns: Push in on the magazine plug locking pin (#15312) and use the long end, which is sticking up, to turn the magazine tube (#14797) counterclockwise about a half turn until it will pull forward. Pull the magazine tube forward as far as it will go. Push forward now on the action slide handle (#1597) and rotate the entire barrel assembly one quarter-turn counterclockwise. The barrel/ magazine tube assembly can be withdrawn forward off the receiver.

The cartridge guide stop screw (lower left) is removed, and then the carrier pin is pushed out. With the hammer cocked, the carrier is pulled out through the bottom.

The action slide hook screw is removed from the right side of the bolt.

3 To disassemble the action: Remove the carrier pin stop screw (#10897) from the rear of the gun; this is just behind and to the left of the hammer. With the hammer down, push down on the carrier (#9597), cock the hammer and using a suitable pin punch, drift out the carrier pin (#10797). Remove the cartridge guide stop screw (#8197) from the lower right side of the receiver. The entire carrier assembly can now be lifted out the bottom of the receiver. You can disengage the breech bolt (#5897) from the action slide hook (#3597) by first removing the action slide hook screw (#3697 located on the lower front of the breech bolt. Using a small screwdriver, pull the action slide hook down, away from the breech bolt. Pull the breech bolt out through the rear of the receiver. Now you can then reach into the receiver and retrieve the action slide hook, being sure to note the position of the action slide hook for reassembly later.

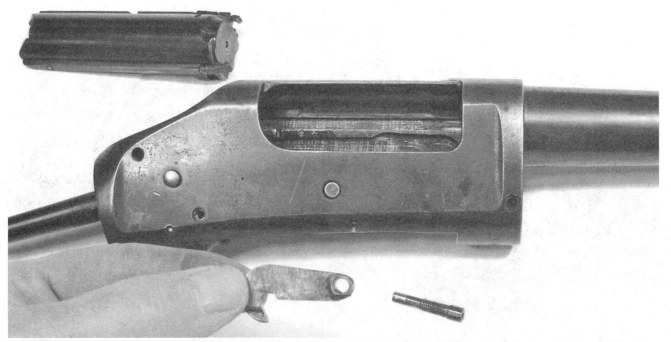

After the action slide hookis disengaged from the bolt, the bolt is pulled out the rear of the action. The gunsmith is holding the action slide hook.

The buttstock is held on with one long bolt, accessible through the hole in the rear of the buttstock.

4 To remove the buttstock and trigger group: Remove the two buttplate screws (#9112) and the buttplate (#7397). Use a large long-shank screwdriver to reach into the center hole in the buttstock (#6297) and unscrew and remove the buttstock bolt along with its washer (#7197). The buttstock can now be pulled off the rear of the receiver (#16897). Drift out the trigger pin (#18297) so the guard bow assembly (#13097) can be pulled straight out the rear of the

receiver. The trigger (#18197) is now loose. A slave pin, the width of the guard and no wider, will be required for reassembling the guard bow assembly back into the receiver. The slave pin should be .125-inch in diameter and .900-inch long.

5 Barrel subassembly disassembly, take-down model: Remove the two magazine plug screws (#15597), being careful to hold your finger over the magazine plug (#15497) because it is under tension

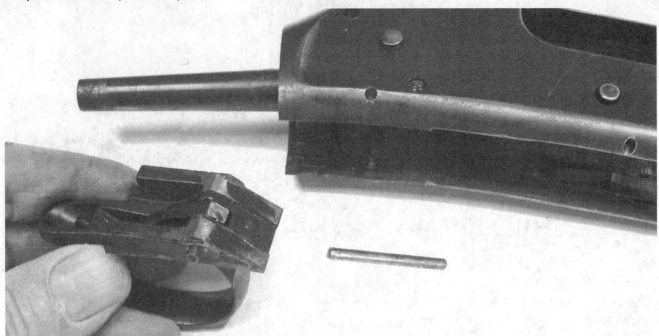

A slave pin just the width of the guard is used to take the place of the trigger pin for assembly. Here the slave pin is left protruding from the side of the guard.

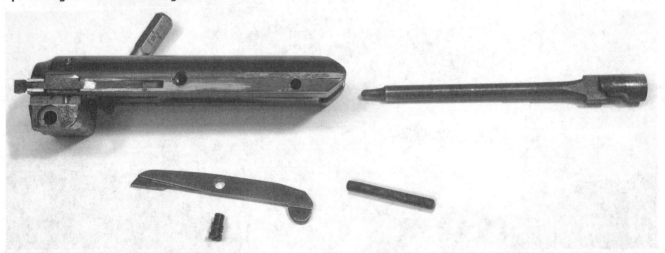

Here is the '97's bolt with the firing pin mechanism removed; the only part not shown is the firing pin lock spring. The left hand extractor is still assembled in the bolt.

toward the front from the magazine spring (#16397). Remove the magazine plug and the magazine plug stop (#15697) from the front of the magazine tube. Make careful note of the position of these parts for reassembly. Remove the two magazine band bushing screws (#14897) and pry the magazine band (#14597) apart slightly. Slide the entire magazine and action slide assembly forward and off the barrel. The magazine band can be slid off toward the front of the magazine tube; be mindful to note how the band and its bushing comes off. Further disassembly is normally not needed and requires a special spanner wrench to remove the action slide sleeve screw cap (#2597).

5a Breech bolt subassembly disassembly: The firing pin (#12497) can be removed by unscrewing the firing pin lock screw (#12797) and removing the firing pin lock (#12697) and its coil spring (#12897) from the bottom of the breech bolt. Next, drive the firing pin stop pin (#12997) out of the breech bolt (#5897) from either side. The firing pin can now be withdrawn from the rear. For normal cleaning and maintenance it is not required that the extractors be removed; however, should removal be necessary: The right hand extractor (#11097) is pivoted to the rear and upwards slightly. As you force the extractor plunger right hand (#11397) to the rear and hold it there with a dental pick or a tiny screwdriver, the right

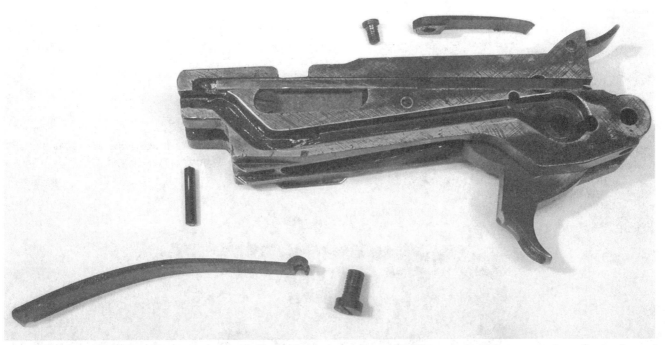

Removing the 1897 mainspring seems very complicated but once you have done it you realize it's very easy to understand.

After the cartridge guide is lifted up as far as it can go, the hammer pin is pushed out and the hammer can be removed from the top. The little part to the lower left is the action slide lock release plunger, which normally lives behind the cartridge guide.

Removing one of the tiny cartridge guide screws requires a strong, skinny screwdriver blade.

This is the 1897 ejector spring and its screw – a very important little part!

hand extractor can now be pivoted forward and pulled straight out of the breech bolt. Use great care: the extractor plunger is under heavy spring tension. Ease it forward and then pull it and its spring (#11497) out of the breech bolt. The left hand extractor (#11197) can be removed by drifting out its pin (#11597) and then lifting the extractor out of its recess.

5b Carrier subassembly disassembly: Remove the sear spring screw (#18097) and the sear spring (#17997). Drift out the sear pin (#17897) and lift the sear (#17797) through the bottom of the carrier. Drift out the mainspring pin (#13797) and loosen the mainspring strain screw (#13697). With the hammer (#13197) all the way forward, use a small punch to drive the mainspring so it will slide toward the front of the carrier (#9597) while reaching up through the sear opening with a small screwdriver to disengage the mainspring from the hammer stirrup (#13397). Lift the cartridge guide (#7797) up as far as it will go and, using an 1/8-inch pin punch, push the hammer pin (#13297) out toward the left side of the carrier and lift the hammer (#13197) out through the top. The action slide lock release plunger can now be lifted out the right side of the carrier. Further disassembly is not normally required.

5c Receiver subassembly disassembly: From the left side of the receiver (#16897) remove the ejector spring screw (#11997) and lift out the ejector spring (#11797). The ejector pin (#12097) can be pushed in from the outside. Note the position of these parts for reassembly. Looking straight up at the bottom of the receiver, remove the left hand cartridge stop screw (#9297) and lift out the cartridge stop and spring, left hand (#8397). Keep this screw with the cartridge stop and put them both in an envelope marked "Left." Remove the right hand cartridge stop screw (#9197) and lift out the cartridge stop, right hand (#8297). Keep this screw together with the right hand cartridge stop. The action slide release plunger pins (#3297) are held in by the action slide release plunger pin springs (#3397). Pry up on the portion of the spring farthest away from the pin to remove its tiny bent head from its hole in the receiver. The spring can be pulled out of the pin and the pin pushed out of the receiver.

REASSEMBLY

Reassemble the shotgun in the reverse order of above.

SECTION V
APPENDIX

ARMS COLLECTOR ORGANIZATIONS IN THE USA

Browning Collectors Association, Scherrle Brennac, 2749 Keith Dr., Villa Ridge, MO 63089 -1929. www.browningcollectors.com. Contact for membership information.

Colt Collectors Association, Karen Green; secretary, 25000 Highland Way, Los Gatos, CA 95030, (408) 353-2658. www.coltcollectorsassoc.com. Contact for membership information.

H&A Arms Society, 1309 Pamela Circle, Delphos, OH 45833. Contact for membership information.

Mannlicher Collectors Association, Don Henry, Exec. Secretary/Treasurer, P.O. Box 7144, Salem, OR 97303. www.lcsmith.org. Contact for membership information.

Marlin Fire Arms Collectors Association, Dick Patterson, 407 Lincoln Bldg., Champaign, IL 61820. www.marlin-collectors.com. Contact for membership information.

Merwin-Hulbert Association, 2503 Kentwood Ct., High Point, N.C. 27265. www.merwinhulbert.com. Contact for membership information.

Remington Society of America, 130 West South Boundary, Perrysburg, OH 43551. (419) 874-5385. www.remingtonsociety.com. Contact for membership information.

Ruger Collectors Association, Inc., P.O. Box 240, Greens Farms, CT 06436.. Contact for membership information.

Smith & Wesson Collectors Association, Sheryle Cheely, 4912 Quail Creek Dr., Great Bend, KS 67530. www.sw-collectors.org. Contact for membership information.

Winchester Arms Collectors Association, Pat Madis, P.O. Box 230, Brownsboro, TX 75756, (903) 852-4027 or fax (903) 852-3029. www.westchestercollector.org. Contact for membership information.

SOME SOURCES FOR HISTORICAL FIREARMS RESEARCH

Browning Firearms: Glen Jensen, Historian, One Browning Place, Morgan, Utah 84050, (800) 333-3288, ext 256. Contact for fees.

Colt Firearms: Kathy Hoyt, Historian, P.O. Box 1868, Hartford, CT 06101, (800) 962-2658. Contact for fees.

"Dope Bag," NRA Publications, 11250 Waples Mill Road, Fairfax, VA 22030. Fee: Free to NRA Members (any firearm evaluated).

Smith & Wesson Firearms: Roy Jinks, Historian, 2100 Roosevelt Ave., Springfield, MA 01102, (413) 781-8300. Contact for fees.

Springfield Research Service (U.S. Military-issue rifles and handguns from post Civil War era): P.O. Box 4181, Silver Springs, MD 20904, (301) 622-4103. Contact for fees. Send SASE with request.

Winchester Firearms (also Marlin & L.C. Smith): Waddy Colvert, Cody Firearms Museum, Buffalo Bill Historical Center, 720 Sheridan Avenue, Cody, WY 82414, (307) 587-4771. Contact for fees.

FIREARMS MANUFACTURERS/ IMPORTERS (HISTORICAL REPRODUCTIONS)

Ballard Rifle & Cartridge Co., 113 W. Yellowstone Ave., Cody, WY 82414, (307) 587-4914

Browning Arms Co., One Browning Pl., Morgan, UT 84050, (801) 876-3331

Cimarron F.A. Company, 105 Winding Oak, Fredericksburg, TX 78624, (210) 997-9090

Colt's Manufacturing Co., P.O. Box 1868, Hartford, CT 06144-1868, (203) 244-1346

Dixie Gunworks, P.O. Box 130, Union City, TN 38281, (901) 885-0561

E.M.F. Company Inc., 1900 E. Warner Ave., Suite 1-D, Santa Ana, CA 92705, (714) 261-6611

European American Armory, P.O. Box 1299, Sharpes, FL 32959, (407) 639-4842

Euroarms of America, Inc., P.O. Box 3277, Winchester, VA 22604, (540) 662-1863

Marlin Firearms Co., 100 Kenna Drive, North Haven, CT 06473, (203) 239-5621

Navy Arms Co. Inc., 815 22nd St., Union City, NJ 07087, (201) 945-2500

New England Firearms, 60 Industrial Row, Gardner, MA 01440, (508) 632-9393

Remington Arms Co. Inc., 870 Remington Drive, Madison, NC 27025-0700, (800) 243-9700

C. Sharps Arms Co., P.O. Box 885, Big Timber, MT 59011, (406) 932-4353

Shiloh Rifle Manufacturing, P.O. Box 279, Big Timber, MT 59011, (406) 932-4454

Stoeger Industries, 17603 Indian Head Hwy., Accokeek, MD 20607, (301) 283-6981

Sturm, Ruger & Co., 200 Ruger Rd., Prescott, AZ 86301, (520) 541-8820

U. S. Fire Arms Mfg. Co., 55 Van Dyke Ave., Hartford, CT 06106, (877) 227-6901

U.S. Repeating Arms Co., 275 Winchester Ave., Morgan, UT 84050, (801) 876-3737

SUGGESTED READING

The Colt Single Action Revolvers, a Shop Manual, Vols I & II. Jerry Kuhnhausen, 2001.

Evolution of the Winchester. R. Bruce McDowell, Armory, 1985.

Flayderman's Guide to Antique American Firearms, 7th ed. Norm Flayderman, K-P Books, 2000.

Gun Digest Book of Exploded Firearms Drawings, 2nd ed, Harold A. Murtz, DBI Books, 1977.

Gun Digest Book of Exploded Gun Drawings. Harold A. Murtz, K-P Books, 2005

Gun Digest Book of Firearms Assembly/Disassembly, Part II, Revolvers. J.B.Wood, K-P Books, 2000

Gun Digest Book of Firearms Assembly/Disassembly, Part V, Shotguns. J.B.Wood, K-P Books, 2002

Gun Digest Book of Firearms Assembly/Disassembly, Sporting Rifles. J.B. Wood, K-P Books, 1997

Gun Parts for Cowboy. VTI Replica Gun Parts Catalog, 2004.

Gunsmithing Guns of the Old West, 2nd Edition. David R. Chicoine, K-P Books, 2004.

Introduction to Modern Gunsmithing. Harold E. MacFarland, Stackpole, 1967.

The Modern Gunsmith. James V. Howe, Bonanza, 1982.

Clyde Baker's Modern Gunsmithing (Revised). Stackpole, 1981.

NRA Guide to Firearms Assembly. NRA Books, 1980.

NRA Illustrated Firearms Assembly Handbook, 6th Printing. NRA Books, 1960.

Numrich Gun Parts World Catalog.

Spare Parts Digest. Davide Pedersoli, 2004.

A Study of Colt Conversions. R. Bruce McDowell, K-P Books, 1997.

The Pitman Notes (Volumes 1-5). Major John Pitman, Thomas Publications, 1992.

Winchester Lever Action Repeating Firearms. Art Pirkle, North Cape, 1994.

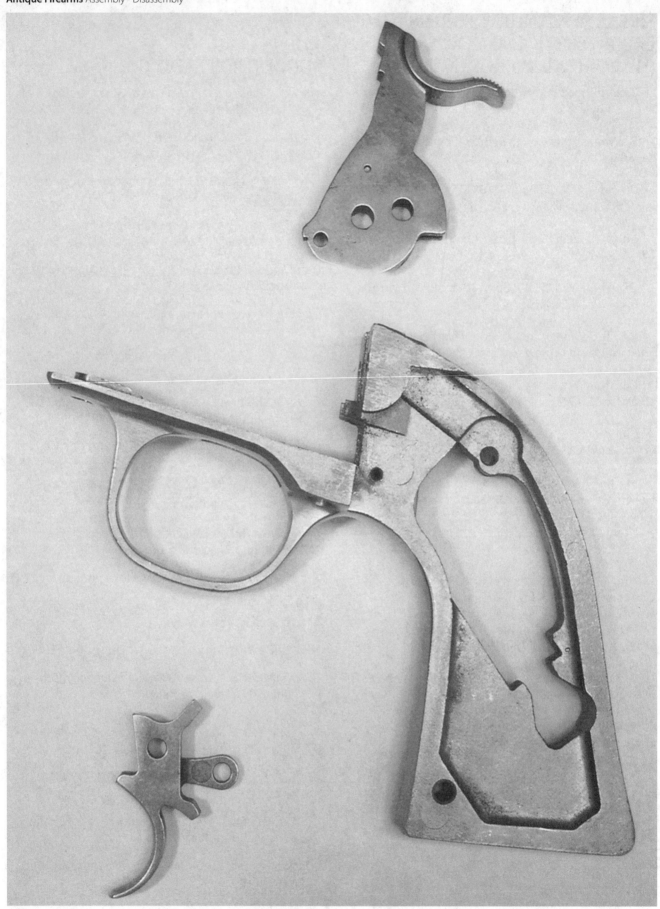

Shown here are the major parts of the very complete Brownells kit that converts a standard New Model Ruger Vaquero into a Bisley model.

SOURCES FOR PARTS AND GUNSMITHING TOOLS
FOR ANTIQUE AND OBSOLETE FIREARMS

Gunsmith Tools and Supplies

Brownells Inc., 200 So. Front St., Montezuma, IA 50171, (800) 741-0015. www.brownells.com.

B-Square Co. Inc., P.O. Box 11281, Ft. Worth, TX 76110, (800) 433-2909.

Dixie Gun Works, Gunpowder Lane, Union City, TN 38281, (731) 885-0700. www.dixiegunworks.com.

Midway USA, 5875 Van Horn Tavern Rd., Columbia, MO 65203, (800) 243-3220. www.midwayusa.com.

Colt Parts

1877, 1878, Lightning rifle: Ed Cox, Circle C X Antiques, P.O.Box 2197, Fernley, NV 89408, (775) 575-6205. www.coltparts.com.

An assortment of Uberti percussion cylinders from VTI Replica Gun Parts, from left: 1849 Pocket .31, 1862 Police .36, 1851 Navy .36, 1860 Army .44 and the huge Walker .44. Author photos.

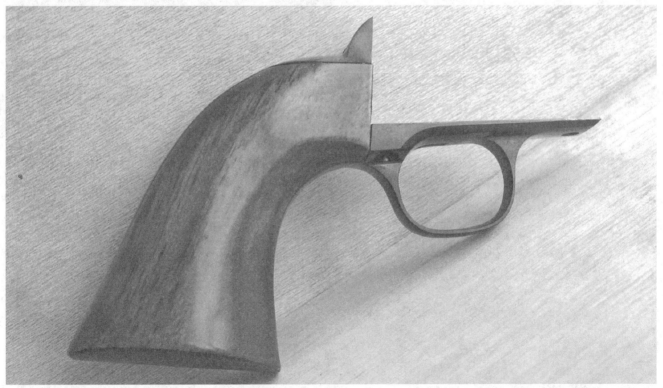

From VTI Replica Gun Parts, these nicely-made all steel grip straps equipped with one piece grip for the 1860 Army. For the person desiring a longer grip, they may also be used on an 1873.

SOURCES FOR PARTS AND GUNSMITHING TOOLS
FOR ANTIQUE AND OBSOLETE FIREARMS

SAA Parts

Smith Enterprise, 1701 West 10th St., Ste.14, Tempe, AZ 85281, (480) 964-1818. www.smithenterprise.com.

Peacemaker Specialists, Ed Janis, P.O. Box 157, Whitmore, CA 96096, (916) 472-3438. www.peacemakerspecialists.com.

Art Pirkle, 1344 W. 17th Place, Yuma, AZ 85364, (520) 783-9108.

Winchester Parts

Buckingham's Winchester Parts, 501 Eaton Brazil Rd., Trenton, TN 38382-9663.

Columbia Precision Parts, P.O. Box 301, Timnath, CO 80547, (303) 686-2865.

Fred Goodwin, Sherman Mills, Maine 04776, (207) 365-4451 (Winchester lever gun parts).

Charles Jones Gun Parts, 110 Sierra Rd., Kerrville, TX 78028, (210) 367-4587.

Art Pirkle, 1344 W. 17th Place, Yuma, AZ 85364, (520) 783-9108.

Western Rifled Arms, P.O. Box 236, Rochester, WA 98579, (360) 273-7716 (Screws & small parts).

Winchester Bob, 143 S. Oakfield Road, Linneus, ME 04730, (207) 532-9206. www.winchesterbob.com.

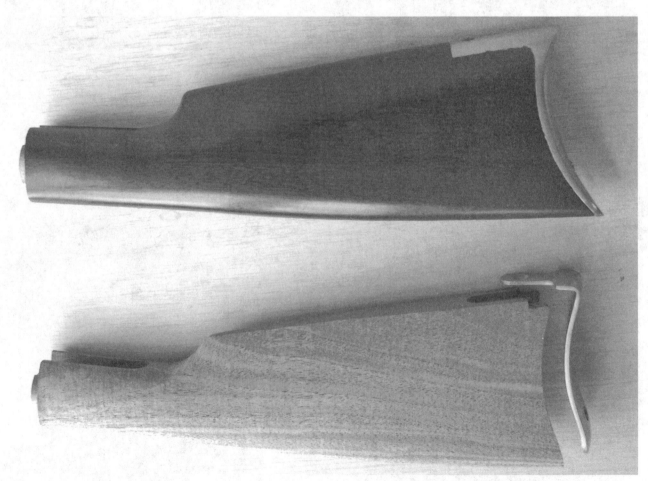

For the popular Uberti-made 1866 and 1873 models with sharply-curved rifle buttstocks, VTI Replica Gun Parts offers replacement butt stocks and butt plates in the faster-handling carbine form (bottom).

Miscellaneous Parts

Ballard, Remington, Stevens, Winchester Screws: Cedar Creek Screw and Machine, P.O. Box, 1531, Woodland, WA 98674.

Colt, Remington and many obsolete firearms: Dixie Gunworks, P.O. Box 130, Union City, TN 38161, (901) 885-0700.

Marlin, Remington, Stevens, Winchester parts & wood: Precision Gun Works, 110 Sierra Rd., Kerrville, TX 78028, (210) 367-4587.

Colt SAA, Ruger Blackhawk: Belt Mountain Enterprises, Box 353, Belgrade, MT 59714. information@beltmountain.com. Fax (406) 388-1396 (custom base pins for Colt & Ruger)

Antique U.S. Military parts: S & S FIREARMS, 74-11 Myrtle Ave, Glendale, NY 11385, (718) 497-1100. info@ssfirearms.com or website www.ssfirearms.com.

Smith & Wesson Top-Break parts, David R. Chicoine, (704) 854-0365, www.oldwestgunsmith.com

Two 1873 Uberti single action hammers. The one on the left has the Uberti hammer block safety while the right hand hammer is a pure Colt clone. From VTI Replica Gun Parts.

SOURCES FOR PARTS AND GUNSMITHING TOOLS FOR ANTIQUE AND OBSOLETE FIREARMS

New and/or Obsolete Gun Parts, All Makes

Bob's Gun Shop, PO Box 200 Royal AR 71968, (501) 767-1970.

Brownells Inc., 200 S. Front St., Montezuma, IA 50171, (641) 623-4000. www.brownells.com.

Jack First Inc., 1201 Turbine Dr., Rapid City, SD 57701, (605) 343-9544. www.1stingunparts.com.

Lee's Gun Parts, 3401 W Pioneer Dr, Suite 2, Irving TX 75061.

Midway USA, 5875 Van Horn Tavern Rd., Columbia, MO 65203, (800) 243-3220. www.midwayusa.com.

Numrich Gun Parts Corp, West Hurley, NY 12491, (914) 679-2417. www.e-gunparts.com.

Poppert's Gunsmithing, PO Box 413, Glenside, PA 19038, (215) 887-2391.

SARCO Inc. PO Box 98, 323 Union Street, Stirling NJ 07980, (908) 647-3800 / Domestic Fax (908) 647-9413 / Int'l Fax (908) 647-3846. info@sarcoinc.com or website www.sarcoinc.com.

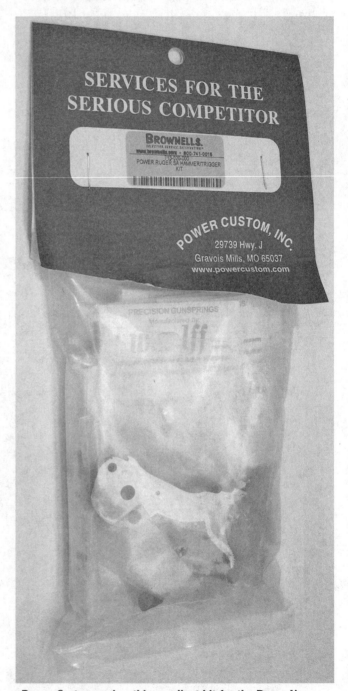

Power Custom makes this excellent kit for the Ruger New Model Vaquero, consisting of a hammer and trigger with factory pre-set pull. From Brownells Inc.

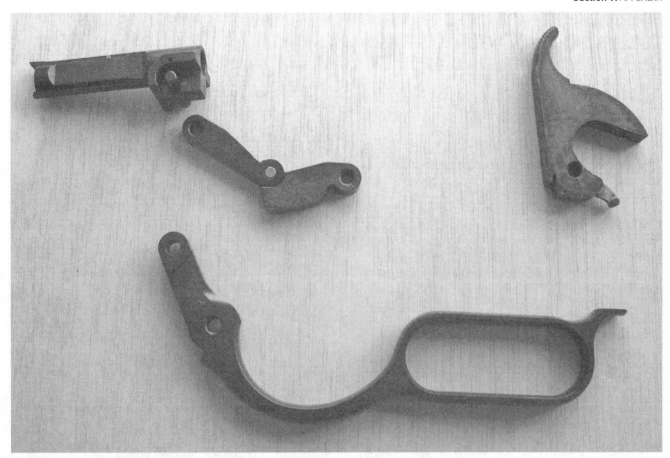

High quality replacement parts for the 1873 Uberti replicas from VTI Replica Gun Parts. Shown here are a set of links, breech bolt, lever and hammer.

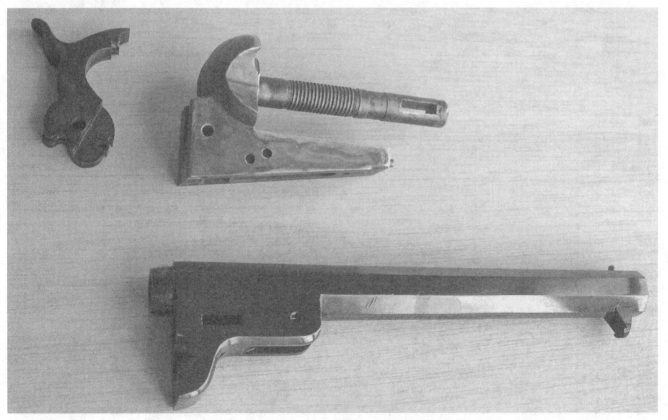

VTI Replica Gun Parts carries all manner of replica parts, even major components including frames and barrels such as these for an 1851 Navy model.

SOURCES FOR PARTS AND GUNSMITHING TOOLS FOR ANTIQUE AND OBSOLETE FIREARMS

Replica Gun Parts

VTI Gun Parts, PO Box 509, Lakeville, CT 06039, (860) 435-8068. mail@vtigunparts.com, www.vtigunparts.com (Pedersoli, Pietta, Uberti, et al). Parts in stock for:

Uberti; Paterson, Walker, 1st, 2nd, 3rd Dragoon, Baby Dragoon, 1849 Pocket, 1849 Wells Fargo, 1851 Navy, 1858 New Army, 1858 Rev Carbine, 1860 Army, 1861 Navy, 1862 Pocket, 1862 Police, 1873 Single Action BP, Rolling Block Pistol, Stallion, 1875

Brownells offers this solid, round-shaped hammer strut kit for Ruger single actions. A drop-in kit, it really does offer smoother, quieter hammer operation.

This is an improved, American-made spring cover (Uberti calls it a ladle) to fit an Uberti Model 1866, offering greater dependability than the original part. From VTI Replica Gun Parts.

Outlaw, 1890 Police, 1873 Single Action & Target, Bisley & Target, Buckhorn, Open Top, Richard Mason, Schofield, Russian, Henry, 1866 Carbine & Rifle & Musket, 1873 Carbine & Rifle & Musket, Revolver Carbine & Target, Rolling Block Carbine & Rifle, 1885 High Wall Carbine & Rifle, Low Wall, Santa Fe Hawkin;

Pietta; including the EMF Great Western II, 1851 Navy, 1858 Remington & Target & SS, Remington

Pocket, 1860 Army, 1861 Navy, Paterson, Smith Carbine, 1873 Single Action, LeMat, Starr Single & Double Action;

Pedersoli; Frontier Rifle, Brown Bess, Kentucky Rifle, 1766 Charleville Musket, 1777 Revolutionaire, 1874 Sharps & Quigley, Springfield Trapdoor Rifle, Carbine & Officer, Rolling Block Rifle; and

IAB Sharps parts (Pedretti).

An array of bolts, triggers and sear & bolt springs to fit single actions, made by Uberti in Italy and available from VTI Replica Gun Parts.

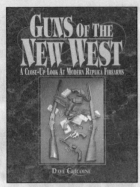
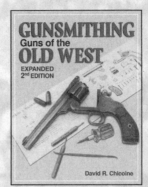